INTERMEDIATE MACROECONOMICS

INTERMEDIATE MACROECONOMICS

Michael R. Darby

Professor of Economics
University of California, Los Angeles

McGraw-Hill Book Company

New York   St. Louis   San Francisco   Auckland   Bogotá   Düsseldorf
Johannesburg   London   Madrid   Mexico   Montreal   New Delhi
Panama   Paris   São Paulo   Singapore   Sydney   Tokyo   Toronto

INTERMEDIATE MACROECONOMICS

Copyright © 1979 by McGraw-Hill, Inc. All rights reserved.
Printed in the United States of America. No part of this publication
may be reproduced, stored in a retrieval system, or transmitted, in any
form or by any means, electronic, mechanical, photocopying, recording, or
otherwise, without the prior written permission of the publisher.

1234567890 DODO 7832109

This book was set in Times Roman. The editors were Bonnie E. Lieberman
and Nancy B. Moore; the designer was Jo Jones; the production
supervisor was Charles Hess. The drawings were done by
Danmark & Michaels, Inc.
R. R. Donnelly & Sons Company was printer and binder.

Library of Congress Cataloging in Publication Data

Darby, Michael R
    Intermediate macroeconomics.

    Includes bibliographies.
    1. Macroeconomics. I. Title.
HB171.5.D216   330   78-10898
ISBN 0-07-015348-5

To David

CONTENTS

PREFACE

Undergraduate macroeconomics texts appear to be the result of a shotgun wedding: an uneasy marriage of recent developments in macroeconomics and the traditional IS-LM model. Recent developments in macroeconomics have been concerned primarily with inflation, money, expectations, and adjustment dynamics. All these topics are awkward if not impossible to analyze within the context of the IS-LM model. As a result undergraduate texts have become quite complex, without adequately presenting the exciting discoveries of the post-Keynesian *and* post-Friedmanian era. This book resolves this impasse by centering the analysis on a dynamic Cambridge equation which is convenient for the analysis of these recent developments. The dynamic analysis is supplemented by the IS-LM model, which provides richer detail for such problems as changes in government spending or autonomous spending. Students may then choose the model most appropriate to the problem at hand just as they choose in microeconomics between the competitive and monopoly models.

We follow here the lead of the author's *Macroeconomics: The Theory of Income, Employment, and the Price Level*, which is in wide use at the advanced undergraduate and beginning graduate levels. The emphasis in the present *Intermediate Macroeconomics* on basic concepts and results permits a non-mathematical presentation, with technical niceties relegated to optional appendixes.

The basic theme of this book is that the macroeconomy fluctuates around a growing equilibrium. The fluctuations result from unexpected changes ("shocks") in monetary and fiscal policy and in behavioral relations and international conditions. The effects of such a change are explained in terms of their short-run impact, of how the long-run growth equilibrium is affected, and of the transition from the short-run toward the long-run. For example, it is shown that differences between the short-run and long-run effects of increased money growth require a transitional period of rising unemployment and inflation rates. The actual position of the economy at any time depends on the short-run impact of recent shocks, the intermediate effects of prior shocks, and the long-run results of yet earlier shocks.

The arrangement of the material is based on this theme. The scene is set in Part One, which introduces the important macroeconomic variables. The long-run equilibrium of the macroeconomy is then developed in Part Two. The fluctuations of the economy around the long-run equilibrium as it adjusts to various shocks is the subject of Part Three. The IS-LM model is introduced in Part Four as a convenient tool for finding the short-run impact of shocks— particularly unexpected changes in fiscal policy and behavioral relations. Part Five is a discussion of how models are used to answer particular problems and includes an illustrative discussion of U.S. macroeconomic history since the 1920s. In Part Six, we examine the issues involved in formulating a stabilization policy strategy in an uncertain world and in choosing long-run goals. This one-step-at-a-time plan has the pedagogical advantage of not presenting a great amount of new material to be digested at any one time.

Learning tools are used in the text to help the student master the material. A What You Will Learn in This Chapter section at the beginning of each chapter provides an agenda of topics to be mastered. Numerical examples are worked through separately where they can contribute to understanding the theoretical concepts. At the end of each chapter, there is a point-by-point summary, a list of concepts to know, problems and exercises, and references for further reading. Some chapters have optional appendixes which cover more advanced material. Answers to selected problems appear in the back of the book. Glossaries of terms and symbols appear there also, as well as capsule reviews of a few mathematical tools which simplify the text.

Many people have contributed to the preparation of this text. The most important of these are my students at UCLA, who provided both the inspiration and the experimental material for this book. Douglas K. Adie, Frederick O. Goddard, Donald G. Heckerman, Wilford L. L'Esperance, Mark E. Schaefer, and M. Holly Shissler read the manuscript in first draft and made many valuable suggestions which substantially improved the final version. Valuable comments and ideas on specific chapters and topics were received from Clive D. Bull, Charles C. Cox, Carl Dahlman, Leslie A. Kent, James W. Moser, John G. Riley, Marius Schwartz, Alan C. Stockman, Charles J. Stokes, Dean G. Taylor, Raburn M. Williams, and J. Richard Zecher. Henrietta Reason typed the manuscript with exceptional speed and accuracy and offered a word of encouragement when it was most needed. My children, Margaret and David, showed a distracted father understanding and patience far beyond their years. All the others who helped me work through specific problems of content or pedagogy—especially colleagues at UCLA, Stanford, and the NBER—are too numerous to mention individually, but collectively contributed a great deal.

Michael R. Darby

INTERMEDIATE
MACROECONOMICS

PART ONE

FOUNDATIONS FOR MACROECONOMIC ANALYSIS

CHAPTER 1

THE ISSUES
OF MACROECONOMIC
ANALYSIS

WHAT YOU WILL LEARN IN THIS CHAPTER
What macroeconomics is ● With what economic
problems it is concerned ● The macroeconomic
approach ● The Keynesian and monetarist
revolutions ● Equivalence of the income-
expenditures and quantity theory presentations ●
How the book is organized

Macroeconomics is about inflation and unemployment. What are they? What causes them? What can be done about them? Macroeconomics is the part of economics that deals with what are for most people the most important issues. Can inflation go on forever or must it end, and is it a necessary part of a modern economy? Will there be another Great Depression, or can something be done to stop it? Must we increase unemployment to reduce inflation? These are real issues about the real world, and that is part of macroeconomics. Hypotheses and theories are constantly confronted with real world data to see if they can pass the test of usefulness. Policies involving billions of dollars and millions of people turn on apparent theoretical niceties, so the scientific debate is often hot. You will get used to that too. One other thing about macroeconomics: it can be exciting and fun.

THE HISTORICAL CHALLENGE

In the last 100 years, the United States has experienced 24 general contractions of business activity. Of these perhaps four were sufficiently severe to earn the title "depression."[1] In a depression, the fraction of the labor force out of work at any one time rises from a normal level of about 5 percent to well over 10

---

[1] Of these, the contractions of 1893–1894 and 1929–1933 were most severe and were followed by a lingering period of all-too-slow recovery. The depressions of 1920–1921 and 1937–1938 were mild only by comparison.

percent and—at the worst—20 percent. Output drops sharply as unemployment rises. The widespread misery leads to universal cries to do something. But
what can be done that does more good than harm?

The other 20 contractions are commonly termed *recessions*. Although not so
economically and socially devastating as depressions, recessions result in a
tragically recurrent waste of human potential. Surely, it seems that we should
be able to do better than this.

Sometimes people think that inflation—like taxes and death—is inevitable.
Yet, from the ratification of the U.S. Constitution in 1789 until 1940, there was
no particular trend in the general level of prices. Sometimes prices would
generally rise for a period of time, but that was sooner or later offset by a
general fall in prices. By 1977, prices were almost 5 times higher on average
than in 1940. Clearly some radical change in the economy must account for the
unprecedented inflation of the last 40 years. But what was this change, and can
price stability be restored to the economy?

THE MACROECONOMIC APPROACH

The basic challenge of macroeconomics is to explain this historical record and
find ways to improve on it. Macroeconomists respond to the challenge by
developing models of the economy which explain the behavior of employment,
output, and the price level in terms of their main determinants. If the behavior
of these determinants, or causes, can be controlled or offset, then the historical
record can be improved upon.

The essential element of the macroeconomic approach is the use of a relatively small number of economic *aggregates* in explaining the economy.
Aggregates are economywide totals or indices of such concepts as employment,
output, prices, and money. Some aggregates measure what concerns us; for
example, the unemployment rate and the price level. Others are included because they describe either the basic determinants or intermediate variables
through which the basic determinants affect the aggregates of chief interest.

Aggregation seems to omit information about the economy which would be
present if we formulated our models in terms of specific industries. But the lost
detail pretty much averages out when we look at the economy as a whole. So
the use of aggregates provides greater clarity of understanding at little cost. Of
course the aggregates used must be chosen, defined, and measured appro-
priately if they are to have these advantages. Chapters 2 and 3 describe the
major aggregates which have been found to work well.

The macroeconomic approach is very much the product of the issues with
which macroeconomists are concerned. The same could be said of the
microeconomic approach and microeconomists. The two major fields of economics in no way conflict because of their differences in approach. Rather they are
complementary. Microeconomists study in detail a particular industry or
group of closely related industries on the assumption that the general level of

prices and income is given. Macroeconomists explore the determination of the general level of prices and income on the assumption that the structure of relative prices and incomes is given. Each group thus takes the work of the other as given in order to have a manageable problem which can yield useful answers to the questions in which they are respectively interested.[2]

CONTROVERSIES IN MACROECONOMICS

Although the roots of macroeconomics can be traced back to the 1700s, the modern field developed in response to the severe depressions which occurred throughout the world in the 1920s and 1930s. The focus at first was exclusively on the problems of depression and unemployment. Systematic examination of inflation came about in the last 20 years as it too came to be recognized as a major economic problem.

For the four decades or so that macroeconomics has existed as a separate field, its history has been marked with heated, often bitter, controversy among people who deeply cared about improving economic conditions but disagreed about how to do it. It is to be hoped that this scientific equivalent of civil war is nearly over, although past wounds may still rankle old warriors. It appears to this author that most of the outstanding issues are empirical questions to be answered by careful analysis of data and not by debate.[3]

A historical perspective on the controversy may help. Through at least the mid-1930s, economists generally agreed that the dominant variable determining the price level and the business cycle was the quantity of money existing in a country. The United States established a central bank—the *Federal Reserve System*, or *Fed* for short—by the Federal Reserve Act of 1913. During the 1920s many economists argued that the Fed's ability to control the money supply eliminated the threats of depression and inflation forever.

The Great Depression of the 1930s was an immense psychological shock to these economists. It was thought that the Fed was doing all it could, and that seemed to be no help at all. Similar conditions existed in Britain. John Maynard Keynes published his *The General Theory of Employment, Interest, and Money* in 1936. This work had a huge, immediate impact. A model was presented which suggested that the quantity of money is not very important—at least during depressions—and that investment, government spending and taxation, and exports are the key variables determining the business cycle. This model, as systematized by Keynes' followers, fairly swept the economic profes-

---

[2] A third group of economists examines the characteristics of a model in which the general level of income and prices is determined simultaneously with their relative structure. Unfortunately these general equilibrium models are so complex that only a limited range of questions can be answered through the use of advanced mathematics. Comparisons with that approach are left to more advanced courses.

[3] Indeed, much of the remaining debate involves claims that the emerging synthesis was really the debater's position all along.

sion. The Keynesian or income-expenditures model was generally accepted by the 1950s.

Some economists remained unconvinced of the ability of the Keynesian model to explain the phenomena observed in the real world. Milton Friedman of the University of Chicago was the acknowledged leader of the group exploring, extending, and testing the older quantity theory of money. Their research had minor effects on the thinking of the economic profession during the 1950s. The details of the basic Keynesian model were altered in response to the quantity theorists' work, but the basic idea remained that the quantity of money which people have does not much affect total spending.

Milton Friedman and Anna Jacobson Schwartz published their own epoch-making book *A Monetary History of the United States, 1867–1960* in 1963. This massive work of scholarship collected data on the money supply and the forces determining it, correlated money supply changes with changes in income and prices, and demonstrated that a modern quantity theory approach could explain macroeconomic events over the nearly hundred years of their study. Particularly important was the demonstration that, claims of monetary ease notwithstanding, the Federal Reserve System initiated and permitted to continue a process which reduced the United States money supply in 1933 to about 70 percent of the level in 1929. The simplest forms of the quantity theory of money would have been sufficient to explain a massive depression. This episode poses the awkward and unanswered question of why the economic profession should have accepted the Federal Reserve officials' self-serving assurances that their monetary policy was expansive and rejected the quantity theory of money which was well documented for many times and for many countries.

The publication of Friedman and Schwartz's book initiated a "monetarist revolution" similar to the Keynesian revolution that occurred following the publication of Keynes' book. The monetarist revolution achieved psychological impact on the basis of a few crucial occasions (1966–1967, 1968, and 1969) when monetary and fiscal policy moved in sharply opposing directions. In each case, well-publicized predictions of monetarist economists proved right while those of Keynesian economists, who emphasized fiscal policy, proved wrong.

The monetarist revolution has not succeeded in achieving the general acceptance once accorded the Keynesian model. Instead there seem to be numerous macroeconomic models, placing greater or lesser emphasis on Keynesian or monetarist elements. This profusion of means of expression seems, however, to mask growing agreement on what is known about the macroeconomy and what issues are to be resolved. The differences between today's Keynesians and monetarists on these points are sufficiently small that the labels have become nearly meaningless.[4]

---

[4] Thomas Mayer recently compiled a list of 12 criteria which might be useful in distinguishing monetarists from Keynesians (The Structure of Monetarism, in two parts, *Kredit und Kapital*, **8**: 191–218, 293–316, Heft 2/3, 1975). While differences of emphasis can be distinguished, none are crucial.

Curiously, as the old controversies die down and macroeconomics enters a post-Keynesian *and* post-Friedmanian era, an array of new issues has presented itself. The field seems younger and fresher than ever.

PEDAGOGICAL APPROACHES

The presentation of macroeconomics is most easily organized around one or the other of two identities: the income-expenditures identity or the Cambridge identity. Either method of presentation can be used to get to the same ultimate conclusion, but not equally easily. It is generally easier to analyze the effects of autonomous changes[5] in one of the major expenditure components by means of the income-expenditures identity. The Cambridge identity generally provides a simpler means of discussing inflation and the effects of changes in the money supply.

---

[5] Autonomous changes refer here to changes due to forces outside the model, such as a political decision.

Figure 1.1 Example of the use of the income-expenditures identity.
Total expenditures $C + I + G$ are graphed as increasing with income, but each dollar increase in income increases expenditures by less than a dollar. The 45° line shows all points at which income and total expenditures are equal as required by the identity. Therefore the intersection E of these two lines determines the equilibrium level of income and expenditures.

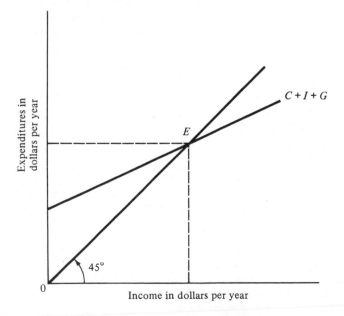

Introductory macroeconomics courses traditionally emphasize autonomous expenditure shocks within the framework of the *income-expenditures identity*. For example, a closed economy might be described as having an income Y which is identically equal[6] to the sum of consumption C, investment I, and government expenditures G:

$$Y \equiv C + I + G \qquad\qquad [1.1]$$

This identity is converted from a tautology to a theory by providing an explanation of $C + I + G$. The simplest explanation is that $C + I + G$—particularly C—increases as Y increases but less than dollar for dollar. Figure 1.1 shows how income is determined by the intersection of the graph of $C + I + G$ with the 45° line. An algebraic solution is discussed in Example 1.1.

An autonomous increase in government expenditures would be illustrated as in Fig. 1.2 by an upward shift in the $C + I + G$ line and a resulting increase in the equilibrium level of income and expenditures. Following this approach,

---

[6] The national income accounts will be reviewed and a more detailed income-expenditures identity presented in Chap. 2.

Figure 1.2 Use of the income-expenditures identity to analyze a change in government expenditures. An autonomous increase in government expenditures shifts the $C + I + G$ line up to $C + I + G'$. As a result, the equilibrium level of income and expenditures increases from that indicated by E to E'.

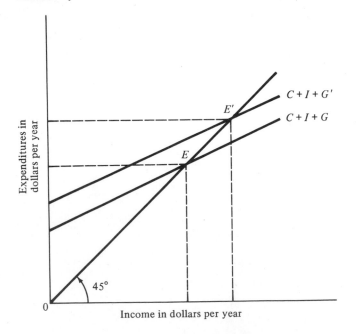

we would next examine how the higher level of income would increase interest rates for a given money stock and how these higher interest rates would shift the $C + I + G$ line. But that is a long story to which we shall return later.

EXAMPLE 1.1

ALGEBRAIC VERSION OF THE INCOME-EXPENDITURES APPROACH

Suppose that the desired level of total expenditures $C + I + G$ increases 50¢ for every $1 increase in income. This can be expressed algebraically by saying that $C + I + G$ is a function of income. For example,

$$C + I + G = \$500 \text{ billion} + 0.5Y$$

This equation may not hold for all conceivable values of Y, but suppose it does within the relevant range of Y values.

Equilibrium income is found by substituting for $C + I + G$ from identity [1.1]:

$$Y = \$500 \text{ billion} + 0.5Y$$

Solving for Y,

$$0.5Y = \$500 \text{ billion}$$

$$Y = \$1,000 \text{ billion}$$

An income of $1,000 billion is an equilibrium because desired expenditures $C + I + G$ will just equal income at that level of income. If income were higher, people would want to spend less than their income. If income were lower than $1,000 billion, people would want to spend more than their income. So $1,000 billion is the equilibrium income.

A quantity theory of money analysis is often organized around the *Cambridge identity*. This identity states that the stock of money M is a fraction[7] ϕ of income:

$$M \equiv \phi Y \qquad [1.2]$$

---

[7] This fraction is often called "the Cambridge k" because of the notation used in the original presentations of the identity. The letter k will be put to other uses so the symbol ϕ (phi) and the term *fluidity* are adopted for the ratio of money to income. The Cambridge identity is equivalent to the income version of the equation of exchange where fluidity is the inverse of income velocity. That is,

$$\text{Income velocity} \equiv \frac{1}{\phi}$$

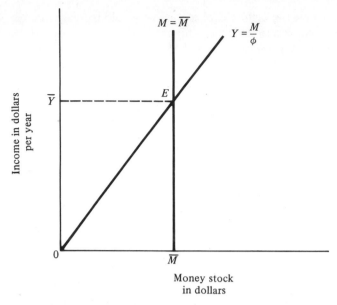

Figure 1.3 Example of the use of the Cambridge identity. The line
labeled $Y = M/\phi$ shows the points at which the Cambridge identity
will hold for the given value of ϕ. The line $M = \overline{M}$ shows the
money stock at a fixed level $\overline{M}$. The point of intersection E
determines the equilibrium income $\overline{Y}$ corresponding to $\overline{M}$.

This identity is converted from a tautology to a theory by explaining the
behavior of ϕ. Suppose, for example, ϕ is a constant. Then, as in Fig. 1.3,
income is proportional to the money stock.

An increase in the money stock would therefore increase income proportionally, as shown in Fig. 1.4. To generalize this approach, we would consider
how the increased income would reduce interest rates for given autonomous
expenditures, and how these lower interest rates would change ϕ and shift the
$Y = M/\phi$ line. But this too is a long story.

One could have started the analysis of the autonomous change in government expenditures by starting with the effect on ϕ in the Cambridge identity.
Or one could have started with the effect of a change in the money stock on
$C + I + G$. A complete analysis will lead to the same final result wherever one
starts; but each problem has a starting place which makes the story easier to
tell.

Similarly, one can start with the long-run equilibrium of the macroeconomy
and then proceed to discuss forces which cause the economy to deviate from
the long-run equilibrium. Or one can start with the short-run equilibrium of
the economy and then see how it moves toward long-run equilibrium. How one
tells the story should not alter the conclusion.

Traditionally, intermediate macroeconomics texts have followed the pattern

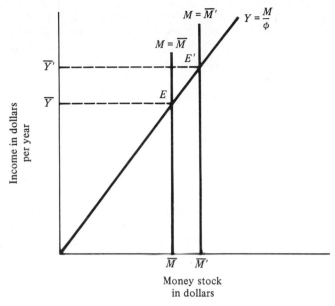

Figure 1.4 Use of the Cambridge identity to analyze a change in the money stock. The Fed's increasing the money stock from $\overline{M}$ to $\overline{M}'$ would be illustrated graphically as a rightward shift in the vertical money line. As a result the equilibrium level of income (and expenditures) increases proportionately from that indicated by E to that indicated by E'.

of introductory texts—that is, have started with a short-run analysis organized around the income-expenditures identity. In this text, the starting point is long-run equilibrium and the Cambridge identity. This makes it pedagogically much easier to incorporate inflation in our model of the macroeconomy. The traditional ordering was developed in the 1940s and 1950s when inflation was a side issue, to the extent that it was considered at all. The approach of this text is also more convenient for explaining the effects of monetary policy; effects now believed to be much more important than formerly thought.

THE PLAN OF THIS BOOK

The first step in macroeconomics is to become familiar with the aggregates which will be used to measure and explain income, employment, and the price level. This is the subject of the remainder of Part One.

These aggregates are first applied in Part Two to examine the long-run moving equilibrium of the macroeconomy. This serves to illustrate the broad trends in the main aggregates. These trends provide the anchor around which the economy swings in response to short-run forces.

In Part Three, the dynamic process of adjustment to macroeconomic shocks is developed. These shocks may be due to monetary or fiscal policy or to instability in the domestic or international economy. They either move the macroeconomy away from long-run equilibrium or alter that equilibrium. In either case the entire response to the shock, as opposed to the short-run impact, is considered.

The traditional Keynesian short-run income-expenditures approach is developed in Part Four. It is used to provide insights into the effects of, and adjustments to, unexpected changes in expenditures.

Part Five provides a brief comparison of the traditional IS-LM model with the dynamic model of Part Three. United States macroeconomic history since the 1920s is then used to show how the models can be applied to understand economic developments.

Macroeconomics serves the goal of improving on the historical record on inflation and unemployment. Part Six is concerned with what can and what cannot be done along these lines. Attempting the impossible has often interfered with achieving the substantial improvement in economic stability which appears within reach.

NOTE TO THE STUDENT

Four separate appendixes are provided following Chap. 15 to make using this book easier. (1) There is a mathematical appendix to review the less familiar mathematical tools. Only high school mathematics is used in the text and references are given to the appendix at points where it may be useful. (2) There are answers to questions selected from those at the end of each chapter. The questions answered in the appendix are preceded by an asterisk. (3) There is a glossary of the technical terms and phrases used. (4) There is a glossary of the symbols—such as Y, C, I, G, and M—used to represent various aggregates.

SUMMARY

1 Macroeconomics attempts to explain the causes of inflation and fluctuations in unemployment and business activity.

2 Macroeconomists look for ways to improve on a record with an average of one recession or depression every 4 years and prices increasing fivefold in less than 40 years.

3 Macroeconomics uses relationships among economywide aggregates to explain movements in the general level of income, prices, and employment.

4 Modern macroeconomics is synthesizing the insights of the Keynesian and monetarist revolutions.

5 Either the income-expenditures or the Cambridge identity can be used as the starting point for a full analysis; but which is simpler and more informative depends on the problem being studied.

CONCEPTS TO KNOW

aggregates   Keynesian revolution
Cambridge identity   macroeconomics
the Fed   monetarist revolution
income-expenditures identity

QUESTIONS AND EXERCISES

*1 (a) Suppose that total expenditures increase 50¢ for every $1 increase in income. Then a $10 billion increase in autonomous expenditures would increase equilibrium income by _____ on the simplest 45°-line version of the income-expenditures approach.

(b) If total expenditures increased instead by 75¢ per $1 increase in income, the $10 billion increase in autonomous expenditures would increase equilibrium income by _____.

2 (a) Suppose that the stock of money is $400 billion and that the public desires to hold an amount of money equal to one-quarter of its annual income. Then the Cambridge identity indicates that equilibrium income is _____.

(b) A $10 billion increase in the stock of money would increase equilibrium income by _____.

(c) If the public desired instead to hold an amount of money equal to one-fifth of its annual income, the $10 billion increase in the stock of money would increase equilibrium income by _____.

3 Identity [1.1] determines income as the sum of C, I, and G. Identity [1.2] determines income given M and ϕ. Since both of these identities hold exactly, C, I, and G and M and ϕ cannot be determined independently. Explain why not.

*4 Monetarists argue that fluctuations in the stock of money have been the main cause of the U.S. business cycle. Does this necessarily imply that they think large fluctuations in government spending would have only trivial effects on unemployment? Explain.

CHAPTER 2

THE MEASUREMENT OF MACROECONOMIC VARIABLES I: THE NATIONAL INCOME ACCOUNTS

WHAT YOU WILL LEARN IN THIS CHAPTER
The circular flows of goods and services and of money ● Equality of income, expenditures, and output ● The principal national income accounts ● Problems in and uses of the national income accounts ● Saving and what it finances

2.1 THE FLOWS OF ECONOMIC ACTIVITY

The first step in understanding macroeconomics is understanding the meaning of the basic macroeconomic terms used to describe the total or average experience of the economy. Microeconomists can appeal to their students' years of experience when they discuss the price and quantity of oranges or flour. It is not so obvious how we can say that the quantity of goods and services produced in the United States was 4 percent higher last year than the year before. If the quantity of every kind of goods and service increased by exactly 4 percent, it would be obvious that any appropriate measure of their total must increase by 4 percent. But some industries expanded much more rapidly than average while others expanded less rapidly or even contracted. How can we average a 5 percent increase in automobile production with a 3 percent increase in production of beer, an 8 percent increase in telephone calls, a 2 percent decrease in production of lumber, and so forth for the hundreds of thousands of different goods and services? Answering that and similar questions is the subject of this chapter.

THE CIRCULAR FLOWS OF ECONOMIC ACTIVITY

To be understandable, definitions must fit into a broad frame of reference. This can be provided for macroeconomics by a general description of the flows of goods and services and payments in the economy. Here we are concerned only

15

with describing the flows among the main economic sectors of the country. Analysis of why these flows are the sizes that they are comes later.

We begin our description by looking at a very simple economy which consists only of households and firms. Households own all the economic resources or *factors of production*. These resources can be aggregated into two groups: the *labor force* or human resources and the *capital stock* or nonhuman resources. Firms rent the use of these resources or *factor services* (also called *inputs*) to carry out the production of *final goods and services* (or *outputs*) which are sold to the households. The owners of firms or *entrepreneurs* receive, as payment for the factor services which they provide, the difference between their sales revenue and their payments for factor services rented from others. This residual is termed *profits.*[1] Competition among potential entrepreneurs assures that these profits will just equal the rental value of factor services provided by the owners. If they were greater some households would stop renting out their

---

[1] Microeconomists distinguish between a normal return to the factors of production owned by the entrepreneurs and an unexpected gain or loss. The latter are sometimes called *pure* or *economic profits* or *losses*. The national income accounts mix these two types of income together as "profits."

Figure 2.1 The circular flows of economic activity in a simple economy. Households sell the services of factors of production to firms for use as inputs to the productive process. The outputs of the productive process (final goods and services) are sold to households for consumption or addition to the stocks of capital of the households. The inner, counterclockwise flows represent the transfers of goods and services. The outer, clockwise flows represent the transfer of money payments. Income, as measured by payments and inputs, exactly equals output, as measured by the value of (payments for) goods and services.

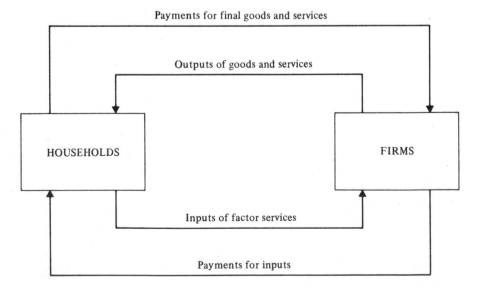

Payments for final goods and services

Outputs of goods and services

HOUSEHOLDS   FIRMS

Inputs of factor services

Payments for inputs

services and become entrepreneurs, thus lowering profits until the returns of firm owners just covered the rental otherwise available. If profits were lower than this amount, some entrepreneurs would switch to renting their factors of production until profits rose to the competitive level.

The flows of economic activity in this simple economy can be described in two equivalent ways: the flow of goods and services and the flow of payments. Payments rendered to the seller just equal the value of the goods and services rendered to the buyer. Thus flows of goods and services in one direction are always matched by flows of money in the opposite direction. Households provide the basic factor services to firms. Firms combine these inputs to the productive process to create final goods and services for sale to the households for consumption and addition to household stocks of capital. The households use their income from the sale of factor services to pay for the goods produced by the firms. The firms use their sales revenue to pay for the factor services provided by the households. Figure 2.1 illustrates this flow of goods and services and counterflow of money payments.

We would measure total income in this simple economy as the total payments for inputs. An obvious way to measure output is by the total value of final goods and services. This weights units of different kinds of goods and services by their marginal value in the marketplace—that is, their price. If one shirt sells for the same amount as five glasses, this measure of output would not be affected by an increase of one shirt and a decrease of five glasses. Firms pay out their entire revenue as rental or profit payments; so income must exactly equal output. Example 2.1 illustrates this point numerically.

EXAMPLE 2.1

CIRCULAR FLOWS OF MONEY
AND OF GOODS AND SERVICES IN A SIMPLIFIED ECONOMY

Suppose that the economy consisted of a labor force of 1000 people, each of whom owned 2 machines. Suppose also that the firms pay an annual wage of $10,000 per person and rental of $1,000 per machine for the use of these resources. One hundred of the labor force serve as entrepreneurs, and the others work for wages.

Each worker would receive $10,000 in wages and $2,000 in rents. Multiplied by 900, this means aggregate wages of $9,000,000 and aggregate rents of $1,800,000. Suppose that the firms are all identical. They must each produce an output worth $120,000 to pay wages of $90,000 to 9 workers, have rents of $18,000 for 18 machines, and have profits (sales revenue less payments for factor services) of $12,000 to compensate the entrepreneur for use of his or her own resources. Aggregate profits are thus 100 times $12,000 or $1,200,000. Aggregate income is

Wages	$ 9,000,000
Rents	1,800,000
Profits	1,200,000
Total income	$12,000,000

This is equal to output, which is 100 times $120,000 or $12,000,000.

The other half of the flow is found by looking at how the people use their income. Suppose they use 10 percent each year to add to the capital stock and consume the rest. Then aggregate expenditures would be

Consumption	$10,800,000
Additions to capital stock	1,200,000
Total expenditures	$12,000,000

So the expenditures of the households provide just enough flows of money for firms to make income payments to finance those expenditures.

Income, output, and expenditures have all been measured at annual rates. If income payments were actually made once a month, a $1 million stock of money would be sufficient to make the monthly payments. This $1 million would then be paid back to the firms as expenditures were made over the course of the month. At the end of the month, the firms would pay out the $1 million in wages, rents, and profits; and the process would begin again. So we cannot infer total income from the stock of money unless we know how frequently it is used to make income payments.

ECONOMIC FLOWS
IN AN ECONOMY WITH FINANCIAL MARKETS

The firms in this simple economy own no resources, but merely rent and combine the services of resources owned by the households. A more accurate description of a modern industrial economy would portray firms as owners of the capital stock of the nation and individuals as the owners of the labor force and of the securities of the firms. Capital refers to all nonhuman factors of production—machines, buildings, and the like—used in producing goods for sale. In a free society, individuals own the rights to the use of their own productive services; therefore firms can only rent labor services from households.

Most firms—as measured by the capital owned—are legally organized as corporations. Corporations have no wealth themselves. The capital owned by a corporation (assets) is exactly offset by claims on the firm (*securities* or liabilities) in the form of debt and residual ownership. The debt of a firm is represented by bonds or other promises to pay certain amounts of dollars at certain dates. Residual ownership or stockholders' equity is represented by stock certificates which confer on their holders a right (in proportion to each holder's fraction of the total number of shares of stock) to the amount by which assets exceed debt. The assets of a corporation frequently include the securities of other corporations. Since the liabilities of any corporation are increased by the amount of any securities of other corporations held, the holding of securities of other corporations cannot alter the equality of the capital stock and the holdings of corporate securities by households. For proprietorships and partnerships, the legal title to capital and the legal responsibility for debts belong to the individual owners. Macroeconomists find it convenient, however, to treat all firms alike, as if they were corporations owning all the capital and issuing equal securities to households.[2]

---

[2] It is quite artificial to think of an individual proprietor issuing himself an ownership certificate for the net worth of his business, but the reduction in wordiness is well worthwhile.

Figure 2.2 The circular flow of economic activity in an economy with financial markets. In this economy, households do not directly own the capital stock or receive its rental payments. All capital is owned by firms. Individuals own the securities of the firms and receive interest and profits on these securities. The securities represent indirect ownership of the capital stock of the firms. The payments of interest and profits are indirect payments of the rental earned by the capital stock. Increases in the capital stock are financed by firms through issuance of new securities.

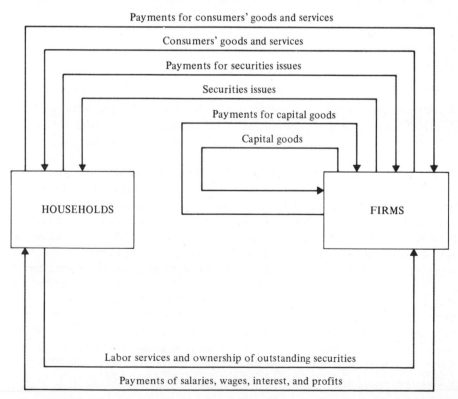

Payments for consumers' goods and services

Consumers' goods and services

Payments for securities issues

Securities issues

Payments for capital goods

Capital goods

HOUSEHOLDS   FIRMS

Labor services and ownership of outstanding securities

Payments of salaries, wages, interest, and profits

Our economy is thus depicted as one in which people hold their nonhuman wealth in the form of securities issued by firms rather than in directly owned capital goods. Firms pay wages and salaries for all labor services provided by householders.[3] Capital services are now provided by the capital stock owned by the firms. The rental value of the capital stock is now received as interest and profit payments to the householders who own the securities of the firms and who finance the capital stock. Total income can be measured as the sum of interest and profits plus salary and wage payments in this economy. This is indicated in the lower part of Fig. 2.2.

The output of final goods and services is no longer sold exclusively to households. Increases in the capital stock or *investment* are now made by firms who purchase capital goods from other firms or from themselves. The firms pay out their entire sales revenue as income, and so must pay for the capital stock by an equal value of *securities issues*, the sale to households of additional securities. This can be done either by actually selling new bonds or stock certificates or by reducing the amount of profits paid out below total profits so that the value of each share of stock is increased. The latter method of "retaining earnings" is most simply thought of as a payment of total profits combined with a sale to the shareholders of securities in the value of the undistributed profits. Total output is again measured by the value of final goods and services or the sum of consumers' spending for goods and services plus the value of investment. Again output and income are identical in value.

THE FLOW OF GOODS AND SERVICES
AND PAYMENTS IN THE UNITED STATES

A reasonably complete description of the flows of economic activity in the United States—or any similar industrialized country—requires the addition of two other economic sectors: government and foreign. We can add them one at a time.

The government sector purchases final goods and services from firms and labor services from households. It uses these to produce government services, which are provided to households and firms. Government services are provided without charge or at arbitrary prices which only rarely cover their cost of production.[4] The bulk of funds required to pay for government purchases is raised from taxes of various kinds paid by households and firms.

Some government payments are treated as negative taxes. These are interest

---

[3] This applies even to labor provided by major shareholders and, formally, to labor provided by proprietors and partners.

[4] Government enterprises which sell their services at market prices roughly commensurate with costs are included in the business sector as firms. Examples would be the Postal Service and municipally owned utilities and bus lines. Surpluses of government enterprise (revenue less purchases) are treated as a tax. Subsidies to government enterprises—or private firms—are treated as a negative tax.

payments on government debt and transfer payments. Because the government capital stock is not used to produce goods sold in the market, national income accountants have so far despaired of estimating its implicit rental return. As a result government output is formally evaluated at the cost of current expenditures for labor services, with goods and services bought from firms treated as final sales. So government interest payments are counted as reductions in taxes instead of as part of total income. Transfer payments are payments made for purposes other than current provision of goods and services. Important examples are welfare, social security, unemployment, and veterans' benefits. They are called transfer payments because they involve taking funds from some individuals and transferring them to others who have provided no goods or services. Since no production occurs, these payments are not included in income or output. They do, however, offset part of the taxes paid by the household and business sectors.

The addition of government to the flow diagram of the economy is made in Fig. 2.3. This involves sales to the government of labor services by households and of goods and services by firms and equal-valued payments by the government. In addition, the government provides government services to households and firms and is paid taxes by both.[5] Unlike firms, the government has no residual owners, so net taxes do not automatically equal government purchases of goods and services from households and firms. The excess of expenditures over taxes or *government deficit* is financed in two ways: government borrowing and money creation. Government borrowing involves selling new issues of government debt in competition with business securities. Some government debt is held by the business sector, but this increases issues of business securities by an equal amount. So net government borrowing—though perhaps channeled through the business sector—ultimately comes from the household sector, as shown in Fig. 2.3. There is no reason for either the deficit or government borrowing to be positive. If the government pays off part of its outstanding debt the direction of flows indicated in Fig. 2.3 will be reversed. Government money creation—which also can be positive or negative—is nowhere explicitly indicated in Fig. 2.3. It is implicit in the excess of the value of government purchases of goods and services over net taxes and borrowing. In the United States the government creates or destroys money through the operation of the Federal Reserve System.[6]

In the economy depicted in Fig. 2.3, total output or final goods and services would equal the sum of consumers' spending, investment, and government purchases of goods and services.[7] Total income would equal payments of sal-

---

[5] Payment of taxes and provision of government services is viewed here in a very literal sense. In a deeper sense, firms cannot bear the burden of a tax or receive the benefit of a government service. Ultimately, only people can. The incidence of government taxes and service to firms—that is, the apportionment of the burden and benefits among the customers, workers, and securities owners of firms—is a microeconomic question of public finance.

[6] See Chap. 3 for details.

[7] Including government purchases of labor services.

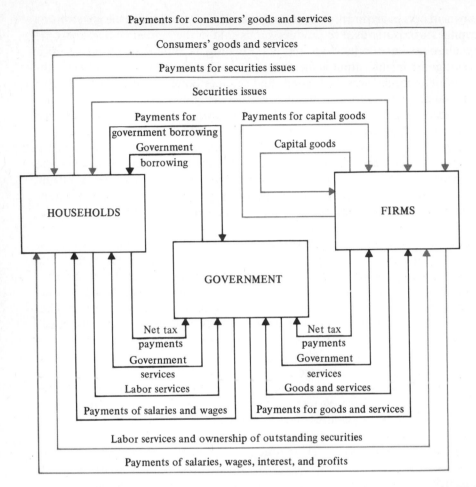

Figure 2.3 The flow of economic activity in an economy with financial markets and government. With the addition of government, households have an additional market for their labor services, and firms have an additional market. The government provides services to and collects taxes from both households and firms, although firms may be more properly said to collect taxes from households for payment to the government. These additional flows of goods and services and of money are indicated in black. Total output is measured as the sum of consumers' spending, investment, and government spending for goods and services. Total income—or claims to output—is equal to business payments of salaries, wages, interest, profits, and taxes plus government payments of salaries and wages. Income and output are equal.

aries and wages by firms and government plus interest, profits, and taxes by firms. Again the arithmetic of the accountants' definitions keeps the value of total income—or claims to output—equal to total output. It is frequently useful to subtract all taxes paid to the government from total income to obtain *private income*. Private income is a measure of the claims to current output accruing to households.

To complete our picture of the major economic flows among sectors we must add our trade with the rest of the world. Although households and government are involved in some direct trade of goods and services with foreigners, we will confine our attention to the main activity in the business sector. All other trade will be consolidated with the trade carried out by firms. Firms both sell goods and services to households, firms, and governments in other countries (*exports*) and buy goods and services from them (*imports*). If exports exceed imports, the amount of goods and services available for domestic use is less than total output. If exports are less than imports, the amount of goods and services available for domestic use exceeds total output. This is so because foreigners are shipping us more goods and services than we are shipping them. If imports and exports are exactly equal, the payments of importing firms for imports will be just sufficient to pay the exporting firms for their exports. The foreign exchange market is a mechanism for canceling such claims on foreigners.[8] The *balance of trade* or *net exports* is defined as the value of exports less the value of imports. If the balance of trade is positive, the difference must be made up by foreigners shipping us a flow of securities worth the difference. These securities may be issued by foreigners or come from their holdings of U.S. securities accumulated previously. Certain exchange rate policies (discussed in Chap. 9) may lead the government to purchase some of this flow of securities from abroad, but that is not important at present in the United States. Instead households (either directly, or indirectly through firms) buy the securities with which foreigners finance their excess of purchases from us over sales to us. Alternatively, if the balance of trade is negative, households reduce their holdings of foreign securities, or foreigners equivalently increase their holdings of American securities.[9] These flows are illustrated in Fig. 2.4.

Total output is defined as the sum of consumers' spending, investment, government spending for goods and services, and net exports. Since income from foreign securities is being included in business revenue, and income paid to foreigners on American securities is deducted from business revenue, net claims to output due to foreign securities will be included in business payments of interest and profits.[10] Total income is therefore still defined as payments of salaries and wages by firms and government plus payments of interest, profits,

---

[8] See Chap. 9 for details.

[9] Interest received on foreign securities is accounted for as payment for an export of (capital) services and interest paid to foreigners is accounted for as an import.

[10] This is a reasonably accurate description of reality. Household holdings of foreign securities are relatively small. Foreign security issues would be largely purchased by firms, which increase their own securities issues by an equal amount. Thus the flows of foreign security issues illustrated in Fig. 2.4 are in fact usually intermediated by firms.

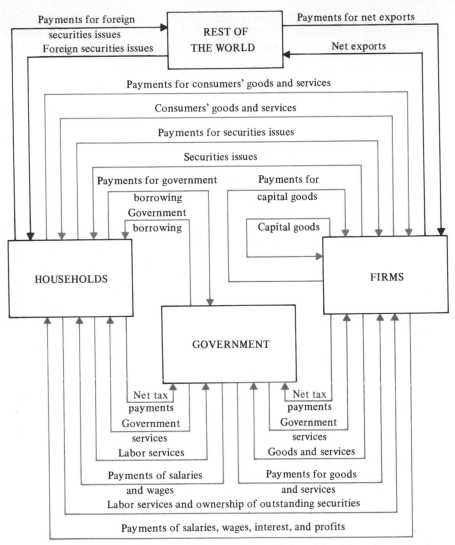

Figure 2.4 The flow of economic activity in an economy with financial markets, international trade, and government. Firms sell net exports to the rest of the world. The rest of the world derives funds to pay for net exports by sales (ultimately to domestic households) of foreign securities or foreign holdings of domestic securities. These additional flows of goods and services and of money are indicated in black. Output consists of sales of goods and services to consumers, to government, to firms for investment, and (on net) to foreigners. Total income, which equals output, is the sum of business payments of salaries, wages, interest, profits, and taxes and government payments of salaries and wages.

and taxes by firms. By the accounting definitions, income and output are equal.

This description of the economy has introduced many concepts in general terms. We can now examine how these and other basic concepts are measured.

2.2   THE MEASUREMENT OF TOTAL INCOME AND OUTPUT

THE PROBLEM OF DOUBLE-COUNTING

The most obvious way to actually compute total output or income would be to add together the total sales of firms—reported on income tax returns—and government expenditures for labor services. Unfortunately this does not work. The reason is that individual firms only rarely produce an entire final good or service. Instead, these final goods and services are produced by a series of firms performing a series of productive processes. That is, a shirt bought by a consumer is actually a "bundle" of products and processes: raw cotton, ginning, spinning, weaving, design, cutting, sewing, transportation, and marketing.[11] In a specialized economy, individual processes are carried out by the firms that can do them most efficiently. The sales revenue of each firm will include both the value of its own output and the value of the raw materials it purchased from other firms. The raw materials of one firm are the finished goods of another, so we use the term intermediate goods and services for products sold by one firm to another. Final goods and services are those sold to *final users*: consumers, government, firms *if for investment*, and foreigners.

An example will help illustrate the issues involved. Let us consider a very simple final product bought by consumers: a loaf of bread. This loaf of bread is a combination of four products: wheat, milling, baking, and marketing. Ignoring other ingredients will keep the example simple, if not very tasty. If one firm carried out all the production processes from growing the wheat to selling the bread to the consumer, the price paid by the consumer, say 50¢, is the value of the final goods and services produced. If each of these steps were instead performed at the same cost by separate firms, we have not changed in any way the goods and services produced. But the total sales of firms are considerably increased. This is illustrated in Table 2.1. The farmer—using only basic inputs for simplicity—produces the wheat required for a loaf of bread at a cost of 25¢, which includes a competitive return on the factors that he owns. He sells this wheat at a price of 25¢ to the miller. The miller converts the wheat into flour at a cost of 8¢. He then sells the flour to the baker at his production cost of 8¢ plus his raw materials cost of 25¢, or a total of 33¢. The baker turns the flour worth 33¢ into bread by using resources which cost 12¢. He sells his loaves of bread in bulk to stores at 45¢ per loaf (33¢ + 12¢). The stores display and market the bread to individual customers, who are happy to pay the 5¢ resource cost of this convenience plus the 45¢ cost of bread bought in large quantities. If we look at the total resource costs of 50¢, we see that they are identical to the price

---

[11] This list is obviously incomplete! Consider the plastic buttons: soy beans, crushing, etc.

Table 2.1 ANALYSIS OF THE VALUE OF THE GOODS AND SERVICES MAKING UP A LOAF OF BREAD

Constituent Product	Type of Firm	Product Sold	Sales Price, e	Resource Costs, e
Wheat	Farm	Wheat	25	25
Milling	Miller	Flour	33	8
Baking	Bakery	Bread in bulk	45	12
Marketing	Store	Distributed bread	50	5
		Totals	153	50

of the final goods sold to the consumer. This is always true, and it enables us to see how to compute the contribution of each firm to total output. The resource cost as measured by the difference between sales revenue and the costs of raw materials used is called the *value added to gross national product* (or *GNP value added*) by each firm.

The basic difficulty with adding up total sales of all firms is the double-counting involved in counting the same constituent product each time it is included in the sales price of a composite product. Thus in our example of the loaf of bread, the total of sales prices includes the value of wheat four times, the value of milling three times, the value of baking twice, and the value of marketing once:

$$25e + (25e + 8e) + (25e + 8e + 12e) + (25e + 8e + 12e + 5e) = 153e$$

There are two alternative approaches to solving this problem of double-counting: The first is to add up the total GNP value added of all firms. The second is to add up total sales of goods and services to final users.

These two approaches come to the same thing, however. If we instruct our national income accountants to add up GNP value added for all firms, they will add up the sales minus the raw materials expenses of each firm. If instead we ask them to total only sales by firms of goods and services to final users, they will total up all sales and then subtract the sales to other than final users—that is, they will subtract the total raw materials expenses of firms, since they represent the only nonfinal uses of goods and services. These two operations are of course arithmetically identical.

GROSS NATIONAL PRODUCT

Gross national product (GNP) is the estimate of the total value at market prices of all goods and services produced in the United States and sold to final users. This would be the sum of total GNP values added by firms plus labor services sold directly by households to the government. The Director of the Office of

Business Economics in the Department of Commerce has provided a well-stated operational definition of how the national income accountants working in his office actually measure GNP:

> National output as the sum of final products can best be characterized from an operational standpoint as the sum of purchases not charged to current expense by business.... To be sure, this operational rule is not profound in expressing the ultimate goals of measurement. But it is important because it tells us in a clear, frank, and unadorned manner what we actually do when we measure the bulk of national product. Recognition of the rule helps to keep our feet on the ground.[12]

The statement of the rule is much easier than its application. It is straightforward enough for the Department of Commerce to add up total sales of firms, subtract total materials expenses, and add purchases of labor from households by all levels of government. But this would not include the value at market prices of all final goods and services produced in the United States.

The most important area of omission is production and consumption within the household sector. It is one thing to simplify a discussion by assuming that all production takes place in firms and quite another to actually expect all production to be listed on the tax returns of firms. Salary and wages paid by one household to another—largely for domestic service—must be added. Production within individual households—housework, child care, do-it-yourself activities—is not priced in the market, so there is no way to place a market value on it. As a result, our measure of output does not reflect all output but only output subject to market transactions. If GNP were to increase because people worked more for the market and did less at home, the value of the increase in market output would be compared with the value of the decrease in home output to compute any net gain or loss. Because of the subjective nature of evaluating home output, national income accountants have wisely chosen to produce an accurate measure of market economic activity alone. This measure can be combined with other, more subjective factors—household production, environmental quality, and the like—determining social welfare, should analysis of a particular problem require it.

One area of household production is partially included in GNP—the services of consumers' durable goods. All durable goods owned by consumers must yield a stream of services over the years sufficient to cover both the depreciation of the value of the goods as they age and the interest or profits which could be earned were the same funds to be used instead to buy securities issued by firms. As a general rule it is argued by national income accountants that these service flows are too intimately related to individual behavior to be included in production. As a result, household purchases of consumers' durable goods such as automobiles, refrigerators, and washing machines are treated for

---

[12] George Jaszi, An Economic Accountant's Ledger, *The Economic Accounts of the United States: Retrospect and Prospect*, supplement to *Survey of Current Business*, July 1971, p. 218.

GNP purposes as if they were consumed when purchased, like restaurant meals.[13] One major exception to this rule is made, however: owner-occupied housing. The large, well-functioning rental market suggests that housing services are easily separated from ownership and provides a solid basis for estimation of a market price for the implicit rental services provided by owner-occupied housing. On this basis, national income accountants *impute* a rental value of owner-occupied housing by estimating its equivalent GNP value added were it rented instead to someone else. In essence, individuals who buy a house are treated as if they had set up a firm which invested in the house, rented it to themselves, and then paid themselves the GNP value added as profits.

National income accountants make three other major imputations for goods and services produced but not explicitly purchased in the market. The first is for salary and wages paid in kind instead of money—largely provision of room and board by an employer. These are treated as if they were money wages which the employee used to buy the room and board. The second imputation is for output consumed by the producer—largely home consumption of crops by farmers. This is valued as if it were sold in the market by the farmer as a firm and bought in the market by the farmer as an individual. The final imputation is for services rendered by financial institutions. Largely for legal reasons, banks and other financial institutions do not pay in full interest on deposits and then charge their depositors in full for services rendered. Instead, large parts of the interest payments and service charges are canceled out and do not show up as revenue on the books of these firms. The national income accountants include in GNP an estimate of the full value of the services actually rendered to and interest earned by depositors.

Some market transactions are not included in GNP. All illegal activity is excluded. This is occasionally justified on the moral ground that if it is illegal, it has no real value even if it does involve the production of goods and services bought by a willing buyer—as, for example, gambling and prostitution[14] as well as drugs. This argument is weak since GNP is supposed to evaluate goods and services at market prices, not some other standard of value. The more practical reason is that there are obviously no good data reported to the government on the GNP value added by illegal production.

Table 2.2 shows the components of United States GNP for 1977 from three points of view: the amounts of production, the amounts of final purchases, and the amounts of claims on output. As you would expect, the bulk of production (almost 85 percent) is carried on in firms, with smaller amounts of GNP value added by government (about 11 percent), by households (3 percent), and by income from foreign investments (0.9 percent). The bulk of purchases of final

---

[13] Allowance for this accounting convention will have to be made later when we analyze in detail the determinants of the size of consumer spending.

[14] These activities are legal in some places, such as parts of Nevada. There the national income accountants apparently recognize a social value.

Table 2.2 THE GROSS NATIONAL PRODUCT OF THE UNITED STATES, 1977

Output[a]			Expenditures[b]			Income[c]		
Where Produced	Amount	% of GNP	Final Purchases	Amount	% of GNP	Received as	Amount	% of GNP
Households	63.0	3.3%	Consumer expenditures	1,210.2	64.0%	Private income[d]	1,309.6	69.3%
Firms	1,604.1	84.9%	Gross investment	294.3	15.6%	Capital consumption	197.0	10.4%
Government	205.8	10.9%	Government expenditures	395.0	20.9%	Net taxes[e]	378.2	20.0%
Rest of the world	17.5	0.9%	Net exports	−9.1	−0.4%	Transfers to foreigners	4.4	0.2%
						Statistical discrepancy	1.2	0.1%
Gross national product	1,890.4	100.0%	Gross national product	1,890.4	100.0%	Gross national product	1,890.4	100.0%

Amounts in billions of dollars. Totals may not add due to rounding.
Source: Calculated from U.S. Dept. of Commerce data in the NBER Data Bank, Feb. 1978.
Notes: [a] Sums of GNP value added for each sector.
[b] Purchases of final goods and services made by each sector.
[c] Claims on output.
[d] Computed as disposable personal income + undistributed corporate profits + wage accruals less disbursements + corporation inventory valuation adjustment − other personal outlays.
[e] Computed as government purchases of goods and services + government surplus (national income and product accounts basis).

goods and services is made by households (64 percent), but there are substantial amounts of business purchases of capital goods (15.6 percent) and government purchases of goods and services (20.9 percent). Net exports (here −0.4 percent) are always relatively very small and can be positive or negative. The two major claims on output (or types of income) are listed as private income (69.3 percent) and net taxes (20.0 percent). The former consists of all rights of individuals to output whether paid out or accrued by firms which they own or by which they are employed. Since personal interest payments are not included in GNP, they are subtracted from interest receipts in arriving at private income. Net taxes are all tax and nontax payments to governments less transfer payments and interest paid on government debt. Transfers to foreigners (0.2 percent) are net gifts (about one-third by households and two-thirds by the federal government) to foreigners. The statistical discrepancy arises because GNP can be computed by totaling values added by each sector of production or by adding up income. Since the sources of data for each calculation are largely different, it is inevitable that a small error creeps in—sometimes positive, sometimes negative. The final claim on output is the *capital consumption allowance*. This refers to the estimated amount of capital goods used up in production both by depreciation due to use and obsolescence and to capital equipment accidentally destroyed.

The requirement for the capital consumption allowance (and the term *gross investment* listed under expenditures) is our warning that GNP still involves considerable double-counting. Investment was defined in Sec. 2.1 as the increase in the capital stock. Gross investment must be as large as the capital consumption allowance just to maintain the capital stock at a constant level. Only to the extent that gross investment exceeds capital consumption does the capital stock increase. Thus investment is equal to gross investment less the capital consumption allowance. GNP value added is based on subtracting raw materials expense to avoid double-counting of production by other firms paid for in the sales price of a firm's product. We should also avoid double-counting of purchases of capital goods to keep the stock of capital goods in its initial condition. The using up of capital goods does not provide any *net* contribution to our ability to either consume or add to wealth, which is the most fundamental definition of income and output.[15] We conclude that gross national product is not an acceptable measure of total income or output.

NET NATIONAL PRODUCT

Net national product (*NNP*) is defined as gross national product less the capital consumption allowance. This can be characterized in three equivalent ways: (1) total purchase of NNP final goods and services, (2) the total contributions of

---

[15] Using up capital is how we are able—as during a war—to consume both privately and publicly a greater amount than current income. But this is done at the cost of reduction in future output because of the reduced capital stock.

Table 2.3 THE NET NATIONAL PRODUCT OF THE UNITED STATES, 1977

Where Produced	Output[a]		Expenditures[b]			Income[c]		
	Amount	% of NNP	Final Purchases	Amount	% of NNP	Received as	Amount	% of NNP
Households	63.0	3.7%	Consumer expenditures	1,210.2	71.5%	Private income[d]	1,309.6	77.3%
Firms	1,407.1	83.1%	Investment	97.3	5.7%	Net taxes[e]	378.2	22.3%
Government	205.8	12.2%	Government expenditures	395.0	23.3%	Transfers to foreigners and statistical discrepancy	5.6	0.3%
Rest of the world	17.5	1.0%	Net exports	−9.1	−0.5%			
Net national product	1,693.4	100.0%	Net national product	1,693.4	100.0%	Net national product	1,693.4	100.0%

Amounts in billions of dollars. Totals may not add due to rounding.
Source: Calculated from U.S. Dept. of Commerce data in the NBER Data Bank, Feb. 1978.
Notes: [a] Sums of NNP values added for each sector.
[b] Purchases of NNP final goods and services made by each sector.
[c] Claims on output.
[d] Computed as disposable personal income + undistributed corporate profits + wage accruals less disbursements + corporation inventory valuation adjustment − other personal outlays.
[e] Computed as government purchases of goods and services + government surplus (national income and product accounts basis).

value added to net national product, and (3) total income or claims to output.
These same approaches were used to analyze GNP.

The first approach applies directly the concepts of final purchases discussed
in Sec. 2.1: *NNP final goods and services* are consumer expenditures, investment, government expenditures, and net exports. The approach is illustrated in
Table 2.3. When Tables 2.2 and 2.3 are compared, it is clear that the only
difference between the expenditures on final goods and services recorded is that
GNP includes gross investment and NNP includes only investment expenditures. Since gross investment equals investment plus capital consumption, it is
clear that NNP equals GNP less the capital consumption allowance.

The second approach is based on adding up NNP values added. *NNP values*

**Figure 2.5 Net national product and gross national product in the post-World War II United
States.** Year-to-year movements of NNP closely mirror movements in GNP so that changes in
either series can be used as an indicator of changes in economic activity.

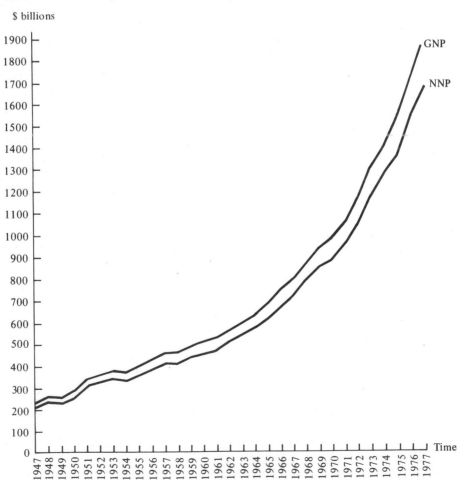

added differ from GNP values added only for firms, where the definition is sales less raw materials and capital consumption expenses. Totaling NNP values added will give results identical to those obtained by totaling GNP values added and subtracting the capital consumption allowance from the total for firms. This is easily seen by comparing Tables 2.2 and 2.3.

The third approach is to add up all claims to output to get total income. The claims are private income, net taxes, transfers to foreigners, and statistical discrepancy. Unlike Table 2.2, Table 2.3 includes under income no entry for capital consumption allowances, which in fact represent no income to anyone.

Throughout the remainder of this book we will use NNP as our empirical measure of total income. Nevertheless, it should be pointed out that the superiority of the NNP concept over the GNP concept is one more of logical consistency than of GNP telling a different story from NNP about the development and year-to-year changes in the level of economic activity. This is illustrated by the close resemblance in Fig. 2.5 of the graphs of NNP and GNP.

CONCEPTUAL PROBLEMS
IN THE USE OF NET NATIONAL PRODUCT

It should not be inferred that NNP is a perfect measure of the underlying concept of total income. There are three remaining areas of difficulty besides those already discussed: (1) capital consumption allowances, (2) residual double-counting of intermediate goods and services, and (3) the valuation of product at market prices. They are discussed here by way of warning that the national income accounts are nothing more—but nothing less—than the best available estimates. We will later have occasion to deal with the practical implications of some of these problems.

The difficulty with the capital consumption allowance is that the estimate is based on data reported on tax returns using an accounting concept that allocates historical costs over time. It would be preferable, though it is impossible, to have a measure of the actual reduction in the capital stock over the period evaluated at current prices. This is mainly a problem when the current prices differ markedly from purchase prices, as occurs under rapid inflations. There is a movement toward adoption of business accounting standards which reflect changes in the value of the dollar because of inflation. This should provide the needed information, otherwise the Department of Commerce soon will have to make its own estimates since rough estimates are clearly better than none at all under current conditions.

Some government services provided to business firms are essentially no different from intermediate products. An obvious—and common—example is the government taking over the maintenance of a factory driveway which was previously maintained by the firm. The firm is charged higher taxes for this service and its output and prices are unaffected. The NNP rises, however, because the cost of maintaining the road is now included both in government

NNP value added and in the NNP value added of the firm (tax payments are not subtracted). It would obviously be desirable to eliminate this double-counting by subtracting the value of government intermediate services for which a tax or nontax fee is charged.[16] It is not at all obvious how to determine this amount; so it remains a problem. The same sort of problem applies to some consumer expenditures which are really costs of working. That is, recorded wages are frequently a payment for an intermediate product consisting of labor and expenses for tools and the like. Some employee expenses are deducted from salaries and wages, but there is no clear place to draw the line—other than what the tax laws happen to make deductible.

The final difficulty—the valuation of goods and services at market prices—brings us back to our original question of how we can combine different amounts of hundreds of thousands of goods and services into a meaningful index of total goods and services. The approach used was to add up their values according to market prices. If one thing sells for ten times what another sells for, then it is valued as equal to ten of the other. This means that the marginal valuation of willing buyers gives us our weights for adding together goods. If prices change, then so do our weights. As a practical matter there is no alternative, and it is not clear that any would be desirable for carrying out the macroeconomist's task of explaining how human behavior determines overall economic activity. For that task it is best to have a measure of economic activity that reflects the actual values placed on goods by the population rather than some alternative standard of social worth. The price which a buyer will consider paying for a product is determined by both the buyer's personal tastes and resources and the supply conditions of the product. It is assumed that these conditions do not change sufficiently rapidly—when averaged over all buyers and all products—to cause any difficulty for macroeconomic analysis. A separate difficulty, analyzed in Chap. 3, is the effect of changes in the overall level of prices or inflation on our measure of income. Special techniques are developed there to measure changes in the overall level of prices and to remove their effects from our measure of output.

2.3 THE ROLE OF SAVING IN THE NATIONAL INCOME ACCOUNTING IDENTITIES

SAVING DEFINED

Saving is the difference between private income and consumer expenditures. Private income measures the amount available to consumers for consumption or addition to their wealth. Consumer expenditures are treated as consumption

---

[16] If the intermediate services provide an implicit subsidy, the price of the firm's output will fall and there will be no double-counting.

in our national income accounts, so the addition to the nonhuman wealth[17] of households, or saving, is measured by the amount of private income not consumed. It is convenient to introduce some symbols for these concepts so that the relations can be described algebraically. Private income is denoted Y_N, consumer expenditures C, and saving S. So our definition of saving is

$$S \equiv Y_N - C \qquad [2.1]$$

The identity sign $(\equiv)$ is used because [2.1] always holds exactly by definition. Macroeconomists generally use identities to indicate such definitional relations and equal signs $(=)$ for relationships based upon how people act (behavioral functions).

This definition of saving as the nonconsumption of private income is very useful in macroeconomic analysis. In our description of the flows of economic activity, we saw that saving is used to purchase both the net securities issues of firms and foreigners and the new issues of government debt and money.[18] Sales of already existing securities, government debt, and government money from one party to another are not a part of saving but merely a transfer of some assets in exchange for other assets.

THE NATIONAL INCOME ACCOUNTING IDENTITIES

The use of saving to finance investment, net exports, and the government deficit is implicit in the national income identities for income and expenditures. Let us include the trivial items of transfers to foreigners and statistical discrepancy in net taxes to keep the analysis simple. Then total income Y is identically equal to the sum of private income and net taxes T (see Table 2.3):

$$Y \equiv Y_N + T \qquad [2.2]$$

Total expenditures, on the other hand, are identically equal to the sum of consumer expenditures, investment I, government expenditures G, and net exports X:

$$Y \equiv C + I + G + X \qquad [2.3]$$

---

[17] Investments in human wealth are in part included in consumer expenditure (tuition, books, etc.) and in part excluded from our measure of income and its components altogether (wages foregone while in school or in an on-the-job training program). Consumers' durable goods are treated as if consumed immediately.

[18] Sometimes saving is divided into personal saving, which is done directly by households, and business saving in which firms (for tax reasons) reinvest part of profits without physically issuing corresponding new securities. This distinction has not proved useful, however, since individuals adjust their personal saving to offset variations in the amount of saving done for them by the firms which they own. In this book, business saving is lumped with personal saving as if firms issued securities to their shareholders in the amount of undistributed profits.

Note that Y can be used interchangeably for total income and total expenditures, since they are merely different names for the same concept.

Substituting [2.2] into [2.3] gives us

$$Y_N + T \equiv C + I + G + X \qquad [2.4]$$

Since private income is the sum of consumer expenditures and saving,

$$C + S + T \equiv C + I + G + X \qquad [2.5]$$

The left-hand side of [2.5] tells us that income is divided between paying for consumer expenditures and taxes and saving. The right-hand side shows that final purchases of goods and services consist of consumer expenditures, investment, government expenditures, and net exports. The two sides must always be equal by the very definitions of the concepts. Subtracting consumer expenditures from both sides and moving net taxes to the right,

$$S \equiv I + G - T + X \qquad [2.6]$$

This equation says that saving is equal to investment plus the government deficit $(G - T)$ plus net exports. This is true by definition. We will frequently refer to this equation in order to check the consistency of a theory which *explains* the actual values of its individual components.

SUMMARY

1 The main flows of economic activity in the United States can be described in terms of four sectors: households, firms, government, and the rest of the world.

2 Households own the labor force and receive wages for its services. They also own securities, debt, and money issued by the other sectors which pay interest and profits to the households.

3 Firms own the capital stock, which they combine with labor services to produce final goods and services purchased by consumers, government, the rest of the world, and by firms for investment in more capital. The capital stock is financed by the securities owned by the household sector.

4 Government provides services to the other sectors, financing its activities by net taxes, borrowing, and issuing new money.

5 Some goods and services produced in the United States are exchanged for those produced in the rest of the world. The difference in value, or net exports, is financed by net issues of foreign securities.

6 Net national product (NNP) is the estimate of total output, total final purchases, and total income of the United States. Gross national product (GNP)

exceeds NNP by the amount of capital consumption; the word gross warns that gross investment is included as a final purchase.

7 Expenditures are the sum of consumer expenditures, investment, government expenditures, and net exports. Income is essentially the sum of private income and net taxes.

8 Saving, the difference between private income and consumer expenditure, finances investment, the government deficit, and net exports.

CONCEPTS TO KNOW

consumer expenditures	net national product (NNP)
factors of production	net taxes
final goods and services	NNP value added
GNP value added	output
government deficit	private income
government expenditures	profits
gross national product (GNP)	saving
inputs	securities
investment	securities issues
net exports	

QUESTIONS AND EXERCISES

1 If you were asked to give a single measure representing 3 pairs of shoes, 7 movie tickets, and 328 paper clips, how would you do it? What about 2 pairs of shoes, 9 movie tickets, and 275 paper clips? Which is bigger? By how much? Does it make a difference what you are going to use the measure for?

2 Why do we say that firms produce output using factor services instead of factors of production?

*3 Profits maintain the equality of output and income. Explain why.

4 Securities issues finance investment, and outstanding securities finance the capital stock. What is the relation of securities issues to outstanding securities? Of investment to the capital stock? Why does the initial statement hold?

5 (a) Why is the amount of securities issues sold to households not reduced if one firm buys the securities of another?

   (b) Certain firms, called intermediaries, specialize in buying the securities of other firms and selling households their own securities. Banks are intermediaries; can you think of others? Do banks increase the amount available to finance investment when they lend to firms?

*6 A company had sales for the year of $2,500,000. Its expenses were

Wages	$1,100,000
Interest	150,000
Taxes	120,000
Depreciation	300,000
Raw materials	750,000
Total expenses	$2,420,000
Net income	80,000
Sales	$2,500,000

(a) What was the company's GNP value added?

(b) What was the company's NNP value added?

7 If a steelmaker buys a coal mine from which it had been buying coal, what happens to total sales? To GNP? To NNP?

8 What happens to NNP if a man marries his housekeeper who continues to perform (almost) identical tasks?

9 Why does the inclusion of the capital consumption allowance in GNP represent double-counting?

10 In Table 2.3, what is the total value of consumer expenditures, investment, and net exports? Could this total exceed private income? Why or why not?

*11 Why is it that firms produce most of the output but do not make most of the final purchases of goods and services?

12 How much was saving in 1977?

REFERENCES FOR FURTHER READING

Kendrick, John W.: "National Income and Product Accounts," in *International Encyclopedia of the Social Sciences*, London: Macmillan, 1968, **11**: 19–34. (A brief introduction to the history and details of the United States National Income and Products Accounts.)

National Accounts Review Committee: *The National Economic Accounts of the United States: Review, Appraisal, and Recommendations*, Washington: GPO, 1958.

Rosen, Sam: *National Income and Other Social Accounts*, New York: Holt, 1972. (This book provides a thorough introduction to the detailed information included in the United States National Income and Product Accounts.)

The Economic Accounts of the United States: Retrospect and Prospect, supplement to *Survey of Current Business*, July 1971.

CHAPTER 3

THE MEASUREMENT OF MACROECONOMIC VARIABLES II: OTHER NATIONAL AGGREGATES

WHAT YOU WILL LEARN IN THIS CHAPTER
How price indices measure the average level of prices ● How price indices are used to remove the effects of inflation from dollar amounts ● The unemployment rate ● Money and how it is supplied ● How business cycles are dated ● Interest rates on various assets ● Continuously compounded interest ● Permanent income as a measure of real wealth

3.1 PRICE INDICES

THE AVERAGE LEVEL OF PRICES

The prices of individual goods and services change frequently—sometimes up, sometimes down. Historically, price changes of individual commodities primarily have reflected changes in the valuation of one commodity as compared with others. These changes in relative prices, studied in microeconomics, are produced by basic forces such as changes in tastes or conditions of production, which produce shifts in supply and demand. Macroeconomists are concerned with explaining the behavior of the average level of prices rather than the behavior of relative prices. At times there is an upward or downward bias superimposed upon changes in relative prices. If this bias is upward, prices which would have risen in its absence rise more, and prices which would have otherwise fallen fall less or even rise, though by less than average. If the bias is instead downward, prices which would otherwise have risen, rise less or even fall, while prices that would have fallen anyway fall more rapidly.

Microeconomists analyze relative price changes by assuming that the average price level is constant or by measuring all prices and costs relative to the average price level. Macroeconomists explain the average price level without reference to the behavior of the relative prices of individual commodities. In this way the two broad areas of economic analysis fit neatly together like two pieces of a puzzle.

The rise and fall of the average level of prices over time creates difficulties for our measure of total income derived as the sum of the quantities times the current prices of final goods and services. The fact that net national product has increased over a particular year does not of itself tell us anything about whether more real goods and services are being produced and made available to satisfy human wants. It could instead be that income rose solely because of the bias imparted by a rising average level of prices. Our primary goal in measuring total income was to develop a weighted average of the actual apples, shirts, automobiles, television repairs, and so forth produced. Although prices provide relative weights for combining the different kinds of goods and services, they distort our measure whenever the average price level changes.

Consider for example an economy in which only three final goods and services (or three commodities) are produced. Different possible quantities and prices are given for 5 years in Table 3.1. In year 0, total income is $4,500:

$$100 \times \$10.00 + 300 \times \$5.00 + 2000 \times \$1.00 = \$4,500$$

In year 1, income has increased to $4,950—an increase of 10 percent

$$\$4,950 - \$4,500 = \$450 \qquad \$450/\$4,500 = 0.10$$

This is exactly how we would want our measure of total goods and services to behave, since the quantity of each commodity increased by 10 percent. In year 2, however, income is also $4,950, but the real output of goods and services is identical to that of year 0. The 10 percent rise in total income is due entirely to the 10 percent increase in each price. It would be desirable to distinguish between these two kinds of increase in the total value of final commodities.

Macroeconomists make this distinction by breaking total income Y into an

Table 3.1 QUANTITIES AND PRICES PRODUCED
IN A THREE-COMMODITY ECONOMY

| Year | Commodity 1 | | Commodity 2 | | Commodity 3 | | Income |
	Quantity	Price	Quantity	Price	Quantity	Price	
0	100	$10.00	300	$5.00	2000	$1.00	$4,500.00
1	110	$10.00	330	$5.00	2200	$1.00	$4,950.00
2	100	$11.00	300	$5.50	2000	$1.10	$4,950.00
3	105	$11.50	315	$5.75	2100	$1.15	$5,433.75
4	95	$11.00	340	$5.00	2100	$1.05	$4,950.00
4a	95	$10.00	340	$5.00	2100	$1.00	$4,750.00
4b	100	$11.00	300	$5.00	2000	$1.05	$4,700.00

index y of the total real quantity of goods and services and another index P of the average level of prices. These indices are defined so that—just as for an individual commodity—quantity times price equals dollar value:

$$yP \equiv Y \qquad\qquad [3.1]$$

Income Y measured in terms of current prices times current quantities is called *nominal income*. The term nominal reminds us that this concept is measured in terms of dollars and so can change because of changes in the value of the dollar. Income as measured by an index of real goods and services is called *real income*. *Price level* is used for the average level of prices. The units in which real income and the price level are measured can be chosen in a completely arbitrary manner so long as they correspond. The most convenient unit for measuring real income is in terms of the average amount of goods and services which could be bought with $1 in a selected base year, or *base-year dollars*, denoted by R$. The selection of a base year is completely arbitrary and only serves to provide a fixed standard for comparing the relative amounts of real income in different years. We have been using year 0 in our example as such a base for comparison. Base-year dollars are also referred to as dollars of constant purchasing power or just constant dollars. The price level for any year is measured consistently as the number of current dollars which it takes to buy the real goods and services which could have been bought with $1 in the base year— current dollars per base-year dollar. The product of real income measured in base-year dollars and the price level measured in current dollars per base-year dollar will indeed be equal to nominal income measured in current dollars.

Let us return to our example and use year 0 as our base year. It will be convenient to use a subscript to denote the value of a variable for the particular year indicated. Thus Y_0 is nominal income in year 0. It is obvious that Y_0 is $4,500, y_0 is R$4,500, and P_0 is $1/R$. This must follow from the definition of base-year dollars as the average amount of goods and services which could be bought with $1 in the base year. In year 1, prices are unchanged so P_1 is $1/R$. Nominal income was computed as $4,950. Real income is easily computed as Y_1/P_1 or R$4,950. As noted previously, real income is thus 10 percent higher in year 1 than in year 0. In year 2, all prices are 10 percent higher so P_2 is $1.10/R$. Dividing nominal income by the price level gives real income y_2 of R$4,500, the same as base-year real income. These examples are very straightforward because only prices change or only output changes. In year 3, all prices are 15 percent higher than in the base year ($P_3 = $1.15/R$), and all quantities are 5 percent higher than in the base year

$$y_3 = 1.05 \times R\$4,500 = R\$4,725$$

The value of nominal income Y_3 computed in Table 3.1 (by summing the values of quantities times current prices) is $5,433.75. This is exactly equal to $y_3 P_3$

($R\$4,725 \times \$1.15/R\$$).[1] So long as *all* prices or *all* quantities are proportional to those of the base year, there is no difficulty in computing the values of P and y. P is the proportional increase in prices and y is the proportional increase in quantities times base-year nominal income.

In a dynamic economy, different prices and different quantities normally change at different rates to reflect the changes in individual conditions of supply and demand. If prices and quantities did not change relative to each other, there would be no problem in measuring real income or the price level, since there would be in effect just one commodity with a single price and quantity. In fact the changes from year 0 to year 4 are more representative of the sort of changes that are observed in any real economy. Some prices go up and some go down. Some quantities go up, some go down. There are two main approaches to dividing such changes into changes in real income and the price level: (1) Compute real income by applying base-year prices to the quantities actually produced. The price level is obtained by dividing nominal income by real income. (2) Compute the price level as the cost at current prices of the base-year quantities divided by the cost of those quantities in the base year. Real income is obtained by dividing nominal income by the price level.[2]

The first approach is actually used by U.S. national income accountants to compute real income. The procedure is illustrated by the line in Table 3.1 labeled 4a. This computes what the nominal income would have been if the same amounts were produced but sold at base-year prices for each commodity. This amount $R\$4,750.00$ is a measure of real income in terms of the actual prices which existed in the base year. The price level is implicit in the values of nominal income and real income so P_4 is $\$4,950/R\$4,750$ or about $\$1.042/R\$$.

The second approach is used to compute many price indices such as the wholesale price index and consumer price index. Line 4b computes the amount which it would cost at year 4 prices to purchase what was actually bought in year 0 for a total cost of $\$4,500$. The price level is the ratio of these amounts $\$4,700/R\$4,500$ or about $\$1.044/R\$$. The corresponding value of real income is

---

[1] Nominal income increases by 20.75 percent here since $(\$5,433.75 - \$4,500.00)/\$4,500.00 = 0.2075$. This exceeds the sum of the percentage increases in the price level and real income because the increase in real income is valued at increased prices. Note however that $1.15 \times 1.05 = 1.2075$.

[2] The price index implied by the first approach is called the *Paasche index*. If P_{ij} and q_{ij} are the price and quantity, respectively, of good i in year j, the Paasche index for year j is

$$P_j = \frac{P_{1j}q_{1j} + P_{2j}q_{2j} + \cdots + P_{nj}q_{nj}}{P_{10}q_{1j} + P_{20}q_{2j} + \cdots + P_{n0}q_{nj}}$$

The price index computed by the second approach is called the *Laspeyres index*. The Laspeyres index for year j is

$$P_j = \frac{P_{1j}q_{10} + P_{2j}q_{20} + \cdots + P_{nj}q_{n0}}{P_{10}q_{10} + P_{20}q_{20} + \cdots + P_{n0}q_{n0}}$$

An examination of the formulas will show that the Paasche index weights prices by the quantities purchased in the current year, while the Laspeyres index weights prices by the quantities purchased in the base year. The microeconomic analysis of alternative price indices is the subject of nearly any intermediate microeconomics text and need not concern us here.

nominal income divided by the price level $4,950/($1.044/R$) or about R$4,739.36. This approach computes the average level of prices relative to the base year by using base-year quantities as weights. The first approach computes the average level of output relative to the base year by using base-year prices as weights.

The two approaches normally do not give very different results. Here real income is estimated to increase from year 0 to year 4 by 5.55 percent with the first method of estimation and by 5.32 percent with the second method. The corresponding increases in the price level are 4.2 percent versus 4.4 percent. More elaborate approaches to averaging price and quantity changes are possible, but not in wide use.

THE IMPLICIT PRICE DEFLATOR FOR GROSS NATIONAL PRODUCT

The most readily available estimate of the overall price level is the *implicit deflator for gross national product* or *GNP deflator*.[3] It is so named because it is implicit in Department of Commerce estimates of nominal GNP and real GNP; these are constructed as nearly as possible by the first method of using base-year prices and current quantities. Since it is impossible to actually use base-year prices for the millions of commodities which are produced, real GNP is estimated by using price indices estimated by using the second approach for very closely related commodities, such as different kinds of wheat or different kinds of automobiles. The nominal value of each narrow commodity group is divided by the price index for that commodity group to get a real value for the commodity group. These are then summed to obtain real GNP. Since changes in relative prices within commodity groups are very small compared to changes in relative prices among commodity groups, this closely approximates the use of base-year prices for each individual commodity. Deflator is an alternative term for price index because dividing nominal income by a price index removes the effects of inflation from nominal income or *deflates* nominal income.

An NNP deflator also exists but is published only irregularly because the Department of Commerce emphasizes the larger concept of GNP. The differences between the two deflators are normally negligible.

CONSUMER PRICE INDEX

The *consumer price index* for all urban consumers (CPI) is a measure of the average level of prices for commodities purchased by urban consumers. Urban consumers constitute about 80 percent of the civilian population. The CPI is

---

[3] The GNP deflator—like most price indices—is usually published in percentage points. The base-year GNP deflator is thus 100 percent and a price level of 1.1 is recorded as 110. The current base year used in the national income and product accounts is 1972.

based on weighting current prices by the average quantities of goods and services purchased by all urban consumers in the base year (currently 1967) and dividing this sum by the cost of those quantities in the base year. The actual quantities used are based on extensive budget surveys carried out in the base year. The approximately 400 most important commodities are sampled monthly by employees of the Bureau of Labor Statistics, which computes and publishes the CPI.

Until recently, the CPI was based on weighting prices by purchases of "moderate income, urban families"—who were defined to make up about half the urban population. This concept is still reported as the "consumer price index for urban wage earners and clerical workers." It should not be confused with the basic CPI.

The CPI is properly used to evaluate the real command of urban families over the goods and services which they purchase. Some commodities are over-represented and others underrepresented from the point of view of all consumers' command over goods and services from a given nominal income.[4]

The CPI is not of particular value in macroeconomic analysis. Its main value arises from the fact that it is available at monthly intervals while the implicit price deflators—like the national income accounts from which they are derived—are available only quarterly. The CPI can be used as an approximate indicator of what is happening to the general level of prices in intraquarter periods.

THE WHOLESALE PRICE INDEX

The *wholesale price index* (WPI) is an index of prices charged to wholesale buyers for industrial and agricultural goods. It thus provides a measure of prices of goods (but not services) in the production and distribution chain, rather than prices to final users. For crude, manufactured, and processed goods, prices at each level of processing are included. Weights are based on relative quantities in the base year (currently 1967). The Bureau of Labor Statistics computes and publishes this index monthly.

An important limitation is that except for goods sold on organized commodity exchanges, price data are taken from list prices reported by sellers. It has been shown[5] that these reported prices vary much less than the prices actually paid after correction for changes in discounts, shipping charges, and the like. For this reason the WPI tends to understate wholesale prices in a boom and overstate them when the economic activity is down.

---

[4] An implicit price deflator for personal consumption expenditures which can serve well for this purpose is computed by the National Income Division of the Department of Commerce, however.
[5] See George J. Stigler and James K. Kindahl, *The Behavior of Industrial Prices*, New York: National Bureau of Economic Research, Inc., 1970.

DEFLATION OF NOMINAL VARIABLES

There are many macroeconomic variables which are originally measured in terms of current dollars. Any such amount is called a *nominal* amount. Important variables measured in nominal terms are private income, saving, and the money stock held by the public. To analyze the behavior of individuals and firms with respect to such variables, it is necessary to remove the effects of inflation from the data by deflating by the price level. The *real* amount x of any nominal variable X is obtained by dividing the nominal amount by the price level at the same time.

$$x \equiv \frac{X}{P} \qquad [3.2]$$

Throughout this book nominal amounts will be represented by capital letters, and real amounts will be represented by lowercase letters.

Deflation by the general price level P converts nominal amounts into base-year dollar amounts on the basis of the average price level of final goods and services. A real amount is thus measured in terms of the average real goods and services which could be purchased with or sold for $1 in the base year. This is precisely what is desired in most cases, but on occasion it will be necessary to take into account temporarily divergent movements in other important price averages such as wholesale prices and investment goods prices.

The price index P can also be used to find the current price or value of $1. The price in dollars of $1 is not very interesting—that price is always $1. The more basic price of a dollar is the real quantity of goods and services which must be sold to obtain a dollar or which can be purchased with a dollar. These goods and services are the alternative to owning a dollar. In terms of base-year dollars, this quantity is computed as $1/P$. For example, if the price level is 1.25 (that is $1.25/R\$1$), then the current value of the dollar is $R\$0.80$ since

$$\frac{\$1}{P} = \frac{\$1}{\$1.25/R\$1} = R\$0.80 \qquad [3.3]$$

This says that goods and services which cost only 80¢ in the base year now cost $1 or, alternatively, that goods and services which could be sold for only 80¢ now bring in $1. In determining the price level, this value is computed for the average basket of final goods and services actually sold. It would not be expected to hold exactly for each and every individual commodity since relative prices change in response to changing conditions of supply and demand in each market.

3.2 LABOR FORCE AND UNEMPLOYMENT

THE LABOR FORCE

The *age-eligible population* is the number of persons 16 years of age and over who are residents of the United States or serving in the armed forces overseas.[6] The age-eligible population is divided into three main components: the civilian labor force, members of the armed forces, and persons not in the labor force.

The *civilian labor force* is the number of civilians who have jobs, are looking for jobs, or are waiting to report to jobs. The *total labor force* is the civilian labor force plus the number of members of the armed services. Persons who are not in the labor force include those who are engaged in housework in their own homes, in school, retired, or disabled, and seasonal workers (during the off season), as well as those who have given up looking for jobs or are not interested in working.

The civilian labor force is divided further into the employed and the unemployed. *Employed persons* are all those who are either at work or have jobs but are not currently working. People are counted as "at work" if they did any work during the week for either pay or profit (self-employed) or worked without pay on a family farm or business for 15 hours or more. Persons with jobs but not at work are those temporarily absent from jobs because of vacation, illness, labor-management disputes, bad weather, or the like. Persons rather than jobs are counted so each person who fits any or several of the requirements is counted as one employed person even if he or she holds two jobs.

Unemployed persons are those who are not employed, were available for work during the week, and either attempted to find jobs within the past four weeks or are waiting to report to jobs after a layoff or to new jobs within 30 days. Basically, the unemployed are those available for and seeking work. This definition is based on objectively observable behavior and so is not subject to the difficulties in determining whether or not a person who is not employed "wants" to be employed. Nearly everyone would "want" to be employed at a wage of $1,000,000 per year, but the unemployed include only those who actively take steps to become employed at a wage which they think might be obtainable.

Other broader definitions of unemployment or "underemployment" can be based on the official measure of unemployment and other data if analysis of a particular problem requires it. But, as in the case of the national income and product accounts, there is much to be said for the government's computing a hard, objective estimate and leaving subjective components to other analysts.

---

[6] Children 15 years and under are considered too young to be eligible for full-time work. Persons confined to institutions are similarly excluded.

METHOD OF ESTIMATION

Unlike the national income and product accounts, there is no base of income tax or similar reports which can be used to estimate the total labor force and its components, with the exception of membership of the armed forces. Instead, a survey of about 50,000 households is conducted for the Bureau of Labor Statistics for one week each month. Well-trained interviewers ask questions designed to classify all members of the household 16 years of age and over according to the strict definitions of employed, unemployed, or not in the labor force.

The survey estimates are by no means perfect but do closely approximate the totals that would be obtained from a complete monthly census of all American households. The Bureau of Labor Statistics also uses the survey data to estimate the number employed and unemployed classified by sex, age, color, marital status, occupation, and other characteristics, and by combinations of these characteristics. The reliability of these estimates deteriorates as their proportion of the total labor force decreases, however. This is true because if there are relatively few individuals with the specified characteristics in the survey sample, there is less likelihood that individual peculiarities of the households actually selected will average out.

THE UNEMPLOYMENT RATE

The *unemployment rate* is computed by dividing the total number of unemployed by the civilian labor force. The unemployment rate estimates the fraction without jobs of all those who desire jobs at a wage that they believe obtainable in the market. This fraction—often quoted in percentage points—is widely publicized and figures prominently in political discussions of the state of the economy.

Unemployment rates are also computed for subgroups as classified by characteristics. The unemployment rate, the white unemployment rate, and even the white male unemployment rate are well estimated by the sample in the sense that over 95 percent of the time the estimates will be within 0.2 or 0.3 percentage points of the actual unemployment rates that would be computed by a complete census of the population. For groups which make up a smaller fraction of the total labor force, a quite substantial margin of error must be allowed. For white females, this margin—using the 95 percent criterion—is currently about 0.3–0.5 percentage points. For a group as small as nonwhite teenagers, the unemployment rate computed currently has a margin of error lying between 4 and 6 percentage points. This means that a much smaller change in the estimated total unemployment rate provides convincing evidence of a change in the true total unemployment rate than would be required for the teenage nonwhite unemployment rate. Thus a change in an unemployment rate which would be very important if it were true must be classified as "statistically insignificant" if it can be reasonably attributed to the peculiarities of the particular samples chosen.[7]

The welfare meaning of the unemployment rate—like the total number unemployed—is quite ambiguous. There are some senses in which it is an overestimate of unused human resources and others in which it is an underestimate. These arguments are much more important—or at least selectively useful—in the political sphere than for macroeconomic analysis. For macroeconomists, the unemployment rate is a useful index with a somewhat arbitrary normal level. The relative size of (statistically significant) deviations of the unemployment rate from this normal level is all that is required.

3.3 MONEY

MONEY AS A PARTICULAR KIND OF ASSET

The term money is used in everyday language in three different ways: income (as, "He makes a lot of money."), wealth ("They have a lot of money."), and a particular type of asset ("She has lots of money in her pocket."). In economics, the term money is used *only* in the sense of a particular type of asset. An *asset* is a form in which wealth is held, such as money, government bonds, or various corporate securities. This means that one can have constant income and wealth, yet increase one's holdings of money by selling some other assets.

Money is defined as those forms of wealth which are in fact generally used to make ultimate payment for goods, services, and debts. Not all forms of money will be acceptable for all transactions: Try to buy a package of gum with a $500 bill.[8] But each form of money must be used in making a wide variety of payments. The precise operational definition used to measure money depends on what actually is used to make payments. At different places and times, money has been gold, seashells, corn, cigarettes, stones, and many other transferable objects.

In the United States today, everyone would agree that currency and coin issued by the federal government should be counted as money. The vast majority of payments, however, are made by transferring deposit claims against commercial banks.[9] A check is a legal order by a depositor to his bank to transfer all his rights in a certain amount of his deposit to the payee of the check. The check itself is not money but merely an instruction to make an ultimate payment by transferring deposit claims. These deposit claims against commercial banks are clearly money also. Deposit claims or *deposits* are a

---

[7] A more complete discussion of these issues is found in Geoffrey H. Moore, On the "Statistical Significance" of Changes in Employment and Unemployment, *Statistical Reporter*, no. 73–9, pp. 137–139, Mar. 1973.

[8] This experiment provides a great excuse to write home for more money.

[9] A commercial bank is a bank which can issue deposits transferable by check.

liability (legal obligation) of the bank to pay to the depositor a certain amount of currency and coin. It is often much easier to transfer these promises than actual currency and coin, so bank deposits have become money also.

It is not clear exactly which bank deposits should be counted as money, however. *Demand deposits* are payable on demand and transferable by check. *Time deposits* are payable only a certain time after notice or on a fixed date and cannot be transferred by check. The actual deposits which are transferred in making payments are thus always demand deposits. On this basis, many economists argue that only demand deposits should be counted as money. Other economists raise a question of the actual as opposed to legal usage of time deposits. With certain exceptions, time deposits have been in fact generally payable on demand and until 1933 were transferable by check. The Banking Acts of 1933 and 1935 attempted to establish a buyers' cartel price of zero by prohibiting payment of interest on demand deposits. As is the usual case with cartels, enforcement quickly breaks down because each member has an incentive to cheat on his fellows—here, by secretly paying a bit more than the cartel price and attracting more profitable deposits. The details will be discussed shortly, but one way of secretly paying interest on demand deposits is to call them time deposits. It is indeed the case that passbook savers do not need to give the required 30- to 90-day notice to obtain currency or to exchange time deposit claims for demand deposit claims. Two recent changes have made it simpler to use time deposits as means of payment: (1) On telephone order, banks can now transfer claims between demand and time deposits so that only a small balance is ever classified as a demand deposit, and the remainder earns interest as a time deposit. (2) Banks in a few states are permitted to offer time deposits subject to "negotiable orders of withdrawal" which have the same effect as checks. If time deposits in commercial banks thus actually are part of the deposits used to make payments, they are money despite the legal fictions of notice for payment and the like. There are clearly some difficult issues of fact here that have not yet been satisfactorily resolved.

There are two main, competing operational measures of the money supply. The *narrow money supply* (universally known as M_1) is the sum of currency, coin, and demand deposits held by the nonbank public. The nonbank public excludes the federal government and commercial banks but includes households, firms, foreigners, states, and local governments. The federal government is excluded because its power to issue new money makes its recorded holdings an accounting artifact without any influence on its behavior. Commercial bank holdings of demand deposits, coin, and currency are excluded to prevent double-counting since these assets support their deposits. The *broad money supply* (M_2) is equal to M_1 plus time deposits at commercial banks except for negotiable certificates of deposit of $100,000 or more ("large CDs"). The exclusion of large CDs is made on the grounds that for these time deposits, the maturity date is actually enforced. There are clearly other time deposits for which legal notice or maturity is enforced by banks, but there is no way to exclude them on the basis of current data.

There are two logically acceptable operational definitions of the U.S. money stock—M_1 and M_2. Probably M_1 is too narrow because it excludes deposits which are in fact used for making payments. However, M_2 probably includes some deposits which are not used for making payments. Lack of data prevents a more refined intermediate concept. The evidence as to which available concept seems to work better in analyzing macroeconomic behavior is still unsettled. The issue is not very important for the purposes of this book because the two data series behave very similarly.[10] When it is necessary to give an empirical definition of money, only M_1 will normally be used for convenience.

THE MONEY SUPPLY PROCESS

The United States presently is on a *fiat standard* in which money consists of pieces of paper and rights to pieces of paper. Formerly the United States was, as some other countries now are, on a *commodity standard* in which money consists of a physical commodity, such as gold, or rights to a certain number of ounces of that commodity. The Federal Reserve System, which issues nearly all money issued by the government, will, in exchange for a $5 bill, issue a new $5 bill, five $1 bills, or some token coins,[11] but does not offer any physical commodity. American money is valuable to a person only because other people will accept it in exchange for valuable goods, and not because of any intrinsic value in and of itself. This is largely true of commodity monies also, but is less obvious because the value of the commodity in nonmonetary uses—such as gold used to make jewelry—will adjust to equal the value in monetary uses. Only if monetary uses are small relative to nonmonetary uses (including monetary uses in other countries) will the value of the money be little affected by the country's demand for money.

The U.S. money supply rests upon the *base money* issued by the federal government. Government-issued money is also called *high-powered money* for reasons which will shortly be obvious. The main issuer of base money is the U.S. central bank, the *Federal Reserve System*. The Federal Reserve System—popularly called the *Fed*—is a quasi-independent agency of the legislative branch of government, which is charged with determining and carrying out monetary policy.[12] Base money is currency, coins, and deposits at the Fed. Deposits at the Fed are owned by commercial banks and are transferable

---

[10] This probably explains why the question is unsettled. The two series are so similar that there are few cases of different predictions to be analyzed statistically.

[11] Token coins are coins whose value as money much exceeds the value of the metal which they contain.

[12] For historical reasons, the Fed formally has commercial banks as stockholders ("members") but the usual prerequisites of ownership such as rights to residual income (profits) and selection of top management are all vested in the government. The Federal Reserve Act of 1913 established an elaborate facade to conceal the fact that it created a central bank which was an unpopular concept at the time.

among the Fed's depositors (members) or payable in currency on demand. In this way, the Fed acts as a "banker's bank."

In a fractional reserve banking system such as exists in the United States, bankers normally hold a small fraction of the value of their deposits as reserves of base money. The remainder of the value of deposits is lent out to earn interest. Banks need hold only a small fraction of their deposits as reserves because demands for payment in base money will be approximately offset by receipts of base money. Net payments of base money are made only to the extent that total deposits decrease. When the receipts and payments of all the depositors of a bank are added together, the net change will normally be small relative to total deposits. Further, much bank lending is in the form of purchases of government and private bonds which can be easily resold to others to replenish a depleted reserve.

Banks increase the stock of money to the extent that their deposits, which are included in the money supply, exceed their reserves, which are excluded from the money supply. If banks did not exist, the stock of money would be increased by the amount of their reserves of base money but decreased by a much larger amount of deposits. This net money creation by banks equals in value their holdings of securities. Bank deposits are loans from the depositors, which are either lent to others or held as base money. Banks are sometimes called financial intermediaries because they intermediate in this way between lenders and borrowers.[13]

The money supply is often described as a multiple of base money:

$$M = \mu B \qquad\qquad [3.4]$$

This multiple μ is called the *money multiplier*. The money multiplier is increased if money creation by banks increases. This occurs in two ways: (1) If the *cash-deposit ratio* of cash held by the public to bank deposits included in the money supply falls, this makes more reserves of high-powered money available to banks. They then expand their lending and money creation in proportion. (2) If the *reserve-deposit ratio* of bank reserves to bank deposits included in the money supply falls, this means that banks are creating more money from a given amount of reserves. Elaborate models of the money multiplier are analyzed in money and banking texts, but it is sufficient for our purposes to note that the money multiplier is a decreasing function of both the cash-deposit ratio and the reserve-deposit ratio.[14]

Changes in the money supply occur because of changes in base money B, in the money multiplier μ, or in both. The money multiplier can change only if the cash-deposit or reserve-deposit ratios change. The cash-deposit ratio is

---

[13] There are many other types of financial intermediaries, but claims against them are not used as money.

[14] That is, the money multiplier moves in the opposite direction when either ratio changes. See Sec. M.2 of the Mathematical Appendix for a review of functions.

normally quite stable, aside from small seasonal fluctuations, and moves only with a gradual trend.[15] Nor is the reserve-deposit ratio normally the source of more than gradual changes in the money multiplier. This ratio is affected by changes in the ratio of demand to time deposits, since smaller reserves are held against the latter than the former; but these changes too occur gradually. The main source of changes in the reserve-deposit ratio is the Fed, which sets the minimum required reserve ratios for various types of bank deposits. A change in required reserve ratios is a very crude policy tool and used only infrequently. Unless there are changes in the Fed's policy, the money multiplier will normally change only gradually. As a result, the control by the Fed of the monetary base is essentially the same thing as control of the money supply.

The Fed has the authority to decide how much money is created by the federal government. For a given government deficit, this determines net government borrowing.[16] New federal, state, and local bonds are in fact issued for the entire amount of the deficit (or retired if there is surplus). The Fed then buys back securities with newly created base money (or sells more securities to destroy base money). Net government borrowing is thus the deficit less base-money creation. The Fed deals primarily in U.S. Treasury securities, but some promissory notes of bankers and international reserve assets (foreign government securities and currencies and gold)[17] are bought and sold. If the Fed lends to a banker or foreign government, *net* government borrowing is decreased just as if the Fed had bought a U.S. Treasury bond.

By using its power to create and destroy the base of the money supply process, the Fed determines the amount of the U.S. money supply. Although this has not always been so—for example, the Fed did not even begin operations until 1914—it is now true.

THE REAL QUANTITY OF MONEY

The measures of money discussed so far are all derived by totaling the value in dollars of a particular class of assets. Since these are current dollar amounts, they are measures of the nominal quantity of money. It is often useful to look instead at the quantity of money in terms of the real goods and services which could be exchanged for it. This *real quantity of money m* is obtained by deflating the nominal quantity of money M by the price level P

$$m = \frac{M}{P}$$ [3.5]

---

[15] A notable exception used to occur during banking panics when people would want to reduce bank deposits because of fear that many banks would become bankrupt. This is analyzed in Chap. 8.
[16] Recall that the government deficit $G - T$ is equal to government borrowing plus government money creation.
[17] Details of transactions in international reserve assets are discussed in Chap. 9.

This measures the quantity of money in terms of base-year dollars, the average amount of final goods and services which could be bought with $1 in the base year.

INTEREST PAYMENTS ON BANK DEPOSITS

Bankers' associations were successful in inserting into the Banking Acts of 1933 and 1935 provisions establishing a cartel pricing scheme for bank deposits. Interest payments on demand deposits were entirely prohibited and the Fed was given authority to establish maximum interest rates on time deposits. Enforcement of the cartel was to be carried out by the Fed and other banking regulatory agencies.[18]

Cartel agreements break down rapidly whenever there are more than a few cartel members. Each individual firm attempts to attract more customers by offering covert price concessions. Bankers cannot pay interest on deposits in a way that the cartel enforcers (here, government bank examiners) will detect and punish. So they use indirect payments such as free services, reduced rates on loans, and so forth. They also find ways to classify as time deposits what are for all intents and purposes demand deposits. In the end no bank attracts business from its competitors, and the price is driven to its competitive level. Each banker bewails the fact that his or her fellow cartel members are such "cheats" and "chiselers" to bring this about.

This competitive process is not perfect, especially for small depositors in small, one-bank towns, but for the bulk of deposits it works out rather well. Nevertheless, there are undeniably some real costs involved in such evasions which could be eliminated by repeal of the cartel legislation. Similar results apply for time deposits whenever the Fed sets the maximum explicit interest rate payable on time deposits below the competitive level.

As can be easily imagined, there are no official data gathered on the true interest rates paid on demand deposits nor on time deposits when the maximum rate is below the competitive rate. Some estimates are implicit in the national income and product accounts.[19] Others have been made by surveying banks,[20] or estimating the competitive equilibrium interest rate.[21] Each of these techniques has its limitations, so that none can be considered generally satisfactory.

---

[18] Needless to say, like all cartels enforced by government regulation, this scheme was sold as being in the public interest to eliminate "unsound, ruinous competition."

[19] See p. 28.

[20] Robert J. Barro and Anthony M. Santomero, Household Money Holdings and the Demand Deposit Rate, *Journal of Money, Credit, and Banking*, 4: 397–413, May 1972.

[21] Benjamin Klein, Competitive Interest Payments on Bank Deposits and the Long-Run Demand for Money, *American Economic Review*, 64: 931–949, Dec. 1974; and Michael R. Darby, The Allocation of Transitory Income Among Consumer Assets, *American Economic Review*, 62: 928–941, Dec. 1972.

3.4 BUSINESS FLUCTUATIONS

INTRODUCTION

One of the main reasons for studying macroeconomics is that there are times when just about everything seems to go wrong. Real income drops quarter after quarter and so does employment. About the only thing that seems to go up is the unemployment rate. This general reversal of the normal growth of the economy is called a *contraction* or more popularly a *recession*. A particularly severe contraction is known as a *depression*. The more usual case of general growth in economic activity is called an *expansion*.

The National Bureau of Economic Research (NBER) is an independent research organization which has pioneered much of the basic collection and analysis of data on business fluctuations. The NBER found it useful to establish consistent dates for expansions and contractions so that the cyclical behavior of the economy could be consistently analyzed. These dates have been universally accepted and it is the NBER—not some government agency—that "officially" declares the beginning and end of a recession.

Business fluctuations have been traditionally called *business cycles*. This name arose because at times there appears to be a regular alternation of expansions and contractions. Nevertheless this pattern of expansion and contraction has never exhibited the regularity of timing necessary for a true "cycle." For example, complete "cycles" of a contraction and expansion have been as short as $1\frac{1}{2}$ years and as long as over 8 years. Nor are business fluctuations self-generating, with each phase caused by the preceding phase. Nevertheless the use of "cycle" for "fluctuation" is well established in the macroeconomic literature and will be used similarly here.

THE NBER'S CLASSIFICATION METHOD

The NBER chronology of expansions and contractions consists of a list of the months and years in which an expansion ends and a contraction begins and in which a contraction ends and an expansion begins. An expansion and the successive contraction is called a *reference cycle*. The month in which an expansion ends and a contraction begins is called a *reference cycle peak*. The month in which a contraction ends and an expansion begins is called a *reference cycle trough*.

Whether the economy is in an expansion or a contraction, some specific measures of economic activity will increase and others will decrease. The NBER has chosen as reference cycle peaks those months in which the majority of measures turn from increasing to decreasing, and vice versa for reference cycle troughs. It is of course true that these many individual measures will normally change direction only when real income changes direction. Using the consensus of individual measures instead of examining only real income is done for two reasons: (1) Real income is available only quarterly, and the use of measures available monthly permits finer dating. (2) The use of many measures obviates the possibility that disaster in one or two industries (for example, a crop failure), which reduces total real income, will be counted as a reference cycle unless its effects spread throughout the economy. Despite this careful distinction, it is true that real income has never declined for *more* than one quarter without fulfilling this criterion for a contraction nor increased without fulfilling the criterion for the onset of an expansion.[22]

Figure 3.1 illustrates the business cycle chronology for the postwar period. This figure graphs real income, the unemployment rate, and an index of industrial production. The periods of contraction are shaded. Note that the scale of the unemployment rate is inverted since an increase in the unemployment rate indicates a decrease in economic activity. Thus expansions are characterized by increasing real income and industrial production and falling or low unemployment rates. Contractions are characterized by decreasing real income and

---

[22] Excluded here are spurious falls in reported real income when the official price index rises rapidly due to the removal of price controls. The catch-up of the official index with economic reality caused a drop in reported real income of almost 13 percent from 1945 to 1947, a period classified as an expansion by the NBER. A similar aberration in the official data occurred in the first half of 1974. See Chap. 13 for details.

Figure 3.1 Business cycles as reflected in real GNP, industrial production and unemployment.
NBER reference cycle peaks are indicated by a *P* and troughs by a *T*. Contractions (shaded) are marked by falling real GNP and industrial production and by rising unemployment rates (scale inverted). Expansions have generally rising real income and industrial production and falling or low unemployment rates.

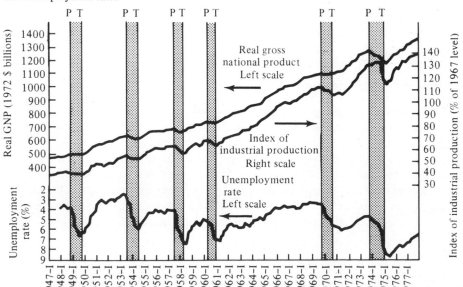

industrial production and rising or high unemployment rates. Many other series could be illustrated with similar results, but these adequately suggest why macroeconomists are interested in explaining business fluctuations.

GROWTH FLUCTUATIONS

The criterion that the majority of indicators of economic activity be decreasing during a contraction conceals fluctuations which are similar in type but less severe than the officially recognized contractions. This concealment occurs because in the United States economic activity normally grows. Slower-than-normal growth reduces real income and employment relative to what they would have been, and the unemployment rate rises, as for example during the latter part of 1959 and again during 1962.

A related difficulty with the NBER's reference cycle approach is that the economy will be characterized by slower-than-normal growth before a peak and after a trough. So if contractions were measured by less-than-normal growth, they would be somewhat longer and expansions would be somewhat shorter than on the NBER definition.

When business fluctuations are analyzed in Part Three of this book, it will appear that comparison of economic activity with its normal or trend level is the more useful approach. At the NBER, Ilse Mintz and others have experimented with an alternative chronology based on growth fluctuations. Nevertheless, the standard NBER chronology doubtless still serves as a useful frame of reference for discussing both the broad and detailed features of business fluctuations.

3.5 INTEREST AND WEALTH

STOCKS AND FLOWS

Macroeconomic aggregates are often referred to as either *stocks* or *flows*. A *flow variable* is an amount measured per unit of time. In this book, the standard unit of time is the year, so flows will be measured per year (per annum). An example of a flow would be a wage of $10,400 per year, regardless of whether it was paid as $200 per week or $866.67 per month.[23] A *stock* is an amount which can be measured without regard to the passage of time. For example, at a certain instant in October 1977 the civilian labor force was 98,100,003 people. The value of a stock at a particular time could be calculated by totaling up the

---

[23] Note that ($200/week) × (52 weeks/year) = $10,400/year and that ($866.67/month) × (12 months/year) = $10,400/year.

numbers or amounts of the things then existing which make up the stock. Flows occur over time and can be observed only by measurements made over a period of time. Income and expenditure concepts are particularly important examples of flows.

National income accountants measure income over quarterly intervals, but report income and its components at annual rates. This is equivalent to observing that someone drove 10 miles in 15 minutes or drove at a speed of 40 miles *per hour*. Income is reported in per annum terms by multiplying the total purchases of final goods and services made in the quarter by four. This converts the quarterly totals into amounts easily comparable with annual totals, or any other periods converted into annual rates.

Flows are computed by dividing periodic totals by the period expressed in years. Shorter observations reduce both numerator and denominator proportionally; so shorter periods neither increase or decrease flows expressed at annual rates. It simplifies many problems to be able to discuss flow variables at a specific point in time rather than over a period of time. This would be roughly the same thing as the current reading on the speedometer in the automobile example. Formally, a flow measured at an instant of time is the ratio of a periodic total to the corresponding arbitrarily small length of time.[24]

The income actually measured over a quarter is simply the average of all these instantaneous measures of incomes. In the same way, if you drive 30 minutes with the speedometer reading 10 miles per hour and 30 minutes with the speedometer reading 20 miles per hour, you will actually cover the average number of miles, 15:

$$\frac{10 \text{ miles}}{\text{hour}} \times 0.5 \text{ hour} + \frac{20 \text{ miles}}{\text{hour}} \times 0.5 \text{ hour} = 15 \text{ miles}$$

THE CONCEPT OF INTEREST

Flows of income are often derived from particular assets, which are stocks. The *interest rate* is the concept by which the income and asset are related. The interest rate on any asset can be defined as the ratio of the flow per annum of income from the asset to the value of the asset. This ratio is measured as a decimal fraction per year—such as 0.10/year, which is usually read as 10 percent per annum. The income flow may be received in money, in goods or services, or in both; it may be received continuously or left to accumulate for a while.

This concept of interest is best illustrated by a series of applications.

---

[24] A second equals 0.00000003170979 year, which is almost arbitrarily small. If NNP were $100 per second, this would be at the rate of $100/0.00000003170979 year = $3,153,600,000/year.

A SINGLE-PAYMENT LOAN

Suppose that a $1,000 loan is for 1 year at 10 percent interest, with interest and principal to be repaid at the end of the year. Then the borrower pays the lender $1,100 ($100 interest plus $1,000 principal) at the end of the year. The income flow is $100 per annum and the interest rate is this $100/year divided by $1,000, or 0.10/year as stated.

For this kind of loan, if L_0 is the amount lent, L_1 the amount of principal and interest due after 1 year, and R the interest rate, then

$$L_1 \equiv (1 + R)L_0 \qquad [3.6]$$

This formula can be used to compute the interest rate R if only L_0 and L_1 are known or to compute L_0 if only L_1 and R are known. This is particularly important for *discount bonds*, which state only that a certain amount will be paid the lender on a certain date. The borrower sells the bond at a discount to the lender. The amount which the lender pays is the amount of the loan L_0, and R is inferred from formula [3.6]. Alternatively, one might have in mind a value of R fixed by competing loans and use this plus L_1 to compute the price paid for a discount bond.

The most important example of discount bonds are *U.S. Treasury bills*. These bills are issued in a minimum denomination of $10,000 and in four different terms to maturity. The *term to maturity* (or just *maturity* for short) of a bond or other loan is the length of time to the final payment. Treasury bills have maturities of 3, 6, 9, and 12 months when they are sold by the government at a weekly auction.

Most of the Treasury bills have a maturity of 3 months. Since the interest rate is at an annual rate, formula [3.6] applies only to discount bonds with maturities of 1 year. For 3-month bills, one gets a quarter of a year's interest. Suppose for example that a $10,000, 3-month bill sold at auction for $9,756.10. Then the interest amount is $10,000.00 - $9,756.10 = $243.90. This quarter year's income is at an annual rate of $975.60 per annum since 4 × $243.90 = $975.60. So the interest rate is ($975.60/year) ÷ $9,756.10 = 0.10/year or 10 percent per annum.

These calculations can be summarized in a formula applicable for periods less than a year. Suppose that the maturity of a single-payment loan is z (in years), the loan is L_0, L_z is the amount paid at maturity, and R is the interest rate, then

$$L_z \equiv (1 + Rz)L_0 \qquad [3.7]$$

In the example of the 3-month bill, L_z was $10,000, R was 0.10/year, z was 0.25 year, and L_0 was $9,756.10. (Check: $10,000 = [1 + (0.10/year)(0.25 year)] × $9,756.10.) The formula [3.6] is a special case of [3.7] where z is 1 year.

Treasury bills can be resold readily if the need arises. The price which will be paid for the bills can be computed by [3.7], based on the remaining term to maturity and the current interest rate implicit in the discounts of bills with similar maturities.

COMPOUND INTEREST

If a person lends (deposits in) a bank $1,000 with 5 percent per annum interest paid quarterly, the bank will pay interest of $12.50 at the end of each quarter.[25] This is like a series of one-quarter single-payment loans in which $1,000 is lent, $1,012.50 repaid, and $1,000 is immediately re-lent. Nothing new is introduced if the depositor leaves the principal on deposit quarter after quarter.

Frequently depositors have the bank add each quarter's interest payments to their deposits. As a result, they earn interest on previous quarters' interest payments. If the deposits are left to acculate for a year, total interest paid will be greater than if interest were paid out quarterly, as illustrated in Example 3.1. The formula for total principal and interest due after n compoundings at intervals of z (a total period of nz) is

$$L_{nz} \equiv (1 + Rz)^n L_0 \qquad [3.8]$$

If we use this formula to compute the amount due after 1 year in Example 3.1, we will obtain

$$L_{(4)(0.25 \text{ year})} \equiv [1 + (0.05/\text{year})(0.25 \text{ year})]^4 (\$1,000)$$

$$L_{1 \text{ year}} \equiv (1.0125)^4 (\$1,000)$$

$$L_{1 \text{ year}} \approx (1.05094)(\$1,000) = \$1,050.94$$

This corresponds to the amount calculated in the example by tediously repeated use of [3.7].

Accumulation of interest on interest will be implicit in the quoted interest rates of loans compounded infrequently. As a result rates quoted on infrequently compounded loans must be a bit higher than on more frequently compounded loans to obtain the same final payment.

EXAMPLE 3.1

COMPOUND INTEREST

Suppose a particular bank paid 5 percent per annum interest, compounded quarterly. This means that at the end of each quarter year, the bank pays 1.25 percent ($\frac{1}{4}$ of 5 percent) of the balance in the account. If $1,000 is

---

[25] Computed as $(0.05/\text{year}) \times (0.25/\text{year}) \times \$1,000 = \$12.50$.

deposited on January 1, the bank pays $12.50 interest at the end of March. If the interest payment is left in the account to compound, then the bank pays $12.66 at the end of June since

$$0.0125 \times \$1{,}012.50 = \$12.66$$

If each quarter's interest is left to accumulate in the account, the interest payments at the end of September and December are $12.81 and $12.97, respectively. The computations are tabulated as

Quarter	Beginning Balance	Interest Payment	Ending Balance
1st	$1,000.00	$12.50	$1,012.50
2d	$1,012.50	$12.66	$1,025.16
3d	$1,025.16	$12.81	$1,037.97
4th	$1,037.97	$12.97	$1,050.94

At the end of the year, the total interest payments of $50.94 can be withdrawn leaving the principal amount of $1,000. This is equivalent to a 1-year single-payment loan paying 5.094 percent per annum.

CONTINUOUS COMPOUNDING

This ambiguity in interest rates can be resolved by converting all interest rates to equivalent *continuously compounded* interest rates. Interest rates are said to be continuously compounded when only an arbitrarily small period of time elapses between successive compoundings.[26] After a period of time z at a continuously compounded interest rate R, the amount of principal and interest due on an initial loan of L_0 is

$$L_z \equiv e^{Rz} L_0 \qquad\qquad [3.9]$$

where e is the base of natural logarithms. Since $e^{0.0488}$ is 1.05, a continuously compounded interest rate of 4.88 percent per annum is equivalent to an annually compounded interest rate of 5 percent per annum.[27] In later chapters,

---

[26] It is obtained mathematically by decreasing z and increasing n in [3.8] so that their product nz is constant and solving for R as z becomes arbitrarily small. This is the source of the formula [3.9].

[27] If R_z is the interest rate for loans compounded each successive period of length z, and R is the equivalent continuously compounded interest rate, they are related by the formulas

$$R_z \equiv \frac{1}{z}(e^R - 1) \qquad R \equiv \frac{1}{z} \log[1 + (R_z)(z)]$$

any interest rates will normally be measured in continuously compounded terms.

The continuously compounded interest rate is used on many savings accounts. It is simple to compute with a calculator and avoids messy approximations when a deposit and accumulated interest is withdrawn after an irregular length of time. This interest rate corresponds to the ratio of the income flow at an instant of time to the asset which yields the flow. Since many assets—factors of production—yield income in the form of a continuous flow of services, the continuously compounded interest rate will prove convenient.

PRESENT VALUES

Identity [3.8] or [3.9] is frequently used to compute the value of an asset now (L_0), which would correspond to a particular future payment and given interest rate. This value now is called the *present value* of the future payment. If the future payment L_z is received after a period of z, and R is continuously compounded, then the present value is

$$L_0 \equiv \frac{L_z}{e^{Rz}} \equiv e^{-Rz}L_z \qquad [3.10]$$

This amount L_0 could be borrowed now and paid back (with accumulated interest) by an amount L_z at the end of a period of z. Alternatively, one would have to lend L_0 now in order to have an amount equal to L_z at the end of a period of z. Dividing an amount z years in the future by e^{Rz} is called *discounting* the amount to obtain the present value.

A MULTIPLE-PAYMENT LOAN

Many assets are claims to a number of payments made at future dates. Important examples are mortgages and long-term bonds. Most such contracts specify some n payments at intervals of z. The total present value of these payments is the sum of the present values of the individual payments.

Suppose for simplicity that a bond promises to pay a "coupon amount" $\bar{L}$ at the end of each of the next n years plus a "face value" of L_n at the end of n years. This corresponds to a typical long-term bond.[28] If we use R here as the interest rate for annual interest payments, then the present value of this bond is

$$L_0 \equiv \frac{\bar{L}}{1+R} + \frac{\bar{L}}{(1+R)^2} + \cdots + \frac{\bar{L}}{(1+R)^n} + \frac{L_n}{(1+R)^n} \qquad [3.11]$$

---

[28] Actually, bond coupons are usually paid semiannually, but this complicates the algebra without affecting the conclusions.

Long-term bonds are usually issued so that their sales price L_0 will equal the face amount L_n. This is done by setting the coupon amounts as $R \cdot L_n$, where R is determined by competing bonds. However, once the bonds are sold, the coupon amounts are fixed. If interest rates on competing bonds increase, a higher R will be used in computing the present values so that the holder of the bonds can sell them only at reduced prices. If interest rates fall, however, the prices of existing bonds will rise. Another name for the interest rate computed by solving [3.11], given the bonds' current price and future payments, is the *yield to maturity*.

PRESENT VALUE OF A PERPETUITY

Some bonds and other forms of wealth yield a constant flow of income forever. For example, consols (short for "consolidated annuities") of the British government promise to pay a certain number of pounds each year forever. Such an asset is termed a *perpetuity*. A perpetuity yielding $\bar{L}$ at the end of each year has the present value

$$L_0 \equiv \sum_{j=1}^{\infty} \frac{\bar{L}}{(1+R)^j} \equiv \bar{L} \sum_{j=1}^{\infty} \frac{1}{(1+R)^j} \qquad [3.12]$$

The infinite sum on the right side of [3.12] equals $1/R$. So the present value of a perpetuity yielding $\bar{L}$ per annum is

$$L_0 \equiv \frac{\bar{L}}{R} \qquad [3.13]$$

If the annually compounded interest rate is 5 percent per annum, a perpetuity paying $100 per year would sell for $100/0.05 = $2,000. It should be noted that [3.13] holds as well for a continuous stream of income at the annual rate $\bar{L}$ if R is interpreted as the continuously compounded interest rate.

AN INDEX OF INTEREST RATES?

There are no broad indices of interest rates. The reason is that financial markets are so closely intertwined and so competitive that a movement in any interest rate is equally reflected in all. So for most purposes, it serves adequately to use the interest rate on 3-month Treasury bills or long-term government bonds as "the" interest rate. We will see, however, that there are certain situations which shift interest rates relative to each other. In these cases it may be important to distinguish between interest rates on various types of assets.

THE WEALTH CONSTRAINT

Individuals make decisions on the basis of the resources available and opportunities open to achieve their basic goals. The opportunities are alternative uses of the total available resources—purchases of clothes substitute at market prices for purchases of food or movie tickets; more total consumption now can be exchanged for less consumption next year. An increase in the total resources available to all individuals will have predictable effects on the quantities of goods and services purchased and on many other aspects of aggregate consumer behavior.

The total resources available to support current and future spending by consumers is called *wealth*. It is desirable to measure nominal wealth in terms of total current dollar value or real wealth in base-year dollars (command over real goods and services). Private wealth is the net present value of all present and future private claims to receive income, less the net present value of private liabilities. After debts are cancelled, private wealth consists of the present value of the factors of production. Whether for the economy as a whole or for a single individual, it is very difficult to measure wealth. Only a fraction of the nonhuman wealth is traded on well-organized markets, such as the New York Stock Exchange, from which the current value can be computed. Worse, human wealth (the present value of an individual's rights in his or her expected future income) cannot be traded at all, and human wealth is about three-quarters of total wealth. As a result, direct estimates of wealth are insufficiently precise for general use in macroeconomic analysis.

PERMANENT INCOME

An alternative concept of the total resources available for present and future consumption is the real private income normally expected from current real wealth. This amount is called *permanent income*. Actual private income will fluctuate around permanent income, but it indicates the average income corresponding to the current real wealth. If it is assumed that the ratio of permanent income to real wealth is a constant r_P, it is statistically possible to infer permanent income and wealth from observed private income and consumer expenditure data.[29] The assumed constancy of r_P appears to work well empirically; Chap. 5 suggests why it should. Since permanent income and wealth are proportional to each other, they can be used almost interchangeably.

The ratio r_P is a real interest rate relating a real income flow to a real wealth stock. Analysis of the difference between nominal and real interest rates is postponed to Part Two.

---

[29] Details are found in Michael R. Darby, The Permanent Income Theory of Consumption—A Restatement, *Quarterly Journal of Economics*, **88**: 228–250, May 1974.

Permanent income y_P can be interpreted as the average yield from real wealth v:

$$y_P \equiv r_P v \qquad\qquad [3.14]$$

Wealth will grow over time due to saving and investment in human capital, and permanent income grows in proportion.

The actual value of real private income fluctuates around permanent income—higher at reference cycle peaks and lower at troughs. Real private income y_N is therefore divided between permanent income and these windfall gains or losses called *transitory income* y_T:

$$y_N \equiv y_P + y_T \qquad\qquad [3.15]$$

These windfalls change wealth so that it grows more rapidly than normal when transitory income is positive and more slowly when y_T is negative. Nonetheless, transitory income will be small relative to real wealth, so that fluctuations in the growth of wealth and permanent income will be small relative to fluctuations in the growth of real private income.[30]

SUMMARY

1 Nominal income as measured in current dollar values is an imperfect measure of economic activity because it confounds increases in the average output of real goods and services with increases in their average prices. Economists solve this problem by dividing nominal income into indices of real income and the price level. These indices are defined relative to an arbitrary base year.

2 Real income is measured in units of the average quantities of final goods and services which could be bought with $1 in the base year (or base-year dollars R$). The price index is measured in units of current dollars per base-year dollar.

3 The age-eligible population is divided into the civilian labor force, members of the armed services, and persons not in the labor force. A monthly survey is used to allocate people between the civilian labor force and those not in the labor force. The civilian labor force is made up of the employed (people with jobs) and the unemployed (those available for and seeking work).

4 The unemployment rate is the ratio of the number unemployed to the civilian labor force.

---

[30] If transitory income is 10 percent of permanent income over a particular year, and permanent income is 10 percent of wealth, then transitory income would add 1 percent $(0.10 \times 0.10 = 0.01)$ to wealth. Permanent income is proportional to wealth, so it too is increased by only 1 percent.

5 Money is a particular type of asset or form of wealth. Money is those assets actually used to make ultimate payment for goods, services, and debts.

6 In the United States, money is measured in two alternative ways: The narrow money supply (M_1) is currency, coin, and demand deposits held by the nonbank public. The broad money supply M_2 is M_1 plus time deposits at commercial banks, with the exception of large negotiable certificates of deposit.

7 The money supply is a multiple of the base money issued by the federal government. Base money is equal to coin and currency plus deposits at the Federal Reserve System.

8 Explicit interest payments are prohibited on demand deposits and limited on time deposits; so banks pay interest in indirect ways such as free services, reduced loan rates, and classifying part of demand deposits as interest-paying time deposits.

9 The National Bureau of Economic Research (NBER) defines a contraction as a period of time during which a majority of specific indicators of economic activity are declining. An expansion is a period in which most of these indicators are rising.

10 Expansions are characterized by rising real income and industrial production and low or declining rates of unemployment. Contractions are characterized by falling real income and industrial production and high or rising rates of unemployment.

11 Flow variables are measured per year. Stock variables are measured without reference to the passage of time.

12 The interest rate on any asset is the ratio of the flow of income from the asset to the value of the asset.

13 The present value of one or more future payments is found by discounting the payments by an amount to allow for compound interest between now and then.

14 There is a large variety of financial assets. The competitive and integrated nature of financial markets assures that interest rates move together except in special circumstances.

15 Permanent income is the amount of real private income normally expected from current real wealth. It serves as a proportional measure of real wealth.

16 Transitory fluctuations in real private income around permanent income cause relatively much smaller fluctuations in permanent income and real wealth.

CONCEPTS TO KNOW

base money	discounting
base-year dollar	expansion
deflation of nominal amounts	fiat standard

flow variable

interest rate

M_1 (narrow money supply)

M_2 (broad money supply)

money

money multiplier

permanent income

perpetuity

present value

price level

real income

stock variable

term to maturity

Treasury bills

unemployment rate

wealth

QUESTIONS AND EXERCISES

1 In an economy with only two final commodities, the following data are observed:

	Commodity 1		Commodity 2	
Year	Quantity	Price, $	Quantity	Price, $
1	1000	1.00	2000	2.00
2	1100	0.80	1900	2.25

Use year 1 as the base year. Compute nominal income, real income, and the price level for years 1 and 2 using base-year prices and current quantities to compute real income. Do the same for base-year quantities and current prices to compute the price level.

*2 (a) Complete the following table:

Year	Y	y	P
1	1000.00		1.000
2	1102.50		1.050
3	1212.75	1050.00	
4	1210.00		1.100

(b) Which year has the highest nominal income? Which year has the highest real income? Which year has the highest price level?

(c) The data listed for Y are measured in billions of dollars per year. In what units are the y data measured? The P data?

3 The wholesale price index is estimated from data on many more commodities than is the consumer price index, yet the CPI is a broader index than is the WPI. In what sense is "broader" used in this statement?

4 If the age-eligible population of 150,000,000 can be divided into 3,000,000 in the armed forces, 85,000,000 employed, 5,000,000 unemployed, and 57,000,000 not in the labor force, what is the unemployment rate?

5 Suggested adjustments to the number unemployed include subtraction of job vacancies, addition of "unemployed equivalents" for people working part-time or in different jobs from those desired, inclusion of "discouraged workers" who do not seek work only because they do not believe there are any jobs at an acceptable wage, and exclusion of those who have refused a job offer. Can you see problems of interpretation and data collection in any of these suggestions?

*6 Can a person with a $10,000 per year income have more money than a person with a $100,000 per year income? Why or why not?

7 Some economists have argued that in some sense credit card accounts (in the amount of the credit limit) are money because they are used to purchase goods and services. A credit card purchase is an exchange of goods and services for a debt (promise to pay) of the cardholder. In what sense is a credit card line of credit not general purchasing power? Does signing a credit card slip make or order an ultimate payment?

8 If a particular bank has deposits included in the money supply of $100 million and holds $14 million in reserves (deposits at the Fed plus vault cash), how much money can this bank be said to have created? What is the meaning of "created" here?

9 Suppose that the Fed raised reserve requirements so that the reserve-deposit ratio rose, other things staying the same. What would happen to the money multiplier? The nominal money supply?

10 If the interest rate on 3-month Treasury bills is quoted as 8 percent per annum, what would be the price of a $10,000 3-month bill?

11 Suppose that a machine worth R$1,000 is used to produce goods worth R$400 per year. It costs R$300 per annum for all other inputs used to produce the goods and R$40 per annum to maintain the machine in like-new condition. What interest rate is earned on the machine?

12 If $1,000 were lent for 4 years at 10 percent per annum, compounded annually, what single interest and principal payment would be due at the end of 4 years?

*13 What is the present value of $100 at the end of 1 year plus $1,100 at the end of 2 years at 10 percent per annum interest, compounded annually?

REFERENCES FOR FURTHER READING

The references to Chap. 2 also deal with the concepts discussed in Sec. 3.1.

Burger, Albert E.: *The Money Supply Process*, Belmont, Calif.: Wadsworth, 1971.

Jordan, Jerry L.: Elements of Money Stock Determination, *Federal Reserve Bank of St. Louis Review,* **51** (10): 10–19, Oct. 1969.

Mitchell, Wesley C.: *What Happens during Business Cycles: A Progress Report,* New York: NBER, 1951.

Moore, Geoffrey H.: *How Full Is Full Employment? And Other Essays on Interpreting the Unemployment Statistics,* Washington: American Enterprise Institute for Public Policy Research, 1973.

PART TWO

LONG-RUN MACROECONOMIC EQUILIBRIUM

Movements in the main macroeconomic variables can be divided into movements in their long-run equilibrium values and movements around these values. The long-run equilibrium movements determine the basic trends of the economy as it grows over time. The short-run movements around the long-run equilibrium are the stuff of business cycles.

Macroeconomic theory must explain both long-run trends and short-run fluctuations. It is easier to learn the theory in steps, however. The chapters in Part Two will concentrate on the forces which shape the long-run equilibrium of the economy. In this discussion we can temporarily leave aside the issues of economic fluctuations. Once the general trends of the economy are known, analysis of business cycles is presented in Part Three.

Macroeconomic theory is expressed by a framework or model which focuses on the main forces by leaving out much unessential detail. The model aims at explaining real income and the price level. Other important variables are initially left in the background because they can be readily inferred by movements in real income and the price level. For example, if real income is below its long-run equilibrium level, the unemployment rate will be high. These variables are studied in detail later.

The long-run equilibrium of the macroeconomy determines both the levels of variables and how they grow over time. Chapter 4 shows how the levels of real income and prices are determined by the resources, technology, institutions, and tastes of the economy. Chapter 5 considers how changes in these basic factors over time will cause growth in real income and the price level.

CHAPTER 4

THE LEVELS
OF INCOME AND PRICES

WHAT YOU WILL LEARN IN THIS CHAPTER
How the long-run equilibrium levels of real income,
labor, real wages, and real capital earnings are
mutually determined ● Investment and saving
equated by the interest rate ● The Fed determines
the nominal supply of money ● The demand for
money ● The long-run equilibrium real quantity of
money fixed by variables determined in the labor,
capital, and goods markets ● The price level
determined by the ratio of the nominal money
supply to the real money demand

4.1 INTRODUCTION

The basic variables to be explained by macroeconomic theory are real income and prices. This chapter discusses the main forces determining their levels. In the next chapter, we will see how gradual changes in the underlying factors cause growth in income and prices. In both chapters the analysis is framed in terms of an economy in long-run equilibrium. *Long-run equilibrium* refers to the position of the economy when the temporary effects of unexpected changes in macroeconomic conditions have been eliminated.[1] It is the position around which the economy fluctuates.

The factors underlying this equilibrium can be divided into two essentially separate groups: the real and the monetary. Although this division—like that between supply and demand in microeconomics—is not perfect, the exceptions are minor enough that the framework captures all the main points.

The main outline can be described simply before a more detailed study is begun. Real income—the total final goods and services produced—is determined by (1) the resources of labor and capital which actually exist, (2) the technology and institutions which govern the possible ways these resources can be combined to produce final output, and (3) tastes which influence both the

---

[1] The temporary effects of these unexpected changes are the subject of Part Three.

composition of goods actually produced and the amount of labor services made available. Market output will be the largest amount that can be produced, given the knowledge and institutions of the society and the resources made available. Total demand will just equal the total amount produced since people must either consume or save, and the interest rate on savings will equate business demand for increased capital to the amount of output not consumed. Monetary factors are negligible in the determination of real income. But one of the institutions underlying the real equilibrium of modern economies is the widespread use of money as a medium of exchange. Prices are quoted in terms of money. The ratios of the prices of individual goods are determined by the real factors, but their general level is determined by monetary factors. The price level adjusts to equate the demand for money with the amount in existence.

In this chapter and the next, government expenditure and taxation will be combined with consumer spending and income. This discussion views the government as essentially a consumer cooperative providing jointly consumed goods and apportioning the costs. Similarly, international trade is ignored as if the United States were a closed economy. These simplifications will be abandoned later to discuss the effects of changes in government spending and taxation and in international trade.

4.2 DETERMINANTS OF REAL INCOME

THE MEANING OF REAL INCOME

Recall from Sec. 3.1 that nominal income Y can be decomposed into an index of real income y and the price level P such that

$$Y \equiv yP \qquad \text{or} \qquad y \equiv \frac{Y}{P} \qquad\qquad [4.1]$$

Real income is expressed in base-year dollars ($R\$$): the average amount of real goods and services which could be bought with $1 in the base year. Real income is an aggregate measure in terms of physical units of all final goods and services produced. It also measures the command over real commodities of all income received.

Real income is a basic measure of output available for satisfying human wants, devoid of the veil of a changing price level. With rapid inflation nominal incomes and prices can double every year, but no one need be any better off for it. When the rate of inflation is negative, both nominal incomes and prices may fall year after year while real incomes steadily rise.

Analysis of the determinants of real income must be the first task of a macroeconomist. In this chapter, a detailed, cross-section analysis of a particular instant of time is presented first.

THE AGGREGATE PRODUCTION FUNCTION

Real income in an economy is determined by the amounts of labor and capital used in production and by the technology and institutions of the economy. All human inputs to the productive process are summed as labor and all produced means of production are called capital. Labor and capital are used here to refer to the flows of labor and capital services (or inputs). The terms *labor force* and *capital stock* will be used in full for the corresponding stock concepts.[2] Labor and capital—like real income—are idealized aggregate indices of the diverse types and qualities of workers on the one hand and machines, buildings, roads, inventories, and the like on the other. The technology and institutions of the society will determine how the labor and capital are combined to produce output. The relationship between the factors of production, labor l and capital k, and the output y produced in an economy at a particular time is summarized by the *aggregate production function*[3] $f(\ )$:

$$y = f(k, l) \tag{4.2}$$

Output is an increasing function of capital and labor. Increases in either or both factors of production will increase output by the amount indicated by the aggregate production function.

The production functions for individual firms which we study in microeconomics are strictly technological statements of the greatest possible amount that could be produced on the basis of the current state of knowledge. The aggregate production function of macroeconomics reflects both these technological possibilities and the further constraints on production due to government laws and regulations, monopoly powers, and other institutional restrictions. Also underlying the aggregate production function is the general composition of output as determined by the individual supply and demand relations for the various goods and services. These underlying conditions are assumed to be constant—or, later, changing over time in carefully specified ways—for our analysis.

Labor is the quality-adjusted number of man hours employed for production. This takes into account both the number of people actually employed and the fraction of time available worked by each. The adjustment for the quality of workers is extremely important since the average level of training has been rising steadily over time in the United States and many other countries. The increase in productivity due to training is said to reflect investment in the stock of human capital. *Human capital stock* is a term for our own total productive capacity. Economists use the term as a reminder that labor, like machine services, flows from a stock which has been built up by past investment. In the

---

[2] Note below, however, that capital input is in fact estimated as proportional to the capital stock.
[3] Functional notation is used to explain how one macroeconomic variable is determined by others. Functions are reviewed in Sec. M.2 of the Mathematical Appendix.

United States, the major portion of labor income—and total national income as well—can be attributed to training as opposed to the return to raw labor. The main forms of investment in human capital are education and, even more important, on-the-job training. An hour of an operating engineer's time may be ten times as productive and ten times as well paid as an hour of raw labor; so each hour of the engineer's time counts ten times as much in our index of labor input as does an hour of raw labor.

Capital, or more precisely *nonhuman capital*, is a quality-adjusted index of the machines, buildings, inventories, and other nonhuman inputs used in production. It would be desirable to have a measure of machine hours similar to the labor index so as to account for the intensity of use. However, since the intensity of capital use does not seem to have any long-run trend—in contrast to the average numbers of hours worked—economists rarely attempt such an intensity adjustment. The capital stock measures only the stock of capital goods used in market production and not those goods, such as private cars, used in direct household production which is not included in income. The capital stock as defined here does not include government-owned capital such as army bases. The value of the services of government-owned capital goods is generally not included in market income aside from its effects on the amount produced by other factors of production. The governmentally provided capital is a factor underlying the position of the aggregate production function, but is not included among the purchased factors of production. Some advanced treatments explicitly include governmentally provided factors of production in the production function. Like labor or real income, capital is an index of widely divergent sorts of things weighted by relative values.

Real income is determined, given the production function, by the amounts of capital and labor used. Therefore, to understand the determination of real income we must examine the demands for and supplies of the factors of production.

THE DEMAND FOR LABOR

The demand for labor is derived from the production function. For a given amount of capital k we can graph the amount of output which will be produced using various amounts of labor. This is done in Fig. 4.1 for k_0, where the subscript denotes a specific value of k. In the relevant range of values for labor, output increases as labor is increased but at a decreasing rate. This is summarized by the *Law of Diminishing Returns:* For fixed values of other inputs, unit increases in the variable factors of production will, at least beyond some point, cause decreasing increases in output. The increase in output per unit increase in labor is given by the slope, $(y_1 - y_0)/(l_1 - l_0)$, of the $y = f(k_0, l)$ line. Diminishing returns are illustrated in Fig. 4.1 by the decreasing slope of this line.

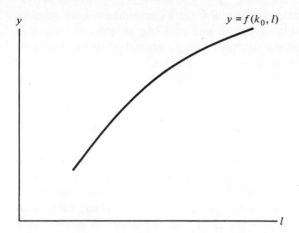

Figure 4.1 Graph of the aggregate production function for a given capital stock k_0. Output y increases with increased labor inputs l, but at a decreasing rate. The increase in output per unit.increase in labor is given by the slope of the $y = f(k_0, l)$ line for each level of labor input. This illustrates the Law of Diminishing Returns.

The increase in total output due to one more unit of labor for each amount of labor is called the marginal product of that amount of labor. Employers will desire to employ more labor whenever the *marginal product* of labor is greater than its cost in wages and less when its marginal product is less than the wage rate. Thus the quantity of labor demanded at each real wage is that for which

Figure 4.2 The demand for labor for a given capital stock k_0. Lower real wage rates w increase the quantity of labor demanded l^d. For larger capital stocks than k_0, the demand curve would be located above and to the right of the $l^d = l^d(w, k_0)$ line.

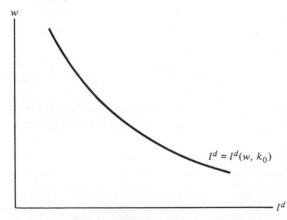

the marginal product of labor equals the real wage.[4] The demand curve relating wages and the quantity of labor is drawn in Fig. 4.2 by plotting the slope of $y = f(k_0, l)$ in Fig. 4.1 against the corresponding amounts of labor. The general form of the demand function is

$$l^d = l^d(w, k) \tag{4.3}$$

Demand for labor is a decreasing function of the real wage rate w since the greater the real wage, the smaller is the labor input that can be profitably employed. Conversely, a lower real wage encourages employers to hire more laborers until the increase in output due to an additional worker ceases to exceed the cost in output terms of the additional worker. Given the real wage, the demand for labor will generally increase with the amount of capital used in combination with labor. The greater capital available per unit of labor allows an additional worker to produce more than if the worker were less well equipped. This is roughly the other side of the Law of Diminishing Returns which states that in the relevant range the marginal product of labor falls as the quantity of labor increases relative to the fixed quantity of capital. Here the marginal product of labor rises as capital is increased relative to a fixed quantity of labor. The Law of Diminishing Returns implies this last statement exactly only for certain types of production functions, but it will generally hold in the range in which economies actually operate.

THE DEMAND FOR CAPITAL

The arguments used to derive the demand for labor can be repeated for the demand for capital. Thus Fig. 4.3 illustrates the output associated with different stocks of capital for a given amount of labor l_0. The *marginal product of capital*, the increase in output due to a unit increase in capital, is equal to the slope of the $y = f(k, l_0)$ line. The demand for capital for the given amount of labor l_0 is graphed in Fig. 4.4 by plotting the slope of the $y = f(k, l_0)$ line and the corresponding capital amounts shown in Fig. 4.3. More generally, the demand for capital is a decreasing function of the real rental rate ρ and an increasing function of the amount of labor used:

$$k^d = k^d(\rho, l) \tag{4.4}$$

The real rental rate of capital corresponds to the real wage rate of labor. Firms normally own the capital which they use, but the real rental rate indicates the

---

[4] Both output and real wages are measured here in base-year dollars per unit of labor, so no adjustment for the price of output is required. A monopolist would equate a fraction (the marginal revenue to price ratio) of the marginal product to the real wage. Including this complication would not affect the conclusions of the analysis; so it is omitted for the sake of simplicity.

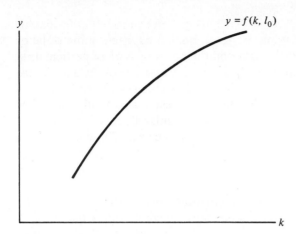

Figure 4.3 Graph of the aggregate production function for a given labor supply l_0. Output y increases with increased capital k, but at a decreasing rate. The increase in output per unit increase in capital is given by the slope of the $y = f(k, l_0)$ line for each level of capital input.

returns to capital received by the firm. These returns are used to pay interest and dividends to the households which finance the capital stock by holding securities issued by firms. The real rental rate is sometimes referred to as the *shadow price of capital*—the price is not seen directly but firms behave as if they paid a real rental rate ρ to use their capital.

Figure 4.4 The demand for capital for a given amount of labor l_0. Lower real rental rates ρ increase the quantity of capital demanded k^d. For larger amounts of labor than l_0, the demand curve would be located above and to the right of the $k^d = k^d(\rho, l_0)$ line.

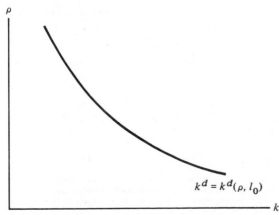

THE SUPPLY OF LABOR

The supply of labor depends upon the total, quality-adjusted, units of labor available in the age-eligible population and their average rate of participation in the labor force. At any point in time the quality and size of the age-eligible population is fixed, so the supply of labor reflects changes in the fraction of units of labor working at the time. Despite our interest in a particular instant of time, we will adjust the fraction working for regular fluctuations over the course of a week, due to holidays, and seasons of the year. These fluctuations and similar ones in income and prices are not of interest to macroeconomists and are removed from the various data series by averaging and seasonal adjustment.

The key determinants of the labor participation rate π are the real wage rate, the average quality of labor q, and the per capita income from capital:

$$\pi = \pi(w, q, \rho k/n) \qquad [4.5]$$

where n is the age-eligible population. The effect of the real wage rate on the participation rate is ambiguous. The participation rate measures the average fraction of time spent actually working,[5] the alternative being leisure—including nonmarket production and educational investment in human capital. A high wage rate increases income and therefore the attractiveness of leisure. In addition high wages relative to the costs of education increase the desirability of staying in school, but wages and costs of education normally move in proportion. Thus, although an increase in the real wages increases the attractiveness of working, it also increases the attractiveness of alternatives to work, and the net effect of an increase in real wages may increase or decrease the participation rate.[6] The effect of the average quality of labor is ambiguous for similar reasons. If we measure q in units of raw labor, the average wage received per year worked—as opposed to unit of labor provided—is wq. So an increase in quality, for a given wage per unit of labor, will also increase the attractiveness of work and at the same time increase per capita income and therefore the attractiveness of leisure. An increase in per capita income from capital increases the attractiveness of leisure, but not of labor, and so reduces the participation rate, given the real wage rate and average quality of the population.

The labor supply is equal to the participation rate times the average quality times the size of the population

$$l^s = \pi(w, q, \rho k/n) \cdot qn \qquad [4.6]$$

---

[5] This use of the term "participation rate" should not be confused with the data collected by the U.S. Department of Labor on the fraction of the population which is in the labor force.

[6] The source of the difficulty is that both leisure and commodities purchased with real income enter into individuals' utility functions. An increase in the wage rate raises the amount of market goods obtained for each hour of leisure foregone. Microeconomists analyze the situation in terms of opposing income and substitution effects.

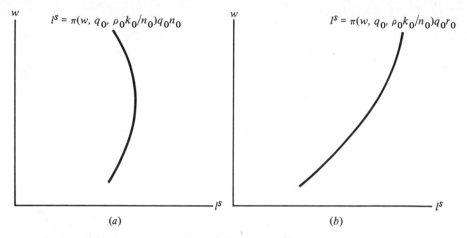

Figure 4.5 Possible labor supply functions. In the case of a backward-bending labor supply curve (a), increases in the real wage above some point reduce the quantity of labor supplied as more leisure is consumed. The supply curve in (b) is one which slopes upward for all wages.

An increase in real wages, other things being equal, may either increase or decrease the quantity of labor supplied, depending upon the exact nature of the underlying tastes. Empirical evidence on the effect of the real wage on the supply of labor is very tenuous. Some studies suggest a *backward-bending supply curve of labor*, as shown in Fig. 4.5(a), while others suggest a positively sloped labor supply curve, as shown in Fig. 4.5(b). Whatever the sign of the net effect, it appears to be small relative to the effect of the real wage on the demand for labor. The total effect on labor supply of an increase in quality, other things being equal, is almost surely positive, with the direct proportional effect of increased quality swamping any possible effect on the participation rate. Similarly, an increase in population, other things being equal, will increase the labor supply both directly and by increasing the participation rate. Increases in either the rental rate or stock of capital or both, other things being equal, will decrease the labor supply.

THE SUPPLY OF CAPITAL

Capital is measured as only those capital goods used in production, and its amount can be changed over time only by the processes of investment and depreciation. Much the same argument could in fact be made about the supply of labor were it not for the relatively easy substitution of leisure for work. The capital stock will be seen to have a very definite desired level at any point in time, and the difference between actual and desired level of capital is an important determinant of the rate of investment. But discussion of changes in the capital stock, like that of changes in the size or quality of the population, is left to the analysis of economic growth and dynamic adjustments in later chapters.

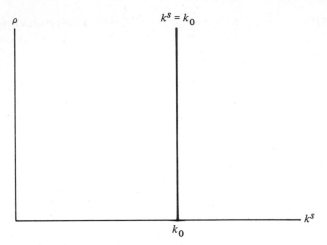

$$k^s = k_0$$

Figure 4.6 The supply curve of capital. The capital stock k is fixed at any point in time. The rental rate, ρ, allocates the available capital among alternative uses but does not affect the amount of capital currently available.

For analysis of the level of income, the supply curve of capital is vertical at the existing amount, say k_0, as illustrated in Fig. 4.6, or algebraically

$$k^s = k_0 \qquad\qquad [4.7]$$

The current rental rate on capital serves to allocate the fixed amount of capital and does not affect the amount available now, but only in the future.

DETERMINATION OF EQUILIBRIUM REAL INCOME

The equilibrium level of real income, the inputs of capital and labor, the real rental rate on capital, and the real wage can be determined from the aggregate production function, the demand and supply functions for labor and capital, and the existing level of the capital stock and size and quality of the age-eligible population. Substituting the existing values and noting that the quantities of capital and labor demanded and supplied equal the quantities used in equilibrium, we have a formal system of five equations and the five unknowns y, k, l, ρ, and w:

$$y = f(k, l) \qquad\qquad [4.8]$$

$$l = l^d(w, k) \qquad\qquad [4.9]$$

$$l = \pi(w, q_0, \rho k/n_0) \cdot q_0 n_0 \qquad\qquad [4.10]$$

$$k = k^d(\rho, l) \qquad\qquad [4.11]$$

$$k = k_0 \qquad\qquad [4.12]$$

These equations are a way of summarizing the millions of individual demand curves, supply curves, and production functions which describe the various markets in the economy. The mathematical solution of this system by substitution can be illustrated graphically.

First the labor market equations [4.9] and [4.10] are graphed in Fig. 4.7, given $k = k_0$. The labor demand curve can be graphed quite simply, since it relates labor only to the real wage w and the given capital stock k_0. The labor supply function, however, explains the quantity of labor supplied by the real wage and the real rental rate on capital ρ, as well as variables given at the time of analysis. The labor supply function can be plotted on the basis of a given value of ρ such as ρ_1 however. If ρ were ρ_1, then the labor market would be in equilibrium at l_1 and w_1. If ρ were instead ρ_2, which is larger than ρ_1, the labor supply function would lie above and to the left of the one for ρ_1. Equilibrium in the labor market if ρ equaled ρ_2 would occur for l_2 and w_2. For every value of ρ, there will be an associated value of l and w. The labor market equilibrium (LE) curve in Fig. 4.8 plots every possible combination of ρ and l for which the labor market is in equilibrium. The LE curve has a negative slope because

Figure 4.7 Derivation of labor market equilibrium curve. The quantity of labor demanded is a function of the real wage w and the given stock of capital k_0. The quantity of labor supplied is a function, aside from given values, of both the real wage and the rental rate on capital, ρ. A supply curve for labor can be drawn for each possible value of ρ. Examples are drawn for the values ρ_1 and ρ_2, where ρ_2 is greater than ρ_1 so that the labor supply curve associated with ρ_2 is above and to the left of the curve for ρ_1. Equilibrium values of labor and the real wage associated with ρ_1 and ρ_2 are l_1, w_1 and l_2, w_2, respectively. A value of l can thus be associated with every value of ρ. Each combination (ρ, l) for which the labor market is in equilibrium is plotted in Fig. 4.8 as the negatively sloped LE curve.

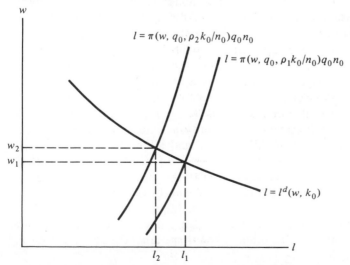

$$l = \pi(w, q_0, \rho_2 k_0/n_0)q_0 n_0$$

$$l = \pi(w, q_0, \rho_1 k_0/n_0)q_0 n_0$$

$$l = l^d(w, k_0)$$

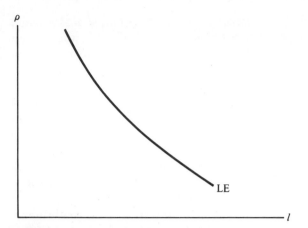

Figure 4.8 The labor market equilibrium or LE curve. The
LE curve shows all combinations of ρ and l for which the
labor market is in equilibrium.

higher values of ρ are associated with smaller values of l as was shown for ρ_1
and ρ_2. The LE curve also can be derived for backward-bending labor supply
curves for which the effect of real wages on the quantity of labor supplied is less
than the effect on the quantity of labor demanded.

The capital market equations are graphed in Fig. 4.9. The capital supply
curve is a vertical line through the existing amount k_0. The capital demand
function explains the quantity of capital demanded, as determined by both the
real rental rate ρ and the labor used l. This function can be plotted for given
values of l such as l_1. If the quantity of labor used is l_1, then the rental rate on
capital must be ρ_1 for the demand for capital to equal the existing supply. If l
were instead l_2, which is larger than l_1, the capital demand function would lie
above and to the right of the one for l_1. Equilibrium in the capital market if l
equaled l_2 would occur if ρ was ρ_2. For every value of l, there will be an
associated value of ρ. The capital market equilibrium (KE) curve in Fig. 4.10
plots every combination of ρ and l for which the capital market is in equilibrium. The KE curve has a positive slope because higher values of l are associated with higher values of ρ as was shown for l_1 and l_2.

The LE curve shows all combinations of ρ and l for which the labor market
is in equilibrium. The KE curve shows all possible values for which the capital
market is in equilibrium. By plotting the LE and KE curves on one graph as
shown in Fig. 4.11, we find the only combination of ρ and l for which both the
labor and capital markets are in equilibrium at the same time. These values, ρ_e
and l_e, are not determined in the capital market or in the labor market
separately, but by the interaction of the two markets. The equilibrium value of
capital is the existing stock k_0. The equilibrium real wage rate and real income
are found by substitution of the other values in the labor demand function and

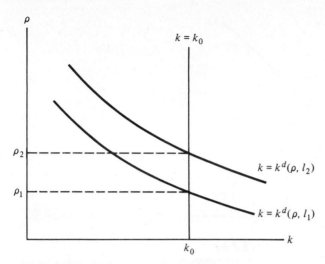

Figure 4.9 Derivation of the capital equilibrium curve. The capital supply is fixed at the existing amount k_0. The quantity of capital demanded is a function of both the real rental rate ρ and the quantity of labor l. A demand curve for capital can be drawn for each possible value of l. Examples are drawn for l_1 and l_2, where l_2 is greater than l_1, so that the capital demand curve associated with l_2 lies above and to the right of the one for l_1. Equilibrium values of the rental rate associated with l_1 and l_2 are ρ_1 and ρ_2, respectively. A value of ρ can thus be associated with every value of l. Each combination (ρ, l) for which the capital market is in equilibrium is plotted in Fig. 4.10 as the positively sloped KE curve.

Figure 4.10 The capital market equilibrium curve, or KE curve. The KE curve shows all combinations of ρ and l for which the capital market is in equilibrium.

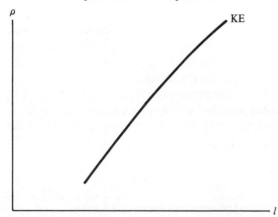

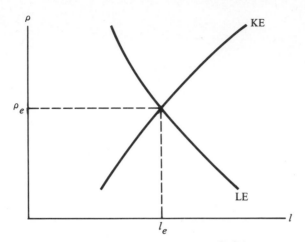

Figure 4.11 Use of the KE and LE curves to find the equilibrium values of ρ and l. The point where the positively sloped KE curve intersects the negatively sloped LE curve shows the only combination of ρ and l for which the capital and labor markets are in simultaneous equilibrium. These values, ρ_e and l_e, are those which will be achieved by the interaction of the supply and demand functions for capital and labor.

aggregate production function.[7] This is shown graphically in Figs. 4.12 and 4.13. Figure 4.12 reproduces the labor demand function for k_0 which was graphed in Fig. 4.7. The equilibrium real wage w_e is the one corresponding to l_e. Figure 4.13 graphs the production function for the existing capital stock k_0. Equilibrium real income y_e is the amount which is produced by the existing capital stock k_0 and the equilibrium quantity of labor l_e.

THE DEMAND FOR OUTPUT

The demand for output did not explicitly enter into the determination of real income. This is because the labor supply function implicitly reflects the choice between market goods and leisure. Income exactly equals output, so that the means of making purchases is just equal to the purchases to be made.

A possible difficulty arises because consumers use their income not only to consume but also to save. The only way that society as a whole can save, in the sense of nonconsumption of income, is to use part of output to add to the capital stock so as to increase future output. That is, society can save only by

---

[7] The LE and KE curves are graphs of two equations obtained by substitution among [4.8] through [4.12] to eliminate three of the unknowns: y, k, and w. The remaining unknowns (l and ρ) having been solved for, they are substituted back into the original equations to obtain the corresponding values of y, k, and w.

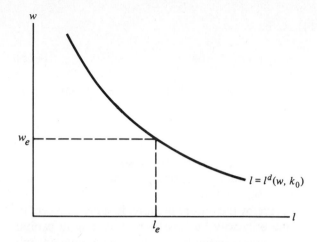

Figure 4.12 Determination of the equilibrium real wage w_e. The equilibrium real wage w_e is the one for which the quantity of labor demanded is equal to the equilibrium amount l_e.

investing. This point is easy to see by dividing output into its two possible uses, real consumption c and real investment i:

$$y \equiv c + i \qquad\qquad [4.13]$$

However, saving s is the portion of income which is not consumed

$$y \equiv c + s \qquad\qquad [4.14]$$

Figure 4.13 Determination of equilibrium real income y_e. The equilibrium real income is the amount produced using k_0 and l_e.

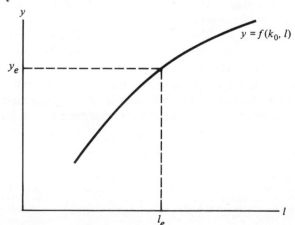

Combining [4.13] and [4.14], we have

$$c + s \equiv c + i \qquad\qquad [4.15]$$

Subtracting consumption from both sides, we obtain the equality of saving and investment:

$$s \equiv i \qquad\qquad [4.16]$$

This is a simplified version of [2.6], corresponding to consolidation of government accounts into the consumer accounts and to neglect of international trade so that net exports are zero.

    This condition is not always true by the nature of individual plans, except in a simple economy in which the only way to save is by investing in capital goods. In modern market economies, individual saving plans—net of any government deficit in the current consolidated accounts—are not automatically identical to the investment plans of firms. Yet, after the fact, net purchases of securities by individuals must exactly equal net issuance of securities by firms to finance investment.[8]

    It is easy to see that the actual amount of real output that is not consumed must equal the actual amount added to the capital stock, but this does not show how the *desired* amount of saving is equated to the *desired* amount of investment. The difference is analogous to the market for corn: the amount supplied must exactly equal the amount demanded in equilibrium, but the desired sales and purchases are equated by the movement of the price of corn. Investment is simply the amount of additional capital demanded and saving the amount of additional capital supplied. We call the demand function and supply function for additional capital the *investment function* and *saving function*, respectively.

    The desired level of investment depends upon the interest rate[9] R that must be paid or foregone to finance new capital, the cost of capital goods, and the expected rental stream to be generated by the new capital. If the rental stream is more than sufficient to cover payments on a loan which covers the cost of the investment, the investment will be made. The number of investments which can cover the loan payments decreases as the rate of interest increases. The cost of capital goods relative to other goods rises or falls when the rate of investment is high or low relative to capacity in the capital goods industry, but these variations are discussed with other disequilibrium behavior in Parts Three and Four. Similarly the state of expectations about the future rental rate on capital

---

[8] See Secs. 2.1 and 2.3 for details.

[9] Strictly speaking, the real interest rate r is applicable to investment and saving decisions. The real interest rate differs from the nominal interest rate R by an amount determined by the expected inflation rate. At a particular instant of time, the expected inflation rate is constant (given) and so does not change saving or investment. The relationship between real and nominal interest rates will be studied in Sec. 5.3 in connection with the inflation rate.

is largely predetermined for the equilibrium discussed in this chapter. It will be seen later that a considerable controversy exists over whether expected future rentals are based essentially on observed past and present rental rates and growth in income, or whether independent moods of optimism and pessimism play an important part in determining investment. For the current discussion of long-run equilibrium, only the effects on expectations from current income and rental rate on capital are included in the investment function:

$$i = i(R, y, \rho) \qquad\qquad [4.17]$$

Investment is a decreasing function of the interest rate R, and an increasing function of income y and rental rate ρ, to the extent that they create expectations of high future rental rates. The values of y and ρ for which the labor and capital markets are in equilibrium were previously determined to be y_e and ρ_e. The investment function for those equilibrium values of y and ρ is graphed in Fig. 4.14.

The saving function, like the investment function, is complicated by expectational factors in disequilibrium. For long-run analysis, we can concentrate on the effects of income and the interest rate. Individuals choose to save because a positive interest rate permits exchange of a dollar's worth of real goods and services now for a larger amount of real goods and services in the future. This exchange of present for future goods is accomplished by saving. Individuals do not choose to save all their income, however, because the more that is saved the less is present consumption relative to future consumption. Saving proceeds

Figure 4.14 The investment function at equilibrium levels of real income and the rental rate on capital. At lower interest rates, investment projects yielding lower expected future rental streams become attractive, so that investment increases. The position of the curve is determined by the investments actually available and the expected returns on those investments.

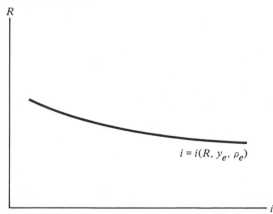

only to the point that the marginal utility of a dollar's worth of consumption now is equated to the marginal utility of the future consumption that could be obtained by saving a dollar. The marginal utility of consumption declines with its level, so this implies that future levels of consumption will exceed current levels in equilibrium. The lower marginal utility associated with higher levels of future consumption just offsets the lower current price, given the interest rate, of future consumption relative to the marginal utility of current consumption. It may be that the utility of the same consumption level in the future is valued less than it is in the present, but saving to increase future consumption relative to more expensive present consumption generally also occurs. The data indicate that for over a century U.S. saving has been a nearly constant fraction of income in long-run equilibrium. This constant, long-run saving ratio is consistent with, but not required by, the economic theory of optimal consumption over time.[10]

The effect of the interest rate on saving is very little understood. In part this reflects the differing impact of various changes that could alter the interest rate. The main reason for our lack of knowledge is that the long-run interest rate, when adjusted for the influence of expected inflation, has changed so very little over time. The effect of an increase in the interest rate is generally thought to be a small increase in the saving rate, but some argue that the effect would be a small decrease analogous to the backward-bending supply curve for labor. It will be assumed that the effect of an increase in the interest rate is a slight

---

[10] See, for example, Milton Friedman, *A Theory of the Consumption Function*, Princeton: Princeton University Press for NBER, 1957; and Paul A. David and John J. Scadding, Private Savings: Ultrarationality, Aggregation, and "Denison's Law," *Journal of Political Economy*, **82**: 225–249, Mar./Apr. 1974. A full discussion of saving would take into account saving to smooth out life-cycle variation in income as well as saving to increase the future level of consumption of oneself and heirs. These details are left for specialized discussions.

Figure 4.15 The saving function at the equilibrium level of income. An increase in the interest rate slightly increases the saving associated with each level of income in long-run equilibrium.

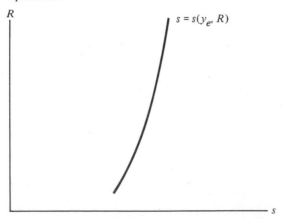

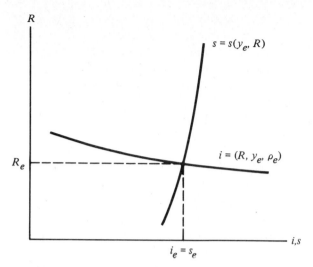

Figure 4.16 Equilibrium of the demand and supply of additional capital goods. The interest rate moves to R_e to equate investment to saving at $i_e = s_e$.

increase in the saving rate, but none of the arguments will be based on this precise shape. The saving function

$$s = s(y, R) \tag{4.18}$$

is illustrated for the equilibrium value of income y_e in Fig. 4.15.

Investment is equated to saving, as required by the equilibrium condition [4.16] by movements in the interest rate. This is illustrated in Fig. 4.16 and Example 4.1. In full moving equilibrium, as discussed in Chap. 5, the interest rate will be equated to the rental rate of capital by the cumulative effects over time of investment on the capital stock.

Movements in the interest rate assure that the total amount demanded will be just equal to total output in equilibrium. In the complete model, decisions of firms and households are made consistent by the operation of three prices: the wage rate w, the rental rate ρ, and the interest rate R. Households will have plans for working, consuming, and saving so that the income earned and its disposition between current and future consumption will be as determined by utility maximization. Net investment will be equated to net savings by adjustment of the rate of interest paid on financial assets.

EXAMPLE 4.1

EQUALIZATION OF INVESTMENT AND SAVING

The (simplified) national income accounting identities show that saving must exactly equal investment at any instant. But comparison of the investment and saving functions illustrated in Figs. 4.14 and 4.15 makes it obvious that desired investment would not equal desired saving for most possible combinations of the determinants y, ρ, and R—real income, real rental rate, and the nominal interest rate. The identity $s \equiv i$ must hold for the combination of y, ρ, and R which actually exists; so these variables adjust to equate saving and investment. In short-run equilibrium all three determinants might vary. But in analyzing long-run equilibrium, real income and the real rental rate will be at their previously derived values y_e and ρ_e, so the interest rate alone adjusts to equate investment and saving.

To see how this works, consider two simple examples of the saving and investment functions [4.18] and [4.17]:

$$s = 0.1y + 100R$$

$$i = 80 + 0.05y + 350\rho - 1000R$$

Saving, investment, and income are measured in billions of base-year dollars per annum; the interest rate is a decimal fraction per annum; and the real rental rate is in base-year dollars per annum. Suppose y_e is R\$1,000 billion per annum and ρ_e is R\$0.04 per annum. Then,

$$s = 0.1 \times 1000 + 100R = 100 + 100R$$

$$i = 80 + 0.05 \times 1000 + 350 \times 0.04 - 1000R$$

$$i = 80 + 50 + 14 - 1000R = 144 - 1000R$$

The values of real saving and real investment which households and firms would want to make depend on the interest rate as given in the table:

R	s	i
0.01	101	134
0.02	102	124
0.03	103	114
0.04	104	104
0.05	105	94
0.06	106	84
0.07	107	74

Only at an interest rate of 0.04 (4 percent) per annum are saving and investment equated. If the interest rate were lower, firms would want to invest more than households would want to finance by saving. If the interest rate were higher, households would want to finance more investment than firms would want to make. So only at an interest rate of 4 percent per annum can the desires of households and firms be reconciled with no excess supply or demand for new securities issues.

SUMMARY OF THE DETERMINATION OF REAL INCOME

Real income is determined by the amount of labor employed with the existing capital stock as the largest amount which can be produced from those factors, given the technological know-how, institutional framework, and composition of output as determined by tastes and relative costs of production. The amount of labor supplied and demanded is such that the marginal output produced by labor has a value equal to the leisure which can be substituted for work. Investment is equated to saving, or nonconsumption of income, by changes in the interest rate which firms pay savers who finance the investments of the firms. In this way, total income just equals the amount of market goods desired for current consumption and for addition to the capital stock to increase future income.

4.3 DETERMINANTS OF THE PRICE LEVEL

NOMINAL INCOME AND THE PRICE LEVEL

One of the most productive institutions in modern market economies is the widespread use of money to avoid barter. *Barter*, direct trade of one commodity for another without the use of money, imposes two special constraints on market exchange: (1) one party must want to buy what the other wants to sell and to sell what the other wants to buy; and (2) purchases must coincide in time with an equal-valued sale. Barter requires the use of much time in searching for the best combination of offers; it also restricts the size and timing of transactions. The costs of making these transactions are greatly reduced by the expression of all prices in terms of units of a single commodity and using that commodity as the second item in each transaction. This commodity, money, serves as an information, guarantee, or rationing device to assure that one cannot buy things worth more than the goods one sells, with a running total kept over time by the level of one's money balance. As a result of the ability to trade with general rights to present or future goods, people are willing to sell when and to whom their output is most valued and to buy when and from whom their purchases are cheapest.

The value of money relative to goods can change substantially with changes in supply or demand conditions for money. The value in terms of money of the goods and services produced will vary inversely with the value of a unit of money in terms of the goods which it can purchase. That is, the price of money in terms of goods is $1/P$, or the amount of goods that it would cost now to buy

$1, the goods being measured in base-year dollars.[11] Nominal income, measured in current dollars, is simply the product of real income and the price index,

$$Y \equiv yP \qquad [4.19]$$

Given the level of real income determined in Sec. 4.2, nominal income (like the price level) varies inversely with the value of money.

The value of money—and thus nominal income—is determined in the same way as that of any other commodity, by its supply and demand.

THE SUPPLY OF MONEY

The American money supply consists of currency and coin which are directly controlled by the Federal Reserve System plus deposits at commercial banks[12] which are indirectly controlled by the Fed. The quantity of money supplied is determined by government monetary policy as explained in Sec. 3.3. The Fed has not always exercised that control in a conscious effort to achieve a particular level of the money supply. Under other monetary systems, the nominal supply of money may be dependent not on governmental policy but on such factors as the amount of gold in the country if gold is the monetary base instead of fiat money issued by the government.

For the analysis of the determination of the price level, it will be assumed that the nominal supply of money is fixed at some value M_0 by the government's monetary policy:

$$M^s = M_0 \qquad [4.20]$$

Similar results can be obtained from more complex money supply models appropriate to other institutional frameworks. The price level is determined for a given value of the nominal money supply. Of considerable interest are the implications of alternative choices of the nominal money supply for the price level.

The supply of money in real terms varies inversely with the price level:

$$m^s = \frac{M_0}{P} \qquad [4.21]$$

The real and nominal supply of money are graphed in panels (a) and (b), respectively, of Fig. 4.17.

---

[11] See the end of Sec. 3.1.
[12] Whether only demand (checking) deposits or all deposits are included depends on whether one is using the narrow (M_1) or broad (M_2) definition of money. This distinction, which is treated in courses in money and banking, will not be made in the general presentation here.

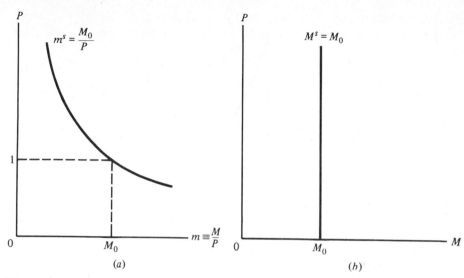

Figure 4.17 Money supply as a function of the price level. The Federal Reserve System determines the nominal amount of money existing as M_0, as shown by a vertical line in (b). The real value of this nominal stock of money is dependent upon the price level, as shown by the rectangular hyperbola in (a).

THE DEMAND FOR MONEY

Money is used to avoid the costs associated with barter. Individuals and firms hold money as an inventory or buffer stock which increases when proceeds from sales are received and decreases when payments for purchases are made. Figure 4.18 illustrates the typical pattern of an individual's money balances. At each payday, money balances jump up and are then gradually spent until next payday. Typically payments will be disproportionately bunched on and right after payday, as indicated by the faster decline of money balances then. If one were certain that no extraordinary expenses would occur, one could spend one's last cent just as pay envelopes were passed out. Most people find this awkward and instead hold a reserve for emergencies. If unusual income is received—such as in the third pay period in Fig. 4.18—people do not immediately spend it on goods or other assets, but hold it until a convenient time arises.

The long-run demand for money refers to the average amount of money which people want to hold. This is made up of two parts: (1) average holdings of money used to separate expenditures from receipts and (2) average holdings of money to serve as a reserve for emergencies.[13] The first part is referred to as

---

[13] At any particular instant people would be willing to hold more or less than this long-run average in order to avoid sudden changes in planned receipts and expenditures. We are here concerned with an economy in long-run equilibrium and can leave these short-run deviations to Part Three.

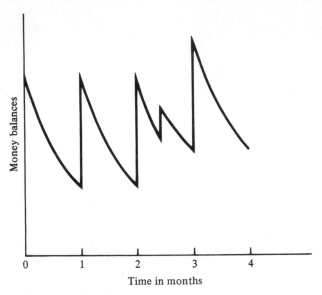

Figure 4.18 Money balances held by a representative individual.
This individual is paid monthly, as indicated by the sudden
increase in money balances at the beginning of each month. The
money is then spent over the course of the month. The faster
decline in money balances in the early part of the month is
because people tend to bunch expenditures after receipts.
Unexpected large receipts or expenditures would cause sharp up
or down changes in money balances similar to the receipt of a
pay check; an example is shown in the third month. The cash
reserve left over just before payday serves as a buffer to absorb
these unexpected money flows temporarily.

the *transactions demand* for money and the second as the *asset demand* for
money. This separation is not hard and fast since one dollar can serve both
purposes, but it does serve to organize our discussion.

The transactions demand for money depends upon the total amount of
receipts or expenditures being made and upon payment practices. Nominal
income is our best, albeit incomplete, measure of total receipts or expenditures
in the economy. It leaves out intermediate and financial transactions, but these
move more or less proportionately. For given payments practices, the transactions demand for money increases proportionately with income, as illustrated
in Fig. 4.19. If payments are made more frequently or expenditures more
closely coordinated with receipts, this reduces the average transactions balances for a given level of income, as shown in Fig. 4.20. It is costly to compute
payrolls more frequently[14] or to plan expenditures more closely. Whether it is

---

[14] Or to buy securities and resell them in the middle of the pay period. This is another way by which the
individual can achieve a pattern like that in panel (*a*) of Fig. 4.20.

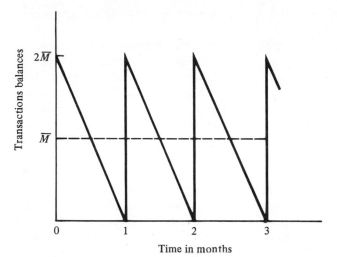

Figure 4.19 Illustration of average transactions balances. In this
example, the individual receives an amount $2\overline{M}$ at the beginning of
each month and spends money at a constant rate between paydays.
The average holdings of transactions balances for a month is the
area of the rectangle under $\overline{M}$—that is, to $\overline{M} \times 1 = \overline{M}$. So in this
case average transactions balances equal one-half of monthly income.

Figure 4.20 Changes in payment practices which reduce average transactions balances. Panel (a)
illustrates how more frequent paydays reduce average transactions balances. Here the same
monthly receipts of $2\overline{M}$ are now received as two payments of $\overline{M}$—one at the beginning and the
other at the middle of the month. This reduces average money holdings by half as compared to
the previous (shaded) pattern reproduced from Fig. 4.19. Panel (b) shows how bunching of
payments after paydays reduces average transactions balances from $\overline{M}$ to M'.

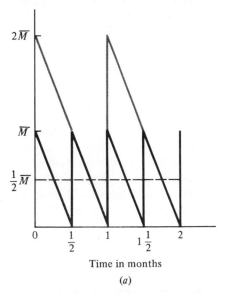

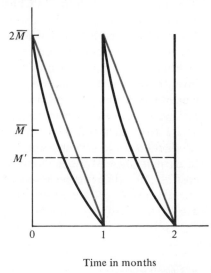

worth the cost depends on what is to be gained by reducing average money holdings.

The gains to reducing money holdings are found by comparing the interest rate paid on money with the interest rates available on alternative assets. The interest rate paid on money is zero for coin and currency and is proportionate to the interest rate on short-term bonds for bank deposits.[15] There are many alternative assets, but we might mention short-term and long-term bonds in particular. Generally, the lower the interest rate on money and the higher the interest rates on alternative assets, the greater is the gain in using payment practices which reduce average transactions balances.

The asset demand for money is more closely related to an individual's nominal wealth than to his current nominal income. Wealth measures the total amount to be apportioned among all assets and indicates the scale of potential emergencies. For an economy in long-run equilibrium however, current nominal income will equal permanent income times the price level. Permanent income was seen in Sec. 3.5 to be proportional to real wealth. So the asset demand for money can also be described as increasing with nominal income. The gains in reducing money holdings are the same for the asset demand as for the transactions demand.

Summing up, the long-run demand for money is an increasing function of nominal income and the interest rate on money and a decreasing function of the interest rates on alternative assets such as short-term and long-term bonds.

It will prove useful to write the demand for money in a form which corresponds to the Cambridge identity:

$$M \equiv \phi y P \qquad\qquad [4.22]$$

This identity was first met in Chap. 1. It defines fluidity ϕ as the ratio of money to income.[16] Fluidity is more widely known as the "Cambridge k" because the symbol k was used instead of ϕ in the original presentations. Since the symbol k is even more commonly used to denote capital, ϕ is adopted here.

Fluidity, the ratio of money to income, is analogous to a firm's ratio of inventories to sales. Both are measured as the length of time (in years) over which transactions can be made at the current rate from the stock of money or inventories. For a firm, new production replaces sales from inventories. The lower its average level of inventories the more frequently must new production come available and the more closely must production be adjusted to current sales. More economical production techniques can be used at the cost of maintaining larger inventories. There will be some optimal level of the average inventory-sales ratio: above this level the costs of additional inventory exceeds the resulting reduction in production costs; below this level the costs

---

[15] The interest rate on deposits will be less than on short-term bonds because a fraction of bank assets are held as zero-interest reserves and because of the costs of intermediation and of evasion of restrictions on deposit interest payments.
[16] The ratio is the same whether real money and income $(M/P)/y$ or nominal money and income M/yP is used.

of carrying additional inventory are less than the resulting reduction in production costs. If actual inventories rise above this desired optimal level, production will be adjusted downward when most convenient until the excess is worked off. Alternatively, low actual inventories will lead, when convenient, to increased production. Similarly, there will be an optimal money-income ratio which balances the costs of additional money holdings against the costs of more frequent payments and more careful planning. Deviations of actual from desired fluidity lead individuals to adjust money receipts and expenditures, when convenient, to move toward the desired level. The term *fluidity* is used because higher levels of this ratio mean that individuals are less tied to particular transaction plans and can more easily smooth over unexpected expenditures and receipts.

Money demand is written in the Cambridge format as

$$M^d = \phi^d(y, R_M, R_S, R_L) \cdot yP \qquad [4.23]$$

This equation states that nominal money demand is a fraction ϕ^d of nominal income $yP \equiv Y$. The fraction is determined by the arguments of the function

$$\phi^d = \phi^d(y, R_M, R_S, R_L) \qquad [4.24]$$

Real income is included as a determinant of desired fluidity ϕ^d because people may want to allocate an increasing or decreasing fraction of their wealth to money holdings as they become wealthier in real terms. Whether ϕ^d in fact increases or decreases with increases in y (as an indicator of real wealth) is uncertain both theoretically and empirically. The effects of interest rates on desired fluidity and nominal money demand are proportional, so desired fluidity is an increasing function of the interest rate on money and a decreasing function of the interest rates on other assets. The desired fluidity function implicitly incorporates the technology for making payments, the institutions, and the tastes existing in the economy. While these may gradually change over time, they are given for the instant of time considered here.

For most problems we can assume that the interest rates on money and other assets are moving in proportion. In that case a compact form of the nominal demand for money is

$$M^D = \phi^d(y, R) \cdot yP \qquad [4.25]$$

Generally the gap between the interest rate on money and the rates on other assets will increase as interest rates in general rise. The net effect of increases in interest rates generally (as indexed by R) will be to decrease desired fluidity and the demand for money. Dividing both sides of [4.25] by P gives us real money demand:

$$m^d \equiv \frac{M^d}{P} = \phi^d(y, R) \cdot y \qquad [4.26]$$

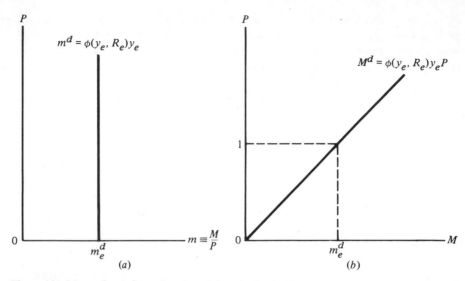

Figure 4.21 Money demand as a function of the price level. The general price level P does not affect the real demand for money graphed in (a). The nominal demand for money increases in proportion to the price level in (b). At $P = 1$, the nominal demand for money is equal in magnitude to the real demand for money m_e^d.

Notice that real money demand is determined by real income and the interest rate only. The equilibrium values of these variables have already been found as y_e and R_e. The real quantity of money demanded is thus fixed as shown in panel (a) of Fig. 4.21. The nominal quantity of money demanded equals the fixed real quantity m_e^d times the price level P. This is graphed in panel (b) of Fig. 4.21.

The real demand for money is completely determined as m_e^d by the real equilibrium of the economy, but the nominal money demand varies directly as the price level.

THE EQUILIBRIUM PRICE LEVEL

The equilibrium price level is determined by the condition that money supply must equal money demand:

$$M^S = M^D \tag{4.27}$$

This can also be written in real terms by dividing both sides of [4.27] by the price level P:

$$m^s = m^d \tag{4.28}$$

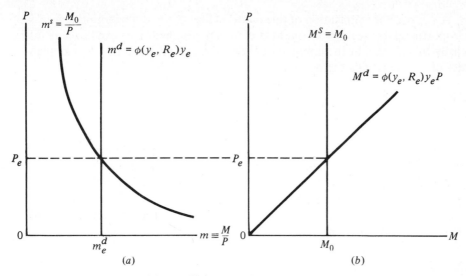

Figure 4.22 Determination of the equilibrium price level. The real conditions underlying the demand for money fix the real amount of money of money demanded at m_e^d. Governmental monetary policy fixes the nominal amount of money supplied. In real terms (a), the quantity of money supplied is equated to the fixed amount demanded at the equilibrium price level P_e. In nominal terms (b), the quantity of money demanded is equated to the fixed amount supplied at the equilibrium price level P_e.

Using the equilibrium values for income y_e and the interest rate R_e determined by the real sector, [4.20], [4.25], and [4.27], or equivalently [4.21], [4.26], and [4.28], are consistent sets of three equations in three unknowns which can be solved for equilibrium money supplied, money demanded, and the price level.

The graphical solution of these equations is presented in Fig. 4.22. Panel (a) depicts the price level changing so that the real supply of money is equated to the real demand for money as determined by real conditions. Panel (b) shows the other side of the coin in nominal terms. Price-level changes adjust the nominal amount of money demanded to the fixed nominal amount supplied. The geometric construction of the graphs assures that the equilibrium price level P_e will be the same for both approaches.

Conditions of demand determine the real quantity of money, conditions of supply determine the nominal quantity of money, and the price level conforms so that the two amounts are equivalent when adjusted by the price level into the same units. Were the price level below the equilibrium level so that the quantity of money supplied exceeded the quantity of money demanded, whether measured in real or nominal terms, there would be increased bids for the fixed amount of goods produced as people attempted to reduce the excess money balances. This would drive the price level upward toward its equilibrium level. Conversely, if the price level were too high so that the quantity of money demanded exceeded the quantity of money supplied, people would reduce their bids and the price level would fall toward its equilibrium level.

An important implication of this model is that the equilibrium price level is proportional to the nominal quantity of money supplied. This can be seen most easily by noting that the nominal quantity of money divided by the real quantity of money equals the price level.

$$P = \frac{M}{m} \qquad [4.29]$$

In equilibrium, the nominal quantity of money is equal to the amount supplied and the real quantity of money equals the fixed real amount demanded. So [4.29] can hold only if a 5 percent increase in the amount of money supplied causes a 5 percent increase in the price level.

Equilibrium nominal income is the product of the equilibrium real income and the equilibrium price level,

$$Y_e = y_e P_e \qquad [4.30]$$

Since real income is fixed by the real conditions of technology, institutions, and tastes, nominal income—like the price level—is proportionate to the nominal quantity of money supplied.

SUMMARY

1 The long-run equilibrium value of real income is determined jointly with the quantity of labor and the real wage rate and real rental rate earned by labor and capital. These variables are mutually determined so that the markets for labor and capital will both be in equilibrium, given the existing capital stock and the possibilities summarized by the aggregate production function.

2 In long-run equilibrium, the desired quantity of investment is equated to the desired quantity of saving by movements in the interest rate. This assures that total expenditures will equal total output and income as required for equilibrium in the market for final goods and services.

3 The nominal quantity of money supplied is determined by the monetary policy of the Federal Reserve System.

4 The real demand for money is an increasing function of real income and a decreasing function of the general level of interest rates.

5 A useful way to write the real demand for money is in terms of a fluidity function times real income. Fluidity is a decreasing function of the nominal interest rate, but either a decreasing or an increasing function of real income. The nominal demand for money is the real demand times the price level.

6 The long-run equilibrium real quantity of money demanded is fixed by the values of real income and the nominal interest rate required for equilibrium in the labor, capital, and goods markets.

7 The long-run equilibrium price level equates the quantity of money demanded and supplied when measured in the same units, either base-year dollars or current dollars. The price level and nominal income are proportionate to the nominal quantity of money supplied.

CONCEPTS TO KNOW

aggregate production function · · · · · · · · long-run equilibrium
asset demand for money · · · · · · · · · · · marginal product
average quality of labor · · · · · · · · · · · nominal demand for money
barter · nominal supply of money
demand for capital · · · · · · · · · · · · · · · real demand for money
demand for labor · · · · · · · · · · · · · · · · real supply of money
desired fluidity · · · · · · · · · · · · · · · · · · real wage rate
fluidity · saving function
investment function · · · · · · · · · · · · · · supply of capital
labor participation rate · · · · · · · · · · · · supply of labor
Law of Diminishing Returns · · · · · · · · · transactions demand for money

QUESTIONS AND EXERCISES

1 If there were an age-eligible population of 120 million people who had an average quality equivalent to six units of raw labor, what would be the rate of labor input if the population actually worked an average of $\frac{1}{4}$ of the time?

2 It is difficult to add different kinds of machines and buildings to obtain a measure of capital. Is this problem conceptually any different from estimating real income or real labor input? Explain why or why not.

3 Part of the rental value of the capital stock accrues to individuals who do not work in any case, such as retired people. Does this eliminate or merely reduce the change in the quantity of labor supplied, other things being equal, if the rental rate on capital somehow increases? Would these people really not work even if the rental rate on capital fell to zero?

4 What is the difference between the labor market equilibrium (LE) curve and the demand curve for labor? What is the difference between the capital market equilibrium (KE) curve and the demand curve for capital?

5 Use the KE and LE curves to analyze the effects of the following situations on real income, real wage rate, real rental rate, and amount of labor used:
   (a) A decrease in the age-eligible population.
   (b) An earthquake which destroys a substantial part of the capital without harming the population.
   (c) An increased taste for leisure as opposed to work.

6 An investment project is expected to yield returns of $10, $10, and $110 at the end of 1, 2, and 3 years, respectively, and nothing thereafter. If the investment costs $100 now, would it be profitable at a market interest rate of 8 percent per annum, compounded annually? 10 percent? 12 percent?

7 Explain why $s = i$ is a condition of equilibrium and does not imply identical saving and investment functions?

*8 Solve the following equations for real saving and real investment:

$$i = 144 - 1000R$$

$$s = 100 + 100R$$

$$s \equiv i$$

Compare your results with Example 4.1.

9 If individuals were free to use money however they wanted, except that they had to hold exactly $100 at noon each Sunday, the economy would be a sort of barter economy. Explain why?

*10 Why is $1/P$ called the price of money instead of R_M?

11 Suppose that the interest rate paid on deposits is a constant fraction of the interest rate on short-term bonds. Show that the gap between the interest rates on short-term bonds and deposits increases as the interest rate on short-term bonds increases. In what sense is this an increase in the cost of holding money instead of short-term bonds?

12 Why do we discuss the real money supply adjusting to equal the fixed real money demand, but talk about the nominal money demand adjusting to equal the fixed nominal money supply? Why are these statements not contradictory?

*13 Consider two alternative states which differ only in the nominal supply of money. Each state is in long-run equilibrium. Denote values of variables which exist in state 1 by a subscript 1 and in state 2 by a subscript 2. In state 1, $M_1 = 200$, $P_1 = 1.25$, $y_1 = 800$. What is Y_1? ϕ_1? In state 2, $M_2 = 300$. What are P_2, y_2, Y_2, ϕ_2? What are M_2/M_1, P_2/P_1, y_2/y_1, Y_2/Y_1, ϕ_2/ϕ_1? What do you conclude?

REFERENCES FOR FURTHER READING

The material in Sec. 4.2 aggregates and generalizes the material found in standard microeconomics texts.

Friedman, Milton: "The Quantity Theory of Money—A Restatement," in Milton Friedman (ed.): *Studies in the Quantity Theory of Money*, Chicago: The University of Chicago Press, 1956.

CHAPTER 5

INCOME AND
THE PRICE LEVEL IN
A GROWING ECONOMY

WHAT YOU WILL LEARN IN THIS CHAPTER
Measures of growth ● Determinants of long-run equilibrium growth in real income and real income per capita ● Effects of increased saving on real income growth ● Determinants of the long-run equilibrium inflation rate ● Effects of inflation on nominal interest rates ● Effects of alternative growth rates of nominal money on real income and the price level

5.1 INTRODUCTION

Rising standards of living, income, and often prices characterize the world's economies. Growth in the equilibrium levels of income and prices occurs because of changes in their underlying determinants. In this chapter, the emphasis is on the steady, gradual changes in these factors that determine the trend or *secular* rates of growth of income and prices over long periods of time. In Part Three, we will study the fluctuations—the booms and busts of the business cycle—which result from fluctuations in the rate of change of the underlying determinants.

MEASURING GROWTH

How is growth measured? We will find two separate but related concepts useful. First, the *rate of change* of a variable expresses the growth per year of that variable in terms of the units by which the variable is measured. For example, the labor force was 95,286,000 persons at the beginning of 1976 and 98,106,000 persons at the end of the year. So the rate of change of the labor force for 1976 was 2,820,000 persons per year. Second, the *growth rate* of a variable expresses growth as a proportion or fraction of the amount of the variable. For example, the 2,820,000 persons per year change in the labor force relative to a beginning level of 95,286,000 persons implies a growth rate of 0.030 per year. Growth rates are often quoted in percentage terms such as 3.0 percent per annum.

The rate of change is computed by subtracting the beginning level of a variable from its value at the end of the period and dividing by the length of the period to convert the change into annual rates. For example, if the real capital stock measured R$1,000 billion 6 months ago and now measures R$1,040 billion, the rate of change is

$$\frac{R\$1,040 \text{ billion} - R\$1,000 \text{ billion}}{0.5 \text{ year}} = \frac{R\$40 \text{ billion}}{0.5 \text{ year}} = \frac{R\$80 \text{ billion}}{1 \text{ year}}$$

That is, the rate of change in the real capital stock over the last 6 months was R$80 billion per annum. For reasons analogous to those discussed in Sec. 3.5 with respect to the compounding of interest, it is convenient to measure the rate of change of a variable at an instant of time. This is the ratio of the change in a variable to the corresponding arbitrarily short period of time.[1] We will denote the rate of change of a variable by preceding the variable with the symbol delta Δ. So Δk is read as the rate of change of the real capital stock.[2] The rate of change computed over any period of time is the average of the rates of change at each instant.

The R$80 billion per annum change in the capital stock was at a rate equal to 8 percent of the initial stock of R$1,000 billion. Often such a percentage or proportional measure of growth is the most useful and meaningful. The growth rate of a variable is the ratio of the rate of change of the variable to its level. As with rates of change, growth rates are measured in this book at an instant of time.[3]

We will denote the growth rate of a variable by preceding the variable with the symbol gamma Γ. So Γk is read as the growth rate of the real capital stock.[4]

---

[1] Mathematically, the rate of change of any variable h at time 0 is

$$\frac{h_z - h_0}{z}$$

where z is arbitrarily small. That is, the rate of change of h is the derivative of h with respect to time.

[2] Similarly, $\Delta(yP)$ is read as the rate of change of the product of real income and the price level.

[3] Mathematically, the growth rate of any variable h at time 0 is

$$\frac{h_z - h_0}{h_0 \cdot z}$$

where z is arbitrarily small. That is, the rate of change of h is the derivative of h with respect to time divided by h.

[4] Similarly $\Gamma(yP)$ is read as the growth rate of the product of real income and the price level.

For any variable h, the growth rate is related to the rate of change by

$$\Gamma h \equiv \frac{\Delta h}{h} \qquad\qquad [5.1]$$

A more detailed discussion of these measures of growth is contained in Sec. M.4 of the Mathematical Appendix.

Two rules on growth rates derived in the Mathematical Appendix are used repeatedly below: (1) The growth rate of a product of two or more variables equals the *sum* of the growth rates of these variables. (2) The growth rate of a ratio of two variables equals the growth rate of the numerator variable minus the growth rate of the denominator variable.

A moving equilibrium or *steady state* refers to an economy in which all economic aggregates—such as income, price level, population, and money supply—are growing at constant rates. If all these growth rates are zero so that all these aggregates have the same value year after year, the steady state is called a *stationary state*. The steady-state growth path of an economy is a useful standard against which the actual current economic performance can be measured.

The underlying factors in a growing economy can be divided into the same two broadly separate classes of real and monetary factors that were useful for analyzing the determination of the levels of income and prices. The separation is usually less clear-cut, however, in an economy characterized by steady-state growth, because current rates of growth will continue into the future and expectations of the future have a pervasive influence.

5.2 DETERMINANTS OF REAL GROWTH

THE PROXIMATE DETERMINANTS OF REAL INCOME GROWTH

Growth in real income occurs through growth in the inputs to the productive process, labor and capital, through changes in the aggregate production function, or both. Although one normally thinks of an upward secular growth in real income, continuing adverse changes—such as those due to the introduction of a fatal disease to an isolated country—may cause negative rates of growth over a period of some time.

In analyzing steady-state growth, basic determinants are separated into two groups: (1) those affected in a predictable way by economic factors and (2) those which are not. The determinants in the first group are said to be *endogenous*, or determined within the economic model based on the given values of the second group of *exogenous* determinants which define the outside conditions to which the economic system adjusts. Much recent history of economic thought is based on reclassifying exogenous determinants as endogenous variables while economists expand their understanding of economic influences on such traditionally "noneconomic variables" as population growth, education, marriage, crime, and legal structures. This expansion of the class of endogenous variables also reflects an expanded technical ability to deal with many factors at the same time, so that previously neglected minor influences no longer need be ignored. Modern models of economic growth have become very complex and mathematically elegant explanations of the reasons behind some generally observed empirical regularities. Only the most basic results are presented here, leaving more detailed discussions to specialized courses.

In most simple growth models the growth rate of labor is assumed to be fixed by noneconomic factors at a constant rate. Using an overbar to denote particular constant values of a variable, this rate is $\overline{\Gamma l}$. If the growth rate of labor is constant and the amount of labor at any point in time is known, it is possible to compute the amount of labor at every other instant.[5] More elaborate models have been developed in which the growth rate of labor is influenced by economic factors. Because essentially the same results are obtained by more complicated methods, it will be assumed in the current presentation that the growth of labor is an exogenously fixed factor to which the economy adjusts. The effects on the economy of alternative growth rates of labor would be a problem in comparative dynamics.[6]

The growth rate of capital Γk is the rate of change in the capital stock Δk divided by the capital stock:

$$\Gamma k \equiv \frac{\Delta k}{k} \qquad\qquad [5.2]$$

If the capital stock is measured in base-year dollars, the rate of change in the capital stock will be equal to the rate of real investment i. Thus,

$$\Gamma k \equiv \frac{i}{k} \qquad\qquad [5.3]$$

That is, the growth rate of capital equals the proportionate rate per annum at which capital is increased by investment.

The simplified national accounting system used in this and the preceding chapter was shown in [4.16] to imply that real saving s and real investment will be equal:

$$s \equiv i \qquad\qquad [5.4]$$

---

[5] As shown in the Mathematical Appendix, if the amount of labor at time 0 is l_0 and the growth rate is $\overline{\Gamma l}$, then the amount of labor at time z is

$$l_z = l_0\, e^{\overline{\Gamma l} z}$$

[6] Comparative dynamics compares two growth equilibriums. Several such comparisons are made in the text. The effect of alternative growth rates of labor is the subject of problem 3 in the Questions and Exercises.

It was also noted in Chap. 4 that real saving can be approximated very well as a constant, say σ, times real income y:

$$s = \sigma y \qquad [5.5]$$

Combining [5.3], [5.4], and [5.5],

$$\Gamma k = \sigma \frac{y}{k} \qquad [5.6]$$

That is, the growth rate of capital equals the saving-income ratio times the ratio of income to capital. The equation is used to endogenously determine the growth rate of capital.

The analysis is greatly simplified by assuming that the aggregate production function $y = f(k, l)$ is homogeneous of the first degree and does not change over the period being studied. The first requirement means that output changes in proportion to changes in capital and labor (constant returns to scale). So if both capital and labor were doubled, income would also be doubled. If the aggregate production function is of this form, it can also be written as

$$y = k \cdot f(1, l/k) \qquad [5.7]$$

Figure 5.1 The output-capital ratio as a function of the labor-capital ratio. For an aggregate production function that is homogeneous of the first degree, the entire production function can be summarized by the production function for a unit of capital and its share of labor l/k. The decreasing slope of the curve reflects the Law of Diminishing Returns.

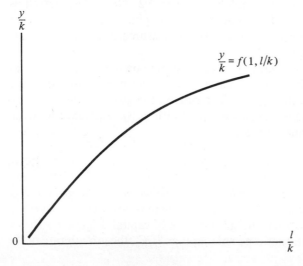

since total output will equal output per unit of capital times the total capital stock. The ratio of output to capital can be found by dividing both sides of [5.7] by k

$$\frac{y}{k} = f(1, \, l/k) \tag{5.8}$$

This ratio is graphed in Fig. 5.1 as a function of the labor-capital ratio. As when the production function was graphed for a given quantity of capital in Chap. 4 (Fig. 4.1), the decreasing slope of the curve reflects the smaller increase in output from a given increase in labor as the ratio of labor to capital increases.

The requirement that the aggregate production function not change over time is not as strong as would first appear. Changes in technology are possible so long as they are embodied in our measures of capital and labor as quality changes. The government-supplied factors of production, implicit in the aggregate production function, will normally increase in proportion with capital and labor; thus, one can act *as if* the production function were an unchanging homogeneous-of-degree-one function of capital and labor alone.

STEADY-STATE REAL EQUILIBRIUM

The growth rate of capital was shown in [5.6] to equal the saving-income ratio σ times the output-capital ratio. Combining this result with [5.8] expresses the growth rate of capital as an increasing function of the labor-capital ratio:

$$\Gamma k = \sigma f(1, \, l/k) \tag{5.9}$$

The graphical interpretation is presented in Fig. 5.2. Note that output is measured in units of base-year dollars per year and capital in units of base-year dollars, consequently the output-capital ratio is measured in per annum units as is the growth rate of capital.

The constant growth rate of labor can be illustrated on the same diagram as a horizontal line intersecting the vertical axis at $\overline{\Gamma l}$ which is measured in per annum units. This is done in Fig. 5.3. The rule on the growth rate of a ratio implies that the growth rate of the labor-capital ratio is the difference between the growth rates of labor and capital:

$$\Gamma(l/k) \equiv \Gamma l - \Gamma k \tag{5.10}$$

The growth rate of the labor-capital ratio is positive whenever the growth rate of labor exceeds the growth rate of capital; its growth is negative whenever the growth rate of labor is less than the growth rate of capital. Figure 5.3 shows that should any labor-capital ratio be smaller than l_e/k_e, the growth rate of the

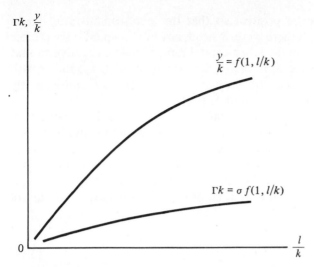

Figure 5.2 Relation of the growth rate of capital to the output-capital ratio. The growth rate of capital is obtained by multiplying the output-capital ratio by the constant fraction σ. Since the output-capital ratio increases, at a diminishing rate, with increases in the labor-capital ratio, so does the growth rate of capital.

Figure 5.3 Determination of real sector growth equilibrium. For any l/k greater than l_e/k_e, Γk exceeds Γl and l/k will be falling toward l_e/k_e. Similarly, for any l/k less than l_e/k_e, Γl exceeds Γk and l/k will be rising toward l_e/k_e. Thus, the economy tends toward l_e/k_e and $\Gamma k = \Gamma l$. Output per unit of capital will therefore tend to y_e/k_e with $\Gamma y = \Gamma k$.

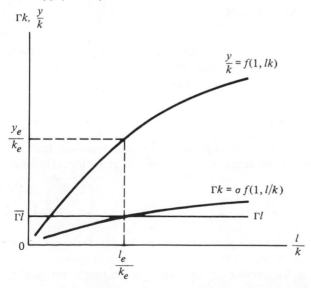

labor-capital ratio would be positive so that the labor-capital ratio would approach l_e/k_e over time. If there were, instead, any labor-capital ratio greater than l_e/k_e, the growth rate of the labor-capital ratio would be negative so that the labor-capital ratio would approach l_e/k_e over time. At l_e/k_e, the growth rate of capital Γk just equals the growth rate of labor, Γl, consequently the labor-capital ratio remains constant $[\Gamma(l/k) = 0]$.

Thus, a stable-equilibrium labor-capital ratio (l_e/k_e) exists. It is maintained when saving is just sufficient to finance new units of capital for use with new units of labor in the same proportion as exists for the previous amounts of labor. Should a macroeconomic shock such as that discussed in Part Three move the economy away from this equilibrium, it will return over time.

Since there is a constant-equilibrium labor-capital ratio, output per unit of capital will also be constant at

$$\frac{y_e}{k_e} = f(1, l_e/k_e) \tag{5.11}$$

as shown in Fig. 5.3. This ratio can be constant only if the growth rate of real income is equal to the growth rate of capital, which in turn equals the constant growth rate of labor. Thus, in full, steady-state equilibrium, it follows that

$$\overline{\Gamma y} = \overline{\Gamma k} = \overline{\Gamma l} \tag{5.12}$$

The endogenous growth rates of real income and capital thus adjust to equal the exogenous constant growth rate of labor.

IMPLICATIONS OF STEADY-STATE
GROWTH FOR THE STANDARD OF LIVING

The *standard of living* is measured by per capita real income, or y/n in terms of the age-eligible population. The growth rate of per capita real income is the difference between the growth rates of real income and population:

$$\Gamma(y/n) \equiv \Gamma y - \Gamma n \tag{5.13}$$

Assuming a constant growth rate of population $\overline{\Gamma n}$ and recalling that the steady-state growth rate of real income equals the constant growth rate of labor $\overline{\Gamma l}$,

$$\overline{\Gamma(y/n)} = \overline{\Gamma l} - \overline{\Gamma n} \tag{5.14}$$

Consequently, per capita real income grows at the rate by which the growth of labor exceeds the growth of population.

The quantity of labor is the product of the participation rate π, the quality index q, and the age-eligible population n; so the growth rate of labor is the sum of the growth rates of these three factors:

$$\Gamma l \equiv \Gamma \pi + \Gamma q + \Gamma n \qquad [5.15]$$

If it is assumed that each of these growth rates is a constant—$\overline{\Gamma \pi}$, $\overline{\Gamma q}$, and $\overline{\Gamma n}$, respectively—substitution in [5.14] shows that

$$\overline{\Gamma(y/n)} = \overline{\Gamma \pi} + \overline{\Gamma q} \qquad [5.16]$$

Thus growth in the standard of living ultimately reflects growth in the labor participation rate and in the average quality of labor.

The participation growth rate reflects trends in the average work week and work life as well as in sex and race participation. The growth rate of average quality reflects the impact of steadily increased education and on-the-job training. In the United States, the distinctly positive trend in the growth rate of the quality of the labor force has been the major contributor to growth in per capita real income. The fact that the growth rate of the standard of living can be increased if the growth rate of participation is increased reminds us that the data of the national income accounts are only one factor which must be combined with evaluations of leisure and social institutions to make a comparison of different economies across time or space.

The distribution of income between labor and capital is also implied by the growth model. A constant labor-capital ratio implies that the steady-state growth of the economy occurs at a single point on the per unit of capital version of the aggregate production function:

$$\frac{y_e}{k_e} = f(1, \, l_e/k_e)$$

As a result, the marginal products of capital and labor—and thus the real rental rate on capital and the real wage of labor—are constants.

The average real interest rate paid on all securities will equal this constant real rental rate per unit of capital.[7] In steady-state equilibrium, firms cannot pay out more than the rental earned on their capital, while competition among firms for financing prevents them from paying less. The real wage as measured per unit of raw labor is also constant, but the average hourly wage of individual workers will rise with their growing average quality.

Since a constant amount is earned per unit of capital and per unit of labor and since capital and labor grow in constant proportion, the ratio of people's total earnings from capital to their total earnings from labor will be constant in

---

[7] Some securities with below-average risk or inconvenience of trading will pay less than average so that those accepting correspondingly less attractive securities can be paid more.

steady-state equilibrium. This, in fact, is found to hold fairly well over long periods of time. In the United States, personal income is derived on average about one-quarter from capital and three-quarters from labor.[8]

A GRAPH OF STEADY-STATE REAL INCOME

In Part Three we will relate short-run cyclical fluctuations to long-run trend behavior by examining graphs over time of the values of variables such as real income. This is easier if the variables are scaled by plotting the (natural) logarithm of their values rather than the values themselves. The reason for this is that the slope of the graph of the logarithm of a variable is equal to the growth rate of the variable. For example, the secular growth rate of real income is a constant $\overline{\Gamma y}$ so the graph of the logarithm of trend real income is a straight line with slope $\overline{\Gamma y}$. Logarithms are used extensively in this book for the purposes of scaling variables—but not for computations. Their properties are reviewed in Sec. M.3 of the Mathematical Appendix.

Panel (a) of Fig. 5.4 graphs the logarithm of the steady-state equilibrium values of real income, log y—the log of steady-state real income, for short. Because it grows at a constant rate $\overline{\Gamma y}$, this graph is a straight line. The term *growth path* is used to refer to such a graph of the logarithm of a variable.

Panel (b) of Fig. 5.4 graphs the corresponding steady-state growth rate of real income $\overline{\Gamma y}$ as a horizontal line at height $\overline{\Gamma y}$. It is easy to graph the growth rate below the growth path of a variable because the former is the slope of the latter.[9]

THE EFFECTS OF THE SAVING-INCOME RATIO ON STEADY-STATE EQUILIBRIUM

A surprising result of the analysis of steady-state equilibrium is that the saving-income ratio σ does not affect the growth rate of real income. The growth rate of real income adjusts to equal the growth rate of labor. The saving-income ratio does, however, generally affect the level of real income at any particular point in time.[10]

The effects of alternative values of the saving-income ratio are analyzed by comparative dynamics. Suppose that two alternatives are compared, σ_0 and σ_1, and that σ_1 is greater than σ_0. All other conditions are assumed equal. This

[8] Irving B. Kravis, Relative Income Shares in Fact and Theory, *American Economic Review*, **49**: 917–949, Dec. 1959.
[9] The slope of the growth path of any variable h is Δ log h. In the Mathematical Appendix it is shown that Δ log $h \equiv \Delta h/h \equiv \Gamma h$. Section M.6 explains how to read slopes from graphs.
[10] It is therefore possible to build neo-Malthusian growth models in which the growth rate of labor depends on the *level* of per capita income so that the saving-income ratio will affect the growth rate of real income. The empirical relevance of such models is far from clear, particularly for developed nations.

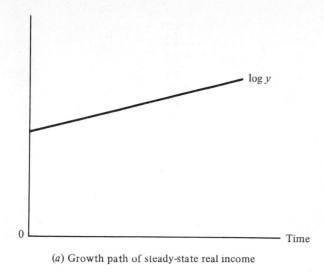

(a) Growth path of steady-state real income

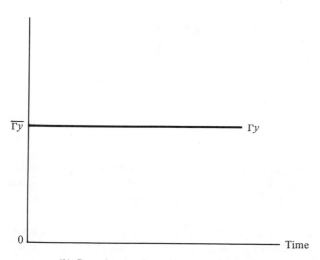

(b) Growth rate of steady-state real income

Figure 5.4 Steady-state real income. Panel (a) graphs the logarithm of the steady-state equilibrium values of real income. Its constant slope is equal to the steady-state growth rate of real income as graphed in panel (b).

means that in each instance there is the same growth rate of labor $\overline{\Gamma l}$ and aggregate production function $f(\ \ )$. Figure 5.5 repeats Fig. 5.3 but with two alternative curves for the growth rate of capital: $\Gamma k = \sigma_0 f(1, l/k)$ and $\Gamma k = \sigma_1 f(1, l, k)$. Equilibrium exists in each case where the growth rate of capital equals the growth rate of labor $\overline{\Gamma l}$. Subscripts 0 and 1 are used to indicate the equilibrium values of variables according to whether the saving

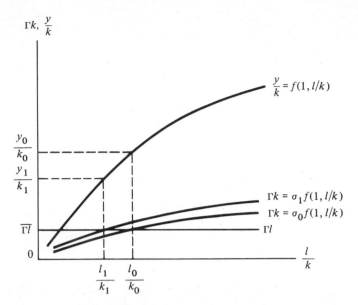

Figure 5.5 The effects of alternative saving-income ratios on steady-state equilibrium. State 0 is characterized by σ_0 and state 1 by σ_1. All other conditions are the same, but σ_1 is greater than σ_0. The resulting equilibria are $l_0/k_0 > l_1/k_1$ and $y_0/k_0 > y_1/k_1$. Although the real income per unit of capital is lower in state 1 than in state 0, the higher total amount of capital and equal amounts of labor imply that real income will be higher in state 1 than in state 0. In each state the growth rate of capital and real income will equal the growth rate of labor $\overline{\Gamma}l$.

ratio is σ_0 or σ_1, respectively. The equilibrium labor-capital ratios are found in Fig. 5.5 to be l_0/k_0 and l_1/k_1. The corresponding equilibrium income-capital ratios are y_0/k_0 and y_1/k_1. Thus, a higher saving-income ratio implies a lower labor-capital ratio.

Since the quantity of labor is exogenously given at any point in time, a lower labor-capital ratio implies that there is more capital with σ_1 than with σ_0. More capital and the same amount of labor imply more output at any point in time.[11]

These results are summarized in Fig. 5.6. The growth paths of y_0 and y_1 are drawn parallel because they have the same growth rate $\overline{\Gamma}l$ and therefore the same slope. At any instant of time, real income is higher in the case with the higher saving-income ratio. But real income grows at the same proportionate rate in both cases.

---

[11] Formally, the same argument used to derive [5.7] yields $y = l \cdot f(k/l, 1)$. At any instant l is the same in both cases ($l_0 = l_1$), but $k_1/l_1 > k_0/l_0$ so $y_1 > y_0$.

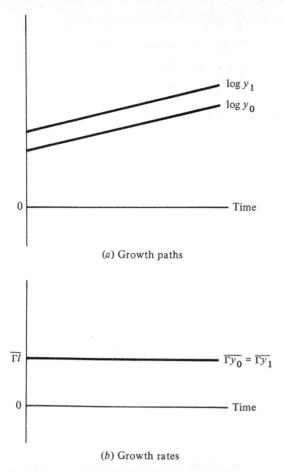

(a) Growth paths

(b) Growth rates

Figure 5.6 Growth paths of real income for alternative saving-income ratios. The growth paths of y_0 and y_1 where $\sigma_0 < \sigma_1$ are illustrated in (a). At any instant, $y_1 > y_0$, but the growth rates are identical and equal to $\overline{\Gamma l}$ [see (b)]. So the growth paths are parallel straight lines with slope $\overline{\Gamma l}$. Note that the quantity $\log(y_1/y_0) \equiv \log y_1 - \log y_0$ is a positive constant, so that y_1/y_0 is a constant ratio with a value greater than 1.

SUMMARY OF THE REAL STEADY-STATE EQUILIBRIUM

Real income grows at a constant rate equal to the growth rate of labor. Capital grows at the same rate. Per capita income grows at the sum of the growth rates of the labor participation rate and the labor quality index. The real rental rate on capital, the real wage rate, and the real interest rate are also constant. Alternative saving-income ratios affect the steady-state level, but not the growth rate, of real income.

5.3 STEADY-STATE GROWTH OF NOMINAL VARIABLES

THE DYNAMIC VERSION OF THE CAMBRIDGE IDENTITY

The growth of nominal variables is most easily analyzed in terms of the Cambridge identity [4.22] which is rewritten here:

$$M \equiv \phi y P \tag{5.17}$$

Nominal money equals the product of fluidity, real income, and the price level. Applying the rule on the growth rate of a product yields the *dynamic Cambridge identity:*

$$\Gamma M \equiv \Gamma \phi + \Gamma y + \Gamma P \tag{5.18}$$

The growth rate of nominal money equals the sum of the growth rates of fluidity, real income, and the price level.

The *inflation rate* is the growth rate of the price level. A statement that the rate of inflation was 6 percent per annum over the last year means that price level is 6 percent higher now than it was a year ago. We can solve [5.18] for the inflation rate:

$$\Gamma P \equiv \Gamma M - \Gamma \phi - \Gamma y \tag{5.19}$$

The inflation rate is explained in terms of the three growth rates on the right-hand side of identity [5.19]: the growth rates of nominal money, fluidity, and real income. Identity [5.19] can be interpreted by recalling that real money equals the product of fluidity and real income, so

$$\Gamma m \equiv \Gamma \phi + \Gamma y \tag{5.20}$$

We see that the rate of inflation is shown in [5.19] to equal the difference between the growth rates of nominal money and real money.[12]

DETERMINATION OF THE RATE OF INFLATION

The growth rate of nominal money is assumed to be determined by the government's monetary policy. This is an extension of our procedure in Chap. 4 where we solved for the price level at an instant of time, given the nominal money supply chosen by the government. We will denote the chosen value of the

---

[12] Recall that the determination of the *level* of the price level was summarized using [4.29] in terms of the ratio of nominal money to real money. Applying the rule on the growth rate of a ratio, the growth rate version of [4.29] is $\Gamma P \equiv \Gamma M - \Gamma m$. This is the same as [5.19] except that Γm is broken down into its component parts here.

growth rate as $\overline{\Gamma M}$ and solve for the corresponding inflation rate. Recall that we are dealing here with the secular trends in nominal money growth and inflation. Short-run fluctuations around these trends will be considered in Part Three. Different trend growth rates of nominal money would imply different rates of inflation, as will be seen below.

The growth rate of real income was determined in Sec. 5.2 to be $\overline{\Gamma y}$. We can use this value directly here.

In long-run equilibrium actual fluidity will equal its desired values. This is equivalent to saying that money demand and supply will be equal. So the growth rate of fluidity can be explained by changes in the factors which determine the desired value of fluidity. Desired fluidity at an instant of time was written in compact form in [4.25] as

$$\phi^d = \phi^d(y, R) \tag{5.21}$$

Real income growth will cause desired fluidity to increase or decrease over time if people want to hold an increasing or decreasing fraction of their wealth as money as they become wealthier.[13] The level of nominal interest rates R will be shown to be constant in steady-state equilibrium. So while the *level* of R affects the *level* of fluidity, interest rate changes are not a contributor to the growth rate of fluidity. Perhaps the most important determinants of the growth rate of fluidity—changes in technical and institutional conditions which affect the use of money in making transactions—are not explicit in [5.21]. As of now we have no good way of measuring these factors. It is observed however that there are long periods, measured in decades, over which the trend growth rate of fluidity appears nearly constant. So we assume that the combined effects of real income growth, institutional changes, and technological progress produce a constant secular growth rate of fluidity $\overline{\Gamma \phi}$.

The steady-state equilibrium rate of inflation is found by substituting these three values into [5.19]:

$$\overline{\Gamma P} = \overline{\Gamma M} - (\overline{\Gamma \phi} + \overline{\Gamma y}) \tag{5.22}$$

This equation says that the inflation rate will be the difference between the growth rate of the nominal money supply determined by monetary policy and the growth rate of real money demand $(\overline{\Gamma \phi} + \overline{\Gamma y})$. This rate of inflation will maintain continuous equality—once in a position of equilibrium—of the supply and demand for money.

---

[13] Formally, if η is the real income elasticity of the demand for real money, then the contribution of real income growth to the fluidity growth rate is $(\eta - 1)\overline{\Gamma y}$. If η exceeds 1 (money is a luxury), then real income growth increases the growth rate of fluidity. If η is less than 1 (money is a necessity), then real income growth decreases the growth rate of fluidity.

AN ALTERNATIVE APPROACH

A more roundabout approach is convenient for graphical analysis—particularly when we examine fluctuations around the long-run equilibrium in Part Three. This approach starts from the nominal income form of the Cambridge identity [1.2]:

$$M \equiv \phi Y \qquad\qquad [5.23]$$

The corresponding dynamic identity is

$$\Gamma M \equiv \Gamma \phi + \Gamma Y \qquad\qquad [5.24]$$

If we substitute the trend growth rates of nominal money and fluidity, the equilibrium growth rate of nominal income is solved as

$$\overline{\Gamma Y} = \overline{\Gamma M} - \overline{\Gamma \phi} \qquad\qquad [5.25]$$

Nominal income grows in equilibrium at a rate equal to the amount by which growth in the nominal money supply exceeds growth in nominal money demand relative to nominal income.

Panel (b) of Fig. 5.7 illustrates the determination of the equilibrium growth rate of nominal income given the growth rates of nominal money and fluidity. First the constant growth rate of money is graphed as a horizontal line at a height of $\overline{\Gamma M}$. Then the constant growth rate of fluidity is graphed as a horizontal line at $\overline{\Gamma \phi}$. It is assumed here that $\overline{\Gamma \phi}$ is negative, because that corresponds to the U.S. experience of the last quarter century.[14] At other times, such as when banks were spreading rapidly during the nineteenth century, different and sometimes positive secular growth rates of fluidity have been observed. Since ΓY is always exactly equal to $\Gamma M - \Gamma \phi$, it is plotted at a height $\overline{\Gamma Y}$ equal to the vertical distance between ΓM and $\Gamma \phi$.

Panel (a) of Fig. 5.7 illustrates the corresponding growth paths of nominal money, fluidity, and nominal income. The growth paths can be drawn by plotting the logarithms of the equilibrium values of nominal money, fluidity, and nominal income for a particular instant of time and then drawing straight lines through these points with slopes equal to $\overline{\Gamma M}$, $\overline{\Gamma \phi}$, and $\overline{\Gamma Y}$, respectively. Starting from an equilibrium value and applying the growth rate of the equilibrium value traces out the growth of the equilibrium value over time.

Two rules on logarithms (corresponding to the two rules on growth rates) make it easy to draw graphs like panel (a) of Fig. 5.7: (1) The logarithm of a

---

[14] This is based on the narrow (M_1) definition of the money supply. Fluidity defined as the ratio of M_2 to nominal income has had an essentially zero growth rate. The difference apparently reflects a gradual shift of transaction balances from what are officially classified as demand deposits to time deposits.

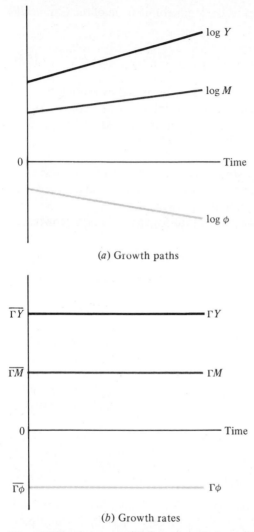

(a) Growth paths

(b) Growth rates

Figure 5.7 Steady-state equilibrium of nominal money, fluidity, and nominal income.
Panel (b) illustrates the constant steady-state equilibrium growth rates of nominal
money and fluidity by horizontal lines at $\overline{\Gamma M}$ and $\overline{\Gamma \phi}$, respectively. The growth
rate of nominal income is the vertical distance between these two lines which is
the constant $\overline{\Gamma Y}$. Panel (a) shows the corresponding growth paths. The log M line is
determined by monetary policy. The log ϕ line is determined by factors affecting
real money demand. The log Y line plots the vertical distance between the log M
and log ϕ lines at each instant. The growth rates in panel (b) are the slopes of the
lines in panel (a).

product of two or more variables equals the *sum* of the logarithms of these
variables. (2) The logarithm of a ratio of two variables equals the logarithm of
the numerator variable minus the logarithm of the denominator variable.

Applying the first rule to [5.23] gives us the logarithmic form of the Cambridge identity:

$$\log M \equiv \log \phi + \log Y \qquad [5.26]$$

Once we draw the growth paths of M and ϕ as determined by monetary policy and forces affecting real money demand, nominal income can be drawn simply at a height equal to the vertical distance between the $\log M$ and $\log \phi$ lines. This height changes over time but it is easy to plot a straight line with two points.

Figure 5.8 adds the graphs of the steady-state growth path and growth rate of nominal income to the corresponding graphs for real income which were presented in Fig. 5.4. The growth path and growth rate of the price level are derived by converting the identity $P \equiv Y/y$ into logarithmic and growth rate forms:

$$\log P \equiv \log Y - \log y \qquad [5.27]$$

$$\Gamma P \equiv \Gamma Y - \Gamma y \qquad [5.28]$$

Panel (*a*) of Fig. 5.8 plots the growth path of the price level as the vertical distance at each instant between the $\log Y$ and $\log y$ lines. Panel (*b*) similarly plots the inflation rate ΓP as the vertical distance between the ΓY and Γy lines. The construction of Figs. 5.7 and 5.8 is such that this roundabout method yields the same inflation rate as the direct solution [5.22].[15] This graphical representation of steady-state equilibrium simplifies the later discussion of short-run fluctuations.

INFLATION AND THE PRICE LEVEL

The concepts of inflation and the price level lend themselves to easy confusion which should be carefully avoided. *Inflation* properly refers to a condition of *rising* prices or a positive rate of inflation. This should not be confused with prices which are *high* relative to past levels. Prices must have risen at some time in the past in order to be high in the present, but ending inflation would simply require a zero growth rate or constant price level, not a return of prices from their high level to some—which?—"normal" level. *Deflation* is a condition of *falling* prices—not low prices—or a negative rate of inflation. The term *rate of deflation* is sometimes used for minus the rate of inflation.

In the discussion in Chap. 4 of the effect of a 10 percent increase in the money supply on the price level, it was shown that the price level would also

---

[15] This is confirmed by substituting [5.25] into [5.28].

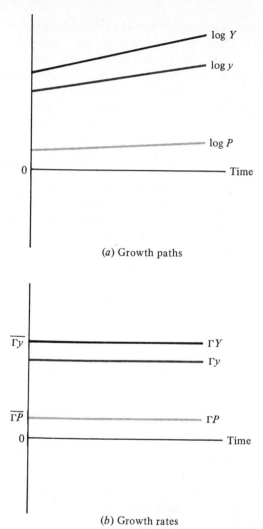

(a) Growth paths

(b) Growth rates

Figure 5.8 Steady-state equilibrium of nominal income, real income, and the price level. Panel (b) reproduces the equilibrium growth rates of nominal income and real income from Figs. 5.7 and 5.4 respectively. The growth rate of the price level is the constant vertical distance $\overline{\Gamma P}$ between the ΓY and Γy lines. Panel (a) reproduces the equilibrium growth paths of nominal income and real income from Figs. 5.7 and 5.4 respectively. The growth path of the price level labeled log P is the vertical distance between log Y and log y at each instant. The growth rates in panel (b) are the slopes of the lines in panel (a).

increase by 10 percent. That result was for a hypothetical comparison of two alternative money supplies at the same point in time. In this chapter we have been considering the actual effects expected to result from changes in the money supply that occur over a time during which the conditions of the real economy will be changing in predictable ways. If the money supply grows by 10 percent *over a year* in an economy in steady-state equilibrium, one must subtract the rate of growth in real income and fluidity to derive the rate of increase in prices over time. For example, if these rates were 3 percent and 1 percent, respectively, the price level would increase by 6 percent. Nevertheless, were the money supply to be 10 percent lower at each point in time—though growing by 10 percent over the year—then the price level at each point in time would be 10 percent lower than in the first case. This latter comparison is made for given points in time for which the conditions of the real economy are the same—a problem in comparative statics.

The rate of inflation, though dependent on the growth rates of real income and fluidity, is essentially a monetary phenomenon in this sense: Changes in the rate of growth in money are matched percentage point for percentage point by changes in the rate of inflation; and changes in the growth rate of the money supply, being subject to government policy, can change widely as compared to the growth rates of the real variables. More generally, inflation results from a more rapid increase in the nominal money supply than in the real money demand.

SPECIAL THEORIES OF INFLATION

The theory of inflation just discussed has been—with the possible exception of the downward sloping demand curve—the most thoroughly tested and documented of economic propositions. Despite the universal conformity of economic experience in different times and different countries to the theory, there is an almost equally universal tendency in each case to attempt to explain inflations at the time they occur by special circumstances rather than by the general rule. Such rationalizations are particularly valued by politicians wishing to bear neither the blame for the costs of reducing the rate of inflation—discussed in Parts Three and Six—nor the blame for the continuation of high rates of monetary growth and inflation.

The special circumstances most widely offered as explanation for the inflation of the 1960s and 1970s are the powers possessed by monopolistic businessmen and unionists to set prices and wages. These powers have been used greedily, it is asserted, thereby causing inflation. Like any popular fallacy, this rationalization is based upon a kernel of truth: Monopoly power due to market closure reduces real income and raises the price level for a given quantity of money relative to the values they would have were markets open to entry. But this is an argument for high, not rising prices. A monopolist may be able to change his price from the profit maximizing one, but only if he is willing to suffer a reduction in income. Only if monopoly power due to market closure is increasing will the rate of growth of income fall and prices rise. So any effect of monopoly on the rate of inflation is associated only with periods of changing degrees of market closure. If market closure increases, the aggregate production function is affected adversely; the reverse is true for a decrease in market closure. There is no evidence of any change in the degree of market closure in the 1960s and 1970s, or of monopolists doing anything other than adjusting their nominal prices to reflect inflation.[16]

INFLATION AND INTEREST RATES

The influence of the inflation rate on interest rates is most easily illustrated by noting that the growth rate of an amount left to continuously compound is the interest rate.[17] If the amount is measured in nominal (dollar) terms, the interest rate is a nominal interest rate. If the amount is measured in real (base-year dollar) terms, the interest rate is a real interest rate. If H is the value of an asset in nominal terms, then $h \equiv H/P$ is the value of the asset in real terms. Using the rule on the growth rate of a ratio, the growth rate of the real value of the asset is the growth rate of its nominal value minus the rate of inflation:

$$r \equiv R - \Gamma P \qquad [5.29]$$

The nominal interest rate R exceeds the real interest rate r by the inflation rate ΓP because the increase in the nominal value of the asset is counted in the nominal but not in the real interest rate.

The average real interest rate in the economy must equal the marginal product of capital.[18] Some security holders may receive more and others less because of differences in risk, but the average must equal the total real income flow divided by the total real value of the capital stock. The marginal product of capital, and hence the real interest rate, is a constant $\bar{r}$ fixed by the conditions of steady-state equilibrium as discussed in Sec. 5.2. The inflation rate was just determined to be $\overline{\Gamma P}$, so we can solve for the nominal interest rate

$$\bar{R} = \bar{r} + \overline{\Gamma P} \qquad [5.30]$$

This equation is often called the *Fisher equation* after Irving Fisher who developed and tested it.

The Fisher equation states that the nominal interest rate quoted on loans

---

[16] Curiously, the only case in modern American history, aside from wars, of an apparent major shift in the aggregate production function was associated with the passage (June 1933) of the National Industrial Recovery Act and the declaration two years later by the Supreme Court that the act was unconstitutional. The act raised prices and wages by closing markets to competition, but the high real income associated by the politicians with high prices did not appear. Instead, industrial production was below that achieved in 1933 before the NIRA until several months after the Supreme Court declaration.

[17] Using formula [3.7] the proportionate increase in a loan L_0 for a period of time z is

$$\frac{L_z - L_0}{L_0 \cdot z} \equiv \frac{(1 + Rz)L_0 - L_0}{L_0 \cdot z} \equiv R$$

If z is arbitrarily small, the left-hand expression is the growth rate of L as formally defined in footnote 3 above, and R is the continuously compounded interest rate.

[18] The marginal product of capital is the real flow of output in base-year dollars per base-year dollar of capital.

expressed in dollars will equal in long-run equilibrium the real interest rate which would be quoted if the inflation rate were zero plus the actual inflation rate. Lenders demand the higher nominal interest rate to offset the declining real value of the nominal principal amount. Borrowers are willing to pay the higher rates because they know that they will be paying back less valuable dollars.

The Fisher equation was developed around the beginning of the twentieth century, when income taxes were negligible. It must be amended now to take account of U.S. tax laws.[19] Under these laws, the nominal interest payment to compensate for the decline in real value of the principal is taxable as income to the lender and deductible from the taxable income of the borrower. This transfers tax liability so that, if the Fisher equation held, after-tax real interest payments would be less than with no inflation. As a result the nominal interest rate will exceed the real interest rate by enough to compensate lenders for both the decline in the real value of the nominal principal and the tax liability transferred. The borrowers in effect reduce their own tax payments and pass the money on to the lenders, who pay it for them. The tax-amended Fisher equation is

$$R \equiv r + \frac{\Gamma P}{1 - \tau} \qquad\qquad [5.31]$$

where τ is the marginal tax rate reflected in the market for interest payments and deductions.[20] This formula is illustrated in Example 5.1. The tax-amended Fisher equation indicates that a positive inflation rate will increase the nominal interest rate above the real interest rate by more than the inflation rate. For example if the tax rate τ was 20 percent, the real interest rate $\bar{r}$ was 3 percent per annum, and the inflation rate $\overline{\Gamma P}$ was 4 percent per annum, the nominal interest rate would be

$$\bar{R} = \frac{0.03}{\text{year}} + \frac{0.04/\text{year}}{1 - 0.20}$$

$$= \frac{0.03}{\text{year}} + \frac{5}{4} \cdot \frac{0.04}{\text{year}}$$

$$= \frac{0.03}{\text{year}} + \frac{0.05}{\text{year}} = \frac{0.08}{\text{year}}$$

or 8 percent per annum.

---

[19] Most countries which have experienced substantial sustained inflations have changed their tax laws to eliminate the tax effect discussed here.

[20] In a positive inflation rate situation, compared with a zero inflation rate case, there is a tendency for taxes on profits to increase due to the use of historical cost depreciation. This would affect the real interest rate in a complicated way. We assume, however, that tax laws are adjusted through accelerated depreciation and changes in nominal tax rates to maintain the same real tax burden. A similar case arises for personal income taxes— people with a given real income are pushed into higher tax brackets because of their rising nominal income. In both cases, politicians love to announce "tax cuts" which in fact just leave the real burden unchanged.

When a borrower and a lender agree on a nominal interest rate, it is the inflation rate which they *expect* to observe over the life of the loan which matters. Once the contract is signed, the nominal interest rate is fixed. If the inflation rate turns out to be higher than expected, the borrower wins and the lender loses, because dollars less valuable than expected are repaid. It works just the opposite if the actual inflation rate is lower than expected. Because we are dealing with an economy in long-run steady-state equilibrium in Part Two, the actual and expected inflation rates will be equal. In Part Three, we will see that this is not always so.

The equilibrium nominal rate of interest can be characterized as a monetary phenomenon much as is the rate of inflation. The influence, however, runs from money-supply growth to the rate of inflation to the expected rate of inflation and finally to the nominal interest rate.

EXAMPLE 5.1

TAXES, INFLATION, AND INTEREST

Suppose that a lender of $1,000 agrees to a nominal interest rate of 5 percent per annum, compounded annually, when the inflation rate is zero. At the end of a year the lender would receive $1,050. If the effective tax rate were 20 percent, then 20 percent or $10 of the nominal interest received ($50) would go to the government. So after taxes only $1,040 would be received by the lender. If the price level were $1.00/R$ at the beginning of the year, it would be the same at the end of the year since the inflation rate is zero. So the real principal would be R$1,000, the real amount repaid after taxes would be R$1,040, and the *after-tax* real interest rate would be

$$\frac{R\$40/\text{year}}{R\$1000} = \frac{0.04}{\text{year}}$$

or 4 percent per annum.

Now suppose that the inflation rate were 4 percent per annum, compounded annually. Formula [5.31] would suggest that the lender should charge a nominal interest rate

$$R = \frac{0.05}{\text{year}} + \frac{0.04/\text{year}}{1 - 0.2}$$

$$R = \frac{0.05}{\text{year}} + \frac{0.04/\text{year}}{0.8}$$

$$R = \frac{0.05}{\text{year}} + \frac{0.05}{\text{year}} = \frac{0.10}{\text{year}}$$

or 10 percent per annum. Let us check the after-tax real interest rate which would be received. The lender would be repaid $1,100. Of the $100 nominal interest payment, $20 would go for taxes, and the after-tax nominal repayment would be $1,080. If the price level grew at 4 percent per annum from $1.00/R$ to $1.04/R$, the real amount lent would be R$1,000 and the real amount repaid would be

$$\frac{\$1,080}{\$1.04/R\$} = R\$1,038.46$$

The after-tax real interest rate would be

$$\frac{R\$38.46/\text{year}}{R\$1,000} = \frac{0.03846}{\text{year}}$$

or about the same as the 4 percent per annum earned in the no-inflation case. The rates would be exactly equal if we used continuously compounded interest rates and growth rates in all the calculations (see Sec. 3.5).

EFFECTS OF NOMINAL MONEY GROWTH ON FLUIDITY

As discussed above, the level of nominal interest rates is constant in steady-state equilibrium. So changes in nominal interest rates are not a source of steady-state growth in fluidity. The level of nominal interest rates does affect the level of fluidity at any instant however. If we consider the comparative dynamics effects of two alternative growth rates of nominal money, then different levels of nominal interest rates and fluidity would be associated with each.

Suppose we compare the steady states associated with $\overline{\Gamma M}_1$ and $\overline{\Gamma M}_0$, for example, where $\overline{\Gamma M}_1$ exceeds $\overline{\Gamma M}_0$. The steady-state values of variables will be denoted by subscripts 1 and 0, respectively. The nominal interest rate $\bar{R}_1$ in Case 1 will be higher than the rate $\bar{R}_0$ in Case 0 with lower nominal money growth. Since fluidity is a decreasing function of the nominal interest rate, fluidity will be lower in Case 1 than in Case 0 at any instant. Thus fluidity grows at the same rate in both cases, but has a lower level at any instant in Case 1 than in Case 0. So the two growth paths will be parallel, with log ϕ_1 always below log ϕ_0. This is illustrated in Fig. 5.9.

A further complicating factor arises because the level of monetary exchange as against barter is one of the factors underlying the aggregate production function. If high interest rates cause people to resort to more barter to economize on money holdings, real income net of the costs of making transactions will be reduced for any level of capital and labor. As a result there will also be a small downward parallel shift in the growth path of real income, as shown in

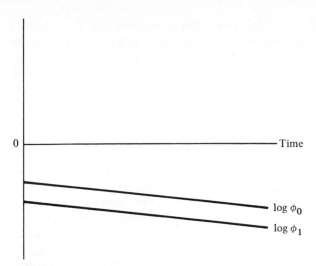

Figure 5.9 Effects of the growth rate of nominal money on the growth path of fluidity. A higher nominal-money growth rate implies higher nominal interest rates in Case 1 than in Case 0. Fluidity is a decreasing function of interest rates so fluidity will be lower in Case 1 than Case 0. The growth rate of fluidity is the same in both cases so the two growth paths have the same slopes (are parallel).

Figure 5.10 Effects of the growth rate of nominal money on the growth path of real income. A high nominal interest rate R_1 will reduce real income below that associated with a low nominal interest rate R_0, as real resources are substituted for real money balances. The growth paths are parallel because the growth rates (slopes) are the same.

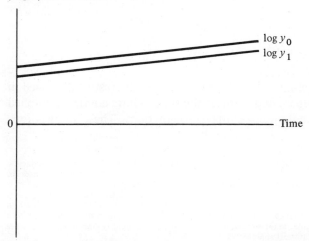

Fig. 5.10.[21] The lower level of income at each point in time reflects the substitution of real resources—to compute payrolls more often, make more trips to the bank, make more detailed plans of cash flow and the like—for the services of real money balances which are free to society at the margin. There may also be a small change up or down in the real rental rate on capital and the real interest rate, but this effect is negligible.

The empirical issues of the size of net negative impacts of increases in interest rates on the desired level of fluidity and on real income are still unsettled.[22] To the extent that banks successfully evade restrictions on interest payments on deposits and so pay competitive interest rates (see Sec. 3.3), the effect of the nominal interest rate on the demand for money as a whole may well be very small. Higher interest rates would tend to decrease the desired ratio of currency to deposits, however. In European hyperinflations, defined by price increases of at least 50 percent per *month*, the reduction in fluidity and real income is very obviously related to the rate of inflation, but this may be due to the breakdown of competitive interest on deposits as part of the general breakdown of debt financing during these periods. For the range of interest rates observed in the 1950s and 1960s in the United States, effects on both fluidity and real income appear small and are neglected entirely in some analyses.

These indirect effects of the rate of growth of the nominal money supply on fluidity and real income break down the strict separation of the real economy from the nominal money supply even in long-run equilibrium. The simple separation of Chap. 4 was based on an implicitly given value of the expected rate of inflation, which is endogenously determined in a steady state. The level of the nominal money supply, given its rate of growth, affects only the price level and not the real economy in long-run equilibrium. This is referred to as the *neutrality* of money. But, the growth rate of the nominal money supply, for a given nominal money supply, *can* affect both the price level and the real economy. If even the growth rate of nominal money does not affect fluidity or real income in long-run equilibrium, money is said to be *superneutral*.

A COMPARATIVE DYNAMICS PROBLEM: SUPERNEUTRAL CASE

A concrete problem is useful to illustrate and organize the results discussed in this chapter. We will compare and contrast the steady-state equilibria implied by two alternative nominal-money-supply growth rates. These implications

---

[21] There may be an offsetting increase in the saving-income ratio, but the effect on the aggregate production function would appear to dominate. This is, however, an open empirical question. See the "References for Further Reading" for literature surveys by Harry Johnson and Allan H. Meltzer.

[22] The difficulty in evaluating the empirical data occurs because actual fluidity is expected for other reasons (discussed in Part Three) to vary over the business cycle in much the same way as it would because of cyclical variations in interest rates. Economists who include some or all of these other reasons in their analyses report a much smaller—or no—influence of interest rates on the long-run desired level of fluidity than do those who leave the alternative forces out of their statistical analyses.

would influence the government's choice of a monetary policy. We will first consider the simpler case of superneutrality in which fluidity and real income are independent of the growth rate of nominal money. Then we can turn to the case in which money is not superneutral.

Suppose that the two proposed nominal-money growth rates are 3 percent and 7 percent per annum. We will use a subscript 0 for steady-state equilibrium values corresponding to the 3 percent per annum growth rate and a subscript 1 for those corresponding to the 7 percent rate. Overbars are used to indicate constant values of the indicated variable. The units (billions of dollars, per year, and so on) of all variables are omitted for compactness. Growth rates are measured in percentage points. So the nominal-money growth rates are written $\overline{\Gamma M_0} = 3\%$ and $\overline{\Gamma M_1} = 7\%$.

Table 5.1 organizes the results of this chapter. The numerical values can be substituted into these formulas to obtain a solution. Some values—the levels and growth rates of money—are given as the basis of the problem. Others are observed to reflect the real resources, tastes, technology, and institutions of the economy. The remaining values can then be derived.

The numerical values of $\overline{\Gamma M_0}$ and $\overline{\Gamma M_1}$ are listed in Table 5.2 as 3 percent and 7 percent. The growth rates of fluidity and real income and the real rate of interest will be the same for both growth rates of the nominal money supply.

Table 5.1 COMPARATIVE DYNAMICS RESULTS:
SUPERNEUTRAL MONEY CASE

Variable	State 0	State 1
Growth rate of nominal money*	$\overline{\Gamma M_0}$	$\overline{\Gamma M_1}$
Growth rate of fluidity†	$\overline{\Gamma \phi}$	$\overline{\Gamma \phi}$
Growth rate of nominal income	$\overline{\Gamma Y_0} = \overline{\Gamma M_0} - \overline{\Gamma \phi}$	$\overline{\Gamma Y_1} = \overline{\Gamma M_1} - \overline{\Gamma \phi}$
Growth rate of real income†	$\overline{\Gamma y}$	$\overline{\Gamma y}$
Inflation rate	$\overline{\Gamma P_0} = \overline{\Gamma Y_0} - \overline{\Gamma y}$	$\overline{\Gamma P_1} = \overline{\Gamma Y_1} - \overline{\Gamma y}$
Real interest rate†	$\bar{r}$	$\bar{r}$
Nominal interest rate	$\bar{R}_0 = \bar{r} + \dfrac{\overline{\Gamma P_0}}{1 - \tau}$	$\bar{R}_1 = \bar{r} + \dfrac{\overline{\Gamma P_1}}{1 - \tau}$
Nominal money*	M_0	M_1
Fluidity†	ϕ_0	$\phi_1 = \phi_0$
Nominal income	$Y_0 = \dfrac{M_0}{\phi_0}$	$Y_1 = Y_0 \dfrac{M_1}{M_0}$
Real income†	y_0	$y_1 = y_0$
Price level	$P_0 = \dfrac{Y_0}{y_0}$	$P_1 = P_0 \dfrac{M_1}{M_0}$

* Assumed for purposes of comparative analysis.
† Determined by the real resources, tastes, technology, and institutions of the economy.

Table 5.2 SOLUTION TO EXAMPLE:
            SUPERNEUTRAL MONEY CASE

Variable	State 0	State 1
Growth rate of nominal money	3%*	7%*
Growth rate of fluidity	−2%*	−2%
Growth rate of nominal income	5%	9%
Growth rate of real income	4%*	4%
Inflation rate	1%	5%
Real interest rate	3%*	3%
Nominal interest rate ($\tau = \frac{1}{3}$)*	4.5%	10.5%
Nominal money	200*	200*
Fluidity	0.2*	0.2
Nominal income	1000	1000
Real income	800*	800
Price level	1.25	1.25

* Given data for solution.

The observed values $\overline{\Gamma\phi} = -2\%$, $\overline{\Gamma y} = 4\%$, and $\bar{r} = 3\%$ are entered in Table 5.2 for state 0 and recopied for state 1.[23] The growth rate of nominal income is computed as the difference between the growth rates of nominal money and fluidity (see [5.25] or Table 5.1):

$$\overline{\Gamma Y}_0 = \overline{\Gamma M}_0 - \overline{\Gamma\phi}_0 = 3\% - (-2\%) = 5\%$$
$$\overline{\Gamma Y}_1 = \overline{\Gamma M}_1 - \overline{\Gamma\phi}_1 = 7\% - (-2\%) = 9\%$$

Note that the difference in the two states' nominal-income growth rates equals the difference in their nominal-money growth rates, $\overline{\Gamma M}_1 - \overline{\Gamma M}_0 = 7\% - 3\% = 4\%$. The difference in the inflation rates is the same amount, since (see [5.28] or Table 5.1):

$$\overline{\Gamma P}_0 = \overline{\Gamma Y}_0 - \overline{\Gamma y}_0 = 5\% - 4\% = 1\%$$

and

$$\overline{\Gamma P}_1 = \overline{\Gamma Y}_1 - \overline{\Gamma y}_1 = 9\% - 4\% = 5\%$$

---

[23] The values approximate those observed in the United States for the 1960s and 1970s. Note that $\overline{\Gamma\phi}_0 = \overline{\Gamma\phi}_1 = \overline{\Gamma\phi}$, $\overline{\Gamma y}_0 = \overline{\Gamma y}_1 = \overline{\Gamma y}$, and $\bar{r}_0 = \bar{r}_1 = \bar{r}$.

Finally, the nominal interest rates can be computed using [5.31] based on the given tax rate of $\frac{1}{3}$:

$$\bar{R}_0 = \bar{r} + \frac{\overline{\Gamma P}_0}{1 - \tau} = 3\% + \frac{1\%}{\frac{2}{3}} = 4.5\%.$$

and

$$R_1 = r + \frac{\overline{\Gamma P}_1}{1 - \tau} = 3\% + \frac{5\%}{\frac{2}{3}} = 10.5\%$$

The difference between the two nominal interest rates will exceed the difference in nominal-money growth rates unless the tax rate τ is zero:

$$\bar{R}_1 - \bar{R}_0 = \frac{1}{1 - \tau}(\overline{\Gamma P}_1 - \overline{\Gamma P}_0) = \frac{1}{1 - \tau}(\overline{\Gamma M}_1 - \overline{\Gamma M}_0)$$

This completes the values for the upper (growth rates and interest rates) portion of Table 5.2. They illustrate the following principle: *Different growth rates of the nominal money supply do not affect the growth rates of fluidity and real income or the real interest rate, but cause identical differences in the rates of growth of nominal income and prices and differences in nominal interest rates $1/(1 - \tau)$ times as large as the difference in nominal-growth rates.*

Panel (b) of Fig. 5.11 illustrates this solution for the first three growth rates in Table 5.2. The growth rate of fluidity is the same value $\overline{\Gamma\phi} = -2\%$ for both states. The growth rates of nominal money are $\overline{\Gamma M}_0 = 3\%$ and $\overline{\Gamma M}_1 = 7\%$. Recall that the growth rate of nominal income is the vertical distance between the growth rates of nominal money and fluidity. This is $\overline{\Gamma Y}_0 = 5\%$ or $\overline{\Gamma Y}_1 = 9\%$, respectively.

Panel (a) of Fig. 5.11 plots the growth paths corresponding to the growth rates in panel (b). The growth path of fluidity is not affected by the growth rate of nominal money in the case of superneutrality. So the same fluidity growth path is drawn for the two states. The growth path of nominal money is steeper in state 1 than in state 0. At the time labeled z, the two nominal money supplies are equal. After z, M_1 exceeds M_0 while before z, M_1 is less than M_0. Since nominal money grows faster in state 1 than in state 0, M_1 must eventually overtake and pass M_0. The growth path of nominal income plots the vertical distance between the growth paths of nominal money and fluidity corresponding to each state. At time z, nominal income is equal for the two states. Afterward, Y_0 is less than Y_1, and before, Y_0 is greater than Y_1.

The general results in Table 5.1 hold for any time at which the steady states are supposed to exist. It is convenient to complete the lower part of Table 5.2 for time z, when the nominal money supplies are equal. Suppose for our calculations that then $M_0 = M_1 = 200$. Suppose also that the value of fluidity in-

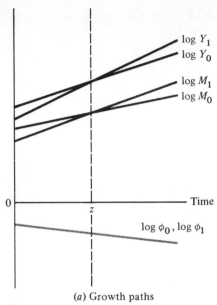

(a) Growth paths

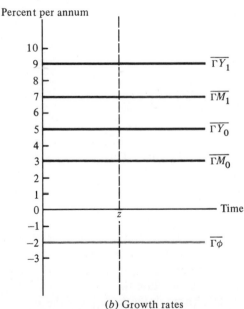

(b) Growth rates

Figure 5.11   Graphical solution for nominal income: superneutral money case. At the instant of time labeled z, the nominal money supplies are equal in the two states 0 and 1 although their growth rates are different. In panel (b), the alternative growth rates of nominal money are plotted as well as the growth rate of fluidity. In each state, the steady-state growth rate of nominal income is found as the vertical distance between the corresponding growth rate of nominal money and the growth rate of fluidity. The higher growth rates of nominal money and nominal income in state 1 than in state 0 are reflected in the steeper slopes of the log M_1 and log Y_1 growth paths as compared with log M_0 and log Y_0, respectively. The nominal-income growth paths equal the vertical distance between the corresponding nominal-money growth path and the fluidity growth path.

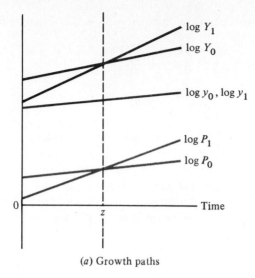

(a) Growth paths

(Percent per annum)

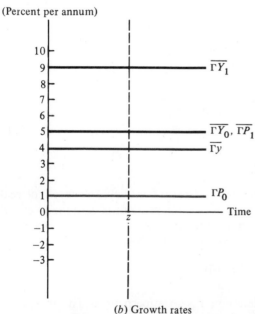

(b) Growth rates

Figure 5.12 Graphical solution for real income and the price level: superneutral money case. The growth rate of real income $\overline{\Gamma y} = 4\%$ is the same in both states as shown in panel (b). The growth rates of nominal income $\overline{\Gamma Y_0} = 5\%$ and $\overline{\Gamma Y_1} = 9\%$ are reproduced from Fig. 5.11. The rate of inflation is the vertical distance between the growth rates of nominal income and real income. In panel (a) the growth path of real income is the same for both states. The alternative growth paths of nominal income are reproduced from Fig. 5.11. The growth paths of the price level equal the vertical distance between the growth paths of nominal income and real income. At time z when the nominal incomes are the same in both states, so are the price levels.

dicated by its steady-state growth path is then $\phi_0 = \phi_1 = 0.2$. Then nominal income is

$$Y_0 = \frac{M_0}{\phi_0} = \frac{200}{0.2} = 1000$$

$$Y_1 = \frac{M_1}{\phi_1} = \frac{200}{0.2} = 1000$$

These three values are entered in Table 5.2 for both states 0 and 1.

Panel (b) of Fig. 5.12 illustrates the division of the growth rate of nominal income into components of real-income growth rate and inflation rate. The real-income growth rate fixed by growth in effective labor supply is $\overline{\Gamma y} = 4\%$ in both cases. The growth rates of nominal income are reproduced from Fig. 5.11 as $\overline{\Gamma Y_0} = 5\%$ and $\overline{\Gamma Y_1} = 9\%$. The rate of inflation is the vertical distance between the growth rates of nominal income and real income, or $\overline{\Gamma P_0} = 1\%$ and $\overline{\Gamma P_1} = 5\%$.

Panel (a) of Fig. 5.12 reproduces the nominal-income growth paths constructed in Fig. 5.11. The real-income growth path is the same for both states 0 and 1. The growth path of the price level plots the vertical distance between the growth paths of nominal income and real income. If the latter growth path indicates that real income at time z is 800, then $y_0 = y_1 = 800$ is entered in Table 5.2. The price level is computed as the ratio of nominal to real income:

$$P_0 = \frac{Y_0}{y_0} = \frac{1000}{800} = 1.25$$

$$P_1 = \frac{Y_1}{y_1} = \frac{1000}{800} = 1.25$$

These entries complete Table 5.2.

Summing up in the case of superneutrality of money, the levels of real variables such as fluidity and real income are independent of *both* the level and growth rate of nominal money. Nominal income and the price level in the two states are in proportion to the nominal money supplies.

A COMPARATIVE DYNAMICS PROBLEM: NON-SUPERNEUTRAL CASE

Let us now turn to the case in which money is not superneutral. The analysis of growth rates and interest rates is unaffected; so those portions of Tables 5.1 and 5.2 and Figs. 5.11 and 5.12 apply without change to this case as well. The only changes occur because the growth paths of fluidity and real income are shifted down. In Table 5.3, these downward shifts are represented by writing ϕ_1 as a fraction γ of ϕ_0 and y_1 as a fraction δ of y_0. As a result nominal income in state 1 will be greater (by a factor of $1/\gamma$) relative to state 0 than would be predicted by the ratio of the nominal money supplies. The price level ratio will be a greater multiple $(1/\gamma\delta)$ of the nominal money ratio because it is increased by both the upward shift in nominal income and the downward shift in real

Table 5.3 COMPARATIVE DYNAMICS RESULTS: NON-SUPERNEUTRAL MONEY CASE

Variable	State 0	State 1
Growth rates and interest rates as in Table 5.1		
Nominal money*	M_0	M_1
Fluidity†,‡	ϕ_0	$\phi_1 = \gamma\phi_0$
Nominal income	$Y_0 = \dfrac{M_0}{\phi_0}$	$Y_1 = Y_0 \dfrac{M_1}{\gamma M_0}$
Real income†,‡	y_0	$y_1 = \delta y_0$
Price level	P_0	$P_1 = P_0 \dfrac{M_1}{\gamma\delta M_0}$

* Assumed for purposes of comparative analysis.
† Determined by real resources, tastes, technology, and institutions of the economy.
‡ As discussed in the text, the parameters γ and δ lie between 0 and 1.

Figure 5.13 Graphical solution for nominal income: non-superneutral money case.
If money is not superneutral, higher nominal-money growth rates cause downward parallel shifts in the fluidity growth path (see Fig. 5.9). This means that the log ϕ_1 line is parallel to but lower than the log ϕ_0 line. The growth paths of nominal money are determined by the government's monetary policy. The growth paths of nominal income plot the vertical distance between the growth paths of nominal money and the corresponding growth paths of fluidity. At time z when the nominal money supplies are the same in both states, nominal income is higher in state 1 than in state 0 by the amount of the downward shift in fluidity. The determination of growth rates is the same as in the superneutral case.

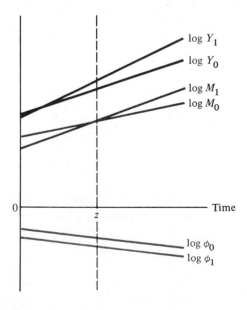

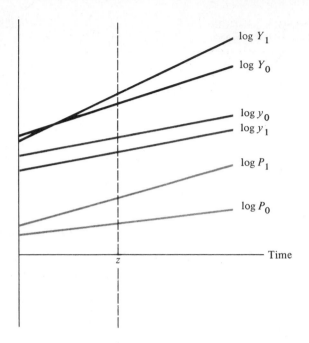

Figure 5.14 Graphical solution for real income and the price level: non-superneutral money case. If money is not superneutral, higher nominal-money growth rates cause downward parallel shifts in the real income path (see Fig. 5.10) as illustrated. The growth paths of nominal income are reproduced from Fig. 5.13. The growth paths of the price level plot the vertical distance between the growth paths of nominal income and the corresponding growth paths of real income. At time z when the nominal money supplies are the same in both states, the log of the price level is higher in state 1 than in state 0 by the *sum* of the downward shift in real income and the upward shift in nominal income. The determination of growth rates is the same as in the superneutral case.

income. Figure 5.13 shows how the downward shift in fluidity causes an upward shift in nominal income. Even though the nominal money supplies are the same at time z, Y_1 then exceeds Y_0. Figure 5.14 shows how this, combined with the downward shift in real income, implies a larger upward shift in the price level.

Suppose that an increase in nominal interest rates from 4.5 percent to 10.5 percent reduced the desired level of fluidity, other things equal, by 25 percent.[24]

---

[24] This corresponds to an interest elasticity of the demand for money equal to about -0.3 which is rather on the high side (in absolute value) of estimates for the postwar United States. If this elasticity were -0.1, the decrease in fluidity would be only about 8 percent.

Table 5.4 SOLUTION TO EXAMPLE:
        NON-SUPERNEUTRAL MONEY CASE

Variable	State 0	State 1
Growth rates and interest rates as in Table 5.2		
Nominal money	200*	200*
Fluidity ($\gamma = 0.75$)*	0.2*	0.15
Nominal income	1000	1333
Real income ($\delta = 0.98$)*	800*	784
Price level	1.25	1.70

* Given data for solution.

Then γ would be 0.75. Nominal income in state 0 is unchanged at 1000, but in state 1,

$$Y_1 = \frac{M_1}{\phi_1} = \frac{M_1}{\gamma\phi_0} = \frac{200}{0.75 \times 0.2} = \frac{200}{0.15} = 1333$$

These values are entered in Table 5.4.

Real income is 800 again in state 0, but suppose that it is decreased by 2 percent ($\delta = 0.98$) in state 1. Then $y_1 = \delta y_0 = 0.98 \times 800 = 784$. The price levels are

$$P_0 = \frac{Y_0}{y_0} = \frac{1000}{800} = 1.25$$

$$P_1 = \frac{Y_1}{y_1} = \frac{1333}{784} = 1.70$$

These results complete Table 5.4. Note that the nominal incomes differ from the ratio of nominal moneys ($\frac{200}{200} = 1$) at time z by a factor $1/\gamma$:

$$\frac{Y_1}{Y_0} = \frac{1333}{1000} = 1.333 = \frac{1}{0.75} = \frac{1}{\gamma}$$

The ratio of the price levels differs from the nominal money ratio by a factor $1/\gamma\delta$ since $P_1/P_0 = 1.70/1.25 = 1.36$ and

$$\frac{1}{\gamma\delta} = \frac{1}{0.75 \times 0.98} = \frac{1}{0.735} = 1.36$$

This is as indicated in Table 5.3.

A COMPARATIVE DYNAMICS PROBLEM: SUMMARY

A higher growth rate of nominal money will thus cause an equal increase in the rate of inflation. If money is superneutral, growth rates of nominal variables and nominal interest rates are affected, but there is no effect on real variables. In particular, the same amount of goods and services are available for consumption and investment. If money is not superneutral, however, the steady-state levels but not growth rates of real variables such as fluidity and real income will be affected. In particular there will be a smaller amount of real goods and services available.[25] The growth paths of nominal income and the price level will not only be steeper—as in the superneutral case—but will also shift upwards.

The strict conditions for superneutrality of money almost surely do not hold. Nonetheless, many economists will analyze a particular problem *as if* money were superneutral, on the grounds that the shifts are negligible complications compared to the changes in the growth rates.[26] Others disagree about this. This debate and the use of simplified models will be explored at length in Part Five.

SUMMARY

1 The rate of change and the growth rate of a variable are alternative measures of its growth per annum—the former in absolute and the latter in proportionate terms.
2 The long-run equilibrium of the economy is characterized as a steady state in which the major macroeconomic variables grow at constant rates.
3 In the steady state the growth rates of real income and capital are equal to the growth rate of labor. Per capita income grows by the sum of the growth rates of labor-force quality and participation of the population.
4 The constant ratio of capital to labor leads to a constant real rental rate on capital, real interest rate, and real wages.
5 The saving-income ratio affects the level but not the growth rate of real income.
6 The inflation rate is determined by the difference between growth rates of the nominal quantity of money supplied and the real quantity of money demanded.
7 The growth rate of the real quantity of money demanded is the sum of the growth rates of desired fluidity and real income. The secular growth rate of

---

[25] A fuller analysis of the choice of a steady-state inflation rate is presented in Sec. 15.4.
[26] This is similar to the use of the perfectly competitive model in microeconomics to analyze problems for which it is not strictly applicable. Frequently a simple understandable analysis which gives an answer correct to within say 5 percent is preferable to a more accurate but much more complicated analysis.

fluidity is determined by the growth of real income and changes in institutions and payments technology; it is constant for long periods of time.

8 Alternatively, the nominal-income growth rate equals the difference between the growth rates of nominal money and fluidity. The inflation rate equals the difference in the growth rates of nominal and real income.

9 The nominal interest rate exceeds the real interest rate by the inflation rate divided by 1 minus the marginal tax rate on interest payments.

10 The steady-state growth rates of nominal variables, but not real variables, are affected by the government's choice of the nominal-money growth rate. If money is superneutral this choice will not affect the levels of real variables, otherwise it will.

11 Where money is not superneutral, higher growth paths of fluidity and real income are associated with lower rates of nominal-money growth and the resulting lower nominal interest rates.

CONCEPTS TO KNOW

deflation	inflation rate
endogenous	nominal interest rate
exogenous	rate of change
Fisher equation	real interest rate
growth path	stationary state
growth rate	steady state
inflation	

QUESTIONS AND EXERCISES

*1 Can you think of any economies, present or past, which would approximate a stationary state? Does a constant population imply a stationary state of no growth?

2 (a) The hypothetical aggregate production function $y = 3k^{1/2}l^{1/2} = 3\sqrt{kl}$ is homogeneous of the first degree. Illustrate this by computing y_0 for $k_0 = 40,000$ and $l_0 = 160,000$ and y_1 for $k_1 = 1$ and $l_0 = 4$ and the ratios y_1/y_0, k_1/k_0, l_1/l_0.

   (b) Divide the production function in part (a) by k and show that output per unit of capital is dependent on the ratio of labor to capital but not on their levels.

*3 Two economies are alike in their aggregate production function and saving-income ratio, but differ in their growth rates of labor which are $\overline{\Gamma l_0}$ in country 0 and $\overline{\Gamma l_1}$ in country 1. Assume $\overline{\Gamma l_0}$ is less than $\overline{\Gamma l_1}$. Use a graph to derive and compare the equilibrium labor-capital ratios in the two countries. Can you tell which country will have the highest income per unit of labor? The highest per capita income? Explain.

4 Does a high level of education imply a higher growth rate of per capita income? Does a rising level of education imply a higher growth rate of per capita income?

5 "Inflation results to the extent that growth in the money supply exceeds growth in real goods and services." Evaluate critically.

6 During the post-World War I German hyperinflation, German central bankers claimed that the inflation could not be blamed on them because they were just meeting the increased demand for money due to increased income. Indeed, they claimed, monetary policy was tight because interest rates were high and money was a smaller fraction of income. What is wrong with this argument?

7 A comparative dynamics problem: Compare the effects of alternative rates of monetary growth by filling in the blanks in the following table.

Variable	State 0	State 1
Growth rate of the money supply	6%	11%
Growth rate of fluidity		
Growth rate of nominal income	5%	
Growth rate of real income		
Growth rate of the price level	2%	
Real interest rate		
Nominal interest rate (tax rate = $\frac{1}{2}$)	8%	

*8 In the comparative dynamics problem of Table 5.2, a 7 percent increase in the money supply over a year would be required for a 5 percent increase in prices. At the end of Chap. 4, the comparative statics analysis demonstrated that "a 5 percent increase in the amount of money supplied causes a 5 percent increase in the price level." Can both statements be correct? Explain.

REFERENCES FOR FURTHER READING

Johnson, Harry G.: "Money in a Neo-Classical One-Sector Growth Model," in *Essays in Monetary Economics,* London: G. Allen, 1967.

Meltzer, Allan H.: Money, Intermediation, and Growth, *Journal of Economic Literature,* **7**: 27–56, Mar. 1969.

Solow, Robert M.: *Growth Theory: An Exposition,* New York: Oxford University Press, 1970.

PART THREE

DYNAMIC ADJUSTMENTS
TO MACROECONOMIC SHOCKS

The smooth steady-state equilibrium of Part Two provides the broad trends about which the economy is constantly fluctuating. Most of the interesting problems in macroeconomics involve these fluctuations in business activity and what can be done to moderate them.

Fluctuations arise because some unexpected event or events either push the economy away from the steady-state equilibrium or change the steady-state equilibrium. These events, called *macroeconomic shocks*, might take the form of a permanent or temporary change in the basic behavioral functions, or a change in the government policy which underlies the steady-state equilibrium. For example, a decision to increase the growth rate of nominal money will change the steady-state equilibrium. It takes time for the economy to adjust to the new steady state, and in the meanwhile wide fluctuations in the growth rates of real income and the price level occur.

The analysis of the adaptations of the economy to macroeconomic shocks is termed *adjustment dynamics*. This is distinct from the comparative dynamics of Chap. 5. Comparative dynamics compares and contrasts the long-run growth equilibrium which would exist in an economy under two alternative sets of conditions. Adjustment dynamics explains how an economy not in steady-state equilibrium gets there. Often the economy is not in steady-state equilibrium, because of a change in underlying conditions; so adjustment dynamics is used to explain how the economy moves from one steady-state equilibrium to another.

Macroeconomic shocks are discussed in three general groups. Chapters 6 and 7 analyze the effects of a change in the growth rate of the nominal money supply. This shock receives separate treatment because of its importance in the real world and because it is a simple case that introduces the forces involved in the dynamic adjustment of the economy to macroeconomic shocks. Chapter 8 studies all other potential macroeconomic shocks which occur within the domestic economy. Chapter 9 relates the American economy to the rest of the world and considers possible shocks affecting the United States from the outside.

CHAPTER 6

EFFECTS OF A MONEY SUPPLY SHOCK ON NOMINAL INCOME

WHAT YOU WILL LEARN IN THIS CHAPTER
Macroeconomic shocks as a source of business fluctuations ● Changes in monetary policy ● Money as a shock absorber ● Cyclical adjustments of the growth rates of fluidity and nominal income ● Why the nominal-income growth rate fluctuates by more than the change in the nominal-money growth rate ● The timing of the adjustment process

6.1 THE NATURE OF MACROECONOMIC SHOCKS

The smooth steady-state economic growth of Part Two is continually interrupted by shocks which either force the economy away from equilibrium or change the equilibrium itself. These shocks lead to a period of adjustment which explains many of the phenomena of the business cycle. We must examine these periods of disequilibrium to understand fluctuations in unemployment, output, and inflation. So analysis of adjustments to shocks is the heart of macroeconomics.

Referring to the period of adjustment after a macroeconomic shock as one of *disequilibrium* is subject to semantic quibbling. It is a period during which the economy is away from its long-run or steady-state equilibrium. But if one takes full account of all the costs of adjustment, the economy can be said to be continuously in short-run equilibrium. So the term disequilibrium is used to refer to the long run here.

Macroeconomic shock is one of those concepts which is hard to define other than by showing how it is used. It is not very satisfying to say that macroeconomic shocks are those things which cause the actual and steady-state equilibrium values of the main macroeconomic variables to diverge. You certainly would not be able to point one out if it were walking down the street. So, while some general properties will be discussed now by way of introduction, for the most part shocks will be defined by listing the most important ones and seeing how they work.

Consider first shocks which change the steady-state growth equilibrium of the macroeconomy. Since we have studied in Part Two the major factors determining the steady-state equilibrium, we know that this kind of shock involves changes in one or more of these factors. Examples would be a change in the growth rate of the nominal money supply or of the labor supply or in the ratio of saving to income. But these changes are shocks primarily because they are unpredictable, so that they cannot be incorporated into the analysis of the steady state. Predictable changes—such as normal growth in the effective units of labor supplied—are incorporated into the steady-state equilibrium and so are not themselves shocks. We shall see later that unpredictability is essential to the nature of shocks because people act in expectation that things will be different from what they turn out to be.

Some shocks have relatively little effect on the steady-state equilibrium, but do cause macroeconomic variables to move away from their steady-state values. For the most part these involve major shifts in expenditures and production from one group of goods to another. The most important example of this sort of shock is an unexpected shift in government expenditures which either increases or decreases output in one industry before offsetting changes occur in other industries. Similar effects would occur in the face of unexpected changes in investment or consumption expenditures or net exports.

The choice of which shock to examine first is largely arbitrary. An unexpected change in the growth path of the nominal money supply will be studied first for several good reasons. First is the monetarist assertion that "money mostly matters" or, less cryptically, that money supply shocks have been the major cause of business cycles historically. Although this assertion is not generally accepted as fact, there is little dispute that money supply shocks have been a very important factor in business fluctuations. A second reason for giving money supply shocks pride of place is pedagogical convenience. It allows us to use what we have just learned in Chap. 5 to see precisely how changes in money supply growth affect the steady-state equilibrium.

The effects of unexpected changes in nominal money supply growth are highlighted by starting from an equilibrium based on one growth rate of the nominal money supply, changing that growth rate, and tracing the adjustment of the economy until the new steady-state equilibrium is achieved. A formal statement of the problem is: Starting from a steady state with a nominal-money-supply growth rate of $\overline{\Gamma M}$, what would be the effects of an unexpected change at time z to a new, different growth rate $\overline{\Gamma M}'$ which is maintained indefinitely thereafter? The final solution when the economy has achieved steady-state growth was contrasted with the initial steady state in the comparative dynamics problem at the end of Chap. 5. Here the concern is with what happens between z and the time when the economy ultimately converges to the new moving equilibrium.

The problem as stated is somewhat artificial, since a change in the nominal-money-supply growth rate usually occurs long before the economy has adjusted to the preceding growth rate change, but all possible initial conditions cannot be considered separately. The influence of initial conditions in reinforcing or offsetting the effects explained here is discussed in Chap. 13 in connection with the actual record of twentieth-century U.S. macroeconomic history.

The stated problem suggests that the Federal Reserve System increases or decreases the rate of growth of the money supply, and all other macroeconomic shocks are excluded. This, however, is impossible because government transactions (with the accounts of the Federal Reserve System and Treasury consolidated) are subject to the budget identity

$$G \equiv T + \Delta B + \Delta D \qquad [6.1]$$

That is, the rate of government spending G is equal to the total of the rate of net taxes T and the rates of change in base money ΔB and in the government debt held by the public ΔD, each of the variables being measured in nominal terms. Changes in base money and the national debt, if positive, are the possible ways to finance an excess of government spending over taxation; if they are negative, these changes are the alternative possible uses of an excess of taxes over government spending. The growth rate of the nominal money supply is the sum of the growth rates of base money and the money multiplier. On the reasonable assumption that the growth rate of the money multiplier is unchanged, the change in the growth rate of the money supply will require an equal change in the growth rate of base money. The growth rate of base money is the rate of change in base money divided by its level to convert the absolute change into proportionate terms:

$$\Gamma B \equiv \frac{\Delta B}{B} \qquad [6.2]$$

For a given amount B of base money outstanding, the change in ΓB must be accomplished by a change in ΔB. The required change in ΔB must be offset by changes in G, T, or ΔD because of the government budget identity.

In this chapter it is assumed that changes in the rate of base-money creation are offset by an opposite change in the rate of increase in government debt. This would correspond to the Fed's increasing the growth rate of the nominal base money by buying government bonds from the public at a faster rate. In Chap. 8, effects of changes in the rate of government spending and taxation, offset by changes in the rate of increase in the national debt, will be discussed. The results of the two chapters can be combined to analyze the effects of an increased growth rate of money, which finances an increased rate of government spending or decreased rate of taxation.

An increase in the growth rate of nominal money is termed a *stimulative monetary policy* for reasons which will soon be obvious. Similarly, a decrease in the nominal-money growth rate is a *restrictive monetary policy*. Sometimes monetary policy is said to be easy if nominal interest rates are low or falling and tight if these rates are high or rising. Section 7.3 will show why the cyclical adjustment of nominal interest rates makes them an unreliable indicator of the direction of monetary policy.

6.2 THE CYCLICAL ADJUSTMENT OF FLUIDITY

CHANGES IN STEADY-STATE GROWTH PATHS

The effects of the monetary shock described in Sec. 6.1 are most readily understood by examining, first, the effects on fluidity and nominal income and, then
in Chap. 7, how fluctuations in nominal income are divided between real
income and the price level. Consider first the case of a stimulative monetary
policy in which the new rate of growth in the money supply $\overline{\Gamma M}'$ is greater than
the old growth rate $\overline{\Gamma M}$.

The actual growth path of the money supply is illustrated in panel (a) of
Fig. 6.1. The increased trend growth rate of the money supply is indicated by
the increased slope of the logarithm of the money supply at z. Panel (b) shows
this directly as a sudden jump at z in the growth rate of the money supply
which is the slope of the log M line in panel (a).

The steady-state growth paths that fluidity and nominal income would
follow if the economy were somehow to immediately and completely adjust to
the new, higher rate of money-supply growth are useful standards for comparison. At the end of Sec. 5.3, this very problem was solved in a slightly different
setting. Up to z, the growth paths desired are the ones which were derived for
state 0 defined by a monetary growth rate $\overline{\Gamma M}_0$. After z, the growth paths for
state 1 defined by $\overline{\Gamma M}_1$ are those sought. The main cyclical effects can be
illustrated by the simpler superneutrality case. So suppose that the long-run
elasticity of the demand for money with respect to the general level of market
interest rates is zero because of the payment of competitive interest rates on
money. The complications of effects of the level of nominal interest rates on the
steady-state level of fluidity are added in an appendix to Chap. 7.

These steady-state growth paths and growth rates are illustrated in panels
(a) and (b), respectively, of Fig. 6.2. A subscript S is used to indicate the current
steady-state value of a variable. An overbar and an overbar with a prime are
used to indicate constant steady-state values before and after z, respectively.
The growth path and growth rates of the nominal money supply are reproduced from Fig. 6.1. The increase in the growth rate of the nominal money
supply has no effect on the steady-state growth path of fluidity.[1] The slope of
the steady-state growth path of nominal income is increased by the amount of
increase in the slope of the growth path of the nominal money supply at time z.

These graphs are easy to construct because the steady-state values must be
consistent with the Cambridge identity $M \equiv \phi Y$, so

$$\log M \equiv \log \phi_S + \log Y_S \qquad [6.3]$$

$$\Gamma M \equiv \Gamma \phi_S + \Gamma Y_S \qquad [6.4]$$

---

[1] Remember that we are considering the superneutrality case in which the long-run elasticity of money demand
with respect to market interest rates is zero.

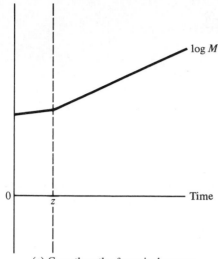

(a) Growth path of nominal money

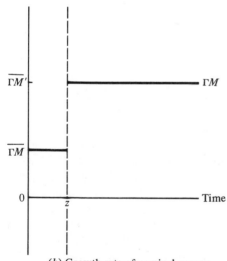

(b) Growth rate of nominal money

Figure 6.1 An increase in the money-supply growth rate at z. At z, monetary policy changes and the growth rate of the money supply is increased from $\overline{\Gamma M}$ to $\overline{\Gamma M}'$. This change is shown in (a) by an increase in the slope of the log M line at z; (b) shows a discontinuous jump at z in the money-supply growth rate from $\overline{\Gamma M}$ to the higher rate $\overline{\Gamma M}'$, which is maintained thereafter.

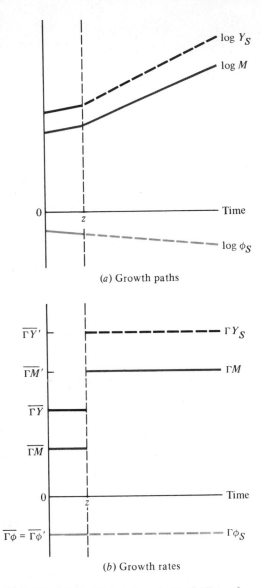

(a) Growth paths

(b) Growth rates

Figure 6.2 Steady-state growth paths for fluidity and nominal income. The steady-state growth path of fluidity is fixed by the conditions of the real economy and not affected by the growth rate of the money supply. The entire increase in the growth rate of the money supply (slope of the log M line) after z is reflected in an equal increase in the steady-state growth rate of nominal income (slope of the log Y_S line).

The growth path of M is the graph of log M against time, and it is determined by the monetary policy which we are studying. The steady-state growth path of fluidity is fixed by real conditions of the economy. So the steady-state growth path of nominal income (the graph of log Y_S) is the vertical distance between the graph of log M and the graph of log ϕ_S.[2] Similarly, the growth rate of Y_S is the vertical distance between ΓM and $\Gamma \phi_S$.

The steady-state growth paths of fluidity and nominal income were drawn as dashed lines after the monetary policy change at z. This is so because the economy adjusts only slowly to the new growth paths after a monetary shock. While this adjustment is going on, the *actual* values of fluidity and nominal income deviate from their steady-state values for a substantial period of time. In the final analysis, the adjustments of the two variables reflect mutual interactions. We shall start our discussion, however, by focusing on the adjustment of fluidity.

THE SHOCK-ABSORBER ROLE OF MONEY

In a period of disequilibrium, it is important to distinguish between the short-run and long-run demand for money. The long-run demand for money underlies the analysis of the steady state in Part Two. This long-run demand totals the average money holdings desired by all the individuals and firms in the economy. Their desired average holdings are chosen given their level of income, expenditure and wealth and the interest rates paid on money and on alternative assets.

If we were to look closely at any particular individual (or firm), we would see his money holdings were rarely at this desired average level. In part, this reflects a normal pattern in which money holdings are above average just after receipt of a paycheck and are then drawn down until replenished by the next paycheck. But most people also use money balances as a sort of shock absorber, so that if the amount or timing of one of their planned receipts or expenditures is changed—or something unexpected comes up—they do not have to alter all their other plans. This is done by just letting money balances rise above normal when money receipts are higher or expenditures lower than expected. If expenditures are higher or receipts lower than expected, money balances would be reduced. In this way, people can use money as a general reserve for unplanned events so that their lives are not disrupted by every surprise.

Of course, if money balances are to serve this shock-absorber purpose they must be eventually replenished either by an offsetting unplanned receipt—such as when a late payment finally arrives—or by changing plans when convenient. For example, one could make a smaller deposit in or even a withdrawal from a savings account, or perhaps delay the purchase of a new refrigerator. Similarly, persistently above-normal money balances will be drawn down and put to

---

[2] Equivalently in Fig. 6.2, add the vertical distance between log ϕ_S and the horizontal axis to log M to obtain log Y_S.

better use, perhaps by making a larger savings deposit or buying the new refrigerator a little earlier.

This short-run variation of money holdings is analogous to the shock absorber of a car. If one drives over a bump (or a dip) the shock absorber compresses (extends) so that the passengers can continue level without much effect from the temporary disturbance. If one goes up a ridge to a higher level of roadway, the shock absorber spreads the adjustment over time as it gradually returns to its normal level. The shock absorber eventually must return to normal, of course, so that it is ready to protect against future shocks.

These short-run fluctuations of individual money holdings around their desired level do not average out during the period of adjustment to a monetary shock. The reason is that the unexpected change in monetary policy means higher money receipts and less money expenditures than planned. When, because of increased money creation, the government borrows less than was anticipated, planned loans of money are frustrated. Most of this money will be immediately lent out elsewhere but this displaces other funds in turn.

Ultimately the excess funds will leak from the financial institutions that first feel the shock to other firms and individuals. This happens as financial institutions increase their loans to (by approving applications faster, for example) and reduce their borrowings from other firms and individuals. These excess money balances are like a hot potato: With the total supply of money determined by the government's policy, if one person reduces his or her money balances by spending more, someone else's money balances are increased. But the attempts of individuals to get rid of excess money balances by spending them on other assets (including consumers' durable goods such as refrigerators and cars) are essential to the adjustment process.

The increased spending by individuals and firms (which find it easier to finance investment) increases spending on final goods and services and hence nominal income. The increased nominal income does not reduce the supply of money, but it does increase the demand for it. Lower interest rates also increase the quantity of money demanded, at least until banks reduce their implicit interest payments on deposits. So the individuals' attempts to reduce the quantity of money held by spending and lending it have the unintended effect of reducing excess money balances by increasing the quantity of money demanded.

IMPLIED SHOCK-ABSORBER ROLE OF FLUIDITY

The discussion so far has been framed in terms of money rather than fluidity, but the two are related arithmetically. Desired fluidity was defined in Chap. 4 as the ratio of (long-run) money demand to income:[3]

$$\phi^d \equiv \frac{M^d}{Y} \qquad\qquad [6.5]$$

---

[3] This ratio may be taken for either real or nominal values since the price level cancels out and $m^d/y \equiv M^d/Y$.

Actual fluidity is the ratio of the nominal quantity of money supplied to nominal income

$$\phi \equiv \frac{M}{Y} \tag{6.6}$$

Taking logarithms and subtracting [6.5] from [6.6] yields

$$\log \phi - \log \phi^d \equiv \log M - \log M^d \tag{6.7}$$

That is, the logarithmic (or proportionate) *excess fluidity* is identical to the logarithmic (proportionate) excess supply of money.[4] Since it is convenient to use logarithmic scaling anyway, the previous discussion of a shock-absorber response first creating and then eliminating an excess money supply holds exactly the same for excess fluidity.

Three separate influences on the growth rate of fluidity have been identified: (1) Fluidity has a normal growth rate as discussed in Chap. 5. (2) Fluidity tends to grow faster (slower) than normal if money grows faster (slower) than expected. (3) Fluidity tends to grow slower (faster) than normal if actual fluidity exceeds (is less than) desired fluidity. These three forces can be combined into a single equation[5]

$$\Gamma\phi = \overline{\Gamma\phi} + (\Gamma M - \Gamma M^*) - \lambda(\log \phi - \log \phi^d) \tag{6.8}$$

The first term on the right-hand side of the equation is the normal steady-state growth rate of fluidity. Using an asterisk to indicate the expected growth rate, the second term is the difference between the actual and expected growth rates of money. This is the "shock" which is added in the first instant to excess money balances and hence fluidity.[6] The third term states that the logarithmic excess fluidity is worked down at a rate λ. The rate λ (in units per annum) measures the speed of adjustment of actual to desired fluidity.[7]

AN ILLUSTRATIVE EXAMPLE

It is useful to work through an example of how an equation such as [6.8] could be used to obtain the response of actual fluidity to a monetary shock. This is done in Fig. 6.3 on the temporary simplifying assumption that desired fluidity is always equal to steady-state fluidity.[8]

---

[4] This result is independent of whether we consider nominal or real money since $\log M - \log M^d \equiv \log m - \log m^d$. See Sec. M.3 of the Mathematical Appendix on the use of logarithmic differences as a measure of proportionate or percentage differences.

[5] This equation omits the effects on the growth rate of fluidity of other shocks discussed in Chaps. 8 and 9.

[6] This is the amount by which the money supply is growing faster than built into spending and receipt plans.

[7] For example, a λ of 0.1/year or 10 percent per annum would indicate a very slow adjustment process. A λ of 20/year, on the other hand, would imply essentially complete adjustment to any past shock within a month.

[8] I am indebted to Professor Douglas K. Adie for suggesting this graphical approach.

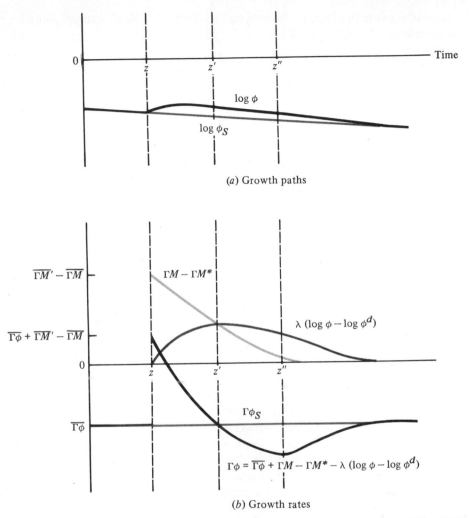

(a) Growth paths

(b) Growth rates

Figure 6.3 Illustration of shock-absorber response of fluidity. The unexpected portion $(\overline{\Gamma M} - \overline{\Gamma M^*})$ of money supply growth is at first the whole increase $\overline{\Gamma M'} - \overline{\Gamma M}$, but expectations and plans adjust over time. The growth path of actual fluidity is plotted using the growth rate $\Gamma \phi$ as the slope. The $\lambda(\log \phi - \log \phi^d)$ is a multiple of the vertical distance between $\log \phi$ and $\log \phi_S$. The actual growth rate $\Gamma \phi$ is plotted by adding to $\overline{\Gamma \phi}$ the vertical difference between the $\Gamma M - \Gamma M^*$ and the $\lambda(\log \phi - \log \phi^d)$ lines. At the time labeled z', $\Gamma M - \Gamma M^*$ equals $\lambda(\log \phi - \log \phi^d)$ so the actual and steady-state growth rates of fluidity are equal. This is when logarithmic excess fluidity is a maximum. At the time z'' the growth rate of fluidity stops falling and begins to rise back to its steady-state level. This occurs when the slopes of the $\Gamma M - \Gamma M^*$ and $\lambda(\log \phi - \log \phi^d)$ lines are equal. The apparent circularity of the graph is eliminated by working iteratively for small intervals of time or by use of more advanced mathematical tools. Note that the rise and fall back of actual relative to steady-state fluidity is reflected in a cyclical adjustment of the growth rate of fluidity.

Consider first the line in panel (b) labeled $\Gamma M - \Gamma M^*$. This is the graph of the unexpected portion of money-supply growth. As time goes on, people will adjust their expectations and spending/receipt plans toward the higher growth rate of the nominal money supply. This is reflected in the decrease over time in unexpected money supply growth. Initially the entire increase $\overline{\Gamma M'} - \overline{\Gamma M}$ is unexpected as indicated at time z.

The actual growth rate of fluidity $\Gamma \phi$ is determined by Eq. [6.8] on the assumption $\phi^d = \phi_S$. Before z the economy is assumed to be in steady-state equilibrium, so actual and steady-state levels and growth rates of fluidity are the same. At z, the growth rate of fluidity accelerates, but only as time passes will the actual *level* of fluidity come to exceed the steady-state level. So at z, the growth rate of fluidity exceeds the steady-state growth rate by the full (unexpected) increase in nominal-money-supply growth $\overline{\Gamma M'} - \overline{\Gamma M}$. This is illustrated by a sharp increase in the slope of the log ϕ line at time z in panel (a). As time progresses, excess fluidity (log ϕ − log ϕ_S) becomes positive. This tends to reduce the growth rate of fluidity as people increase their spending in an attempt to get rid of excess money holding.

We can work back and forth between panels (a) and (b) by: (1) computing the growth rate of fluidity by adding to $\overline{\Gamma \phi}$ the vertical difference between the $\Gamma M - \Gamma M^*$ line and the $\lambda(\log \phi - \log \phi^d)$ line, (2) then using this as the slope of the log ϕ line in panel (a) for a brief interval, (3) then plotting λ times the value of log ϕ − log ϕ_S after this interval as the next point on the $\lambda(\log \phi - \log \phi^d)$ line in panel (b), and then returning to step (1). Needless to say, there are easier ways to solve this problem in practice. A numerical solution is provided in Example 6.1.

EXAMPLE 6.1

AN ARITHMETIC ANALYSIS OF FLUIDITY ADJUSTMENT

As an alternative to the graphical solution of Fig. 6.3, the adjustment of fluidity can be derived arithmetically. Suppose for our example that $\lambda = 0.5$ per annum and $\overline{\Gamma \phi} = -0.03$ per annum so that Eq. [6.8] can be written as

$$\Gamma \phi = \frac{-0.03}{\text{year}} + (\Gamma M - \Gamma M^*) - \frac{0.5}{\text{year}} (\log \phi - \log \phi^d)$$

Suppose also that ΓM were increased from 2 to 4 percent per annum and expected money supply growth shifts up by 0.25 percentage point each quarter until it moves from 2 to 4 percent per annum.

The problem is solved by use of a table:

Quarter	Expected Nominal Money Growth ΓM^*	Money Growth Shock $\Gamma M - \Gamma M^*$	Logarithmic Excess Fluidity $\log \phi - \log \phi^d$	Actual Fluidity Growth $\Gamma \phi$	Rate of Change in Logarithmic Excess Fluidity $\Gamma \phi - \overline{\Gamma \phi}$	Quarterly Change in Logarithmic Excess Fluidity $(\Gamma \phi - \overline{\Gamma \phi})(0.25 \text{ year})$
1	0.0200	0.0200	0	−0.0100	0.0200	0.00500
2	0.0225	0.0175	0.00500	−0.0150	0.0150	0.00375
3	0.0250	0.0150	0.00875	−0.0194	0.0106	0.00266
4	0.0275	0.0125	0.01141	−0.0232	0.0068	0.00170
5	0.0300	0.0100	0.01311	−0.0266	0.0034	0.00086
6	0.0325	0.0075	0.01397	−0.0295	0.0005	0.00013
7	0.0350	0.0050	0.01410	−0.0320	−0.0020	−0.00051
8	0.0375	0.0025	0.01359	−0.0343	−0.0043	−0.00107
9	0.0400	0	0.01252	−0.0363	−0.0063	−0.00156
10	0.0400	0	0.01096	−0.0355	−0.0055	−0.00137
11	0.0400	0	0.00959	−0.0348	−0.0048	−0.00120
12	0.0400	0	0.00839	−0.0342	−0.0042	−0.00105
...	...	...	...	...	...	...
16	0.0400	0	0.00492	−0.0325	−0.0025	−0.00063
...	...	...	...	...	...	...
30	0.0400	0	0.00076	−0.0304	−0.0004	−0.00010
...	...	...	...	...	...	...
∞	0.0400	0	0	−0.0300	0	0

The first column keeps track of time elapsed in quarters from the change in monetary policy. The second column gives the expected nominal-money-supply growth rate and the third column gives the difference between the actual and this expected rate. The fourth column gives the logarithmic difference between actual and desired fluidity, which is initially zero. Using the equation, the first quarter growth rate of fluidity is calculated as

$$\Gamma \phi = \frac{-0.03}{\text{year}} + \frac{0.0200}{\text{year}} - \frac{0.5}{\text{year}}(0) = \frac{-0.0100}{\text{year}}$$

or −1 percent per annum. This value is entered in the fifth column for quarter 1.

We calculate logarithmic excess fluidity $\log \phi - \log \phi^d$ at the beginning of the second quarter by use of the fact that $\Gamma \phi - \overline{\Gamma \phi}$ is its rate of change per annum.[a] During the first quarter, this rate of change $\Gamma \phi - \overline{\Gamma \phi}$ is (−0.01/year) − (−0.03/year) = 0.02/year which is entered in the sixth column. So during the first quarter year, excess fluidity will increase from zero by (0.02/year)(0.25 year) = 0.005, which goes in the

---

[a] Note that $\Delta(\log \phi - \log \phi^d) \equiv \Delta \log \phi - \Delta \log \phi^d = \Gamma \phi - \overline{\Gamma \phi}$.

right-hand column. This value is also entered for the beginning of the second quarter in the fourth column of the table. Put differently, actual fluidity grows 2 percent per annum faster than desired fluidity, so actual fluidity will exceed desired fluidity by $\frac{1}{2}$ percent or 0.005 at the end of the quarter. The growth rate of fluidity for the second quarter is then computed as

$$\Gamma\phi = \frac{-0.03}{\text{year}} + \frac{0.0175}{\text{year}} - \frac{0.5}{\text{year}}(0.00500) = \frac{-0.0150}{\text{year}}$$

or -1.5 percent per annum.

The increase in logarithmic excess fluidity during the second quarter is found by multiplying $\Gamma\phi - \overline{\Gamma\phi}$ by the 0.25 year elapsed to obtain $(0.015/\text{year})(0.25 \text{ year}) = 0.00375$. So logarithmic excess fluidity at the beginning of the third quarter is $0.00500 + 0.00375 = 0.00875$ or 0.875 percent. This is entered in the fourth column of the table.

The table repeats the calculations over and over. Note that after six quarters, the fluidity growth rate falls below the steady-state rate of -3 percent per annum and remains below it until the excess fluidity is eliminated. Once the difference between actual and expected nominal-money-supply growth is eliminated, this is accomplished by a gradual reduction of excess fluidity at a rate of 12.5 percent per quarter (the λ value of 0.5, or 50 percent per annum, equals 12.5 percent per quarter). This particular form of the adjustment equation implies that it would take literally forever to return completely to long-run equilibrium. But excess fluidity is reduced to 0.5 percent after 4 years and to three-quarters of a tenth of a percent after $7\frac{1}{2}$ years, which surely qualifies as an "essentially complete" adjustment. The higher the value of λ actually existing in the economy, the faster will the economy converge to the long-run steady-state equilibrium.

A few points should be noted for future use. First, there is a time z' in the adjustment period (where the $\Gamma M - \Gamma M^*$ and $\lambda(\log \phi - \log \phi^d)$ lines intersect) at which the actual and steady-state growth rates of fluidity are equal. Before this time actual fluidity rises relative to its steady-state value and afterward falls back toward it. During the period following this time, the actual growth rate of fluidity is less than the steady-state growth rate. This cyclical adjustment is required by the arithmetic of the process: At z and at the end of the adjustment process actual and steady-state fluidity are equal, so they must have had the same average growth rate in the interim. Therefore, if actual fluidity first grows faster than steady-state fluidity it must later grow less rapidly so things will average out.[9]

---

[9] Students familiar with integral calculus can prove that the area between the $\Gamma\phi$ and $\Gamma\phi_s$ line when $\Gamma\phi$ exceeds $\Gamma\phi_s$ is equal to the corresponding area when $\Gamma\phi$ is less than $\Gamma\phi_s$.

This last point can be illustrated by thinking of two cars driving along together at 40 miles per hour. If the first car speeds up to 60 for an hour while the second car continues at 40, then the first car must slow down to 20 for an hour to allow the second car to catch up. Similar cyclical adjustment patterns for growth rates are common for the various aggregates.

The cyclical pattern of fluidity growth in Fig. 6.3 captures the main features of the adjustment to a monetary shock. It does not take account, however, of differences between desired and steady-state fluidity during the adjustment period. We will see in Chap. 7 that the responses of real income and interest rates to a monetary shock cause desired fluidity to be less than steady-state fluidity in the latter stages of adjustment to an increased money growth. This can add a few complications to the adjustment pattern. However, these fluctuations in desired fluidity—although detectable statistically—do not appear to be important empirically except for deep depressions such as the 1930s.[10] So we can proceed using this cyclical adjustment process as a good approximation, but will consider a more complicated adjustment in Chap. 7.

6.3 THE CYCLICAL ADJUSTMENT OF NOMINAL INCOME

THE NOMINAL INCOME ADJUSTMENT
IMPLIED BY THE FLUIDITY ADJUSTMENT

The adjustment pattern of nominal income to the monetary shock can be inferred directly from the adjustment of fluidity. Monetary policy determines the nominal money supply M, so the Cambridge identity $M \equiv \phi Y$ can be solved for nominal income, given fluidity ϕ. This is most readily done by use of graphs.

For constructing graphs, it is handy to relate the actual values to steady-state values[11]

$$\log Y - \log Y_S \equiv -(\log \phi - \log \phi_S) \qquad [6.9]$$

$$\Gamma Y - \Gamma Y_S \equiv -(\Gamma \phi - \Gamma \phi_S) \qquad [6.10]$$

That is, the differences (whether measured in logarithms or growth rates) between the actual and steady-state values of nominal income are identical except for sign to those for fluidity. Figure 6.4 reproduces the steady-state growth paths and growth rates of nominal money, fluidity, and nominal income from Fig. 6.2. It then superimposes the cyclical adjustment of actual fluidity relative

---

[10] This statement is based upon estimates of models quite similar to that in this chapter by Matthew S. Goldberg and Thom B. Thurston, Monetarism, Overshooting, and the Procyclical Movement of Velocity, *Economic Inquiry*, **15**: 26–32, Jan. 1977; and by Dean Taylor, Friedman's Dynamic Models: Empirical Tests, *Journal of Monetary Economics*, **2**: 531–538, Nov. 1976.

[11] These relations are derived by subtracting [6.3] and [6.4] from the logarithmic ($\log M \equiv \log \phi + \log Y$) and growth rate ($\Gamma M \equiv \Gamma \phi + \Gamma Y$) forms of the Cambridge identity, respectively.

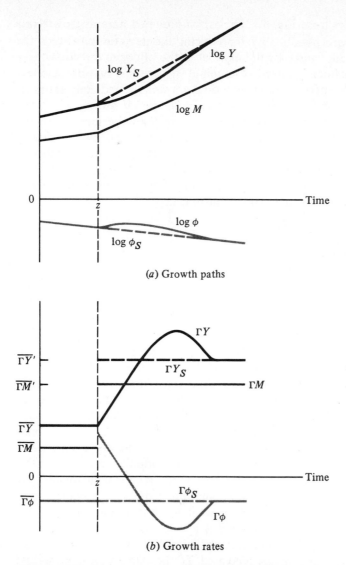

(a) Growth paths

(b) Growth rates

Figure 6.4 Adjustment pattern of nominal income and fluidity. The figure reproduces the steady-state growth paths and growth rates of nominal money, nominal income, and fluidity from Fig. 6.2 and the adjustment pattern of actual fluidity from Fig. 6.3. The adjustment pattern of actual versus steady-state nominal income is graphed, using the Cambridge identity, as the reverse of that for fluidity. The initial inertia in the actual growth path of nominal income requires a catch-up period during which the gap between actual and steady-state nominal income is closed. The actual growth rate of nominal income overshoots its steady-state value during this period.

to steady-state fluidity from Fig. 6.3. The actual growth path and growth rate of nominal income are obtained by reproducing the deviations between the actual and steady-state values for fluidity, but in the opposite direction.

The implied adjustment pattern of nominal income has two notable features: (1) The nominal-income growth rate does not shift immediately at time z, but accelerates over time. (2) There is a *catch-up period* during which the nominal-income growth rate is increased by more than the increase in the nominal-money-supply growth rate. This is referred to as *overshooting* in the growth rate of nominal income. This cyclical pattern in the growth rate occurs because the steady-state growth path tilts upward while actual nominal-income growth displays inertia, continuing at first along the previous steady-state growth path. So a catch-up must occur.

DIRECT ANALYSIS
OF THE NOMINAL INCOME ADJUSTMENT

Although the nominal income adjustment can thus be inferred from the fluidity adjustment pattern, fresh insight is gained by seeing how spending changes bring about this pattern.

Spending plans in the aggregate will normally grow at the same rate as nominal income is expected to grow. This is necessary for plans to be consistent with the expectations on which they are based, since income and expenditures are identically equal in the aggregate. Using the Cambridge identity this normal planned growth would equal $\Gamma M^* - \overline{\Gamma \phi}$ where ΓM^* is the expected money supply growth implicit in expenditure and receipt plans.

During the adjustment period, people will attempt to reduce their money balances, which are growing faster than the quantity of money demanded at current levels of income and interest rates. Each individual attempts to do this by spending more money than he or she is receiving. Of course the total supply of money is set by government policy and cannot be reduced by passing it from hand to hand. Individuals will primarily want to convert the excess money balances into other assets with higher yields of interest payments or services. To the extent that they purchase consumers' durable goods, expenditures for final goods and services are directly increased. To the extent that they increase their purchases of financial assets, market interest rates are lowered and the incentives for firms to invest are increased, and so expenditures on final goods and services are indirectly increased. Of course as final expenditures and income increase, this will encourage further increased expenditures by consumers and increased investment by firms along the lines of multiplier-accelerator models familiar from introductory macroeconomics courses.[12] This

---

[12] This further increase in spending will increase interest rates, reducing investment, and so forth. A thorough study of this aspect of the transmission mechanism is delayed until Chap. 11. For now it is sufficient to relate increased spending to excess of money supply over the quantity of money demanded at current income and interest rates.

additional spending need not be immediately translated into output and income increases, however, if firms at first meet the increased demand out of inventories and only increase production as higher sales persist.[13]

The growth rate of nominal income is thus related to normal planned growth and to attempts to spend excess money balances. A formal description would be

$$\Gamma Y = (\Gamma M^* - \overline{\Gamma\phi}) + \lambda(\log \phi - \log \phi^d) \qquad [6.11]$$

where use has been made of the identity $\log M - \log M^d \equiv \log \phi - \log \phi^d$. Equation [6.11] says that nominal income growth is equal to the amount by which expected nominal-money-supply growth exceeds the trend growth rate of fluidity[14] plus a multiple λ of the logarithmic excess money balances. This means that an initially unexpected increase in the nominal-money-supply growth rate does not affect nominal income growth until it increases expected money supply growth or creates excess money balances. Equation [6.11] can be derived by using [6.8] to substitute for $\Gamma\phi$ in the identity $\Gamma Y \equiv \Gamma M - \Gamma\phi$, so the two alternative dynamic equations [6.8] and [6.11] are just different ways of saying the same thing.[15]

Return to Fig. 6.4 in light of the present discussion. At first (time z) the expected nominal-money-supply growth rate would equal the original lower growth rate $\overline{\Gamma M}$ and there would not yet be any excess money balances. So the growth rate of nominal income would be unchanged, and nominal income would proceed along its original steady-state growth path, not the new steeper one. As time passes, expected nominal-money-supply growth adjusts toward its higher actual value, and this causes the nominal-income growth rate to increase. Also, since nominal income growth lags behind nominal money growth, nominal money balances grow faster than the demand for them and attempts to spend the resulting excess money balances also increase nominal income growth.

The interaction of increases in expected money growth and excess money balances in causing the characteristic overshooting of the nominal-income growth rate is illustrated in Fig. 6.5 which corresponds to panel (b) of Fig. 6.4. The smooth increase in expected nominal-money-supply growth ΓM^* would imply a corresponding smooth increase in the nominal-income growth rate ΓY,

---

[13] Using national income accounts NNP data, this will lengthen the initial period in which the growth rate of nominal income is unchanged and the fluidity growth rate is increased by the full increase in money supply growth.

[14] This amount $\Gamma M^* - \overline{\Gamma\phi}$ is the normal planned growth in nominal income.

[15] The derivation is

$$\Gamma Y \equiv \Gamma M - \Gamma\phi$$
$$\Gamma Y = \Gamma M - \overline{\Gamma\phi} - (\Gamma M - \Gamma M^*) + \lambda(\log \phi - \log \phi^d)$$
$$\Gamma Y = (\Gamma M^* - \overline{\Gamma\phi}) + \lambda(\log \phi - \log \phi^d)$$

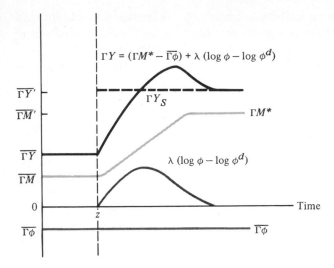

Figure 6.5 Overshooting of the nominal-income growth rate.
Nominal income grows by the difference between expected
nominal-money-supply growth and trend fluidity growth plus λ
times logarithmic excess fluidity. Logarithmic excess fluidity
measures the proportionate excess money supply. The first part is
given by the vertical distance between ΓM^* and $\overline{\Gamma\phi}$ and the second
part by the height of $\lambda(\log \phi - \log \phi^d)$ above the time axis. Here
$\log \phi - \log \phi^d$ is taken from panel (a) of Fig. 6.4, but it could be
derived by a procedure similar to that used in Fig. 6.3.

except for the excess money or excess fluidity effect. The excess fluidity is built
up while the actual nominal-income growth rate is less than its steady-state
rate. It adds to the nominal-income growth rate until the excess is finally
worked off when the actual level of nominal income catches up with its steady-
state level. Example 6.2 provides a numerical solution to this adjustment
process.

EXAMPLE 6.2

AN ARITHMETIC ANALYSIS
OF NOMINAL INCOME ADJUSTMENT

Instead of using the graphical approach in Fig. 6.5, the adjustment of
nominal income to a monetary shock can be derived arithmetically.
Suppose for this example that $\lambda = 0.5$ per annum and $\overline{\Gamma\phi} = -0.03$ per
annum (the same values as used in Example 6.1). Then Eq. [6.11]
can be written as

$$\Gamma Y = (\Gamma M^* - \overline{\Gamma\phi}) + \frac{0.5}{\text{year}} (\log \phi - \log \phi^d)$$

We again suppose that the monetary shock is an unexpected increase of ΓM from 2 to 4 percent per annum and that expected ΓM shifts up by 0.25 percentage point until it reaches 4 percent per annum.

The problem is solved by this table:

Quarter	Normal Planned Nominal Income Growth $\Gamma M^* - \overline{\Gamma\phi}$	Logarithmic Excess Fluidity $\log\phi - \log\phi^d$	Actual Nominal Income Growth ΓY	Rate of Change in Logarithmic Excess Fluidity $\Gamma\phi - \overline{\Gamma\phi}$	Quarterly Change in Logarithmic Excess Fluidity $(\Gamma\phi - \overline{\Gamma\phi})(0.25 \text{ year})$
1	0.0500	0	0.0500	0.0200	0.00500
2	0.0525	0.00500	0.0550	0.0150	0.00375
3	0.0550	0.00875	0.0594	0.0106	0.00266
4	0.0575	0.01141	0.0632	0.0068	0.00170
5	0.0600	0.01311	0.0666	0.0034	0.00086
6	0.0625	0.01397	0.0695	0.0005	0.00013
7	0.0650	0.01410	0.0720	−0.0020	−0.00051
8	0.0675	0.01359	0.0743	−0.0043	−0.00107
9	0.0700	0.01252	0.0763	−0.0063	−0.00156
10	0.0700	0.01096	0.0755	−0.0055	−0.00137
11	0.0700	0.00959	0.0748	−0.0048	−0.00120
12	0.0700	0.00839	0.0742	−0.0042	−0.00105
...	...	...	...	...	...
16	0.0700	0.00492	0.0725	−0.0025	−0.00063
...	...	...	...	...	...
30	0.0700	0.00076	0.0704	−0.0004	−0.00010
...	...	...	...	...	...
∞	0.0700	0	0.0700	0	0

The first column keeps track of time in quarters from the change in monetary policy. The second column gives the normal planned growth in nominal income or $\Gamma M^* - \overline{\Gamma\phi}$. This number $\Gamma M^* + (0.03/\text{year})$ starts at 0.05/year and then increases with ΓM^* at 0.25 percentage point per quarter up to 0.07/year. The logarithmic difference between actual and desired fluidity (third column) is initially zero. Using our equation, the first growth rate of nominal income is calculated as

$$\Gamma Y = \frac{0.0500}{\text{year}} + \frac{0.5}{\text{year}}(0) = \frac{0.0500}{\text{year}}$$

or 5 percent per annum. This is the old steady-state growth rate of nominal income corresponding to a 2 percent per annum ΓM. It is entered in the fourth column of the table.

We need $\Gamma\phi - \overline{\Gamma\phi}$ to calculate $\log\phi - \log\phi^d$ for the beginning of the second quarter. By the Cambridge identity $\Gamma\phi \equiv \Gamma M - \Gamma Y$, so for this example

$$\Gamma\phi - \overline{\Gamma\phi} = \Gamma M - \Gamma Y - \overline{\Gamma\phi} = \frac{0.04}{\text{year}} - \Gamma Y - \left(\frac{-0.03}{\text{year}}\right)$$

$$\Gamma\phi - \overline{\Gamma\phi} = \frac{0.07}{\text{year}} - \Gamma Y$$

So during the first quarter, $\Gamma\phi - \overline{\Gamma\phi} = 0.02/\text{year}$. This 2 percent per annum faster growth of actual than desired fluidity will cause a gap of $(0.02/\text{year})(0.25 \text{ year}) = 0.005$ or 0.5 percent at the end of the first quarter as noted in the sixth column. This proportionate (or logarithmic) gap is entered in the third column for the beginning of the second quarter.

Second quarter nominal income growth is the

$$\Gamma Y = \frac{0.0525}{\text{year}} + \frac{0.5}{\text{year}}(0.005) = \frac{0.055}{\text{year}}$$

or 5.5 percent per annum. The corresponding $\Gamma\phi - \overline{\Gamma\phi}$ of 0.015/year implies that logarithmic excess fluidity increases by $(0.015/\text{year})(0.25 \text{ year}) = 0.00375$. So logarithmic excess fluidity at the beginning of the third quarter is $0.00500 + 0.00375 = 0.00875$ or 0.875 percent. This is entered in the third column of the table. The table reports the results of repeating these calculations over and over.

Note that it takes six quarters for actual nominal income growth to catch up to the new steady-state growth rate of 7 percent per annum (0.07/year). At this point actual fluidity exceeds steady-state fluidity by 1.4 percent. By reference to Eq. [6.9], this implies that actual nominal income is 1.4 percent less than steady-state nominal income. During the remainder of the adjustment period, this gap is gradually eliminated.

Comparing the tables in Examples 6.1 and 6.2, it is clear that they are mutually consistent. The values of ΓY could be found from Example 6.1 as $\Gamma Y = \Gamma M - \Gamma\phi = (0.04/\text{year}) - \Gamma\phi$. Or using the table in this exercise, we could find the growth rate of fluidity as $\Gamma\phi = \Gamma M - \Gamma Y$. This confirms that Eqs. [6.8] and [6.11] are mathematically equivalent.

Summing up, the cyclical adjustment patterns of the nominal-income and fluidity growth rates illustrated in Fig. 6.4 are mutually consistent and under-standable either on a shock-absorber model of fluidity or on the view that nominal income growth reflects normal expected growth plus attempts to spend excess money balances. The gradual adjustment of nominal income from its old to its new steady-state growth path requires fluidity to temporarily deviate from its unchanged growth path.

A USEFUL PHYSICAL ANALOGY

The process of adjustment can be clarified by a simple physical analogy. Figure 6.6 shows a somewhat peculiar train consisting only of an engine and a boxcar joined together by a long shock absorber.[16] This shock absorber has springs which allow it to lengthen or shorten with sudden changes in force on it, but the springs will thereafter gradually return the shock absorber to its normal length.

The engine, shock absorber, and boxcar are identified with the nominal money supply, fluidity, and nominal income, respectively. Suppose that the train is proceeding smoothly along level ground at a speed of 40 miles per hour. If the engineer increases the speed of the engine to 50 mph, the shock absorber stretches at first beyond its normal length. But increased force is applied to the boxcar as the shock absorber lengthens and the boxcar begins to speed up. When the speed of the boxcar reaches 50 mph, the shock absorber stops stretching. But the force of the springs will tend to return the shock absorber to its normal length, and so the boxcar will speed up faster than 50 mph for a while. The adjustment of the shock absorber to normal length can be smooth or it can fluctuate—first too long, then too short, and so forth. But the economy appears adequately represented by a smooth adjustment. Once the train has adjusted to the new speed, both engine and boxcar have increased their speed by the same amount, and the shock absorber has returned to normal length.

---

[16] The caboose will be added in Chap. 7!

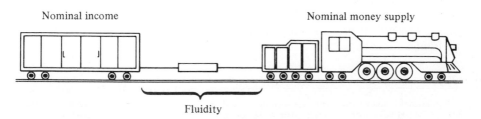

Nominal income   Nominal money supply

Fluidity

Figure 6.6 Train analogy to adjustment of fluidity and nominal income. The speed of the boxcar is determined in the long run by the speed of the engine. If the engine suddenly accelerates, however, at first the shock absorber stretches (fluidity increases) and the boxcar (nominal income) only gradually speeds up. There must be a period—when the shock absorber returns to its normal length—during which the boxcar's speed is increased by more than the engine's.

Physical analogies are never perfect[17] and cannot substitute for a careful study of the economic forces which determine the adjustment of fluidity and nominal income. But the train is better than most and does focus our attention on the adjustment to changes in the long-run equilibrium. So we will return to our railroad almost as often as in a game of Monopoly.

THE TIMING OF THE ADJUSTMENT PROCESS

The timing of the adjustment process remains a very open empirical issue. The statistical issues in reconciling the timing patterns implicit in various specific mathematical models are beyond the scope of this text. Suffice it to say that the cumulative effects of a "normal-sized"[18] change in monetary policy become quite apparent between two and four quarters of a year after the policy change. On some estimates the adjustment process is essentially completed within 3 years or less. Other estimates indicate that this takes 5 years or more.[19] The timing of the adjustment process would be influenced by the initial conditions and by the absolute size of the change in monetary growth rate. Large changes in the growth rate of the nominal money supply are reflected in large changes in the actual growth path of nominal income, which are much more quickly noticeable than are small changes.

The initial lag between the change in monetary policy and a significant impact on nominal income is as long as it is because unplanned inventory changes occur. The initial increase in spending on final (mainly durable) goods is largely met by sales from inventories rather than by increased output or prices. The resulting unintended *dis*investment in inventories held by firms offsets the increase in spending until firms increase production to restore inventories to their normal levels. In terms of the train analogy of Fig. 6.6, the long shock absorber could be replaced by two shorter shock absorbers and an intermediate boxcar labeled final spending. The details of this spending-inventory transmission process can normally be left in the background, however.

Recent refinements of the empirical definition of a monetary shock as unexpected nominal-money-supply growth provide hope of more precise estimates of the adjustment-process timing in the future. We must wait for that hope to be fulfilled.

---

[17] For example, steady-state fluidity has been drawn with a negative trend. To account for this, the shock absorber would have to have a steadily decreasing "normal" length. This would imply a faster speed for the boxcar than for the engine, of course.

[18] That is, changes in the nominal-money-supply growth rate such as have occurred in the past—say about 3 to 6 percentage points per annum.

[19] The timing relationships are best estimated within models which allow for the effects of other macroeconomic shocks, so the citations of the empirical literature will be delayed to a more general discussion in Chap. 8. This controversy does not divide monetarists from Keynesians, since some of each school are found on either side of the long versus short lags debate.

EFFECTS ON FLUIDITY AND NOMINAL INCOME OF AN UNEXPECTED DECREASE IN NOMINAL-MONEY-SUPPLY GROWTH

If the unexpected change from $\overline{\Gamma M}$ to $\overline{\Gamma M}'$ had represented a decrease in the nominal-money-supply growth rate instead of an increase, the effects would have been just reversed. The decrease in the growth rate of the nominal money supply does not affect the growth rate of nominal income at first. As nominal income proceeds initially along its old growth path, actual money balances fall relative to the quantity of money demanded, and fluidity falls below its steady-state level. This is illustrated in Fig. 6.7. As people decrease their spending in an attempt to rebuild their money holdings and in response to falling expected nominal-money-supply growth, the growth rate of nominal income begins to fall. This is reflected in an increasing growth rate of fluidity. The initially too-rapid growth in nominal income must be offset by a period of *undershooting*, in which the nominal-income growth rate is decreased by more than the decrease in the nominal-money-supply growth rate. This period of undershooting is needed to close the gap between actual and steady-state nominal income. The gap between actual and steady-state fluidity is simultaneously eliminated. It would take about 6 to 12 months for the decrease in the nominal-income growth rate to be apparent, and perhaps 3 to 5 years for the adjustment process to be essentially complete.

SUMMARY

1 A monetary shock—an unexpected change in the growth rate of the nominal money supply—initiates an adjustment process to a new steady-state equilibrium. This chapter concentrates on an increase in the nominal-money-supply growth rate—a stimulative monetary policy.

2 The increase in the growth rate of nominal money is matched in the steady-state growth rate of nominal income, but the steady-state growth rate of fluidity is unchanged.

3 The actual growth rate of nominal income is slow to change, as fluidity acts as a shock absorber. This shock-absorber response means that actual fluidity first rises rapidly relative to steady-state fluidity, and then slows to gradually close the gap. Alternatively, nominal income gradually adjusts from the old to the new steeper steady-state growth path. This adjustment involves a cyclical overshooting of the nominal-income growth rate during the catch-up period in which the gap between actual and steady-state nominal income is closed.

4 The timing of the adjustment process remains an open empirical question, but notable effects on nominal income growth are normal within 6 to 12 months, and the process probably takes 3 to 5 years to complete.

5 An unexpected decrease in the nominal-money-supply growth rate—or a restrictive monetary policy—has the reverse effects on nominal income and

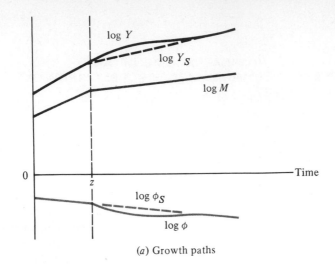

(a) Growth paths

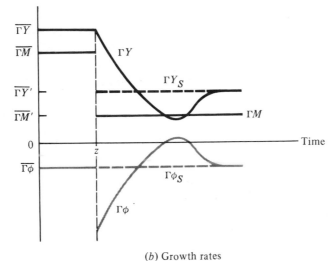

(b) Growth rates

Figure 6.7 Adjustment of nominal income and fluidity to reduced nominal-money-supply growth. If the unexpected change in the nominal-money-supply growth rate from $\overline{\Gamma M}$ to $\overline{\Gamma M}'$ were a decrease, the adjustment patterns of fluidity and nominal income would be reversed from the case of an increase (compare Fig. 6.4). A reduction in the nominal-money-supply growth rate causes an equal reduction in the steady-state growth rate of nominal income. Actual nominal income initially at time z continues along the old steady-state growth path. So the actual growth rate of fluidity is reduced at first by the amount of the decrease in nominal-money-supply growth. Actual nominal income gradually adjusts to the new, less steep steady-state growth path. Undershooting of the nominal-income growth rate $\overline{\Gamma Y}$ is required to make up for the initially too rapid growth. This undershooting may involve negative actual nominal-income growth rates even if the steady-state nominal-income growth rate is positive. No such negative $\overline{\Gamma Y}$'s occur in the particular case drawn, however.

fluidity. As nominal income gradually adjusts downward to the new, less steep steady-state growth path, there is a period of undershooting during which the nominal-income growth rate falls by more than the decrease in nominal-money-supply growth.

6 The analogy of engine and boxcar joined by a shock absorber (nominal money supply, nominal income, and fluidity) illustrates the adjustment process.

CONCEPTS TO KNOW

catch-up period
excess fluidity
macroeconomic shocks
overshooting

restrictive monetary policy
stimulative monetary policy
undershooting

QUESTIONS AND EXERCISES

1 (a) If the money-multiplier growth rate averaged −2 percent per annum, the Fed would have to increase base money at a _____ growth rate to achieve a 4 percent per annum growth rate of the nominal money supply.

(b) If the Fed wished to increase the growth rate of the nominal money supply from 4 percent to 8 percent per annum for a year, this would require *additional* open market purchases of about _____ worth of government securities during the year, assuming that $B = \$100$ billion and $\mu = 2.5$ at the beginning of the year.

*2 (a) Suppose that at the end of 1985 the economy were in long-run equilibrium, with a 4 percent per annum nominal-money-supply growth rate and a −1 percent per annum fluidity growth rate. The corresponding nominal-income growth rate would be _____.

(b) If an unexpected change in monetary policy then increased ΓM to 8 percent per annum, the new steady-state nominal-income growth rate would be _____.

(c) Suppose that from the end of 1985 to the end of 1987, the average growth rate of nominal income were 7 percent per annum. To achieve long-run equilibrium by the end of the next 2 years, the average growth rate of nominal income would have to be _____ from the end of 1987 to the end of 1989. This would imply an average ΓY of _____ from the end of 1985 to the end of 1989.

3 Use the train analogy to discuss an unexpected reduction in the growth rate of the nominal money supply.

4 In Figs. 6.3 and 6.4 and Example 6.1, the highest value of excess logarithmic fluidity (measured as $\log \phi - \log \phi^d$) occurs as the actual fluidity growth rate equals the steady-state fluidity growth rate during the middle of the adjustment process. Explain why.

REFERENCES FOR FURTHER READING

Darby, Michael R.:　The Allocation of Transitory Income among Consumers' Assets, *American Economic Review*, **62**:928–941, Dec. 1972.

Friedman, Milton:　*A Theoretical Framework for Monetary Analysis*, New York: NBER, 1971, pp. 1–48.

————: The Lag in the Effect of Monetary Policy, *Journal of Political Economy*, **69**:447–466, Oct. 1961.

Goldberg, Matthew S., and **Thurston, Thom B.:** Monetarism, Overshooting, and the Procyclical Movement of Velocity, *Economic Inquiry*, **15**:26–32, Jan. 1977.

Taylor, Dean:　Friedman's Dynamic Models: Empirical Tests, *Journal of Monetary Economics*, **2**:531–538, 1976.

CHAPTER 7

EFFECTS OF A MONEY SUPPLY SHOCK ON REAL INCOME AND THE PRICE LEVEL

WHAT YOU WILL LEARN IN THIS CHAPTER
Okun's law relating real income and unemployment
● The transitory effects of a monetary shock on real income ● Overshooting and undershooting in the adjustment of the inflation rate to a monetary shock ● Stagflation and cost-push inflation as a phase of adjustment to a monetary shock ● The cyclical adjustment of interest rates

7.1 EFFECTS ON REAL INCOME AND THE PRICE LEVEL: A SUPPLY AND DEMAND APPROACH

Nominal income is the product of real income and the price level. The adjustment of nominal income to a monetary shock can be decomposed into the adjustments of these two components. The adjustment of real income traces out cyclical fluctuations around the trend growth path of real income. These fluctuations are associated with abnormally low or high unemployment rates. The adjustment of the price level is characterized by large fluctuations in the inflation rate. Simple statements relating the inflation rate to real income growth or unemployment are the macroeconomist's philosophers' stone: much sought after but always disappointing in application. The essential fuller description is the subject of this chapter.

Two different approaches will be used to illuminate the adjustment process. First we will examine a series of short periods to see how increases in nominal spending would affect real output, employment, and the price level. We then turn to a continuous dynamic approach similar to that used in Chap. 6. This approach clarifies the relationship of real income, the price level, and nominal income and their cumulative adjustments.

The chapter concludes with an analysis of the cyclical adjustment of interest rates to monetary policy changes. This adjustment pattern—besides being interesting for itself—will be used later in discussing monetary policy when the Fed attempted to offset interest rate changes. Two appendixes add the minor wrinkles required to take account of the non-superneutrality of money and of differences between desired and steady-state fluidity during the adjustment period.

THE LINKAGE BETWEEN REAL OUTPUT AND UNEMPLOYMENT

Short-run movements in real output and the unemployment rate are very closely linked. Increases (decreases) in the unemployment rate are associated with abnormally low (high) real-income growth rates. This empirical relationship is referred to as *Okun's law*.[1] A formal mathematical statement of Okun's law is

$$\Delta u = -a(\Gamma y - \overline{\Gamma y}) \tag{7.1}$$

That is, the rate of change per annum in the unemployment rate is inversely proportional to the difference between the actual and trend (or steady-state) growth rates of real income. The factor of proportionality indicated here by a is about one-third for the United States. So a 1 percentage point drop in the unemployment rate over a year would be associated with a real-income growth rate over the year about 3 percentage points per annum higher than normal. Note that a 1 percentage point drop in the unemployment rate *over 6 months* would be associated with about 6 percentage points per annum above normal real income growth.[2]

Okun's law is presented here as an empirical but not a causal relationship. That is, the forces which determine real income growth also simultaneously determine the unemployment rate. There are of course influences running from unemployment to output and from output to unemployment, but the empirical association reflects other influences as well. For example, when the unemployment rate is high, the average hours worked by those employed and the average hours during which plant and equipment are used tend to be low. All these lower the flow of labor and capital services and hence (given the aggregate production function) real output, which is identical to real income.

This relationship—although not perfect—has held up quite well in the postwar U.S. data.[3] It is frequently useful to look at an alternate form of Okun's

---

[1] The original statement of the "law" was by Arthur M. Okun, Potential GNP: Its Measurement and Significance, *1962 Proceedings of the Business and Economic Statistics Section of the American Statistical Association*, pp. 98–104.

[2] If u drops from say 6 to 5 percent in 6 months, this is a rate of change of -0.01 per half year or -0.02/year, which would imply $\Gamma y - \overline{\Gamma y}$ was about 0.06/year or 6 percent per annum over the same period.

[3] The only notable exceptions are during the 1945–1947 and 1971–1974 price control periods, which apparently reflect problems in the reported data rather than in Okun's law. This is discussed further in Chap. 13. Statistically, quarter-to-quarter changes in the real-income growth rate explain 50 to 60 percent of the quarter-to-quarter changes in the unemployment rate.

law which relates deviations of unemployment from normal to deviations of real income from normal

$$u - \bar{u} = -a(\log y - \log y_S) \qquad [7.2]$$

This says that the deviations of the unemployment rate from normal will be opposite in sign and about one-third the magnitude of the proportionate deviations of real income from normal.[4] For example, if the normal unemployment rate were 5 percent and real income were 4.5 percent above normal, the actual unemployment rate would be about 3.5 percent.[5]

In this chapter, we will keep the discussion manageable by concentrating on the level and growth rate of real income. The corresponding behavior of the unemployment rate can be adequately inferred for now from the behavior of real income: If actual real income is above (below) its steady-state level, the unemployment rate is abnormally low (high). If the actual real-income growth rate is faster (slower) than its steady-state rate, the unemployment rate is falling (rising). The empirical correspondence is not perfect, but it is much simpler to deal with real income first and then concentrate separately on the unemployment rate in Chap. 14.

AGGREGATE SUPPLY AND DEMAND

The effects of a stimulative monetary policy on real output and the price level can be studied in terms of shifts in aggregate supply and demand curves. How this can be done is indicated in a general way before going into the details of why these shifts occur.

The basic idea is that real income and the price level are inversely related, given current conditions (including especially monetary policy), just as are quantity sold and price in the demand curve for an individual industry.[6] An *aggregate demand curve* relating the average price level and real income for some short period is labeled D in Fig. 7.1. There is a corresponding *aggregate supply curve* labeled S. Their intersection determines real income and the price level for the particular period and conditions for which they are drawn.

---

[4] Variations in real income relative to trend explain statistically about 85 percent of quarterly variations in the level of the unemployment rate. Note that taking rates of change in [7.2] yields $\Delta u - \Delta \bar{u} = -a(\Delta \log y - \Delta \log y_S)$ which, given an approximately constant normal unemployment rate ($\Delta \bar{u} = 0$), corresponds to [7.1].

[5] That is, $u - 0.05 \approx -\frac{1}{3}(0.045)$

$$u \approx 0.05 - 0.015 = 0.035 \text{ or } 3.5 \text{ percent}$$

[6] Nominal income ($Y \equiv yP$) corresponds to revenue for an industry demand curve. If nominal income were fixed, regardless of how it were divided between real income and the price level, the aggregate demand curve would be unit-elastic. (That is, the elasticity of real income with respect to the price level would be -1; see Sec. M.5 of the Mathematical Appendix, on elasticities.) Actually the aggregate demand curve appears to be somewhat elastic (an elasticity less than -1 in algebraic value), but that does not matter for the current discussion. A formal derivation of the aggregate demand curve will be outlined in Chap. 11.

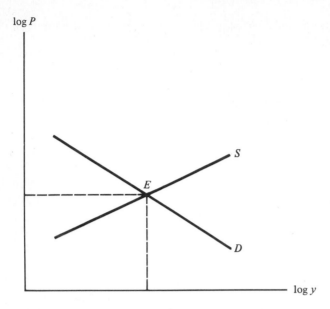

Figure 7.1 Determination of real income and the price level by aggregate demand and supply curves. The negatively sloped aggregate demand curve shows the real expenditures which would be made at alternative price levels. The aggregate supply curve shows the real output which would be produced at alternative price levels. Their intersection E determines the price level and real income for the short period and conditions for which the curves are drawn.

To see how the curves work, suppose for a minute that the economy were in a steady-state equilibrium with positive growth rates of both real income and the price level. In that case, both the aggregate supply and demand curves would shift upward each period at the steady-state rate of inflation and to the right at the growth rate of real income. This is illustrated in Fig. 7.2. Because the curves shift together, their intersections move in the same way. So long as the steady-state equilibrium continues, the period-to-period change in the *logarithms* of real income and the price level will be constants.[7] This is illustrated by the straight-line expansion path E traced out by the intersections of the successive periods' aggregate supply and demand curves. Note that, except for changes in *relative* demand or cost conditions, exactly the same picture would emerge for successive periods in any particular industry.

In what follows, we will be mainly interested in fluctuations of real income around its steady-state level. It is these fluctuations (measured as $\log y - \log y_S$) which cause the unemployment rate to deviate from normal according

---

[7] These constants are the respective growth rates times the length in years of the short periods for which the curves are drawn.

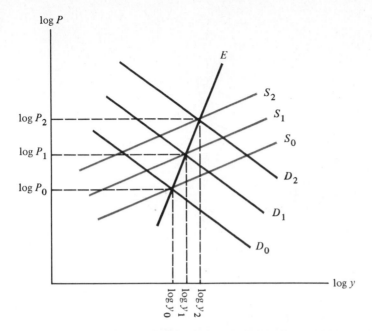

Figure 7.2 Shifts in aggregate supply and demand curves for successive periods in a steady-state equilibrium. This figure shows the shifts in aggregate supply and demand curves for the three successive periods 0, 1, 2. In a steady-state equilibrium, both curves shift up each period by the steady-state rate of inflation $\overline{\Gamma P}$ times the length of the period and to the right by the steady-state growth rate of income $\overline{\Gamma y}$ times the length of the period. Therefore the intersections of the curves move up and over by the same amounts. This is shown by the constant increases in log y and log P between periods or the straight-line expansion path E. The slope of E is $\overline{\Gamma P}/\overline{\Gamma y}$.

to Okun's law [7.2]. Figure 7.3 reproduces Fig. 7.2, except with actual real income measured relative to steady-state real income. The steady-state expansion path labeled E becomes a vertical line through 0 on the horizontal axis.

AGGREGATE DEMAND AND SUPPLY SHIFTS DUE TO A MONETARY SHOCK

Let us now return to our monetary shock—an increase in the nominal-money-supply growth rate from $\overline{\Gamma M}$ to $\overline{\Gamma M'}$ at time z. It is handy to have for comparison what shifts in aggregate supply and demand would occur if the economy immediately followed the new steady-state equilibrium. This is done in panel (a) of Fig. 7.4. The increased nominal-money-supply growth is assumed to begin at the end of period 1. Thereafter, the steady-state aggregate supply and demand curves shift up more each period because the steady-state rate of

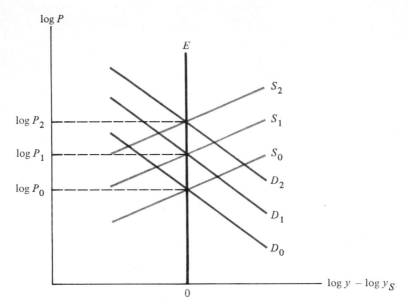

Figure 7.3 Shifts in steady-state aggregate supply and demand curves with real income deviation measure. This figure reproduces Fig. 7.2 except that actual real income y is here measured as a logarithmic deviation from steady-state real income. This eliminates the rightward part of the shifts. So both aggregate demand and supply curves shift up each period by $\overline{\Gamma P}$ times the length of the period. This upward shift equals $\log P_1 - \log P_0 = \log P_2 - \log P_1 = \cdots$. The steady-state expansion path is the vertical line E.

inflation is increased by the same amount $\overline{\Gamma M'} - \overline{\Gamma M}$ as the nominal-money-supply growth rate is increased as shown in Chap. 5. The logarithmic change in the price level over the previous period correspondingly increases from $\log P_1 - \log P_0$ to $\log P_2 - \log P_1$ and continues constant in the following periods. The growth rate of nominal wages will increase by the same amount as the inflation rate, so the growth rate of real wages and the supply of labor is unaffected in steady-state equilibrium.

Panel (b) of Fig. 7.4 illustrates how shifts in the actual aggregate supply and demand curves can be used to trace out the actual adjustment process for real income and the price level. During periods 0 and 1, monetary policy has not yet been changed, so actual and steady-state values are identical. The adjustment process proper occurs in the two periods labeled 2 and 3.

The shifts in the aggregate demand and supply curves reflect two empirical generalizations: (1) Shifts in actual aggregate demand initially lag behind more rapid shifts in the steady-state aggregate demand curve, but then catch up. (2) Shifts in the actual aggregate supply curve at first lag behind more rapid shifts in the actual aggregate *demand* curve, but then catch up.

The first principle is illustrated by the fact that actual D_2 is shifted up from D_1 by less than the shift in the steady-state panel (a) although by more than D_1

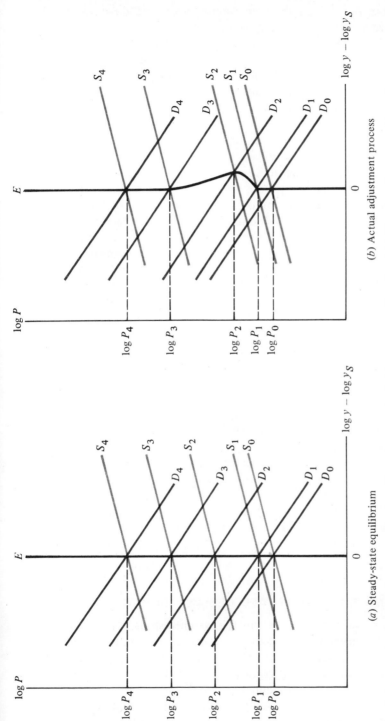

(a) Steady-state equilibrium

(b) Actual adjustment process

Figure 7.4 Comparison of steady-state and actual adjustment to a stimulative monetary policy. Panel (*a*) illustrates the more rapid steady-state inflation rate $\overline{\Gamma P}'$ associated with the increased nominal-money-supply growth rate $\overline{\Gamma M}'$ beginning at the end of period 1. The upward shift in steady-state aggregate supply and demand curves equals the steady-state inflation rate times the length of the period. So the more rapid increase in log P after period 1 reflects the fact that $\overline{\Gamma P}'$ exceeds $\overline{\Gamma P}$ by $\overline{\Gamma M}' - \overline{\Gamma M}$. In panel (*b*), the upward shift in the actual aggregate demand curve is initially less than in the steady-state aggregate demand curve [compare panel (*a*)]. Thereafter, the actual upward shift exceeds that in the steady-state aggregate demand curve so that the actual catches up with the steady-state aggregate demand curve. Continuing with panel (*b*), in period 2 the upward shift in the actual aggregate supply curve lags behind the increased upward shift in the actual aggregate demand curve. In period 3, however, a more rapid upward shift in the actual aggregate supply curve allows it to catch up to the actual aggregate demand curve and the steady-state aggregate supply curve. Examination of the actual expansion path E in panel (*b*) shows a temporary increase in actual real income relative to steady-state real income. The actual rate of inflation at first lags behind the increased steady-state inflation rate and then overshoots it while the actual price level catches up to the steady-state price level.

175

was shifted up from D_0. Actual D_3 then catches up to steady-state D_3 by shifting up by more than the new steady-state shift.

The second empirical generalization is illustrated by the fact that the actual upward shift in S_2 from S_1 is only a little more than S_1 was shifted up from S_0. Actual aggregate supply then catches up with actual aggregate demand by the large upward shift to S_3. Comparing panels (a) and (b) of Fig. 7.4, we can see that actual aggregate supply also catches up with steady-state aggregate supply in period 3.

Let us now see what Fig. 7.4 tells us about the adjustments of actual real income and the price level. First, as to real income: Actual real income grows relative to steady-state real income in the early part of the adjustment process and then falls back to equal steady-state real income in the latter part. The corresponding movement in the unemployment rate suggested by Okun's law [7.2] is that the unemployment rate falls initially and then rises back to normal. Next, as to the price level: At first the inflation rate (which is proportional to the change in log P over the previous period) accelerates less than the steady-state rate. So the actual price level in period 2 is considerably below the steady-state price level. This is seen by comparing log P_2 in panel (b) with panel (a). Later the actual rate of inflation exceeds the steady-state rate until the actual price level catches up with the steady-state price level. The use of a larger number of shorter periods would provide more detail on the adjustment of real income and the price level. Unfortunately the diagrams become rather messy, so that detail will be postponed to the continuous dynamic analysis of Sec. 7.2.

In sum, during the process of adjustment to a stimulative monetary policy, actual real income first rises relative to steady-state real income and then falls back to its steady-state expansion path. The rate of inflation lags behind the increased steady-state rate of inflation at first and then overshoots the new steady-state rate as the actual price level catches up with the steady-state price level. Needless to say, the early period of rapid real income growth, falling unemployment rates, and little-increased inflation rates is politically popular. The remainder of the adjustment period (slow or negative real income growth, rising unemployment rates, and overshooting inflation rates) is a time for politicians to give specious excuses.

REASONS BEHIND THE AGGREGATE DEMAND SHIFTS

It is time to redeem our pledge to see why the assumed shifts in the aggregate demand and supply curves would occur. Look first at the aggregate demand curve. The empirical generalization (assumption) underlying the shifts depicted in Fig. 7.4 was: Shifts in actual aggregate demand initially lag behind more rapid shifts in the steady-state aggregate demand curve, but then catch up. To see why this would be so, the connection between the aggregate demand curve and nominal income must be clear.

For any point on the aggregate demand curve, nominal income Y is simply the product of the indicated price level P and real income y by the definition of y.[8] This corresponds to price times quantity equals revenue, for an ordinary (microeconomic) industry demand curve. On the current approach, nominal income is determined simultaneously with real income and the price level by the intersection of the aggregate demand and supply curves (see Fig. 7.1). In Chap. 6, we analyzed the adjustment of nominal income to a stimulative monetary policy without explicit reference to how the nominal income changes were divided between real income and the price level. This is strictly valid only if the aggregate demand curve is unit-elastic.[9]

There is indirect evidence[10] that the aggregate demand curve is somewhat elastic. This means that the position of the aggregate supply curve would enter into the determination of nominal income. These effects appear small, however, relative to the forces shifting the aggregate demand curve. So we continue the provisional assumption that we can examine the adjustment of real income and the price level, given the adjustment of nominal income. The analysis of the details of the simultaneous determination of nominal income, real income, and the price level is left to Appendix A to this chapter.

On this basis, the shifts in the aggregate demand curve are period-by-period snapshots of the adjustment of nominal income discussed in Chap. 6. We saw there that the initial slowness of people to adjust their spending plans meant that nominal income growth is first slow relative to the increased steady-state growth rate. Then the nominal-income growth rate accelerates and overshoots the new steady-state growth rate during the period in which actual catches up to steady-state nominal income. Since the upward shifts in the aggregate demand curve are proportional to the corresponding average growth rate of nominal income for the period, the basic empirical generalization is just a restatement of Chap. 6.

REASONS BEHIND THE AGGREGATE SUPPLY SHIFTS

The aggregate supply curve shows how variations in cost conditions induced by variations in output would be reflected in the price level during the period. Costs will increase with output both because (1) marginal costs increase for

---

[8] Since we have been using logarithmic scales, the graphical indication of log Y is the sum of the lines perpendicular to the vertical and horizontal axes (log y and log P, respectively). The elasticity of the aggregate demand curve is simply 1 divided by the slope of the aggregate demand curve.

[9] If the aggregate demand curve is unit-elastic, the same nominal income corresponds to every combination of real income and the price level on the given aggregate demand curve.

[10] The indirect evidence is primarily the low real income elasticities estimated for short-run real-money demand functions. These reflect both gradual adjustment to long-run desired real money balances and the relatively weak impact of temporary changes in real income which do not correspond to proportional changes in real wealth. The slope of the aggregate demand curve can be interpreted as -1 divided by the sum of (a) the income elasticity of the short-run demand for money and (b) the corresponding interest elasticity times the ratio of the percentage changes in the interest rate and real income. Most estimates indicate that the interest-elasticity effect is too little to bring the sum up to 1, so -1 divided by the sum is less than -1 in algebraic value.

given amounts of capital, nominal wages of labor, and prices of intermediate goods, and because (2) a general increase in employment of labor and purchases of intermediate goods will raise their wages and prices, respectively.

To discuss shifts in the aggregate supply curve, we have to consider its height at some particular real output level. The steady-state real output seems a natural choice. So shifts in the aggregate supply curve reflect factors which determine the nominal wage rate and prices of intermediate goods at that output. The initial tendency of the aggregate supply curve to shift up, as in the old steady state, is due to (1) initially small changes in the nominal-wage growth rate and (2) time required for unexpected cost increases to work through the various stages of production and distribution to the prices of final goods and services. The initial stickiness in nominal wage growth is explained below in terms of job search strategy. The time for cost increases to work through the system is related to the price-setting behavior of firms.

Firms can increase real output only by increasing their employment of factors of production. In part this is done by varying the work weeks of labor and capital.[11] But the number of workers employed also varies, as was seen in discussing Okun's law. Employment is increased both because firms reduce the rate at which they fire or lay off workers, and because firms increase the rate at which they hire new workers. To see how this affects the growth rate of the nominal wage, we will touch briefly on topics explored in depth in Chap. 14.

An unemployed worker must search for a new job because information about the opportunities available is costly. The job seeker must actually go from firm to firm until receipt of an offer of a nominal wage which seems acceptable when compared with the expected costs and benefits of further search. If the probability of receiving an acceptable offer is underestimated because of an unusually high demand for new employees, the average worker will consider it good fortune to find a good wage offer after less-than-usual search. If the job seeker had known how easy it actually was to obtain such an offer, he or she probably would have searched longer for a higher wage. Initially then, firms can increase employment at little increase in wages over what would have been expected under the old steady state. As time goes on, workers adjust their expectations of what is available by way of job offers, and so nominal wages grow more rapidly.

Other factors make the growth rate of nominal wages initially slow to adjust—or "sticky." The most important of these are explicit and implicit contracts which have terms quoted in nominal wages. Explicit contracts, usually negotiated through labor unions, cover a bit less than a quarter of the labor force. But many nonunionized employers implicitly offer terms of employment which keep nominal wages relatively stable in good times and bad as

---

[11] The 40-hour work week is about as standard for plant as for employees. Apparently—except for very capital intensive industries—it is cheaper to have machines idle than to pay the wage premiums required to man them at "off" hours. See Gordon C. Winston, The Theory of Capital Utilization and Idleness, *Journal of Economic Literature*, **12**: 1301–1320, Dec. 1974.

much as union contracts do explicitly. When the contractual wage initially lags behind, the next contract will provide for a catch-up in nominal wages as well as for any increase in the expected future growth rate of nominal wages.

So wage growth is initially slow to adjust to an increased demand for labor because of being tied to an expected nominal wage rate. This expected nominal wage rate is reflected both in the search behavior of unemployed workers and in labor contracts. As expectations adjust to reality, however, the expected nominal wage rate will have a catch-up period in which it grows more rapidly even than in the new steady-state equilibrium.

In the long run, changes in nominal wage rates are reflected proportionally in the price level. The price level must reflect the costs of the factors of production. Labor income (inclusive of taxes on it) makes up three-quarters to four-fifths of all factor costs. The remainder is the return on capital (inclusive of taxes), but this return is itself proportionate to the nominal wage rate.[12] Unexpected changes in nominal wages take time to be fully reflected in the aggregate supply curve, however, because of the price-setting behavior of firms.

Most firms set a price for a considerable period of time and vary their inventories and output or (for distributors) purchases within that period to sell the quantity demanded at that price. If nominal wages or prices of goods purchased by the firms increase more (or less) than expected, these cost changes are not immediately reflected in the firms' prices. The reasons for this price-setting behavior are still a controversial area of research, but they seem to involve risk sharing and the costs of communicating information. The fact that these practices exist implies further initial stickiness in the growth rate of the price level of final goods and services and an eventual catch-up period as cost increases are passed through.[13]

Thus the initial tendency of shifts in the actual aggregate supply curve to lag behind shifts in the aggregate demand curve is explained in terms of (1) the stickiness of the nominal-wage growth rate and (2) the time taken for unexpected cost increases to pass through the chain of production and distribution. As expectations of nominal wages and costs adjust, there is a catch-up period in which the upward shifts in the actual aggregate supply curve would exceed those in the aggregate demand curve. Finally wages and prices grow at more rapid rates with no effect on real income, real wages, or employment. So unexpected increases in aggregate demand appear to affect prices of final goods and services mainly by bidding up wages and capital costs, which are then passed through as price increases.

---

[12] The return on capital equals the real interest rate times the value of capital. In long-run equilibrium, the value of capital equals the number of hours required to construct the capital (accumulated at the real rate of interest) multiplied by the nominal wage rate. So given an invariant real interest rate in the long run, the return on capital is proportionate to the nominal wage rate.

[13] This is illustrated by the fact that prices of basic goods included in the wholesale price index respond to monetary shocks at about the same time as output. But the prices of final goods and services take another 6 to 12 months to show a significant response.

AGGREGATE SUPPLY AND DEMAND SHIFTS UNDER A RESTRICTIVE MONETARY POLICY

Suppose the change in monetary policy had been restrictive instead of stimulative. That is, suppose that the new nominal-money-supply growth rate $\overline{\Gamma M}'$ were less than the old $\overline{\Gamma M}$. Then the converse of the reasons just discussed would suggest two generalizations about the shifts in the aggregate demand and supply curves: (1) Shifts in actual aggregate demand initially exceed the reduced shifts in the steady-state aggregate demand curve, but then the shifts in actual aggregate demand will be less than in steady-state aggregate demand during the catch-up period. (2) Shifts in the actual aggregate supply curve will at first exceed the reduced shifts in the actual aggregate demand curve, but this will be reversed during the catch-up period.

Panel (a) of Fig. 7.5 shows the shifts in aggregate supply and demand which would occur were the economy immediately to adjust to the reduced nominal-money-supply growth. Panel (b) illustrates the shifts in the actual aggregate demand and supply curves. At first, actual D_2 is shifted up from D_1 by more than the shift in the steady-state panel (a), although by less than D_1 was shifted up from D_0. Actual D_3 then shifts by less than the reduced steady-state shift in D_3 in the latter part of the adjustment period, so that steady-state aggregate demand catches up with actual aggregate demand. For some values of $\overline{\Gamma M}$ and $\overline{\Gamma M}'$, actual aggregate demand would in fact shift down. The actual upward shift in S_2 from S_1 is only a little less than S_1 was shifted up from S_0. Actual aggregate demand then catches up to actual aggregate supply in the latter part of the adjustment period because of the smaller upward shift (as illustrated) or larger fall in actual aggregate supply. Actual and steady-state aggregate supply are again equated at the end of the adjustment process. Since the actual curves at first shifted too fast, the catch-up period involves slowing down to let the steady-state catch up. Figure 7.5 shows that real income falls relative to steady-state real income in the early part of the adjustment process. It then rises back during the latter recovery part to equal steady-state real income. The rate of inflation initially decelerates by less than the steady-state rate. So the actual price level in period 2 is considerably higher than the steady-state price level. Later the actual inflation rate is much lower than the steady-state rate until the steady-state price level catches up with the actual price level. It is not illustrated here, but the catch-up might involve downward shifts and falling prices even if the new steady-state rate of inflation is positive.

Summarizing, a restrictive monetary policy implies an adjustment process in which real income first falls relative to steady-state real income and then rises back to its steady-state expansion path. This would correspond to the unemployment rate first rising above normal and then falling back. The rate of inflation initially exceeds the reduced steady-state rate of inflation and then undershoots the new steady-state rate as the actual price level adjusts to the lower steady-state price level. The early period of slow or negative real income growth and rising unemployment with little reduction in the inflation rate makes it politically dangerous to implement a monetary policy aimed at permanently reducing the inflation rate.

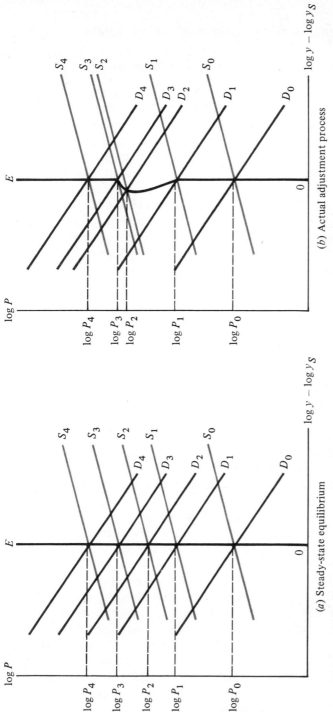

(a) Steady-state equilibrium

(b) Actual adjustment process

Figure 7.5 Comparison of steady-state and actual adjustment to a restrictive monetary policy. Panel (a) illustrates the less rapid steady-state inflation rate $\overline{IP}'$ associated with the decreased nominal-money-supply growth rate $\overline{IM}'$ beginning at the end of period 1. The upward shift in steady-state aggregate supply and demand curves equals the steady-state inflation rate times the length of the period. So the less rapid increase in $\log P$ after period 1 reflects the fact that $\overline{IP}'$ is less than $\overline{IP}$ by $\overline{IM} - \overline{IM}'$. In panel (b), the upward shift in the actual aggregate demand curve is initially greater than in the steady-state aggregate demand curve [compare panel (a)]. Thereafter, the actual upward shift is less than that in the steady-state aggregate demand curve so that the steady state catches up with the actual aggregate demand curve. Continuing with panel (b), at first the upward shift in the actual aggregate supply curve exceeds the reduced shift in the actual aggregate demand curve. In period 3, however, a less rapid upward shift in the actual aggregate supply curve allows the actual aggregate demand curve to catch up. Shifts in both actual curves are enough less than in the steady-state curves that the steady-state aggregate supply and demand curves catch up to the actual curves during the latter periods. The actual expansion path E in panel (b) shows a temporary decrease in actual real income relative to steady-state real income. The actual rate of inflation at first exceeds the reduced steady-state inflation rate and then undershoots it as the actual price level adjusts to the lower steady-state price level during the catch-up period.

181

7.2 EFFECTS ON REAL INCOME AND THE PRICE LEVEL: A DYNAMIC VERSION

A DYNAMIC RESTATEMENT OF THE ADJUSTMENT PROCESS

The period-by-period aggregate supply and demand analysis provides considerable insight into the effects of a monetary shock on real income and the price level. There is an alternative continuous dynamic approach which illustrates the same ideas in a way which some people find simpler. This approach also has the advantage of being readily integrated with the analysis of Chap. 6.

Figure 7.6 reproduces from Fig. 6.2 the steady-state growth path of nominal income in the case of a stimulative monetary policy which increases nominal-money-supply growth from $\overline{\Gamma M}$ to $\overline{\Gamma M}'$ at time z. The effects of alternative nominal-money-supply growth rates on the steady-state growth paths of real income and the price level were considered in Sec. 5.3. On the assumption that money is superneutral,[14] nominal-money-supply growth does not affect the steady-state growth path of real income as illustrated in Fig. 7.6. So the entire change in the growth path of nominal income reflects the increased growth rate of the price level. This figure is constructed to be consistent with the definitional identities

$$\log Y \equiv \log y + \log P \qquad [7.3]$$

$$\Gamma Y \equiv \Gamma y + \Gamma P \qquad [7.4]$$

That is, adding the vertical heights of the real income and price level graphs gives the height of the nominal income graph in both panels (a) and (b).

Figure 7.6 is reproduced in Fig. 7.7, with the steady-state values after z indicated by dashed lines since actual values deviate from steady-state values during the period of adjustment. The nominal-income adjustment pattern studied in Chap. 6 is reproduced from Fig. 6.4. So the only lines in Fig. 7.7 remaining to be explained are the indicated actual adjustments of real income and the price level.

Actual real income at first grows relative to steady-state real income and then falls back to the steady-state growth path as indicated in panel (a) of Fig. 7.7. This plots against time the real income adjustment derived by shifting aggregate supply and demand curves and plotted against prices in Fig. 7.4. The actual growth rate of real income plotted in panel (b) is the slope of this actual growth path. Actual real income grows relative to steady-state real income while the actual growth rate Γy exceeds the steady-state growth rate $\overline{\Gamma y}$. During the period in which actual real income is falling relative to steady-state real income, the actual growth rate Γy must be less than the steady-state growth rate $\overline{\Gamma y}$ and may—as pictured here—be negative for a while. Over the whole adjustment period the average actual real-income growth rate will equal the steady-state rate $\overline{\Gamma y}$—the high early real income growth is offset by low real income growth during the catch-up period.

---

[14] Appendix B to this chapter considers the case in which money is not superneutral.

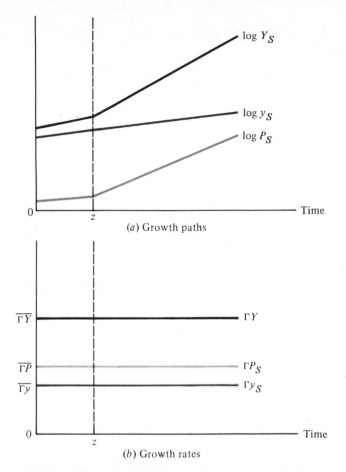

(a) Growth paths

(b) Growth rates

Figure 7.6 Steady-state growth paths for nominal income, real income, and the price level. The steady-state growth path and growth rate of nominal income corresponding to an increased nominal-money-supply growth at time z is reproduced from Fig. 6.2. The change in monetary policy does not affect real steady-state values— including real income. So the increase in the nominal-income growth rate corresponds to an equal increase in the inflation rate ΓP which is the slope of the growth path of the price level.

The adjustment of the price level can also be viewed as plotting against time the results derived period by period in a version of Fig. 7.4 drawn for many short periods. At first the price level continues along the old steady-state growth path and then gradually adjusts upwards to the new steeper steady-state growth path. The actual rate of inflation ΓP plotted in panel (b) is simply the slope of this growth path. Since at first the actual inflation rate is less than the increased steady-state rate $\overline{\Gamma P'}$, it must exceed $\overline{\Gamma P'}$ during the period in which the actual price level closes the gap and catches up to the steady-state price level.

Alternatively, the price-level growth path (or growth rate) could be said to

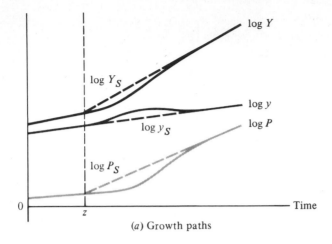

(a) Growth paths

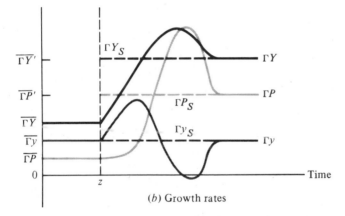

(b) Growth rates

Figure 7.7 Adjustment of real income and the price level to increased nominal-money-supply growth. The steady-state growth paths and growth rates of Fig. 7.6 are reproduced here with dashed lines after the monetary policy change at time z. The adjustment pattern of nominal income is repeated from Fig. 6.4 where it was shown that the gradual adjustment to the new steeper growth path implied that the actual growth rate of nominal income ΓY overshoots the increased steady-state rate $\overline{\Gamma Y}'$ during a catch-up period. The tendency for actual real income initially to rise relative to steady-state real income and then to fall back is a restatement of the results derived period by period in Fig. 7.4. The slope of the actual log y graph is the actual growth rate of real income. The gradual adjustment of the price level to the new steeper steady-state growth path (and implied overshooting of the actual inflation rate ΓP during the catch-up period) also restates the results of Fig. 7.4. Because of the identities [7.3] and [7.4], the graphs of any one of the variables is implied by the graphs of the other two.

be determined as the difference between the nominal-income and real-income growth paths (growth rates). This is required by identities [7.3] and [7.4]. Or we could say that the real-income adjustment pattern is implicit in the adjustment patterns of nominal income and the price level. Since nominal income and its division into real income and the price level are simultaneously and consistently determined in the economy, we can infer the adjustment pattern of any one of these variables from the other two.

The basic pattern is that an unexpected increase in nominal-money-supply growth leads to an unexpected increase in nominal income growth. At first almost the entire unexpected increase in nominal income represents an increase in real income since the price level is nearly unaffected. As time goes on the difference between actual and expected nominal-income growth rates will eventually decrease, and firms will try to make up for past slow price growth.

RATIONALE OF THE ADJUSTMENT PROCESS

In Fig. 7.7, the adjustment of real income and the price level to a stimulative monetary policy is presented in the context of the economy's evolution over time. It is natural to recast in similar terms the reasons for this adjustment pattern occurring.

The basic idea is that most sellers decide on a price at which they will sell and then sell what they can at that price. These decisions are changed from time to time on the basis of actual past costs, expected changes in costs, and expected demand. The current actual growth rate of nominal income has little if any impact on how these factors change now, and hence on the current growth rate of the price level. Current growth in nominal income will, however, influence these factors, and hence the inflation rate in the future, by influencing the actual and expected changes in costs and expected demand. So the inflation rate adapts with a lag to changes in the nominal-income growth rate. When costs increase more rapidly than anticipated, these cost increases will be incorporated into the inflation rate when firms make up for their past errors. The fact that sellers of labor have nominal wage demands tied to expected nominal wages further slows the adjustment of the price level. It does so by slowing the adjustment of costs to unanticipated increases in demand for the given labor and capital resources of the economy.

With sellers setting prices and selling to meet demand, unanticipated growth in nominal income must be met by increased real output of final goods and services. This is simply the other side of the price-setting coin. The quicker are all prices readjusted in the face of unanticipated changes in aggregate demand, the less will be the temporary effect on real income.[15]

---

[15] In the terms of Sec. 7.1, this more frequent setting of prices would mean that the aggregate supply curve displays a smaller initial lag behind unanticipated shifts in the aggregate demand curve. Robert E. Lucas has argued that the frequency with which prices will be adjusted depends on the degree to which aggregate demand is predictable. Where aggregate demand is relatively unpredictable, unexpected changes in aggregate demand have smaller and shorter-lived effects on real output. The evidence from a cross section of countries supports his theoretical arguments. See Robert E. Lucas, Some International Evidence on Output-Inflation Tradeoffs, *American Economic Review*, **63**:326–334, June 1973.

It may be helpful to summarize the forces operating on the growth rates of real income and the price level in mathematical terms. Equations [6.8] and [6.11] provided similar summaries of the forces influencing the growth rates of fluidity and nominal income.

Such an illustrative equation for real income would be

$$\Gamma y = \overline{\Gamma y} + (\Gamma Y - \Gamma Y^*) - \beta(\log y - \log y_S) \qquad [7.5]$$

This equation says that the real-income growth rate equals its steady-state growth rate $\overline{\Gamma y}$ plus any unexpected nominal income growth $(\Gamma Y - \Gamma Y^*)$ less a multiple β of the logarithmic difference between actual and steady-state real income.[16] So real income is supposed to grow at its normal rate except that sellers (1) meet unanticipated increases (or decreases) in growth in expenditures by adjusting output and (2) attempt to correct past errors which caused output to be above normal because prices were set too low for actual demand.

The corresponding[17] equation for the inflation rate is

$$\Gamma P = (\Gamma Y^* - \overline{\Gamma y}) + \beta(\log y - \log y_S) \qquad [7.6]$$

That is, the rate of inflation equals the amount by which the expected nominal-income growth rate exceeds steady-state real income plus a multiple β of the logarithmic difference between actual and steady-state real income. The difference between the expected nominal-income growth rate and steady-state real-income growth rate represents the inflation rate which would be expected to be consistent with normal growth in real output. Sellers would adjust their prices up (down) from this rate to make up for past pricing errors which had led to real output being above (below) its normal level.

Either of these dynamic equations [7.5] and [7.6] can be combined with the nominal-income growth rate equation [6.11] and an appropriate assumption about the expected nominal-income growth rate ΓY^*. These equations could then be used to derive the adjustment pattern illustrated in Fig. 7.7 as in Example 7.1.

EXAMPLE 7.1

AN ARITHMETIC ANALYSIS OF
REAL INCOME AND PRICE LEVEL ADJUSTMENT

The effects of a stimulative monetary policy on real income and the price level can be derived arithmetically in terms of Eqs. [6.11] and [7.5]. We will continue Example 6.2, where an unexpected increase in ΓM

---

[16] An asterisk again indicates an expected growth rate. Supply shocks such as strikes are omitted from the equation but will be considered in Chap. 8. The coefficient β (beta) has units of 1/year and indicates the speed with which real income adjusts to steady-state real income.

[17] That is, Eq. [7.6] can be derived by substituting [7.5] into the definitional identity $\Gamma P \equiv \Gamma Y - \Gamma y$.

from 2 percent to 4 percent per annum was considered. The actual nominal-income growth rate was derived there on certain assumptions, and this rate is entered in the second column of the table below. The first column keeps track of time in quarters from the change in monetary policy. For convenience, suppose that the coefficient β in Eq. [7.5] is 1 per annum and $\Gamma y = 0.03$ per annum. So the real-income growth rate is computed as

$$\Gamma y = \frac{0.03}{\text{year}} + (\Gamma Y - \Gamma Y^*) - \frac{1}{\text{year}} (\log y - \log y_s)$$

Suppose for this example that the expected nominal-income growth rate ΓY^* is a simple average of the actual and expected growth rates from the previous quarter. In this way the expected growth rate adapts to the actual growth rate over time without being completely dominated by the latest quarter. The initial quarter ΓY^* would be 5 percent per annum to correspond to the initial steady-state ΓY.

Now the actual real-income growth rate for quarter 1 is computed by plugging into our formula, using the fact that $\log y = \log y_s$ initially

$$\Gamma y = \frac{0.03}{\text{year}} + \frac{0.0500}{\text{year}} - \frac{0.0500}{\text{year}} - \frac{1}{\text{year}}(0) = \frac{0.03}{\text{year}}$$

Quarter	Actual Nominal-Income Growth ΓY	Expected Nominal-Income Growth ΓY^*	Logarithmic Excess Real Income $\log y - \log y_s$	Actual Real Income Growth Γy	Actual Inflation Rate ΓP	Rate of Change in Logarithmic Excess Real Income $\Gamma y - \overline{\Gamma y}$
1	0.0500	0.0500	0	0.0300	0.0200	0
2	0.0550	0.0500	0	0.0350	0.0200	0.0050
3	0.0594	0.0525	0.00125	0.0357	0.0237	0.0057
4	0.0632	0.0560	0.00266	0.0345	0.0287	0.0045
5	0.0666	0.0596	0.00380	0.0332	0.0334	0.0032
6	0.0695	0.0631	0.00460	0.0318	0.0377	0.0018
7	0.0720	0.0663	0.00505	0.0307	0.0413	0.0007
8	0.0743	0.0692	0.00521	0.0299	0.0444	−0.0001
9	0.0763	0.0718	0.00518	0.0293	0.0470	−0.0007
10	0.0755	0.0740	0.00501	0.0265	0.0490	−0.0035
11	0.0748	0.0748	0.00413	0.0259	0.0489	−0.0041
12	0.0742	0.0748	0.00310	0.0263	0.0479	−0.0037
...	...	...	...	...	...	...
16	0.0725	0.0732	0.00042	0.0289	0.0436	−0.0011
...	...	...	...	...	...	...
30	0.0704	0.0705	−0.00018	0.0301	0.0403	0.0001
...	...	...	...	...	...	...
∞	0.0700	0.0700	0	0.0300	0.0400	0

So during the first period no change in Γy results since ΓY has not yet changed. This is entered in the fifth column of the table. The sixth column is calculated according to $\Gamma P \equiv \Gamma Y - \Gamma y$, so $\Gamma P = (0.05/\text{year}) - (0.03/\text{year}) = 0.02/\text{year}$, as indicated. This of course is the old steady-state inflation rate $\overline{\Gamma P}$. Since the actual and steady-state real-income growth rates are identical, there is no change in the logarithmic difference between actual and real income as entered in column 7. This implies that $\log y - \log y_s$ remains 0 at the beginning of the second quarter, as indicated in column 4. Further, the average of the actual and expected first quarter nominal-income growth rates is 0.0500, and this is entered for the second quarter ΓY^* in column 3.

In the second quarter, actual nominal income growth begins to accelerate in response to the stimulative monetary policy. Substituting,

$$\Gamma y = \frac{0.03}{\text{year}} + \frac{0.0550}{\text{year}} - \frac{0.0500}{\text{year}} - \frac{1}{\text{year}}(0) = \frac{0.0350}{\text{year}}$$

or 3.5 percent per annum. The inflation rate is $\overline{\Gamma P} = (0.0550/\text{year}) - (0.0350/\text{year}) = -0.0200/\text{year}$. So real income growth increases by the full amount of the unexpected increase in nominal income, with no initial effect on the growth rate of the price level.

The rate of change in $\log y - \log y_s$ is $\Delta \log y - \Delta \log y_s \equiv \Gamma y - \overline{\Gamma y} = (0.0350/\text{year}) - (0.0300/\text{year}) = 0.0050/\text{year}$. Over a quarter this would imply an increase of $(0.0050/\text{year})(0.25 \text{ year}) = 0.00125$. This is added to zero and entered in column 4 for the beginning of the third quarter. The expected nominal-income growth rate for the third quarter is

$$\frac{(0.0550/\text{year}) + (0.0500/\text{year})}{2} = \frac{0.0525}{\text{year}}$$

and this is entered in column 3.

To find the third quarter real-income growth rate,

$$\Gamma y = \frac{0.03}{\text{year}} + \frac{0.0594}{\text{year}} - \frac{0.0525}{\text{year}} - \frac{1}{\text{year}}(0.00125)$$

$$= \frac{0.03}{\text{year}} + \frac{0.0069}{\text{year}} - \frac{0.00125}{\text{year}} = \frac{0.03565}{\text{year}}$$

or 3.57 percent per annum. So the increase in real income growth due to the unexpected nominal income growth of 0.69 percent per annum is partially offset by firms adjusting output (and prices) to correct for past errors at a rate of -0.125 percent per annum. The rate of inflation is increased to $\Gamma P = (0.0594/\text{year}) - (0.0357/\text{year}) = 0.0237/\text{year}$ or 2.37

percent per annum. This could be equivalently derived by substitution into Eq. [7.6] as

$$\Gamma P = \frac{0.0525}{\text{year}} - \frac{0.03}{\text{year}} + \frac{1}{\text{year}}(0.00125) = \frac{0.02375}{\text{year}}$$

or 2.37 percent per annum. This higher inflation rate is seen to reflect the increased expected nominal income growth built into the price setting of sellers, plus an attempt to make up for past pricing errors.

The remainder of the table is derived by repeating these operations over and over. Note that the rate of inflation begins to overshoot the new steady-state rate $\overline{\Gamma P}' = 0.04$/year in the seventh quarter. Similarly, the real-income growth rate drops below normal beginning in the eighth quarter. In this example, the economy begins to approach the long-run equilibrium growth rates of real income and the price level by the twelfth quarter and is most of the way there for real income by the sixteenth quarter. In the thirtieth quarter, the adjustment process is complete for all practical purposes.

FORMATION OF EXPECTATIONS

The formation of expected values such as ΓM^* and ΓY^* is the subject of much current theoretical and empirical research. Advanced statistical techniques are essential in the empirical work, since expected values cannot be observed directly but must be inferred from the effects of expectations upon observed behavior. In terms of the present analysis, this is a largely technical issue of the precise measurement of a monetary shock. When we turn to the analysis of stabilization policy in Part Six, however, the very feasibility of stabilization policy will turn on the Fed's access to information not used by the public in forming their expected growth rates of nominal money and nominal income.

Views on how expectations are formed range from fairly simple extrapolations of the recent history of the variable itself to elaborate statistical models incorporating the behavior of a variety of information sources. For our current purposes, it is sufficient to note that the expected values must converge to the actual values as the economy approaches steady-state equilibrium.

RETURN TO THE TRAIN ANALOGY

The caboose can now be added to the train analogy of Sec. 6.3. The train illustrated in Fig. 7.8 now consists of an engine, a boxcar, and a caboose, connected by long shock absorbers. The shock absorbers lengthen or shorten with sudden changes in force, but their springs thereafter gradually return the shock absorbers to their normal length.

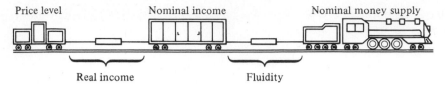

Real income   Fluidity

Figure 7.8 Train analogy to adjustment of real income and the price level. The speeds of the boxcar and caboose are determined in the long run by the speed of the engine. If the engine suddenly accelerates, however, the first shock absorber initially stretches (fluidity increases) and the boxcar (nominal income) only gradually speeds up. The increased speed of the boxcar stretches the second shock absorber (real income increases) and finally the caboose (price level) gradually speeds up. The boxcar's speed must be increased by more than the engine's while the first shock absorber returns to its normal length. The caboose's speed must be increased by more than the boxcar's while the second shock absorber returns to its normal length.

The engine, boxcar, and their connecting shock absorber are identified as before with the nominal money supply, nominal income, and fluidity. The caboose and other shock absorber now represent the price level and real income. Fluidity and real income must either have no trend growth themselves or else be measured relative to their steady-state levels, with the normal length of the shock absorber representing equality of the actual and steady-state levels.

Suppose that the train is proceeding smoothly along level ground at a speed of 40 miles per hour. If the engineer suddenly increases the speed of the engine to 50 mph, the first shock absorber stretches at first beyond its normal length. But increased force is applied to the boxcar as the shock absorber lengthens, and the boxcar begins to speed up and must for a bit even go faster than 50 mph while the shock absorber returns to its normal length. This represents the shock absorber response of fluidity (first increasing and then returning to normal in face of a stimulative monetary policy) and the initial inertia[18] and eventual overshooting of the growth rate of nominal income.

As the boxcar speeds up, the caboose at first continues at 40 mph and the second shock absorber stretches. Note that this initial stretching of the shock absorber occurs simultaneously with—*not* after—the increased speed of the boxcar: With the caboose continuing at the same speed, an increased speed of the boxcar implies that the distance between them begins to increase. Then the increased force exerted by the second shock absorber begins to speed up the caboose. The caboose must go faster than the boxcar for a while—just as the boxcar must go faster than the engine—while the second shock absorber returns to its normal length.

This illustrates how the increase in nominal-income growth due to a stimulative monetary policy is reflected in a temporary increase in real income

---

[18] Inertia is defined as resistance to acceleration or deceleration. It means that bodies do not change their speed except in response to outside forces.

relative to normal, which is then gradually eliminated. This increase occurs because of the initial inertia in the growth rate of the price level. The rate of inflation must overshoot as the price level catches up.

These adjustments can be smooth or fluctuating, with the shock absorbers first too long then too short, and so forth. The adjustment of the caboose and the second shock absorber could have a significant effect on the adjustment of the boxcar and first shock absorber. All these complications have been omitted because they seem to be of negligible importance for the U.S. economy.

TIMING OF THE ADJUSTMENT PROCESS

As observed in Chap. 6, empirical studies of the timing of the adjustment process still have a rough-and-ready pioneering quality, although substantial progress is being made of late. The initial change in nominal income growth is almost entirely a reflection of increased real income growth with no change in the inflation rate. This is normally apparent about two to four quarters after the policy change. Effects on the growth rates of wholesale prices of basic commodities and of nominal wages also becomes noticeable about then. But the inflation rate—the growth rate of the price level of final goods and services—does not normally show much movement until about five to seven quarters after the monetary policy change. For this reason the inflation rate is said to lag behind real income growth by about three-quarters of a year.

The length of time required to reach essentially full adjustment remains very much an open question. Three to five years is not a bad answer in terms of most of the evidence, but it could well be a shorter or a longer period.

EFFECTS ON REAL INCOME AND THE PRICE LEVEL OF AN UNEXPECTED DECREASE IN NOMINAL-MONEY-SUPPLY GROWTH

If the change from $\overline{\Gamma M}$ to $\overline{\Gamma M}'$ were a decrease in the nominal-money-supply growth rate instead of an increase, the effects would be reversed, as discussed at the end of Sec. 7.1. The restrictive monetary policy has little initial effect on the growth rate of nominal income, but soon it turns down. Because the rate of inflation is sticky and little affected at first, the decreased growth rate of nominal income corresponds to a decreased and perhaps negative growth rate of real income. This is illustrated in Fig. 7.9. Over time, falling *expected* nominal-income growth rates and attempts to correct past pricing errors lead to the inflation rate falling to and, for a while, past the reduced steady-state inflation rate $\overline{\Gamma P}'$. In the figure, this catch-up period includes a period of deflation (falling prices). Whether this actually occurred would depend on the size of the reduction in the nominal-money-supply growth rate and the level of $\overline{\Gamma P}'$. As sellers correct their pricing errors, which originally were reflected in actual real income's fall relative to steady-state real income, real income will rise back

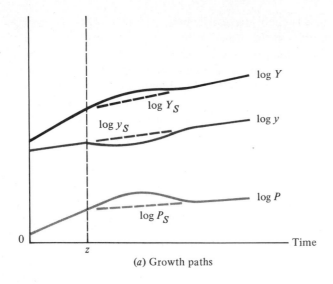

(a) Growth paths

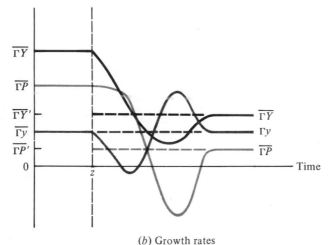

(b) Growth rates

Figure 7.9 Adjustment of real income and the price level to decreased nominal-money-supply growth. An unexpected reduction in the nominal-money-supply growth rate from $\overline{\Gamma M}$ to $\overline{\Gamma M}'$ causes an adjustment pattern of real income and the price level which is reversed from the case of an increase (compare Fig. 7.7). The steady-state growth rates of nominal income and the price level both fall by $\overline{\Gamma M} - \overline{\Gamma M}'$. The adjustment pattern of nominal income is repeated from Fig. 6.7. Because the actual inflation rate ΓP is slow to change, the reduced nominal-income growth rate initially corresponds to a matching fall in the real-income growth rate. As sellers' expectations adjust to slower growth in nominal spending and as they attempt to make up for past pricing errors, the inflation rate falls and for a while undershoots the reduced steady-state rate $\overline{\Gamma P}'$. This pattern is implied by the gradual adjustment of the price level from the old to the new, less steeply sloped growth path. The recovery period is characterized by above-normal real-income growth rates and sharply reduced inflation rates.

toward normal. The actual real-income growth rate will exceed the steady-state rate $\overline{\Gamma y}$ during this recovery period.

The initial period of low and negative real income growth, and so rising unemployment rates, is the classical pattern of a monetary recession. The following recovery period is characterized by above-normal real income growth as the unemployment rate falls back toward normal, and by a sharply reduced inflation rate. In terms of timing, the real-income slowdown is normally apparent 6 to 12 months after the start of the restrictive policy. Perhaps 3 to 5 years are required for complete adjustment.

STAGFLATION, COST-PUSH INFLATION, AND EXPECTATIONS

The term *stagflation* is used by different economists to refer to somewhat different phenomena. Three possible definitions are (1) high inflation rates relative to the recent past and slow real income growth; (2) high inflation rates and a below-normal *level* of real income and above-normal unemployment rate; and (3) rising inflation rates and unemployment and falling real-income growth rates. Each of these phenomena appear puzzling to those who expect inflation rates to move in the opposite direction from unemployment.[19] They can be understood, however, in terms of the economy's adjustments over time to monetary shocks.

Considered by the first definition, stagflation is a necessary part of the adjustment of real income and the price level to a stimulative monetary policy. It corresponds to the catch-up during the latter half of the adjustment period in Fig. 7.7. Stagflation according to the third definition occurs during about the third quarter of the illustrated adjustment period.

The second definition of stagflation appears a paradox to those who, by analogy to simple microeconomic models, expect reductions in demand to reduce prices. But the prices in an industry supply and demand diagram are relative prices—the price of the good divided by the price level. To apply the analogy to the aggregate price level one should say that an unexpected reduction in aggregate demand growth would cause real income and the price level to be lower than they otherwise would have been. But this need hardly entail a drop in the price level. If the economy were in a steady-state equilibrium with a high inflation rate, then a restrictive monetary policy would lead to above-normal unemployment rates while the rate of inflation was still high.

Cost-push inflation is a term used to suggest that the inflation rate is increased by rapid increases in cost disproportionate to increases in demand. In other words, the aggregate supply curve is shifting upwards faster than the aggregate demand curve. In a dynamic context, this does not differ in cause

---

[19] This negative "Phillips curve" relation is discussed at length in Chap. 14.

from *demand-pull inflation* which is the opposite situation. Each occurs in response to a single unexpected change in the nominal-money-supply growth rate. If the unexpected change is an increase, we see (Fig. 7.4) demand-pull followed by cost-push inflation. At first prices and costs lag behind their increased steady-state growth rates and later they catch up. It is so much nonsense to attribute the latter (but not the former) to greedy unionists or businessmen. If the nominal-money-supply growth rate is decreased, then it can be said that cost-push inflation is followed by demand-pull inflation (see Fig. 7.5).

A unifying theme is the concept of the expected nominal-money-supply growth rate. So long as a nominal-money-supply growth rate is expected and built into all spending and price-setting plans, costs, wages, aggregate supply, and aggregate demand will all rise smoothly together with no effect on real income or employment. It is not that prices and wages instantaneously adjust to expected nominal-money-supply changes. Rather plans and contracts are made in anticipation of the expected changes so that the price and wage changes can occur simultaneously. Effects on real income and employment due to unexpected nominal-money-supply growth occur because expectations, and hence plans and contracts, were inappropriate and it takes time to correct things.

7.3 THE CYCLICAL ADJUSTMENT OF INTEREST RATES

STEADY-STATE EFFECTS OF INTEREST RATES

The tax-amended Fisher equation [5.31] states that the nominal interest rate exceeds the real interest rate by $1/(1 - \tau)$ times the expected rate of inflation ΓP^* where τ is the marginal income tax rate applicable to borrowers and lenders. In Chap. 5, we saw that the steady-state real interest rate can be taken as unaffected by the nominal-money-supply growth rate. So the steady-state real interest rate would be given as $\bar{r}$ both before and after the increase at time z from $\overline{\Gamma M}$ to $\overline{\Gamma M}'$. In steady-state equilibrium, actual and expected inflation rates are equal to the steady-state inflation rates—that is, the $\overline{\Gamma P}$ before z and $\overline{\Gamma P}'$ afterward. Therefore, the steady-state nominal interest rate before z is

$$\bar{R} = \bar{r} + \frac{\overline{\Gamma P}}{1 - \tau} \tag{7.7}$$

After z, the steady-state nominal interest rate is

$$\bar{R}' = \bar{r} + \frac{\overline{\Gamma P}'}{1 - \tau} \tag{7.8}$$

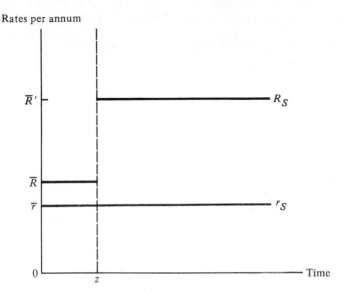

Figure 7.10 Steady-state nominal and real interest rates. An increase in the nominal-money-supply growth rate at time z does not affect the steady-state real interest rate which is constant at $\bar{r}$. It does cause the steady-state inflation rate to increase from $\overline{\Gamma P}$ to $\overline{\Gamma P'}$. Therefore the steady-state nominal interest rate increases from $\bar{R} = \bar{r} + \overline{\Gamma P}/(1 - \tau)$ to $\bar{R}' = \bar{r} + \overline{\Gamma P'}/(1 - \tau)$, where τ is the marginal tax on lenders and borrowers.

As was discussed in the previous section, the increase in the steady-state inflation rate $(\overline{\Gamma P'} - \overline{\Gamma P})$ is equal to the increase in the nominal-money-supply growth rate $(\overline{\Gamma M'} - \overline{\Gamma M})$. This implies[20] that the increase in the steady-state nominal interest rate $(\bar{R}' - \bar{R})$ is equal to $1/(1 - \tau)$ times the increase in the nominal-money-supply growth rate. That is,

$$\bar{R}' = \bar{R} + \frac{\overline{\Gamma M'} - \overline{\Gamma M}}{1 - \tau} \qquad [7.9]$$

Since the marginal tax rate τ lies between 0 and 1, the increase in the steady-state nominal interest rate will generally exceed the increase in the nominal-money-supply growth rate. This is illustrated in Example 7.2.

The steady-state values of the nominal and real interest rates are graphed in Fig. 7.10. The steady-state real interest rate stays constant at $\bar{r}$. The increase at z in the nominal-money-supply growth rate causes the steady-state nominal interest rate to rise from $\bar{R}$ to $\bar{R}'$.

[20] Subtract Eq. [7.7] from [7.8] and substitute $\overline{\Gamma M'} - \overline{\Gamma M}$ for $\overline{\Gamma P'} - \overline{\Gamma P}$.

EXAMPLE 7.2

EFFECTS ON STEADY-STATE NOMINAL INTEREST RATES

Suppose that the nominal-money-supply growth rate were increased by 4 percentage points from 1 percent to 5 percent per annum and that the steady-state inflation rate increased from 0 to 4 percent per annum as a result. If the marginal tax rate τ were 20 percent, this would imply a 5 percentage point increase in the nominal interest rate. The calculation is

$$\bar{R}' = \bar{R} + \frac{0.04/\text{year}}{1 - 0.2} = \bar{R} + \frac{0.05}{\text{year}}$$

An alternative calculation would be to start from the original nominal interest rate—say it is 3 percent per annum. Of course, the definition of the real interest rate is the nominal interest rate corrected for inflation, and in this particular case there is no inflation to correct for. Then the steady-state nominal interest rate after time z is

$$\bar{R}' = \bar{r} + \frac{\overline{\Gamma P'}}{1 - \tau} = \frac{0.03}{\text{year}} + \frac{0.04/\text{year}}{1 - 0.2} = \frac{0.08}{\text{year}}$$

or 8 percent per annum. This is—as computed directly above—an increase of 5 percent per annum in the steady-state nominal interest rate.

ADJUSTMENT TO A STIMULATIVE MONETARY POLICY

The process of adjustment of the nominal interest rate to an increase in nominal-money-supply growth shows an interesting cyclical pattern. The nominal interest rate initially declines, but this decline is soon reversed. The nominal interest rate then rises back to and above its original level, eventually approaching the new steady-state level $\bar{R}'$. This adjustment pattern of R is illustrated graphically in Fig. 7.11.

Since the nominal interest rate R is the sum of the real interest rate r and the tax-adjusted inflation rate $\Gamma P^*/(1 - \tau)$, the adjustment pattern of R is explained in terms of these factors.[21] Fluctuations in the real interest rate r appear to dominate the early part of the adjustment process.

---

[21] This section integrates a vast theoretical and empirical literature. A few of the most important references are to Irving Fisher, *The Theory of Interest*, New York: Macmillan, 1930; Milton Friedman, "Factors Affecting the Level of Interest," in D. P. Jacobs and R. T. Pratt, eds., *Saving and Residential Financing: 1968 Conference Proceedings*, Chicago: United States Savings and Loan League, 1968; Phillip Cagan and Arthur Gandolfi, The Lag in Monetary Policy as Implied by the Time Pattern of Interest Rates, *American Economic Review, Papers and Proceedings*, **59**: 277–284, May 1969; William E. Gibson, Interest Rates and Monetary Policy, *Journal of Political Economy*, **78**: 431–455, May/June 1970; William P. Yohe and Denis S. Karnosky, Interest Rates and Price Level Changes, 1952–69, *Federal Reserve Bank of St. Louis Review*, **51**(12): 18–29, Dec. 1969; Thomas J. Sargent, Anticipated Inflation and the Nominal Rate of Interest, *Quarterly Journal of Economics*, **86**: 212–226, May 1972; Michael R. Darby, The Financial and Tax Effects of Monetary Policy on Interest Rates, *Economic Inquiry*, **13**: 266–276, June 1975; Jack Carr, James E. Pesando, and Lawrence B. Smith, Tax Effects, Price Expectations and the Nominal Rate of Interest, *Economic Inquiry*, **14**: 259–269, June 1976; and Thomas F. Cargill, Direct Evidence of the Darby Hypothesis for the United States, *Economic Inquiry*, **15**: 132–134, Jan. 1977.

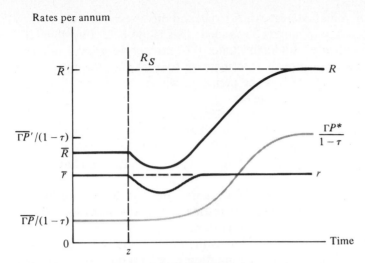

Figure 7.11 Cyclical adjustment of interest rates to an increase in the nominal-money-supply growth rate. Immediately after the start of the stimulative monetary policy at z, the liquidity effect is dominant, and the real and nominal interest rates r and R fall. As real-income and later price-level growth rates accelerate, the income effect begins to offset the liquidity effect and the initial fall in interest rates is reversed. As the tax-adjusted expected inflation rate $\Gamma P^*/(1 - \tau)$ finally increases, the nominal interest rate increases relative to the real interest rate due to the expectations effect.

Movements in the real interest rate are explained in terms of the liquidity effect and the income effect. The liquidity effect refers to the tendency of the price of bonds to be driven up by the reduced rate of issuance of new government bonds to the public[22] and the increased demand for nonmoney forms of wealth as a use for excess cash balances. An increase in the price of existing bonds is the same thing as a decrease in the nominal interest rate. Since the actual and expected inflation rates will not yet be affected, this fall in the nominal interest rate is also a fall in the real interest rate. The income effect refers to the tendency of increases in real income and ultimately the price level to absorb excess cash balances and offset the reduction in interest rates due to the liquidity effect.

The argument can be restated by writing nominal money demand as the product of the real money-demand function and the price level

$$M^d = m^d(y, R) \cdot P \qquad [7.9]$$

An increased growth rate of the nominal money supply will induce faster growth in the nominal quantity of money demanded. At first the growth rates of the real income and the price level are little affected so that growing pressure

---

[22] Recall that the increased growth rate of the money supply is brought about by a reduced rate of issuance of government bonds.

is exerted on the nominal interest rate R to fall and thereby cause faster growth in the nominal quantity of money demanded. This is the period in which the liquidity effect is said to be dominant. Later the real-income growth rate and ultimately the price-level growth rate increase so that the pressure on the interest rate is eliminated. This is the period in which the (nominal) income effect grows to offset the liquidity effect.

As the actual inflation rate rises the expected inflation rate will also begin to rise, although more slowly. A gradual upward adjustment of the (tax-adjusted) expected inflation rate is indicated in Fig. 7.11. When this expectation effect[23] is added to the real interest rate, the adjustment pattern of the nominal interest rate is obtained.

This general pattern seems to hold for nominal interest rates on all sorts of bonds and loans, but there are some interesting differences. For example, the adjustment to the new steady-state equilibrium appears to be much faster for nominal interest rates on short-term bonds than on long-term bonds. This is sensible, because the relevant expected inflation rate for a bond is the average expected rate over the term of the bond. People will pay relatively more attention to recent inflation history than to long-term inflation trends for a 90-day Treasury bill than for a 20-year government bond. The size of the cyclical fluctuation in long-term real interest rates is similarly smaller than that for rates on short-term bonds. The nominal interest rates on marketable securities such as Treasury bills fall temporarily relative to those on bank loans of similar maturity, because banks tend to act as price setters on loan rates, only gradually adjusting them when the average interest rate earned on marketable securities varies. Some apparent differences in empirical studies are merely reflections of different timing and magnitudes for the adjustment pattern of different measures of "the" nominal interest rate.

During this adjustment period, actual inflation rates will typically exceed the expected inflation rates used in determining the interest rates. As a result those who owe money on net will win, and those who are owed money on net will lose from the unexpected inflation. This is so because debtors repay creditors dollars less valuable than expected in terms of the goods and services which the dollars can buy. In countries where inflation rates are particularly unpredictable, loans are frequently contracted which use price indices to adjust all amounts owed for the actual rate of inflation.

TIMING OF THE ADJUSTMENT PROCESS

Twentieth-century U.S. data suggest that the initial period of falling nominal interest rates lasts about two to three quarters of a year. The nominal interest rate would normally rise back to its original level by the fifth or sixth quarter after the change in the nominal-money-supply growth rate.

---

[23] The expectation effect is sometimes called the *Fisher effect* after Irving Fisher, who developed the theoretical analysis.

It should be noted that the magnitude of the initial fall in the nominal interest rate does not seem to be large. Even for nominal interest rates on negotiable short-term securities, the maximum fall is only an eighth or less of the increase in the nominal-money-supply growth rate.[24] So a 4 percentage point increase in $\overline{\Gamma M}$ (say, from 2 to 6 percent per annum) would cause short-term interest rates to drop by no more than $\frac{1}{2}$ a percentage point, say from 5 to 4.5 percent per annum. Interest rates on bank loans and long-term securities would typically fall less.

Considerable uncertainty—and dispute—exists about how long it would take to reach full steady-state equilibrium. Some evidence on short-term interest rates implies that it takes only a couple of years after the inflation rate has converged to the new steady-state rate. This would be some 5 to 7 years after the initial change in monetary policy. For long-term interest rates, other evidence suggests that full adjustment takes 20 to 30 years. These estimates are not necessarily in conflict, of course, because a longer history may be relevant to forming expectations about the average inflation rate over the term of a long-term bond. Expected inflation rates appear to adjust more rapidly in economies with large, frequent changes in the nominal-money-supply growth rate.

CYCLICAL ADJUSTMENT TO A RESTRICTIVE MONETARY POLICY

The effects of a decreased nominal-money-supply growth rate are just the opposite of the effects of stimulative monetary policy. As illustrated in Fig. 7.12, the steady-state nominal interest rate falls by $1/(1 - \tau)$ times the decrease in the nominal-money-supply growth rate. At first the liquidity effect is dominant, and the nominal interest rate rises for 6 to 9 months. Thereafter the income effect begins to offset the liquidity effect, and finally the expectations effect reduces the nominal interest rate further. It historically takes about 15 to 18 months after the change in monetary policy for the nominal interest rate to fall back to its original level. The subsequent gradual fall to the new steady-state nominal interest rate is measured in years or decades, depending on the particular nominal interest rate examined. During the period in which expected inflation typically exceeds actual inflation, net creditors win and net debtors lose.

CENTRAL BANK POLICY AND INTEREST RATE ADJUSTMENTS

Central bankers have traditionally emphasized the initial period in which the liquidity effect is dominant. As a result, they would decrease the nominal-money-supply growth rate to increase interest rates, or increase it when they

---

[24] This is the deepest fall estimated for various techniques and periods by Cagan and Gandolfi, op. cit., p. 281.

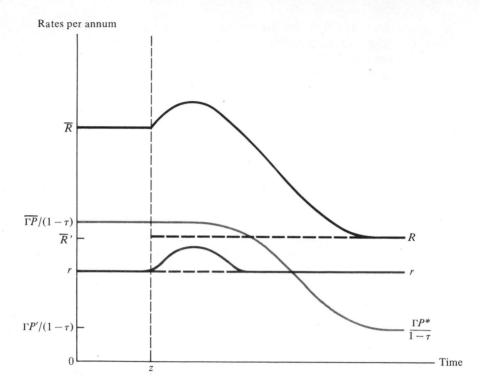

Figure 7.12 Cyclical adjustment of interest rates to a decrease in the nominal-money-supply growth rate. Immediately after the start of the restrictive monetary policy at z, the liquidity effect is dominant, and the real and nominal interest rates r and R rise. As real-income and later price-level growth rates decelerate, the income effect begins to offset the liquidity effect and the initial rise in interest rates is reversed. As the tax-adjusted expected inflation rate $\Gamma P^*/(1 - \tau)$ finally decreases, the nominal interest rate decreases relative to the real interest rate due to the expectations effect.

wished to lower interest rates. This works fine over a short period, but when long-continued is self-defeating.

Suppose for example the Fed wished to decrease the interest rate from 6 percent to 5.5 percent per annum. It could do so at first by increasing ΓM sufficiently. But this would tend to wear off after a while, so further increases in ΓM would be required as time went on. The Fed behaves like a dog chasing its tail. Soon inflation begins to accelerate, and it becomes impossible to continue the reduced nominal-interest-rate goal. If the Fed then increases its interest rate target, the process is reversed downward.

In recent years, major central banks have begun to abandon trying to control interest rates. Instead they formulate policy in terms of a nominal-money-supply growth rate. In many cases, traditional habits die hard, however. For example, the Fed each month tries to achieve its desired nominal-money-supply growth rate by choosing an appropriate interest rate.

SUMMARY

1 Okun's law describes the empirical correlation between the unemployment rate and real income: When actual real income exceeds (is less than) steady-state real income, the unemployment rate will be below (above) normal.

2 The effects of monetary policy on real income and the price level can be described either by shifting aggregate demand and supply curves or in terms of a continuous dynamic adjustment process.

3 A stimulative monetary policy (an increase in the nominal-money-supply growth rate) is seen to cause a temporary increase in real income relative to an unchanged steady-state growth path. The inflation rate is initially slow to increase and so overshoots the increased steady-state inflation rate during a catch-up period.

4 This pattern occurs because sellers set prices at a level expected to be optimal and vary the quantities sold to meet demand at the set price. Ultimately, increased demand for the given labor and capital resources bids up their prices and so increases costs and prices of goods and services generally.

5 A restrictive monetary policy causes a temporary decrease in actual real income relative to its steady-state growth path, while the inflation rate is slow to adjust downward. This is the typical monetary recession. Later the inflation rate undershoots and real income recovers during a catch-up period.

6 Real income effects are typically noticeable about 6 to 12 months after a change in monetary policy, with noticeable changes in the inflation rate occurring about 15 to 21 months after the policy change. Complete adjustment takes perhaps 3 to 5 years.

7 The cyclical adjustment of interest rates to monetary policy is explained in terms of liquidity, income, and expectation effects. A stimulative monetary policy causes interest rates to fall for 6 to 9 months and then rise to and (after 15 to 18 months) above their original level. The pattern is reversed for a restrictive monetary policy.

8 Historically, central banks have engaged in self-defeating policies of attempting to keep interest rates low by increasing nominal-money-supply growth rates.

CONCEPTS TO KNOW

aggregate demand curve   Okun's law

aggregate supply curve   stagflation

cost-push inflation

QUESTIONS AND EXERCISES

1 (*a*) If real income dropped by 2.5 percent one year (compared with a normal increase of 3.5 percent), what do you predict would happen to the unemployment rate, based on U.S. experience?

 (*b*) If real income were 2 percent above its trend growth path, the unemployment rate would be about _____ percentage points below normal.

2 Explain how aggregate demand affects costs by bidding up wages of labor and rental rates on capital.

3 Suppose that a restrictive monetary policy had reduced actual real income to 6 percent below its steady-state level and the price level was 4 percent above its steady-state level. If the steady-state growth rates of real income and inflation were 3 percent and 2 percent per annum, respectively, over the next 2 years, and steady-state equilibrium were reached at the end of those 2 years, what would be the average Γy and ΓP during this recovery period?

*4 Real income is temporarily increased by a stimulative monetary policy because sellers take actions that they would not take if they were aware of true conditions. Evaluate.

5 Use the train analogy to discuss the adjustment of real income and the price level to an unexpected reduction in the nominal-money-supply growth rate.

6 Explain why the initial effect on the nominal interest rate of a change in the nominal-money-supply growth rate is opposite to the long-run effect.

REFERENCES FOR FURTHER READING

Friedman, Milton, and **Anna J. Schwartz:** Money and Business Cycles, *Review of Economics and Statistics,* **45:** 32–64, Feb. 1963 (Supp.).

Lucas, Robert E., Jr.: "Understanding Business Cycles," in K. Brunner and A. Meltzer (eds.), *Carnegie-Rochester Conference Series,* **5:** 7–29, 1977.

Trends and Fluctuations in Monetary Growth, *Federal Reserve Bank of St. Louis Review,* **54**(9): 6–10, Sept. 1972. Highly recommended for illustrating the application of the theory to the real world.

CHAPTER 7, APPENDIX A

CYCLICAL FLUCTUATIONS IN DESIRED FLUIDITY

Chapters 6 and 7 have proceeded by assuming that desired and steady-state fluidity are equal. This assumption simplifies the analysis while providing an empirically useful "first approximation" of the adjustment process. It is similar to analyzing a falling body *as if* it were in a vacuum: For most purposes it works fine, but not for exceptional cases such as a falling feather. In this appendix, the more complicated case in which desired fluidity deviates from steady state is considered. The differences are empirically important primarily for such exceptional cases as the Great Depression, but fresh insight into the transmission process will be gained from the exercise.

Deviations of actual from steady-state fluidity have been empirically important only in the adjustment to sharply reduced nominal-money-supply growth rates. So our analysis is limited to the case of a restrictive monetary policy. The reader can supply the corresponding arguments for a stimulative monetary policy.

In Chap. 6, we saw that spending would increase more slowly than otherwise, or fall, if people had less money than they desired to hold. The idea was that people would reduce their spending on assets other than money—directly reducing consumer durable goods expenditures and indirectly reducing investment expenditures. The amount of money which people desire to hold is determined by the money-demand function:

$$m^d = m^d(y, R) \tag{7.10}$$

That is, the real quantity of money demanded m^d is an increasing function of real income y and a decreasing function of the nominal interest rate R.

Remember that the logarithmic difference between actual and desired fluidity is identical to the logarithmic difference between actual and desired real money[25]

$$\log \phi - \log \phi^d \equiv \log m - \log m^d \tag{7.11}$$

This follows from the definition of the desired fluidity function

$$\phi^d = \phi^d(y, R) \equiv \frac{m^d(y, R)}{y} \tag{7.12}$$

Unless real income and the nominal interest rate are at their steady-state levels, desired fluidity (and the real quantity of money demanded) will differ from its steady-state level. Since the analysis of Chap. 7 shows that a monetary shock causes y and R to deviate from their steady-state values during the adjustment process, their effects on ϕ^d should be taken into account.

REAL INCOME EFFECTS ON DESIRED FLUIDITY

Consider first the effects of deviations in real income. It is important to distinguish here between permanent income and transitory income. Permanent income is proportional to wealth, and so movements in permanent income

---

[25] And the logarithmic difference between actual and desired real money is identical to the logarithmic difference between actual and desired nominal money, or $\log m - \log m^d \equiv \log M - \log M^d$.

correspond to movements in wealth.[26] Transitory income is the difference between current real income and permanent income—the normal income stream from current wealth. The deviations of actual real income from steady-state real income change wealth little, and so are primarily fluctuations in the transitory component of real income.

These fluctuations in transitory income do affect the quantity of money demanded, but not by as much as would have been the case if permanent income (and wealth) had changed. Formally, the elasticity of real money demand with respect to real income is greater than zero but much less than one, if permanent income is held constant. This means that negative transitory income equal to 5 percent of permanent income would decrease real money demand by a smaller percentage, say 1 percent. Desired fluidity ϕ^d is the ratio of real money demand to real income (m^d/y), so decreases in the transitory component of real income decrease the denominator proportionately more than the numerator, and desired fluidity rises.[27] Summing up: When actual real income falls relative to steady-state real income, desired fluidity rises relative to steady-state fluidity, other things being equal.

INTEREST RATE EFFECTS ON DESIRED FLUIDITY

Other things are not equal during the adjustment process, however, because of the cyclical adjustment of interest rates. In response to a restrictive monetary policy, interest rates at first rise but after a while fall back to, and eventually below, their initial level as discussed in Sec. 7.3. Again it is important to see how short-term fluctuations in R have different effects on real money demand than in steady-state equilibrium.

To see this, write the more complete money-demand function of Chap. 4

$$m^d = m^d(y, R_M, R_S, R_L) \qquad [7.13]$$

This states that real money demand is an increasing function of real income y and the nominal yield on money R_M and a decreasing function of the nominal yields on short-term and long-term securities R_S and R_L. If all these yields move in normal proportion, it is appropriate to use a single composite interest rate R. Short-run fluctuations in R have different implications from long-run changes in R. This is so because the yields on money and long-term securities adjust gradually to changes in short-term yields. The yield on long-term securi-

---

[26] See Sec. 3.5 for details.

[27] Suppose real income is transitorily decreased 5 percent from R\$1000 to R\$950 billion, and this decreases the real quantity of money demanded by 1 percent from R\$200 to R\$198 billion. Then desired fluidity rises by 4 percent from R\$200/R\$1000 = 0.200 to R\$198/R\$950 = 0.208. Formally the elasticity of desired fluidity with respect to real income (permanent income held constant) is −1 plus the corresponding real income elasticity of real money demand.

ties R_L has little impact on money demand empirically, so we can concentrate on movements in R_S and R_M.

The initial slowness of R_M to adjust to the increased yield on short-term securities decreases the relative attractiveness of money, and hence money demand, in the early part of the period. This is eliminated—and perhaps for a while reversed—as short-term rates fall back and the yield on money adjusts.

THE ADJUSTMENT PROCESS

Combining both the interest rate and real income effects for a restrictive monetary policy, desired fluidity initially falls relative to steady-state fluidity when only the initial interest rate effect is operative. Desired fluidity soon rises above steady-state fluidity as the initial rise in R_S relative to R_M is eliminated, and real income falls relative to steady-state real income. This pattern is illustrated in Fig. 7.13.

Figure 7.14 shows the adjustment process for actual fluidity and nominal income, given that fluidity adjusts to this desired level rather than to the steady-state level. The only substantive differences from Fig. 6.7 arise because

Figure 7.13 Cyclical adjustment of desired fluidity to a restrictive monetary policy. A decreased growth rate of the nominal money supply leads to an initial decrease in desired relative to steady-state fluidity as the yield on short-term securities rises relative to the yield on money. Later, as real income decreases more than in proportion to the induced decrease in real money demand, desired fluidity rises above the steady-state fluidity growth path.

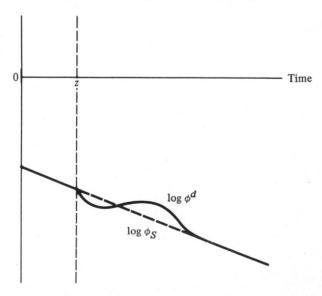

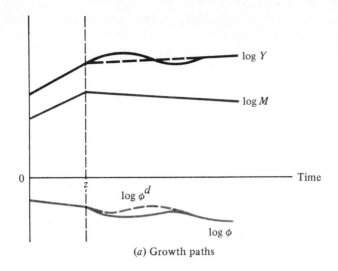

(a) Growth paths

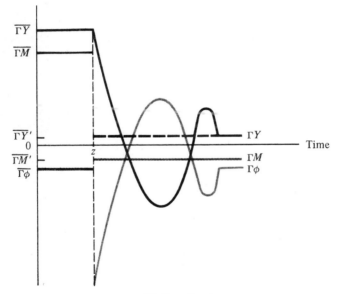

(b) Growth rates

**Figure 7.14 Adjustment to a restrictive monetary policy where
desired and steady-state fluidity differ.** The effects of a restrictive
monetary policy on the growth path of desired fluidity are
reproduced from Fig. 7.13 in panel (a). Actual fluidity is shown
adjusting over time to desired fluidity. The implied actual growth
path of nominal income drops below the (less steep) steady-state
growth path during the latter part of the adjustment process when
actual fluidity exceeds steady-state fluidity. The slopes of the growth
paths in panel (a) are the growth rates as drawn in panel (b). The
adjustment process shows a second catch-up period for the growth
rates of fluidity and nominal income. (Compare Fig. 6.7.)

actual fluidity during the latter stages of the adjustment process is above steady-state fluidity, and nominal income therefore falls below steady-state nominal income. So the induced rise in fluidity makes the contraction worse by causing nominal income to fall further than otherwise. A second catch-up period is implied for the growth rates of fluidity and nominal income. This occurs as real income rises back to its unchanged steady-state growth path so that the difference between actual and desired fluidity is eliminated.

These effects on nominal income would make for a greater fall and more rapid recovery of real income than would have taken place otherwise, but the basic pattern of real income and price level adjustment would not be substantially altered.[28]

The rise in fluidity during depressions has often been used by central bankers to deny responsibility for the effects of a reduced nominal-money-supply growth rate. "Look," they say, "the money supply is high relative to income, and interest rates are low; so we have been following an easy-money policy and cannot be blamed for the depression." But low interest rates and high fluidity can indicate either the beginning of a stimulative monetary policy *or* the later stages of a restrictive monetary policy. So the evidence of "easy money" is specious.

CHAPTER 7, APPENDIX B

THE CASE OF NON-SUPERNEUTRAL MONEY

Chapters 6 and 7 have so far assumed that the interest elasticity of the demand for money is negligible in the long run, so that money is superneutral. This assumption greatly simplifies the exposition without making any substantial difference in the analysis of the cyclical adjustment to a monetary shock. Nevertheless, the preponderance of the empirical evidence implies some long-run negative relationship between the level of interest rates and the real quantity of money demanded. As will be seen below, allowance for this fact does have some interesting implications for the price level.

Consider first the effects of a stimulative monetary policy on the steady-state growth paths of fluidity and nominal income. This problem was solved in a slightly different form at the end of Sec. 5.3 and the results are reproduced in Fig. 7.15. The higher nominal-money-supply growth rate $\overline{\Gamma M}'$ after time z implies higher steady-state inflation rates and nominal interest rates and therefore lower levels of fluidity in long-run equilibrium. Since the steady-state growth rate of fluidity is unaffected, the steady-state growth path of fluidity is shifted down, parallel to the old growth path in panel (a). This implies an initial

---

[28] Cyclical adjustments of Γy and ΓP more complicated than those previously illustrated may occur, but there is insufficient evidence to describe the details of the adjustment process that finely.

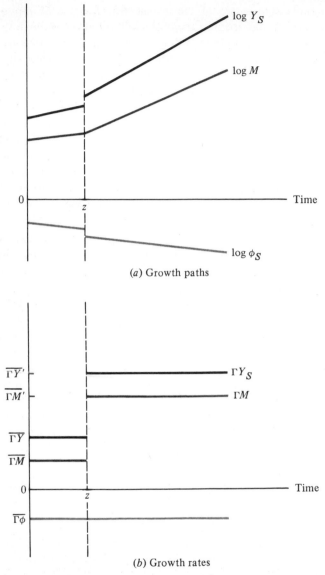

(a) Growth paths

(b) Growth rates

Figure 7.15 Steady-state growth paths of fluidity and nominal income with interest-elastic demand for money. The higher steady-state nominal interest rates associated with the increased nominal-money-supply growth rate reduces the steady-state level but not growth rate of fluidity after z. This occurs because real money demand is reduced relative to any given real income. It is illustrated in panel (a) by a parallel downward shift in the log ϕ_S line. This shifts the log Y_S line up by the same amount while the slope of the log Y_S line is increased by the same amount as the slope of the log M line. These slopes are the steady-state growth rates graphed in panel (b). Panel (b) is identical to the superneutral case with zero long-run interest elasticity of money demand (Fig. 6.2) because the shifts in the growth paths at the instant z cannot be indicated graphically.

jump in the steady-state growth path of nominal income, as well as the increased slope previously considered. Panel (a) of Fig. 7.15 differs from panel (a) of Fig. 6.2 only in the downward parallel shift in the growth path of fluidity after z and corresponding upward parallel shift in the nominal-income growth path. Panel (b) of Fig. 7.15 showing the growth rates is drawn identically to panel (b) in Fig. 6.2. The steady-state growth rates are not affected by whether or not real money demand is interest-elastic. However, there is no indication of the jumps in the steady-state growth paths of fluidity and nominal income at time z.[29]

The adjustment process differs from that discussed in Chap. 6 in two main respects: (1) It is lengthened by the gradual upward adjustment of the expected inflation rate and hence nominal interest rates. This slow increase in nominal interest rates gradually decreases desired fluidity toward the lower steady-state growth path. During the long adjustment period, the effects are the same as if the steady-state growth rate of fluidity had decreased slightly. (2) The average growth rates of nominal income and fluidity over the entire adjustment period do not equal their steady-state values. The average growth rate of fluidity will be lower by the decrease in log ϕ_S at z, divided by the length of the adjustment period. This slower growth is required to get down to the lower steady-state fluidity growth path.[30] The average nominal-income growth rate during the adjustment process is increased by the same amount for the same reasons.

Figure 7.16 illustrates these differences. The complete adjustment process is not drawn because the long gradual adjustment of fluidity and nominal income would require compressing the time scale so much that the early cyclical adjustments would be hard to see. In any case, the actual growth paths of fluidity and nominal income gradually approach their steady-state growth paths in the latter stages of adjustment. The catch-up periods for $\Gamma\phi$ and ΓY are now elongated to allow for these gradual adjustments in the level.

A parallel downward shift in the steady-state growth path of real income was associated with higher rates of nominal-money-supply growth in Sec. 5.3. The empirical evidence on this effect is meager, but it is almost surely much smaller in magnitude than the fluidity shift. Figure 7.17 shows the steady-state results. The upward shift in the nominal-income growth path is reproduced from Fig. 7.15. An (exaggerated) downward parallel shift is shown for the growth path of real income. The growth path of the price level is the difference between these other growth paths, so it shifts up at z by the amount of the upward shift in the nominal-income growth path plus the downward shift in the real-income growth path. The steady-state growth rates are unaffected—

---

[29] At the instant z, the steady-state growth rates of fluidity and nominal income are $-\infty$ and $+\infty$, respectively. There is no way to indicate that graphically.

[30] Suppose that the nominal-money-supply growth rate were increased enough that steady-state fluidity was decreased by 10 percent. If it took 10 years to achieve full adjustment, the average growth rate of fluidity would be 0.1/10 years = 0.01/year or 1 percent per annum below the steady-state growth rate during the adjustment period.

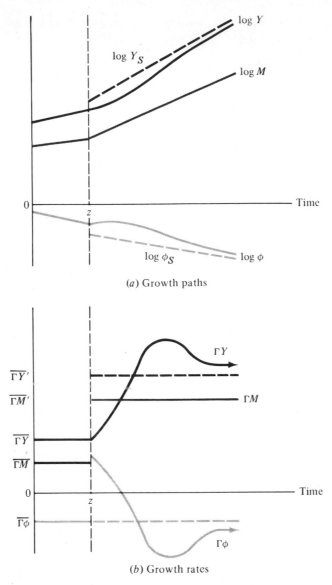

(a) Growth paths

(b) Growth rates

Figure 7.16 Adjustments of fluidity and nominal income with interest-elastic demand for money. The adjustments of fluidity and nominal income to a stimulative monetary policy are very similar whether or not there is a substantial long-run interest elasticity of money demand. (Compare Fig. 6.4.) However, if money is interest-elastic in the long run, the adjustment process is prolonged by a period (not completely drawn here) in which actual fluidity gradually adjusts down to steady-state fluidity and nominal income gradually adjusts up to steady-state nominal income. This long gradual adjustment period (which is hard to distinguish from a temporarily lower steady-state fluidity growth rate) occurs because of the slow adjustment of expected inflation and nominal interest rates.

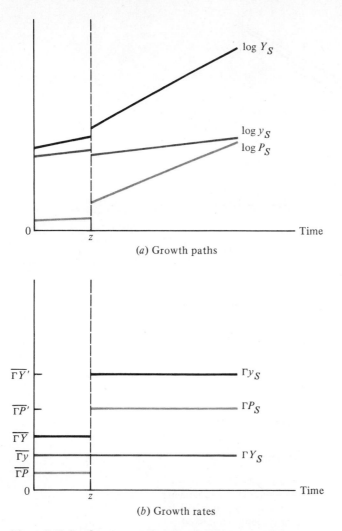

(a) Growth paths

(b) Growth rates

Figure 7.17 Steady-state growth paths of real income and the price level with interest-elastic demand for money. The steady-state growth path of nominal income is reproduced in panel (a) from Fig. 7.15. A downward parallel shift in the real-income growth path indicates the reduction in the level—but not growth rate—of real income associated with reduced usage of money at higher nominal-money-supply growth rates. The steady-state growth path of the price level is the difference between the log Y and log y lines. It shifts up by the upward shift in log Y plus the downward shift in log y. The steady-state growth rates in panel (b) are not affected except at the instant z. (Compare Fig. 7.6.)

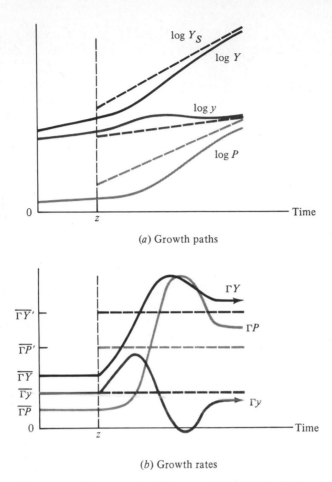

(a) Growth paths

(b) Growth rates

**Figure 7.18 Adjustments of real income and the price level with
interest-elastic demand for money.** As with fluidity and nominal
income, the adjustment pattern of real income and the price level
are not changed much by allowing for the long-run interest
elasticity of money demand. The period is protracted by the
gradual convergence of the actual real income growth path to
the lower steady-state growth path. This period does not indicate
rising unemployment but rather the increasing use of labor and
capital to make transactions instead of to produce goods. The
rate of inflation is above steady state to accommodate the above-
steady-state growth rate of nominal spending and below-steady-
state growth rate of real output.

except at the instant z—so panel (b) of Fig. 7.17 is identical to panel (b) of
Fig. 7.6 drawn for the no-interest-rate-elasticity case.

The adjustment of real income would be virtually unaffected except that the
actual real-income growth rate will remain slightly less than the steady-state
growth rate for a protracted period. The more rapid nominal income growth

due to the below-steady-state growth rate in fluidity would be expected during this period and so be fully reflected in the growth rate of the price level. This adjustment process is illustrated in Fig. 7.18.

It is straightforward to include the complications of Appendix A or to analyze a restrictive monetary policy; so those cases are left as an exercise for the reader.

The conclusions to be drawn from this appendix are that the interest elasticity of money demand reinforces the inflationary effects of a stimulative monetary policy with an upward shift in the price level, but otherwise the adjustment process is pretty much the same as in the simpler case.

CHAPTER 8

EFFECTS OF FISCAL AND OTHER DOMESTIC SHOCKS

WHAT YOU WILL LEARN IN THIS CHAPTER
Different kinds of macroeconomic shocks ● Effects of the level of real government spending on the steady-state equilibrium ● How government spending can crowd out private spending ● How the economy adjusts to unexpected changes in real government spending ● Adjustment to unexpected changes in taxes ● Changes in the money multiplier, money demand, and investment demand as sources of demand shocks

8.1 TYPES OF MACROECONOMIC SHOCKS

A CLASSIFICATION SCHEME

Macroeconomic shocks have their initial impact either on the aggregate demand for goods and services or on the aggregate supply. Thus they are termed either *demand shocks* or *supply shocks*. For large industrial economies, fluctuations in real income, unemployment, and inflation are almost exclusively related to demand shocks. Accordingly our discussion will concentrate on these shocks, although supply shocks will be considered further in Sec. 8.4.

Demand shocks by definition cause unexpected changes in aggregate demand as measured by the growth rate of nominal expenditures ΓY. That is, they change the rate at which the aggregate demand curve shifts outward. But the dynamic form of the Cambridge equation implies that the growth rate of nominal expenditures is equal to the difference between the growth rates of the nominal money supply and fluidity:

$$\Gamma Y \equiv \Gamma M - \Gamma \phi \qquad [8.1]$$

So a demand shock must operate by causing unexpected changes in the growth rate of the nominal money supply, of fluidity, or of both. No unexpected change in aggregate demand can occur otherwise. If a demand shock changes the nominal-money-supply growth rate, the shock is termed a *monetary shock*. A demand shock which occurs with an unchanged nominal-money-supply growth path is termed a *nonmonetary demand shock*. As seen in Chap. 6, a monetary shock will normally involve changes in the growth rates of *both* the nominal money supply and fluidity. A nonmonetary demand shock, however, acts only through changes in the growth rate of fluidity since the growth rate of nominal money is unchanged.

Demand shocks can also be classified by whether they are the result of a government policy decision or of an unexpected shift in macroeconomic behavioral functions. These will be termed *policy* and *behavioral* demand shocks, respectively. Behavioral demand shocks are also referred to as *autonomous* demand shocks in the macroeconomic literature. Table 8.1 classifies the types of demand shocks within the domestic economy which have been of major concern to macroeconomists.

The various actions of the central bank which influence the growth rate of the nominal money supply are collectively referred to as *monetary policy*. Nonmonetary macroeconomic policy is divided into fiscal policy and debt policy. *Fiscal policy* refers to the decisions which determine the aggregate levels of expenditures on goods and services and of taxes. *Debt policy* refers to the decisions which determine the maturity structure of the government debt.[1] Decisions of the many state and local governments are individually too small to have a noticeable effect on fiscal or debt policy. The federal government—which actively considers the macroeconomic impact of its large spending, taxing, and borrowing—dominates these policies. Although once thought powerful, debt policy is almost entirely neutralized by changes in the maturity

---

[1] The maturity structure refers to the fraction of total value of government bonds outstanding represented by each different term to maturity. The term to maturity of a bond is the length of time remaining until the principal is due.

Table 8.1 CLASSIFICATION SCHEME FOR DEMAND SHOCKS

Source of Demand Shock	Nature of Demand Shock	
	Monetary	Nonmonetary
Policy	Decisions which determine growth rate of base money and influence growth rate of the money multiplier	Decisions on government expenditures for real goods and services, the level of taxation, and maturity structure of government debt
Behavioral or autonomous	Banking panics	Shifts in investment demand, real money demand, and consumer expenditure function

structure of private borrowing and lending.[2] So we limit our discussion of nonmonetary policy shocks to fiscal policy.

The remainder of this section and Secs. 8.2 and 8.3 will discuss the nature and effects of fiscal policy. Behavioral or autonomous demand shocks are similar in effect to the corresponding policy shocks. Section 8.4 deals with them as well as with supply shocks.

THE GOVERNMENT BUDGET IDENTITY AGAIN

The government budget identity [6.1] relates total government expenditures for goods and services to the ways in which they may be financed. Rewriting it here:

$$G \equiv T + \Delta D + \Delta B \qquad\qquad [8.2]$$

That is, nominal government expenditures are identically equal to the sum of nominal taxes T, the rate of change in nominal government debt ΔD, and the rate of change in nominal base money ΔB. The difference between expenditures and taxes—the amount financed by money creation and debt issuance—is the government *deficit*. Expenditures, revenues, and borrowings of state and local governments are consolidated with those of the federal government.

Fiscal policy is defined in terms of decisions about government expenditures and taxes which leave the nominal-money-supply growth rate unchanged. If a change in G or T were offset by a change in ΔB, the growth rate of the nominal money supply would indeed be affected. So our analysis of fiscal shocks assumes that any increase in government spending or decrease in taxes is financed by an equal increase in government borrowing ΔD.

TRENDS IN GOVERNMENT SPENDING AND TAXES

Government spending for goods and services has grown slowly but steadily as a fraction of net national product, with the exception of temporary wartime increases. This pattern of growth is illustrated in Table 8.2.

---

[2] From 1961 until 1965, the Fed and Treasury attempted to increase the interest rate on short-term bonds relative to that on long-term bonds in what was called "Operation Twist." This involved replacing long-term government bonds with short-term Treasury bills. While short-term rates did rise relative to long-term rates, the rise was similar to that experienced in other postwar business expansions. This is consistent with the view that private lenders and borrowers compete away any advantage or disadvantage in making a series of short-term loans versus one long-term bond. The literature on the term structure of interest rates is immense. Key references are to David Meiselman, *The Term Structure of Interest Rates*, Englewood Cliffs, N.J.: Prentice-Hall, Inc., 1962; Reuben A. Kessel, *The Cyclical Behavior of the Term Structure of Interest Rates*, NBER Occasional Paper No. 91, New York: Columbia University Press, 1965; and Burton G. Malkiel, *The Term Structure of Interest Rates: Expectations and Behavior Patterns*, Princeton: Princeton University Press, 1966. Important unsuccessful attempts to find an effect of debt policy are Franco Modigliani and Richard Sutch, Debt Management and the Term Structure of Interest Rates: An Empirical Analysis of Recent Experience, *Journal of Political Economy*, **75:** 569–589, Aug. 1967; and Michael E. Echols and Jan Walter Elliott, Rational Expectations in a Disequilibrium Model of the Term Structure, *American Economic Review*, **66:** 28–44, Mar. 1976.

**Table 8.2 GOVERNMENT EXPENDITURE FOR GOODS
AND SERVICES: TOTAL RELATIVE TO NNP
AND FEDERAL SHARE OF TOTALS**

Years	G/Y	Share of Federal Expenditures in G
1869–78	0.056	n.a.
1879–88	0.048	n.a.
1890	0.056	n.a.
1895	0.062	n.a.
1900	0.067	n.a.
1905	0.067	n.a.
1910	0.068	n.a.
1915	0.080	n.a.
1920	0.074	n.a.
1925	0.087	n.a.
1930	0.117	0.163
1935	0.157	0.295
1940	0.156	0.429
1945	0.414	0.901
1950	0.147	0.486
1955	0.206	0.593
1960	0.219	0.535
1965	0.219	0.486
1970	0.246	0.437
1975	0.248	0.364
1977	0.233	0.368

The data for 1869–1888 are averages for the indicated decades.
Sources: 1869–1925: John Kendrick, *Productivity Trends in the United
States*, Princeton: Princeton University Press for the NBER, 1961;
1930–1970: *The National Income and Product Accounts of the United
States, 1929–74*; 1975 and 1977: *Survey of Current Business*, July 1978.

The federal government currently accounts for between a third and a half of
total government spending—that is, for about 10 percent of NNP.

Government expenditures on goods and services are largely determined by
the public's demand for them given their cost in taxes. The political process is
surely more complex than private markets, but spending appears to respond to
public desires in a stable and predictable manner. This places a limit on the
extent to which real government spending can be varied over a year for reasons
of macroeconomic policy. As a practical matter, a change in real *federal*
government spending amounting to 10 percent of its normal level is as big a
change as seems feasible except in wartime. This would amount to an increase
or decrease in real government spending equal to about 1 percent of NNP.

Similar statements could be made about real taxes net of transfers. Taxes are the primary means of financing the desired level of government spending, although borrowing has been increasingly used during recent recessions.[3]

8.2 EFFECTS OF CHANGES IN GOVERNMENT SPENDING

AN INCREASE IN GOVERNMENT SPENDING

Macroeconomic policymakers sometimes propose to increase the growth rate of nominal income by an unexpected increase in real government spending. We will examine how this policy works by assuming that monetary and tax policies are unchanged. So the increased spending is financed by increased borrowing. It would be unusual in practice for policymakers to concentrate only on government spending, but more complex policy mixtures can be readily considered once the effects of the pure individual policies are known.

In principle, the effects of the increase in government spending depends on exactly what goods and services expenditures are increased. For example, an increase in government spending and borrowing for hydroelectric dams may exactly replace private investment and financing. Similarly, if the government institutes a housing program by buying houses for people and issuing them transferable leases, then government bonds would just replace private mortgages. In neither of these cases would one expect to detect any effect on total income, but only on how national income accountants divide it. If government hires more people to serve as social workers, however, there is no obvious automatic, equal decline in the private demand for social workers. It would be tedious to examine the effects of each possible sort of increase in government expenditures, so fiscal policy is assumed to raise or lower spending in a mixture of programs as might actually occur. Thus a temporary increase in real government spending involves some programs which directly replace private investment and financing, others for which there is no competing private provision, and many intermediate projects.

THE SIMPLE MULTIPLIER APPROACH

The simple multiplier approach to analyzing an increase in real government spending is standard fare in introductory economics courses. The argument is that the increased level of government spending will increase aggregate expenditures $C + I + G$ by an equal amount. But aggregate income is equal to

---

[3] Since 1975 large government deficits amounting to up to 19 percent of spending have been financed by borrowing and base-money creation. These reported deficits are partially an illusion, because the government does not allow for inflation in its bookkeeping. The real value of the government debt and base money falls by the inflation rate times their real levels, so nominal borrowing and base-money creation in this amount just keep things even. In 1976, the rate of inflation was 4.75 percent per annum, and total government debt and base money was about $673 billion. So about $32 billion of the reported $36 billion deficit was an illusion due to inflation.

expenditures so income is increased, and this in turn increases consumer expenditures. This increases income further, and the process continues until income is increased by a multiple of the original increase in government expenditures. This increase in income is usually illustrated by a diagram like Fig. 1.2 in Chap. 1.

Although familiar, this approach leaves out a great deal. In particular it omits the fact that an increased nominal-income growth rate implies an increased growth rate of the nominal quantity of money demanded. Since the growth rate of the nominal money supply is unchanged[4] this creates a growing excess demand for money. Ultimately this excess demand must be eliminated by offsetting changes in private expenditure growth (which reduce nominal income growth) or increases in interest rates (which reduce the quantity of money demanded) or both.

LONG-RUN EFFECTS OF INCREASED GOVERNMENT SPENDING

As with a monetary shock, it is useful to start our analysis at the end rather than at the beginning. That is, to see what are the effects on the steady-state equilibrium of an increased level of real government spending. These effects are the subject of a continuing debate. The issues involved can be understood best in terms of the model of steady-state growth presented in Chap. 5.

We saw in Chap. 5 that the steady-state growth path of real income is determined by the growth path of labor, the aggregate production function, and the ratio of real investment to real income. Unexpected changes in real government spending will temporarily affect the unemployment rate, and hence labor supply, during the period of adjustment. But in the long run, the level of real government spending will not significantly affect the labor supply or its growth rate. The steady-state growth rate of real income is equal to the growth rate of labor, so it too is unchanged. Therefore any effects on steady-state real income must change its level but not its growth rate—that is, must take the form of parallel shifts in the real-income growth path.

Some economists argue that increased government production will necessarily cause an adverse change in the aggregate production because the government is less efficient than the private sector. Others take just the opposite view. Neither side has mustered much evidence for an effect one way or the other, so this possibility will be neglected as uncertain and unproven.

Real income effects will occur if there is a change in the fraction of income invested. This would not occur if the increased government spending replaced

---

[4] While the government is spending more money it is also borrowing more, so the total amount of money in the hands of the public is unaffected.

some private investment with an equal amount of government investment.[5] It is generally supposed that increased government spending will partially replace private investment with government consumption. Thus increased government spending would decrease the total fraction of real income which is invested. It was shown in Figs. 5.5 and 5.6 that a lower value of this fraction σ implies a downward parallel shift in the growth path of real income. That is, the level of real income is lower at each instant of time, but the steady-state growth rate of real income is unaffected.

If the fraction of income invested is reduced, there will also be a shift in the growth path of fluidity unless money is superneutral. This occurs because capital then becomes more scarce relative to labor. This increases the marginal product of capital and hence the real interest rate. The expected inflation rate is not affected, so the nominal interest rate will be increased by the same amount as the real interest rate. This increase in the nominal interest rate has effects on fluidity and real income similar to those illustrated in Figs. 5.9 and 5.10, where the nominal interest rate is increased due to an increase in the growth rates of nominal money and the price level. That is, the higher level of nominal interest rates will reduce the steady-state levels (but not growth rates) of fluidity and real income. This secondary reduction in the growth path of real income would be in addition to the initial reduction due to a lower investment-income ratio.

In sum, the increased level of real government spending has effects depending on whether or not total private and government investment is reduced relative to income. If the total investment-income ratio is unchanged, the steady-state equilibrium is also unchanged. If the total investment-income ratio is reduced, there will be a downward parallel shift in the growth path of real income. If money is not superneutral, the downward real income shift would be accompanied by a downward parallel shift in the growth path of fluidity. We saw at the end of Chap. 5 that such downward parallel shifts in fluidity and real income imply an upward parallel shift in the growth path of the price level. That is, the rate of inflation is unaffected, but the price level will be increased by a percentage equal to the sum of the percentage decreases in fluidity and real income.

In our analysis of the adjustment process, we will initially focus on the simpler case in which the steady-state equilibrium is unchanged. The appendix to this chapter provides an analysis taking account of parallel shifts in the growth paths of fluidity, real income, and the price level. Many economists believe that these shifts are trivial in size and so use the simpler case as a good working approximation.

---

[5] If individuals are fully rational and do not wish to transfer resources to themselves from future generations, it can be shown that they will adjust their private consumption and saving to achieve this equality. See for example Robert J. Barro, Are Government Bonds Net Wealth? *Journal of Political Economy*, **82**: 1095–1117, July/Aug. 1974; Levis A. Kochin, Are Future Taxes Anticipated by Consumers? *Journal of Money, Credit and Banking*, **6**: 385–394, Aug. 1974. Few economists believe that these perfect adjustments fully occur.

CROWDING OUT

Reductions in private expenditures may offset all or part of the increase in government expenditures. This process is often described as government expenditures *crowding out* private expenditures. Crowding out occurs to some extent if total income and expenditures increase less than government expenditures so that the government's decision to buy more reduces private spending.

It is useful to distinguish between nominal crowding out and real crowding out. Complete *nominal crowding out* occurs if the increase in real government expenditures leaves nominal income unchanged—each dollar increase in nominal government expenditures is matched by a dollar decrease in nominal private expenditures. Complete *real crowding out* occurs if the increase in real government expenditures leaves real income unchanged—each base-year dollar increase in real government expenditures is matched by a base-year dollar decrease in real private expenditures.

Partial nominal (or real) crowding out occurs if nominal (real) income increases less than the increase in nominal (real) government expenditures so that nominal (real) private expenditures are decreased, but by a smaller amount than in complete crowding out. The steady-state analysis suggests that real crowding out may be more than complete in the long run, since real income may fall so that real private expenditures are reduced by more than real government expenditures are increased.

The extent—and perhaps existence—of crowding out varies over the adjustment process. Crowding out is generally more nearly complete in the long run than in the first year or so of the adjustment process.

AN OUTLINE OF THE ADJUSTMENT PROCESS

The unexpected increase in the level of real government spending will involve both increased government employment and increased purchases of goods and services from private firms. This will directly increase output and income, although at first the increased purchases will result largely in reduced inventories rather than increased production. Later, production of these goods will be increased to meet the increased demand and rebuild inventories.

As nominal income rises, so does the nominal quantity of money demanded. The nominal supply of money is unaffected. Increased income will lead consumers to want to increase their expenditures and this will offset any tendency to reduce consumer expenditures because of an excess demand for money. Instead consumers would wish to reduce their holdings of securities to finance increased money holdings and consumer expenditures. The desire of consumers generally to sell securities will drive down their price. A lower price on an existing bond is an increase in the market interest rate. This increase in the market interest rate does two things: (1) it reduces the quantity of money demanded, and (2) it reduces the amount of investment which firms desire to make, which in turn tends to reduce income and money demand. So the attempts of individuals to increase their money holdings by selling securities to each other do serve to reconcile the quantity of money demanded to the amount supplied. Interest rate adjustments are more important and investment adjustments less important initially than later. As time goes on, reductions in private expenditures (mainly investment) offset an increasing amount of the increase in government expenditures.

This process can be summarized in terms of crowding out. During the first year or so when the bulk of the process occurs, the price level would be virtually unaffected so that it is not necessary to distinguish between nominal and real crowding out. Initially there is considerable partial crowding out as sales from inventories reduce the inventory component of investment. As time progresses, the extent of crowding out falls as production for government increases faster than production for investment in plant, equipment, and housing falls. There is a point at which private expenditures are either hardly reduced or perhaps even somewhat increased.[6] Past this peak increase in income, decreases in private expenditures are dominant and nominal, and real income falls.

Figures 8.1 and 8.2 illustrate this adjustment pattern on the simplifying assumption that the shifts in the fluidity and real-income growth paths are negligible. A more complete analysis taking into account possibly substantial steady-state shifts is presented in the appendix of this chapter. In Fig. 8.1, the nominal-income growth rate is initially sharply increased as government employment is rapidly increased after time z. Rapid growth is continued as private production of government goods is increased more rapidly than investment production falls. This rapid growth in nominal income is reflected in a below steady-state growth rate of fluidity. As investment is further reduced, the growth rate of nominal income falls below the steady-state growth rate in a catch-up period during which actual nominal income falls back to its steady-state level. Figure 8.2 shows the same pattern occurring for real income on the assumption that the adjustment process occurs sufficiently rapidly that effects on the price level are negligible. If this were not so, the temporary increase in actual relative to steady-state nominal income would be reflected in similar temporary increases in *both* real income and the price level.

The adjustment process reflects the interaction of a large number of behavioral responses to the unexpected change in real government spending. A formal analysis of these interactions for a short period will be discussed in Chap. 11 using the IS-LM model developed there.

---

[6] Here we are closest to the result of the simple multiplier analysis.

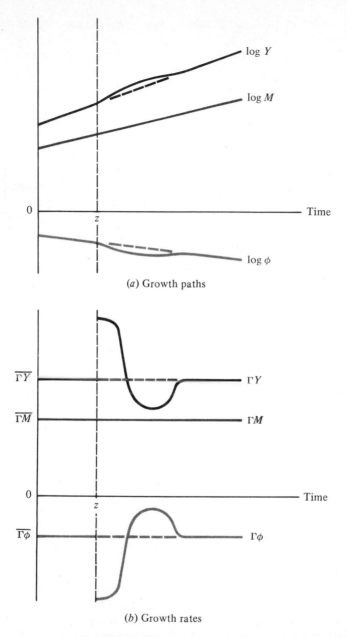

(a) Growth paths

(b) Growth rates

Figure 8.1 Adjustment of fluidity and nominal income to increased real government spending. An unexpected increase in real government spending at time z causes actual nominal income to grow faster than steady-state nominal income for a while and then fall back during a catch-up period. This pattern is precisely reversed for fluidity. In the case illustrated here the long-run effects on the steady-state growth paths are assumed negligible. It is debatable whether the peak increase in actual relative to steady-state nominal income is somewhat greater than the dollar increase in nominal government spending (multiplier effect) or less than that amount (partial crowding out).

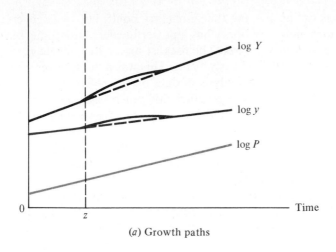

(*a*) Growth paths

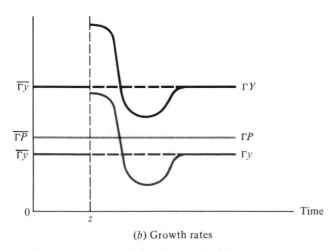

(*b*) Growth rates

Figure 8.2 Adjustment of real income to increased real government spending. On the assumptions that the effects both on steady-state growth paths and on the actual growth path of the price level are negligible, the bulge in nominal income (reproduced from Fig. 8.1) is all due to a bulge in real income. Thus the pattern of an initially high growth rate followed by a below-steady-state growth rate is identical for both nominal and real income. A small transitory bulge in the price level probably occurs but most of the adjustment process is reflected in real income.

EMPIRICAL EVIDENCE ON THE ADJUSTMENT PROCESS

Until recently, there was a wide divergence of opinion about the effects of fiscal and monetary policy on nominal income. *Fiscalists* generally argued that changes in government spending—and taxation as discussed in Sec. 8.3—have large multiplier effects on income, but that monetary policy has weak effects. *Monetarists* argued that monetary policy has a powerful effect on income, but that fiscal policy is comparatively weak. The fiscalist-monetarist debate raged hot and heavy during the 1960s and early 1970s. This was a debate over what the real world is like; so statistical analysis of data on the U.S. economy has now pretty much ended it. At least there is sufficiently general agreement on the size of the effects that the remaining differences do not suggest qualitatively different views of the macroeconomy.

There are always problems in using historical as opposed to experimental data for statistical analysis. These problems can be lumped together as spurious correlation and direction of causation.

Spurious correlation arises when two variables display similar movements not because of the effects of one on the other, but because of the effects on both of a third variable not considered in the analysis. There are statistical techniques for estimating the effects of one variable on another in the presence of influences from other variables, but they work only if the other variables are correctly identified. The remaining areas of debate arise primarily from disagreement over exactly which other variables to control for.

Statistical analysis cannot tell us which of two related variables is the cause and which is the effect, or whether each has effects on the other. Three approaches have been used to try to pin down the direction of causality: (1) a historical analysis of the exact causality of particular changes in monetary and fiscal policy, (2) tests of relationships for long periods and different countries so that widely different institutions determine monetary and fiscal policy, and (3) statistical analysis of timing relationships between policy changes and nominal income changes.

Analyses using a wide variety of techniques arrive at qualitatively similar results on the magnitude and timing of the effects of fiscal and monetary policy.[7] The timing and substantial size of the effects of monetary policy have been previously discussed in Chaps. 6 and 7, while the effects of changes in taxes will be discussed in Sec. 8.3. So the current discussion can be restricted to the effects of changes in government spending, even though the statistical esti-

---

[7] Some of the most important of recent empirical studies are Leonall C. Andersen and Jerry L. Jordan, Monetary and Fiscal Actions: A Test of Their Relative Importance in Economic Stabilization, *Federal Reserve Bank of St. Louis Review*, **50**(11): 11–24, Nov. 1968; see also comment and reply on this paper in the same *Review*, **51**(4): 6–16, Apr. 1969; Michael W. Keran, Monetary and Fiscal Influences on Economic Activity: The Historical Evidence, *Federal Reserve Bank of St. Louis Review*, **51**(11): 5–24, Nov. 1969; Michael W. Keran, Monetary and Fiscal Influences on Economic Activity: The Foreign Experience, *Federal Reserve Bank of St. Louis Review*, **52**(2): 16–28, Feb. 1970; E. Gerald Corrigan, The Measurement and Importance of Fiscal Policy Changes, *Federal Reserve Bank of New York Monthly Review*, **52**(6): 133–145, June 1970; Christopher A. Sims, Money, Income, and Causality, *American Economic Review*, **62**: 540–552, Sept. 1972; and Peter Schmidt and Roger N. Waud, The Almon Lag Technique and the Monetary Versus Fiscal Policy Debate, *Journal of the American Statistical Association*, **68**: 11–19, Mar. 1973; Franco Modigliani and Albert Ando, "Impacts of Fiscal Actions on Aggregate Income and the Monetarist Controversy: Theory and Evidence," in Jerome L. Stein, ed., *Monetarism*, Studies in Monetary Economics, vol. 1, Amsterdam: North-Holland Publishing Co., 1976; Ettore F. Infante and Jerome L. Stein, Does Fiscal Policy Matter? *Journal of Monetary Economics*, **2**: 473–500, Nov. 1976; and Benjamin M. Friedman, Even the St. Louis Model Now Believes in Fiscal Policy, *Journal of Money, Credit, and Banking*, **9**: 365–367, May 1977.

mation of the effects of monetary and fiscal policy must be performed simultaneously.

The effects on nominal and real income of an increase in government expenditures apparently build up over a period of 6 months to a year or so. At their peak, nominal income is increased about 1 dollar per dollar of increase in nominal government expenditures. But the evidence is consistent with anything from mild partial crowding out (say only a $0.60 increase in Y per $1 increase in G) to a small multiplier effect (as much as a $1.50 increase in Y per $1 increase in G). Similar statements apply to real income and real government expenditures measured in base-year dollars.

After this peak is passed, the effects of increased government spending on income wear off about as rapidly as they build up—aside from any long-run steady-state effects. That is, the entire adjustment process is essentially complete 1 to 2 years after government spending is increased.

As discussed above, there is no general agreement on whether the increased government spending financed by borrowing significantly reduces total investment, capital, and real income in the long run. If it does, this would imply higher interest rates, lower fluidity, and higher nominal income in the steady state. These effects are presumably small relative to those found for the adjustment process, but there is little empirical evidence one way or the other.

EFFECTS OF A DECREASE IN GOVERNMENT SPENDING

An unexpected decrease in the level of government spending and borrowing has effects opposite to those of an increase. Since the shock comes from government spending being less than anticipated, even a small increase in government spending counts as a decrease relative to the amount expected.

In the long run, private expenditures will rise in whole or in part to offset the decrease in government expenditures. But in the short run lower government expenditures will fall faster than private expenditures rise, and private expenditures may even fall at some time during the adjustment process. Generally, the unexpected decrease in government spending will cause a temporary fall in the level of nominal and real income relative to the previous steady state. In the long run, there may be no noticeable effect on nominal income, real income, the price level, and fluidity, or there may be permanent downward parallel shifts in the growth paths of nominal income and the price level and permanent upward parallel shifts in the growth paths of real income and fluidity.

REVERSAL OF CHANGES IN GOVERNMENT SPENDING

Our analysis of changes in real government spending has been on the assumption that the changes are a permanent change in level—that is, that the growth path of real government spending is permanently shifted up or down. This assumption is questionable in view of the discussion in Sec. 8.1, which related the level of government expenditures to the desires of the electorate.

An alternative characterization of government-spending shocks would be to suppose that the unexpected changes in spending are gradually offset as time passes. On this view fiscal policy can temporarily speed up or slow down increases in real government spending, without affecting the long-term trend. If the offset to the original changes in the level of government spending occurs in a gradual and predictable fashion, the short-run (adjustment process) effects will be negligible. Further any steady-state effects of the original change will be eliminated when the offset is complete.

The empirical analyses discussed above have not been formulated to distinguish between these alternative characterizations of changes in real government spending. This would be very difficult to do with the available data, and the estimated adjustment process may reflect some gradual offset of unexpected changes in real government spending.

INFLUENCE OF THE BUSINESS CYCLE

The effects of changes in government spending financed by borrowing were highlighted by comparison with a steady-state equilibrium, which the economy would otherwise follow. At times real government spending might be increased to move actual real income temporarily above steady-state real income—for example, just before an election. But advocates of fiscal policy would argue that the proper use of increased government spending is to speed recovery from a recession.[8] Questions arise about whether the effects of increased real government spending depend on the nature and severity of the recession and whether the effects are desirable.

Robert Clower and Axel Leijonhufvud have argued that during sufficiently severe recessions the effects of changes in government spending are larger than in more normal times. This is based on a belief that consumption becomes more responsive to changes in income during depressions or severe recessions.[9] This may be the case, but there is little empirical evidence one way or the other. In any case, this does not appear to be a significant problem for the relatively mild cyclical fluctuations observed in the United States since World War II.

The main effects of increased real government spending are fast acting and temporary. These are very desirable features in terms of eliminating a recession. If the unexpected increase in real government spending were properly timed, it would increase the growth rate of real income when it would otherwise decline.

---

[8] Chapter 15 discusses some of the problems in actually increasing real government spending before the recession is over. Here we are concerned with the effects of such a policy, not with its feasibility.

[9] Their argument is motivated by the idea that a depression will exhaust many consumers' buffer stocks of liquid assets so that they must reduce their expenditures dollar for dollar with reductions in income. For details, see Axel Leijonhufvud, Effective Demand Failures, *Swedish Journal of Economics*, **75**: 27–48, Mar. 1973.

Later the declining effects of the increase on real income would be offset by normal recovery of the economy. So unexpected increases in real government spending could fill in what would otherwise be a gap between actual and steady-state real income. This feature makes changes in real government spending a potentially valuable tool to stabilize the economy.

SUMMING UP

Unexpected borrowing-financed changes in the level of government spending cause movements in income in the same direction. The main effects on income are relatively short-lived: they build up and then wear off over a period of a year or two. The peak effect is on the order of a $0.60 to $1.50 (or base-year dollar) increase in income for each dollar (base-year dollar) increase in government spending. Some economists believe that there is a substantial effect on the steady state because higher levels of government spending reduce total private and government investment. If so, there would be downward shifts in steady-state fluidity and real income and upward shifts in nominal income and the price level. However, the change in fiscal policy might well be reversed before any such steady-state effects became important.

8.3   EFFECTS OF CHANGES IN TAXATION

CHANGES IN TAXATION

We now turn to the other tool of fiscal policy—changes in taxation. As with changes in government spending and monetary policy, we assume that changes in taxes are offset by equal changes in borrowing so that the government budget identity holds. That is, reductions in taxes are financed by equal increases in borrowing, and increases in taxes finance equal reductions in borrowing. So here we take real government spending and money supply growth as givens and ask what are the effects of alternative mixes of taxation and borrowing.[10]

---

[10] Effects on the price level could in principle change the total amount to be financed by taxes and borrowing. We have given the real level of government spending g and the rate of change of nominal base money ΔB. So the amount to be financed by real taxes t and by deflated nominal borrowing $\Delta D/P$ is

$$g - \frac{\Delta B}{P} \equiv t + \frac{\Delta D}{P}$$

Thus any effects of taxation on the price level will affect the amount which must be borrowed. These price-level effects appear to be empirically negligible and are not considered further. The term *deflated nominal borrowing* is used because the rate of change in the real debt (real borrowing Δd) is reduced if inflation is positive ($\Delta d = \Delta D/P - \Gamma P \cdot d$), as discussed in footnote 3 above.

As with government spending changes, the effects of a tax reduction may depend on just what taxes are reduced or transfer payments increased.[11] The details of alternative mixes of taxes and transfers to achieve a given net level of taxes must be left to specialized courses in public finance. We consider here a typical general tax change reflecting such changes in individual taxes and transfers as might normally occur. A tax reduction is first considered in detail.

MAJOR CHANNELS FOR TAX-REDUCTION EFFECTS

The effect of a tax reduction on consumer expenditures is generally supposed to be the main channel by which tax changes influence the macroeconomy. A simple multiplier analysis, for example, would argue that ,a tax reduction increases consumer spending for any given level of real income y. This is because real consumer expenditures c are supposed to be an increasing function of real (net after-tax) private income $y_N = y - t$. This increase in c would imply a multiplied increase in $y = c + i + g$ in the multiplier analysis. As with changes in government expenditures, the simple multiplier analysis is seriously incomplete. But the key first step in a more sophisticated analysis is that the tax reduction increases real private income for any given real income, and this increases consumer expenditures. The size of this first step is a source of considerable controversy. It is examined in detail below.

A second channel through which the tax reduction might influence the macroeconomy is the demand for money. The idea is that the amount of money which the public will want to hold depends on private income and private wealth. If so, a tax reduction will increase the real quantity of money demanded for any given real income and nominal interest rate because the tax reduction increases private income. The importance of this channel is subject to dispute as well.

A final channel of influence on the macroeconomy is through incentive effects on the labor supply and aggregate production function. The idea is that taxation of income and output leads workers to work less and to consume more (untaxed) leisure and firms to produce less efficiently. So a tax reduction would reduce this deadweight loss and shift the growth path of real income upwards. The theory is well established in public finance, but macroeconomists have generally neglected this incentive effect on the grounds that the feasible variations in taxes for *fiscal policy purposes* are too small to significantly shift real income. That tradition is followed here, but recent wide swings in the government deficit and lack of empirical evidence suggest that it be followed with some caution.

---

[11] Remember from Chap. 2 that our concept of taxes is gross taxes *less* government transfer and interest payments.

THE CONSUMER-EXPENDITURE EFFECT

If data over a long period of time are examined, consumer expenditures appear to be proportional to real net private income. This long-run relation was expressed in Chap. 5 by the assumption that saving is a constant fraction σ of real private income.[12] Since real saving plus real consumer expenditures equal real private income, this long-run relation can be expressed as: Real consumer expenditures are a constant fraction $1 - \sigma$ of real private income. The long-run value of σ is about 0.1, so the long-run effect of a $R\$1$ billion increase in private income would be to increase real consumer expenditures by $R\$0.9$ billion. It is generally agreed that a $R\$1$ billion tax reduction will increase consumer expenditures by less than $R\$0.9$ billion, but there the agreement ends. Some economists argue that a $R\$1$ billion tax reduction (particularly a temporary one) would have no significant effect on consumer expenditures. Others estimate effects upward to a $R\$0.9$ billion increase in consumer expenditures.

One area of dispute is the differential effects of changes in permanent and transitory income.[13] Permanent income y_P was defined in Chap. 3 as the normal real private income to be expected from the current real wealth. Transitory income y_T equals actual real private income less permanent income. Transitory income measures the rate at which current windfalls—for good or ill—are changing wealth. In data for a long period, the movement of actual real private income is dominated by the steady-state growth of permanent income. The simple proportional relation reflects the effects of permanent income[14] on consumer expenditures. But changes in transitory income are important in the case of a tax reduction.

Some economists argued that the distinction between permanent and transitory income was unimportant because permanent income adapted to actual real net private income so rapidly that over a year's time they were practically identical. The statistical evidence offered in support of this position has been shown to be strongly biased by an inconsistency between the theory and the data used. Corrected estimates indicate a rather small effect of transitory income on permanent income. Further, each $R\$1$ billion change in transitory income induces about a $R\$0.4$ billion change in consumer expenditures.[15] Thus transitory income increases have about half the effect of permanent income increases on consumer expenditures. The bulk of the effect of transitory income on consumer expenditures is due to changes in expenditures on durable goods. Purchases of consumers' durable goods are a form of saving as viewed by the consumers, although not by our national income accountants.

---

[12] The government sector is compressed into the private sector in the simple neoclassical growth model, so there was no distinction between real income and real private income in Chap. 5.

[13] A formal short-run consumer-expenditure function will be discussed in Chap. 10.

[14] And factors which grow with permanent income as seen in Chap. 10.

[15] See Michael R. Darby, The Permanent Income Theory of Consumption—A Restatement, *Quarterly Journal of Economics*, **88:** 228–250, May 1974; and Michael R. Darby, Postwar U.S. Consumption, Consumer Expenditures, and Saving, *American Economic Review*, **65:** 217–222, May 1975.

These estimates suggest that an unexpected tax reduction would initially increase real consumer expenditures by R$0.4 billion. This amount would gradually increase to R$0.9 billion as the tax reduction came to be fully reflected in permanent income.

The basic conception of a permanent tax reduction financed by a permanent increase in borrowing is unacceptable to many economists. They would argue that this has undesirable long-run properties and has not been observed historically. The only relevant tax reduction for fiscal policy purposes is a temporary one which would have a smaller effect.

A few economists would take this argument one step farther. They would argue that future gross taxes must be increased to pay the higher interest payments implied by increased government borrowing. Because the increased borrowing equals the present value of future taxes, consumers will see that they are really no better off and so not increase their consumption. But if consumers viewed the purchase of durable goods as one way to save, then consumer expenditures would still increase. The distinction between *consumption* (the use of goods and services) and consumer expenditures (the purchase of goods and services) suggests that consumer expenditures will be increased by a tax reduction even if consumers fully anticipate future tax increases.

In sum, an unexpected tax reduction apparently increases consumer expenditures for a given real income by about one-third to one-half the amount of the tax reduction. The remainder of the tax reduction would be reflected in increased saving as illustrated in Example 8.1. This induced increase in consumer expenditures—and government borrowing relative to saving—is analogous to an equal increase in government spending financed by borrowing.

EXAMPLE 8.1

INCREASE IN CONSUMER EXPENDITURES AND BORROWING RELATIVE TO SAVING DUE TO A TAX REDUCTION

Suppose that consumer expenditures are increased by 40¢ per dollar of tax reduction. Suppose also that before a tax reduction, real taxes were R$300 billion per annum, consumer expenditures were R$900 billion per annum, and saving was R$100 billion per annum. So real (net after-tax) private income was

$$y_N = c + s = \frac{R\$900 \text{ billion}}{\text{year}} + \frac{R\$100 \text{ billion}}{\text{year}} = \frac{R\$1{,}000 \text{ billion}}{\text{year}}$$

Real income was similarly

$$y = y_N + t = \frac{R\$1{,}000 \text{ billion}}{\text{year}} + \frac{R\$300 \text{ billion}}{\text{year}} = \frac{R\$1{,}300 \text{ billion}}{\text{year}}$$

If taxes were reduced by 10 percent or R$30 billion per annum and real income did not change, then consumer expenditures would increase by

$$0.4 \frac{R\$30 \text{ billion}}{\text{year}} = \frac{R\$12 \text{ billion}}{\text{year}}$$

Real net private income would be increased by R$30 billion per annum to R$1030 billion per annum. So saving would be increased to

$$\frac{R\$1,030 \text{ billion}}{\text{year}} - \frac{R\$912 \text{ billion}}{\text{year}} = \frac{R\$118 \text{ billion}}{\text{year}}$$

This saving increase of R$18 billion per annum would finance purchase of R$18 billion per annum in additional issues of government bonds. This leaves a net increase in government borrowing over saving of R$12 billion per annum, which is the amount of the increase in consumer expenditures. Either real investment and net exports must fall by this amount (complete crowding out) or else real income must rise in order for the national income accounting identities to hold.

EFFECTS ON MONEY DEMAND

Unlike increased government spending financed by borrowing, a tax reduction may increase the quantity of money demanded even without any increase in real income. This occurs if real private income is a determinant of the demand for money. The resulting tendency for fluidity to rise implies a fall in nominal income which works in the opposite direction from the increase in consumer expenditures.

The money-demand effect of a tax reduction was overlooked until recently.[16] Both real private income and real income have been used successfully in statistical studies. There is not yet any real evidence on whether one, the other, or both income concepts are properly included in money-demand functions. Economists who emphasize the transactions demand for money include only real income—as the better estimate of the work to be done by money. Economists who view money in part as a store of value would expect real private income to play a role in the demand for money.

---

[16] The first published analysis appears to be James M. Holmes and David J. Smyth, The Specification of the Demand for Money and the Tax Multiplier, *Journal of Political Economy*, **80**: 179–185, Jan./Feb. 1972. A formal analysis is the subject of Exercise 12.3 below.

THE ADJUSTMENT PROCESS

The traditional analysis of a tax reduction financed by borrowing is that the effects are identical to a smaller increase in government spending financed by borrowing. Empirical evidence to support the theoretical (or any other) effects is slim.[17] Three explanations suggest themselves: (1) Historically, tax reductions financed by borrowing have been fairly small except during wars. The effects on nominal and real income would be even smaller and quite hard to detect in the data. So while tax reductions (or increases) work as they are supposed to, they have never really been tried. (2) Consumers expect that a tax reduction will be succeeded by a tax increase and do not increase their purchases of consumers' durable goods as they normally do when transitory income is increased. So the change in taxes has no effect on any class of expenditures. (3) The stimulative effect of a tax reduction on consumer expenditures is offset by its restrictive money-demand effect. Consumer expenditures are increased, but investment plus net exports falls as rapidly.

SUMMING UP

The effects of unexpected tax changes are quite unsettled. Some economists believe strongly that a tax reduction (or increase) will have identical effects to a government spending increase (decrease) amounting to one-third to one-half as much. Other economists believe equally strongly that tax changes—unlike government spending changes—have no effects on nominal and real income. Obviously each group stresses certain theoretical hypotheses and neglects others. One cannot even be sure that the truth lies between the extremes, since the money-demand effect—if important—means that a tax reduction could even reduce nominal and real income.

There is much to be said for an agnostic position—aware of the arguments and awaiting more empirical evidence to decide on the effectiveness of tax changes. The traditional presumption remains that a tax reduction increases nominal and real income during the adjustment process. But even a 10 percent reduction in net federal taxes would increase nominal and real income by no more than 1 percent at the peak and probably considerably less.[18]

BALANCED-BUDGET FISCAL POLICIES

The budget of the federal government is said to be *balanced* if the federal deficit (borrowing plus money creation) is zero. This concept can also be applied to

---

[17] See footnote 7 above for references.

[18] A 10 percent reduction in net federal taxes would be about 1 percent of NNP. If this caused an increase in consumer expenditures equal to $\frac{1}{2}$ percent of NNP and if the peak increase in NNP were as much as twice this amount, this would be a 1 percent increase in NNP. If consumer expenditures increased by only a third of the tax reduction and the peak NNP increase were equal to this amount, we would be talking about a $\frac{1}{3}$ percent peak increase in nominal and real income. This amount might be reduced further by consumer anticipation of future tax increases or by the money-demand effect.

the aggregate of all governments. Fiscal policy which leaves the deficit unchanged—that is, equal changes in government spending and taxes—is called *balanced-budget fiscal policy* whatever the actual level of the deficit.

A balanced-budget increase in real government spending and taxes can be thought of as an increase in government spending financed by increased borrowing and an equal increase in taxes that finances decreased borrowing. Similarly, a balanced-budget decrease in real government spending and taxes consists of a decrease in government spending that finances decreased borrowing and of an equal decrease in taxes financed by increased borrowing. The effects are therefore obtained by combining the previous analyses of unexpected changes in real government expenditures and taxes.

In the traditional view, the impulse from the increased (decreased) real government expenditures is lessened by a third to a half by the offsetting decrease (increase) in real consumer expenditures.[19] The offsetting change in real consumer expenditures is induced by the change in taxes. So the overall effects on nominal and real income of a balanced-budget increase (decrease) in real government expenditures follow the same pattern but are only a half to two-thirds as large as for a borrowing-financed increase (decrease).

Those who do not think that changes in the mix of taxes and borrowing make any difference for nominal and real income would argue that balanced-budget and borrowing-financed changes in real government spending have equal effects on nominal and real income. The actual behavior of the macroeconomy may lie anywhere between these views,[20] but the evidence is still too slender—at least for this author—to guess just where.

SEPARATION OF EFFECTS OF FISCAL AND MONETARY POLICIES

As will be seen in Chap. 13, pure fiscal policy with a constant growth rate in the money supply is actually quite rare. A stimulative fiscal policy is normally combined with a stimulative monetary policy (increased growth rate of the money supply) which finances part of the increased government spending or decreased taxation. The exceptions, though rare, in which only pure fiscal or monetary policy is operative or in which monetary and fiscal policies operate in opposite directions provide the best evidence we have on the separate effects of monetary and fiscal policies.

The usual pattern of reinforcing monetary and fiscal policies has led to an understandable confusion of the *effects* of monetary and fiscal policies. Changes in government spending or taxation are debated in Congress and

---

[19] "Balanced-budget multipliers" of 1 are often derived in introductory courses using the simple multiplier approach. The arithmetic exercise unfortunately tells us little about the real world and is best forgotten.

[20] Actually, if the money-demand effect of a tax change is strong enough, a balanced-budget change in real government spending could have even larger effects on nominal and real income than a borrowing-financed change.

widely publicized. Much less publicity accrues to the Fed's administrative decisions which determine the rate of growth of the money supply. A purely discretionary Fed decision to partially finance an increase in government spending or reduction in taxation by say, increasing the growth rate of the money supply by 3 percentage points may have a much greater effect than the original fiscal policy. If the distinction between the two effects is not kept carefully in mind, it is natural but erroneous to attribute the sum of the effects of monetary and fiscal policies to the much more dramatic change in fiscal policy.

8.4 OTHER POTENTIAL DOMESTIC MACROECONOMIC SHOCKS

SHIFTS IN BEHAVIORAL FUNCTIONS AS A SOURCE OF MACROECONOMIC SHOCKS

So far we have discussed macroeconomic shocks connected with government decisions: changes in the growth rate of the money supply or, more precisely, changes in the growth rate of high-powered money, and changes in the growth paths of government spending and taxation. This section considers macroeconomic shocks which might arise in the private sector of the economy. These shocks would involve sudden changes in the basic behavioral relationships: the money multiplier, the demand for money function, the investment function, the consumer-expenditure function, the aggregate production function, and the supply function for labor. A shift in the first of these would be classified as a monetary shock, in any of the next three as a nonmonetary demand shock, and in the last two as a supply shock.

A change in the value of a behavioral function—for example, a change in the desired quantity of real investment—can reflect changes in the arguments of the function or a change in the function itself. An example of the former sort of change, a *movement along the function*, would be the increase in the desired quantity of real investment which results from a decrease in the interest rate, with the other arguments of the investment function unchanged. An example of the latter sort of change, *a shift in the function*, would be a change in the desired quantity of real investment with *all* the arguments of the investment function unchanged.

A difficulty with this distinction is that one economist's shift in a behavioral function is simply a movement along another economist's more complete behavioral function. Carrying the investment function example a step further, an economist who omits transitory income from his specification (or mathematical description) of the investment function will note a shift in his estimated investment function whenever transitory income changes. Economists who include transitory income in their estimated investment function will call these changes in real investment a movement along the investment function. More generally, as a philosophical matter, stating that there was a shift in one of our behavioral functions is the same thing as saying that there was a movement along the true, complete behavioral function due to a change in an argument of which we are unaware or neglectful because of our ignorance or inability to measure.

From the standpoint of macroeconomic shocks, we are interested in sudden shifts in behavioral functions which occur because of changes in any factor not systematically determined within the macroeconomic model. Much of the current debate among macroeconomists questions whether or not apparent shifts in behavioral functions—particularly the investment function—are due to changes in factors properly determined within the macroeconomic model. Particularly important for decisions about investment in a capital commodity yielding services over many years are expectations of the future real rental rates to be received. If these expectations change only in response to changes in such factors as present and past rental rates on capital, real income, and nominal money supply growth, these apparent shifts in the investment function are induced by macroeconomic shocks and are not themselves sources of macroeconomic shocks. The apparent shifts just pinpoint part of the model requiring more work to explain the details of the way in which, say, monetary and fiscal policy changes affect real income and the price level. If, however, there are important factors affecting expectations which are not given or determined in macroeconomic models, then changes in those factors will be sources of macroeconomic shocks. The only ultimate way to settle this debate is to find a reliable way to measure and explain expectations and see whether or not there are important neglected factors.

We now turn to a discussion of the potential size of shifts in the individual behavioral functions and, where appropriate, the effects of such shifts.

CHANGES IN THE MONEY MULTIPLIER

Nominal money can be written as the product of the money multiplier and nominal base money B:

$$M \equiv \mu B \qquad [8.3]$$

So the growth rate of the nominal money is the sum of the growth rates of the money multiplier and nominal base money

$$\Gamma M \equiv \Gamma \mu + \Gamma B \qquad [8.4]$$

So far in this book we have assumed that the money-multiplier growth rate was some given constant. In that case *changes* in the growth rates of the nominal money and nominal base money are equal. This is a generally good representation of the economy, but there are two important exceptions.[21]

First, the Federal Reserve System can change the fraction of bank deposits which member banks must hold in the form of base money (reserves). In Sec. 3.3 it was noted that increases (decreases) in the reserve-deposit ratio decrease (increase) the money multiplier. Normally banks hold only the amount of reserves which they are required to, so the reserve-deposit ratio changes in lock-step with the required reserve ratio.[22] Fairly small reserve requirement changes can cause large sudden shifts in the nominal-money growth path. The Fed rarely uses such a crude tool. When it does, offsetting changes in nominal base money are simultaneously made to leave the nominal money supply unaffected. The one time that changes in reserve requirements caused an important monetary policy shock occurred between August 1936 and May 1937. During this period, the Board of Governors of the Federal Reserve System used its newly acquired power to set reserve requirements by doubling them in a series of steps. The resulting sharp decline in the growth rate of the money supply as the money multiplier fell was sufficient to stop the recovery from the Great Depression and begin the severe recession of 1937–1938.[23]

Through the 1930s, banking panics were the most important source of macroeconomic shocks. Banking panics started when, through mismanagement or mischance, a major bank went bankrupt. Rumors would spread that other banks which had held deposits in the closed bank would go bankrupt as a result. A *run* on these banks would occur in which depositors would line up demanding their funds in base money. Since banks held only a small fraction of their deposits in reserves of base money, they could pay off their depositors only if they could borrow or buy base money from others on the strength of their loans and investments. In a panic, this was often not possible and the bank would have to close, which threatened other banks in turn.

In Sec. 3.3 we saw that the money multiplier falls when either the cash-deposit or reserve-deposit ratio rises. In a banking panic, the public wants a higher cash-deposit ratio because of doubt about the safety of bank deposits, so that the money multiplier falls. If the central bank does not step in and supply more base money, the money supply must fall as well. This reduction in the money supply is spread over time as banks at first dip into their reserves and

---

[21] There are also two minor exceptions: (1) There are pronounced seasonal movements in the money multiplier primarily due to seasonal variations in the cash-deposit ratio. (2) An increased (decreased) growth rate of nominal base money causes a temporary increase (decrease) in the money multiplier relative to its trend. This is due to unexpected money supply changes being held primarily as deposits, so an unexpected increase in base money decreases the cash-deposit ratio. Both of these exceptions are easily allowed for in the day-to-day conduct of monetary policy by the central bank.

[22] For example, in 1976 excess reserves (that is, actual minus required reserves) averaged $219 million or only 0.6 percent of total reserves.

[23] Because of effects on the demand for money (by altering the ratio of interest rates paid on bank deposits to those on short-term bonds), changes in the money supply achieved through changes in the reserve-deposit ratio will have smaller effects on aggregate demand than would the same changes caused by changes in base money. A thorough analysis of these differential effects must be left to courses in money and banking. Similar changes can be achieved by varying the amount of U.S. Treasury deposits at commercial banks, since they affect required reserves but are not part of the money supply.

the reserve-deposit ratio is temporarily reduced. Later bankers try to liquidate their loans and investments as rapidly as possible to achieve the desired reserve-deposit ratio. In severe panics, banks as a group would suspend payments of deposits in base money to give themselves time to liquidate their loans and investments, and then reopen with reduced deposits (loans would be paid off in, or sold for, deposits) commensurate with their abilities to pay out base money.

As a result of a panic, there would be a very large decrease in the rate of growth of the money supply (which would average a negative number of large size) over a few months. After that, monetary growth would resume. Over a period of some years, doubts about the ability of banks to pay depositors recede, and the money multiplier returns to its original growth path. Although the data are very imprecise for the periods in which panics occurred in the United States, the broad effects are quite clear and are as expected from the discussion in Chaps. 6 and 7. Soon after the start of the panic, nominal income fell sharply in response to the fall in the money supply. The dramatic fall in nominal income affected both real income and the price level, though the effect on real income was apparently considerably smaller when the country was primarily agrarian than it would be today. Real income would recover to its steady-state growth path over the next few years, with slower recoveries in money supply, nominal income, and the price level.[24]

Recurrent episodes of panic and its aftermath no longer occur in the United States or most other industrialized countries. In the United States, bankruptcies of even large banks no longer lead to panics because the Federal Deposit Insurance Corporation was established in 1934. The FDIC nominally insures deposits up to $40,000, but in fact effectively insures all deposits—with rare exceptions—in order to avoid providing large depositors with an incentive to start a run on a bank. Some other countries prevent panics by instructing the central bank to lend freely as an emergency "lender of last resort" so that increases in base money offset decreases in the money multiplier. The Federal Reserve Act of 1913 which established the Federal Reserve System instructed our central bank to do the same, but it nevertheless failed to do so in the banking panics of 1930, 1931, and 1933. As a result of the unreliability of the Fed, Congress established the FDIC.

Sudden changes in the money multiplier other than those due to changes in Fed policy are no longer a major source of macroeconomic shocks.

CHANGES IN THE DEMAND FOR MONEY

The steady-state growth path of fluidity reflects the growth of real income, of communications and payment technology, and of substitutes for the use of money. However a radical technological or institutional innovation can cause a

---

[24] In practice, this process was speeded by increases in the stock of base money under the international gold standard then operative. International complications are discussed in Chap. 9.

sudden change in the steady-state growth path of fluidity. For example, in 1975 and 1976 a series of new laws, regulations, and court rulings greatly expanded the ability of individuals and firms to use explicitly interest-bearing time deposits at commercial banks as transactions balances.[25] This avoids the difficulty of roundabout implicit interest payments on demand deposits. As a result the demand for money on the M_1 (currency plus demand deposits) fell considerably as some billions of dollars in transactions balances were reclassified from demand to time deposits. At the same time the demand for money on the M_2 (M_1 plus time deposits) definition was probably somewhat increased since elimination of waste involved in implicit interest payments increases the net interest on deposits in terms of value to the customer.[26]

Suppose that the Fed had maintained a constant growth rate of the nominal money supply defined as M_1 despite the downward shift in the demand for money so defined. This would build up excess money balances similarly to an unexpected increase in the nominal-money-supply growth rate as analyzed in Chaps. 6 and 7. Desired fluidity changes in proportion to the real quantity of money demanded for a given real income. So shifts in the money-demand function can be interpreted as changing the steady-state growth path of fluidity with the same effects as a change in the growth path of the nominal money supply of the same size but opposite sign.

The 1975–1976 experience is the exception that proves the rule. During the preceding 25 years the rapid growth of savings and loan associations and the spread of credit cards reduced the steady-state growth rate of fluidity. The trend growth rate of fluidity was much lower than it was before World War II. The trend growth rate of fluidity was remarkably steady within this period, however.

Although sudden changes in the steady-state growth rate of fluidity may be an occasional source of macroeconomic disturbances, they are exceptional. For long periods of time no such major technological or institutional innovations occur, and changes in the steady-state growth rate of fluidity are negligible.

CHANGES IN INVESTMENT DEMAND

Keynesian economists traditionally have argued that investment demand is very unstable because the expectations of businessmen about future returns from investment are very fragile and unstable. If there is a general feeling of

---

[25] Most publicity has been given to the NOW (negotiable order of withdrawal) accounts which pay explicit interest on a checkable account. NOW accounts are limited to a few states, however. Much more important in dollar terms are rulings which (1) permit commercial banks to transfer funds between checking and saving accounts upon telephone order from the customer and (2) permit business saving accounts up to $150,000. So a business (or individual) can now deposit its receipts into its explicitly interest-paying saving account and transfer funds to its checking account only as checks are written.

[26] At the same time, a reduction in market interest rates relative to the (unchanged) maximum payable on savings accounts induced a switch from large marketable certificates of deposit (CDs), which are excluded from M_1 and M_2, into savings accounts, which are included in M_2. Offsetting this in part was the grant of permission to mutual savings banks to issue NOW accounts. See Jean M. Lovati, The Growing Similarity among Financial Institutions, *Federal Reserve Bank of St. Louis Review*, **59**(10): 2–11, Oct. 1977.

optimism in which future prospects are viewed through rose-colored glasses, investment demand will be high. If, conversely, entrepreneurs are generally gloomy, then investment demand will be lower. Sudden "autonomous" shifts in investment demand (financed by borrowing) are equivalent in short-run effect to an equal shift in real government spending financed by borrowing. The steady-state effects are ultimately nil as expectations must eventually adjust to the real rate of return which can be earned. But a wave of optimism, like an unexpected increase in real government expenditures, would cause a temporary increase in nominal and real income relative to their steady-state growth paths.

One of the major questions in macroeconomics is whether substantial shifts in expectations occur frequently because of unexplainable changes in mood, or whether such changes in expectations as occur are due to other macroeconomic shocks. If the changes in expectations are truly autonomous, then the observed large cyclical variation in real investment would be a *cause* of business cycles. If, instead, expectations change because of other macroeconomic shocks, then the cyclical variation in real investment is simply part of the transmission—a symptom—of the basic causes of business cycles. There is no clear consensus yet on the empirical importance of autonomous shifts in investment demand. The strongest negative evidence is similar to Sherlock Holmes's clue of the dog that did not bark.[27] That is, there seems to be no period in which investment demand shifts in the absence of other macroeconomic shocks, as seen for example in Chap. 13.

CHANGES IN OTHER BEHAVIORAL FUNCTIONS

The aggregate production function, the supply function of labor, and the consumer expenditure function do not appear to be important sources of macroeconomic shocks in the United States.[28]

The aggregate production function could significantly vary from year to year in a small agricultural country. Those complications due to the random effects of weather can be safely neglected when averaged over the United States as a whole. For certain states, weather conditions may nevertheless have a greater influence in determining state real income than moderate monetary and fiscal policy actions. Major strikes—such as in the automobile or steel industry—have noticeable but very short-lived effects on nominal and real income. Changes in the terms on which exports can be traded for imports (really an international shock) are treated by some authors as a shift in the aggregate production function. Except for small, specialized countries these terms-of-trade changes tend to be small with negligible effects.

Though expected nominal wages enter the short-run labor-supply function, there is no suggestion that these expectations are determined by anything other

---

[27] If a stranger was prowling about at night, why did the dog not bark?
[28] Minor exceptions to this statement will be noted in Chap. 13.

than present and past conditions. Changes in the trend growth rate of the labor supply occur much too gradually to count as a macroeconomic shock.

The consumer-expenditure function was originally difficult for economists to describe well. Steady work over the last 40 years has culminated in recent advances which leave little room for any significant shifts in the consumer-expenditure function.

SUMMARY OF BEHAVIORAL SHIFTS
AS SOURCES OF MACROECONOMIC SHOCKS

There are only three behavioral functions which have been—at least arguably—significant sources of macroeconomic shocks: (1) the money multiplier, (2) the money-demand function, and (3) the investment function. The money multiplier was formerly a major source of shocks because of the instability of the fractional reserve banking system, but the FDIC changed all that. Now sudden changes in the money multiplier reflect Fed policy actions. There appear to be rare changes in the steady-state growth path of fluidity. Changes in the money multiplier and in the demand for money operate in a manner closely analogous to changes in high-powered money, which are offset by changes in government borrowing. However, decreases in the demand for money have effects on aggregate demand which are equivalent to those caused by increases in the supply of money. Changes in the investment function due to random changes in expectations would have short-run effects on aggregate demand equivalent to a temporary change in government spending and borrowing. An increase in investment demand increases investment, however, while an increase in government spending decreases investment.

With the exception of policy effects on the money multiplier, we are discussing shocks due to random or unknown causes. The only effective way to get an idea of the relative importance of such shocks is to examine the empirical record, as in Chap. 13.

SUMMARY

1 Macroeconomic shocks can be classified as demand or supply shocks. Demand shocks are described as monetary or nonmonetary and as policy or behavioral (autonomous).

2 Fiscal policy determines the level of government spending and taxes for a given nominal-money-supply growth rate. Real government spending and taxes have trend growth paths determined by the tastes, income, and institutions of the society. Fiscal policy can alter—at least temporarily—the actual levels of spending and taxes around these trend growth paths.

3 A borrowing-financed increase in real government spending does not affect the steady-state equilibrium unless total government and private investment is reduced relative to income. If the total investment-income ratio is reduced, the tendency is for the growth paths of real income and fluidity to shift down and of nominal income and the price level to shift up.

4 Increased government expenditures may cause decreases in private expenditures. This crowding out is expressed in both nominal and real terms and may be complete or partial.

5 During the adjustment to an unexpected increase in real government expenditures, actual nominal and real income temporarily rise relative to their steady-state values. At the peak, private spending appears to be little if any decreased and—on some estimates—is increased. During the catch-up period, nominal and real income fall back to their (possibly shifted) steady-state growth paths. Unexpected decreases in real government spending have the opposite effects.

6 A borrowing-financed tax reduction acts to increase consumer spending by a third to a half of the amount of the reduction. Tax reductions are traditionally analyzed as having about the same effects as a government expenditure increase about a third or half as large. The lack of much empirical confirmation of these effects can be explained by the small size of tax changes which have occurred, by the reluctance of consumers to change their expenditures for a temporary tax cut, and by a neglected offsetting change in money demand.

7 A balanced-budget increase in government spending and taxes is traditionally expected to have a somewhat smaller effect than an equal borrowing-financed increase in government spending.

8 Macroeconomic shocks due to shifts in behavioral functions have been concentrated in the money multiplier, demand-for-money function, and investment function. Whether or not shifts in the investment function are a major cause of business cycles is the subject of a continuing debate.

CONCEPTS TO KNOW

autonomous demand shock	monetary shock
balanced budget	nominal crowding out
balanced-budget fiscal policy	nonmonetary demand shock
behavioral demand shock	policy demand shock
debt policy	real crowding out
demand shock	run on a bank
fiscal policy	supply shock
government deficit	

QUESTIONS AND EXERCISES

1 Why does the government budget identity include the *levels* of government spending and taxes and the *rates of change* of base money and government debt?

*2 If nominal income is increased by 80 percent of an increase in government spending 6 months after the beginning of a pure fiscal policy, and at that time federal government spending is $110 billion instead of the $100 billion that it would have been otherwise, how much will nominal income be if it would have been $1,000 billion in the absence of the policy? This is a _____ percent increase in government spending and a _____ percent increase in nominal income.

3 How would the federal government temporarily increase its real spending on *goods and services* by 10 percent over what it would otherwise have been? How much time do you think that it would take to get these programs started? Does it seem sensible to shift resources into producing these goods and services and then a year or two later to stop buying these goods and services?

*4 Why would we expect the effect of a tax decrease financed by borrowing to have smaller effects on nominal income than an equal increase in government spending and borrowing?

5 Why might the increase in private income associated with a tax cut financed by borrowing increase the demand for money in the short run? In the long run?

6 For much of its existence, Federal Reserve policy was couched in terms of maintaining a certain interest rate on short-term securities until a new interest rate was chosen. This was done by buying back government bonds (issued by the Treasury) with new high-powered money if the interest rate rose above target and selling government bonds and so withdrawing high-powered money if the interest rate fell below target. What would this policy do to growth of the money supply if government spending and borrowing were increased? Reduced? (*Hint:* What happens to the interest rate if real government spending is increased with the nominal-money-supply growth rate constant?)

7 Why are gradual shifts in behavioral functions incorporated in the analysis of steady-state equilibrium instead of being treated as macroeconomic shocks?

*8 Banking panics often increased the desired reserve-deposit ratio of bankers, who felt the threat of panics more keenly for some years afterwards. As the actual reserve-deposit ratio was adjusted to the new desired reserve-deposit ratio, what would be the effect on the money multiplier?

9 Detail the process by which an increase in investment demand increases interest rates and nominal income.

REFERENCES FOR FURTHER READING

Andersen, Leonall C., and Jerry L. Jordan: Monetary and Fiscal Actions: A Test of Their Relative Importance in Economic Stabilization, *Federal Reserve Bank of St. Louis Review,* **50** (11): 11–24, Nov. 1968.

Carlson, Keith M., and Roger W. Spencer: Crowding Out and Its Critics, *Federal Reserve Bank of St. Louis Review,* **57** (12): 2–17, Dec. 1975.

Haberler, Gottfried: "Monetary and Real Factors Affecting Economic Stability: A Critique of Certain Tendencies in Modern Economic Theory," as abridged in Robert Aaron Gordon and Lawrence R. Klein (eds.), *Readings in Business Cycles,* Homewood, Ill.: Irwin for the American Economic Association, 1965.

Modigliani, Franco: Long-Run Implications of Alternative Fiscal Policies and the Burden of the National Debt, *Economic Journal,* **71:** 730–755, Dec. 1961.

U.S. Council of Economic Advisers Staff Memorandum: "Financing a Federal Deficit," in Warren L. Smith and Ronald L. Teigen (eds.), *Readings in Money, National Income, and Stabilization Policy,* 3d ed., Homewood, Ill.: Irwin, 1974.

CHAPTER 8, APPENDIX

GOVERNMENT SPENDING EFFECTS ON STEADY-STATE EQUILIBRIUM

If an upward shift in the growth path of real government spending reduces the ratio of total private and government investment to income, the steady state will be changed. As discussed in Sec. 8.2, there will be downward parallel shifts in the growth paths of real income and (except in the case of superneutrality) fluidity and resulting upward shifts in the growth paths of nominal income and the price level. Figures 8.3 and 8.4 illustrate these effects for a borrowing-financed increase in government spending at time z.

Figures 8.5 and 8.6 combine the adjustment process illustrated in Figs. 8.1 and 8.2 with a gradual adjustment to the new steady-state equilibrium which was illustrated in Figs. 8.3 and 8.4. The change in the total investment-income ratio only gradually reduces the capital stock relative to its previous growth path. So the whole adjustment period is divided into an early part dominated by the temporary effects and a later part dominated by slow movement toward the new steady-state equilibrium. Few macroeconomists would expect a fiscal policy to be continued so long that the new steady state would be reached.

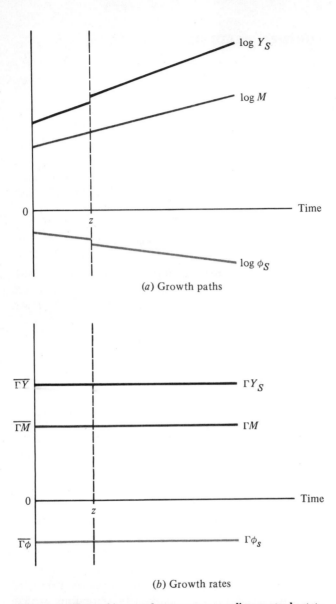

(a) Growth paths

(b) Growth rates

**Figure 8.3 Effects of increased government spending on steady-state
nominal income and fluidity.** Panel (*a*) illustrates the downward
shift in the growth path of steady-state fluidity ϕ_S due to an
increased level of real and nominal interest rates. The growth path
of the nominal money supply M is unaffected by the increase in
real government spending. In view of the Cambridge identity, the
growth path of steady-state nominal income Y_S must shift up by
the amount of the downward shift in fluidity. The steady-state
growth rates in panel (*b*) are not affected except at the instant z.

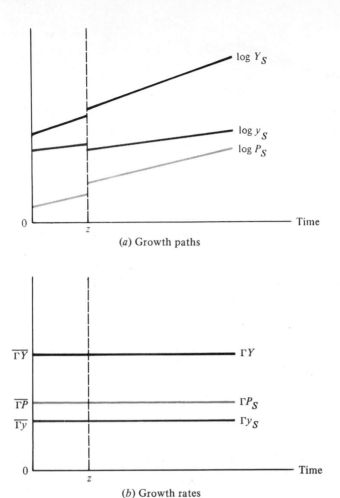

(a) Growth paths

(b) Growth rates

Figure 8.4 Effects of increased real government spending on steady-state income and the price level. Panel (a) reproduces the upward shift in the growth path of steady-state nominal income Y_S from Fig. 8.3. The downward shift in the growth path of steady-state real income is due to the decrease in the total investment-income ratio and to the use of resources in transactions due to reduced real money balances. The definition $\log P \equiv \log Y - \log y$ implies that the growth path of the steady-state price level P_S shifts upward by the amount of the upward shift in $\log Y_S$ plus the downward shift in $\log y_S$. The steady-state growth rates in panel (b) are not affected except at the instant z.

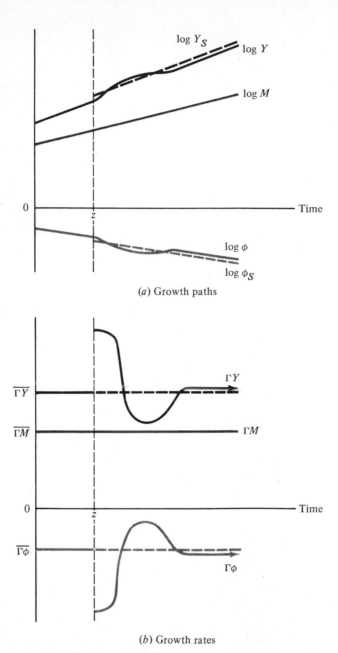

(a) Growth paths

(b) Growth rates

**Figure 8.5 Adjustment of fluidity and nominal income to increased
real government spending with steady-state effects.** This figure
combines the short-run temporary increase in nominal income
(decrease in fluidity) from Fig. 8.1 with a gradual adjustment
toward the new steady-state equilibrium reproduced from Fig. 8.3.
The figure illustrates a rapid short-run adjustment process compared
with the long, gradual adjustment toward the new steady state.

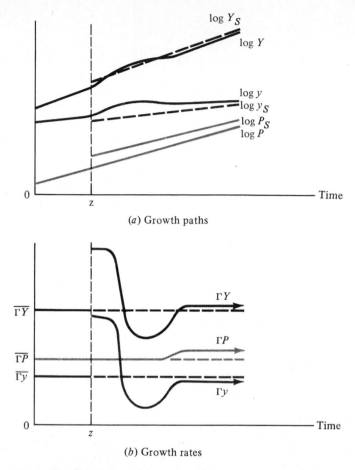

(a) Growth paths

(b) Growth rates

Figure 8.6 Adjustment of real income and the price level to increased real government spending with steady-state effects. The graphs of the nominal-income growth path and growth rate are reproduced from Fig. 8.5. The illustrated growth path and growth rate of real income combines the temporary short-run adjustment process of Fig. 8.2 with a gradual adjustment toward the new steady-state equilibrium. The short-run adjustment process is illustrated as essentially complete before the gradual adjustment toward the upward shifted steady-state price level sets in. As noted previously, some minor price-level movements may in fact occur during the short-run adjustment process.

CHAPTER 9

INTERNATIONAL TRADE AND FINANCIAL ARRANGEMENTS

WHAT YOU WILL LEARN IN THIS CHAPTER
How foreign exchange markets eliminate barter in international trade ● How the exchange rate equates the supply of and demand for dollars in exchange for foreign money ● Alternative exchange rate systems ● Effects of foreign shocks on the domestic economy ● Implications of alternative exchange rate systems for monetary policy

9.1 FOREIGN EXCHANGE MARKETS

Fluctuations in foreign economies are transmitted through international trade and financial arrangements to the domestic economy. There they act as shocks with temporary effects on nominal and real income. Furthermore, certain exchange rate policies greatly limit the freedom of the central bank to carry out monetary policy. For both these reasons, macroeconomists must be concerned with international trade and finance.

WHY DO WE HAVE INTERNATIONAL FINANCIAL ARRANGEMENTS?

The basic function of money is to eliminate barter. This works very well when sellers and buyers are residents of the same country. If commodities are exchanged for money, the most willing buyers can always buy from the most willing sellers, regardless of whether the sellers want to buy what the buyers sell. Sometimes the buyers who value a commodity most and the sellers who can produce it most cheaply are in different countries. Simple monetary exchange is impossible because the buyer's money, say dollars, is not money to the seller and the seller's money, say pounds, is not money to the buyer. So they must either engage in barter or not trade at all.

International financial arrangements arose as a means of extending the benefits of money in eliminating barter to international transactions. This is done by making it possible for buyers to pay in their money and sellers to receive payment in their money. Do international exchange markets actually transform dollar bills into pound notes by some magic process? No, they just make individuals in each country who buy from foreigners pay those who sell to foreigners. This section and the next will discuss the mechanics of this process and how it is that these two totals happen to be equal. When looked at from this point of view, international finance turns out to be not so mysterious as it would appear from romanticized newspaper stories. Although they are not mysterious, the details of international finance are numerous and must be left largely to specialized works.[1] This chapter emphasizes only the key facets for macroeconomic analysis.

TRADE BETWEEN TWO COUNTRIES

Most of the basic principles of international finance are illustrated by a simple world of only two countries trading with each other. This example will serve as an introduction to the discussion of many countries trading in the complicated patterns observed in the real world. The two countries will be called America and Britain and their moneys called dollars ($) and pounds (£), respectively. The exchange rate E between pounds and dollars is £0.40/$; that is, $1 can be purchased with or can purchase £0.40. How this exchange rate is determined will be discussed later.

A British chemical firm wishes to buy a computer and finds that the best combination of characteristics and price is offered by an American-manufactured machine priced at $2,500,000. The British chemical firm would like to make a payment of the equivalent sum in British money, £1,000,000 [$2,500,000 × (£0.40/$)]. The American computer manufacturer would like to receive payment in American money, $2,500,000. The transaction is completed by the chemical firm writing a check for £1,000,000 on its British bank. Either the chemical firm or the computer firm (depending on the sales contracts) pays a tiny commission to sell the £1,000,000 deposit at a British bank for a $2,500,000 deposit at an American bank. The deposit at the American bank is then transferred through the American banking system to the account of the computer firm.

This transaction is all very simple, except that one not-so-minor point was left out: Who sold the $2,500,000 for £1,000,000? Say at the same time an American department store bought £1,000,000 worth of sweaters from a British woolens firm. Just as with the computer sale, each firm would like to exchange goods for its own country's money. Since the moneys are different, $2,500,000 of the department store's bank deposit must be sold for a £1,000,000 British bank deposit which can be transferred to the account of the woolens firm. The

---

[1] Such as the book by H. Robert Heller listed in the references for this chapter.

seller of the $2,500,000 for £1,000,000 is provided by this sweater sale. In effect, the department store pays $2,500,000 to the computer firm, and the chemical firm pays £1,000,000 to the woolens firm.

This offsetting of amounts due to foreigners against amounts due from foreigners is what foreign exchange markets are all about. *Foreign exchange markets* are places where the money of one country is exchanged for the money of other countries. Most exchanges involve transfer of rights to bank deposits, though actual currency is also traded. With modern telegraphic communications, such markets are effectively combined into a single worldwide foreign exchange market. As illustrated in Fig. 9.1, goods and services flow from each country's exporters (sellers) to the other country's importers (buyers). Money flows from each country's importers to its own exporters.

It may be that the value owed American exporters exceeds the value owed by American importers; that is, nominal net exports or the balance of trade is positive. Since the British importers owe the amount due to American exporters and the British exporters are owed the amount due from American importers, British nominal net exports are equal to minus American nominal net exports when converted into the same monetary units by the exchange rate.

In the assumed situation of a positive American balance of trade (or *trade surplus*) and a negative British balance of trade (or *trade deficit*), more dollars appear to be received than paid and fewer pounds paid than received. The

Figure 9.1 International flows of goods and payments. Amounts owed to foreigners are matched with amounts owed by foreigners in the foreign exchange market. This permits payments of dollars to be made from American importers to American exporters and payments of pounds to be made from British importers to British exporters. Commodities are shipped from American exporters to British importers and from British exporters to American importers.

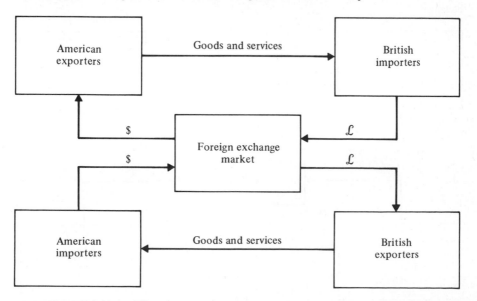

difference arises because an important class of international transactions has been omitted: international capital flows. *International capital flows* refer to the purchase by the residents of one country of securities owned or newly issued by residents of another country. This may be in the form of a long-term loan to finance a sale of real capital goods, such as machines for a new automobile plant, but there is no necessary or usual connection. The term *international securities flows* would be more descriptive, but is not used in the literature. Figure 9.2 illustrates both types of international transactions, the sales of real goods and services and the sales of securities representing rights to future payments. *Net capital outflows, CO,* the value of securities bought less the value of securities sold, must exactly equal net exports for each country. If this is true, the total amount of dollars paid by American buyers will just equal the total amount of dollars received by American sellers. Similarly, the total pounds paid and received by British buyers and sellers will be equal.

An example will illustrate how this works. Suppose that American exporters sell $10 billion (£4 billion) worth of goods and services to British importers, while American importers buy $7.5 billion (£3 billion) worth of goods and services from British exporters. Then America has a trade surplus of $2.5 billion (£1 billion) and Britain has a trade deficit of £1 billion ($2.5 billion). The difference is made up by capital flows in which Americans buy $6 billion (£2.4 billion) worth of British securities while Britons buy £1.4 billion ($3.5 billion) worth of American securities. This is a net capital outflow of $2.5 billion for America and −£1 billion for Britain. These capital outflows

Figure 9.2 International finance of trade and capital flows. Both commodities and securities are traded. Net international capital outflows must exactly equal net exports so that the total value of goods, services, and securities sold exactly equals the total value of goods, services, and securities bought.

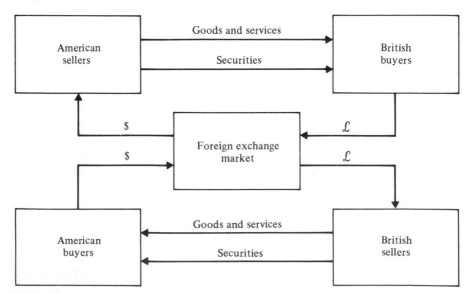

exactly equal net exports in each case. The total dollars offered for pounds by American purchasers of British goods, services, and securities ($7.5 billion + $6 billion = $13.5 billion) exactly equal the total dollars demanded for pounds by American sellers ($10 billion + $3.5 billion = $13.5 billion). The same equality holds for the £5.4 billion offered and demanded.

One wonders how the foreign exchange market equates net exports with net capital outflows. Since foreign exchange transactions always involve a seller and a buyer, the transactions of sellers of dollars for pounds must always equal those of the buyers of dollars for pounds after all is said and done. The question is why people will desire to sell and buy exactly equal amounts. As with the case for the demand and supply of peanut butter or any other commodity, the price will adjust until the amount willingly sold exactly equals the amount willingly bought at the market price. The price in the foreign exchange market is the exchange rate E.

DETERMINANTS OF NOMINAL NET EXPORTS

American nominal net exports are a decreasing function of the exchange rate.[2] This is so because a fall in the exchange rate makes American goods cheaper to the British in terms of pounds while British goods are made more expensive to American buyers in terms of dollars.[3] Such a relation is illustrated in Fig. 9.3. The net export curve has a negative or downward slope to show that net exports are a decreasing function of the exchange rate. The net export curve can be drawn either for short-run changes in the exchange rate or for long-run adjustments to changes in the exchange rate continuing over extended periods of time. Net exports will be more responsive in the long run because this will allow time for the establishment of commercial relationships (for example, automobile dealerships selling foreign cars) and construction of plants in the country with increasing exports and the depreciation of plants in the country with reduced exports.

Among the most important "other things constant" which underlie the nominal net export curve are the levels of prices P and real income y in America and Britain. Foreign prices and real income (here British) will be denoted by a subscript F as P_F and y_F respectively. Nominal net exports can be written in functional form as

$$X = P \cdot x\left(\frac{EP}{P_F}, y, y_F\right)$$

[9.1]

---

[2] British net exports are an increasing function of the exchange rate, but a decreasing function of the British exchange rate defined as the number of dollars per pound ($1/E$).

[3] These facts alone are not enough to unambiguously indicate that nominal net exports will increase with a decrease in the exchange rate. This ambiguity arises because the induced increase in import prices in dollars conceivably could be sufficiently great to offset the fall in the quantity of imports and the rise in the dollar price and quantity of exports. This does not appear to be more than a hypothetical curiosity judging from the actual behavior of nominal net exports.

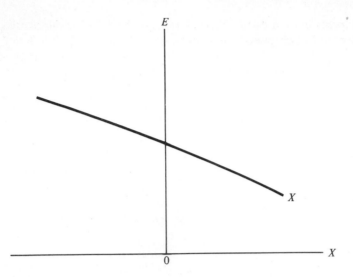

Figure 9.3 Relationship of nominal net exports to the exchange rate. A decrease in the exchange rate (£/$), other things being equal, will increase American nominal net exports because American goods are cheaper to British buyers and British goods are more expensive to American buyers. Similarly, higher exchange rates reduce nominal net exports. The level of nominal net exports will be more responsive to exchange rate changes (that is, the net export curve will be flatter) in the long run, when sellers and buyers have had time to adjust fully, than in the short run.

The function $x(\ )$ determines real net exports measured in base-year dollars per annum. Multiplication by the American price level converts this into the nominal net exports measured in dollars per annum. The discussion in the previous paragraph of the effects of changes in the exchange rate applies to any change in the relative prices of domestic and foreign goods. This is measured more generally by EP/P_F; so $x(\ )$ is a decreasing function of this *purchasing power ratio*. An increase in American real income y will decrease net export demand by increasing domestic demand for foreign goods (imports). An increase in British real income y_F will similarly increase British imports, and British imports are American exports. So real net exports are a decreasing function of American real income and an increasing function of foreign real income.

DETERMINANTS OF NOMINAL NET CAPITAL OUTFLOWS

There is not yet any generally accepted theory of the determination of nominal net capital flows. This may reflect the important role of expectations in the decision to lend or borrow abroad. Besides the usual considerations in any such transaction within a country, questions of political stability and control or expropriation of foreign investments arise in the international arena. Political decisions on trade, tariff, and exchange rate policies can create huge gains or losses on foreign investments. The influence of these unique factors creates a formidable statistical problem, which has not yet been satisfactorily solved. However, a number of factors have been identified which determine nominal net capital outflows for a given state of expectations.

In the steady state, net capital outflows serve to transfer capital from countries with relatively high saving-income ratios to those with lower ratios.[4] This movement of capital tends to equalize the real returns to capital and labor in various countries. For example the real interest rate rises in the high-saving countries and falls in the low-saving countries.[5] The equalization is rarely complete because of the political hazards of investing in foreign countries. This implies a gap (risk premium) between the real interest rate earned at home and the corresponding rate which would be earned abroad if the returns were in fact paid to foreign investors. Each country will have a normal real net capital outflow relative to its real income—positive if it is financing foreign capital accumulation and negative if foreigners finance part of its own capital accumulation. Changes in political risk or national saving-income ratios would alter these steady-state ratios of net capital outflows to income.

Suppose that an American is considering whether to lend abroad or at home. By lending at home, a nominal interest rate R would be earned. If instead the American were to lend abroad, the nominal interest rate earned in terms of dollars would depend not only on the foreign nominal interest rate, but also on changes in the exchange rate. A single-payment foreign loan, for example, involves first exchanging dollars for pounds at the exchange rate and then later exchanging the principal and interest paid in pounds back into dollars. If the exchange rate falls over the term of the loan, one gets more dollars per pound repaid than were paid per pound lent. This increases the effective nominal interest rate in terms of dollars, as illustrated in Example 9.1. Similarly, a rising exchange rate reduces the effective nominal interest rate in terms of dollars. For continuously compounded rates, the effective dollar nominal interest rate on a foreign loan is the difference $R_F - \Gamma E$ between the foreign nominal interest rate and the growth rate of the exchange rate.[6]

---

[4] Generalizing the neoclassical growth model of Chap. 5 to open economies requires advanced mathematics so that only the basic results can be outlined here. References are to James A. Hanson and Phillip A. Neher, The Neoclassical Theorem Once Again: Closed and Open Economies, *American Economic Review*, **57**: 869–879, Sept. 1967; and Phillip A. Neher, *Economic Growth and Development: A Mathematical Introduction*, New York: John Wiley & Sons, 1971, pp. 257–282.

[5] By the more efficient allocation of capital, both foreign investors and local residents of a poor country gain. However, the workers' gains are partially at the expense of the local owners of capital. The latter groups frequently stage "nationalist" campaigns to prevent foreign investment from "exploiting the workers" (by raising their wages!).

[6] Consider a loan of H pounds at a continuously compounded nominal interest rate R_F. The value of this loan in dollars is H/E. The growth rate of H/E is equal to its continuously compounded interest rate. Using the rule on the growth rate of ratios, this is $R_F - \Gamma E$.

EXAMPLE 9.1

DOLLAR RETURNS ON A FOREIGN LOAN

An American lends a Briton £1,000 for 1 year at 10 percent per annum, compounded annually. Suppose that the exchange rate is £0.40/$ when the loan is made and £0.38/$ when it is repaid. The amount of dollars lent is

$$\frac{£1,000}{£0.40/\$} = \$2,500.00$$

The principal and interest repaid is £1,000 × 1.10 = £1,100. When converted back to dollars this is

$$\frac{£1,100}{£0.38/\$} = \$2,894.74$$

In terms of dollars, $2,500.00 was lent and $2,894.74 was repaid. The effective interest receipt is $394.74. The effective dollar nominal interest rate on the loan is computed as

$$\frac{\$394.74}{\$2,500.00} = 0.158$$

or 15.8 percent compounded annually. This is approximately equal to foreign nominal interest rate (10 percent) minus the growth rate of the exchange rate (−5 percent). The equality is exact only if the computations are based on continuously compounded interest and growth rates.

The difference between the nominal interest rate in dollars earned or paid on foreign and on domestic securities is $R_F - \Gamma E - R$. In deciding between domestic and foreign securities, individuals will compare the expected amount of this difference with the risk involved in making the foreign loan. The two nominal interest rates are known at the time the decision is made. But the growth rate of the exchange rate is not known and must be replaced with its expected value ΓE^*.[7] An increase in this difference would induce real net capital outflows to take advantage of the increased foreign yield. The higher is the current exchange rate, other things being equal, the lower is its expected

---

[7] It is often possible to contract to sell or buy foreign money in the future at an agreed exchange rate. These "futures contracts" transfer the burden of predicting future exchange rates to specialists but do not eliminate the basic economic uncertainty.

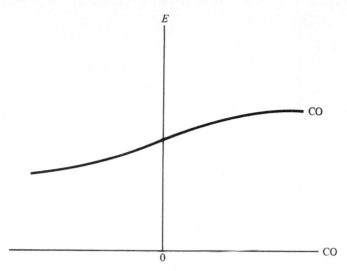

Figure 9.4 Relationship of nominal net capital outflows to the exchange rate. An increase in the exchange rate E, for given expected future exchange rates and domestic and foreign interest rates, makes foreign securities more attractive when they are compared to American securities. This occurs because the expected fall in the exchange rate provides an extra return to foreign securities in terms of dollars.

growth rate. This is because the current exchange rate is increased relative to expectations of its future values. So higher current exchange rates tend to increase $R_F - \Gamma E^* - R$ and therefore increase net capital outflows as illustrated in Fig. 9.4.

EQUILIBRIUM FOR TWO-COUNTRY TRADE

If the dollars willingly offered in exchange for pounds are to equal the dollars demanded in exchange for pounds, the exchange rate must be such that desired nominal net exports equal desired nominal net capital outflows. This occurs at the point of intersection in Fig. 9.5 of the nominal net export and nominal capital outflow curves. At the equilibrium exchange rate $\bar{E}$, the values of desired nominal net exports and nominal net capital outflows are equal at $\overline{X} = \overline{CO}$. In the case illustrated, there is a positive balance of trade (trade surplus) and positive net capital outflows (positive net purchases of foreign securities). In this case, Americans on net find it advantageous to provide some current goods and services to the British in return for claims on future British goods and services. This position could instead be reversed with the British acquiring securities from Americans on net.

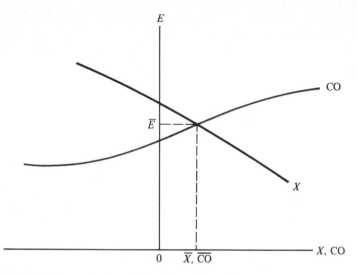

Figure 9.5 Determination of the values of the exchange rate, nominal net exports, and nominal capital outflows. The exchange rate adjusts to equate the desired levels of nominal net exports and nominal net capital outflows. The equilibrium exchange rate is $\bar{E}$ and equilibrium nominal net exports are $\bar{X}$. Equilibrium nominal net capital outflows are $\overline{CO} = \bar{X}$. The value of $\bar{X} = \overline{CO}$ can be positive, zero, or negative in steady-state equilibrium.

In steady-state equilibrium, the actual and expected growth rate of the exchange rate will equal the difference between the foreign and domestic steady-state inflation rates, $\overline{\Gamma P}_F - \overline{\Gamma P}$. This growth rate $\overline{\Gamma E}$ is such that the purchasing power ratio will be constant.[8] Details are left to specialized courses.

TRADE AMONG MANY COUNTRIES

More complex patterns of trade are possible when the number of countries involved is increased beyond two. The reason for this is that the most willing foreign buyers of American goods, services, and securities and the most willing foreign sellers of goods, services, and securities to Americans are not evenly distributed throughout the world. Instead, Americans may buy automobiles from Japan and stock certificates from Brazil and pay for these by selling computers to Britain and wheat to India. Each of these countries will in turn be net buyers from some countries and net sellers to other countries.

---

[8] The purchasing power ratio EP/P_F will grow in the steady state at the rate $\overline{\Gamma E} + \overline{\Gamma P} - \overline{\Gamma P}_F = \overline{\Gamma P}_F - \overline{\Gamma P} + \overline{\Gamma P} - \overline{\Gamma P}_F = 0$.

For each country, however, the foreign exchange market permits such variation so long as the nominal value of net exports to all countries equals the nominal value of net capital outflows to (security purchases from) all countries. This can be alternatively stated as requiring only that the value of all sales to foreigners of goods, services, and securities equal the value of all purchases from foreigners of goods, services, and securities. This is because total sales of each money must equal total purchases, but it is not necessary that total sales of each money equal total purchases in exchange for each of the other moneys individually.

An example for three countries will make the situation clear. Assume trade takes place among America, Britain, and Japan. The exchange rate of pounds for dollars is $E_B = £0.40/\$$ and the exchange rate of Japanese yen ($¥$) for dollars is $E_J = ¥300/\$$. Note that it is not necessary to state the exchange rate of yen for pounds explicitly as this can be computed as $E_J/E_B = (¥300/\$)/(£0.40/\$) = ¥300/£0.40 = ¥750/£$. Table 9.1 presents hypothetical data on nominal net exports and nominal net capital outflows for each country both on an overall basis and in terms of trade with each country. For example, overall America has a trade deficit of \$15 billion paid for by a net capital outflow of $-\$15$ billion. That is, Americans are selling less goods and services to foreigners than they are buying. These goods are paid for by, on net, selling more American securities to foreigners in the amount of \$15 billion. Since these two amounts are equal, the total amount of dollars offered for foreign moneys by buyers from foreigners is equal to the total amount of dollars received for foreign moneys by sellers to foreigners. American net exports can be broken down into $-\$5$ billion with Britain and $-\$10$ billion with Japan. Net capital outflows are $+\$25$ billion and $-\$40$ billion respectively; that is, America is a net buyer of British securities while Japan buys even more American securities. The differences of $-\$30$ billion and $+\$30$ billion are the excess of dollars demanded over dollars supplied in exchange for pounds and the excess of dollars demanded over dollars supplied in exchange for yen, respectively. Their

Table 9.1 THREE-COUNTRY EXAMPLE OF INTERNATIONAL PAYMENTS

Country		Overall	To America	To Britain	To Japan
America	Net exports	$-\$15$	...	$-\$\ 5$	$-\$10$
	Net capital outflows	$-\$15$	...	$+\$25$	$-\$40$
	Difference	0	...	$-\$30$	$+\$30$
Britain	Net exports	$-£18$	$+£\ 2$	...	$-£20$
	Net capital outflows	$-£18$	$-£10$	...	$-£\ 8$
	Difference	0	$+£12$	...	$-£12$
Japan	Net exports	$+¥18,000$	$+¥\ 3,000$	$+¥15,000$	...
	Net capital outflows	$+¥18,000$	$+¥12,000$	$+¥\ 6,000$	...
	Difference	0	$-¥\ 9,000$	$+¥\ 9,000$	...

Note: All amounts in billions. Exchange rates are £0.40/\$, ¥300/\$, and ¥750/£.

sum is of course zero as required for the total amount of dollars demanded to equal the total amount of dollars supplied. Note that each amount in the by-country breakdown of any country is necessarily repeated with opposite sign and converted by the exchange rate in the by-country breakdown of the other country. Thus net exports of Britain to America are $-(-\$5$ billion) $\times$ ($£0.40/\$$) $= +£2$ billion. This must happen because a sale from one country to another is by definition a purchase by the second country from the first.

In this example, Americans are offering on net ¥9,000 billion for $30 billion and offering $30 billion for £12 billion. The dollar amounts are equal, but who will take the yen and provide the pounds? Since total net exports equal total net capital outflows, there must be a demand for exactly the amount of yen supplied and a supply of exactly the amount of pounds demanded.[9] This is shown in Table 9.1 by the differences of $-£12$ billion and $+¥9,000$ for Japanese-British payments. British purchasers and Japanese sellers are offering on net £12 billion for ¥9,000 billion. Specialists, called *arbitrageurs*, buy the ¥9,000 for $30 billion and simultaneously both sell the ¥9,000 for £12 billion and sell the £12 billion for $30 billion. The incentive for this transaction is in fact offered by the exchange rate of yen for pounds being slightly lower than implied by E_J/E_B say ¥749.9/£ instead of ¥750/£. That difference of 0.013 percent would provide an annual gross income to arbitrageurs of $4,000,000.[10] Compared to the billions involved, $4,000,000 is negligible, but it can pay for the salaries, telephone bills, and paperwork to keep enough arbitrageurs in business to make the foreign exchange market work quite smoothly.

Broadening trade to all the countries in the world changes none of these principles. So long as the nominal net exports of each country equal the nominal net capital outflows, there will always be a sequence of transactions by which arbitrageurs can eliminate any inequality of a country's payments to other countries individually.

EQUILIBRIUM FOR TRADE AMONG MANY COUNTRIES

With many countries, equality of nominal net exports with nominal net capital outflows for each country is achieved by the simultaneous adjustment of all exchange rates. For macroeconomists interested in analyzing only the influence of the " rest of the world " on a single economy, this detail is superfluous and aggregate measures of real income, average price level, and average exchange rate for the rest of the world will serve quite well. The symbols y_F, P_F, and E_F will be adopted for these " rest of the world " aggregates. Thus Fig. 9.5 serves to

---

[9] This must be true because the overall difference for each country is zero and the difference between each pair of countries enters both countries' accounts.

[10] This is found by computing the profit on the pounds for yen transaction: ¥9,000 billion/(¥749.9/£) $- £12$ billion $= £12.0016$ billion $- £12$ billion $= £1.6$ million. In dollars, this is £1.6 million/($£0.40/\$$) $= \$4$ million. All these amounts are flows measured at annual rates.

illustrate the determination of net exports and the average exchange rate in this more general case also. The statements made about " Britain " in the two-country case apply more generally to America and the aggregate " Rest of the World."

9.2 EXCHANGE RATE SYSTEMS

TYPES OF EXCHANGE RATE SYSTEMS

The term *floating exchange rates* is applied to exchange rates determined in markets free of government intervention. The main elements of this system were presented in the previous section. Starting in 1973, the international financial arrangements among major trading nations can be generally characterized as a floating exchange rate system.[11] Smaller countries still generally link their currencies to the currency of a major trading nation through the other exchange rate systems discussed below.

Floating exchange rates were exceptional during the period from World War II to 1973.[12] During this period there was an international agreement to maintain exchange rates in terms of dollars at certain announced levels, plus or minus 1 percent. These levels were changed from time to time. This agreement was usually referred to as the Bretton Woods Agreement because it was signed at Bretton Woods, New Hampshire (1944). The Bretton Woods Agreement established a system of *pegged exchange rates* because foreign governments took actions—explained shortly—to assure that the exchange rate for their currency would fluctuate around the announced or pegged exchange rate.

Some countries are linked by *fixed exchange rates* or a *unified monetary system*. Fixed exchange rates are similar to pegged exchange rates in the sense that exchange rates fluctuate only within a very narrow band around an announced exchange rate. They differ fundamentally however in two ways: (1) a unified monetary system has an automatic device linking the money supplies of the countries involved; and (2) the exchange rates cannot be changed so long as the system exists.

EQUILIBRIUM UNDER UNIFIED MONETARY SYSTEMS

The principal difference between a unified monetary system and a system of pegged or floating exchange rates is that it is indeed possible to convert the money of one country into the money of another country at a fixed exchange

---

[11] Intervention by central banks has continued to some extent in an attempt to " moderate day-to-day fluctuations " in exchange rates. This speculative activity by the government has led to the characterization of the system as a "dirty float." (See the discussion of speculation at the end of this section.)
[12] The most important exception in terms of length of time and size of country was Canada. Details of the more remote history of international financial arrangements are beyond the scope of this book.

rate. If, for example, there are only two countries involved, there is no reason that the total sales of each country to the other should equal the total purchases from the other country. The difference can be made up by converting one money to the other and shipping it.

A trivial but illuminating example arises from treating California as one country and the rest of the United States as another country. If Californians purchase more from other Americans than they sell at the exchange rate of one Californian dollar to the dollar, the exchange rate will not rise. Californians will simply transfer Californian dollars out of the state to pay their bills. The transfer is made by shipping base money. Note that this will not continue indefinitely however, since Californians would run out of money. Instead the reduction of the California money supply will lead to a bit higher interest rates in California in the short run, attracting loans from out of state. In the longer run California aggregate demand will be a bit lower than it otherwise would have been so California prices will drop slightly relative to other American prices, and California's nominal net exports curve will shift up until the California money supply stops decreasing relative to the total American money supply. These adjustments take place so quickly and automatically that no one has cause to remark on them. They serve to keep the value of the dollar similar throughout the country.

Precisely the same situation applies less trivially for Panama and Liberia. The currency units of these countries are defined in terms of American dollars and, except for coinage, dollars actually circulate there. The same is true for the British pound in the Republic of Ireland.

A historically important unified monetary system existed under the gold standard. National monetary units were defined as certain weights of pure gold. The value of an ounce of gold would be kept constant throughout the system by melting of gold coins of one country where prices were high and shipping them to a place where prices were lower. The system could be broken if the government of a country redefined the weight of gold equal to a unit of its currency.

Under most unified monetary systems there are slight fluctuations of exchange rates around the conversion or *central rate* to cover the cost of shipping and converting one money to another. The Federal Reserve System subsidizes these costs in the United States, so there are no longer domestic exchange rates between, say, Chicago and New York. But the right to a dollar in a Panamanian bank can and does exchange for slightly more or less than the right to one dollar in a New York bank. Under the gold standard, the costs of converting and shipping gold from one country to another could amount to 1 to 2 percent of the amount shipped.

The determination of exchange rates where there are shipping and conversion costs is illustrated in Fig. 9.6. The central rate E_c is determined by the ratio at which one money can be converted into another. The *upper rate* E_u equals the central rate plus shipping and conversion costs measured in foreign mon-

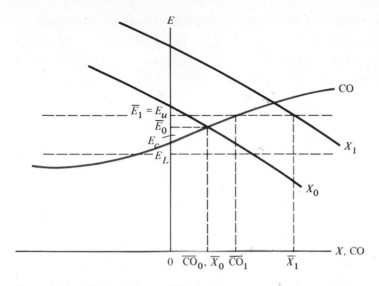

Figure 9.6 Equilibrium under a unified monetary system. Under a unified monetary system, money is converted and shipped whenever the exchange rate would otherwise rise above the upper rate E_u or fall below the lower rate E_L. This occurs because, outside of these rates, it is cheaper to convert and ship money than to pay for net purchases by buying foreign exchange. In Case 0, the equilibrium exchange rate $\bar{E}_0$ is determined in the usual way with nominal net exports $\bar{E}_0$ equal to nominal net capital outflows $\overline{CO}_0$. In Case 1, with a higher net export curve the exchange rate would rise above the upper rate E_u if no money were converted and shipped by foreigners. In this case, nominal net exports $\bar{X}_1$ exceed nominal net capital flows $\overline{CO}_1$ at the equilibrium exchange rate $\bar{E}_1 = E_u$. The difference or balance of payments surplus is paid by foreigners' shipping $\bar{X}_1 - \overline{CO}_1$ in money. The balance of payments can be zero, positive, or negative.

etary units per domestic unit. The *lower rate E_L* is the central rate less these shipping and conversion costs. If, as for nominal net export curve X_0, the exchange rate determined by the equality of net exports and net capital outflows lies between E_u and E_L, that rate, here $\bar{E}_0$, will be the exchange rate. If that rate is above the upper rate, the exchange rate will equal the upper rate, as for the net export curve X_1. Nominal net exports will exceed nominal net capital outflows and the difference $X - CO$ is called the *balance of payments*. In this case the balance of payments is positive (or *in surplus*) and it is paid by importing base money from the foreign country. If the exchange rate at $X = CO$ happens to be less than the lower rate E_L, the balance of payments will be negative. The excess of nominal net capital outflows over nominal net exports will be paid by exporting base money to the foreign country.

EQUILIBRIUM UNDER THE PEGGED EXCHANGE RATE SYSTEM

The pegged exchange rate system was aimed at approximating the unified monetary system which existed under the gold standard. Indeed the system was euphemistically called the " gold exchange standard." Central, upper, and lower rates were announced and central banks in foreign countries would sell dollar securities for their own money if the upper rate was reached and buy dollar securities with their own money if the lower rate was reached. The foreign central banks thus provided whatever capital flows were necessary to equate net capital outflows and net exports between the upper and lower rate. Net capital outflows on private and central bank accounts were accounted separately, with the American balance of payments equal to net purchases by foreign central banks of dollar-denominated securities plus any net sales by the American monetary authorities of foreign securities or gold to assist foreign central banks.

Gold entered the picture because between 1946 and 1968 the United States would buy gold from foreign central banks or sell it to them at $35 per ounce. Central banks could use dollars to buy gold from the Fed instead of dollar-denominated securities. The idea was that the requirement to buy or sell gold would keep the dollar's value fixed in terms of gold while other moneys were fixed in terms of dollars.

The determination of equilibrium under the pegged exchange rate system is identical to that under a unified monetary standard if nominal net capital outflows CO are interpreted as referring to private capital flows only, and the balance of payments are interpreted as net central bank capital and gold outflows. The two main differences between the pegged exchange rate system and a unified monetary system are: (1) Countries could offset (*sterilize*) the effects of their balance of payments on their monetary base by selling their own securities for their own money if they were buying dollar securities with their own money, and vice versa. (2) Countries could change announced exchange rates whenever a balance of payments surplus or deficit became too bother-some. Consequently, foreign central banks would not let their money supplies passively adjust to the American balance of payments. Some (most notably Britain) would desire a faster rate of monetary growth and raise the pegged exchange rate (depreciate their currency) from time to time. Others (notably Germany) would desire a lower rate of monetary growth and lower the pegged exchange rate (appreciate their currency) on occasion. This led to huge private capital flows whenever it became obvious that the rates would soon be changed. These huge capital flows can occur only under a pegged exchange rate system. Under either a unified monetary system or a floating exchange rate system, small, frequent adjustments in the relative money supplies or exchange rates, respectively, keep the system in equilibrium.[13] The delayed adjustments

---

[13] A banking panic which suddenly reduced the money supply and raised the interest rates in one country would cause large net capital *inflows* to finance a large balance of payments surplus needed to restore the money supply under the gold standard.

of the pegged exchange rate system presented private individuals with a "sure bet," and the resulting capital flows led to the eventual destruction of the system.

THE RESERVE-CURRENCY COUNTRY

Under the Bretton Woods system of pegged exchange rates, other countries committed themselves to intervene in the foreign exchange market to maintain the exchange rate of their currency for the U.S. dollar within an announced band. The U.S. dollar was called the *reserve currency*. This term was used because the bulk of central bank foreign exchange reserves was held in securities denominated in U.S. dollars such as U.S. Treasury bills.

This system has quite different monetary implications for the reserve-currency country (the United States) and the non-reserve-currency countries. Suppose for example that a non-reserve-currency country were running a balance of payments surplus. Its central bank would then buy dollar securities with newly issued base money. This is like an open market operation except that foreign rather than domestic securities are purchased. If the central bank did not want its money supply to change in response to its balance of payments, it could sterilize the money supply effect by simultaneously selling an equal amount of its domestic securities.[14] But there is a direct, an automatic, effect of the balance of payments on the nominal money supply of a non-reserve-currency country under pegged exchange rates.

There is no such automatic linkage between the balance of payments and money of the reserve-currency country. Insofar as the foreign central banks did all the buying and selling of dollar securities, there was no effect on the U.S. money supply. There were two exceptions however: (1) The Fed would sometimes accommodate or assist foreign central banks in their pegging operations by lending them new U.S. base money or by selling some foreign securities for U.S. base money. (2) If the foreign central banks exchanged U.S. base money for gold, our base money was reduced unless the Fed sterilized the effects. The decision of France to accumulate gold instead of dollar securities led to the first unofficial, then official, abandonment of the U.S. linkage to gold. Instead we made explicit that our money is purely a managed fiat standard: one dollar bill is convertible on demand only into another dollar bill and not into any commodity at a fixed price.

Because the United States has long been in fact a reserve-currency country on a fiat standard, its monetary policy can be determined by the Fed and analyzed by macroeconomists independently of the balance of payments. If we

---

[14] Some economists who advocate the monetary approach to the balance of payments (see Sec. 9.4 below) doubt the ability of non-reserve-currency countries to sterilize their balance of payments. Except perhaps for the smallest and most open of such countries, this does not seem to present problems in the short run. It does prove impossible over long periods, however, as discussed in Sec. 9.4. This section is based on Michael R. Darby, The Monetary Approach to the Balance of Payments: Two Specious Assumptions, *Economic Inquiry*, in press.

turn to analysis of a non-reserve-currency country, the case may be much different.

This distinction between reserve-currency and non-reserve-currency countries is not applicable to either a floating or a fixed exchange rate system. In the former case there is no balance of payments to affect base money, and under a unified monetary system there are automatic base-money effects for all countries. It is as if with floating rates every country has the independence of a reserve-currency country and under fixed rates no country has.[15]

9.3 EFFECTS OF INTERNATIONAL SHOCKS ON AGGREGATE DEMAND

RESPONSE OF NET EXPORTS TO AN INTERNATIONAL SHOCK UNDER A FLOATING EXCHANGE RATE SYSTEM

Unexpected changes in foreign real income and price level affect the domestic economy by shifting the net export curve. All such shocks arising from a nation's international trade are termed international shocks. Thus, one country's domestic shock, say a change in the nominal-money-supply growth rate, causes an international shock to each of its trading partners.

The impact of international shocks is easy to illustrate. First consider the current situation of a floating exchange rate system. A foreign monetary shock which increases y_F relative to its steady-state growth path will shift the nominal and real net export curves upward. This occurs because of the resulting increased foreign demand for American goods. This is most conveniently illustrated by graphing the real net export curve and the real capital outflows curve as shown in Fig. 9.7. In this figure, the curve labeled x_0 indicates what the real net export curve would have been in the absence of the international shock. The curve labeled x_1 indicates the real net export curve. Real net exports are increased by the amount $\bar{x}_1 - \bar{x}_0$ and real capital outflows (or net borrowing by foreigners) are increased by the equal amount $\overline{co}_1 - \overline{co}_0$. This is nearly equivalent to an equal increase in real government expenditures financed by increased government borrowing.

The analysis of international shocks is somewhat different from that presented for government spending because of their more gradual nature. The government can fairly suddenly shift spending above (or below) its previous steady-state growth path. This is not characteristic of the response of real income to macroeconomic shocks, however. Since international shocks are a reflection of the response of foreign real income to foreign macroeconomic

---

[15] For a unified monetary system based on a fiat reserve currency such as the United States and Panama, the reserve-currency country can independently determine monetary policy for the *whole* system and thus indirectly for the reserve-currency country.

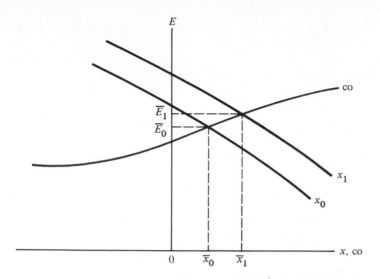

Figure 9.7 Effect of an increase in real net export demand on real net exports. An outward shift in the real net export curve due to an increase in foreign real income increases the exchange rate from $\bar{E}_0$ to $\bar{E}_1$ and real net exports from $\bar{x}_0$ to $\bar{x}_1$. The increase in real net capital outflows (net foreign borrowing) will equal the increase in real net exports.

shocks, a gradual rise in net export demand relative to normal is to be expected. This more gradual rise would apparently reduce the portion of the change in net exports which could be labeled unexpected. It is of course only the unexpected changes in real net exports—just as in real government spending—which would induce substantial changes in real income. Very little empirical work has yet been done in this area. Indirect evidence is inconclusive but consistent with an adjustment pattern similar to unexpected borrowing-financed changes in real government spending. This was illustrated in Figs. 8.1 and 8.2 (for what corresponds to increased real net exports) as a temporary rise in nominal and real income relative to an unchanged steady-state equilibrium. Here the increased real net exports are crowding out real investment and consumer expenditures.

A sudden shift in the real net capital outflow curve—due, for example, to fears that a new government will expropriate capital in a country—will also affect real net exports. Figure 9.8 illustrates how such fears would shift the net real capital outflow curve of the country involved down and to the right. As a result, the exchange rate falls and net exports rise. People try to shift their investment abroad, but they can do so only if they accept less foreign money for each unit of domestic money. At the same time, there would likely be shifts in the real investment function and perhaps the consumer expenditure function; so the total macroeconomic effect would be difficult to predict.

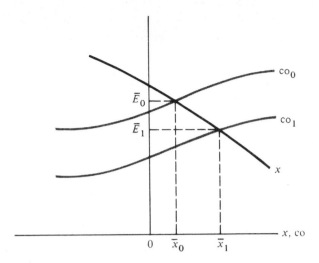

Figure 9.8 Effect of an adverse shift in expectations. Fears of
political instability or other changes which reduce the expected
future exchange rate (foreign money per unit of domestic money),
or otherwise reduce the expected return to foreign investors, shift
the real net capital outflow down and to the right as from co_0 to
co_1. This results in an increase in real net exports from $\bar{x}_0$ to $\bar{x}_1$
and an immediate fall in the exchange rate from $\bar{E}_0$ to $\bar{E}_1$. Put
differently, to get capital out of the country, real net exports
must increase. This is accomplished by a fall in the exchange rate
so that it becomes profitable to export more and import less.

ADJUSTMENT TO INTERNATIONAL SHOCKS
UNDER PEGGED EXCHANGE RATES AND STERILIZATION

Under a pegged exchange rate system, the impact of shifts in real net export
demand on aggregate demand will be, if anything, larger than under floating
exchange rate systems. This occurs because whenever the shift in net export
demand would increase the exchange rate E above the upper rate E_u (or
decrease it below the lower rate E_L), the central banks step in and supply
whatever government net capital outflows are needed over private net capital
outflows to equate net capital outflows to net exports at E_u (or E_L). This
permits a greater expansion (or contraction) of net exports than would occur
under floating exchange rates (compare Figs. 9.6 and 9.7).

   We assume here—as in the floating case—that there are no repercussions on
the nominal money supply. For the United States this would require that the
Fed sterilize any gold flows (when they occurred) or assistance to foreign
central banks in maintaining the pegged exchange rate. All the other government capital flows, it will be recalled, affect foreign but not U.S. base money. If
we were considering a non-reserve-currency country, this would require that its

central bank sterilize the effects on its base money of its foreign exchange market operations. This latter task might not be possible on a sustained basis, as discussed in Sec. 9.4.

PEGGED EXCHANGE RATES
WITH NO OR INCOMPLETE STERILIZATION

The central bank of a country running a balance-of-payments deficit or surplus might allow all or part of the direct effect on base money to occur. In this case, the effect of international shocks through changes in real net exports is reinforced by changes in the same direction in nominal money. This money supply effect would always occur for a unified monetary system. This secondary monetary impact might well have a temporary effect on real income larger than the direct effect. As with the case of increased real government expenditures financed by increased base-money creation, most of the attention would be paid to the dramatic balance of trade figures rather than to the induced changes in nominal money. For this reason, the separate effects of the international shock and the money creation are often confused.

9.4 MONEY SUPPLY GROWTH
AND LONG-RUN INTERNATIONAL EQUILIBRIUM
UNDER ALTERNATIVE EXCHANGE RATE SYSTEMS

THE PURCHASING POWER PARITY THEOREM

The purchasing power ratio EP/P_F will have a particular *purchasing-power parity* value consistent with given conditions and a particular steady-state balance of payments to income ratio.[16] Shifts in the given conditions are normally so small relative to changes in price levels and exchange rate that this parity value can be taken as a constant. Thus, to maintain a given balance of payments to income ratio, the following condition must hold on average:

$$\Gamma E + \Gamma P = \Gamma P_F \qquad [9.2]$$

That is, the growth rate of the exchange rate plus the inflation rate must equal the foreign inflation rate. If the foreign inflation rate were higher than this sum, the purchasing power ratio would grow above its parity value, and the balance of payments surplus would become large as domestic goods became cheap relative to foreign goods. If the sum on the left-hand side of [9.2] exceeded the foreign inflation rate, then the balance of payments deficit would grow large as foreign goods became increasingly cheap compared to domestic goods.

---

[16] Among the conditions determining this parity value are tariffs or other barriers to trade and relative saving-income ratios. Details are left to specialized courses in international finance.

No country can choose the foreign inflation rate, but it can choose either its own inflation rate or the growth rate of its exchange rate.[17] One having been chosen, the other is implied by the purchasing power parity condition [9.2].

THE MONETARY APPROACH TO THE BALANCE OF PAYMENTS OF A NON-RESERVE-CURRENCY COUNTRY

The monetary approach to the balance of payments (MABP) has been widely used in recent years.[18] This approach is most directly applicable to a small non-reserve-currency country which maintains a pegged exchange rate and makes no attempt to sterilize the monetary effects of its balance of payments.

The approach is based on the fact that the steady-state growth rate of real money is determined by demand conditions, as shown in Chap. 5. The steady-state inflation rate must equal the inflation rate of the reserve-currency country in view of [9.2]. This means that the growth rate of nominal money must equal their sum:

$$\overline{\Gamma M} = (\overline{\Gamma \phi_S} + \overline{\Gamma y_S}) + \overline{\Gamma P_F} \qquad [9.3]$$

This just reverses the analysis of Chap. 5 because the inflation rate is determining the nominal-money-supply growth rate. The nominal-money growth rate adjusts to the value determined in [9.3] because: (1) If ΓM exceeded $\overline{\Gamma M}$, a balance of payments deficit would result, and this would reduce the growth in nominal money. (2) If ΓM were less than $\overline{\Gamma M}$, a balance of payments surplus would increase the growth of nominal money. Unlike the cases in Chaps. 4 through 8, the balance of payments provides the economy with a way to adjust the nominal quantity of money supplied to the amount demanded.

The only role for a central bank is to decide (given $\overline{\Gamma M}$ and the growth rate of the money multiplier) how much of the growth in nominal base money should be provided by the purchase of domestic securities. The rest will be provided by the central bank purchases of foreign securities for reserves to maintain the pegged exchange rate. If, for example, a country wanted to run a large balance of payments surplus, it would provide little base-money growth through open market operations. The rest of the base-money growth would come from purchases of reserve-currency securities with new base money as required to maintain the exchange rate.

---

[17] Actually, if an exchange rate goal is chosen it is almost always a zero growth in the exchange rate for a particular currency such as the U.S. dollar—that is, a fixed exchange rate.

[18] The main writings are collected in Jacob A. Frenkel and Harry G. Johnsons (eds.), *The Monetary Approach to the Balance of Payments*, Toronto: University of Toronto Press, 1976. The literature is reviewed in Marina v. N. Whitman, Global Monetarism and the Monetary Approach to the Balance of Payments, *Brookings Papers on Economic Activity*, 1975(3): 491–536; and Stephen P. Magee, The Empirical Evidence on the Monetary Approach to the Balance of Payments and Exchange Rates, *American Economic Review, Papers and Proceedings*, **66**: 163–170; May 1976.

THE RESERVE-CURRENCY COUNTRY UNDER PEGGED EXCHANGE RATES

Since the reserve-currency country does not attempt to maintain a pegged exchange rate, it is free to choose its own inflation rate. When the United States increased its trend growth rate of nominal money in the late 1960s and early 1970s (see Chap. 13), this led after a time to overshooting in the U.S. inflation rate. This overshooting inflation rate led to very large balance of payments surpluses in the countries which pegged their exchange rates to the dollars. Most such countries experienced rapid nominal money growth followed by accelerating inflation. This experience led eventually to abandonment of the Bretton Woods system of pegged exchange rates.

FLOATING EXCHANGE RATES

Under the floating exchange rate system which replaced the Bretton Woods system, each country can choose a growth rate of its nominal money supply consistent with its own desired rate of inflation. The value of its money will rise in terms of the money of a country with more rapid inflation and fall in terms of a country with less rapid inflation. The differences in the rate of inflation will be reflected in both the expected rate of change in the exchange rate and the differences in nominal interest rates so that there is no net effect on real capital flows.

SUMMARY

1 Foreign exchange markets eliminate barter in international transactions by canceling amounts due to foreigners against amounts due from foreigners. In effect, a country's buyers from foreigners pay its sellers to foreigners.
2 There are three main alternative foreign exchange rate systems: (a) floating exchange rate systems, (b) pegged exchange rate systems, and (c) unified monetary systems or fixed exchange rate systems.
3 A floating exchange rate system is currently dominant. Under this system, exchange rates adjust so that a country's desired nominal net exports equal its desired nominal net capital outflows.
4 Under a unified monetary system, net exports need not equal net capital outflows if at the exchange rate it is feasible to convert and ship base money from one country to the others to make up for any difference (balance of payments).
5 Under a pegged exchange rate system, central bank capital flows provide a means of bridging a difference between private nominal net capital outflows and nominal net exports. These net government capital outflows are the balance of payments.

6 Foreign booms and recessions cause international shocks to the domestic economy by shifting the real net export curve up or down, respectively. The effect is similar to a gradual increase (or decrease) in real government spending financed by borrowing—a temporary increase (decrease) in nominal and real income relative to their steady-state growth paths.

7 The direct impacts of shifts in real net export demand are amplified under pegged exchange rates (assuming sterilization is incomplete) and under fixed exchange rates by a similar change in the growth rate of nominal money.

8 A country can choose and achieve either an inflation rate goal or a growth rate of the exchange rate goal, but not both independently.

9 A non-reserve-currency country which maintains a constant exchange rate against a reserve country must accept the reserve country's inflation rate in the long run. The non-reserve-currency country's central bank determines its balance of payments by how much base money growth it provides through domestic open market and discounting operations.

CONCEPTS TO KNOW

balance of payments	purchasing-power parity
balance of trade	purchasing-power ratio
fixed exchange rates	reserve currency
floating exchange rates	sterilization
foreign exchange markets	trade surplus or deficit
net capital outflows	unified monetary system
pegged exchange rates	

QUESTIONS AND EXERCISES

1 In the absence of foreign exchange markets, why would there be barter involved in a sale of woolens by a British firm to an American firm for $1,000,000?

2 Why is the equality of nominal net exports and nominal net capital outflows equivalent to the equality of the quantities of dollars supplied and demanded in the foreign exchange market?

*3 What are the units of the purchasing power ratio EP/P_F? In what sense is this a measure of the relative quantity of real goods and services which could be bought abroad compared with the quantity that could be bought in America for a given amount of money? Why would increases in this ratio tend to increase American imports and reduce American exports?

4 Other things being equal, what would be the effect of an increase in the expected future exchange rate on the current exchange rate and net exports under floating exchange rates? Under pegged exchange rates? Why

is the expected growth rate of the exchange rate subject to sudden, large changes under pegged exchange rates more than under floating exchange rates?

5 In Table 9.1, are the figures given for Japanese net exports and net capital outflows to Britain consistent with the British figures for Japan? Why or why not?

*6 Is it a cause for any particular notice or concern under floating exchange rates if Japan exports more to America than it imports from America? Why or why not? Is it a cause for any particular notice or concern if you buy more from your local supermarket than you sell to it? Why or why not?

7 Under floating exchange rates, the balance of payments is always zero. Why? Why is it impossible to have a "balance of payments problem" under floating exchange rates?

8 If the city of Columbus, Ohio, were to secede from the United States and establish its own money, there would be a great deal of "international trade" between Columbus and the United States. Under floating exchange rates, would changes in the American money-supply growth rate cause significant macroeconomic shocks for Columbus? Would changes in the Columbus money-supply growth rate cause significant macroeconomic shocks for the United States? Why would the absolute size of the shocks be similar but the sizes relative to income be dissimilar? Does this have any application to the United States and Canada?

9 (a) Show that large shifts in the (private) net capital outflows curve have less effect on net exports under pegged exchange rates than under floating exchange rates.

(b) Show that large shifts in the net exports curve have less effect on net exports under floating exchange rates than under pegged exchange rates.

10 American net exports are affected by domestic as well as international shocks; show why. If this were not true, there would be no international shocks. Why? Why are data on actual real net exports insufficient to pinpoint international shocks?

11 Analyze the effect of a reduction in the growth rate of the Canadian money supply on American real income under floating exchange rates.

*12 Can monetary policy be used to select the trend rate of inflation in a small, open economy under floating exchange rates independent of the rates of inflation in its large trading partners?

REFERENCES FOR FURTHER READING

Friedman, Milton: "The Case for Flexible Exchange Rates," in *Essays in Positive Economics*, Chicago: University of Chicago Press, 1953.

————: "Free Exchange Rates *and* The Political Economy of International Monetary Arrangements," in *Dollars and Deficits*, Englewood Cliffs, N.J.: Prentice-Hall, 1968.

Heller, H. Robert: *International Monetary Economics*, Englewood Cliffs, N.J.: Prentice-Hall, 1974.

Machlup, Fritz: "The Theory of Foreign Exchanges," as reprinted in Howard S. Ellis and Lloyd A. Metzler (eds.), *Readings in the Theory of International Trade*, Homewood, Ill.: Irwin, for the American Economic Association, 1950.

Whitman, Marina v. N.: Global Monetarism and the Monetary Approach to the Balance of Payments, *Brookings Papers on Economic Activity*, 1975(3): 491–536.

Yeager, Leland B.: *International Monetary Relations: Theory, History, and Policy*, New York: Harper & Row, 1966.

PART FOUR

THE KEYNESIAN MODEL

Part Three presented one approach to analyzing the short-run impact of macroeconomic shocks upon the economy. A very important alternative, the Keynesian model, is the subject of Part Four. The dynamic monetary model of Part Three readily illustrates the effects of changes in money supply and demand conditions upon the economy. The Keynesian model is particularly useful for understanding the initial effects of unexpected changes in fiscal policy or investment or export demand. A complete analysis using one approach gives the same answer as a complete analysis with the other, but typically one or the other will highlight the factors important for a particular problem in a convenient way. So each model contributes to our total understanding of the macroeconomy.

The Keynesian model discussed in Part Four is the standard macroeconomic model adopted by the followers of John Maynard Keynes along lines suggested by Sir John Hicks. It is also referred to as the IS-LM or income-expenditures model. While the model is rooted in the work of Keynes, neither all the weaknesses nor all the strengths of the model apply to Keynes' own thought.

The Keynesian model is a comparative statics model of aggregate demand. It explains in great detail certain aspects of short-run adjustment which are subsumed in the dynamic monetary model. In order to focus such attention on some features of the economy, other features are assumed constant. As time progresses, many initially negligible influences become substantial. Eventually so many forces are shifting the curves that the model no longer serves to clarify. Similar confusion arises even in the short-run analysis of a few interesting problems. It is hardly surprising that a specialized tool is better at some jobs than at others.

Chapter 10 explains the basic elements used to build the Keynesian model. Most are familiar from earlier chapters, but there are some differences of emphasis. These elements are integrated into a model of income determination in Chap. 11. The model is used to analyze the short-run effects of fiscal and monetary policies and other macroeconomic shocks.

CHAPTER 10

THE KEYNESIAN BUILDING BLOCKS

WHAT YOU WILL LEARN IN THIS CHAPTER
The short period, constant price level, and quantity adjustment mechanism form the viewpoint for Keynesian analysis ● Elements of consumer expenditure theory ● The Keynesian consumption function ● How tax changes affect consumer expenditures ● The investment-demand function ● The aggregate expenditure function ● Keynesian analysis of money demand and supply

10.1 UNDERLYING ASSUMPTIONS

THE KEYNESIAN APPROACH

The Keynesian approach to income determination is one of aggregate demand. Individual components of total expenditures are analyzed separately and then added together to obtain the total. Consistency of the total with conditions underlying the individual components and with the demand and supply of money is then obtained. This chapter undertakes the first part of the task—the analysis of the expenditure components. The basic elements are put together in Chap. 11.

There are three basic assumptions that underlie the Keynesian model: (1) There is a short period of time within which the economy adjusts to the equilibrium described by the model, a period which is so short that changes in the existing stocks are negligible. (2) The price level is given. (3) A quantity adjustment mechanism exists by which the comparative static equilibrium can be reached.

THE SHORT PERIOD ASSUMPTION

Strictly speaking, the Keynesian model is a model of comparative statics. A comparative statics analysis compares alternative equilibria at the same instant of time. In that instant, the effects of flows on stocks are nil. For example, it makes no difference to the stock of capital whether investment at that instant is $100 billion or $200 billion per annum. No time elapses so there is no change in capital. This greatly simplifies the analysis since the values of all stocks can be omitted from explicit consideration.

No one supposes that adjustment to changed conditions could in fact occur instantaneously. But it is assumed that the adjustment is completed over some short period—such as one-quarter or at most one-half year—in which the effects of different flows on stocks is negligible. The analysis can then be applied again in the next period. Large-scale computerized versions of the model take explicit account of the effects of some flows on stocks from period to period, but as a practical matter the properties of these models cannot be described analytically.[1]

Perhaps the shortness of the short period is a bit overdone in terms of other evidence on the timing of adjustments to macroeconomic shocks, but the idea is doubtless a usable approximation even for periods of a year.

THE CONSTANT PRICE LEVEL

It is a matter of logical necessity that the price level is given for the analysis. Unless the price level or some similar variable—such as the nominal wage rate—is fixed, there are an infinite number of solutions to the Keynesian model. For expositional purposes it is easiest to assume that prices are given.

The assumption is sensible for an instant of time. The growth rate of prices may well be sticky enough that the price level can be treated as if it were given for any single short period.

A useful way to view this assumption is that the Keynesian aggregate supply curve is a horizontal line at a height of $\log \bar{P}$. This means that the only interesting point on the aggregate demand curve is the one at $\log P = \log \bar{P}$. The Keynesian model analyzes what equilibrium income y_e will be associated with $\bar{P}$ on the aggregate demand curve as in Fig. 10.1.

The horizontal aggregate supply can be viewed as an extreme version of the aggregate supply curve discussed in Chap. 7. It is probably a reasonably accurate approximation for a very short period. In the strict Keynesian model, however, it makes no difference to the future positions of the aggregate supply curve where the current aggregate demand and supply curves intersect.

Because abundant unutilized resources are assumed, the Keynesian analysis sometimes has been called "depression economics." In particular, the horizontal aggregate supply curve was often rationalized by the assertion that prices are very sticky downward and do not fall in the face of unemployed resources.[2]

---

[1] The implications of a computer model are usually found by putting in alternative assumptions and waiting to see what the computer grinds out.

[2] Note however that the price level fell by 22 percent from 1929 to 1933.

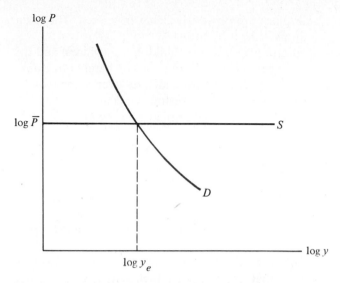

Figure 10.1 Graphical representation of the constant price level assumption. The Keynesian assumption of a constant price level is represented by a horizontal aggregate supply curve at height $\log \bar{P}$. Any amount demanded will be produced at the given price level by employing a corresponding amount of otherwise unemployed resources. Only the point ($\log y_e$, $\log \bar{P}$) on the aggregate demand curve is of interest, and so the model is solved for that point alone. It is sometimes assumed that there is some maximum level of real income at which the aggregate supply curve becomes vertical, but the Keynesian model is inapplicable if that level of income is reached.

Since the price level is fixed, the distinction between nominal and real magnitudes becomes superfluous. No theory, just arithmetic, is required to relate nominal to real magnitudes.

THE QUANTITY ADJUSTMENT MECHANISM

The quantity adjustment mechanism is the means by which the quantity of output is adjusted to equality with total expenditures. The basic hypothesis is that firms will increase production if demand for their output at the fixed price exceeds the amount actually produced and will reduce production if the quantity demanded is less than the quantity produced.

Suppose, for example, that total *planned* expenditures are $1,020 billion per annum when output is only $1,000 billion per annum. Actual expenditures must always exactly equal output which is identical to income. But this means that actual expenditures are $1,000 billion per annum, or $20 billion less than planned expenditures. Some plans are obviously being frustrated. The main frustrated plans are found in investment by firms.

Investment can be divided into investment in buildings, machines, and the like or *fixed investment* and changes in the stock of goods on hand or *inventory investment*. The $20 billion excess of planned expenditures over output will be met by selling out inventories. So inventory investment occurs at a rate $20 billion per annum less than planned so that other planned expenditures can be made.

Firms do not want their inventories to grow so slowly—or to decline—so they hire more workers and put idle capital to work to produce more goods. This increases output and income toward the planned level of expenditures. The higher level of income will generally raise expenditure plans but by an amount less than the increase in income. So the difference between planned expenditures and income narrows. The process continues until planned expenditures equal actual expenditures.

Consider the initial example in which planned expenditures exceed original output by $20 billion. Suppose that firms increase their output by the whole amount by which planned inventory investment exceeds the actual inventory investment. In the next round, output will be $1,020 billion per annum. But the $20 billion increase in output may increase the desired level of planned expenditures. Suppose that they increase by 20 percent of the increase in output, that is, to $1,024 billion per annum ($1,020 billion + 0.2 × $20 billion = $1,024 billion). Then, planned expenditures still exceed actual expenditures by $4 billion. This is noted as Round 1 in Table 10.1. If firms then again increase output by this difference, output increases to $1,024 billion per annum and planned expenditures to $1,024.8 billion per annum. This process continues as noted in Table 10.1 until planned and actual expenditures are equal at $1,025 billion per annum.

An increase in income on net might, however, decrease planned expendi-

Table 10.1 EXAMPLE OF THE OPERATION OF THE QUANTITY ADJUSTMENT MECHANISM

Round Number	Output = Income = Actual Expenditures	Planned Expenditures	Unplanned Investment
0	1000	1020	− 20
1	1020	1024	− 4
2	1024	1024.8	− 0.8
3	1024.8	1024.96	− 0.16
…	…	…	…
∞	1025	1025	0

Note: In this example it is assumed that an increase in income increases the level of planned expenditures by 20 percent of the increase in income.

Table 10.2 EXAMPLE OF THE OPERATION OF THE QUANTITY ADJUSTMENT MECHANISM

Round Number	Output = Income = Actual Expenditures	Planned Expenditures	Unplanned Investment
0	1000	1020	− 20
1	1020	1016	+ 4
2	1016	1016.8	− 0.8
3	1016.8	1016.64	+ 0.16
...	...	...	...
∞	$1016\frac{2}{3}$	$1016\frac{2}{3}$	0

Note: In this example it is assumed that an increase in income decreases the level of planned expenditures by 20 percent of the increase in income.

tures. It will be seen in Chap. 11 that this can occur because an increase in income increases money demand relative to money supply. The process of quantity adjustment works much the same way. Table 10.2 records the process if planned expenditures *decrease* by 20 percent of any increase in income. In Round 1, output is increased to \$1,020 billion per annum, but this reduces planned expenditures to \$1,016 billion per annum (\$1,020 billion − 0.2 × \$20 billion = \$1,016 billion). As a result, there is an unplanned inventory investment of + \$4 billion per annum and output would be cut back. Eventually, actual and planned expenditures are equal at \$1,016.67 billion.

The process is reversed if planned expenditures are less than actual expenditures. So long as the change (whether an increase or decrease) in planned expenditures is less than the change in income, the process will converge from either direction to a single equilibrium in which planned expenditures equal actual expenditures.

This rigid step adjustment of output to the full amount of unplanned inventory changes is at best a caricature of the gradual adjustment process that actually occurs. The dynamic implications of such a mechanical approach should not be taken too seriously. For example, the oscillatory adjustment in Table 10.2 would not be likely to occur. As income gradually increased, planned expenditures would gradually decrease until the two were equal.[3] But some such quantity adjustment mechanism is indeed required.

A quantity adjustment mechanism is not explicit in a formal comparative statics analysis based on the Keynesian model. It is implicitly assumed, however, that some such mechanism is in operation and works with sufficient rapidity that the equilibria described by the formal analysis will adequately describe actual income over some short period.

---

[3] Interestingly, gradual adjustment makes any negative impact of income changes on planned expenditures stable, but positive impacts are stable only if an increase in income of R\$1 increases planned expenditures by less than R\$1.

10.2 THE CONSUMPTION FUNCTION

Aggregate expenditures can be divided into four main categories: consumer expenditures c, investment i, government expenditures g, and net exports x:[4]

$$y \equiv c + i + g + x \qquad\qquad [10.1]$$

All variables refer to the instant—or short period—of time being analyzed. It was seen in Table 2.3 that consumer expenditures constitute a considerable majority of aggregate expenditures. The explanation of consumer expenditures is the first task of a macroeconomic model based on the explanation of individual expenditure components.

AN INTRODUCTION TO CONSUMER EXPENDITURES THEORY[5]

Keynes did not distinguish between consumer expenditures and the consumption of service flows. Failure to make this distinction has been the source of much confusion. *Consumption of service flows* (or *consumption*) is the idealized concept of price theory which measures the use of goods and services. Consumers attempt to maximize their lifetime utility in allocating their wealth between current consumption and future consumption and bequests. *Consumer expenditures* refer to all market purchases of goods and services. The difference arises because of semidurable and durable goods such as clothing, automobiles, and dishwashers. Consumer expenditures include automobiles, for example, when they are purchased by consumers. Consumption, in contrast, includes the automobile services which flow over time from the consumers' stock of automobiles. That is, consumption excludes purchases of durable and semidurable goods but includes their implicit rental value.

Consumption can be defined as current purchases of nondurable goods and services plus the implicit rental value (depreciation and real interest) of the stock of consumer durable and semidurable goods. That is, consumption is found by subtracting purchases of durable and semidurable goods from consumer expenditures and adding back their implicit rental value.

Use $\hat{c}$ to stand for consumption and Ω for the stock of consumer durable and semidurable goods. Consumer expenditures exceed consumption by the

---

[4] This is a real-magnitude version of [2.3].

[5] The discussion of this subsection draws heavily on the ideas and estimates presented in Michael R. Darby, Postwar U.S. Consumption, Consumer Expenditures, and Saving, *American Economic Review*, **65**: 217–222, May 1975. More advanced treatments of some of the issues discussed in the text are found in Michael R. Darby, The Permanent Income Theory of Consumption—A Restatement, *Quarterly Journal of Economics*, **88**: 228–250, May 1974; and Michael R. Darby, The Allocation of Transitory Income among Consumers' Assets, *American Economic Review*, **62**: 928–941, Dec. 1972.

amount that the rate of increase in this stock exceeds the imputed real interest yield on it:

$$c = \hat{c} + \Delta\Omega - r\Omega \qquad [10.2]$$

Consumer expenditure theory attempts to explain consumption $\hat{c}$ and the rate of change in the stock of consumer durable and semidurable goods (for short, the rate of change in durables) $\Delta\Omega$. The level of the stock of durables is the sum of past rates of change in durables and therefore does not require a separate explanation.

Consumption behavior is relatively easy to explain and understand. Simply put, consumption is a constant fraction of permanent income.[6] This statement rests on two substantive empirical generalizations: (1) consumption depends on permanent income, not current income, and (2) the fraction of permanent income devoted to consumption neither rises nor falls as permanent income increases over time.

Good or bad luck as measured by transitory income y_T, the difference between actual income and permanent income, affects consumption. It does this, however, only over time by affecting the basic constraint of wealth which is measured here by permanent income. The present value of planned present and future real consumption will just equal the amount available to spend—current real wealth. The windfall gain or loss measured by transitory income is a flow which increases real wealth and permanent income over time. So transitory income affects consumption in all future periods, but not current consumption. This is the reason behind the first empirical generalization above.

It is sometimes argued that the fraction of income consumed will decrease as wealth increases because "needs" or wants become less pressing as wealth increases. This is bad logic however, because the consumption-saving decision involves the comparison of the values of current and future consumption. The poor may in some sense place a greater psychological value on present consumption than the rich, but they will also put a greater value on increasing next year's consumption than will the rich. There is no reason to expect the relative valuation of present to future consumption to be any greater in the one case than in the other.

A number of factors affect the rate of change in durables $\Delta\Omega$. An individual views his or her stock of durables as a form of wealth which yields consumption services. In full equilibrium, there will be a desired ratio of these stocks to wealth or permanent income. This ratio depends on the demand for these consumption services. If, however, an individual is in disequilibrium because of windfall gains or losses (transitory income) or excess money holdings, speeding or retarding durables purchases is a convenient means of adjustment. So he or

---

[6] Recall that permanent income y_P is the normal real private income to be expected from the current real wealth.

she will alter the rate of change in durables from that which just covers the desired increase due to growth of permanent income. Possibly offsetting or reinforcing these influences on the rate of change of durables would be the gradual elimination of any excess or deficiency of actual compared to long-run desired stocks of durable and semidurable goods. Thus the rate of change of durables will increase if permanent income y_P, transitory income y_T, or excess real money holdings $m - m^d$ are increased and decrease if they are decreased. Increases in the stock of consumers' durable and semidurable goods Ω will decrease the rate of change in durables and vice versa.

We can use this reasoning and Eq. [10.2] to write a general *consumer-expenditure function*:

$$c = c(y_P, y_T, m - m^d, \Omega) \tag{10.3}$$

Again, total consumer expenditures increase with increases in permanent income, transitory income, and excess real money holdings, but with decreases in the current stock of consumers' durables.

For situations of full equilibrium, transitory income and excess money balances are zero, and stocks of consumers' durables and permanent income increase in constant proportion. In that case, consumer expenditures (like consumption) are proportional to permanent and actual real private income. This is the average relationship actually observed over long periods of time. It is *not* a behavioral relationship which explains how changes in current real private income affect real consumer spending however. An increase in real private income immediately affects only the transitory income $(y_T = y_N - y_P)$ argument of the consumer-expenditure function. But each dollar change in transitory income causes only about a \$0.40 change in consumer expenditures. This is much less than would be predicted by the long-run ratio of consumer expenditures to private income. This ratio $(1 - \sigma)$ is about 0.9.

THE SHORT-RUN KEYNESIAN CONSUMPTION FUNCTION

Keynes' (imprecise) use of the term consumption for consumer expenditures led him to call his short-run consumer-expenditure function a consumption function. That traditional name will be used here also to avoid confusion in outside readings.

Keynes hypothesized a consumption function of elegant simplicity:

> The fundamental psychological law ... is that men are disposed, as a rule and on average, to increase their consumption as their income increases, but not by as much as the increase in their income.[7]

---

[7] John Maynard Keynes, *The General Theory of Employment, Interest, and Money*, New York: Harcourt, Brace, 1936, p. 96.

In functional notation, this is expressed as

$$c = c_K(y_N) \qquad [10.4]$$

where consumer expenditures are an increasing function of (net after-tax) private income such that $(c_1 - c_0)/(y_{N1} - y_{N0})$ is less than one. This ratio of the change in consumer expenditures to the change in income is known as the *marginal propensity to consume* (MPC).

Note that it is assumed that private income y_N is the relevant income for determining consumers' expenditures. Private income measures the amount actually available to consumers for either spending or adding to wealth. Its value is found by subtracting taxes t from total income:

$$y_N \equiv y - t \qquad [10.5]$$

RELATIONSHIP OF THE KEYNESIAN CONSUMPTION FUNCTION TO THE CONSUMER-EXPENDITURE FUNCTION

The Keynesian consumption function is much simpler than the consumer-expenditure function [10.3]. The simplification is justified by the short period of analysis within which stocks are effectively fixed.

Substituting the definition of transitory income $(y_T \equiv y_N - y_P)$ into the consumer-expenditure function, we get

$$c = c(y_P, y_N - y_P, m - m^d, \Omega) \qquad [10.6]$$

Within the short period of analysis, permanent income y_P and the consumer durables stock Ω are fixed and so do not change consumer expenditures. The excess money supply $m - m^d$ has traditionally been assumed to be zero or to have negligible effects. This assumption will be continued for now, but will be considered further in Chap. 12. So the only variable in [10.6] which changes consumer expenditures within the short period is private income just as in the Keynesian consumption function [10.4]. The omitted variables determine the form and position of the function $c_K(\cdot)$. In succeeding periods, changes in y_P and Ω cause shifts in the Keynesian consumption function but movements along the consumer-expenditure function.

THE TREATMENT OF TAXES IN KEYNESIAN ANALYSIS

It is expositionally simpler if the definition of private income is substituted for private income in the short-run consumption function:

$$c_t = c_K(y - t) \qquad [10.7]$$

This eliminates possible confusion of private and total income.

The usual assumption is that the real burden of taxes (net of transfers) is held constant for purposes of analysis unless explicitly changed. An equally plausible assumption that taxes vary with total income is sometimes used. There is not much substantive difference in the analysis; consequently the simpler assumption of constant taxes will be followed.

One of the interesting questions considered in this framework is how fiscal policy in the form of tax changes will affect total income. The key point is how alternative amounts of taxes affect consumer spending. That can be considered now.

Figure 10.2 illustrates the short-run consumption function for the alternative taxes t_0 and t_1 where t_1 exceeds t_0. Income must be $t_1 - t_0$ higher in Case 1 than in Case 0 at the same level of consumer expenditures. This is clear in view of [10.7] and the fact that

$$(y + t_1 - t_0) - t_1 = y - t_0 \qquad [10.8]$$

Thus, an increase in taxes shifts the consumption function that amount to the right in the yc plane.

The shift in the consumption function due to a change in taxes can also be described as a vertical shift in the consumption function. The vertical distance between the curves is of interest in this regard because it measures the difference in consumer expenditures at the same level of total income. The MPC is

Figure 10.2 Alternative real taxes and the Keynesian consumption function. An increase in taxes from t_0 to t_1 shifts the consumption function to the right by $t_1 - t_0$. Since consumption is a function of private income $y_N \equiv y - t$, income must increase by just enough to make up for the tax increase if consumption is to be unchanged.

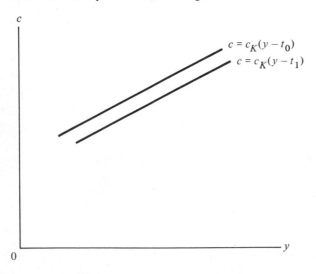

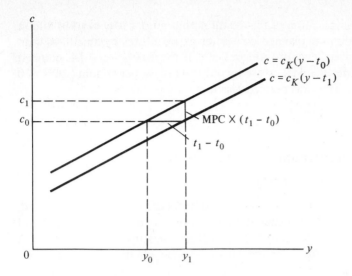

Figure 10.3 The vertical shift in the Keynesian consumption function due to a change in real taxes. The effect of a tax increase from t_0 to t_1 is to shift the consumption function to the right by $t_1 - t_0$. Therefore, if $c_K(y_0 - t_0) = c_0$ and $y_1 = y_0 + t_1 - t_0$, $c_K(y_1 - t_1) = c_0$. But by the definition of the marginal propensity to consume as the slope of the consumption function, $(c_1 - c_0)/(y_1 - y_0) = \text{MPC}$. So $c_1 - c_0 = \text{MPC} \cdot (t_1 - t_0)$. The vertical shift in the consumption function is $c_K(y_1 - t_1) - c_K(y_1 - t_0) = c_0 - c_1 = -\text{MPC} \cdot (t_1 - t_0)$. Hence, consumer spending for a given level of income changes by the marginal propensity to consume multiplied by minus the changes in taxes.

by definition the slope of the short-run consumption fuction. Consider the triangle drawn in Fig. 10.3. Here y_1 exceeds y_0 by $t_1 - t_0$. Assuming taxes of t_0, c_0 corresponds to y_0 and c_1 to y_1. Now

$$\frac{c_1 - c_0}{y_1 - y_0} = \text{MPC}$$

$$c_1 - c_0 = \text{MPC} \cdot (y_1 - y_0)$$

$$c_1 - c_0 = \text{MPC} \cdot (t_1 - t_0) \qquad [10.9]$$

If taxes are t_1 instead, c_0 corresponds to an income of y_1. And so, the vertical distance between the short-run consumption functions corresponding to t_0 and t_1 is equal to the MPC times the difference in taxes.[8] This is the *decrease* in consumption for a given income corresponding to an *increase* in taxes; therefore, consumer expenditures are a decreasing function of taxes.

---

[8] This result holds exactly only if the short-run consumption function is a straight line with constant MPC in the region of interest. An equivalent result for the long-run consumption function was derived in Sec. 8.3.

The substantive implication of this result is that a tax cut of say $10 billion per annum would increase planned consumer expenditures by much less than that amount at a given level of total income. If the MPC were 0.4, planned consumer expenditures would increase by only $4 billion per annum (0.4 × $10 billion = $4 billion). This was derived less formally in Sec. 8.3.

10.3 OTHER EXPENDITURE COMPONENTS

KEYNESIAN INVESTMENT ANALYSIS

Investment is normally only about 8 percent of total income.[9] Keynes believed, however, that variations in investment demand were a very important cause of business fluctuations. It is certainly true that there are substantial variations in the investment-income ratio over the business cycle whether these variations are cause or effect.

There is a variety of approaches—largely overlapping—to deriving the Keynesian investment-demand function. Almost all approaches are simple elaborations of the basic investment function presented in Sec. 4.2. Perhaps the simplest approach relates investment to changes in the desired stock of capital.

Investment is the rate of change in the stock of capital, so investment demand is derived from changes in the demand for capital.[10] The desired stock of capital, for given conditions, is that stock at which the real rental rate received on capital just covers the cost of financing capital. If the real rental rate on capital were greater than the cost of financing capital, firms would have an incentive to increase the capital stock. If the real rental rate were less than the cost of financing capital, firms would want to reduce the capital stock by not replacing worn-out machines. The higher the amount of capital relative to labor, the lower will be the real rental rate earned on capital, and vice versa. So these adjustments will tend, other things being equal, to move the stock of capital toward an amount at which the real rental rate on capital just equals the cost of financing capital.

In the aggregate, the cost of financing capital is measured by the real interest rate.[11] Given the expected rate of inflation, it is permissible to use changes in the nominal rate of interest as a measure of changes in the cost of financing capital. Since lower desired capital stocks are associated, other things being equal, with higher costs of financing capital, and vice versa, it follows that the stock demand for capital is a decreasing function of the nominal interest rate.

---

[9] See for example Table 2.3.

[10] In microeconomic terms, the demand for capital is a demand to hold a stock, while investment demand is a demand to alter the stock held.

[11] In a strict Keynesian model, no explicit distinction is made between the nominal and real interest rate. It is nonetheless implicit in what Keynes refered to as the "state of long-term expectation" and is widely used by recent Keynesians.

The most important " other thing " in determining the rental rate earned by a given quantity of capital is the amount of labor used with the capital. Within the short period of analysis, variations in the amount of labor employed are uniquely associated with the level of real income. So the level of employment can be measured by the level of real income—higher employment corresponding to higher real income. Given the nominal interest rate and other factors, increases in real income will increase the desired capital stock and decreases in real income will decrease the desired capital stock. So the stock demand for capital is an increasing function of real income.

The nominal interest rate and real income are the only explicit arguments of the Keynesian investment-demand function. In functional notation the desired capital stock k^d is determined as

$$k^d = k^d(R, y) \qquad [10.10]$$

where k^d is a decreasing function of the nominal interest rate R and an increasing function of real income y. Changes in any other factor affecting the desired capital stock would be represented as a shift or change in the function $k^d(\ )$.

Investment is the rate of change in capital. The desired level of investment will reflect the expected rate of change in the desired capital stock and any difference between the current actual capital stock and desired capital stock.

The desired capital stock is expected to expand over time as the labor force and real income grow. Existing firms undertake expansion and new firms steadily enter. This normal growth in the capital stock provides a base or normal level of investment. Indeed, contracts are often made months or even years in advance, so that there is normally a cost involved in varying the actual rate of investment away from this normal rate in a short period, whether up or down.

If the currently desired capital stock differs from the actual capital stock, firms will want to increase or decrease the rate of investment from the normal rate.[12] The precise rate at which firms want to adjust actual capital stock toward desired capital stock will be affected by the costs of varying the rate of investment and the extent to which the current level of employment is extrapolated into the future.

The conclusion to be drawn is that investment is an increasing function of both the normal rate of investment and of desired capital stock minus actual capital stock. But, for the short period being analyzed, both the normal rate of investment and the actual capital stock are fixed by the existing conditions. Thus, for the purposes of Keynesian analysis, the only endogenous variables

---

[12] If the difference between the current actual capital stock and desired capital stock were attributed to factors that would not extend to the next short period, this would not occur. A change in the expected rate of change in the desired capital stock would completely offset the effect of the difference between the current actual and desired capital stocks. In the text, expectations are assumed to extrapolate current conditions at least partially into the future.

which affect investment are those which affect the desired capital stock: the nominal interest rate and real income. Increases in the desired capital stock increase investment, and decreases in the desired capital stock decrease investment. Therefore, the investment-demand function can be stated as

$$i = i(R, y) \qquad\qquad [10.11]$$

where investment is a decreasing function of the interest rate R and an increasing function of real income y.

The graphical representation of investment demand in the yi plane is shown in Fig. 10.4. The upward slope of the investment function for any given interest rate shows that investment is an increasing function of real income. For any level of income, investment is higher for R_0 than for R_1, because R_0 is less than R_1 and investment is a decreasing function of the nominal interest rate.

Figure 10.4 The investment-demand function. Investment is a decreasing function of the nominal interest rate and an increasing function of real income. That investment is an increasing function of real income is illustrated by the positive slope of the investment function when graphed for a given nominal interest rate R_0 in the yi plane. That investment is a decreasing function of the nominal interest rate is shown by the fact that the investment-demand function for R_1, where R_1 exceeds R_0, lies below the investment-demand function for R_0.

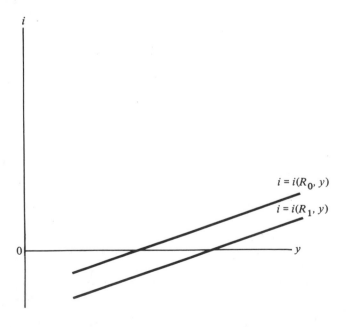

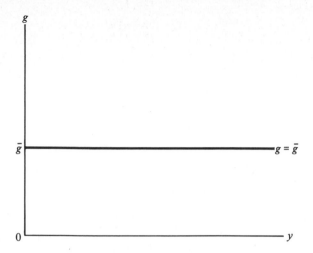

Figure 10.5 The government-expenditure function. The government-expenditure function is a constant function $g = \bar{g}$. This is graphed as a horizontal line in the yg plane at height $\bar{g}$.

GOVERNMENT EXPENDITURES

Government expenditures for real goods and services are currently about one-quarter of total income. Their determination in the Keynesian model presents no particular difficulties. Since government expenditures are subject to the discretion of government officials, they are treated as exogenously given by fiscal policy. That is, government expenditures are simply a constant g. A comparative statics analysis might be used to consider two alternative levels of government expenditures, however. Figure 10.5 illustrates government expenditures in the yg plane for a particular value $\bar{g}$.

NET EXPORTS

Real net exports make up a tiny, possibly negative fraction of total expenditures in the United States. The variability of net exports can be substantial, however, particularly in countries with an extensive international trade.

On the Keynesian view all prices are given, so the only factors affecting real net exports are domestic real income and foreign real income. Foreign real income is exogenous to the model, so foreign purchases (American exports) are fixed. American purchases from abroad (imports) increase with income, however. This happens because part of consumer expenditures and investment, which increase with real income, are for foreign goods.

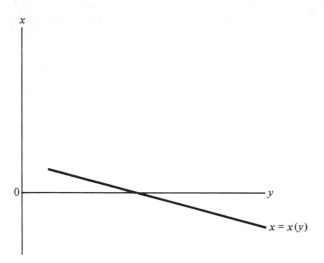

Figure 10.6 The net-exports function. Net exports are a
decreasing function of real income. This is illustrated by a
negative slope for the graph of the net-exports function in the yx
plane.

Increases in real income decrease net exports (exports less imports), and
decreases in real income increase net exports. In functional notation,

$$x = x(y) \tag{10.12}$$

where net exports are a decreasing function of real income. This is illustrated in
the yx plane in Fig. 10.6.

THE AGGREGATE EXPENDITURE FUNCTION

Aggregate expenditures are the sum of consumer expenditures, investment,
government expenditures, and net exports:

$$c + i + g + x = c_K(y - t) + i(R, y) + g + x(y) \tag{10.13}$$

Using the symbol a for aggregate expenditures $(c + i + g + x)$, the aggregate
expenditure function is

$$a = a(y, R; g, t) \tag{10.14}$$

The nature of the aggregate expenditure function is deduced from the component functions on the right-hand side of [10.13]. Consumption and investment

are increasing functions of real income, while net exports are a decreasing function of real income. But net exports decrease with an increase in real income only because a *part* of the increase in consumer expenditures and investment is used to buy foreign goods. This part cancels out, and the remainder of the increase in consumer expenditures and investment causes aggregate expenditures to increase. Thus, aggregate expenditures are an increasing function of real income. The only effect of the nominal interest rate on aggregate expenditures is through the investment-demand function. And so, aggregate expenditures are a decreasing function of the nominal interest rate. Real government expenditures and taxes are fixed for the model but included explicitly in the function because they frequently figure in comparative statics problems. An increase in real government expenditures increases aggregate expenditures by the same amount, other things being equal. Similarly, an increase in real taxes decreases aggregate expenditures by the amount of the increase times the marginal propensity to consume.

The aggregate expenditure function can be derived graphically, as shown in Fig. 10.7. On the same axes, all four components of aggregate expenditures are graphed as functions of real income. They are then added vertically to obtain aggregate expenditures as a function of real income.

Figure 10.7 The aggregate expenditure function. The aggregate expenditure function for given values R_0, g, and t is derived by vertically summing the expenditure functions corresponding to those values for consumer expenditures, investment, government expenditures, and net exports. This illustrates desired or planned aggregate expenditures as an increasing function of real income.

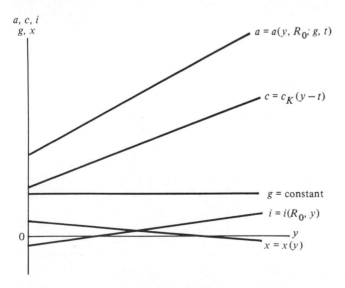

10.4 KEYNESIAN MONEY DEMAND AND SUPPLY

KEYNESIAN MONEY DEMAND

Keynesian real money demand is determined by the level of real income and the nominal interest rate.[13] It is assumed that there is no interest paid on money—not even bank deposits—so that the nominal interest rate measures the interest foregone if money is held instead of bonds. "Bond" is used in Keynesian discussions as a collective term for all nonmoney financial assets.

In functional notation,

$$m^d = m^d(y, R) \qquad [10.15]$$

Real money demand is an increasing function of real income. This is true because income is a measure of the level of transactions taking place and also of the wealth of moneyholders—that is, a measure of the work to be done by money and of the wealth constraint on asset holdings. The level of total income

---

[13] This can be viewed as a simplification of a more general money-demand function such as that discussed in Parts Two and Three of this book. The effect of any omitted variables is implicit in the functional form of money demand.

Figure 10.8 The money-demand function. Keynesian money demand is an increasing function of real income and a decreasing function of the nominal interest rate; (a) illustrates the graph of money demand in the mR plane for a given real income y_0. It has a negative slope because increases in the nominal interest rate reduce the amount of real money demanded. In (b), money demand is graphed in the my plane for a given level of the nominal interest rate R_0. Since increases in real income increase the real quantity of money demanded, the graph is positively sloped.

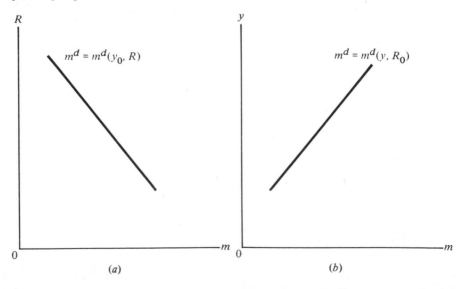

$$m^d = m^d(y_0, R)$$

$$m^d = m^d(y, R_0)$$

(a)   (b)

is clearly a better indicator of transactions than wealth, however. The interest rate measures the alternative return available on holding bonds instead of money. At higher rates of interest, bonds would be more attractive relative to money, so more bonds and less money would be held. The same transactions could be made with lower average money holdings, but only by undertaking the costs of more frequent buying and selling of bonds or otherwise synchronizing receipts and expenditures of money.[14]

Money demand can be graphed in the mR plane for a given value of y [see Fig. 10.8(a)] or in the my plane for a given value of R [Fig. 10.8(b)]. In the first instance, the effects of alternative levels of income are indicated by the placement of the demand curve: Higher incomes shift the demand curve to the right, since more money would be demanded at each level of interest. Similarly, lower incomes shift the demand curve to the left. In panel (b), lower interest rates shift the demand curve to the right, since more money would be demanded at each level of income. Higher interest rates would shift the graph to the left.

THE LIQUIDITY TRAP

A very special hypothesis of Keynes, one still retained by some of his followers, is known as the liquidity trap. The hypothesis is that there is some positive interest rate at which the demand for money becomes infinitely elastic. This means that the money-demand curve in the mR plane becomes horizontal at a minimum interest rate R^{min}, as illustrated in Fig. 10.9. The horizontal portion of the demand for money curve is called the *liquidity trap*.

It is supposed that if the interest rate declined at all below R^{min}, all bonds would be sold and people would want to hold money only. At exactly R^{min}, people are indifferent between any combination of money and bonds so long as they hold at least the minimum amount of money consistent with R^{min}.

Keynes attributed this minimum interest rate to the operation of the speculative motive for holding money. The *speculative motive* refers to the desire to hold money instead of interest-bearing bonds because bond prices are expected to fall. There is some interest rate greater than zero, Keynes argued, below which everyone would agree that interest rates must rise and hence bond prices must fall. At any rate below that, no one would want to hold bonds, and so money demand would become unlimited.

However, unless expectations about interest rates are practically unanimous, there will not be a point at which everyone suddenly switches from money to bonds. Instead, a normal, downward-sloping demand curve for

---

[14] The classic analyses are William J. Baumol, The Transactions Demand for Cash: An Inventory Theoretic Approach, *Quarterly Journal of Economics*, **66**: 545–556, Nov. 1952; and James Tobin, The Interest-Elasticity of Transactions Demand for Cash, *Review of Economics and Statistics*, **38**: 241–247, Aug. 1956.

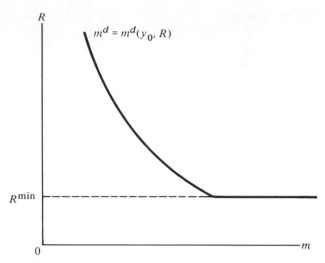

Figure 10.9 The money-demand function with a liquidity trap. If the liquidity trap exists, there is some low but positive nominal interest rate R^{min} at which the elasticity of the demand for money with respect to the nominal interest rate becomes infinite. This is illustrated by a horizontal demand curve in the mR plane at R^{min} and real income y_0. An increase in real income shifts the demand function to the right but does not change R^{min}.

money would emerge for the community as a whole.[15] Consequently, this argument provided no logical necessity for the existence of the liquidity trap.

An alternative explanation of the speculative motive was proposed by James Tobin.[16] He suggested that people have to be paid to accept the risk of holding bonds which can fluctuate in price. Generally, the higher the interest rate, the greater the risk that will be accepted. Only under special assumptions, however, does this approach imply the existence of a liquidity trap.

Both Keynes' and Tobin's arguments provide reasons for people to shift from long-term bonds as interest rates decline, but it is not clear why people would shift into money instead of short-term bonds. Short-term bonds provide a practically risk-free return, which, in the Keynesian model, money does not.

---

[15] A more convincing argument for a relatively interest-elastic demand for money function is based on the term-structure of interest rates. Long-term rates are identified as "the" interest rates and these interest rates are "little" affected by current short-term rates. This occurs because expected future short-term rates are the dominant factor in explaining long-term interest rates, and expected future short-term rates are little affected by current short-term rates. If the demand for money is a function of short-term interest rates, and small variations in the long-term interest rate are caused by large variations in the short-term interest rate, large changes in the demand for money would be associated empirically with small, short-period changes in the long-term interest rate. Over time, long-term and short-term interest rates return to their normal relationship, so this is only a temporary phenomenon.

[16] James Tobin, Liquidity Preference as Behavior towards Risk, *Review of Economics Studies*, **25**: 65–86, Feb. 1958.

Perhaps the best argument for the liquidity trap at a positive rate of interest is that short-term bond yields cannot decline to so low a level that they do not cover the transaction costs of buying them and collecting the amount due.

Keynes himself never claimed that the liquidity trap had ever been encountered in the real world. Nor is there any empirical evidence indicating that it has ever been encountered. Perhaps the very short-run increase in fluidity immediately following an increase in the money supply could be viewed as a temporary liquidity trap. That interpretation is a bit strained, because these increases reflect differences in actual money balances and long-run demand, or disequilibrium, rather than movements along the long-run demand for money function.

Nor is the existence of a liquidity trap necessary or sufficient for the major Keynesian propositions. It merely permits an expositional simplification and unduly extreme statements on the relative effectiveness of fiscal and monetary policy. Lacking both necessity and evidence, the liquidity trap has been abandoned by many Keynesians.

THE SUPPLY OF MONEY

Like real government expenditures, the nominal supply of money is determined by decisions of government officials. Therefore, the nominal money supply is treated as exogenously given by monetary policy. That is, the nominal money supply is simply a constant

$$M^S = M \qquad [10.16]$$

The given price level assumption enters at this point. Since the price level is fixed at some particular value $\bar{P}$, it is possible to say that control over the nominal money supply is equivalent to control over the real money supply.

$$m^S = \frac{M^S}{\bar{P}} = \frac{M}{\bar{P}} = m \qquad [10.17]$$

Note that, in the Keynesian model, the rigidity of prices assures that supply conditions determine real money balances. This differs from the dynamic model in which adjustment (over time) in the price level allows conditions of money demand to determine real money balances.

SUMMARY

1 The Keynesian approach to macroeconomics investigates intensively the determinants of a single point on the aggregate demand schedule. This chapter presents basic elements which are combined in a unified model in Chap. 11.

2 There are three sorts of basic elements used in the Keynesian analysis: (*a*) Underlying assumptions set the framework within which the analysis is carried out. (*b*) Functions determining the components and total of aggregate expenditures explain aggregate expenditures as a function of real income, nominal interest rate, and some exogenously given variables. (*c*) Money demand and supply are also functions of real income, nominal interest rate, and some exogenously given variables.

3 The underlying assumptions are that the analysis is a static one applied to a short period, that the price level is given for the period, and that a quantity adjustment mechanism moves the economy to the static equilibrium within the short period.

4 The major components of aggregate expenditures are consumer expenditures, investment, government spending, and net exports.

5 Consumer expenditures are an increasing function of private income (total income less taxes). A change in the assumed level of taxes changes consumer spending for a given level of income by minus the marginal propensity to consume times the change in taxes.

6 Investment is a decreasing function of the nominal interest rate, given the expected inflation rate, and an increasing function of real income. Government expenditures are exogenously given, like taxes, by fiscal policy. Net exports are a decreasing function of real income.

7 Aggregate expenditures are an increasing function of real income and a decreasing function of the nominal interest rate.

8 Generally, real money demand is an increasing function of real income and a decreasing function of the nominal interest rate. Some Keynesian economists hypothesize that a liquidity trap with infinitely elastic money demand exists at a positive rate of interest, but this is neither required for the Keynesian model nor observed empirically.

9 Since the price level is given and the nominal money supply is subject to government control, monetary policy can be taken to determine the real money supply.

CONCEPTS TO KNOW

aggregate expenditure function
constant price level
consumer-expenditure function
consumption function
consumption of service flows
fixed investment
inventory investment

liquidity trap
marginal propensity to consume (MPC)
quantity adjustment mechanism
short-period assumption
speculative motive

QUESTIONS AND EXERCISES

*1 If investment is R\$100 billion per annum and the capital stock is initially R\$3,000 billion, how much would the capital stock be worth after 1 year? After $\frac{1}{2}$ year? After $\frac{1}{4}$ year? Why does the assumption of a "short period" make a constant capital stock and positive rate of investment compatible?

2 "The Keynesian approach to macroeconomics investigates intensively the determinants of a single point on the aggregate demand schedule." Why can the aggregate supply schedule and all the other points on the aggregate demand schedule be neglected?

*3 (a) Suppose that the consumption function is $c = R\$500$ billion/year $+ 0.3y$. If $i + g + x$ were somehow fixed at R\$500 billion per annum, at what level of real income would $c + i + g + x = y$?

(b) Suppose that $i + g + x$ were instead fixed at R\$600 billion per annum. At what level of real income would $c + i + g + x = y$?

(c) What is the value of the marginal propensity to consume in the assumed consumption function? Why might $1/(1 - \text{MPC})$ be called the simple income multiplier of changes in $i + g + x$?

4 (a) Omitting the units of coefficients, suppose the investment-demand function can be written as $i = 20 + 0.1y - 500R$. If real income is measured in billions of base-year dollars per annum and the interest rate as a decimal fraction per annum, what units must be applied to the coefficients 20, 0.1, and 500?

(b) Complete the following table:

R	y	i
0.03	1000	
0.04	1000	
0.05	1000	
0.03	1100	
0.04	1100	
0.05	1100	

(c) Do the figures in the table in part (b) show the correct general properties for an investment-demand function? Why?

5 Why is the effect of an increase in income on net exports less in absolute amount than the effect on $c + i$?

6 According to [10.1], aggregate expenditures equal real income. How then can aggregate expenditures be a function of real income? (*Hint:* The quantity demanded and supplied of a commodity are always equal. How can the demand and supply functions be different?)

*7 Why might short-period changes in real income be associated with smaller changes in real money demand than if they were to persist over a long period of time?

8 Why might short-period changes in the long-term interest rate be associated with larger changes in real money demand than if they were to persist over a long period of time?

REFERENCES FOR FURTHER READING

References are given at the end of Chap. 11, as most of them refer to these topics in the context of the model presented there.

CHAPTER 11

THE COMPLETE KEYNESIAN MODEL

WHAT YOU WILL LEARN IN THIS CHAPTER
How the IS curve portrays equilibrium in the goods
market ● How the LM curve portrays equilibrium in
the money market ● The intersection of the IS and
LM curves determines short-run equilibrium real
income and nominal interest rate ● Factors which
shift the IS and LM curves ● Short-run effects of
fiscal and monetary policy ● Derivation of the
aggregate demand curve

11.1 THE IS-LM MODEL

THE IS-LM APPROACH

The IS-LM model shows how real income and the nominal interest rate adjust
so that the desired level of aggregate expenditures equals real income at the
same time that the real quantity of money demanded equals the amount
supplied. This model, developed by Sir John Hicks,[1] is thus a useful graphical
device for determining the short-period equilibrium of the economy and the
impact of various macroeconomic shocks. The approach is a familiar one for
economists. Determinants of equilibrium are divided into two largely separate
groups—the income-expenditures sector and the monetary sector. Each sector
is summarized by a single equation or line in the *yr* plane. This can be done
because the only variables which directly affect both the income-expenditures
and monetary sectors simultaneously are real income and the nominal interest
rate. One line shows all combinations of real income and the nominal interest
rate for which the income-expenditures sector is in equilibrium. The other
shows all combinations of the same variables in which the monetary sector is in
equilibrium. So the intersection of the two lines is the only combination of real
income and the nominal interest rate for which both sectors are in equilibrium.

   This approach follows the familiar pattern of supply and demand analysis.

---

[1] John R. Hicks, Mr. Keynes and the "Classics"; A Suggested Interpretation, *Econometrica*, **5:** 147–159, Apr.
1937.

There all the factors affecting the output of a particular commodity are grouped according to whether they affect the amount offered for sale (supply) or the amount purchased (demand).[2] Normally the only common factors are quantity and price. Therefore, the supply and demand curves are drawn in the quantity-price plane. Their intersection is the only combination of price and quantity at which the market is in equilibrium. The same mode of analysis was used in Chap. 4 to derive and use the labor market (LE) and capital market equilibrium (KE) curves.

THE BASIC KEYNESIAN EQUATIONS

The Keynesian model can be solved by the set of five equations [11.1] through [11.5] listed and described in Table 11.1. The five unknown (endogenous) variables that must be simultaneously determined by this system of five equations are real income y, the nominal interest rate R, aggregate expenditures a, real quantity of money demanded m^d, and real quantity of money supplied m^s. The three exogenous policy variables—real government spending g, real taxes t, and deflated nominal money m—enter the system explicitly, but they are fixed in determining any particular solution of the model. All other factors which affect the solution do so by changing (shifting) either of the behavioral relations [11.1] and [11.3]. Since there are five equations and five unknowns, a unique solution is possible.

Equation [11.1] is the aggregate expenditure function. Equation [11.3] is the money-demand function. Equation [11.4] sets money supply at the amount exogenously given by monetary policy. These three relations were considered in Chap. 10.

Equations [11.2] and [11.5] are the conditions of equilibrium in the income-expenditures sector and the monetary sector, respectively. In Chap. 2 it was seen that aggregate expenditures—the sum of consumer expenditures, investment, government expenditures, and net exports—are exactly equal to total

---

[2] If this division cannot be made, as when the same factors affect costs of production and demand for the product, the analysis is messy and inconclusive. It will be seen that the same is true at times for the IS-LM model.

Table 11.1 THE BASIC KEYNESIAN EQUATIONS

Equation	Description	Number
$a = a(y, R; g, t)$	Aggregate expenditures	[11.1]
$a = y$	Income-expenditures equilibrium	[11.2]
$m^d = m^d(y, R)$	Demand for money	[11.3]
$m^s = m$	Supply of money	[11.4]
$m^d = m^s$	Monetary equilibrium	[11.5]

income after all is said and done. Equation [11.2] assures that this occurs for the desired or planned level of aggregate expenditures determined in [11.1]. Similarly, [11.5] assures that the quantity of money demanded will equal the quantity of money supplied.

The model as stated explicitly assures that there is equilibrium in the markets for goods and money. But what about the third Keynesian market—the market for bonds? The equilibrium of this market is implied by equilibrium in the other markets. This is true because people can plan to buy more bonds than are issued only if they also plan to spend less income than they receive, decrease money balances below the amount supplied, or both. These are the only sources of funds to buy the bonds. Similarly, if people plan to buy fewer bonds than are issued, they must plan to spend more than they receive as income or increase money balances. But in the equilibrium defined by [11.1] through [11.5], people plan to spend just as much income as they receive and to hold just as much money as is supplied. Therefore, it must be true that the demand and supply of bonds are also in equilibrium. The aggregate expenditure and money-demand and -supply functions implicitly reflect the associated effects of bond demand and supply.

It may be possible to solve Eqs. [11.1] through [11.5], but the fact that there is one equation for each unknown is not sufficient to guarantee that a unique solution will exist. This would not occur if some of the equations were either redundant or inconsistent. To show that a unique solution in fact exists, it is necessary to turn to a graphical analysis.

THE DERIVATION OF THE IS CURVE

Equations [11.1] and [11.2] can be combined to describe the equilibrium of the income-expenditures sector:

$$a(y, R; g, t) - y = 0 \qquad\qquad [11.6]$$

This equation states that in equilibrium the excess demand for goods must be zero. This is true because $a(y, R; g, t)$ is the amount of goods demanded and y is the amount of goods actually produced. Equation [11.6] is called an *implicit function* of real income and the interest rate because the functional relationship between the two is implied by requiring y and R to vary so that the excess demand for goods remains zero. This equation defines the income-expenditures equilibrium or IS curve.[3]

The graphical derivation of the IS curve is a two-step procedure. The first step involves graphing the aggregate expenditure function in the ya plane for a

---

[3] The name IS was adopted because of early Keynesian emphasis on the relation of investment and saving in a model excluding government spending and net exports.

given interest rate R_0, as shown in Fig. 11.1. The aggregate expenditure function is an increasing function of real income but with a slope less than unity.
The only level of income consistent with the given interest rate R_0 and the
condition that aggregate expenditures equal income is y_0. Consider a second
interest rate, R_1, which is less than R_0. Since aggregate expenditures are a
decreasing function of the nominal interest rate, the aggregate expenditure
curve for R_1 will be everywhere above the curve for R_0 as drawn in Fig. 11.2.
Consequently the equilibrium level of real income y_1 for R_1 is higher than the
level y_0 for R_0. This statement is true for every combination of nominal interest
rates.

This argument proves that the locus of all points in the yR plane for which
the goods market is in equilibrium must be negatively sloping. Thus the IS
curve, as defined by [11.6], has a negative slope, as shown in Fig. 11.3. The
curve could actually be derived by finding the real income corresponding to
every possible interest rate or by solving [11.6] for y as a (decreasing) function
of R:

$$y = \text{IS}(R) \tag{11.7}$$

**Figure 11.1 Determination of equilibrium real income for a
given nominal interest rate R_0.** The aggregate expenditure
function for the given interest rate R_0 is graphed as $a =
a(y, R_0; g, t)$. The slope is less than 1 because a R\$1 increase
in real income increases aggregate expenditures by less than
R\$1, other things being equal. The other line, labeled 45°, is drawn
through the origin with slope equal to 1. It is the locus of all
points for which $a = y$—that is, all points with zero excess
demand for goods. Real income $y_0 = a_0$ is therefore the only
level of real income consistent with a nominal interest rate
of R_0 and equilibrium in the goods market.

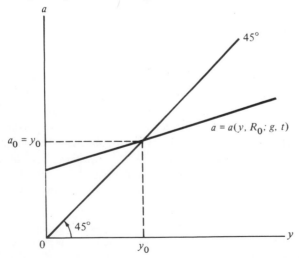

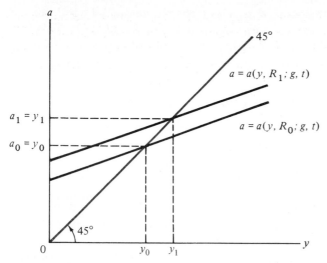

Figure 11.2 The effect of alternative interest rates on equilibrium real income. Interest rate R_0 is greater than R_1. Since aggregate expenditures are a decreasing function of the nominal interest rate, the aggregate expenditure curve for R_1 will lie everywhere above the one for R_0. So the level of equilibrium real income y_1 implied by interest rate R_1 exceeds the level y_0 implied by R_0. In terms of goods market equilibrium, lower interest rates are associated with higher levels of real income.

Figure 11.3 The income-expenditures equilibrium or IS curve. The IS curve plots all combinations of real income y and the nominal interest rate R for which income and expenditures are equal. This curve has a negative slope because lower interest rates are associated with higher levels of income. The IS curve is the graph of [11.6].

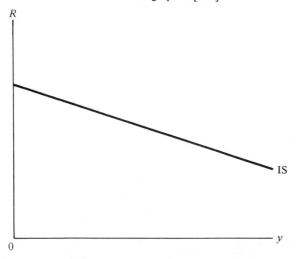

Note that the greater the effect of a given change in nominal interest rates on aggregate expenditures, the less steeply sloped will be the IS curve. This happens because small decreases in R will be associated with larger increases in y.

THE DERIVATION OF THE LM CURVE

Equations [11.3], [11.4], and [11.5] are combined to describe the equilibrium of the monetary sector

$$m^d(y, R) - m = 0 \qquad\qquad [11.8]$$

Equation [11.8] states that in equilibrium the excess demand for money must be zero. The function $m^d(y, R)$ determines the demand for real money, and m is the amount of money supplied, as determined by the government. This equation implies a functional relationship for the values of real income and the nominal interest rate which are consistent with equilibrium in the money market. So [11.8] defines the monetary equilibrium or LM curve.[4]

---

[4] This name arose because Keynes referred to the money-demand function as the liquidity preference function (L) and the money supply as M.

Figure 11.4 Determination of equilibrium nominal interest rate for a given real income y_0. If the money market is to be in equilibrium, money demand $m^d = m^d(y, R)$ must equal money supply $m^s = m$. This occurs only at the intersection of the money demand and money supply curves. If real income were y_0, the money market would be in equilibrium only at an interest rate of R_0.

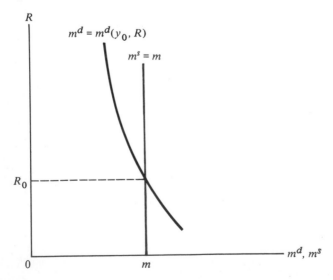

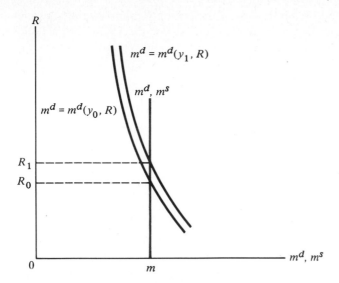

Figure 11.5 The effect of alternative real incomes on the equilibrium interest rate. Real income y_1 is greater than y_0. Since real money demand is an increasing function of real income, the demand curve for y_1 lies to the right of the demand curve for y_0. Hence, the equilibrium nominal interest rate R_1 implied by real income y_1 exceeds the rate R_0 implied by y_0. In terms of money market equilibrium, higher nominal interest rates are associated with higher levels of real income.

The slope of the LM curve is established by a graphical technique similar to that used for the IS curve. The money-demand function for a given real income y_0 is graphed in Fig. 11.4. The curve is negatively sloped because real money demand is a decreasing function of the interest rate. The supply of real money is a vertical line at m. Supply and demand are equal—excess demand is zero—at the point (m, R_0) where the supply and demand curves intersect.

Consider a second real income y_1 which is greater than y_0. Since money demand is an increasing function of real income, the money demand curve for y_1 will lie everywhere to the right of the money demand curve for y_0. As shown in Fig. 11.5, this graph implies that the nominal interest rate R_1 associated with y_1 is greater than the nominal interest rate R_0 associated with y_0 and indicates that higher levels of real income are associated with higher interest rates if the money market is to remain in equilibrium.

Thus the locus of all points in the yR plane for which the money market is in equilibrium must be positively sloping. This is the LM curve, defined by [11.8] and illustrated in Fig. 11.6. The LM curve could be derived by plotting the nominal interest rate corresponding to every possible real income or by solving [11.8] for R as an (increasing) function of y;

$$R = \text{LM}(y) \qquad [11.9]$$

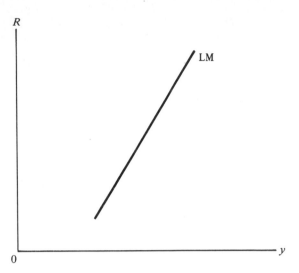

Figure 11.6 The monetary equilibrium or LM curve. The
LM curve plots all combinations of real income y and the
nominal interest rate R for which real money demand and
real money supply are equal. This curve has a positive
slope because higher levels of the nominal interest rate are
associated with higher levels of real income. The LM curve
is the graph of [11.8].

The greater the increase in money demand for a given increase in real income
and the smaller the decrease in money demand for a given increase in the
nominal interest rate, the steeper will be the slope of the LM curve. This follows
because small increases in y will be associated with larger increases in the
interest rate.

SPECIAL CASES OF THE LM CURVE

Two extreme cases of money demand are often discussed: perfectly interest-
inelastic money demand and the liquidity trap. If either of these occur in the
relevant range of real incomes and nominal interest rates, the LM curve will
not be positively sloped.

In the case of perfectly interest-inelastic money demand, changes in interest
rates have no effect on money demand. So the money demand curve is a
vertical line in the mR plane. For one and only one level of real income, money
demand and supply will coincide regardless of the interest rate, as shown in
Fig. 11.7(*a*). Thus, the LM curve will be a vertical line at that level of real
income, as shown in (*b*) of that figure.

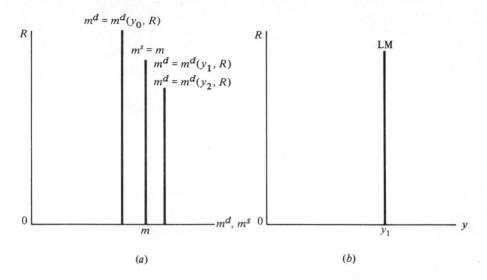

Figure 11.7 The LM curve in the presence of perfectly interest-inelastic real money demand. If real money demand is perfectly inelastic with respect to the nominal interest rate, the real-money-demand curve is a vertical line determined by the level of real income alone. For real income y_1 in (a), this vertical line and the real-money-supply curve coincide, and so any interest rate R whatsoever and real income y_1 imply equilibrium in the money market. If real income were lower, say y_0, real money demand would be shifted to the left and there is no interest rate at which real money demand and real money supply are equal. Similarly, levels of real income higher than y_1, such as y_2, imply that real money demand is higher than real money supply for all interest rates. Hence, the LM curve is a vertical line through y_1, as illustrated in (b).

In the case of the liquidity trap, the money demand curve becomes infinitely interest elastic (horizontal) at some positive interest rate R^{min}. Although increases in real income still shift money demand to the right, the liquidity trap portions will partially overlap, as shown in Fig. 11.8(a). Consequently different real incomes may be associated with the same nominal interest rate R^{min} as long as the money supply is large enough to intersect both demand curves in their liquidity trap portions. This leads to an LM curve characterized [as in Fig. 11.8(b)] by a horizontal portion at R^{min} for low levels of real income and a positively sloped portion for higher levels of real income.

DETERMINATION OF EQUILIBRIUM
REAL INCOME AND NOMINAL INTEREST RATE

The IS curve gives all possible combinations of real income and the nominal interest rate for which the goods market is in equilibrium. The LM curve gives all such combinations for which the money market is in equilibrium. If both are

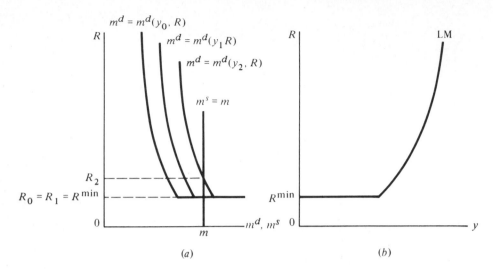

Figure 11.8 The LM curve in the presence of a liquidity trap. At real income y_0, the money supply curve in (*a*) intersects the liquidity trap portion of the money demand curve, and so $R_0 = R^{min}$. Any lower level of income would also be associated with R^{min}. An increase in real income from y_0 to y_1 shifts the demand curve to the right. In this instance, the shift is too small to change the interest rate, therefore $R_1 = R^{min}$. For sufficiently high levels of real income such as y_2, however, the supply curve intersects the demand for money out of the liquidity trap, and higher levels of income are associated with higher nominal interest rates. In this region the LM curve has the characteristic positive slope. All real incomes sufficiently low for money supply to intersect money demand in the liquidity trap will be associated with a single interest rate R^{min}. Consequently, the portion of the LM curve corresponding to these lower levels of income is horizontal at height R^{min}. The LM curve in (*b*) is thus horizontal for low levels of real income and positively sloped for higher levels.

graphed on the same axes, as in Fig. 11.9, their intersection at E or (y_e, R_e) is the only combination of real income and nominal interest rate at which the goods market and money market[5] are simultaneously in equilibrium.

The complete solution values to the original set of five equations—[11.1] through [11.5]—can now be given as y_e, R_e, $a_e = y_e$, $m^s = m$, and $m^d = m$. Given the negative slope of the IS curve and the positive (or nonnegative) slope of the LM curve, there cannot be more than one solution.[6] This one solution will in fact exist so long as there is either no liquidity trap or the IS curve intersects the vertical axis above R^{min}. The empirical evidence suggests that this has always been the case.

---

[5] And hence the bond market.
[6] More elaborate versions of the IS-LM model assume that it is possible that a R$1 increase in real income might increase desired aggregate expenditures by more than R$1 in which case the IS curve could be upward-sloping and multiple solutions could exist. These complications are neglected here on empirical grounds.

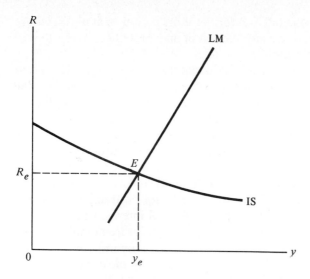

Figure 11.9 Determination of the equilibrium real income and nominal interest rate. The intersection E of the IS and LM curves, or (y_e, R_e), is the only point at which the goods market and the money market are simultaneously in equilibrium. So y_e and R_e are unique solution values for the set of equations [11.1] through [11.5].

This solution shows the results of a particular set of given conditions. The strength of the model is its ability to provide definite comparisons of the results associated with alternative given conditions. These comparative static analyses are the subject of the following sections.

11.2 EFFECTS OF SHIFTS IN THE INCOME-EXPENDITURES SECTOR

TYPES OF SHIFTS IN THE AGGREGATE EXPENDITURE FUNCTION

Shifts in the aggregate expenditure function must be caused by shifts in one or more of the component expenditure functions explaining consumer expenditures, investment, government expenditures, and net exports. Most emphasis has historically been placed on shifts in the investment-demand function, in government expenditures, and in the consumption function due to tax changes.

Since expectations and plans are given for the short period of analysis, we are considering the effects within the short period of unexpected changes—that is, the initial impact of macroeconomic shocks.

The position of the investment-demand function was believed by Keynes to depend on the unstable state of long-term expectation. He argued that the psychology of businessmen was subject to sudden changes between optimism and pessimism over the future returns to current investments.

These changes in expectations might reflect changes in belief about future real rental rates on capital or about the expected rate of inflation by which the expected real interest rate is derived from the nominal interest rate. Higher expected future real rental rates would most likely reflect higher expected future sales. This would make current investment more attractive. So would higher expected rates of inflation for a given nominal interest rate, since this lowers the real interest rate. Increased optimism about future nominal returns to investment—whether because of higher real returns or inflation—will increase the desired amount of investment for given values of the nominal interest rate and real income. Conversely, increased pessimism will shift the investment function downward.

The empirical question is whether expectations of business executives concerning future returns to investment are largely ephemeral, as suggested by Keynes, or firmly rooted in reality, as suggested by Keynes' critics. The evidence is not sufficient to provide any clear-cut answer on the magnitude of exogenous shifts in investment demand.

Government expenditures are set by fiscal policy and can be changed at will. So it is in principle possible to offset a shift in investment demand by an opposite shift in government expenditure.[7]

An alternative form of fiscal policy is to change real taxes and so induce shifts in the consumption function. Higher taxes shift the consumption function downward, and lower taxes shift the consumption function upward.

Exogenous shifts in the consumption function or net export function are conceivable, but they are not of much empirical interest for the United States. Such shifts affect real income through shifting the aggregate expenditure function in precisely the same way as a similar shift in the investment-demand function; therefore, no separate exposition is necessary.

Summing up, higher levels of investor optimism and government expenditures and lower levels of taxes are associated with higher values of the aggregate expenditure function for any given combination of real income and nominal interest rates. All shifts in the income-expenditure sector operate through their effect on the aggregate expenditure function.

---

[7] As will be seen in Chap. 15, this in fact requires the ability to alter government expenditures instantaneously or to predict sufficiently in advance what future shifts in investment demand will occur.

THE EFFECTS OF ALTERNATIVE EXPENDITURE FUNCTIONS

Consider two alternative aggregate expenditure functions:

$$a = a_0(y, R; g_0, t_0) \qquad\qquad [11.10]$$

$$a = a_1(y, R; g_1, t_1) \qquad\qquad [11.11]$$

Assume that for any given values of real income and the nominal interest rate, the aggregate expenditure function denoted by 0 implies lower desired aggregate expenditures than the alternative function denoted by 1. For the current analysis, it is irrelevant whether this difference arises because of differences in the functional relationships themselves, in the exogenous values of g or t, or in some combination. Table 11.2 gives examples of the changes in basic conditions which might cause aggregate expenditures to rise or fall.

For any given value of the interest rate, say $\overline{R}$, the aggregate expenditure function 1 will lie above the aggregate expenditure function 0 when they are graphed in the ya plane. This graph, shown in Fig. 11.10, implies that for any given interest rate there will be a higher equilibrium real income in Case 1 than in Case 0.

The IS curve is the locus of all points in the yR plane for which the goods market is in equilibrium. It was just seen that for any R, a higher equilibrium value of y occurs in Case 1 than in Case 0. Thus the IS curve for Case 1 (IS_1) lies to the right of the IS curve for Case 0 (IS_0), as shown in Fig. 11.11.

Table 11.2 SOURCES OF CHANGES IN DESIRED AGGREGATE EXPENDITURES FOR GIVEN REAL INCOME AND NOMINAL INTEREST RATE

Factors Which Would Increase Desired Aggregate Expenditures	Factors Which Would Decrease Desired Aggregate Expenditures
An increase in real government expenditures financed by borrowing	A decrease in real government expenditures financing reduced borrowing
A decrease in real taxes financed by borrowing	An increase in real taxes financing reduced borrowing
An autonomous upward shift in investment demand due to more favorable expectations	An autonomous downward shift in investment demand due to less favorable expectations
An autonomous upward shift in the consumption function	An autonomous downward shift in the consumption function
An autonomous upward shift in net exports due, for example, to increased foreign real income	An autonomous downward shift in net exports due, for example, to decreased foreign real income

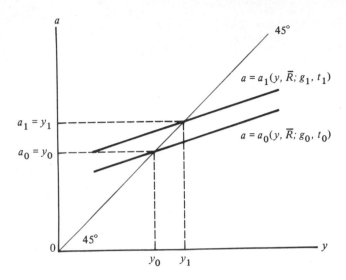

Figure 11.10 Effects of alternative aggregate expenditure functions on equilibrium real income for a given interest rate $\bar{R}$. For any nominal interest rate $\bar{R}$, the aggregate expenditure function denoted by 1 lies above the function denoted by 0. The condition for equilibrium in the goods market—that planned real aggregate expenditures equal real income—occurs where the aggregate expenditure function intersects the 45° line. So the equilibrium value of real income in Case 1, y_1, is higher than the equilibrium value in Case 0, y_0. In the simplest case of a parallel upward shift, it can be shown that the difference in equilibrium real income equals the difference in desired aggregate expenditures for $(y_0, \bar{R})$ divided by 1 minus the slope of the aggregate expenditure function.

The effect of alternative aggregate expenditure functions on equilibrium real income and nominal interest rate is found by combining the alternative IS curves with the LM curve. Since the money market is unaffected by the factors altering the aggregate expenditure function, the LM curve is the same for either case. Figure 11.12 shows that Case 1 implies higher equilibrium values of both real income and the nominal interest rate than Case 0. The increase in nominal interest rates from R_0 to R_1 reduces the amount of investment, other things being equal. So equilibrium income is increased less than would be the case if the interest rate were unchanged. The degree to which each changes reflects the magnitude of the shift in the IS curve and the slopes of both the IS and LM curves.

In the special case of a vertical LM curve (see Fig. 11.7), the shift in the IS curve from Case 0 to Case 1 would increase the nominal interest rate but not affect real income, as illustrated in Fig. 11.13. This case would imply complete *short-run* real (and nominal) crowding out of private expenditures by government expenditures. An increase in real government expenditures financed by

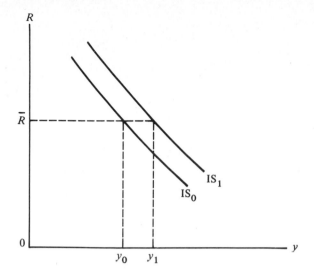

Figure 11.11 Implications of alternative aggregate expenditure functions for the IS curve. There is a higher equilibrium value of real income y in the goods market for any nominal interest rate R in Case 1 than in Case 0. It was seen, for example, in Fig. 11.10 that the interest rate $\overline{R}$ implied equilibrium income y_0 for the lower aggregate expenditures function and y_1 for the higher aggregate expenditure function. By the definition of the IS curve as the locus of equilibrium points for the goods market, the IS curve for Case 1 (IS_1) must lie to the right of the IS curve for Case 0 (IS_0).

borrowing would drive up the nominal interest rate until real investment was reduced by an equal amount. In the case of Fig. 11.12, the rise in the nominal interest rate reduced real money demand relative to real income (that is, reduced fluidity) so that real income increased. In the case of Fig. 11.13, real money demand is assumed unaffected by the nominal interest rate so money demand and supply can be equal only at one value of real income. Complete short-run crowding out does not appear consistent with the empirical evidence discussed in Sec. 8.2.

SUMMARY OF THE EFFECTS OF SHIFTS IN THE INCOME-EXPENDITURES SECTOR

Shifts in any of the functions determining the components of aggregate expenditures will alter the aggregate expenditure function. Keynesian economists generally believe that investment demand is subject to large shifts as a result of

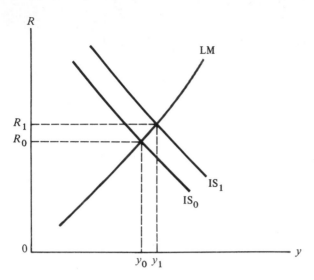

**Figure 11.12 Implications of alternative IS curves for equilibrium
real incomes and nominal interest rates.** IS_1 lies to the right of
and above IS_0 because the aggregate expenditure function for
Case 1 is greater than it is for Case 0. Since the LM curve is
positively sloped, the equilibrium point (y_1, R_1) for Case 1 lies
above and to the right of the equilibrium point (y_0, R_0) for
Case 0. These equilibrium incomes y_0 and y_1 allow for changes
in the equilibrium nominal interest rate and so differ from the
incomes derived for a given $\bar{R}$ in Figs. 11.10 and 11.11. The
increase in R from R_0 to R_1 makes for a smaller increase in
income. For a given slope of the IS curves and a given horizontal
distance between them, the flatter (more nearly horizontal) the
LM curve, the greater will be the difference in real income and
the less will be the difference in interest rates. For a given slope
of the LM curve and a given horizontal distance between the
IS curves, the flatter (more nearly horizontal) the IS curve, the
less will be the differences in real income and the less will be
the difference in nominal interest rates. For given slopes of
the IS and LM curves, the greater the horizontal distance
between the IS curves, the greater will be the differences in
both real income and nominal interest rates. (See Exercises 5, 6,
and 7 for the proofs of these three propositions.)

the state of expectations. Other important shifts occur because of fiscal policy:
changes in government expenditures and in the consumption function due to
tax changes. Higher levels of investor optimism and government expenditures
or lower levels of taxes are associated with higher aggregate expenditure functions. A higher aggregate expenditure function shifts the IS curve to the right
and thereby increases equilibrium real income and nominal interest rate.

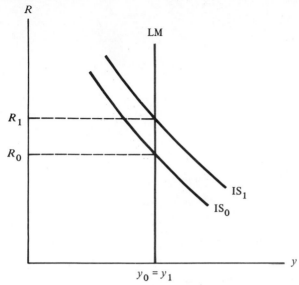

Figure 11.13 **Implications of alternative IS curve in the special case of a vertical LM curve.** If the LM curve were vertical, the position of the IS curve would not affect real income. The nominal interest rate is higher in Case 1 than in Case 0, but there is no corresponding increase in real income. Only at $y_0 = y_1$ will the demand for money equal the amount supplied.

11.3 EFFECTS OF SHIFTS IN THE MONETARY SECTOR

THE EFFECTS OF MONETARY POLICY

Monetary policy is characterized by the choice of the real money supply m. Alternative monetary policies can be represented by the alternative money-supply functions

$$m^s = m_0 \qquad\qquad [11.12]$$

$$m^s = m_1 \qquad\qquad [11.13]$$

Assume that m_1 is greater than m_0.

The effects of the alternative monetary policies on the position of the LM curve are analyzed in Fig. 11.14. For a given nominal interest rate, higher levels of real income must be associated with a money supply of m_1 than with m_0 if the money market is to be in equilibrium.[8] So the LM curve LM_1 for money

---

[8] An exception would be in the instance of the liquidity trap, in which case money demand and supply can be equal for different money supplies and the same real income and interest rate.

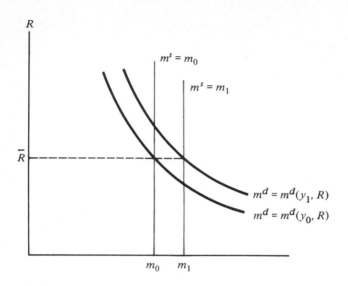

Figure 11.14 The effects of alternative monetary policies on the position of the LM curve. Consider any given nominal interest rate, say $\bar{R}$. There will be some real income y_0 for which real money demand $m^d(y_0, \bar{R})$ equals real money supply at m_0. This is a point on the LM$_0$ curve corresponding to real money supply m_0. There will also be some larger real income y_1 at which real money demand $m^d(y_1, \bar{R})$ equals money supply at m_1. This is a point on the LM$_1$ curve corresponding to real money supply m_1. So the LM curves for higher real money supplies lie to the right of the LM curves for lower real money supplies. If the liquidity trap exists, $\bar{R}$ would have to be chosen greater than or equal to the minimum nominal interest rate R^{min}. At R^{min}, there would be a range of lower income levels at which LM$_0$ and LM$_1$ coincided.

supply m_1 lies to the right of the LM curve LM$_0$ for money supply m_0. The change in money supply has no direct effect on the aggregate expenditure function in the Keynesian model; therefore the IS curve is unchanged. Figure 11.15 shows that higher money supplies imply higher levels of real income and lower interest rates. The decrease in nominal interest rates from R_0 to R_1 increases the quantity of money demanded, other things being equal. So equilibrium income increases less to equate money supply and demand than would be the case if the interest rate were unchanged.

If, however, the IS curve were to intersect LM$_0$ in a horizontal portion corresponding to the liquidity trap, it would intersect LM$_1$ at the same point as seen in Fig. 11.16. Many Keynesian economists used this special case as a working approximation until well into the 1960s. If real money demand were horizontal—or nearly so—in the relevant range, monetary policy would be

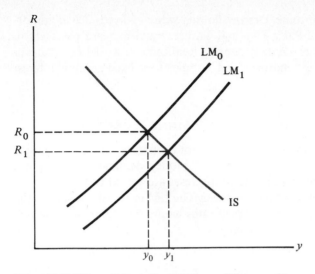

Figure 11.15 Effects of alternative monetary policies on real income and the nominal interest rate. A real money supply of m_0 is associated with LM_0. A higher real money supply m_1 would be associated with some LM curve LM_1, to the right of LM_0. The equilibrium points are (y_0, R_0) for m_0 and (y_1, R_1) for m_1. These equilibrium incomes y_0 and y_1 allow for changes in the equilibrium nominal interest rate and so differ from the incomes derived for a given $\overline{R}$ in Fig. 11.14. The decrease in R from R_0 to R_1 makes for a smaller increase in income. Consequently higher money supplies correspond to higher levels of real income and lower levels of interest rates.

Figure 11.16 Effects of alternative monetary policies in the liquidity trap region. If the IS curve and LM_0 intersect in the horizontal or liquidity trap region, an increase in money supply from m_0 to m_1 would not alter either real income or the interest rate. This is true because the horizontal portion of LM_1 would include the entire horizontal portion of LM_0.

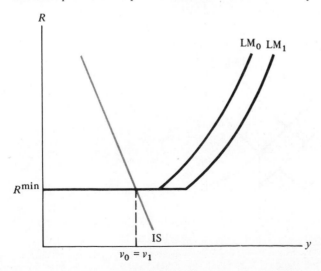

impotent to increase real income. Desired fluidity, which played such an important role in the analysis of Parts Two and Three, would increase passively to
offset any increases in the real money supply. Real income would be whatever
equated desired aggregate expenditures and income at the fixed nominal interest
rate R^{min}.

EFFECTS OF SHIFTS IN THE MONEY-DEMAND FUNCTION

Instability in the money-demand function has not been important in Keynesian
analysis. A hypothetical decrease in the real money demand for any given
combination of real income and nominal interest rate would be equivalent to
an increase in the real money supply, however. The LM curve would shift to the
right, real income would rise, and interest rates would fall. An increase in real
money demand would have opposite effects.

FINANCING INCREASED
GOVERNMENT EXPENDITURES BY MONEY CREATION

It is normally assumed that changes in government expenditures, taxes, or
(base) money creation are offset by changes in borrowing. Suppose an increase
in government spending totaling $10 billion over a short period were financed

**Figure 11.17 Effect of financing increased government
expenditure by money creation.** Increased government
expenditure shifts the IS curve to the right from IS_0 to IS_1.
Increased money supply shifts the LM curve to the right from
LM_0 to LM_1. Real income must be increased from y_0 to y_1.
Whether the equilibrium nominal interest rate increases or
decreases is uncertain, depending on the precise shifts in the IS
and LM curves.

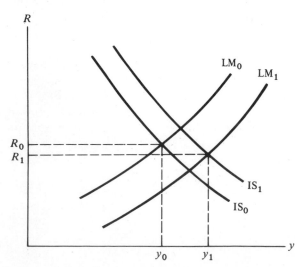

instead by $10 billion of base money. If the money multiplier were 2.5, this would cause a $25 billion increase in the money supply.

If the IS curve, in the absence of the spending increase, were IS_0, the new IS curve, IS_1, would lie to the right of IS_0. Similarly, the new LM curve, LM_1, would lie to the right of the LM curve, LM_0, which would otherwise exist. Figure 11.17 demonstrates that real income is unambiguously increased by the higher levels of government spending and money creation. Whether the nominal interest rate increases or decreases is uncertain, depending on the size of the slopes and shifts in the IS and LM curves.

The possible number of combinations of different sources of shifts in the IS and LM curves is large and need not be worked through here. The solutions always follow the same pattern: First determine the shifts, if any, in the IS and LM curves and then compare the two equilibria.

DERIVATION OF THE AGGREGATE DEMAND CURVE

The aggregate demand curve was used in Chap. 7 to illustrate the relation in a short period of time between real income and the price level viewed in terms of the demand for output. This curve can be derived easily by use of the IS-LM model.

The IS-LM model determines the equilibrium real income—in terms of demand for output—for a given price level P. If we find this real income for all possible price levels, then we have traced out the aggregate demand curve. This aggregate demand curve is based on the conditions used to derive the IS and LM curves, including monetary and fiscal policy. Changes in these conditions would cause the aggregate demand curve to shift.

The only way in which the price level enters the IS-LM model is in converting the nominal quantity of money M determined by the Fed into a real quantity of money m. So if we compare two price levels P_0 and P_1 (where P_0 is greater than P_1) for a given M, the only difference is in Eq. [11.4] which sets $m^s = m_0 = M/P_0$ in Case 0 and $m^s = m_1 = M/P_1$ in Case 1. Since P_0 is greater than P_1, m_0 is less than m_1. This is the case analyzed in Figs. 11.14 and 11.15 except that the difference between m_0 and m_1 is due to different price levels instead of different nominal quantities of money. We saw in Fig. 11.15 that y_0 is less than y_1. So higher price levels cause lower equilibrium real incomes. This is the reason that the aggregate demand curve has a negative slope. The details of the aggregate demand approach are left to advanced texts.

SUMMARY

1 The IS-LM model is used to find the values of real income and the nominal interest rate at which the goods market and the money market are simultaneously in equilibrium.

2 The negatively sloped IS curve gives all combinations of real income and the nominal interest rate for which desired expenditures equal real income.

3 The positively sloped LM curve gives all combinations of real income and the nominal interest rate for which real money demand equals the amount supplied.

4 The intersection of the IS and LM curves is the unique point at which both the goods market and the money market are in equilibrium.

5 Any factor tending to increase aggregate expenditures for each combination of real income and the nominal interest rate tends to shift the IS curve to the right. The most important of these factors, from the Keynesian point of view, are increases in investor optimism, increases in government expenditure, and decreases in taxes.

6 Any factor shifting the IS curve to the right tends to increase both real income and the nominal interest rate. Just the opposite is true for decreases in investor optimism or government spending and increases in taxes.

7 Increases in the real money supply shift the LM curve to the right. Such a shift increases real income and decreases the nominal interest rate. In the special case of the liquidity trap, increases in the real money supply can leave real income and the nominal interest rate unchanged. Decreases in the money supply decrease real income and increase the nominal interest rate, except perhaps for the case of the liquidity trap.

8 Shifts in various functions or policy variables may be combined to achieve offsetting or reinforcing effects.

9 The negatively sloped aggregate demand curve can be derived by assuming different given price levels for the IS-LM analysis.

CONCEPTS TO KNOW

goods market   LM curve

IS curve   money market

QUESTIONS AND EXERCISES

*1 (a) In Chap. 10, it was asserted that either the assumption of a given price level or some substitute was required for the logical completeness of the Keynesian model. Suppose that this assumption was abandoned so that Fed control over the nominal money supply was not equivalent to control over the real money supply. Then [11.4] would be replaced with $M^s = M$. Could the model be solved for a unique solution? Why?

   (b) Suppose that the equation $m^s = M^s/P$ is added also. Can the model be solved for a unique solution? Why? Can the model be solved for real income as a function of the price level? Why? What would such a functional relationship between real income and the price level be called in the terminology of Chap. 7?

2 (a) Suppose that the aggregate expenditure function is

$$a = 1000 + g - 0.4t + 0.6y - 100R$$

where a, g, t, and y are in R\$ billions per annum and R is in percentage points per annum. If $g = R\$105$ billion per annum and $t = R\$100$ billion per annum, complete this table of points on the IS curve:

R	1%	2%	3%	4%	5%
y					

(b) Use the points in the table to draw an IS curve on graph paper.
3 Why is the IS curve flatter, other things being equal, if given changes in the nominal interest rate cause larger changes in investment demand? (*Hint:* An example may help. Substitute

$$a = 1250 + g - 0.4t + 0.6y - 200R$$

for the aggregate expenditure function of Exercise 2. Compare the implied IS curves.)
*4 (a) Show the effects of a decline in investor optimism on real income and the nominal interest rate.
(b) What would happen to the nominal interest rate if monetary policy could be and was used to offset the effect on real income? What about the use of fiscal policy?
5 Suppose a \$10 billion increase in real government spending would shift the IS curve to the right by \$20 billion. Compare the effects on real income and the nominal interest rate according to whether the LM curve is flat or steep. What is the commonsense reason for these differences?
6 The same increase in government spending considered in Exercise 5 is assumed. Compare the effects on real income and the nominal interest rate according to whether the IS curve is flat or steep. What is the common-sense reason for these differences?
7 The \$10 billion increase in government spending of Exercise 5 and a \$20 billion increase are both being considered. Compare the effects on real income and the nominal interest rate of the two policy changes. What is the common sense reason for these differences?
8 Along the lines of Fig. 11.14, derive the effects of alternative real money supplies on the LM curve with a liquidity trap portion.
9 Show that a decrease in money demand for any given level of real income and the nominal interest rate would shift the LM curve to the right.

*10 In a *strict* comparative statics model, it makes no sense to talk about a $10 billion increase in real base money financing a $10 billion increase in the rate of government expenditure. Why? Why might it be permissible to consider changes in the stock of money over the "short period" even though the effects of investment on capital are neglected as trivial?

REFERENCES FOR FURTHER READING

Dernburg, Thomas F., and Duncan M. McDougall: *Macroeconomics*, 5th ed., New York: McGraw-Hill, 1976. (This is one of the most popular, purely Keynesian textbooks.)

Hicks, John R.: Mr. Keynes and the "Classics"; A Suggested Interpretation, *Econometrica*, **5:** 147–159, Apr. 1937.

Keynes, John Maynard: *The General Theory of Employment, Interest, and Money*, New York: Harcourt, Brace, 1936.

Smith, Warren L.: A Graphical Exposition of the Complete Keynesian System, *Southern Economic Journal*, **23:** 115–125, Oct. 1956.

PART FIVE

THE USE OF MODELS TO ANALYZE THE MACROECONOMY

Parts Two, Three, and Four have been devoted to macroeconomic theory. Theory comprises the body of tested hypotheses and models which are useful for understanding how the economy has worked and for predicting how the economy will respond to various changes.

A model will be useful if it readily gives correct answers to interesting questions. It may be that it is awkward or misleading when other interesting questions are proposed. In that situation, economists will match their model to the question asked. In microeconomics, the competitive market model is used for some problems, the monopoly model for others, and more complex models in those special cases where it is worth the trouble to use them. Macroeconomists similarly choose among the neoclassical model of steady-state growth (Part Two), the dynamic model of adjustments to shocks (Part Three), and the Keynesian model (Part Four), depending on the question being studied.

The neoclassical growth model is used to analyze issues involving the broad trends in the economy. Here business fluctuations will average out so that it is appropriate to use a model which takes as given a growing, normal amount of labor.

The dynamic and Keynesian approaches are more directly competitive (or complementary) because they are applied to similar situations. Both approaches are used to analyze the effects of macroeconomic shocks. The Keynesian model provides more theoretical detail and so has more implications as to the initial impact effects of macroeconomic shocks. The dynamic model analyzes the effects on a more limited set of variables over the entire adjustment process.

The sharpness of the short-period Keynesian analysis derives from certain special assumptions that do not hold in certain cases. These assumptions are not made in the dynamic model and can be avoided in the Keynesian model at the cost of complicating the analysis. The Keynesian IS-LM approach can be used to analyze the full adjustment process by taking account of the implied shifts in the IS and LM curves from period to period due to changes in expectations, capital stock, the price level, and so forth. The dynamic approach can provide more detail by addition of various equations and restrictions. But rather than use an awkward tool which can—with great care and effort—do everything, macroeconomists normally select whichever model is most appropriate to the problem at hand. As in microeconomics, the selection of the appropriate model is more of an art than a science.

Chapter 12 deals with one set of issues in selecting an appropriate model—how the dynamic and Keynesian models coincide and how they differ. Historically this comparison has been made in terms of differences in views about the nature of the world between the two groups who developed the approaches, monetarists and Keynesians, respectively. As empirical research has narrowed the differences in views, there is much greater readiness to use the model appropriate to the problem without undue concern about the labels.

Chapter 13 illustrates the use of macroeconomic theory by analyzing the last half century of U.S. macroeconomic history. This serves to show which questions are important in the real world and how macroeconomic models can be used to formulate answers to them. Of course, what questions are important depends on the interests and purposes of the analyst.

CHAPTER 12

COMPARISON OF THE KEYNESIAN AND DYNAMIC MODELS

WHAT YOU WILL LEARN IN THIS CHAPTER
Considerations in choosing a model appropriate to
the question asked ● How special assumptions in
the Keynesian model can be relaxed ● The role of
the real balance effect in reconciling Keynesian and
monetarist results ● The controversy over the
stability and elasticity of investment demand

12.1 INTRODUCTION

Recently economists have begun to use either a Keynesian or a dynamic (monetarist) approach, according to which is appropriate to the particular problem at hand. Previously, monetarist economists or Keynesian economists would normally use their respective models to analyze any problem. Not surprisingly, given their development, each model tends to be most useful for analyzing the problems originally most interesting to their developers: the Keynesian model for the short-run effects of changes in investment demand and fiscal policy and the dynamic model for the process of broad adjustment to monetary shocks.

In choosing which model to use, it is important to know just what question is of interest. Normally if the Keynesian model provides an answer to the question and if the question is consistent with the simplifying assumptions of the model, the Keynesian model would be used since it provides more detailed information. If these conditions do not hold, then it may be possible to use a generalized IS-LM model which will provide the correct answer more readily than a full-scale dynamic analysis. After a point, the dynamic model is easier, surer, and more informative than shifting IS and LM curves back and forth.

The monetarist-Keynesian debates have served to identify the special assumptions in the Keynesian model and the sort of questions for which these assumptions cause difficulties. These issues will be discussed in Sec. 12.2. Further, different views on how the economy operates as a whole do lead economists to disagree about which model is most appropriate for certain problems. The nature and implications of these differences are the subjects of Sec. 12.3.

12.2   ISSUES CONCERNING
THE INDIVIDUAL KEYNESIAN BUILDING BLOCKS

THE MARGINAL PROPENSITY TO CONSUME

The main problem with the simple Keynesian consumption function is that it squares relatively poorly with the data. Keynes' "fundamental psychological law" explains only part of the actual changes in consumer expenditures. The debate over the consumption function has revolved around two issues: the size of the marginal propensity to consume and the impact of real money balances on consumption. The former is discussed here and the latter below.

Early Keynesians thought the marginal propensity to consume (MPC) was quite high—well over 0.5 and in the range of 0.6 or 0.7. This view arose from fitting a simple linear consumption function to the available national income accounts data from 1929 up to the beginning of World War II. Figure 12.1 shows the data for real consumer expenditures c and real disposable personal income dpy[1] for 1929 through 1941. A typical consumption function, as estimated from these data, is

$$c = 31.4 + 0.73dpy \qquad [12.1]$$

This consumption function is the straight line in Fig. 12.1.

As more data became available both back into the nineteenth century and in the post-World War II era, it was apparent that the simple linear consumption function was an inadequate description of consumer expenditures over time. A more accurate description would be $c = 0.9dpy$. This disparity between the long-period time series and the data for the 1930s was shown to reflect statistical biases caused by the omission of wealth or permanent income from the consumption function.[2] The estimated 0.73 coefficient of current disposable personal income is an average of the coefficients of permanent income (0.9) and transitory income (0.3 or 0.4). This explanation was questioned by some Keynesians in a series of papers. The papers were shown by Darby to suffer from a statistical bias also.[3]

The inclusion of permanent income in the consumption function poses no basic difficulty for the Keynesian model. Permanent income—as a measure of wealth—can be taken as fixed for the short period of analysis so that variations in current income correspond to variations in transitory income. There will be

---

[1] Disposable personal income measures only cash income receipts of individuals and not accrued income such as undistributed corporate profits. It was nevertheless widely used until recently in estimating consumption functions.

[2] Milton Friedman, *A Theory of the Consumption Function*, Princeton: Princeton University Press for NBER, 1957; and Franco Modigliani and Richard Brumberg, "Utility Analysis and the Consumption Function: An Interpretation of Cross-Section Data," in Kenneth K. Kurihara (ed.), *Post-Keynesian Economics*. New Brunswick: Rutgers University Press, 1954.

[3] Michael R. Darby, The Permanent Income Theory of Consumption—A Restatement, *Quarterly Journal of Economics*, **88**: 228–250, May 1974.

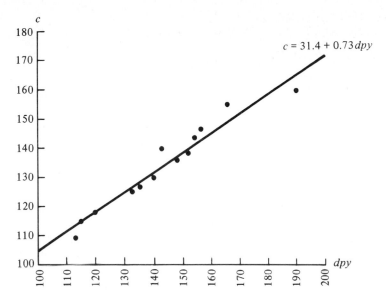

Figure 12.1 Real consumer expenditures and real disposable personal income, 1929–1941. The dots represent the values of real consumer expenditures and real disposable personal income for the 13 years 1929–1941. The linear Keynesian consumption function fitted to this data is shown by the solid line $c = 31.4 + 0.73dpy$. Because variations in measured dpy were partly due to variations in transitory income, and because changes in transitory income have smaller effects on consumer expenditures than do changes in permanent income, the estimated MPC is less than the long-run value of 0.9. It is, however, greater than the short-run value of 0.3 or 0.4. Both c and dpy are measured in billions of 1958 dollars. *Data source*: U.S. Bureau of Economic Analysis, *Long Term Economic Growth*, 1860–1970, Washington: GPO, 1973, pp. 184, 188.

some effect of income during the current period on future consumption—so that a dynamic element is introduced—but this is not of great concern for most problems.[4]

The fact that the ratio of consumer expenditures to income does not decline over time is fatal to one of the predictions of early Keynesians. They argued, following Keynes, that saving would become a larger and larger fraction of income as income rose. The interest rate would have to decline progressively to increase investment sufficiently to maintain full employment. Eventually, the interest rate could fall no further because of the liquidity trap and full employment could no longer be maintained. This *secular stagnation thesis* was the basis of Keynesian predictions of worsened post-World War II depression.

---

[4] Further discussion of the consumption function is found in Secs. 8.3 and 10.2.

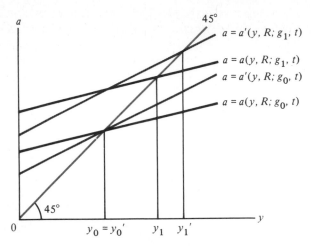

Figure 12.2 Shifts in and the slope of the IS curve for alternative slopes of the aggregate expenditure function. The two aggregate expenditure functions $a = a(y, R; g, t)$ and $a = a'(y, R; g, t)$ differ only in their slope. For purposes of comparison, it is assumed that for the given values R, g_0, and t, equilibrium real income is the same for both functions at $y_0 = y_0'$. Suppose that real government expenditures were instead g_1, which is greater than g_0. This would shift both aggregate expenditure functions up vertically by $g_1 - g_0$. The new equilibrium real income y_1' in the case of the steeper aggregate expenditure function exceeds the corresponding value y_1 for the less steeply sloped function. Hence, the lower the slope of the aggregate expenditure function the smaller is the change in the equilibrium real income. The conclusion is that any shock which shifts the aggregate expenditure function causes a smaller shift in the IS curve if the slope of the aggregate expenditure function is lower than that caused if the slope is high. The same diagram can be used to show that the lower the slope of the aggregate expenditure function, the steeper the IS curve. Suppose that the upward shift in the aggregate expenditure function occurred because the interest rate was reduced rather than because of higher government expenditures. We see that a larger change in income occurs for a given interest rate change if the slope of the aggregate expenditure curve is higher. This means that the IS curve is steeper if the slope of the aggregate expenditure curve is low than it is if the slope is high.

The fault lay, of course, in confusing the short-period and long-run consumption functions.

In terms of short-period analysis, the effect of a lower MPC is to reduce the slope of the aggregate expenditure function in the ya plane. This happens because a R\$1 increase in real income induces a smaller increase in consumer expenditures. The lower the slope of the aggregate expenditure function, the less does a given shift in the function shift the IS curve, as shown in Fig. 12.2.

Conversely, the IS curve is also steeper, a condition which reduces the effects on real income of monetary shocks. The reduced estimate of the MPC thus increases the estimated stability of the economy in response to various macroeconomic shocks. But the basic structure of the Keynesian IS-LM model is unchanged in the short period.

THE REAL BALANCE EFFECT

The tendency for consumer expenditures to increase, other things being equal, with increases in the real amount of money (or "real money balances") in the economy is referred to as the *real balance effect*. It was specifically assumed (Sec. 10.2) in formulating the standard IS-LM model that the real balance effect is negligible. If we allow instead for a substantial real balance effect, changes in money supply directly affect aggregate expenditures. Thus the neat separation of goods (IS) and money (LM) markets breaks down. This is important in the analysis of certain problems.

There are two main reasons why real money balances affect real consumer expenditures: (1) Real money balances are a component of wealth which does not yield a stream of market income and so is excluded from such measures of wealth as permanent income. Consumer expenditures are a function of this total wealth, however. So higher levels of real money will be associated with higher real consumer expenditures, other things being equal.[5] (2) The balance-sheet view (stressed in Part Three of this book) observes that many items of consumer expenditure are durable and semidurable goods which are substitutes for money in the allocation of the wealth of a household. Real money demand is a function of variables (real income and the interest rate) already in the aggregate expenditure function. So changes in real money balances, for given y and R values, will represent changes in the excess money supply. The real money balance effects on consumer expenditures operate primarily as a short-run adjustment process in this view.[6]

---

[5] The earliest discussions of the real balance effect in terms of total wealth were by Gottfried Haberler, *Prosperity and Depression*, 2d ed., Geneva: League of Nations, 1939; and Arthur C. Pigou, The Classical Stationary State, *Economic Journal*, **53**: 343–351, Dec. 1943. The theoretical implications were worked out in detail by Don Patinkin, *Money, Interest, and Prices*, Evanston: Row, Peterson & Company, 1956. The real balance effect is of historical interest in that its recognition eliminated the theoretical possibility of Keynes' "underemployment equilibrium." Keynes had argued that falling prices which increase real money balances would not affect equilibrium income if the economy were in the liquidity trap portion of the LM curve (see Fig. 11.16). However the real balance effect implies that as prices fall the IS curve will shift to the right until employment returns to its normal level.

[6] The balance-sheet approach was suggested by Milton Friedman and Anna Schwartz and pursued by Karl Brunner and Alan Meltzer in numerous articles. The approach is substantially identical to that of James Tobin and his students, although there are important expositional differences. Some recent empirical estimates of the effect of real money balances on consumer expenditures are in Michael R. Darby, Postwar U.S. Consumption, Consumer Expenditures, and Saving, *American Economic Review*, **65**: 217–222, May 1975. The estimates there suggest that—for given values of permanent income, transitory income, and the stock of consumers' durables—an $R\$1$ billion increase in real money balances will cause an increase in real consumer expenditures of some $R\$650$ million to $R\$800$ million per annum. The total wealth view could explain an increase of perhaps $R\$100$ million, so the balance-sheet or substitution effect appears to be dominant.

Recognition of the real balance effect means that the simple IS-LM model of Part Four is inapplicable to problems in which the real quantity of money is changed, as in monetary policy or price level changes. In these cases, many economists use an extended IS-LM approach which allows for the real balance effect. If increases in real money balances in fact lead people to increase real consumer expenditures at a given level of real income and the nominal interest rate, they cause an upward shift in the aggregate expenditure function and hence a shift to the right in the IS curve. The effects on real income and the nominal interest rate of an increase in the real money supply, including the direct effect on consumer expenditures, are illustrated in Fig. 12.3. The effect on real income is reinforced by the shift in the IS curve, so that monetary policy is stronger than would otherwise be the case. The effects on nominal interest rates

Figure 12.3 The effects of alternative real money supplies in the presence of direct effects on consumer expenditures. The real money supply is higher in Case 1 than it is in Case 0. The LM curve for Case 1 (LM_1) lies to the right of the LM curve for Case 0 (LM_0) for the usual reasons. The IS curve for Case 1 (IS_1) also lies to the right of the IS curve for Case 0 (IS_0). This is true because increased real money balances shift the aggregate expenditure function upward. Equilibrium real income y_1 is higher in Case 1 than equilibrium real income y_0 in Case 0. The effect on the nominal interest rate is ambiguous, depending on the relative size of the shifts in the IS and LM curves. In the case illustrated, for example, the equilibrium nominal interest rate declines with increased real money balances. If the shift in the IS curve were to exceed the shift in the LM curve, however, the nominal interest rate would rise.

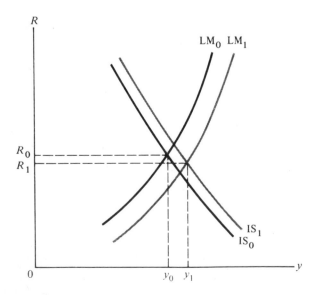

become ambiguous, however, since R rises or falls as the IS curve shifts more or less than the LM curve. In the long run (steady state), the price level would rise in proportion to the increase in nominal money so that the shifts in the IS and LM curves would be eliminated.

These ambiguous results for nominal interest rates are not surprising. Clear results in comparative statics usually occur only when changes in conditions affect only one of the two separate groups of determinants. Since changes in the real money supply affect both the money market and the goods market, offsetting effects can occur.

Allowance for the real balance effect on consumer expenditures complicates the short-period IS-LM model but does not make it unusable.

THE CONTROVERSY OVER INVESTMENT DEMAND

Undoubtedly, over the course of a business cycle, real investment displays the greatest relative fluctuation of any expenditure component. There is considerable continuing controversy over whether this fluctuation in investment is simply an effect of the business cycle or is itself an important cause of business cycles.

The essence of Keynes' message was that business cycles are reflections of sudden and unpredictable shifts in the investment-demand function. This function was supposed to be unstable, shifting with ephemeral waves of optimism and pessimism among investors. This hypothesis is still a viable one as substantial unexplained fluctuations remain in empirical investment-demand functions.[7]

Monetarists interpret the fluctuations in investment quite differently. To them, the cyclical variations in investment are primarily movements along a stable, interest-elastic, investment-demand function. Further, changes in investor psychology do not just happen, but reflect changes in objective conditions in the economy. Consequently, such shifts in the investment function as do occur are not random disturbances but one of the means by which the true disturbances—such as a change in the growth rate of the nominal money supply—affect the economy. For example, an unexpected reduction in the growth rate of the nominal money supply might cause investors to expect accurately that a recession would occur and that the rate of inflation would decrease. This would indeed reduce the current level of investment for a given nominal interest rate and real income, but this shift is in no way a random cause of business fluctuations.

---

[7] The investment-demand literature has been recently reviewed by Dale W. Jorgenson, Econometric Studies of Investment Behavior: A Survey, *Journal of Economic Literature*, **9**: 1111–1147, Dec. 1971. A rather different view of the state of the literature is presented by Robert Eisner, Econometric Studies of Investment Behavior: A Comment, *Economic Inquiry*, **12**: 91–104, Mar. 1974.

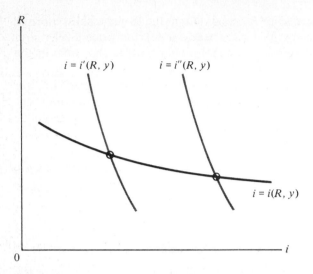

Figure 12.4 Alternative explanations of observed fluctuations in real investment. The two small circles represent hypothetically observed combinations of real investment and the nominal interest rate for a given real income y. These points could both lie on the same flat (highly interest-elastic) investment-demand function $i = i(R, y)$ or on two steeper (less interest-elastic) investment-demand functions $i = i'(R, y)$ and $i = i''(R, y)$. Keynesians tend to attribute changes in real investment to such shifts in the investment-demand function, while monetarists are more likely to view the changes as movements along a stable, flatter investment-demand function.

Figure 12.4 illustrates how fluctuations in real investment can be alternatively viewed as due to movements along a more interest-elastic real investment-demand function or shifts in a less interest-elastic function. Small circles represent two hypothetically observed levels of real investment and nominal interest rates for a given level of real income y. It could be that these points lie on a single relatively interest-elastic investment-demand function, $i = i(R, y)$. Alternatively, these points could lie on two different and less interest-elastic investment-demand functions $i = i'(R, y)$ and $i = i''(R, y)$.

The shifts in investment demand reflect some variables not explicitly included in the investment-demand function or held constant for the period of analysis.[8] The key omitted variable is generally believed to be the state of investors' expectations. Whether these expectations are formed independently

---

[8] Changes in the capital stock would shift the simple investment-demand function, but this presents no difficulties for the IS-LM model because the capital stock is fixed for the short period of analysis.

of economic conditions (à la Keynes) or in response to other economic conditions is crucial. If expectations are formed independently (or "exogenously") of economic conditions, then they can be taken as given, as in the standard IS-LM model. We cannot explain the causes of shifts in investment demand then—only their effects. If expectations are based instead on the economic variables in our model (are "endogenous"), then the omission of the effects of these variables on investment by way of expectations is a potential source of error in the IS-LM model.

Suppose for example that businessmen cut back investment spending, other things being equal, whenever their economists predicted a recession on the basis of reduced real money supply. This would have just the same effect on aggregate expenditures as the real balance effect operating on consumer expenditures. Much of the monetarist-Keynesian debate turned on just this issue: whether increases in the money supply affected investment not only through changes in interest rates but also through expectations, *or* whether exogenous shifts in investment demand increased income and hence the demand for money, with the supply of money being passively increased by the central bank. Studies of the formation of expectations are one of the major areas of current macroeconomic research. The results of this research should help resolve this controversy.

Meanwhile monetarist economists argue that since the behavior of nominal and real income can be adequately explained by monetary and fiscal variables without reference to shifts in investment demand, changes in expectations are endogenous to the system. Keynesians argue that this is in part illusory, because of passive adjustments of money supply to changes in money demand induced by exogenous shifts in investors' expectations. While this author is persuaded for now by the monetarist evidence, there is much work to be done before a final conclusion is possible.

The related questions of the interest elasticity of the investment-demand function and the nature of shifts in this function are important for the analysis of macroeconomic policy. On the one hand, if investment demand is not very elastic with respect to the nominal interest rate, large decreases in R will shift the aggregate expenditure curve up only slightly in the ya plane. Hence, smaller interest elasticities of investment demand are associated with smaller changes in the level of real income required for goods market equilibrium if there is a given decrease in the nominal interest rate. This means that the IS curve is steeper as the interest elasticity of investment demand becomes smaller, as illustrated in Fig. 12.5. Later on, this will be seen to indicate that monetary sector shocks have a smaller effect on equilibrium real income and that income-expenditures sector shocks have a greater effect on real income than would be the case if the IS curves were less steep. Whether or not there are significant spontaneous shifts in investment demand is the key to whether or not government policy to offset these shifts might be desirable. If there are significant induced shifts in investment demand from other macroeconomic shocks, the model should be reformulated to take these influences into account.

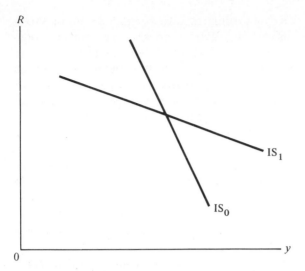

Figure 12.5 Effect of alternative interest elasticities of investment demand on the slope of the IS curve. The more elastic the investment-demand function with respect to the nominal interest rate, other things being equal, the flatter is the IS curve. This is true because a given change in the nominal interest rate will cause a greater change in the value of the aggregate expenditure function the more interest-elastic is investment demand. Thus, IS_0 is drawn according to the Keynesian view of small interest elasticity, and IS_1 represents the monetarist position of a larger interest elasticity of investment demand.

THE MONEY-DEMAND FUNCTION

At times during the monetarist-Keynesian debate, the interest elasticity of real money demand appeared to be "the" issue. It will be seen in Sec. 12.3 that this emphasis was misplaced, but some discussion is in order. The original positions can be characterized as high or infinite interest elasticity of demand on the Keynesian side and low or zero interest elasticity of demand on the monetarist side.

The Keynesian position particularly emphasized the speculative motive for holding money balances, as well as the incentive provided by the interest rate for economizing on money balances through closer synchronization of receipts and expenditures of money.

The theoretical basis for the speculative demand for money has been considerably weakened by subsequent analysis. Firmly held interest-rate expectations were seen to be theoretically invalid and were replaced with uncertainty. Even the uncertainty view does not imply the "speculative" effects of a decrease in the nominal interest rate if the variability of the interest rate is proportional to the level of the rate. In any case, the speculative motive applies to holdings of long-term versus short-term bonds—not money. Some sense can be made of the speculative effect by attributing it to fluctuations in the short-term interest rate which are only slightly reflected in movements of the long-term interest rate.

The theoretical basis of the interest elasticity of the demand for money is on sounder ground. The most important challenge here is to the view that the nominal interest rate on bank deposits is zero. If banks effectively pay interest on deposits,[9] then it is incorrect to view even the short-term nominal interest rate as the cost of holding money instead of bonds. A rise in short-term interest rates will be matched in whole or part by a rise in implicit interest rates on deposits so that the net change in the cost of holding money may be trivial.

The empirical evidence is mixed. Most estimates of the demand for money have placed the interest elasticity of the demand for money between -1 and -0.1. It should be observed that (M_1) fluidity declined by 59.9 percent from the end of 1946 to the end of 1974. During the same period, nominal interest rates on 3-month Treasury bills rose by 1836.8 percent and on long-term government bonds by 216.4 percent. Even if no allowance is made for the growth of money substitutes discussed in this context on page 358, there is not much room left for a large interest elasticity of the demand for real money.[10]

Let us recall, from Chap. 11, that for less interest-elastic money-demand functions, the LM curve is steeper, since larger increases in the nominal interest rate would be required to offset the effect on money demand of a given increase in real income. A steeper LM curve will be seen to indicate that monetary sector shocks have a larger effect on equilibrium real income and that income-expenditures sector shocks have a smaller effect on real income than would be the case if the LM curve were less steep.

At this point, the discussion in Chap. 8 on the possible increase in the real demand for money caused by a tax reduction is apropos. The problem arises because total income is not clearly superior to private income in the determination of the demand for money. Indeed, private income would be more closely related to the wealth constraint on money holdings and perhaps to transactions to be made by private holders of real money. The money-demand function could be rewritten as an increasing function of both total and private income

$$m^d = m^d(y, y - t, R) \qquad [12.2]$$

This means that a tax reduction increases private income and therefore the demand for money. This shifts the LM curve to the left. A shift to the left in the LM curve and a shift to the right in the IS curve leave the effect on real income ambiguous, although the nominal interest rate must increase.[11] As with the real balance effect, this modification is not fatal to the IS-LM model. It does complicate it however.

---

[9] See the discussion and references on page 358.
[10] Note that $-0.599/18.368 = -0.03$ and $-0.599/2.164 \doteq -0.28$.
[11] See Exercise 3 at the end of this chapter. A similar analysis is made by James M. Holmes and David J. Smyth, The Specification of the Demand for Money and the Tax Multiplier, *Journal of Political Economy*, **80:** 179–185, Jan./Feb. 1972.

12.3 COMPARISON OF THE COMPLETE MODELS

DIFFERENCES CONCERNING THE EMPIRICAL MAGNITUDES WITHIN THE IS-LM MODEL

The differences discussed in the previous section are primarily concerned with empirical magnitudes which define the precise nature of the IS and LM curves and how shocks shift them.

Figure 12.6 shows the standard comparison between the monetarist position (*a*) and the Keynesian position (*b*). The steeper slope of the monetarist LM curve reflects the monetarist view that money demand is less interest-elastic than supposed by most of the economists who consider themselves Keynesians. The slope of the monetarist IS curve is usually drawn to be less steep than that of the Keynesian IS curve. There is much overlap in these views, however. Keynesians are likely to suppose that the interest elasticity of investment demand is less than the monetarists would expect.[12] This value would make for

---

[12] This is certainly not universal. Robert Hall has recently argued that the most plausible ranges for the slopes of the IS and LM curves imply relatively small effects of fiscal policy and large effects of monetary policy. This conclusion was not accepted readily by his fellow Keynesians, however. See Robert E. Hall, Investment, Interest Rates, and the Effects of Stabilization Policies, *Brookings Papers on Economic Activity*, 1977(1): 61–103 and the comments and discussion on pages 104–121.

Figure 12.6 The slopes of the IS and LM curves from the monetarist and Keynesian viewpoints. Monetarists generally suppose that the IS curve is flatter and the LM curve is steeper as in (*a*) than the Keynesian visualization of these curves (*b*). This distinction cannot always be made, however, and is not necessary to the positions taken. In the monetarist (*a*) a given horizontal shift in the LM curve will have a greater effect on real income than in the Keynesian (*b*). A given horizontal shift in the IS curve will have the greatest effect on real income in the Keynesian (*b*).

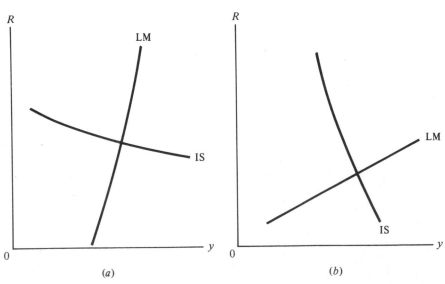

(*a*)   (*b*)

a steeper IS curve, of course. Conversely, monetarists generally suppose that there is a smaller slope of the aggregate expenditure curve and this notion also would make for a steeper IS curve, other things being equal.

Given the relative slopes of the IS and LM curves in panels (a) and (b), the following conclusions can be drawn. (1) A given horizontal shift in the IS curve has a larger effect on equilibrium real income in the Keynesian case than in the monetarist case. (2) A given horizontal shift in the LM curve has a larger effect on equilibrium real income in the monetarist case than in the Keynesian case.

The more nearly the world approaches the Keynesian case (b), the more generally useful will be the IS-LM model as compared to an analysis based on the dynamic Cambridge equation. This is because there will be more variation in fluidity and income in response to nonmonetary shocks. If instead fluidity varies relatively little, as in the monetarist case (a), the Cambridge equation is sufficient for most purposes, and the IS-LM model need be used only if the behavior of interest rates is required. The historical record on variations in fluidity is summarized in Sec. 13.3.

THE RELEVANT PERIOD OF ANALYSIS

The short-period assumption greatly simplifies the IS-LM model. In studying problems which consider effects over an extended period of time, the IS-LM analysis can be used only if one allows for the changes which occur over time. These changes shift the consumption function, the investment-demand function, and the money-demand function. Further changes in government spending, taxes, money supply, and the price level must be allowed for. It becomes rather awkward to handle all these shifts simultaneously. It is attempted, but with limited success.[13]

A more interesting question is: Over how long a "short period" is the IS-LM model a workable approximation? Six months to a year is probably a pretty fair limit. Certainly over 2 years' time, there are substantial effects on prices, expectations, and capital stock, which cannot be neglected. So when a longer horizon is important, the dynamic model of Part Three is more useful.

FLUIDITY AND THE IS-LM APPROACH

The supply of money is given within the IS-LM model. So any changes in income which occur within the model imply changes in the ratio of money to income—that is, in fluidity. Fluidity is not explicit in the IS-LM model but can be readily calculated as the ratio of real money to real income.

---

[13] The most successful attempts to use the IS-LM approach to analyze the adjustment process involve large-scale econometric models in electronic computers. Those models have received mixed reviews and are clearly beyond the scope of this book.

In analyzing historical or current events, one useful approach is to use the dynamic Cambridge equation approach to establish the broad movements in fluidity, nominal income, real income, and the price level implied by monetary policy. The implied growth rates of fluidity, nominal income, and real income can then be adjusted up or down as implied by the IS-LM model for particular years in which substantial nonmonetary shocks occur. This will be illustrated in Chap. 13.

THE STATE OF THE MONETARIST-KEYNESIAN DEBATE

The monetarist-Keynesian debate is not yet dead, but it is certainly quieter than before. There are new theoretical issues to be resolved, which have little if any relation to the monetarist-Keynesian debate. These issues are discussed in other chapters of this book. Currently, the monetarist-Keynesian debate seems little concerned with theoretical issues, somewhat concerned with the empirical magnitudes of such parameters as the interest elasticities of real investment and real money demand, and most basically involved with the stability of the private sector of the economy.

Stability of the private sector has two components: (1) The relative unimportance of behavioral or autonomous shocks as a source of business fluctuations. (2) A speedy adjustment to long-run equilibrium after a macroeconomic shock has occurred. Generally monetarists argue that these characteristics are accurate descriptions of the macroeconomy, while Keynesians believe they are less accurate.

That is, the typical monetarist would say that the economy (1) is characterized by negligible business fluctuations in the absence of monetary and fiscal policy shocks and (2) ameliorates the disturbances of the policy shocks which do occur. Keynesians would typically think of the economy as randomly fluctuating and slow to self-correct except for the wise intervention of monetary and fiscal policy. Even these differences in world view or gestalt are matters of emphasis and subject to resolution by continued research.

The near conclusion of the monetarist-Keynesian debate and the emerging theoretical synthesis has opened up many new topics for research—topics which had been pushed aside in the excitement of the earlier debate. Topics such as expectations formation, international economic linkages, and optimal labor contracts provide a rich menu for research which will substantially extend our knowledge of the macroeconomy.

SUMMARY

1 The standard IS-LM model, an extended version, or a dynamic Cambridge equation analysis is used according to which is the simplest way to answer the question at hand.

2 The IS-LM model (or an extended version) is generally most useful for questions of the short-run effect of changes in the components of the aggregate expenditure function.

3 The dynamic analysis is generally most useful where intermediate and long-run effects are important and for monetary shocks.

4 The real balance effect means that the IS curve shifts to the right with increases in real money; this partially breaks down the separation of the money and goods markets. A similar linkage may operate through the effect of the real money supply on businessmen's expectations, and hence investment demand.

5 Generally monetarists believe that the IS curve is flatter and that the LM curve is steeper than do most Keynesians. The more nearly correct is the monetarist view, the less informative is the IS-LM model vis-à-vis the dynamic Cambridge equation approach.

6 The IS-LM model can be used to adjust for the effects of nonmonetary shocks the income and fluidity growth rates predicted by a dynamic analysis of monetary policy.

7 A theoretical synthesis is emerging from the monetarist-Keynesian debate. The remaining debate is largely concerned with the sources of macroeconomic shocks and the speed with which the economy adjusts to them.

CONCEPTS TO KNOW

real balance effect   stability of the private sector

secular stagnation thesis

QUESTIONS AND EXERCISES

1 (a) Suppose the consumption function could be approximated by $c = 0.9y_P + 0.4y_T$. Suppose in year 0, current private income is $y_N = R\$100$ billion and permanent income y_P is the same amount. Transitory income is measured here as $y_T = y_N - y_P$. Suppose that in year 1, $y_N = R\$110$ billion and $y_P = R\$104$ billion. Compute $(c_1 - c_0)/(y_{1N} - y_{0N})$. Why is this number not the short-period MPC? What would be the effect on consumer expenditures if y_N were $R\$110$ billion in year 0? What would be the effect on consumer expenditures if y_N were $R\$104$ billion in year 1?

(b) Can you suggest why over long periods of time the ratio of total change in consumer expenditures to total change in real private income would converge to 0.9?

2 Use the IS-LM model to derive the short-period effects on real income and the nominal interest rate of a decrease in the real money supply in the presence of the real balance effect.

*3 Show the effect of a tax reduction on real income and the nominal interest rate if the real demand for money is an increasing function of *both* private and total income. Suppose there is no net effect on real income, what happens to the level of consumer expenditures and investment? How is this implied by the consumption function and the investment-demand function?

4 Show that a given horizontal shift in the LM curve has a greater effect on real income in panel (*a*) of Fig. 12.6 than in panel (*b*).

5 Show that a given horizontal shift in the IS curve has a smaller effect on real income in panel (*a*) of Fig. 12.6 than in panel (*b*).

*6 (*a*) Suppose that the IS-LM model is used to show that for $g = R\$250$ billion per annum, $t = R\$250$ billion per annum, and $m = R\$200$ billion, $y = R\$1,000$ billion per annum. What is the value of fluidity?

(*b*) Suppose that for $g = R\$260$ billion per annum, $t = R\$250$ billion per annum, and $m = R\$200$ billion, $y = R\$1,010$ billion per annum. How is the increased real government spending relative to (*a*) financed? What is the value of fluidity now?

(*c*) The $R\$10$ billion per annum increase in real government spending therefore caused a _____ percent fall in fluidity and rise in real income.

7 Show that a falling price level would eventually increase equilibrium real income even if the IS curve initially crossed the liquidity trap portion of the LM curve. (*Hint:* See footnote 5.)

REFERENCES FOR FURTHER READING

Andersen, Leonall C.:   The State of the Monetarist Debate, *Federal Reserve Bank of St. Louis Review*, **55**(9): 2–8, Sept. 1973; and Commentary by Lawrence R. Klein and Karl Brunner, *ibid.*, pp. 9–14.

Friedman, Milton, et al.:   *Milton Friedman's Monetary Framework: A Debate with His Critics*, R. J. Gordon (ed.), Chicago: University of Chicago Press, 1974. (Many of the basic issues of this chapter are involved in Friedman's "Comments on the Critics"; areas of particular interest may be pursued from the references cited there.)

Hall, Robert E.:   Investment, Interest Rates, and the Effects of Stabilization Policies, *Brookings Papers on Economic Activity*, 1977 (1): 61–103; and Comments and Discussion, *ibid.*, pp. 104–121.

Laidler, David E.:   *The Demand for Money: Theories and Evidence*, 2d ed., New York: Dun-Donnelley, 1977.

Leijonhufvud, Axel: *On Keynesian Economics and the Economics of Keynes*, London: Oxford University Press, 1968.

Stein, Jerome L. (ed.):   *Monetarism*, Amsterdam: North-Holland, 1976.

CHAPTER 13

THE IMPACT OF MACROECONOMIC SHOCKS ON THE AMERICAN ECONOMY

WHAT YOU WILL LEARN IN THIS CHAPTER
How macroeconomic theory can explain U.S. macroeconomic history ● The causes of the Great Depression ● The dominance of nominal money growth in explaining variations in the secular trends in nominal income and price level growth ● The interaction of monetary and nonmonetary shocks in determining year-to-year fluctuations in the growth rates of nominal income, real income, and the price level

13.1 THE HISTORICAL RECORD: THE GREAT DEPRESSION THROUGH WORLD WAR II

SETTING THE STAGE

The tools of macroeconomic analysis can most fully be appreciated by applying them to the study of recent macroeconomic experience. This study will provide a grasp of the effects of simultaneous and serial macroeconomic shocks and of the relative importance of different types of macroeconomic shocks. Dates are provided to illustrate the timing relationships rather than for any historical interest.

A study of macroeconomic experience is limited by data—as well as space—to relatively recent times. Before 1929, data series exist only for the broadest macroeconomic variables and are unreliable for detailed information. The early data can provide valuable insights[1] but are not well suited to the current

---

[1] This is shown in Milton Friedman and Anna Jacobson Schwartz, *A Monetary History of the United States, 1867–1960*, Princeton: Princeton University Press for NBER, 1963. Much of the discussion in this section and the next depends on this book. Other data sources for figures given in the text are Milton Friedman and Anna Jacobson Schwartz, *Monetary Statistics of the United States*, New York: NBER, 1970; *The National Income and Product Accounts of the United States, 1929–1974*, 1976 Supplement to *The Survey of Current Business;* and U.S. Bureau of Economic Analysis, *Long Term Economic Growth, 1860–1970*, Washington: GPO, 1973. Nominal income is measured here—for reasons of consistency over the whole period—by gross national product and the price level by the GNP deflator.

illustrative purposes. The data on the national income accounts of the federal government, drawn from basic source records, begin in 1929. Complete quarterly data as described in Chaps. 2 and 3 are available beginning with 1947.

This section will concentrate on the period of reliable data from 1929 through 1946. This very interesting period includes the Great Depression of 1929–1933, the recovery of 1933–1937, the severe recession of 1937–1938, the subsequent recovery and World War II. The next section will discuss the economy in the postwar era.

The dynamic nature of macroeconomic problems requires that some information be given about what was going on before 1929. The period from 1923 through 1928 was characterized by moderate fluctuations in the growth rate of the nominal money supply around an average rate of 4.4 percent per annum. The definition of nominal money supply used in this section is the broad money supply (M_2) because the distinction between demand and time deposits was blurred by banks until the Banking Acts of 1933 and 1935;[2] so M_2 is the only nominal-money-supply definition which is consistent throughout the period.

Between 1923 and 1928, there were two sequences consisting of a significant decrease in the money-supply growth rate followed in about a year by an increased growth rate. The decreases in growth rates started near the beginning of both 1923 and 1926 and caused the contractions of 1923–1924 and 1926–1927, respectively. Nevertheless, the fluctuations were small by previous standards, and the period as a whole was thought to reflect improved skill and ability on the part of the Federal Reserve System.

The average growth rate of fluidity during the period was nearly zero (-0.1 percent per annum). The average growth rate of nominal income (4.5 percent per annum) differed from the growth rate of nominal money (4.4 percent per annum) by only this small amount. The average growth rate in real income was 4.2 percent per annum and that in the price level was 0.3 percent per annum.[3] The period immediately preceding the Great Depression closely resembled the 1950s: Nominal-money growth rate fluctuations were large enough to cause recessions, but not so large as to cause any widespread, continuing macroeconomic problems.

There have been frequent attempts by noneconomists to find reasons for the Great Depression in the period leading up to 1929. Some of these specious arguments will be discussed below, but it should be stated here that there was no basic unsoundness in the economy in 1929 any more than there was in 1959. An argument can be made that the 1920s led to the 1930s in another way however: The Federal Reserve System misunderstood what was happening in

---

[2] See Sec. 3.3 for details.
[3] This average growth rate of real income exceeds the trend growth rate of about 3.1 percent per annum because the recovery from the severe 1920–1921 recession is included.

the 1920s and applied that faulty understanding to dealing with the 1930s. The results were nothing short of disastrous.

THE START OF THE GREAT DEPRESSION

The Great Depression started in a very undramatic fashion. The Fed had become concerned with what it supposed was undue speculation in the stock market. This was attributed to unsound "speculative fever" and "easy credit," and the Fed became determined to purge these supposed evils from the system. In early 1928, the Fed embarked on a restrictive monetary policy by selling government securities and raising the discount rate at which it would buy the promissory notes of member banks. This resulted in slight declines in base money and in the money supply from April 1928 through November 1930—the latter at an average growth rate of -1.4 percent per annum.

This decrease of almost 6 percentage points in the growth rate of the money supply compared to the previous average should, after a lag, cause a sharp decrease in the growth of aggregate demand. The contraction began, in fact, during the summer of 1929, as the decline in fluidity due to the initial monetary shock slowed and reversed. This early part of the contraction from 1929 to 1930 was in no way different from the sharp recession that would be expected from a 6 percentage point decrease in the nominal-money-supply growth rate.

What of the famous stock market crash of October 1929? There is little to choose between it and similar falls such as those occurring near the beginning of the 1937–1938 and 1969–1970 recessions. It is mainly remarkable for having marked the peak in view of the large fall in stock prices which occurred during 1931 and 1932. During 1930, the average stock price was about 5.5 percent *higher* than it had been in 1928 and only 19.2 percent lower than the 1929 average.

THE COLLAPSE OF THE BANKING SYSTEM

Through November of 1930, the recession was severe, but certainly not so severe as to be classed as a depression. The Fed had begun a mild reversal of policy in October 1929 by lowering discount rates and purchasing government bonds in the open market. In addition, gold was flowing into the country from abroad as net exports rose. This gold was purchased by the government with new base money at the fixed exchange rate of $20.67 per ounce. The decline in discount rates was not as large as the decline in market interest rates on short-term government bonds, however. So the net effect was a reduction in member bank borrowing even greater than the increased holdings of government bonds and gold. This mild reduction in nominal base money was the source of the mild reduction in the nominal money supply.

In November and December of 1930, the whole character of the contraction was changed by the emergence of a genuine banking panic of the type which the Fed was established to prevent.[4] During November, a rash of rural bank failures in the Midwest shook confidence in the banking system. The cash-deposit ratio began to rise, causing the money supply to fall and interest rates to rise as banks sold bonds and other earning assets to reduce deposits. Runs became common and banks could turn only to the Fed when holdings of readily marketable securities were exhausted and only loans to customers were left as assets. Amazingly, the Fed displayed little understanding of the " lender of last resort " role of a central bank in preventing the cumulative psychology of panic. Instead, banks were viewed as failing because of " bad management " and the Fed did not encourage banks to borrow during a run. As a result, 256 banks with deposits of $180,000,000 failed during November 1930. The panic became severe after the failure on December 11, 1930, of the Bank of United States.

The Bank of United States was a commercial bank, but the name was suggestive of some sort of official status to many people. It had deposits of over $200,000,000 and was a member of the Federal Reserve System and the New York Clearing House. For a while, the Fed and the other Clearing House banks supported a plan to save the Bank of United States, but once the Clearing House banks withdrew, the Fed chose to allow the Bank to fail. The failure shook confidence in both banks and the Fed, and a total of 352 banks with deposits of $370,000,000 failed during December.

The important impact of the banking panic was the increase in the cash-deposit and reserve-deposit ratios. This caused the money multiplier to drop sharply so that the small increase in nominal base money permitted by the Fed was insufficient to offset the decline in the money multiplier. The nominal-money-supply growth rate during November, December, and January averaged − 12 percent per annum.

The situation appeared to stabilize in January 1931 and the Fed reduced nominal base money during February by selling government securities. The money multiplier stopped falling and even rose slightly so that the nominal money supply rose during February.

In March 1931, runs and bank failures resumed and continued intermittently until March 1933. The Fed took little corrective action, and the cash-deposit and reserve-deposit ratios rose as crisis followed crisis. Between March 1931 and March 1933, the cash-deposit ratio rose from 0.0964 to 0.2252 and the reserve-deposit ratio rose from 0.0807 to 0.1188. As a result, the money multi-

---

[4] See pages 238–239 for an analysis of a bank panic. In essence, the bulk of bank assets consists of nonmarketable loans which cannot be sold to pay off depositors after base-money reserves and marketable securities are exhausted. Selling of marketable securities by money banks during a crisis lowers the price of the securities and makes all banks more prone to failure. Most, if not all, of the deposits in closed banks were eventually paid off under bankruptcy proceedings as the nonmarketable loans were collected, but the delay was costly and well worth avoiding. The costs of bankruptcy proceedings and sacrifice sales of assets could easily absorb enough assets of a sound bank that depositors were not repaid in full. Further, the contraction caused by a panic can bankrupt otherwise sound borrowers from the bank.

Table 13.1 **GROWTH RATES OF THE BROAD MONEY SUPPLY (M_2) 1928–1933**

Period	Growth Rate
April 1928 to April 1929	-1.0%
April 1929 to April 1930	-0.9%
April 1930 to April 1931	-4.3%
April 1931 to April 1932	-19.0%
April 1932 to April 1933	-15.9%

Source: Calculated from data in Milton Friedman and Anna Jacobson Schwartz, *Monetary Statistics of the United States*, New York: NBER, 1970, pp. 24–29.

plier μ fell from 6.278 to 3.720, a fall of some 41 percent. The Fed increased nominal base money over the same period by only 18.7 percent. The net fall in the nominal money supply was 29.7 percent, that is, at an average annual growth rate of -17.6 percent per annum.

Through March 1933, the pattern of monetary policy was one of falling nominal-money-supply growth rates. As would be expected, the cumulative effect on the economy of this series of restrictive shocks was devastating. Over the period from the money supply peak at April 1928 to the money supply trough of April 1933, the average growth rate of the nominal money supply was -8.2 percent per annum. Table 13.1 illustrates the pattern of deceleration concealed by this average. The growth rate of the nominal money supply drops from -0.9 percent per annum over the first two years to -4.3 percent, -19.0 percent, and -15.9 percent per annum over the next three years. On the basis of the available annual data, the average growth rate of nominal income from 1928 to 1933 was -11.1 percent per annum. This was divided between an average growth rate of real income of -6.0 percent and an average rate of inflation of -5.1 percent. As the monetary growth rate did not fall further and even increased slightly between April 1932 and April 1933—though it was still at an unexpectedly low rate—the restorative powers of adjustment in the economy began to emerge. In the summer of 1932, the growth rate of real income apparently rose to about zero, and by March 1933 was strongly positive.[5] Such a huge, cumulative fall in real income reflected a drastic fall in employment. Available estimates of the unemployment rate increase from about $3\frac{1}{4}$ percent in 1929 to 21–25 percent in 1932 and 1933. The behavior of fluidity also was as would be expected. During the first year or so after the April 1928 decrease in ΓM, fluidity fell. Then fluidity rose back to and past its steady-state growth

---

[5] This is inferred from such data as the index of industrial production, since only annual data on real income are available. Real income for 1932 was 71 percent of 1929 real income. For 1933, the figure was 69.5 percent.

path.[6] This is the most important example of the cyclical adjustment in the level of fluidity discussed in Appendix 7A. It occurred because the large fall in real income was proportionately much larger than the induced fall in real money demand. The rise in fluidity intensified the reduction in nominal income due to the reduction in ΓM (refer back to Fig. 7.14).

No mention has been made of fiscal policy or other nonmonetary macroeconomic shocks during this period. During 1930 and 1931, fiscal policy was actually very expansive due to a large increase in real government spending and borrowing relative to their low levels. In 1932, taxes were increased and government expenditures reduced, and then in 1933 real federal expenditures were sharply increased, but real state and local expenditures were reduced by more. The small effects through changing desired fluidity resulting from these and any other nonmonetary shocks are difficult to detect given the overwhelming monetary shock and the limited data. Keynesian economists have emphasized falling investment demand as a macroeconomic shock, but given the relative constancy of consumer and government expenditures, monetary policy must operate primarily by reducing investment if real income is to fall.

A fascinating question which has been posed by Friedman and Schwartz[7] is "Why was monetary policy so inept?" As with any such question of "might have beens," there are many possible answers. Friedman and Schwartz suggested that the main cause was the power vacuum and struggle within the Federal Reserve System following the death of Governor Benjamin Strong in 1928. Other explanations include (1) the Fed's obsession with "unsound stock market speculation" and the general virtues of a "cleansing deflation"; (2) the Fed's practice of sterilizing gold flows so that gold inflows were not allowed to increase base money; (3) a general lack of understanding of monetary theory on the part of Fed officials; and (4) the Fed's being accustomed to bank failures due to mismanagement in the 1920s and thinking bank failures during the crises also reflected mismanagement. As fascinating as these arguments are, they are largely irrelevant to the goal of understanding how macroeconomic shocks affect the economy.[8]

The continuing 1930–1933 monetary crises pointed out a peculiarity of the banking system established by the Federal Reserve Act of 1913. Before the Act, crises were short-lived because all banks in concert temporarily restricted convertibility of deposits into currency until after the panic had subsided, but otherwise continued their usual financial operations. The banks did not close. The fall in the nominal money supply was sharp but was soon followed by a recovery. Under the Federal Reserve Act restricted convertibility was prohibited as outmoded so that this catharsis, or cleansing crisis, did not occur.

---

[6] In 1929, fluidity was about 6 percent below the 1928 level. At the 1932 peak, fluidity rose to 44 percent above the 1928 level. Fluidity in 1933 was down to 33 percent above the 1928 level. These figures reflect relatively constant real money balances demanded and drastically falling real income.

[7] Friedman and Schwartz, *Monetary History*, pp. 407–419.

[8] Chapter 15 on stabilization policy will return to the question of the ability of an independent central bank to stabilize the economy.

This was fine so long as the Fed did what it was supposed to do and lent freely to banks facing runs. But when the Fed failed in this duty, the contagion of panic easily spread from one bank to others.

THE BANKING HOLIDAY OF 1933

Another peak in the pattern of bank failures was reached in January 1933. As panic spread, many states declared bank holidays, closing the banks in their states. By March 4, 1933, when the New York bank holiday began, most other states had already closed their banks. Finally on March 6, 1933, President Roosevelt closed all banks. Thus, the Fed—which was established to prevent panics from leading to restrictions on bank payments of currency—had, by its failure to act, caused the most severe and widespread banking suspension in American history.

Beginning March 13th, banks were permitted to reopen upon license from the Secretary of the Treasury.[9] Only clearly "sound" banks were licensed to reopen. This certification by the newly elected administration restored some confidence in the banking system. On March 15, 1933, 68.6 percent of the banks with 87.3 percent of the nation's total deposits were licensed and open. About half of the unlicensed banks, with one-quarter of the unlicensed bank deposits on March 15, 1933, were reopened by the end of 1933.

The Banking Holiday and licensing served the same cathartic function that restriction of bank payments of currency had served before the Federal Reserve System was established. With a measure of public confidence in the banking system restored, the cash-deposit ratio began falling instead of rising.

THE EXPANSION OF 1933–1937

The bottoming out of real income begun during the summer of 1932 became a definite recovery by early 1933. The recovery was materially hastened by a stimulative monetary shock in the form of an increase in the growth rate of the money supply. Comparison of Tables 13.2 and 13.1 illustrates the large increase in ΓM. The reasons for the reversal in the growth rate of the money supply were twofold: (1) an increased—though still negative—growth rate of the money multiplier and (2) an increased growth rate of base money.

The increased growth rate of the money multiplier is attributable to the changed growth rate of the cash-deposit ratio from positive to negative. Confidence in the reopened banks steadily grew, and as confidence grew the cash-deposit ratio desired by the public fell back toward its normal level.

---

[9] Licenses were issued by state banking officials for banks which were not members of the Federal Reserve System.

Table 13.2 **GROWTH RATES OF THE**
BROAD MONEY SUPPLY (M_2)
1933–1937

Period	Growth Rate
April 1933 to April 1934	8.3%
April 1934 to April 1935	12.6%
April 1935 to April 1936	10.5%
April 1936 to April 1937	7.9%

Source: Calculated from data in Milton Friedman and
Anna Jacobson Schwartz, *Monetary Statistics of the
United States,* New York: NBER, 1970, pp. 28–31.

An important factor in restoring public confidence was the establishment of the Federal Deposit Insurance Corporation in 1934. The enormous value of the FDIC in preventing runs and panics is based more on its actual operation than on its legal contract with depositors. The federal government has no legal liability to bail out the FDIC if its reserves are exhausted by a bank panic, and this was a real possibility in the early years. Further, depositors are insured only up to a specified sum.[10] A very large fraction—usually between one-third and one-half—of bank deposits are thus uninsured. The holders of these deposits would appear quite sufficient to create a run which could cause almost any bank to fail. In operation, the FDIC has eliminated most of the incentive for a run so that cumulative panics have become a thing of the past. This is true because the FDIC rarely allows a bank actually to go bankrupt so that the insurance limits apply. Instead, the FDIC arranges a merger of a mismanaged bank into a well-managed bank and compensates the good bank for any losses incurred in the takeover.

More than offsetting the fall in the cash-deposit ratio was the rise in the reserve-deposit ratio. Bankers had been rapidly increasing their reserve-deposit ratio since it became apparent that the banker who relied on the Fed for borrowing during a panic was very likely to fail, and this increase continued until the summer of 1935.[11] The net effect of the rising reserve-deposit ratio and falling cash-deposit ratio was an average growth rate of the money multiplier μ of -1.6 percent per annum between April 1933 and April 1936. This compared to an average $\Gamma\mu$ of -20.7 percent per annum between October 1930 and April 1933.

---

[10] This was $2,500 on January 1, 1934, raised to $5,000 on July 1, 1934, and maintained there until 1950. Currently the liability limit is $40,000.

[11] From October 1930 to April 1933 the reserve-deposit ratio rose at an average growth rate of 16.3 percent. From April 1933 to June 1935, the growth rate was 19.7 percent. From June 1935 through July 1936, there was no particular trend up or down. The Fed's published figures on bank reserves classified the large fraction which were not required as "excess," even though the evidence shows that they were not so regarded by the banks.

Between April 1933 and January 1934 the United States raised in steps the price at which it would buy or sell gold from $20.67 to $35.00 per ounce. At this high price much gold was purchased with new base money. The Fed had lapsed into almost complete inactivity even with regard to sterilization. So the gold purchases raised base money almost dollar for dollar. As a result the growth rate of base money between April 1933 and April 1936 was 12.2 percent per annum. The net effect on money supply growth is detailed in Table 13.2.

The resulting recovery in real income was highly dramatic. The average growth rate of real income between 1933 and 1937 was 9.0 percent per annum. Despite this very rapid recovery, real income in 1937 was only about the same as in 1929. If real income had grown at the long-run trend growth rate of about 3.1 percent per annum from 1929 on, real income in 1937 would have been about 28 percent higher than in 1929. In other words, 1937 real income was about 22 percent below the estimated steady-state level. Four years of reductions in real income were just made up by the increases of the next 4 years. So even a 43 percent rise in real income over only 4 years was disappointing. Figure 13.1 compares the actual growth path of real income for 1929–1946 with the estimated steady-state growth path. Another way to look at it is that from 1929 to 1937 the civilian labor force rose by 12.6 percent but employment rose by only 5.7 percent. As a result the unemployment rate rose by some 6 percentage points to about 9.2 percent.[12] While this was a great improvement relative to the over 20 percent rates of 1932 and 1933, it was still high compared with a normal rate of around 5 percent.

In part the "slow" recovery can be attributed to certain ill-advised legislation which adversely affected the aggregate production function.[13] The analysis of these structural changes must be left to economic histories. A more generally operative factor played an important role, however. Between 1929 and 1933, there was considerable disinvestment in capital instead of the normal increase. Saving normally falls during contractions. This occurs because the short-run MPC is about 0.4, which implies that saving $(y_N - c)$ is reduced R$0.60 for each R$1 transitory decrease in private income y_N. In the Great Depression,

---

[12] The labor force data quoted in the text here and below for 1934–1943 are based on Stanley Lebergott's updated version of his original estimates for the Bureau of Labor Statistics (BLS) as corrected by Darby to the current definitions of employment and unemployment. See Michael R. Darby, Three-and-a-Half Million U.S. Employees Have Been Mislaid; Or, An Explanation of Unemployment, 1934–1941, *Journal of Political Economy*, **84:** 1–16, Feb. 1976. In both Lebergott's BLS and later estimates, the emergency government labor force (employees of contracyclical government works programs such as the Works Progress Administration) were not counted as regular government employees and so were counted as unemployed when unemployment was estimated by subtracting employment from the labor force. Implicitly, a definition of unemployment as the difference between the labor force and "regular" (noncontracyclical) jobs was used instead of unemployment as the number of people without work who are looking for it. On this special definition, any contracyclical government employment which *increases* total employment by a smaller amount will increase reported unemployment! For the years indicated, unemployment was overstated in terms of the standard definition by about 2–3.5 million people and the unemployment rate by 4–7 percentage points. These data masked the speed and strength of the return of the unemployment rate toward normal levels in the period after the 1933 reference cycle trough.

[13] The National Industrial Recovery Act, minimum wage laws, and similar legislation granted new or increased monopoly power to favored groups in the economy.

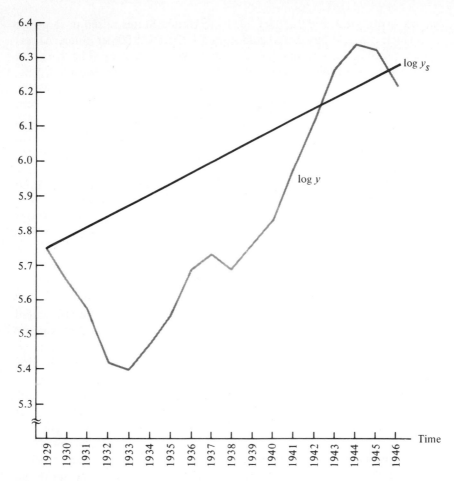

Figure 13.1 Actual and estimated steady-state real income growth paths, 1929–1946. The actual growth path of the logarithm of real income is compared to the straight-line steady-state growth path. The latter was estimated by applying a 3.1 percent per annum trend growth rate to 1929 real GNP. The actual real GNP data are suspect for 1942–1946 because of World War II and price controls.

the fall in transitory income was so great that the saving-income ratio fell from a normal 10 percent to 0.1, − 10.7, and − 10.4 percent in 1931, 1932, and 1933, respectively. Because of rising government deficits, real investment fell more to − 5.5, − 15.6, and − 14.6 percent of private income, respectively. Using 1972 as a base, net investment from 1929 through 1933 totaled − R$35.5 billion compared to the approximately R$100 billion capital accumulation that would have been expected if the Depression had not occurred. The fact that the capital stock was below equilibrium would cause capital to grow more rapidly than labor until the equilibrium labor-capital ratio was reachieved.[14] Until this adjustment was completed, however, real income (and real wages) would be below the steady-state growth path.

SUMMING UP THE GREAT DEPRESSION AND RECOVERY

The Great Depression was primarily the result of a series of monetary shocks. In early 1928, Fed policy reduced the growth rate of the money supply because of concern over "undue speculation" on the stock market. The result had all the appearances of a classic recession beginning in the summer of 1929 and continuing into 1930. In October of 1930, the Fed permitted a banking crisis to get started which recurred in waves until the Banking Holiday of 1933. The Fed had both the power and responsibility to prevent banking panics, but it failed to do so. The resulting large negative growth rate in the money multiplier caused a further sharp fall in the growth rate of the money supply. Further decreases in real income resulted, and recovery did not resume in earnest until early 1933. Rising public confidence in banks after the Banking Holiday nearly offset the continuing efforts of banks to build up reserves in case of renewed crises. The rise in the price of gold, from \$20.67 to \$35 per ounce, led to large government gold purchases. This caused base money to increase rapidly. The resulting large increase in the growth rate of the money supply greatly facilitated the rapid recovery of real income. By 1937, real income had returned to the level of 1929, but this was 20 to 25 percent below the steady-state value of real income. The difference can be attributed to both a level of capital that was below equilibrium—because of low investment during the Depression—and special factors related to New Deal legislation.

THE RECESSION OF 1937–1938 AND RECOVERY OF 1938–1941

Incredibly, the Fed was finally stirred in 1936 by the specter of inflation. The "reinflation" caused by the restoration of the money supply was at an average rate of inflation of 2.8 percent per annum between 1933 and 1936. The price level was still 15.6 percent below the 1929 level. Nevertheless, because banks had accumulated supposedly "excess" reserves, the Fed felt moved to use its newly granted power to change reserve requirements. Reserve requirements were doubled in steps between August 1936 and May 1937. As a result, the average growth rate of the nominal money supply between July 1936 and April 1938 was only 0.8 percent per annum.[15] In April 1938, reserve requirements

---

[14] Refer to the analysis of long-run equilibrium in a growing economy (Sec. 5.2).

[15] Since banks were holding more than the legal requirements in reserves, the rise in requirements caused a gradual adjustment in the reserve-deposit ratio. *Required* reserves could be used to meet a run only in proportion to reductions in deposits; so the excess of reserves over requirements provided the desired cushion against panics.

were reduced and money supply growth increased to an average rate of 10.0 percent per annum through December 1941.

The recovery from the Depression was interrupted by the 1937–1938 contraction caused by the 1936–1938 reduction in nominal-money-supply growth. Nevertheless, by 1941 real income was 29.5 percent above the 1929 level or only 10.7 percent below the steady-state level of real income.[16] Taken as a whole, the average growth rate of real income from 1937 through 1941 was 6.5 percent per annum, about twice the steady-state growth rate.

THE WAR YEARS, 1942–1946

The years of World War II present interesting problems for macroeconomists, but are not of much use for current illustrative purposes. Too many changes are combined with very unreliable data so that general principles are hopelessly veiled. For example, price controls and black markets make both price level and real income data very suspect. Price controls were removed in mid-1946 and a large jump in the price index measured the degree to which the price index was out of touch with reality. Nor is it safe to assume that the composition of real income or the labor supply function were unaffected by the World War! War spending was financed in part by increased money creation as the Fed purchased government securities to the extent necessary to maintain low interest rates. The resulting price increases imposed an effective tax on holders of money.

13.2 THE HISTORICAL RECORD: THE POSTWAR ERA

AN OVERVIEW

The postwar period can be divided into two distinct parts: (1) The first contains the period up to 1962 during which the country returned to a pattern of economic equilibrium disturbed by occasional recessions. During this period, there was no persistent tendency for the growth rate of the nominal money supply to increase or decrease over time. (2) Since 1962, there has been a clearly rising trend in the growth rate of the money supply. During most of this period, the economy was experiencing a new stimulative monetary shock before adjustment to the previous one was completed.

---

[16] As estimated by applying a 3.1 percent trend growth rate to 1929 real income. This reflected both a low capital stock and an unemployment rate of about 6 percent. Furthermore, many people had received less education and on-the-job training than normal during the 1930s; so the labor force was of lower average quality than it otherwise would have been. Some economists refer to this as a below-normal level of human capital.

The first period is mainly remarkable for a rather repetitive series of mild business cycles primarily related to moderate changes in the growth of the money supply. Each is independent but similar to the others. The second period is of especial interest because it has several dramatic points at which fiscal policy moves in one direction and monetary policy in the opposite direction. This permits comparison of the relative power of monetary and fiscal policy.

In this section, the money supply definition used will be the narrow money supply (M_1). Very similar statements could be made about the broad money supply (M_2). As discussed in Chap. 3, the empirical and theoretical evidence presents no clear-cut choice between the two definitions.

MACROECONOMIC TRENDS, 1947–1962

The 16 years 1947–1962 are characterized by a constant trend growth rate of the nominal money supply of 1.9 percent per annum. The actual growth path of the nominal money supply fluctuated around its trend growth path but not by far. Variations in the growth rate occurred, but were always reversed within a year or two so that differences did not cumulate long.

The average growth rate of fluidity was -4.1 percent per annum and that of nominal income was 6.0 percent per annum. These trends are not consistent throughout the period, however. Fluidity had risen sharply during World War II, and it fell back at an average growth rate of -6.3 percent per annum between 1947 and 1951. Thereafter, the average growth rate of fluidity was -3.1 percent per annum and the average growth rate of nominal income was 4.8 percent per annum.

The growth in nominal income was divided between an average rate of inflation of 2.4 percent per annum and an average growth of real income of 3.6 percent per annum. The data are highly suspect in the middle of the period because of the Korean War and associated price controls which likely resulted in a temporary overstatement of real income and understatement of the price level.

The rapid average growth rate of real income can be most easily understood in terms of the growth model of Chap. 5. During the Great Depression, real income fell far below its steady-state growth path and was about 10 percent below it in 1941. Much of the production of capital goods purchased by the government during World War II was converted to the production of private goods, but real income in 1947 was still 13 percent below its steady-state level as estimated by 1929 real income extrapolated at 3.1 percent per annum. This difference was due, not to unemployment of resources, but to the fact that resources—particularly physical and human capital—were below their steady-state growth paths because of low investment rates during the 1930s and World War II. As these resources grew more rapidly than normal to catch up with their steady-state growth paths, real income grew more rapidly to catch up with its steady-state growth path. By 1962, half of the percentage difference between real income and its steady-state growth path was eliminated.[17]

This discussion illustrates the difference between natural-employment real income and steady-state real income. *Natural-employment real income* is the level of real income which would exist if the unemployment rate were at its natural level.[18] Steady-state real income requires also that the level of resources currently available be on their long-run growth paths. The adjustment of real resources to long-term growth paths appears to be a very slow process compared to the adjustment of real income to natural-employment real income.

The explanation of the negative growth rate of fluidity in the postwar period has been the subject of continuing controversy among macroeconomists. An important cause has doubtless been the introduction and steady growth of money substitutes such as savings and loan accounts. These substitutes have resulted mainly from the limitations on interest payment on commercial bank deposits. It is suggestive that fluidity has fallen at a much slower rate for the broad definition of money, for which the interest rate restrictions are less important. Another probable influence has been the rising trend of interest rates. Between 1947 and 1951 the average growth rate of interest rates on Treasury bills was 30.3 percent per annum; it was 4.6 percent per annum between 1951 and 1962—an overall increase from a bill rate of 0.38 percent per annum at the beginning of 1947 to 2.86 percent per annum at the end of 1962. Even if the long-run interest elasticity of the demand for money is very low, an increase of interest rates to seven and one-half times the original level could significantly lower the growth rate of fluidity in the interim.

THE REBIRTH OF MONETARY POLICY

The Fed came out of World War II with a continuing commitment to support the prices of government securities by buying and selling all the securities offered at certain *pegged interest rates*. A policy of maintaining pegged interest rates implies that nominal-money-supply growth will be whatever is necessary, given other economic conditions, to maintain the peg. Such a policy can lead to runaway inflations if the peg is maintained below the interest rate which would otherwise exist, and to runaway deflations if the peg is too high. If for example the peg were too low, private investors would be unwilling to buy all the government securities, so the Fed would have to buy some of them with newly issued base money. This would ultimately raise the level of market interest rates via the (inflation) expectation effect. As the Fed increased the rate at which it bought government securities with base money, runaway inflation would result.

---

[17] It will be seen later that all the difference was eliminated by 1965, and since then the growth rate of real income has averaged about 3 percent per annum.

[18] This is sometimes referred to as "full-employment real income." But one's idea of the unemployment rate which corresponds to "full employment" may differ from the natural rate.

As it happened, the pegged rates were generally about right up until the start of the Korean War. The interest rate peg for long-term government bonds was maintained until then at 2.5 percent per annum. This historically low nominal interest rate was acceptable because of widespread expectations of renewed, worsened depression. In view of a negative expected inflation rate, 2.5 percent was an attractive yield and average nominal-money-supply growth was only a bit over 2 percent per annum.

The beginning of the Korean War in June 1950 eliminated these expectations quickly, and Fed purchases of securities and creation of nominal base money increased rapidly. After a dramatic confrontation with the Treasury and the President, Fed freedom to determine monetary policy without regard to any support prices was announced in the Treasury–Federal Reserve Accord of March 1951.

Despite the accord, Fed policy up through the late 1960s continued to be formulated in terms of pegging the level of interest rates. The Fed also used such phrases as " credit conditions " and "feel and tone of the market," but it pretty much boiled down to an unannounced interest rate peg which the Fed changed from time to time. Unfortunately, the Fed judged its policy as stimulative or restrictive (or *easy* or *tight*) according to whether the pegged interest rates were low or high by historic standards. This will translate into high or low growth rates of nominal money, respectively, only if the nominal interest rate which would otherwise exist remains constant. If this does not roughly hold, particularly as during the 1930s and again in the late 1960s and early 1970s, the result can be rapid deflation or inflation.

Milder nonmonetary shocks will also affect the rate of interest which would exist for a given growth rate of the money supply. If money supply growth adjusts instead of interest rates because of pegging, changes in money supply growth will amplify the effects of nonmonetary shocks. This possible synchronization of shocks has led to much controversy in analysis of the effects of stabilization policy during the postwar period.[19] For this reason, macroeconomists particularly study points at which the Fed changed the interest rate peg by large amounts to offset the effects of fiscal policy or other macroeconomic shocks. These cases provide the clearest opportunity to measure the separate impact of monetary and other shocks in the postwar era.

CYCLICAL CHANGES, 1947–1962

The National Bureau of Economic Research (NBER) chronology includes four contractions between 1947 and 1962, as noted in Table 13.3. During each of these contractions the growth rate of real income not only slowed, but became negative.

The immediate cause of the 1948–1949 recession was a sharp decrease in the

---

[19] See Chap. 15.

**Table 13.3 NBER REFERENCE CYCLE CHRONOL-
OGY, 1947–1962**

November 1948	Peak	
		11-month contraction
October 1949	Trough	
		45-month expansion
July 1953	Peak	
		13-month contraction
August 1954	Trough	
		35-month expansion
July 1957	Peak	
		9-month contraction
April 1958	Trough	
		25-month expansion
May 1960	Peak	
		9-month contraction
February 1961	Trough	

growth rate of the money supply engineered by Fed policy. The pattern of interest rates pegged by the Fed throughout World War II had been set on the basis of an anomalous pattern existing in 1941. The interest rate pegs varied from 0.375 percent per annum on 3-month Treasury bills up to 2.5 percent on long-term government bonds. This sort of spread can exist in the market only when short-term interest rates are expected to rise sharply. As a result, the Fed found itself selling off its long-term government bonds and buying short-term Treasury bills as fast as they were issued. Between the summer of 1947 and the autumn of 1948 the pegged interest rate on short-term government securities was gradually raised to a more realistic 1.125 percent per annum on 3-month Treasury bills. Although the longest-term government bonds were still pegged at 2.5 percent per annum, there had been a substantial increase in the average pegged rate.

At the higher average pegged rate, the equilibium growth rate of the money supply was noticeably lowered. Between January 1948 and January 1949, the average growth rate of the money supply was only − 1.1 percent per annum compared to a 3.5 percent growth rate the previous year. Fiscal policy on the other hand was, if anything, stimulative through the third quarter of 1949, with rising federal expenditures and falling budget surpluses.

Monetary policy during this period is a bit obscured by increases in reserve requirements during 1948 and decreases during 1949. These changes have little effect under a pegged interest rate policy other than to determine how the growth of the nominal money supply will be split between growth in nominal base money and money multiplier. The nominal-money-supply growth rate has to be whatever is consistent with the pegged interest rates and economic conditions.

The contraction (and the decrease in the growth rate of the nominal money supply) was a bit milder than the 1929–1933 contraction in its first year. Unlike the earlier episode, the growth rate of the nominal money supply did not continue to fall. Instead the Fed lowered interest rates below (raised security prices above) the officially pegged level a bit and nominal-money-supply growth rose slightly to 0.0 percent during 1949. The normal return of real income to its natural-employment level was sufficiently strong to overcome a switch to restrictive fiscal policy beginning in the third quarter of 1949 and continuing until the start of the Korean War.

The Fed increased interest rates somewhat during the Korean War, but not by nearly enough to offset the rise in interest rates implied by the rise in the expected inflation rate and government deficit financing. The average growth rate of the nominal money supply was 4.5 percent per annum during 1950, 1951, and 1952. By the beginning of 1953, rising concern about inflation convinced the Fed to adopt a restrictive monetary policy, and it raised the pegged rate on long-term bonds from about 2.75 to 3.25 percent per annum. As a result, the growth rate of the money supply fell to about 1.1 percent per annum during 1953. This was combined with a restrictive fiscal shock due to the end of the Korean War in the third quarter of 1953, and the 1953–1954 recession followed.

The growth rate of the nominal money supply increased in early 1954,[20] to an average rate of 2.7 percent per annum for the year. The combination of monetary stimulus and normal recovery from the recession made 1955 a boom year of rapid recovery. By mid-1955 the economy had apparently surpassed the natural-employment level. Real income growth then slowed while the price level adjusted upward during 1956. This is the characteristic pattern of increased money supply growth followed with a lag by increased real income growth, followed in turn by a more rapid rate of inflation.

The growth rate of the nominal money supply gradually decreased to 2.2 percent for 1955, 1.2 percent for 1956, and −0.7 percent per annum for 1957 in the face of rising interest rates. Growth slowed in 1956 and the recession of 1957–1958 began July 1957.

In November 1957, Fed policy was reversed, with interest pegs lowered through April 1958. The resulting growth rate of the money supply from January 1958 to August 1959 was 4.1 percent per annum. In May 1958 the Fed began to move the interest rate peg upward as the economy recovered. A strike in the steel industry during the summer of 1959 reduced the demand for credit as inventories were drawn down. In itself, the steel strike would have had transient effects. Combined with the Fed's suddenly "too high" interest rate peg, it led to a decline in the growth rate of the money supply to −1.7 percent per annum between July 1959 and June 1960. The recession beginning in May 1960, can thus be related to the unintended impact on the money supply of the previous year's steel strike. The Fed realized at the beginning of 1960 that its interest rate peg was incorrect for current conditions and lowered it sharply

---

[20] The Fed had gradually reduced pegged interest rates since June 1953, but not by enough to offset the fall in the interest rate which would have accompanied the end of the Korean War spending. In January and February, the Fed pushed the Treasury bill rate down by almost two-thirds of a percentage point. The regularity with whic` Fed policy changes with the year is remarkable. Perhaps it reflects New Year's resolutions.

over the first half of the year. Money supply growth resumed in June 1960, strengthening the expansion begun the previous month. The recovery and expansion continued through and beyond 1962.[21]

SUMMING UP THE EXPERIENCE FROM 1947 THROUGH 1962

The broad trend of real income growth was very rapid by long-term historical standards—a growth rate of 3.6 percent per annum compared to the historic trend for the century of 3.0 to 3.2 percent per annum. This meant that real income in 1962 was about 8 percent higher than it would have been had it grown from 1947 at the historic rates. Conversely, the capital-labor ratio in 1947 was very low because of low rates of investment between 1929 and 1946. An even higher growth rate of real income could have been hoped for during the period of increasing capital-labor ratios. Growth may have been slowed by recurrent mild recessions caused by a stop-go monetary policy which mainly resulted from the Fed's reacting with a lag to the ill effects of its previous policy. On occasion, changes in monetary policy were the unintended byproduct of determining policy in terms of interest rates instead of the growth rate of the money supply. Except for the variations in real government spending associated with the Korean War, fiscal and behavioral shocks do not seem to have been significant in magnitude.

MACROECONOMIC TRENDS, 1963–1977

As a whole, the period 1963–1977 can be characterized as a period of increasing growth rates of the money supply. The acceleration was interrupted by three changes of direction: the second half of 1966, 1969, and 1973–1975. Table 13.4 presents the behavior of the growth rates of nominal money and other macroeconomic variables. The average growth rate of the nominal money supply for 1963–1966 was 3.8 percent per annum. This growth rate averaged 5.7 percent in 1967–1971, 6.1 percent in 1972–1977, and 5.4 percent per annum for the whole period 1963–1977.

The average growth rates of fluidity and nominal income for the whole period were −2.9 percent and 8.2 percent per annum, respectively. The growth rate of nominal income was divided between a 3.5 percent growth in real income and a 4.7 percent rate of inflation. The high real income growth was concentrated in the early part of the period, and since 1966 this growth has

---

[21] The NBER growth cycle chronology, however, records a downturn in April 1962 and an upturn in March 1963, corresponding with a lag to variations in nominal-money-supply growth.

Table 13.4 GROWTH RATES OF MAJOR MICROECONOMIC VARIABLES, 1963–1977

Year	Money	Fluidity	Nominal Income	Real Income	Price Level
1963	3.6%	−2.8%	6.4%	5.0%	1.5%
1964	4.5%	−1.2%	5.7%	4.3%	1.4%
1965	4.6%	−5.3%	9.9%	7.4%	2.5%
1966	2.5%	−5.3%	7.9%	4.2%	3.7%
1967	6.4%	0.5%	5.9%	2.8%	3.1%
1968	7.7%	−1.1%	8.9%	4.1%	4.7%
1969	3.2%	−3.2%	6.3%	1.2%	5.1%
1970	5.0%	0.6%	4.4%	−0.6%	5.0%
1971	6.3%	−2.8%	9.1%	4.5%	4.6%
1972	8.7%	−2.4%	11.1%	7.0%	4.1%
1973	5.8%	−4.8%	10.6%	3.3%	7.2%
1974	4.4%	−2.5%	6.9%	−3.5%	10.4%
1975	4.1%	−5.7%	9.7%	2.5%	7.2%
1976	6.0%	−3.3%	9.2%	4.6%	4.6%
1977	7.4%	−3.7%	11.1%	5.5%	5.6%

Sources: Calculated from data in *NBER Data Bank*, May 1978.

been at a much slower average rate of 3.0 percent. The rate of inflation, in contrast, generally has been accelerating.

By the end of 1965, real income had finally achieved the steady-state growth path of real income extrapolated from 1929 at 3.1 percent per annum. This was achieved by reducing the unemployment rate to—and later less than—4 percent when the natural rate was between 4.5 and 5 percent. As capital continued to rise, the steady-state real income growth path could be achieved with levels of unemployment nearer to the natural-employment rate. It must be emphasized that a 3.1 percent per annum growth rate of real income is no more than a historical average used to estimate the underlying concept. Though it seems to work fairly well in explaining long-run trends in the economy, this may reflect historical accidents.

DATA PROBLEMS, 1963–1977

There are two sources of difficulty in analyzing data on the national income accounts: the Vietnamese War and the price and wage control program of August 1971 through April 1974.

The Vietnamese War has no well-defined dates. In terms of the size of the armed forces and expenditures, the war started in 1966 and faded out during

1970 and 1971. During the interim, real income was probably overstated be-cause of the shift in output mix.[22]

The price control program of 1971–1974 may have actually increased full-employment real income slightly by acting to temporarily reduce monopoly power of the unions. Most of the apparent impact in the data is probably due to cheating which reduced the price index relative to the true price level. Darby has estimated that the price index was reduced between 3 and 4.5 percent at the peak impact in late 1972.[23] This difference increased the rate of inflation during 1973 and the first half of 1974, as discussed below.

CYCLICAL CHANGES, 1963–1977

The relatively steady acceleration of money supply growth until 1969 provided no reference cycle peaks or troughs until November 1969.[24] Nevertheless, the adjustment period is of considerable interest.

The growth rate of the nominal money supply increased by 2 percentage points in 1963 and by another percentage point in 1964. The growth rate of fluidity in these years was about 1 percent per annum higher than the −3 percent trend previously observed. Nominal money growth was constant in 1965, and fluidity adjusted back to its trend level by the end of the year. The implied large increase in nominal income was primarily apparent in a large increase in real income. Nominal-money-supply growth stopped during the last half of 1966, initially mainly reducing the growth rate of fluidity. Also reducing the growth rate of fluidity during this year was the stimulative fiscal policy implied by the United States entry in force into the Vietnamese War. At the end of 1966, fluidity was about 2.6 percent below its trend level as extrapolated from 1962 at −3 percent per annum.

The accelerating growth rate of the nominal money supply had come about because the Fed pegged interest rates at a low level to stimulate the economy. As interest rates tended to rise, the Fed " leaned against the wind " by increas-ing the rate of nominal money creation. The accelerating inflation that resulted finally convinced the Fed that it must tighten. As a result, the nominal money supply was constant from June 1966 to January 1967. At the first evidence of slowing industrial production, the Fed stepped on the money accelerator and the nominal money supply grew at an even higher rate than before.

The pause in money supply growth caused the so-called minirecession

---

[22] The unemployment rate was similarly lowered relative to similar economic conditions in peacetime by the practice of drafting teenage males, particularly those searching for a job. Teenage males normally provide a large fraction of unemployed persons. This lowering tends to occur whenever there is a war.

[23] Michael R. Darby, "Price and Wage Controls: The First Two Years" and "Price and Wage Controls: Further Evidence," in K. Brunner and A. Meltzer (eds.), *Carnegie-Rochester Conference Series*, vol. II, Amsterdam: North-Holland, 1976.

[24] The NBER growth cycle chronology records a downturn in June 1966 and an upturn in October 1967. The first half of 1967 is widely known as the *minirecession* although it is not an official reference cycle contraction.

during the first half of 1967. Real income was constant during the first quarter and then increased slightly during the second quarter of 1967. The impact of the minirecession on the economy was trivial, but it did have a significant impact on economic thought. In the ferment following the publication of Friedman and Schwartz's *Monetary History of the United States, 1867–1960*, it provided a sharp contrast between the widely publicized predictions of Friedman, Schwartz, and other "monetarists" and those of prominent Keynesians who were labeled "fiscalists" because of their belief in the power of fiscal policy. The monetarists predicted a sharp drop in the growth rate of real income because of the previous drop in the growth rate of the money supply. Fiscalists predicted further rapid growth of real income because of further rapid increases in real government spending largely financed by borrowing. After the events, study of the views and evidence of the monetarists became more compelling.

During 1967, fluidity rose sharply, relative to the -3 percent trend, due to adjustment upward from the low 1966 level and to the 4 percent per annum increase in the growth rate of the money supply. The relatively high growth rate increased fluidity to about 0.9 percent above its trend growth path. Put another way, the average growth rate of nominal income between the last quarters of 1962 and 1967 equaled the growth rate of the money supply plus 2.8 percent per annum due to a -2.8 percent per annum average growth rate of fluidity.

The growth rate of the money supply increased further during 1968 to 7.7 percent per annum. The acceleration of money supply growth during 1967 and the first half of 1968 had caused monetarists to predict continued rapid growth of nominal income in the last half of 1968. The fiscalists predicted a slow-down or recession because of a very large tax increase passed in June 1968. The tax increase, together with the cessation of growth of real government spending, did in fact stop the normal fall in fluidity during the second half of 1968, but this was not enough to outweigh the money supply acceleration. Monetarist views became more influential. In particular the Fed, which had engineered the money supply acceleration because of fears of fiscal "overkill," began a slow process of deemphasizing interest rate pegs and introducing money supply growth as the guide to open market operations.

Accelerating inflation was widely believed to have been an important issue in the Democratic loss of the Presidency in 1968. Beginning in January 1969, the Fed reduced the growth rate of the money supply to 3.2 percent per annum. Fiscal policy continued restrictive during 1969, and so had a neutral effect on the growth rate of fluidity. The NBER dates the beginning of the recession at November 1969. It is a measure of the acceleration of money supply growth since 1962 that by 1969 a 3.2 percent per annum growth rate of the money supply was a restrictive monetary policy.

The recession of 1969–1970[25] was widely viewed as further evidence of the

---

[25] The trough is dated at November 1970.

dominance of monetary policy. This is, however, an overstatement since fluidity grew in 1970 at a rate 3.6 percent greater than trend even though it started from a level of 2.6 percent above the trend level. Fiscal policy involved a −1.9 percent per annum growth rate of real government expenditures (the same as for 1969) and also a much larger tax cut, reversing the 1968 tax surcharge so that the government deficit increased sharply. An apparently important influence was a sharp fall in the expected rate of inflation brought about by the Fed's willingness to reduce money supply growth and cause a recession. Many borrowers and lenders believed—erroneously as it turned out—the claims by federal officials that monetary restraint would be maintained until inflation was eliminated. In combination with the normal cyclical fall in real interest rates, short-term interest rates fell by 3 percentage points (from 7.82 to 4.87 percent per annum) during 1970. The effect on the demand for money apparently significantly worsened the recession.

Fluidity was reverting to trend at a growth rate of −4.2 percent per annum during the first half of 1971. The so-called Economic Stabilization Program (ESP) announced by President Nixon on August 15, 1971, stopped and for a while reversed that process, at least in the official data. Fluidity growth was a bit above trend for the rest of 1971 and 1972.[26]

Although popularly termed wage and price controls, the ESP controls generally permitted prices to rise in proportion to costs (just as in a steady-state inflation) and only applied to some wages.[27] The wage controls were effective only for union wages, so that the ESP turned out to be little more than an antitrust program for unions. As the normal loss of real income due to the monopoly power of unions is generally estimated to be somewhat less than 1 percent of GNP, an increase of $\frac{1}{2}$ percent of GNP is likely a high estimate of real income gains from ESP after allowance is made for the waste of misallocation in a few industries under special rules and for administrative costs.

Reported real income in the first quarter of 1973 was nevertheless about 4 percent higher than could be accounted for by applying Okun's law to normal growth and the 0.9 percentage point decline in the unemployment rate from the second (pre-ESP) quarter of 1971. Either alchemy had been at work, or firms had responded to the incentives to lie downward about their prices and especially to reduce the quality of their goods. About $1\frac{1}{2}$ percentage points of this apparent understatement of the price level (and overstatement of real income) was worked off by the third quarter of 1973 under Phase III. Controls were then reformulated to place a real constraint on prices as well as wages. The increasing economic dislocations quickly led business executives to join unionists in opposing the ESP. The controls were gradually removed beginning in January 1974, with final abolition in April 1974.

---

[26] This effect on the official data seems to be quite usual during price controls. See Juan T. Toribio, "On the Monetary Effects of Repressed Inflation," Ph.D. dissertation, University of Chicago, 1970.

[27] By July 1972, the wages of 56 percent of the labor force had been exempted from the controls program. This discussion summarizes the material cited previously in footnote 23.

Table 13.5 GROWTH RATES OF COMPONENTS OF NOMINAL INCOME CORRECTED FOR ESTIMATED MISREPORTING DUE TO ESP, 1971–1974

Year	Nominal Income	Real Income	Price Level
1971	9.1%	4.4%	4.7%
1972	11.1%	4.7%	6.4%
1973	10.6%	4.6%	6.0%
1974	6.9%	−2.7%	9.6%

Source: Computed from quarterly data in Michael R. Darby, "Wage and Price Controls: Further Evidence," in K. Brunner and A. Meltzer (eds.), *Carnegie-Rochester Conference Series*, vol. II, Amsterdam: North-Holland, 1976.

By using the normal Okun's law relation of real income to changes in unemployment, estimates of real income have been made. These estimates are used in Table 13.5 to present a division of the growth rate of nominal income alternative to that in the official data reported in Table 13.4.

From December 1971 through June 1973, the Fed—apparently less concerned about inflation because of the ESP—accelerated money supply growth to an average rate of 8.0 percent per annum. As the ESP came unhinged in 1973 under this monetary pressure,[28] the Fed cut money supply growth to 4.6 percent per annum from June 1973 to December 1973, 6.0 percent per annum for the next six months, and 1.3 percent per annum from June 1974 to January 1975.[29] Thus, a recession would have been anticipated beginning about the second quarter of 1974 and worsening late in 1974 due to the near cessation of monetary growth in the last half of 1974.

The establishment in late 1973 of an oil cartel and a temporary embargo on Arabian oil sales to the United States somewhat complicated the picture. On the basis of the quarterly data underlying Table 13.5,[30] the oil embargo had about the same impact on the economy as a major strike. That is, the corrected real income data indicate that compared to the fourth quarter of 1973, real income was about 0.7 percent lower in the first quarter of 1974 but 0.1 percent higher in the second quarter. Two quarters growth would normally imply

---

[28] An almost 8 percent per annum steady-state inflation rate was implied.

[29] The erratic monetary growth rate in 1974 did not reflect policy but occurred because the Fed's operating instructions were formulated in terms of a monthly peg for the federal funds rate on interbank loans. The peg was estimated to imply the Fed's nominal-money-supply growth target. The risk premium on federal funds over Treasury bills rose from 2.5 to 5.4 percentage points from December 1973 to July 1974 because of fears for bank solvency after several large bank failures. As the risk premium rose, the federal funds rate peg was underestimated and nominal-money-supply growth was above the Fed's goal. From July 1974 to January 1975, the risk premium declined to 0.9 percentage point and the federal funds rate peg was overestimated. Thus the nominal-money-supply growth rate was below target.

[30] Similar inferences are implied by such indicators as industrial production and employment which do not involve deflation by the estimated price index.

about a 1.5 percent increase in real income; hence, the second quarter of 1974 shows both some remaining effects of the establishment of the oil cartel and the beginnings of the recession due to the cut in money supply growth. The corrected data show real income growth rates of -1.5 and -9.5 percent per annum for the third and fourth quarters of 1974, respectively.

The official data show a 1.5 percent fall in real income from the fourth quarter of 1973 to the second quarter of 1974. This reflects in part the ending of the ESP and overstatement of real income. But even allowing for that, real-income growth was practically nil, mainly because of the oil embargo and cartel. The remainder of 1974 corresponds to the classical pattern of a monetary contradiction.

No interpretation of the 1971–1974 period can be taken as gospel in view of the serious data problems. It is well to review where the economy was at the close of this period relative to steady-state extrapolations from 1962. Fluidity was high, some 5.8 percent higher than would have been predicted by applying a -3 percent per annum growth rate. Real income on the other hand was low—some 4 to 5 percent below the natural-employment level.[31] While low levels of real income would increase desired fluidity (see Appendix 7A), most of the excess fluidity seems to have been due to the effects of the price control program.

Between 1974 and 1977, fluidity growth was below normal (despite accelerating nominal money growth in 1976 and 1977) so that actual fluidity exceeded the trend estimate of steady-state fluidity by only 2.1 percent by the end of 1977. Similarly, fast real-income growth eliminated over 3 percent of the deficit in real income. Thus overall 1975–1977 can be characterized as a period of convergence to steady-state equilibrium. As can be seen by reference to Table 13.4, accelerating nominal money growth in 1976 and 1977 has set the stage for another round of accelerating inflation.

13.3 THE RELATIVE IMPORTANCE OF SOURCES OF MACROECONOMIC SHOCKS

Our survey of recent macroeconomic history provides perspective on the monetarist proposition that fluctuations in the growth rate of the nominal money supply have been the major source of American business fluctuations.

Recall that the growth rate of nominal income equals the growth rate of nominal money less the growth rate of fluidity,

$$\Gamma Y \equiv \Gamma M - \Gamma \phi \qquad [13.1]$$

---

[31] By 1974 the capital stock adjustment from the low level following the 1930s and World War II was complete. So differences between natural-employment and steady-state real income were negligible.

So fluctuations in nominal income must reflect fluctuations in the difference between the growth rates of nominal money and fluidity. In the very shortest run, unexpected changes in nominal money growth are reflected in fluidity growth with no effect on nominal income. Over time however, fluidity adjusts back toward its trend as the original money shock is transmitted to nominal income growth. Nonmonetary shocks quite independently influence the growth rate of fluidity, and hence induce fluctuations in nominal income for a given growth rate of nominal money. The question posed by the monetarist proposition is the magnitude of these independent fluctuations in the growth rates of fluidity and nominal income relative to those due to fluctuations in the nominal-money growth rate.

Obviously this is a historical question. If one were to examine a period in which the Fed maintained a constant nominal-money growth rate, all fluctuations would be due to nonmonetary shocks. If monetary policy were very erratic, it would dominate the effects of nonmonetary shocks.

As we have examined this particular historical period, we have seen that variations in nominal-money growth are more directly translated into variations in nominal-income growth for data averaged over longer periods than in the case of short periods. For short periods, such as a year or less, there are substantial (up to 3 or 4 percentage points) variations in the growth rate of fluidity. Perhaps half of these fluctuations in fluidity can be attributed to adjustment to monetary shocks. The rest would be the independent influence on the nominal-income growth rate of nonmonetary shocks. Thus we can say that for broad trends in the growth rate of nominal income (and the price level), the growth rate of nominal money is nearly all that matters. This is because of the relatively very stable trend growth rate of fluidity (and real income). For shorter periods, both monetary and nonmonetary shocks have been important, although the monetary shocks have been the senior partner during the period as a whole.

SUMMARY

1 The Fed instituted a restrictive monetary policy in the spring of 1928 because of concern about high stock market prices. The resulting contraction started in the summer of 1929. The recession of 1929–1930 became a depression after the onset of a banking panic in late 1930, which recurred in waves until the Banking Holiday of 1933. Because the Fed abdicated its responsibility to stop panics, the growth rate of the nominal money supply decreased sharply through spring 1932 and then recovered only slightly during the following year.
2 Nominal-money-supply growth resumed in 1933 and continued until the summer of 1936. The Fed then stopped money supply growth until the spring of 1938 by doubling reserve requirements. The rapid recovery after 1933 was then interrupted by the severe recession of 1937–1938. Recovery then

resumed and continued until the start of World War II. Data through the war years are very unreliable, but it is clear that unemployment of resources was practically eliminated during the war.

3 In 1947, the economy was characterized by a low capital-labor ratio because of reduced real investment during the 1930s and the war years. Though deflationary expectations kept unemployment very low—it was easy to find a "good job"—real income was also low compared with 1929 real income projected at the 3.1 percent per annum long-run trend. This provided a base for exceptionally fast growth through the mid-1960s.

4 The growth of the economy between 1947 and 1962 was interrupted by four mild contractions due to monetary shocks and the Korean War. Nevertheless, the real-income growth rate averaged 3.6 percent per annum during this period. Money supply growth fluctuated mildly around a 1.9 percent growth rate, and the rate of inflation averaged 2.4 percent because of a negative trend growth rate in fluidity (-4.1 percent per annum).

5 Between 1963 and 1977, the average growth rate of the money supply increased sharply with fluctuations around the rising trend. In the early part of the period, the acceleration in money supply growth was reflected mainly in increased real-income growth. As the economy adjusted to rapid increases in money, the rate of inflation rose sharply and real-income growth slowed. After 1965, real income fluctuated around a 3.1 percent per annum trend line drawn from 1929.

6 The Economic Stabilization Program of 1971–1974 caused an understatement of the rate of inflation in 1971 and 1972 and a corresponding overstatement in 1973 and 1974.

7 The overall growth in nominal income and the price level from 1962 to 1977 was almost exactly what would have been predicted from the actual growth in nominal money and the secular trend growth rates of fluidity and real income.

8 The historical record seems to indicate dominance of monetary shocks—and war—in determining macroeconomic behavior over periods of a year or more, but a considerable range of influence within a period of a year or so for other macroeconomic shocks.

CONCEPTS TO KNOW

natural-employment real income   pegged interest rates

QUESTIONS AND EXERCISES

*1 During the Great Depression, Fed officials claimed that the depression could not be blamed on them because the fall in the money supply was only as necessary to meet the fall in money demand due to falling income and to

prevent credit conditions from becoming sloppy. Indeed, they claimed that monetary policy was easy because interest rates on Treasury securities were low and money was a larger fraction of income. What is wrong with this argument?

2 Why can a bank go bankrupt during a panic and then have sufficient assets to pay off all depositors with something left over for the stockholders?

3 A great advantage of Federal Deposit Insurance is that it reduces the probability of bank failure—the thing insured against. To achieve this reduction why is it important that insurance limits are rarely applied?

4 The Fed's withdrawal between 1933 and 1937 from money creation—other than issuing base money to pay for Treasury gold purchases—temporarily put the United States on a quasi-gold standard. How would this cause rapid monetary growth between 1933 and 1936?

*5 If the Fed were to try to maintain a low interest rate peg with rapid base-money creation, why would the growth rate of base money have to be increased over time? (*Hint:* What happens to the expected rate of inflation?)

6 If federal expenditures are rising and budget surpluses are falling, what can be inferred about federal taxes?

7 Use [13.1] to explain why nonmonetary shocks are analyzed as affecting the growth rate of fluidity.

REFERENCES FOR FURTHER READING

Friedman, Milton, and Anna Jacobson Schwartz: *A Monetary History of the United States, 1867–1960,* Princeton University Press for NBER, 1963, esp. chaps. 7–11.

——— **and Walter W. Heller:** *Monetary vs. Fiscal Policy,* New York: Norton, 1969.

Sprinkel, Beryl W.: *Money and Markets: A Monetarist View,* Homewood, Ill.: Irwin, 1971, esp. chaps. 1, 5, and 7.

Stein, Herbert: *The Fiscal Revolution in America,* University of Chicago Press, 1969.

PART SIX

MACROECONOMIC POLICY

The most important application of macroeconomic theory is found in the formulation and evaluation of the macroeconomic policy of the federal government. Here macroeconomics discloses what can be done and what cannot be done. It also indicates the means by which possible alternatives can be achieved.

Politicians regularly promise to achieve what cannot possibly be achieved in the area of unemployment and inflation. Chapter 14 examines why workers and other resources are unemployed from time to time. The relationship between unemployment and inflation is then studied. This analysis shows that policy based on an oversimplified short-run model can lead—and has led—to the quite unintended long-run effect of accelerating inflation.

Policy is concerned with more than just unemployment and inflation, however. Chapter 15 considers a wide range of macroeconomic goals. It is often true that more of one goal means less of another and difficult choices must be made in formulating or evaluating policy. On those choices informed individuals can reasonably differ. But the choices should be made with an understanding of what can be chosen. Attempts to attain unattainable goals may be noble but end in unfortunate results for the economy. Macroeconomics does not yet have all the answers to important policy questions, but it does have some and is looking for more.

CHAPTER 14

UNEMPLOYMENT
AND INFLATION

WHAT YOU WILL LEARN IN THIS CHAPTER
The nature of unemployment ● Determinants of the
normal level of the unemployment rate ●
Determinants of cyclical variations in the
unemployment rate—layoffs and search ● Dangers in
using the Phillips curve analysis to trade off a
higher inflation rate for a lower unemployment
rate ● The fallacies in discussions of the wage-price
spiral and job creation

14.1 DETERMINATION OF THE UNEMPLOYMENT RATE

WHAT IS UNEMPLOYMENT?

Unemployment is an experience which is common to all economic resources. It occurs when the owner of the resource searches for a better offer than the best offer received for the employment of the resource.[1]

A period of search for higher-valued employments of particular people or machines is nearly universal. It occurs because information is required to match resources with potential employers particularly desirous of their individual characteristics. This information is costly to produce. Its efficient production frequently involves holding the resource idle while its owner searches out potential employers to see whether they are interested, and at what price.[2]

Resources can be unemployed when they first enter the market and are searching for their best use or between uses when their value in the prior use falls below their value—as perceived by their owner—in other uses. The first sort of unemployment is connected with gross investment in either human or

---

[1] This chapter is largely based on a stream of literature growing out of the seminal papers by George J. Stigler, The Economics of Information, *Journal of Political Economy*, **69**: 213–225, June 1961, and Information in the Labor Market, *Journal of Political Economy*, **70**: 94–105, Oct. 1962. Other key references are to Edmund S. Phelps, et al., *Microeconomic Foundations of Employment and Information Theory*, New York: W. W. Norton and Co., Inc., 1970; and Robert E. Lucas, Jr., Some International Evidence on Output-Inflation Tradeoffs, *American Economic Review*, **63**: 326–334, June 1973.

[2] It is sometimes efficient to keep the resource partially or wholly employed while searching for a higher-valued use. In this case the search period would not involve any unemployment as conventionally measured.

nonhuman capital. New workers, buildings, or machines either replace old workers, buildings, or machines or add to the total stock. In either case, there is usually a period of search for an employer willing to pay an attractive price. The second sort of unemployment is normally connected with changes in the conditions of production or demand for particular products and serves to shift resources from less valued to more valued uses. Thus, temporarily unemployed resources are part of the process of adjustment to change.

This section will be primarily concerned with the determination of the unemployment rate of labor associated with these normal patterns of search for most valued uses. Unemployment normally due to the entry of new workers into the civilian labor force and to changes in relative demand and supply conditions is sometimes called *frictional unemployment*. Fluctuations of the unemployment rate around this normal rate due to business cycles—*cyclical unemployment*—will be discussed in the following section.[3]

It is unfortunate to be forced to search for a new job because one's value in the old job fell through no fault of one's own. There are significant costs of search—foregone earnings, advertising, travel, and the like. This is true not only for a worker but also for the owner of a factory building or machine. Nevertheless, the costs of reallocating resources must be borne by their owners.[4]

Individuals choosing a profession or a potential investment are faced with a range of risks. Opportunities with a smaller risk of unemployment also yield lower average rates of return. In this way, the individuals making risky, specialized investments are compensated for doing so. Whatever the expected compensation for risk, the individuals who make unwise or unlucky choices will deeply regret it.

HOW PEOPLE BECOME UNEMPLOYED

An individual may become unemployed either voluntarily (a *quit*) or involuntarily (a *firing*). In the voluntary case, the individual believes his time would be better spent searching full time for a job than continuing to work at the wage paid by his employer. In the involuntary case, the employer is unwilling to continue to employ the worker at the agreed—or any other reasonable—wage. The old firm may not be willing to pay a wage acceptable to the worker either because the worker is not satisfactorily performing the duties expected, or because changing supply or demand conditions have reduced the demand for

---

[3] Cyclical unemployment could be either positive or negative. In the 1950s the term "structural unemployment" was popular for severe cases of frictional unemployment in which the value of a particular specialized skill became nearly worthless. Investors in any kind of very specialized capital always run the risk of being wiped out by a major shift in demand or supply conditions.

[4] Unemployment compensation, welfare, and income taxation transfer part of the risks and rights of ownership of human capital to the government. People drawing unemployment compensation or welfare can be forced to search for and accept jobs.

labor of the firm. There is no easy way to match reasons for leaving against whether the separation was voluntary or involuntary.

When there is a large, sudden decrease in the demand for the product of a firm, the firm will often lay off employees. A *layoff* is the firing of a group of employees who are eligible to be rehired if demand conditions improve. In some industries there are seasonal layoffs which are almost like unpaid vacations. Salaries in those industries must be higher to compensate for the period in which employees expect to be idle or working at jobs that are not as well paid.

THE UNEMPLOYMENT RATE

Among quits, firings, and layoffs, there is a steady flow of previously employed individuals beginning the search for new jobs. To these must be added the stream of new entrants—people leaving school and the military, or others who had temporarily left the labor force.[5] About 60 percent of unemployed persons quit or were dismissed from previous jobs, the remaining 40 percent are entering—or reentering—the civilian labor force. In a normal year, a number equal to about 25 percent of the civilian labor force will begin the search for new jobs. This search takes an average of about 10 weeks or 0.2 year. So, in a normal year one would expect about 5 percent of the civilian labor force to be unemployed on any given day $(0.25 \times 0.2 = 0.05 = 5$ percent$)$.

The normal unemployment rate is thus the product of the normal search flow and search duration. The *search flow* is the annual flow of people beginning search, expressed as a fraction of the civilian labor force. The *search duration* is the average length of time in years that unemployed people can expect to spend searching for new jobs. For example, if over the course of a year 25 million people became unemployed out of a labor force of 100 million, the search flow would be (25 million people/year)/(100 million people) = 0.25/year. If these people took an average of 10.4 weeks to locate new jobs, the search duration would be 0.2 year. The unemployment rate u would be given by

$$u = (\text{search flow}) \times (\text{search duration}) \qquad [14.1]$$

$$= \left(\frac{0.25}{\text{year}}\right) \times (0.2 \text{ year}) = 0.05 = 5 \text{ percent}$$

That is, although 25 million people will become unemployed over the course of a year, only 5 million (5 percent of the labor force) will be unemployed at any one time.

The normal unemployment rate thus depends on the factors that determine the normal levels of the search flow and search duration. In the absence of

---

[5] There are substantial numbers of short-term entrants such as students looking for summer jobs. These seasonal factors can be corrected for in the data and neglected here.

business fluctuations, the search flow is determined by very slow-moving factors of demography—the number of new entrants—and the normal frequency of shifts in industry demand and supply. For example, the baby famine of the 1930s made for a lower normal search flow in the 1950s. In the 1960s and early 1970s, the baby boom of about 1945–1955 and the increasing participation of women raised the ratio of new entrants into the civilian labor force. This in turn would increase the normal search flow and normal unemployment rate. The normal search flow is determined in a sufficiently stable way by factors outside the scope of macroeconomics that it can be taken as given. The analysis of the normal unemployment rate has therefore focused on the determination of the normal search duration.

THE PROBLEM OF UNCERTAINTY

The key element underlying search and unemployment generally is that information is a valuable commodity which is costly to produce. In any kind of economy, information on the most valued use of a specialized productive resource is expensive. This is particularly the case for an individual worker with individual abilities and individual values for various working conditions included in the total employment package.

Much of the richness of the search process must be lost in any manageable model that reduces each job offer down to a single number, which will be called the nominal wage W. This nominal wage stands not only for the actual money compensation, but also for the money value of working conditions, expected duration and risk of employment, and any other fringe benefits or costs of accepting a particular job offer.

Almost no one is unemployed because he can find literally no job at any wage whatsoever. There are always low-wage, unattractive jobs available, but they may bear no resemblance to the sort of job and wage that an individual expects or even to the unemployment benefits that are available. So people will try to do better, and that is where search comes in.

An unemployed person searching for a new job invests his time and other resources in an attempt to increase his future income stream by obtaining a higher wage. The situation is one of uncertainty because he has no way of knowing whether a particular firm will offer a high wage, a low wage, or no wage at all.

The likelihood of the various possible outcomes of an uncertain event is measured by the probability of each outcome. Probability may be thought of as the relative frequency with which an event would occur in a very large number of trials. For example, if the worker were to somehow visit a million firms and note each wage offer (including zero) received, the probability of each wage offer would be the number of times that offer was received divided by a million.

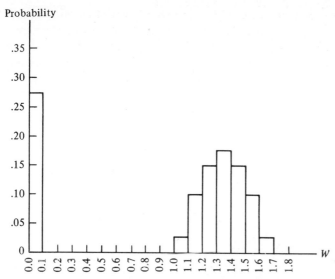

Figure 14.1 Example of graphical representation of probabilities. The heights of the bars represent the probability (or relative frequency) of a wage offer as great as the number to the left of a bar, but lower than the number to its right. Thus, the probability that a particular wage offer is at least 1.1 but less than 1.2 is 0.10. The probability of receiving any offer greater than 1.4 is proportional to the area under the bars to the right of 1.4.

The sum of the probabilities of all possible outcomes always equals 1 (here, 1,000,000/1,000,000 = 1).

Probability can be graphed as illustrated in Fig. 14.1. The most probable wage offer is zero (probability 0.275), but it is more likely that some other wage offer will be received (probability 0.725). The bars are drawn to show the probability of receiving a wage offer as great as the number indicated but less than the next number. The probability of receiving an offer 1.4 or greater is found by summing the bars from 1.4 to the right (0.15 + 0.10 + 0.025 = 0.275). It is more usual to divide the possible wages into arbitrarily small groupings (for example, as great as 1.000 but less than 1.0001) so that the bars do not change much from one wage group to the next. Only the tops of the bars are then drawn as a nearly smooth probability curve or *distribution*. Figure 14.2 illustrates the expected distribution of wages. The probability of receiving no offer (0) cannot be graphed conveniently, but is indicated by the thick vertical axis and the size of the bell-shaped curve. The probability of receiving a wage offer greater than or equal to any given W is still proportional to the area under the wage distribution to the right of that W.

Probability

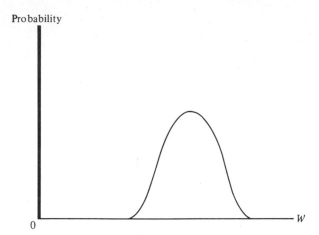

0 W

Figure 14.2 The expected distribution of wage offers. The
probability of receiving a wage offer between any two values—
say W_0 and W_1—is found by determining the area under the
bell-shaped distribution curve between W_0 and W_1. The
probability of receiving a zero wage offer is awkward to graph,
but is indicated by the thick vertical axis and the entire area
under the bell-shaped distribution curve—the larger the area,
the smaller is the probability of a zero wage offer.

THE PROCESS OF SEARCH

An individual worker contemplating searching for a new job must choose a
strategy. It can be shown by advanced analytical techniques that the optimal
strategy is *sequential search.*[6] Sequential search involves choosing a reservation
wage W_r and visiting plants until an offer greater than or equal to W_r is obtained. By following this procedure, a worker who is lucky enough to find a
good job ($W \geq W_r$) quickly will not waste time on further search. Nor will an
unlucky worker give up looking for a good job just because of a string of bad
luck.[7]

The reservation wage is chosen so that the expected marginal value of
further search is just equated to the expected marginal cost of further search.
The marginal value of further search is the present value of the increase in
wage obtained, and this decreases in the relevant range with increases in the
wage turned down. The most important cost of further search is the wages
given up (net of any unemployment benefits) and this will increase with the
wage offer turned down. So some optimal reservation wage will divide offers
into those which are and are not acceptable.

---

[6] See J. J. McCall, Economics of Information and Job Search, *Quarterly Journal of Economics,* **84:** 113–126, Feb.
1970; and S. A. Lippman and J. J. McCall, The Economics of Job Search: A Survey, *Economic Inquiry* (in two
parts), **14:** 155–189, 347–368, June and Sept. 1976.
[7] The reservation wage may be adjusted somewhat over time as search provides new information about the wage
distribution and uses resources. These complications can be neglected in the current qualitative discussion.

Probability

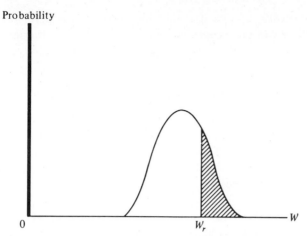

0 W_r W

Figure 14.3 Probability of receiving a job offer at the reservation wage or better. The probability $\mathscr{P}$ of receiving an acceptable wage offer is measured by the shaded area under the wage distribution curve to the right of the reservation wage W_r.

The sequential search strategy is illustrated in Fig. 14.3. The probability $\mathscr{P}$ of receiving an acceptable job offer of W_r or better on a particular visit to a firm is measured by the shaded area to the right of W_r. It can be shown that the average number of firms visited by a worker until an acceptable job is found is equal to $1/\mathscr{P}$.[8]

The average search duration equals the average length of time between visits times the average number of visits. For example, suppose that unemployed workers average a visit to one firm each working day; the average length of time per visit is 0.004 year. Assume also that the reservation wage is set so that on average only 1 visit out of 50 results in an acceptable offer ($\mathscr{P} = 0.02$). Then the average duration of search would be 0.004 year/0.02 = 0.2 year, which was the value used in the earlier example.[9]

In sum, the search duration is the ratio of the average length of time per firm visit to the probability that a visit results in an acceptable job offer. Notice

---

[8] The proof is as follows:

$$\text{Average no. of visits} = 1 \cdot \mathscr{P} + 2(1 - \mathscr{P})\mathscr{P} + 3(1 - \mathscr{P})^2\mathscr{P} + \cdots$$
$$= \mathscr{P}[1 + 2(1 - \mathscr{P}) + 3(1 - \mathscr{P})^2 + \cdots]$$
$$= \mathscr{P}[1 - (1 - \mathscr{P})]^{-2}$$
$$= \mathscr{P}/\mathscr{P}^2$$
$$= 1/\mathscr{P}$$

[9] Most people would find an acceptable job by the end of 7 weeks, but the average would be raised by those who were very unlucky.

particularly that search duration and so the unemployment rate is inversely proportional to the probability of an acceptable job offer: A higher probability implies a lower unemployment rate, other things being equal, and vice versa.

THE NATURAL RATE OF UNEMPLOYMENT

The *natural unemployment rate* is the normal rate of unemployment due to the normal process of entry into the labor force and reallocation of workers from firm to firm and industry to industry. This is the rate to which the economy tends in the absence of macroeconomic shocks. The tendency of unemployment to return to its normal rate underlies the tendency of real income toward natural-employment income.

There is much more agreement about what the U.S. natural unemployment rate was in the past than about what it is now. In the 1950s the natural unemployment rate was about 4 or 4.25 percent. This gradually increased through 1975 by about a percentage point due to the demographic forces discussed previously.[10] Some economists believe that substantially liberalized unemployment benefits—and the elimination of the military draft—have so reduced the costs of search that the natural unemployment rate is now 6.5 or 7 percent. Others are skeptical that these changes could increase the natural unemployment rate beyond 5.5 to 6 percent. Only time and further research will resolve this debate.

Students should be careful not to view the natural rate of unemployment—or the associated concept of natural-employment income—as a sort of goal. The temptation to apply these terms to arbitrary goals, or to make the goals what the natural rate is, has been irresistible at times for government economists. The terms should not be so abused. The natural rate of unemployment is implied by the optimal amount of search by the individuals involved *given* the distribution of wages available and the costs of search. These underlying conditions may induce either too much or too little search when total costs and benefits of search are considered.

For example, income taxes imply that individuals do not obtain the whole benefits of increased wages due to further search; so that they would tend to search too little—if benefits to other taxpayers are counted. In contrast, income taxes and unemployment benefits reduce the cost of search to the individual— but not to the economy—in terms of forgone income; so that search would tend to be too long. The list can be extended to many other factors bearing on the costs and benefits of search. In each case, however, macroeconomics does not really enter. Rather, essentially microeconomic allocative problems are involved in any workable attempts to alter the natural rate of unemployment.

---

[10] The increased ratio of new entrants to civilian labor force increases not only the normal search flow but also the normal search duration. The latter effect occurs because new and recent entrants take longer to find jobs on average than those who have learned a particular trade. This was first noted by Geoffrey H. Moore, *How Full Is Full Employment?* Washington: American Enterprise Institute for Public Policy Research, 1973, pp. 27–29.

This negative bit of knowledge—that changing the natural unemployment rate requires microeconomic not macroeconomic tools—is extremely valuable. Any government policy formulated that neglects this rule can lead to disastrous results, as will be seen in Sec. 14.3.

14.2 THE EXPECTED RATE OF INFLATION AND THE SHIFTING PHILLIPS CURVE

INTRODUCTION

The economic analysis of cyclical unemployment is still at an early stage. At present, various facets of the problem are reasonably understood, but their relative importance in explaining cyclical variations in unemployment is still subject to lively debate. Much research is being devoted to this problem, but a reasonably complete model backed by solid empirical evidence continues to elude macroeconomists. The following discussion presents—tentatively—the main elements in the emerging theory. The common thread in this discussion is that cyclical unemployment results from faulty anticipations. These incorrect anticipations cannot persist indefinitely; so cyclical fluctuations around the natural rate of unemployment are transitory phenomena.

The unemployed can be divided into two main categories: those who are actively searching for new jobs and those who are awaiting recall from a temporary layoff. Those on temporary layoff are not a significant factor in explaining the natural unemployment rate. But many economists (most notably Martin Feldstein) believe fluctuations in the number on temporary layoff are the most important source of variations in the actual unemployment rate around its normal level. Others emphasize variations in the number actively searching and argue that those on temporary layoff behave in a similar manner. The approaches are complementary and both will be presented here.

WHY ARE THERE TEMPORARY LAYOFFS?

Temporary layoffs are similar to a mass vacation at times when a firm's demand for labor is relatively low due either to seasonal factors or to excessive inventories of finished goods. They make sense if the value of labor to the firm falls below the value to the workers of their time on layoff. The idea is that prospective employees consider the benefits of working for a particular firm over a long period of time. A firm which uses temporary layoffs must attract workers by making up for the difference between lost wages and the value of the leisure while on layoff. This difference can be made up by higher wages while working, unemployment benefits,[11] and the like.

---

[11] Unemployment benefits are nearly all paid by the individual firm. But to the extent that the cost is shifted to other taxpayers, this provides an additional incentive to use temporary layoffs.

Some economists attribute temporary layoffs to the obvious advantages of maintaining stable wages. So, the argument goes, the quantity of labor employed varies when the derived demand for labor shifts. This argument apparently ignores the long-term nature of employment connoted by a *temporary* layoff. For a long-term relationship, the issues of stable wages and stable employment are largely separate.[12]

Of course temporary layoffs differ from permanent layoffs which are believed to represent a permanent reduction in the size of the firm's labor force in the face of a permanent reduction in demand. Those on permanent layoff are considered with those who are actively searching for new jobs.

CHANGES IN THE NUMBERS ON LAYOFF

A faster-than-expected increase in aggregate demand for goods and services will reduce the number on layoff. The increase in aggregate demand will offset some fall in relative demand for particular goods and services. So fewer firms than normal will have excessive inventories of finished goods. Fewer firms will lay off workers, and more than usual will recall workers previously laid off. On the other hand, slower-than-anticipated increases in aggregate demand will cause more excessive inventories to build up at the price set. Temporary layoffs will increase, and firms will be slow to recall those previously laid off.

Thus variations in temporary layoffs are a way of correcting for unplanned investment or disinvestment in inventories. This unplanned investment or disinvestment is a result of past errors in anticipating the increase in aggregate demand. When the inventories are restored to normal levels, so are the number on temporary layoff and this short-run effect on the unemployment rate is eliminated.

SOURCES OF VARIATION IN SEARCH UNEMPLOYMENT

Whether the number of unemployed who are actively searching for new jobs rises or falls depends on whether people are beginning the search for jobs at a faster or slower rate than unemployed people are taking jobs. The search flow is the rate (per annum as a fraction of the civilian labor force) that people are starting to look for jobs. The *search unemployment rate* is the ratio of those

---

[12] Suppose that the quality of labor normally employed is worth $5 per hour to a firm except during July when it is worth $3 per hour. If July leisure is worth less than $3 per hour to the employees, they should be employed year around. It is a matter of indifference to the firm whether it pays $5 per hour for 11 months and $3 per hour in July or $4.83 per hour all year $[(\$5)(\frac{11}{12}) + (\$3)(\frac{1}{12}) = \$4.83]$. If stable wages are otherwise preferable, they could be paid. But the firm should remember that $1.83 of the July wage is not the cost of July labor but rather of labor during the other 11 months.

unemployed actively searching for jobs to the civilian labor force.[13] The ratio of the search unemployment rate to the search duration gives the rate (per annum as a fraction of the civilian labor force) that unemployed people are taking new jobs. For example, if the search unemployment rate were 6 percent and the search duration were 0.3 year, then people would be taking jobs at a rate of 20 percent of the labor force per annum (.06/0.3 year = 0.2/year). If the search flow were higher, say 30 percent of the labor force per annum, then more people would begin looking for jobs each day than would take jobs, and the search unemployment rate would rise over time.

The search unemployment rate rises (falls) whenever the search flow is greater (less) than the ratio of the search unemployment rate to search duration.[14] Equation [14.1] related the normal unemployment rate to the product of the normal values of the search flow and search duration. This neglects any temporary-layoff unemployment and applies only to cases where the unemployment rate is not changing, such as a steady-state equilibrium. Cyclical increases (decreases) in the search unemployment rate are due to factors which temporarily increase (decrease) the current values of the search flow and search duration above their normal levels.

FACTORS AFFECTING THE SEARCH DURATION

Macroeconomic shocks which lead to unplanned investment or disinvestment in inventories will cause firms to take such short-run measures as temporary layoffs and adjustments of the work week. To the extent that the effects of unanticipated aggregate demand changes are expected to persist, firms will make more permanent adjustments in their number of employees. For example, after an unexpected acceleration in aggregate demand growth, firms will attempt to hire more workers and will do so in part by increasing nominal wages offered for each quality of labor.

The resulting shift in wage offers will change the actual wage distribution relative to the expected wage distribution which underlies the strategy of searching workers. This shift will take two forms: (1) the probability of being offered a job on a particular firm visit is increased and (2) the average offer actually made will be higher.

This is illustrated in Fig. 14.4. The area under the actual wage distribution is larger than the expected wage distribution and shifted to the right of the area under it. Since individual workers select a reservation wage W_r on the basis of the expected wage distribution, there will be a marked effect on the average search duration. If the actual and expected wage distributions were identical,

---

[13] The search unemployment rate plus a similarly defined temporary-layoff unemployment rate would equal the total unemployment rate.

[14] This neglects a trivial (about 0.1 percentage point) allowance for growth in the civilian labor force.

Probability

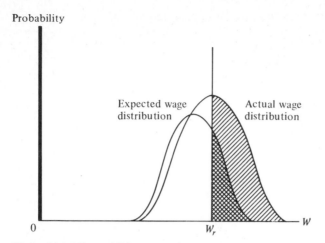

Figure 14.4 **Effects of differences in expected and actual wage distributions on probability of an acceptable job offer.** A stimulative macroeconomic shock causes the actual wage distribution to be larger and shifted to the right of the expected wage distribution. The reservation wage is set at W_r on the basis of the expected wage distribution. The expected probability of an acceptable job offer is measured by the heavily shaded area under the expected wage distribution curve and to the right of the reservation wage. The actual probability is much larger, being the entire area under the actual wage distribution curve to the right of the reservation wage.

the probability of an acceptable wage offer would be measured by the heavily shaded area under the expected wage distribution. In the case at hand, the actual probability $\mathscr{P}$ of an acceptable wage offer is measured by the whole larger area under the actual wage distribution. The actual search duration is inversely proportional to the probability $\mathscr{P}$, so a larger value of $\mathscr{P}$ directly implies a lower average duration of search.

When aggregate demand increases more rapidly than expected, the actual wage distribution shifts up relative to the expected wage distribution; so the actual search duration falls. The reverse also holds: If aggregate demand increases less rapidly than expected, the actual wage distribution shifts down relative to the expected wage distribution; so the actual search duration rises. In the first case, it appears remarkably easy—on average—to get a "good job." In the second case, it seems very difficult to find a "good job." So factors which cause an unexpected increase (decrease) in aggregate demand decrease (increase) the search duration relative to its normal value. This causes the search unemployment rate to fall (rise); thus an important determinant of cyclical fluctuations in the unemployment rate is variation in the actual wage distribution around the expected wage distribution.

FACTORS AFFECTING THE SEARCH FLOW

A faster-than-expected increase in aggregate demand will have the effect of reducing the number of permanent involuntary separations (layoffs and firings). Fewer firms than usual will find it advantageous to reduce their number of employees through permanent layoffs. Workers who would normally be fired as not worth the wage will be kept on in a tight labor market—a labor market in which workers are scarce at the level of wages previously anticipated.

This effect is most noticeable for firms which hire labor subject to a union or minimum wage floor. The wage floor will be only intermittently changed, and can get out of line with market wages between changes. The floors—if effective—artificially raise wages paid by the firm so that the firm could easily obtain more workers if it desired. This happens because the floors raise the wage paid above the going rate for the specified quality of labor. Changes in labor demand by such a firm does not result in any change in wages, but only in the quantity demanded, as illustrated in Fig. 14.5. On the other hand, if lower-than-anticipated aggregate demand lowers the derived demand for labor by

Figure 14.5 Effect of change in demand for labor by a firm subject to union or minimum wage floor. At the wage floor W_u, the firm can obtain as much labor as it desires. If the firm is faced with a fall in relative demand for its product there will be a corresponding fall from D_1 to D_2 in the derived demand for labor. This implies a reduction in the quantity of labor from l_1 to l_2, largely through permanent layoffs. If an increase in aggregate demand just offsets the fall in relative demand, so that the demand for labor remained at D_1, there would be no layoffs. Conversely, a fall in aggregate demand could lower the derived demand for labor from D_1 to D_2 and thereby cause the firm to lay off workers even though there was no change in relative demand.

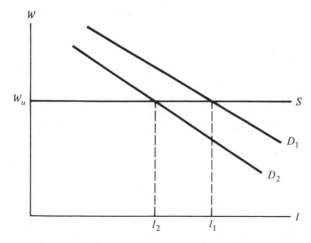

these firms, they will be forced to lay off workers. After a while the floors will be reset by contract or law to about the same position relative to going levels of wages, but in the interim there will be unanticipated employment effects.

Permanent involuntary separations tend to fall when a macroeconomic shock increases the growth of aggregate demand and to rise when a macroeconomic shock decreases the growth of aggregate demand. There is some offset in the rate of voluntary separations, but a similar rise and fall is implied for the actual search flow.

A substantial force partially offsetting this cyclical pattern has been labeled the *discouraged-encouraged worker phenomenon*. This refers to the fact that the civilian labor force grows a bit less rapidly than usual in recessions and more rapidly in booms. A lower rate of new entrants decreases the search flow and a higher rate tends to increase this flow. The factors tending to increase the search flow in a recession clearly dominate the discouraged worker phenomenon and the factors reducing the search flow in a boom more than offset any effect of encouraged workers on this flow.

The causes of the discouraged-encouraged worker phenomenon remain obscure. Significant factors may include: (1) During a boom or recession, the expected wage distribution will adjust upward or downward—though not by as much as the actual wage distribution. Until the price level adjusts, this represents a faster or slower than normal increase in real wages. (2) Widespread publicity about the ease or difficulty of finding a " good job " may encourage or discourage, respectively, individuals to enter or remain in the labor force at that particular time where there are attractive alternatives—such as school, housework, and retirement.

War of course drastically reduces the search flow by sharply reducing—or postponing until peacetime—the rate of net entry into the *civilian* labor force through conscripted and voluntary enlistments. The vast range of unique structural changes that occur during wars do not permit many such generalizations.

CYCLICAL FLUCTUATIONS IN UNEMPLOYMENT RATES

Both the temporary-layoff and search components of the unemployment rate are seen to fall when aggregate demand grows more rapidly than anticipated. Less-than-anticipated growth conversely increases both components of the unemployment rate.

Consider for example, a restrictive monetary policy, which will reduce consumer expenditures and investment so that sales to final purchasers fall relative to output. This difference is made up by an unintended investment in inventories. As firms come to realize that their estimate of the optimal price was too high, they will want to reduce the rate of output permanently, given the cost conditions.[15] They will want to achieve an additional temporary reduction in

---

[15] This is the early part of the adjustment period in which cost conditions (and the aggregate supply curve) are not yet affected.

the rate of output until inventories are worked down to their desired level. Some firms can and do accomplish this entirely through a temporary reduction in employees' work weeks—a part-time temporary layoff that does not get recorded in the unemployment statistics. Others resort to temporary layoffs, which increase the unemployment rate until the workers are recalled. The permanent reduction in the number of employees increases both the search flow and the search duration until expectations and costs adjust to the now lower growth of aggregate demand. Refer back to Fig. 3.1 for a graphic illustration of the sharp increases in the unemployment rate during recessions and the subsequent reversion to normal levels.

Cyclical fluctuations in the unemployment rate all rest on faulty anticipations. Faulty anticipations of the growth of aggregate demand lead to unplanned inventory investment and temporary layoffs. Faulty anticipations of the distribution of nominal wages lead to unintended variations in the average length of time spent searching for jobs. Faulty anticipations generally make costs at a level inappropriate to the derived aggregate demand for resources.

A pattern of incorrect anticipations cannot persist indefinitely, and as these expectations adjust toward actuality, the unemployment rate returns to the natural unemployment rate. This process is frequently discussed by reference to a graphical device called the Phillips curve.

THE PHILLIPS CURVE

The Phillips curve is a line which estimates the statistical relationship between the unemployment rate and the growth rate of nominal wages ΓW for a particular period of time. A hypothetical example is given in Fig. 14.6. The Phillips curve itself is labeled PC and the actual data used to estimate the Phillips curve are indicated by dots. The Phillips curve was originally introduced by A. W. Phillips as a means of describing data for certain periods of British economic history.[16]

The points will generally be closer to an estimated Phillips curve if the expected growth rate of nominal wages is relatively constant over the period. In that case, the growth rate of nominal wages will serve as a proxy for the difference between the actual and expected growth rate of wages. Whenever ΓW is above the expected growth rate unemployment will tend to be low, and whenever ΓW is below the expected growth rate unemployment will be high.

---

[16] A. W. Phillips, The Relation between Unemployment and the Rate of Change of Money Wage Rates in the United Kingdom, 1861–1957, *Economica*, **25**: 283–299, Nov. 1958. A neglected article dealing with a similar relationship between the unemployment rate and the inflation rate was published earlier by Irving Fisher, A Statistical Relation between Unemployment and Price Changes, *International Labor Review*, **13**: 785–792, June 1926; reprinted posthumously as I Discovered the Phillips Curve, *Journal of Political Economy*, **81**: 496–502, Mar./Apr. 1973. The literature on the Phillips curve and its variants is surveyed in Milton Friedman, Nobel Lecture: Inflation and Unemployment, *Journal of Political Economy*, **85**: 451–472, June 1977. Friedman was one of the first economists to point out that the Phillips curve was a transitory phenomenon due to faulty expectations.

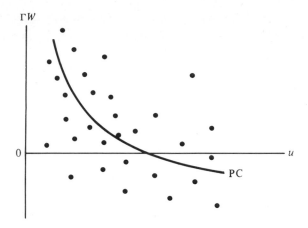

Figure 14.6 A hypothetical Phillips curve. The Phillips curve
PC is a line which estimates or summarizes the average
statistical relationship between the unemployment rate u and
the growth rate of nominal wages ΓW over a particular
period of time. The observed combinations of u and ΓW used
to estimate the Phillips curve are indicated by the dots.

This point is sometimes made by using $\Gamma W - \Gamma W^*$ as the label for the vertical
axis where ΓW^* is the expected growth rate of wages.

As it happened, Phillips analyzed data for which the Phillips curve provided
a good " fit." During most of the period England was on a gold standard which
provided a very stable trend growth path of nominal wages.[17] When applied to
other data, the results have been mixed at best. It is clear that the Phillips curve
cannot be viewed as a stable relationship either across countries or at different
times in the same country.

14.3 THE USE OF MONETARY POLICY
TO INFLUENCE EMPLOYMENT AND REAL INCOME

THE APPARENT TRADEOFF
BETWEEN UNEMPLOYMENT AND INFLATION

Unfortunately, before the "shiftiness" of the Phillips curve became apparent, a
very influential article appeared.[18] This article suggested that since the growth
rate of wages normally exceeds the inflation rate by the trend growth rate of
productivity—approximately the labor quality adjustment factor q—a quasi-

---

[17] A stable growth path of nominal wages means that unusually slow ΓW as due to a banking panic, implies a
later unusually fast ΓW. The resulting cyclical variation in ΓW^* was actually evident in a cyclical pattern of the
data points when identified by years.
[18] Paul A. Samuelson and Robert M. Solow, Analytical Aspects of Anti-Inflation Policy, *American Economic
Review,* **50**: 177–194, May 1960.

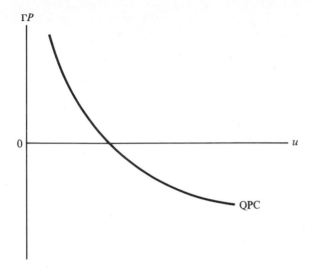

**Figure 14.7 A hypothetical quasi-Phillips curve relating the
unemployment and inflation rates.** A quasi-Phillips curve is an
estimate of the statistical relationship between the
unemployment rate and the rate of inflation over a particular
period of time.

Phillips curve could be drawn relating the unemployment rate and the rate of
inflation. An example is drawn in Fig. 14.7.

The argument continued on the provisional assumption that the quasi-
Phillips curve was a stable, nonshifting relationship which gave the possible
combinations of the values of unemployment and inflation rates that could be
chosen by macroeconomic policymakers. The quasi-Phillips curve thus provides a menu of the possible tradeoffs between reductions in the unemployment
rate and increases in the rate of inflation. For most of the 1960s, the idea of the
tradeoff was very popular.[19]

The tradeoff analysis is illustrated by Fig. 14.8. If the economy happened to
have an unemployment rate of 5 percent and an inflation rate of 1 percent, the
unemployment rate could be lowered to about 3.5 percent in exchange for a 2
percentage point increase in the inflation rate. Conversely, the rate of inflation
could be reduced to zero, but only at the cost of increasing the unemployment
rate to 6 percent. This argument assumed that the tradeoff was permanent.

In fact, the rate of growth of nominal prices, or, more properly, nominal
wages, must be compared with the expected growth rate. If the tradeoff of a
higher rate of inflation for a lower unemployment rate is attempted, the ex-

---

[19] A tradeoff analysis using a stable quasi-Phillips curve is still seen on occasion in the popular press. The
analysis has just the right mix of complexity and elegance to be extremely seductive, especially when printed with
a four-color diagram.

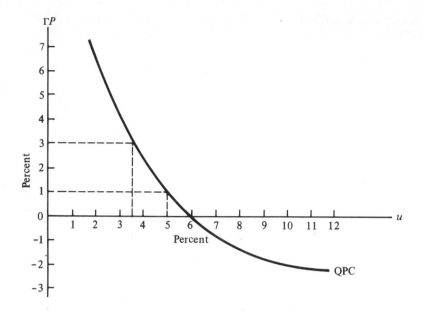

Figure 14.8 An example of tradeoff analysis based on the assumption of a stable quasi-Phillips curve. Suppose that the economy is currently experiencing a 5 percent unemployment rate and a 1 percent rate of inflation. Also suppose that recent data have been used to statistically estimate the illustrated quasi-Phillips curve. If the quasi-Phillips curve is stable, any point on it can be chosen and maintained indefinitely by monetary and fiscal policy. For example, it might be decided that a 3.5 percent unemployment rate and a 3 percent rate of inflation was optimal. This would involve trading off a 2 percentage point increase in the inflation rate to obtain a 1.5 percentage point decrease in the unemployment rate. Conversely, to eliminate inflation would require a 1 percentage point increase in the unemployment rate from 5 to 6 percent.

pected growth rate of wages will rise over time and the unemployment rate will tend to rise back toward the natural rate of unemployment. The tradeoff actually available is a temporary decrease in the unemployment rate in exchange for a future permanent increase in the rate of inflation. Alternatively a future permanent decrease in the rate of inflation can be obtained only at a cost of a temporary increase in the unemployment rate.

Nevertheless, the Fed might attempt the tradeoff suggested by the tradeoff analysis based on a stable quasi-Phillips curve. Two possible rules for determining nominal-money-supply growth are consistent with such an attempt. (1) Increase the trend growth rate of the money supply by two percentage points and hold it there. (2) Increase the growth rate of the money supply whenever the unemployment rate rises above 3.5 percent. If the quasi-Phillips curve really were stable, the two policies would be equivalent since a 2 percentage point increase in the rate of inflation would result in either case (see Fig. 14.8). The actual effects of the policies will be much different, however.

THE EFFECTS ON UNEMPLOYMENT OF A 2 PERCENTAGE POINT INCREASE IN THE GROWTH RATE OF MONEY

A 2 percentage point increase in the growth rate of money will eventually cause a 2 percentage point increase in the rate of inflation and a concomitant 2 percentage point increase in the growth rate of nominal wages. Immediately after the policy begins, however, there will be at first virtually no effects, and then there will be effects on the unemployment rate and growth rate of nominal wages with little effect on the rate of inflation. The tradeoff will seem even better than in the estimated quasi-Phillips curve (QPC_0 in Fig. 14.9).

With the passage of time, the increased growth rate of wages—and other resource prices—begins to show up in the growth rate of the price level. As the

Figure 14.9 Effects on unemployment and inflation of a fixed increase in the growth rate of the money supply. If the Fed decides to take advantage of the apparent tradeoff indicated by the quasi-Phillips curve QPC_0 by increasing the growth rate of the money supply by 2 percentage points, the actual path of the unemployment and inflation rates will be approximately as indicated by the dotted line. During the first 2 years or so, the actual tradeoff will be better than indicated by the estimated quasi-Phillips curve. Then, as prices and wage expectations adjust, the tradeoff will steadily worsen until the rate of inflation temporarily rises above 3 percent per annum and the unemployment rate rises back toward the natural unemployment rate (assumed here to be 5 percent). If the growth rate of the money supply is maintained 2 percentage points higher than the initial trend, the expected rate of inflation will rise from 1 percent per annum to 3 percent per annum. Associated with this rise is a new quasi-Phillips curve, QPC_1, 2 percentage points above QPC_0.

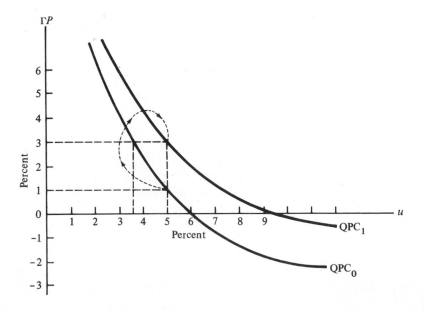

price level catches up, workers gradually become aware of the rapid growth in nominal wages that has occurred, and expected wages begin to catch up with actual wages. Union contracts and minimum wages also catch up. As a result the rate of unemployment rises in the face of accelerating inflation. The apparent tradeoff between inflation and unemployment worsens until there is a new quasi-Phillips curve (QPC_1) 2 percentage points above the old quasi-Phillips curve.

Assuming that the natural rate of unemployment is 5 percent, the economy will then return to natural-employment equilibrium with a 2 percentage point increase in the rate of growth of money, prices, and nominal income, but with real factors unaffected. This is the process underlying the dynamic adjustments discussed in Chap. 7.

THE EFFECTS OF INCREASING THE GROWTH RATE OF THE MONEY SUPPLY AS REQUIRED TO MAINTAIN AN UNEMPLOYMENT GOAL

This policy might start out in the same way with a 2 percentage point increase in the growth rate of the money supply. As expectations of workers, unions, and legislators adjust to the more rapid growth rate of nominal wages and the quasi-Phillips curve starts shifting upward, the unemployment rate will begin to rise above the 3.5 percent goal. Under the assumed rule, the Fed will respond by a further increase in the growth rate of the money supply. This causes wages to actually increase at a sufficiently greater rate to offset their increased expected growth rate. But the expected growth rate will continue to adjust toward reality so that the Fed must continually increase the growth rate of the money supply.

The accelerating growth rate in the money supply implies accelerating growth rates of wages and prices (see Fig. 14.10). Before long, people catch on to the acceleration of the growth rate of nominal wages and adjust their expectations. The Fed must then accelerate the rate at which it accelerates money supply growth. People catch on, and the process continues until the rate of inflation is infinity or a change in government forces a new monetary policy.

THE INABILITY OF MONETARY POLICY TO MAINTAIN AN UNEMPLOYMENT GOAL

No unemployment rate other than the natural rate can be maintained indefinitely by the use of monetary policy. Stated another way, the long-run quasi-Phillips curve is a vertical line through the natural rate of unemployment. See Fig. 14.11.

The inability of the growth rate of the nominal money supply to affect the unemployment rate in the long run is by no means surprising. The nominal money supply is a nominal variable—a variable expressed in money values.

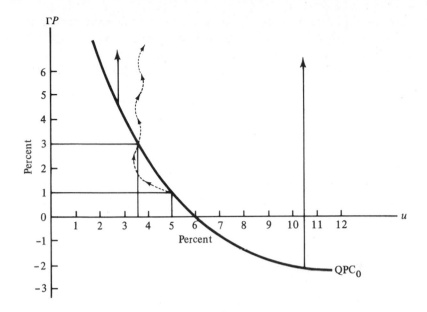

**Figure 14.10 Effects of an attempt by the Fed to maintain an unemployment-rate
goal lower than the natural rate.** If the Fed were to attempt to maintain an
unemployment rate of 3.5 percent when the natural unemployment rate is 5
percent, monetary policy could begin as for Fig. 14.9. The actual paths of the
unemployment and inflation rates are indicated by the dotted line. Later, the Fed
would find that a 2 percentage point increase in the growth rate of the money
supply is no longer enough as prices and expectations begin to adjust. Further
increases in the growth rate of the money supply would lead to further increases
in the rate of inflation and the expected growth rate of wages. Soon,
acceleration of the rate at which the Fed accelerates money supply growth is
required to maintain a 3.5 percent unemployment rate. The quasi-Phillips curve
continually shifts up and the process continues until the rate of inflation becomes
infinite or the policy is changed.

Control over a nominal variable cannot be used to control real variables except
for the period of dynamic adjustment.[20] The unemployment rate is the ratio of
two real variables—the number unemployed and the civilian labor force—and
thus itself is definitely a real variable.

The idea of a stable quasi-Phillips curve reflects a general ignorance of
economic conditions in other times and places. No particular relationship has
been found between the trend rate of inflation and the average rate of unemployment in a country. Reasons which are proposed for a nonvertical, long-run,
quasi-Phillips curve all are based on what has been the recent history of nominal wages in a particular country.

---

[20] This neglects the possible effects through a nonzero elasticity of the real demand for money with respect to the
nominal interest rate. These effects can be safely ignored in a discussion of the American unemployment rate.

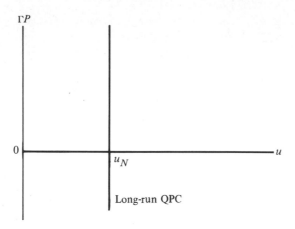

Figure 14.11 The long-run quasi-Phillips curve. The only
unemployment rate which can exist in long-run
equilibrium is the natural unemployment rate u_N,
whatever the rate of inflation. This is illustrated by a
vertical, long-run quasi-Phillips curve through u_N.

For example, it is argued that workers will be happier and less likely to quit
with rising nominal wages than with constant or falling wages. This is true now,
but after a period of adjustment people realize that constant wages and falling
prices make for a rising standard of living and that no better wages are available elsewhere.

THE WAGE-PRICE SPIRAL

There are often discussions of a wage-price spiral, cost-push inflation, and
similar concepts which are inconsistent with the explanation of inflation as an
essentially monetary phenomenon. The basic idea is that unions drive up wages
through unreasonable demands. Prices are then raised to cover the increased
costs, and this causes unions to demand more wage increases to make up for
higher prices, and so forth. The story can as easily be started with greedy
business executives, depending on one's political prejudices. The wage-price
spiral idea is ideal for the politician, since it shifts blame from government
policy, where it belongs, to greedy business executives and unionists. Better, the
business executives and unionists are kept busy denouncing each other for
starting it, so that there is little time left for the dull task of denouncing
government monetary policy.

As with most popular myths, there is an element of truth in this one too. The
latter part of the process of adjustment to an increased rate of money supply
growth looks very much like the wage-price spiral. Union wages rise less
rapidly than nonunion wages in the first year or two of a stimulative monetary

shock, and therefore must rise more rapidly later to catch up. Nonunion wages, though not set by contract, are sticky because of the impact of expected nominal wages on searching workers. Consequently, about the same time, nonunion wages will grow a bit more rapidly too. As unemployment rises and real income falls back to its steady-state growth path, the rate of inflation will rise above the new higher steady-state rate. It is easy to overlook what happened at the start of the boom a year or more before when wages were sticky and real income rose. Hence, the increased growth rate of prices and wages in the face of rising unemployment appears to be a puzzle which can only be explained as some sort of cost-push, wage-price spiral.

The same sort of idea is sometimes applied to the first year or two of a restrictive monetary policy. Despite a lower growth rate of aggregate demand, at first prices and wages—especially union wages—will continue to grow at a rate only slightly less than expected so that the unemployment rate rises and the growth rate of real income falls. The problem is then asserted to be unreasonable union demands that are out of touch with reality. Later when unemployment falls and the rate of inflation falls temporarily below its new lower steady-state rate, politicians are eager to accept credit for wise government policy. Being an arm of the legislative branch of government, the Fed not surprisingly changes its public views on the ability of monetary policy to control the economy according to current economic conditions.

A curious combination of popular belief in the wage-price spiral and a sophisticated argument on wage expectations led to the imposition of wage and price controls in August 1971. The argument on wage expectations was that wage controls would lower the expected wage distribution and thereby speed the adjustment to a steady state consistent with a lower growth rate of the nominal money supply. Thus inflation could be reduced without the political cost of a temporary increase in unemployment. The argument sounded nice on paper, but the Fed increased the growth rate of the money supply instead of decreasing it.[21] The controls—it will be recalled from Chap. 13—did manage to increase the growth of fluidity temporarily, but they collapsed during 1973 as inefficiencies mounted, and they were entirely abolished in April 1974.

JOB CREATION

Government officials frequently claim that this program or that will reduce the unemployment rate by creating so many jobs. To appraise what effect, if any, the program will have on the unemployment rate, one must know what happens to other employment as a result of the program and its financing. This question was analyzed in terms of real government expenditures and total real output in Chaps. 8 and 11. There it was seen that *unexpected* increases in real

---

[21] See Table 13.4, page 363.

government spending temporarily increase total real output at the peak by somewhere between $\frac{1}{2}$ and $1\frac{1}{2}$ times the unexpected increase. Corresponding effects on employment could be predicted.

It is important to recall that the long-run effect of public employment is to crowd out an equal amount of private employment. So ultimately the public program must be judged on its own merits since it "destroys" as many private jobs as it "creates" public ones. This does not say that fiscal policy is necessarily unwise, only that it must be carefully analyzed.

SUMMARY

1 The owners of unemployed resources search for an offer superior to any previous offer. Periods of unemployment are natural for all kinds of resources in a changing economy.

2 The normal level of the unemployment rate is approximately equal to the product of the normal levels of the search flow and search duration (both defined here *inclusive* of workers on temporary layoffs).

3 Normal search flow depends on demographic trends and industry supply and demand shifts.

4 The search duration is implied by the average probability that a visit to a firm will result in a wage offer as good as or better than the reservation wage of an unemployed worker. Unemployed workers set the reservation wage on the basis of the expected wage distribution so that the marginal costs and benefits of further search are equated.

5 The unemployment rate tends to return to the natural unemployment rate in the absence of macroeconomic shocks.

6 Cyclical fluctuations in the unemployment rate are due to cyclical fluctuations in the number of people on temporary layoffs and in the number of other people actively searching for a new job.

7 Temporary layoffs are used to eliminate excessive inventories built up by sales at a lower level than anticipated. When aggregate demand grows at a slower (faster) rate than anticipated, excessive inventories will be more (less) prevalent than normal so that temporary layoffs increase (decrease).

8 When aggregate demand growth is less (greater) than anticipated, the search unemployment rate rises above (falls below) normal because of increases (decreases) in both search duration and search flow.

9 Thus both the temporary-layoff and search components of the unemployment rate are increased by a restrictive macroeconomic shock and decreased by a stimulative macroeconomic shock.

10 A Phillips curve is a statistical description of the relation between the growth rate of nominal wages and the unemployment rate for a particular period. A quasi-Phillips curve is a similar relation for the rate of inflation and the unemployment rate. Both curves shift with the expected growth rates of wages and prices.

11 A temporary decrease in unemployment can be traded for a permanent increase in the rate of inflation. A temporary increase in unemployment is required to achieve a permanent decrease in inflation.

12 Control over the nominal money supply cannot be used indefinitely to achieve an arbitrary unemployment goal.

13 The wage-price spiral is a misconception of what occurs at certain points in the dynamic adjustment to macroeconomic shocks.

14 "Job creation" projects should be analyzed as a particular type of fiscal policy which may crowd out some other employment in the short run and surely will do so in the long run.

CONCEPTS TO KNOW

cyclical unemployment

discouraged-encouraged worker phenomenon

firing

frictional unemployment

layoff

natural unemployment rate

Phillips curve

quasi-Phillips curve

quit

search duration

search flow

search unemployment rate

sequential search

temporary layoff

QUESTIONS AND EXERCISES

1 Why is unemployment of resources a characteristic of any ongoing, changing economy? Why do governments impose restrictions on people's freedom to choose jobs when they establish social insurance programs which partially reimburse unemployed workers for lost wages?

2 Why is the search flow measured in per annum units?

3 If the probability of an unsuccessful visit to a firm drops from 0.98 to 0.97, what happens to the average search duration?

*4 (a) For what type of industries would you expect large unexpected changes in inventories and regular use of temporary layoffs? Can you cite major industries which actually use temporary layoffs?

(b) Why might employees on temporary layoff have an unusually high reservation wage for employers other than their last one? What does this do to the expected duration of search? Might it be worthwhile not to engage in search at all?

*5 (a) Suppose that when computed for active searches only, the normal search duration is 0.2 year and the normal search flow is 0.2 per annum. What is the normal level of the search unemployment rate?

(b) If the search duration suddenly increased to 0.3 year with the search flow unchanged, what would be the immediate effect on the rate at which people accept new jobs? Why would this cause the search unemployment rate to rise? How far would it rise?

(c) What would happen if the search flow had suddenly increased to 0.25 per annum at the same time that the search duration increased to 0.3 year?

6 A stimulative monetary policy decreases unemployment in the short run by making people think they are better off than they really are. What political temptations does this imply if monetary policy is not subject to the constraints of constitution, law, public debate, or commodity standard?

7 What would the Phillips curve look like in a country which had experienced large, frequent changes in the growth of the money supply? Explain how a technique such as expressing all wages as a number times the consumer price index ("indexing") would come into use in such a country.

REFERENCES FOR FURTHER READING

Francis, Darryl R.: Inflation, Recession—What's a Policymaker to Do? *Federal Reserve Bank of St. Louis Review,* **56** (11): 3–7, Nov. 1974.

Friedman, Milton: Nobel Lecture: Inflation and Unemployment, *Journal of Political Economy,* **85:** 451–472, June 1977.

Moore, Geoffrey H.: *How Full Is Full Employment?* Washington: American Enterprise Institute for Public Policy Research, 1973.

Phelps, Edmund S., et al.: *Microeconomic Foundations of Employment and Inflation Theory,* New York: Norton, 1970.

CHAPTER 15

MACROECONOMIC GOALS AND POLICY

WHAT YOU WILL LEARN IN THIS CHAPTER
Macroeconomic theory is used to find the
implications of alternative policies ● Criteria for a
successful stabilization strategy ● The debate over
what strategies meet these criteria ● Policies which
affect the real steady-state equilibrium are primarily
microeconomic in nature ● The steady-state inflation
rate is determined by the choice of the trend
nominal-money growth rate

15.1 MACROECONOMIC GOALS

MACROECONOMICS, GOALS, AND POLICY

The federal government sets U.S. macroeconomic policy. Our central bank, the
Federal Reserve System, determines the money supply, given the predictable
responses of the banking system. Federal spending, taxation, and laws similarly
are the key source of fiscal shocks. Just as the Fed works through the banks and
influences their behavior through such tools as reserve requirements, so does
the federal government determine total government spending and taxes, given
the behavior of the state and local governments as influenced by federal law
and regulations. In both cases, federal control is not really absolute, but federal
decisions are so dominant that the difference is negligible.

There are two views as to how decisions on macroeconomic policy are
made: (1) The social welfare view assumes that the President, Congress, and
other government officials who set macroeconomic policy attempt to maximize
the social welfare of the country, given the macroeconomic possibilities which
are available. (2) The cynical view assumes that the government policymakers
act in their own self-interest and will place too much weight on short-term costs
and benefits of policies and too little on long-term costs and benefits which
occur after the next election. As a matter of descriptive accuracy, there is an
element of truth in both views. For the citizen who wishes to evaluate the

performance of elected officials, the policy implied by the social welfare view provides a yardstick. So it will be emphasized here.[1]

People will disagree about which macroeconomic policy maximizes social welfare. Often this is due to disagreement on the importance of conflicting goals. For example, a goal of reduced inflation was seen in Chap. 14 to be possible only at the cost of a temporary increase in unemployment which would conflict with a goal of a normal unemployment rate. Decisions of how much of which goal to give up depend upon individual valuation of the goals. Different individuals will have different values and would make different choices. The author can make no special claims for his values, so appraisals of alternative policies are left to each reader.

Nevertheless, macroeconomics has much to say on these questions. People can place the same valuations on unemployment and inflation and yet come to radically different conclusions on macroeconomic policy if they disagree on the implications of policies for inflation and unemployment rates. A person who thinks that a stable quasi-Phillips curve exists is likely to prefer a higher inflation rate than a person with identical values who thinks that there is only a temporary reduction in the unemployment rate in exchange for a permanent increase in the inflation rate. Indeed, a deeper understanding of the process by which the cyclical unemployment rate is decreased may change a person's value judgment by altering the perceived implications of a reduction in unemployment.

Similarly, in appraising a particular macroeconomic policy actually selected by government, disagreements can arise because of either differences over the implications of possible policy alternatives or differences in the valuation of those implications. In this case, also, careful macroeconomic analysis can reduce the range of disagreement and even prevent the actual adoption of disastrous policies.

MACROECONOMIC GOALS

The first step in the analysis of alternative policies is to identify the macroeconomic variables which measure the main public concerns. The most important macroeconomic issues were summarized by the Employment Act of 1946 as "maximum employment, production, and purchasing power." Legislative and administrative history identifies other, subsidiary concerns which have in fact

---

[1] If officials fall short of our yardstick, two things can be done. One is to "throw the rascals out" at the next election in hopes that this will provide an incentive to new policymakers to do better. Another is to enact laws and create institutions which reduce their incentives or ability to choose the wrong policies.

shaped macroeconomic policy—such as the balance of payments, interest rates, economic efficiency, economic growth, and environmental quality.

These concerns must be translated into much more specific goals. The actual goals cluster into three separate groups: those dealing with the stabilization of the economy in or near steady-state equilibrium, those dealing with the desired values of real steady-state variables, and those dealing with desired values of nominal steady-state variables.

A general definition of stabilization is keeping the economy in or near steady-state equilibrium. More simply, business cycles are to be reduced or avoided. Fluctuations in the growth rate of real income and the price level are to be reduced, as are the associated cyclical fluctuations in the unemployment rate, industrial production rate, interest rate, and the like. What is desired is a stable, predictable background of the aggregate economy. This permits individuals to make long-term plans and contracts without added risks of massive unemployment or unexpected changes in the price level. The possibilities of stabilization policy are analyzed in Sec. 15.2.

People are concerned not only with keeping the economy in steady-state equilibrium but also about *which* steady-state equilibrium. The key real macroeconomic variables are the growth path of real income and the natural unemployment rate. The main question is what—if anything—macroeconomic policies can do to raise the level or growth rate of real income or to lower the natural rate of unemployment. It is also important to consider the relation of the growth path of real income to other factors important to our well being such as leisure (the participation rate) and environmental quality.

Macroeconomic policies have a particularly important role in determining the steady-state values of nominal variables. The key nominal steady-state variable is the trend inflation rate. The rise in the trend inflation rate since the early 1960s has attracted much public attention and, indeed, outrage. In part, this reflects objection to any change in the inflation rate and so has to do with the stabilization goal. There is, however, a separate objection to high trend rates of inflation. Subsidiary goals with respect to the steady-state values of nominal variables involve the balance of payments and the level of nominal interest rates. Since balance of payments problems can occur only under pegged exchange rates, a more basic and general variable is the trend growth rate of the average foreign-exchange rate.

15.2 STABILIZATION POLICY

STRATEGIES FOR POLICY

It is widely agreed that it is socially desirable to increase the stability of the economy. That is, it would be desirable to reduce the uncertainty and dislocation due to recurrent business cycles. This is done by adopting policies which reduce the extent to which the economy fluctuates around its steady-state equilibrium.[2]

The contribution of macroeconomic policy to economic stability must be considered within the context of an overall strategy. When a football coach calls a run instead of a pass on third down and seven, the team is less likely to make the first down.[3] But it may still be a good call in the broader context of the game and season since it will make it easier to pass in the future. Similarly macroeconomic policy must be evaluated in terms of overall strategy rather than case by case.

A strategy aims to stabilize the economy by offsetting the effects of macroeconomic shocks arising in the private economy. The strategy will stabilize the economy only if: (1) the effects to be offset can be predicted with sufficient accuracy and foresight that macroeconomic policy will on average move the economy in the opposite direction; and (2) the effects of the policy are not so large as to add more instability to the economy than they offset.

These two conditions can be illustrated by thinking of a free-swinging pendulum where the vertical position is the steady-state equilibrium. The shocks that occur in the private economy would be represented by occasional blows of a hammer. Those blows would cause the pendulum to fluctuate around its equilibrium. If one were very quick to respond or had inside information on when the blows would occur, one could hit the pendulum in the direction opposite to its movement and offset the blows of the first hammer more often than not. Of course if you hit too hard or at the wrong time with the second hammer you add to the fluctuations of the pendulum.

These are the elements of a successful stabilization strategy: It offsets those private shocks which can be recognized either as they occur or soon enough thereafter to enable an offsetting policy response; the policy responses are commensurate with the expected private-shock effects to be offset—a heavy-handed policy is worse than none at all. The problem is to find the strategy which does this best.

Economists are divided into three main schools of thought: (1) those who desire a relatively active use of macroeconomic policy to offset private sector

---

[2] A precise measure of economic stability is required for the formal analysis of stabilization policy. The statistical concept of the variance of actual nominal income (or real income or unemployment) around its steady-state level has been popular in the literature. Key studies of stabilization policy include Milton Friedman, "The Effects of a Full-Employment Policy on Economic Stability: A Formal Analysis," in *Essays in Positive Economics*, Chicago: University of Chicago Press, 1953; Milton Friedman, The Role of Monetary Policy, *American Economic Review*, **58:** 1–17, Mar. 1968; William Poole, Optimal Choice of Monetary Policy in a Simple Stochastic Macro Model, *Quarterly Journal of Economics*, **84:** 197–216, May 1970; Board of Governors of the Federal Reserve System, *Open Market Policies and Operating Procedures—Staff Studies*, Washington: Board of Governors, 1971; J. Phillip Cooper and Stanley Fischer, Simultations of Monetary Rules in the FRB-MIT-Penn Model, *Journal of Money, Credit, and Banking*, **4:** 384–396, May 1972; Thomas J. Sargent and Neil Wallace, " Rational " Expectations, the Optimal Monetary Instrument, and the Optimal Money Supply Rule, *Journal of Political Economy*, **83:** 241–254, Apr. 1975; and Robert E. Lucas, Jr., "Econometric Policy Evaluation: A Critique," in K. Brunner and A. Meltzer (eds.), *The Phillips Curve and Labor Markets*, Carnegie-Rochester Conference Series on Public Policy, vol. 1, Amsterdam: North-Holland, 1976.

[3] Except in the case of certain quarterbacks best forgotten.

shocks, (2) those who want relatively limited use of macroeconomic policy, and (3) those who believe any stabilization strategy is at best ineffective.

The first group of policy activists believes that the private economy is characterized by a variety of shocks which have large and long-lasting effects and that these effects can be offset by macroeconomic policy. This is closely allied to the traditional Keynesian view of the economy.

Those who argue for a limited use of macroeconomic policy generally believe that the private economy is not a source of shocks with large or persistent effects. An exception is normally made for changes in the money multiplier. These views are popular with monetarist economists. They urge that the Fed offset money multiplier changes so that a constant nominal-money-supply growth rate is maintained, but that otherwise macroeconomic policy not be used.

The third group points out that only unanticipated changes in money, government spending, or taxes will affect real income or unemployment. Any predictable policy response to observed macroeconomic developments will be anticipated and so ineffective. If an unpredictable element is added to policy, this will only make things worse. This view, associated with work by Lucas, Sargent, and Wallace on rational expectations, will be considered first.

THE LUCAS-SARGENT-WALLACE POLICY SKEPTICISM

If stabilization policy is at best ineffective, the best one can do is to avoid surprises. This view is based on two hypotheses: (1) Only unanticipated policy shocks will have any effect on real income and employment. (2) Any systematic policy response to observed macroeconomic variables can be predicted and therefore will be anticipated. Given these two hypotheses, a stabilization strategy will either have no effect on the economy's stability or else—if the strategy causes any surprises—will decrease its stability.

If the policymakers respond to information not used in forming anticipations of macroeconomic policy, then it is possible that they can stabilize the economy. There are two reasons to expect that this occurs. First the macroeconomic variables to which policy responds may be observed *after* the relevant time for forming anticipations. If shocks must be predicted a year in advance to have no effect on real income, then policy changes based on more recent information can affect real income. Second, the policymakers may use more information than is used by private individuals and firms in forming anticipations. This could be due to confidentiality, but more likely reflects the fact that using the information just would not be worth the cost to any individual.[4] So there appears to be substantial latitude for a systematic macroeconomic strategy to either stabilize or destabilize the economy.

---

[4] See Michael R. Darby, Rational Expectations under Conditions of Costly Information, *Journal of Finance*, **31:** 889–895, June 1976.

POLICY ACTIVISM AND POLICY RESTRAINT

Macroeconomists generally believe that a systematic policy strategy will affect the economy. Some strategies will in fact add to the stability of the economy while others will reduce it. The policy activists believe that frequent adjustments in monetary or fiscal policy or both are the heart of the best stabilization strategy. Those who desire policy restraint argue that frequent changes in macroeconomic policy in fact destabilize the economy.

Timing is the essence of the debate. Activists argue that macroeconomic policymakers can react rapidly and with measured force to private-sector shocks. Thus the macroeconomic policy shocks will on average cancel part of the effects of private-sector shocks and stabilize the economy. Those who prefer a relatively steady policy argue that this cancellation will not occur because private-sector shocks have short-lived effects which will be over before a policy change is made and its effects felt. These economists believe that past policy activism has been the major source of economic *instability* in the period since World War II. The Fed for example has a long history of taking " dramatic action " against inflation by reducing the growth rate of base money, and then reversing itself to take " dramatic action " against the unemployment increase that results from the previous action. This cycle of slamming on the brakes and then the accelerator has been repeated so often that it is referred to as the Fed's *stop-go policy*.

The proper uses of monetary and fiscal policy in a stabilization strategy involve somewhat different issues; so they are considered separately below. The question of the stability of the private economy is important for both, however. The smaller and briefer are the effects of private-sector shocks, the less is the role for any activist macroeconomic policy.

ROLES FOR MONETARY POLICY IN STABILIZATION

Stabilization will clearly result from offsetting the effects on the money supply of fluctuations in the money multiplier. This is a case in which policymakers can almost immediately recognize the occurrence of a private-sector shock and make an almost exactly offsetting policy change. So it is generally agreed that the Fed should offset the effects on the nominal money supply of money multiplier fluctuations. This can be done by varying the growth rate of nominal base money or changing reserve requirements or doing both.

Beyond this, agreement on the role of monetary policy breaks down. There are three popular approaches: (1) Stabilize the growth rate of the nominal money supply at some constant trend rate $\overline{\Gamma M}$. (2) Stabilize the levels of nominal interest rates. (3) Vary the growth rate of the nominal money supply around a trend growth rate $\overline{\Gamma M}$, as warranted by conditions.

THE CONSTANT-GROWTH-RATE STRATEGY

This is the simplest approach to monetary policy: Choose a desired nominal-money-supply growth rate on the basis of its steady-state effects and maintain the actual growth rate constant at that desired rate. No one who urges this policy would argue against a stimulative increase in monetary growth should the country suffer a major recession. They do not believe that this will occur, however, since they attribute past major recessions to past fluctuations in the nominal-money-supply growth rate. Otherwise, monetary policy has effects over such a long period compared to the transient effects of private-sector shocks[5] that only negligible fluctuations in the nominal-money-supply growth rate could contribute to stabilization.

Under a constant nominal-money-supply growth rate rule, nominal-income growth will fluctuate only due to shocks which cause the growth rate of fluidity to fluctuate. In the postwar United States, the fluidity growth rate has fluctuated around trend by as much as plus or minus 3 or 4 percentage points. Proponents of the constant-growth-rate rule argue that most of this fluctuation has been due to fluctuations in the growth rate of the money supply. Thus they argue that with a constant growth rate of the nominal money supply the fluctuations in the annual growth rates of fluidity and nominal income would be no more than plus or minus 1.5 to 2 percentage points.

THE CONSTANT-INTEREST-RATE STRATEGY

The traditional central bank policy has been to stabilize nominal interest rates rather than the growth rate of the money supply. The traditional emphasis on attempts to moderate movements in the level of interest rates may be associated with a tendency for central bankers to model their behavior after that of commercial banks. This is natural because many central bank employees receive their basic training as employees of commercial banks. Commercial banks tend to follow a form of inventory behavior with infrequent changes in interest rates paid on deposits and charged on loans.

A stable-interest-rate policy works well so long as the only other macroeconomic shocks are associated with the money-demand function and the money multiplier. A constant level of nominal interest rates in that case implies no effect on aggregate demand from monetary shocks. The growth rate of the nominal money supply will adjust to that implied by the pegged level of interest rates and the growth in demand for money. Fluctuations in the growth of demand for money are met by fluctuations in the growth rate of nominal money so that growth in the nominal money supply rather than nominal income adjusts to fluctuations in the growth rate of desired fluidity.

---

[5] Private-sector shocks other than money-multiplier fluctuations, that is.

A stable-interest-rate policy and stable policy for growth rate of the nominal money supply are essentially identical in eliminating shocks due to deviations of the money multiplier from trend—though the explicit money supply policy works better with respect to banking panics.[6] A stable-interest-rate policy increases overall stability if shocks due to money demand alone are considered. However, we may recall from Chap. 13 that pegged interest rates lead to the growth rate of the nominal money supply being adjusted to greatly strengthen any real sector shock—whether investment, fiscal policy, international trade, or consumption. A slowed increase in demand in any of these sectors would tend to reduce interest rates if the growth rate of nominal money were constant. Instead, under pegged interest rates, the growth rate of nominal money is reduced to keep the interest rate up. This can turn a minor "blip" into a full-scale recession.

Worse, the decreased growth rate of the nominal money supply can increase the interest rate only temporarily. As it begins to fall after 6 to 9 months, further decreases in the growth rate of the nominal money supply are required, and these further destabilize the economy. The process works in reverse if increased nominal-money-supply growth is used in an attempt to hold the nominal interest rate down to a pegged level. The explosive possibilities are closely analogous to those when monetary policy is used in an attempt to set the unemployment rate below or above the natural rate.

A pegged-interest-rate policy can be viewed as an alternative to a policy for constant growth rate of nominal money; such a policy is more stabilizing in the face of money-demand shocks and less stabilizing—indeed explosive—in the face of real shocks. It is of course an empirical question as to which kinds of shocks are more important. For the United States, that question seems pretty well settled against the policy of attempting to peg nominal interest rates. Autonomous fluctuations in the growth of demand for money seem very small indeed compared to the cumulative processes initiated by real shocks under pegged interest rates. In fact, the attempts to peg nominal interest rates break down, and the pegs change—a macroeconomic shock. So the range of variation in nominal interest rates under a strategy aimed at stabilizing interest rates appears paradoxically to be greater over a period of years than would occur under a constant-nominal-money-growth-rate strategy. The Fed has been gradually abandoning interest-rate stabilization in setting monetary policy since the late 1960s.

THE VARIABLE-GROWTH-RATE STRATEGY

A more robust contender with the constant-nominal-money-growth-rate strategy is a constant trend growth rate with stabilizing deviations. The idea is to stimulate the economy when it is sluggish and restrain it when it is otherwise

---

[6] Changes in risk premiums on different types of loans make the operation of an interest rate peg uncertain during a panic.

stimulated. If this is to work, it is necessary that the deviations of nominal income due to nominal-money-growth deviations on average offset nominal-income deviations due to autonomous shocks. Further, the nominal-money-growth deviations must not be so large that they become a more important source of instability than the shocks they are to offset.

The ability to select nominal-money-supply-growth deviations which are on average stabilizing is a matter of question because of the lags in the effect of monetary policy on aggregate demand. A monetary shock has significant effects on aggregate demand for a period beginning about 6 months later and continuing for 3 years or more. It is not an easy task to predict now what the autonomous shocks will be like over the next 3 or 4 years. If, however, autonomous shocks also tend to persist over a considerable period of time, it is possible to use current conditions to predict at least part of the future period. Since data are not available for truly current conditions but at best for conditions of 1 to 4 months ago, the task is yet more difficult. If, for example, autonomous shocks typically affected nominal income for a total of five quarters, offsetting monetary policies could cause offsetting deviations in nominal income for one or two quarters. It is widely, though not universally, believed that this necessary condition for improvement over a constant-nominal-money-supply growth is met.

A second question is how great is the variance of nominal income remaining under a constant-nominal-money-growth strategy. If this variance is very small, there is little to be gained from further refinements and something to lose in allowing the Fed to deviate from the trend growth rate. The deviations in nominal-money-supply growth may easily be too large and cause net destabilization. The smaller the remaining variance under constant-nominal-money-supply growth, the smaller are the average deviations which can be stabilizing.

THE DEBATE OVER STRATEGIES FOR MONETARY POLICY

There are many economists who believe that given our current state of knowledge, the best that can be done by way of active monetary policy is stabilizing the growth rate of the nominal money supply. They argue that the main source of business fluctuations has been variations in the growth rate of the nominal money supply and that, where such variations in nominal-money-supply growth have been prevented, there have been in fact no significant business fluctuations. In this view, "fine-tuning" of monetary policy is unnecessary and likely to be carried too far.

A great many other economists believe that it is possible to do somewhat better by varying nominal-money-supply growth around a stable trend according to current conditions.[7] Under these plans the nominal-money-supply

---

[7] This requires that stimulative policies and restrictive policies must eventually be canceled out so that the actual growth path of the nominal money supply does not drift away from the trend growth path.

growth rate is decreased if nominal income is above its desired steady-state growth path and increased if it is below that growth path. As a matter of logic, it has been demonstrated that for *small* adjustments in the growth rate of the nominal money supply this sort of strategy yields some improvement over a constant-growth-rate strategy in the stability of a statistical model of the economy.

The debate continues, however. Statistical models of the economy and the economy are two different things, critics of the variable-growth-rate strategy point out. In the real economy, policy shocks have been the main source of economic instability despite their stated goal of stabilizing the economy.[8] Critics of the constant-growth-rate strategy reply that past errors of heavy handed policymakers are to be condemned, but should not prevent us from doing what can be done now.

A related question is the debate over "rules versus authorities." A constant growth rate of the nominal money supply could be easily enacted by statute. If the Fed is instead given independent authority to determine the growth rate of the nominal money supply—as is now the case—it is subject to many political pressures to stimulate the economy near election time, with disastrous results for economic stability. It would, however, be possible to frame an explicit law determining the growth rate of the nominal money supply under a variable-growth-rate strategy, so this presents no real issues for that choice. The strength of an authority is that it can look more deeply into current circumstances, but the weakness is the potential for overemphasis of the "uniqueness" of current conditions and for political abuse.

THE FEASIBILITY OF ACTIVE FISCAL POLICY

Two possible tools of fiscal policy exist: government spending and taxation. The debate over the possible contribution to stability of active manipulation of these tools is quite as sharp as that over the possibility of increasing stability through varying the growth rate of the money supply.

Two separate issues are the subject of debate: (1) Do these tools of fiscal policy have a significant effect on the growth rate of nominal income? (2) If they do, can they be altered sufficiently rapidly that stabilization can in fact occur? If fiscal policy has no effect, even temporarily, on nominal income, then it certainly cannot be used to promote—or harm—the aggregate stability of the economy. If fiscal policy does have some effects on nominal income, it is possibly but not necessarily true that fiscal policy can stabilize the economy. The main issue of debate differs for the two policy tools.

Very few economists will disagree that deviations from the trend growth

---

[8] This apparently reflects the inability of policymakers to restrain their actions to the small variations which could do some good. See Levis A. Kochin, Judging Stabilization Policies, Research Paper No. 7211, Federal Reserve Bank of New York, December 1972.

path in government spending for goods and services have significant, though perhaps temporary effects on aggregate demand.[9] The absolute size of the effect—the " bang per buck "—is still subject to considerable disagreement. The size of the effect is important to the evaluation of the efficiency but not of the possibility of stabilizing variations in government spending.

Unlike monetary policy which can be altered practically instantaneously, variations in the rate of government spending require considerable time to accomplish. After the decision is made to buy more or less goods and services, it takes time to decide precisely which ones, to increase or decrease orders accordingly, and so forth. This lag between decision and action may more than offset any advantages of fiscal policy in terms of the relatively short span of time over which the policy has effects. In order that the fiscal policy actually stabilize the economy, there must be reasonably accurate predictions of autonomous shocks occurring when the policy takes effect. If this is on the order of a year in the future, it is not surprising that this task may prove impossible. In that case, the required negative correlation between policy and autonomous shocks fails, and stabilizing policy based on varying government spending is impossible. Various schemes of standby projects have been proposed to reduce the lag between decision and action, but none have yet passed the test of political feasibility.

A considerable problem with active stabilization through variations in federal spending is the relatively large variations in federal spending required to obtain relatively small variations in nominal income. Such large variations in federal spending may themselves imply waste much greater than the value of any reduction in instability. There is no agreement yet on what—if any— magnitudes are involved. Politicians will undoubtedly continue to cut programs that they oppose in any case "in order to fight inflation" and to add programs that they support anyway "in order to fight unemployment."

Variations in taxation were long thought to offer an attractive alternative to variations in government spending. Since consumer spending is currently about 10 times as large as federal spending, tax-induced variations in consumer spending involve relatively smaller changes than do equal dollar changes in federal spending. They would therefore be likely to be accomplished more quickly and with less waste. The tax and transfer payment[10] laws indeed automatically adjust taxation to current conditions. This would all appear to make tax variation an effective instrument of stabilization policy. Unfortunately, there is a question about whether short-run variations in taxation affect nominal income. As was discussed in Chap. 8, there is little theoretical or empirical reason to expect an effect one way or the other. So the feasibility of stabilization through variation in taxes is not supported by the evidence.

---

[9] See the discussion of the empirical evidence on this point in Sec. 8.2.
[10] Remember that taxes are here counted net of transfer payments.

REVIEW OF THE ISSUES FOR STABILIZATION POLICY

For stabilization policy to be effective, it must be possible to take policy actions which will offset fluctuations in nominal income that are due to autonomous shocks. This presents policymakers with the severe problem of predicting the effects of autonomous shocks over the period during which the effects of current policy decisions on nominal income occur. This task is relatively easy for autonomous shocks to the money multiplier. These shocks have effects almost entirely through their influence on the growth rate of the nominal money supply. Monetary policy which eliminates the resulting effects on the growth rate of the nominal money supply automatically cancels the effects of autonomous shocks and stabilizes the economy.

Other sources of autonomous shocks have no such reliable early warning system. Policymakers must either successfully predict—on average—the net influence of these shocks and other policy shocks in the period over which current policy takes effect or else they must abandon further stabilization entirely.

Some economists argue that as a practical matter instability in the growth rate of the nominal money supply has been the only reason for significant fluctuations in the growth of aggregate demand. The small fluctuations—no more than 1.5 or 2 percent per annum—that would remain under a constant growth rate of the nominal money supply are best left to work themselves out.

Other economists (who may or may not think the first group overoptimistic with respect to the magnitude of the remaining fluctuations) believe that it is possible to improve the stability of the economy further.

One traditional alternative to a strategy of stable nominal-money-supply growth, the stable-interest-rate strategy, is superior only with respect to autonomous shocks in the demand for money and much inferior to a stable nominal-money-supply growth rate in the face of other autonomous shocks. So this alternative does not have much to offer as a stabilization strategy.

More attractive strategies are slight variations in the growth rate of the nominal money supply around a stable trend or variations in the growth rate of real government spending (or both) in accordance with current conditions. These strategies can work only if current conditions provide enough information that these policy shocks can on average offset the remaining autonomous shocks. The long period over which monetary policy has effects and the long period required to change the growth rate of real government spending raise substantial problems for macroeconomists' predictive abilities. Most macroeconomists have sufficient confidence in their current predictive abilities to believe that this hurdle is surmountable and improved stabilization is possible. Whether this is in fact true and whether the benefits of further active stabilization policy beyond maintaining a constant growth rate of the nominal money supply are worth the costs remain very much unsettled issues.

15.3 MACROECONOMIC POLICY AND REAL STEADY-STATE VARIABLES

INFLUENCING THE INVESTMENT-INCOME RATIO BY FISCAL POLICY

There are three basic variables which determine the growth path of real income: the investment-income ratio, the growth rate of labor, and the aggregate production function. Any policy influencing the steady-state growth path of real income must operate through one or more of these variables.

Governments interested in promoting economic development have often chosen to increase the ratio of investment to income, $i/y = \sigma$, through the use of fiscal policy. The simplest way to increase the investment-income ratio is to increase the real government surplus.[11] Rewriting [2.0] in real terms,

$$i = s + (t - g) - x \qquad [15.1]$$

Real investment equals real saving plus the real budget surplus less real capital outflows x. The idea is that saving finances new security issues by firms, government, and foreigners. If the government borrows less or even redeems some of its outstanding securities, more saving will be available to finance investment by firms.

It was seen in Sec. 8.3 that increases in the government surplus will reduce saving somewhat. This reduction is generally less than the increase in the surplus, however, so that investment is increased.[12]

In Chap. 5, it was shown that a higher investment-income ratio implies a higher steady-state level—but not growth rate—of real income at each instant. Fiscal policy can therefore be used to permanently increase the level of real income and temporarily—during the adjustment period—increase the growth rate of real income.

The use of government surpluses to raise real income is not without costs, however. If the government increases the investment-income ratio through fiscal policy, the immediate result is less private and government spending for goods and services yielding current satisfaction—on this broad definition, less consumption. So long as this policy is not carried too far,[13] consumption will, after some future date, always be higher than it would otherwise have been. So there is a potential tradeoff of increased future consumption for a period of decreased consumption. Alternatively, increased present consumption can be obtained, but only at the cost of lower future consumption—as in the case of

---

[11] Remember that the real government surplus is the difference between real government taxes and spending, $t - g$. A decrease in the government deficit is an increase in the government surplus.

[12] If international capital markets were sufficiently free, practically all of the increase in $s + (t - g)$ would go into increased real capital outflows so that foreign investment would be increased but not our own capital and output. Nevertheless our income would increase due to higher earnings on foreign securities and the main conclusions below hold.

[13] That is, so long as the real interest rate exceeds the real-income growth rate.

debt financing of wars—by reducing the government surplus or increasing the government deficit.

The direction and the degree of such a tradeoff are matters of individual value judgment. A government budget balanced except for capital investments is sometimes used as a benchmark. Larger government surpluses imply less current and more future consumption than would be desired by individual savers. Smaller government surpluses imply more current and less future consumption than would be desired by individual savers. Thus a larger or smaller surplus would be justified on the basis of a belief that individuals undervalue or overvalue their future consumption and that of their heirs.

On this analysis, the use of taxation to finance what are in effect capital investments by the government is nearly equivalent to an equal government surplus where all capital is privately owned.[14] The incentives on private and bureaucratic investors are somewhat different so that the investment projects may differ in efficiency, but otherwise the two approaches are equivalent.

MICROECONOMIC POLICIES AND STEADY-STATE REAL EQUILIBRIUM

Most policies substantially affecting steady-state real equilibrium are not at all macroeconomic policies. It may even be stretching the term to call the policies dealing with population or environmental quality microeconomic policies. An analysis of microeconomic policy is beyond the scope of a macroeconomics book, but a brief discussion of some macroeconomic implications is in order.

A great many discussions of the macroeconomic implications of various microeconomic policies are seriously flawed by a thorough confusion of growth rates and levels. Policies which do not affect the growth rate of labor can change the steady-state level but not the growth rate of real income. In the period of adjustment immediately following such a policy change, the growth rate of real income will be higher or lower than the steady-state rate in order to effect the transition to a higher or lower growth path. This is only temporary, however, and thereafter the growth rate is unchanged.

A frequent proposal is to increase real income by reducing government grants of monopoly to businesses and unions. Such a policy would shift upward the aggregate production function in the sense that more real output would be obtained from given quantities of labor and capital. This happens because labor and capital will be put to more valued uses. The effect on the growth path of real income is found in Fig. 15.1. The steady-state growth rate of real income is unchanged at the growth rate of labor Γl. The level of real income at each

---

[14] The government's failure to keep full accounts of government assets may obscure the meaning here. Suppose instead the government issued bonds equivalent to its capital stock and levied taxes sufficient to cover current expenses, depreciation, and interest. Net government investment would then be covered by new borrowing. Alternatively, the government could lease capital goods from private owners—as is done for example with many post offices—and balance the budget including rental payments (that is, depreciation and interest) with all borrowing done by private firms.

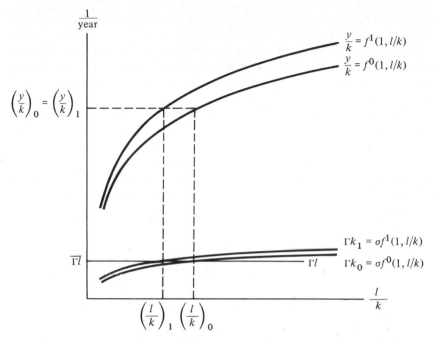

Figure 15.1 Effects of alternative aggregate production functions on steady-state equilibrium. The production function $y/k = f^1(1, l/k)$ exceeds the alternative $y/k = f^0(1, l/k)$ for every positive value of the labor-capital ratio. The growth rate of income is fixed at $\overline{\Gamma l}$, but the labor-capital ratio is less in state 1 than it is in state 0. The income-capital ratio is the same in each case at $\Gamma l/\sigma$. Real income in state 1 exceeds real income in state 0 because there is more capital and the same amount of labor in state 1 and because given amounts of capital and labor produce more output in state 1 than in state 0.

instant of time is increased, however, because more output is produced by given amounts of capital and labor and because the amount of capital is in fact increased at each instant. A complete analysis of the removal of monopoly powers would require microeconomic theory as some groups win and others lose. The point here is that removal of monopoly power is a source of a once-and-for-all increase in real income and not of *continuing* increased growth of real income.

Many popular writers have seen a conflict between improvement of environmental quality and the continuation of economic growth. This dichotomy, too, is mistaken. What is proposed is that pollution of the environment as a result of the productive process be limited. This is done by preventing firms and individuals from using those productive processes which cause pollution. Other, less productive processes will be substituted. Thus the aggregate production function shifts down as less real output is produced from any quantity of capital and labor. This is just the reverse of the previous instance. It is seen from Fig. 15.1 that the steady-state growth rate of real income is unchanged, but the steady-state level of real income at each instant of time is lower because less is produced from given amounts of capital and labor, and less capital will exist. This reduction of market goods and services may be more or less than balanced by the improvement in environmental quality, but that is another question. The growth rate of real income is slowed only temporarily during the period of adjustment.

The macroeconomic implications of alternative growth paths of population, participation, and average quality of the labor force have been analyzed in detail in the text and problems of Chap. 5. That analysis will not be repeated here. It is important to observe that changes in the steady-state growth rate of real income are obtained only through changes in the factors underlying the growth rate of labor. Other changes affect the level but not the growth rate of real income.

ARE THERE LIMITS TO REAL GROWTH?

At least since 1798 when Thomas R. Malthus published his pamphlet *An Essay on the Principle of Population*, there have been recurrent prophecies of the imminent cessation of economic growth. The basic idea is always the same. Some particular type of resource is assumed to be absolutely necessary for economic production. This resource is available only in fixed, or nearly fixed, supply. Hence, it is argued, soon all of this resource will be used or used up, and output must stop growing or fall, respectively. Predictions of cessation within 5 years enjoy more notoriety but provide a less steady source of income to the predictor than a less immediate date.

The reason that the prophets of doom always prove wrong is that the "absolute necessity" never really is. Increasing demand raises the price of the increasingly scarce resource and thus encourages its conservation and the discovery of substitutes. This has happened in every case. Doom is implied only if man is unable to adjust and adapt to changing conditions. It might happen, one supposes, but the force of history runs against the possibility.

15.4 MACROECONOMIC POLICY AND NOMINAL STEADY-STATE VARIABLES

CONTROLLING THE STEADY-STATE INFLATION RATE

Recently, much public concern has been focused on the inflation rate. This concern is natural in the face of accelerating inflation in the decade beginning with 1965. It is perhaps surprising to reflect that controlling the steady-state inflation rate is a relatively easy task for macroeconomic policy. It takes no great sophistication or technical expertise to compute the trend growth rate of real demand for money. Add the desired steady-state inflation rate to that number and the answer is the required trend growth rate of the nominal money supply.

It is remarkably easy to control the inflation rate as long as the Federal Reserve System carries out its duties to maintain the required trend growth rate of the nominal money supply. During the 1960s the Fed instead chased unmaintainable goals of low unemployment and interest rates with accelerating nominal-money-supply growth. And so the attainable good was lost for the unattainable better.

There are three issues connected with the steady-state inflation rate: the implications of alternative rates; the costs and benefits of moving from one rate to another; and the costs and benefits of variable steady-state inflation rates.

THE IMPLICATIONS OF
ALTERNATIVE STEADY-STATE INFLATION RATES

Macroeconomics provides no well-established body of empirical evidence on the real implications of alternative steady-state inflation rates. The hardest part of any scientific research is asking the right questions. At least until recently, the questions examined in research on inflation have not been well constructed.

The layman always finds it hard to understand why macroeconomists should have trouble explaining the effects of inflation when everyone knows it is bad. The problem is that what "everyone" knows is wrong with inflation either does not withstand examination or has to do with the effects of changing the inflation rate from that which is anticipated. The implications of alternative fully anticipated steady-state inflation rates require more careful thought.

The first observation is that the levels of prices and nominal incomes are irrelevant to human satisfaction so long as a rise or fall in prices is reflected in a proportionate rise or fall in incomes. There is no reason to be any more or less happy with an income of $10,000 per annum than with $100,000 per annum if prices are ten times higher in the latter than in the former case. It is of no importance whether we reckon our accounts in dollars or dimes so long as the real work done and goods received are the same.

Therefore, there is no obvious reason why one should feel any better or worse if one's income increases at 8 percent per annum with a 6 percent rate of inflation than if the figures were 2 and 0 percent, respectively. In each case, the actual growth in command over real goods and services is the same 2 percent per annum. There seems to be an illusory feeling by some people that in the first case the 8 percent increase in income is "rightfully theirs" and that inflation robs them of their hard-earned gains. But this is a false reason for opposing high inflation, since the average growth rate of real per capita income in the United States is determined by real factors at a bit under 2 percent per annum. The inflation rate merely provides a base to which must be added the real income gains—or losses—to obtain dollar gains.

Nor are problems of unfairly hurting retired people and other net creditors receiving fixed money income applicable. Nominal interest rates adjust to eliminate any advantage to debtors or creditors. Arbitrary transfers of wealth occur only when the steady-state inflation rate is unexpectedly changed, as discussed further below.

The choice among steady-state inflation rates must be based on comparison of the associated real implications. Unless different steady-state inflation rates imply some different real magnitudes there is no reason to select one inflation rate over another.

Three sorts of real implications appear important: costs involved in economizing on money balances, costs involved in alternative means of financing government, and effects on the investment-income ratio.[15]

Government money creation substitutes for other methods of financing government expenditures. Higher growth rates of nominal base money cause higher inflation rates but also, up to some point, yield higher revenues to the government. This revenue from base-money creation is sometimes imprecisely referred to as the inflationary tax on base money. The real expenditures financed by the tax equal the rate of change in nominal base money divided by the price level:

$$\frac{\Delta B}{P} = \frac{\Delta B}{B}\frac{B}{P} = \Gamma B \cdot b \qquad [15.2]$$

Hence the real revenue from money creation can be thought of as the growth rate of nominal base money times real base money. From the taxation viewpoint, the tax rate is ΓB and the tax base is b. So long as the tax base does not shrink too rapidly, increases in the tax rate ΓB and therefore the inflation rate increase government revenue. This higher revenue can be used to reduce other taxes. These other taxes will have involved costs from administration, avoidance, and distortion,[16] which are avoided at higher revenues from money creation.

Against these costs must be balanced the costs from administration, avoidance, and distortion due to the new tax. These are primarily related to misallocation of resources in an attempt to economize on holdings of base money. Partially, this is accomplished by more extensive use of bank deposits for transactions in which currency would otherwise be cheaper than checks. Bank deposits only use base money for fractional reserves. Indeed the Fed in effect pays at least partial interest on bank reserves through such activities as free check-clearing services, subsidized lending facilities, and the like. There may

---

[15] If the rate of inflation is substantially greater or less than zero, the costs of changing prices, adjusting accounts for the effects of inflation, and similar calculations would appear to be sufficient to noticeably reduce the level of real income.

[16] For example, the income tax alters the value to the individual of work and leisure so that he works less than he would in the absence of the tax.

also be a reduction in the total demand for money as resources are used to match expenditures and receipts more closely so that average money balances are reduced.

Consequently, the elimination of overt taxes tends to shift the production function upward while the increase in the inflationary tax tends to shift the production function downward. There is no clear evidence about the nature of the net effect. Unless the demand for money is substantially interest elastic, the amounts involved are likely to be rather small in any case. For example, base money in 1977 averaged about $123 billion and grew at about 8 percent per annum. The total revenue from money creation was therefore about $10 billion. If the difference in the costs associated with the alternative types of taxes were as great as 10 percent of total revenues, the waste difference would be only $1 billion. This amount—which is surely a high estimate—comes to about one-half of a tenth of a percent (0.05 percent) of total income. While the sums involved are well worth looking into, they are not substantial enough to have any detectable effect on aggregate real income in the range experienced in the United States.

Some authors have placed great emphasis on possible effects on the investment-income ratio. It is argued that so long as the growth rate of real money balances is positive, lower steady-state values of fluidity imply higher investment-income ratios. The idea is that consumers perceive growth in real base money as both income and saving. Hence lower levels of fluidity for a given money multiplier imply that less perceived saving will take place in the form of increased real base-money balances. Although this idea has spawned many elegant papers, the practical interest is slight. For the United States, the entire sum involved is about 0.02 percent of income or 0.3 percent of total investment.[17] Further, any such effects are easily offset by a slight alteration in the growth rate of the real national debt.

Choice of a steady-state rate of inflation is simultaneously the choice of the steady-state level of nominal interest rates and the steady-state growth rate of the average foreign-exchange rate. There is no particular advantage to low or high nominal interest rates where the differences reflect only differences in the inflation rate. Nor is it obvious why anyone would care whether the growth rate of the average exchange rate is positive, zero, or negative where the growth rate merely reflects the difference between the American rate of inflation and the average rate of inflation for the rest of the world. Such changes in the

---

[17] These computations are based on 1977 data and the trend growth rate of real base money from 1953 through 1977 of 0.3 percent per annum. The reduction in saving due to growth in base money is

$$(1 - \sigma)\Gamma b \cdot b \approx (0.9)(0.003/\text{year}) \times (R\$123 \text{ billion}) = R\$0.33 \text{ billion per annum}$$

where 1977 is the base year. Investment for 1977 was $R\$97.3$ billion per annum, hence $R\$0.33$ billion$/R\$97.3$ billion $= 0.003$. Net national product was $R\$1,693.4$ billion per annum, consequently $R\$0.33$ billion$/R\$1,693.4$ billion $= 0.0002$.

exchange rate do not affect the prices of foreign goods relative to American goods either within or outside the United States; so there is no effect on real exports and imports.

In sum, there is little hard evidence to suggest that any one constant inflation rate is better than another. Calculations made for the United States suggest that for moderate inflation rates, say between 0 and 10 percent per annum, the gain or loss from the choice of any particular steady-state inflation rate is not likely to be as great as one tenth of a percent (0.001) of total income. The question of whether a little inflation is a good or bad thing remains open. For example, the calculation costs associated with any nonzero inflation rate have not been measured yet, and could turn out to be large at much lower absolute rates of inflation than so far supposed. The analysis of Chap. 14 should be recalled, since it was seen there that no *constant* inflation rate can affect the natural rate of unemployment, so no benefits can be expected there. There is no clear reason to choose any particular moderate inflation rate because of its steady-state implications.

This analysis applies only to an open inflation not encumbered with government price controls, usury laws, or other artificial constraints on the adjustment of prices. Attempts at suppression, whether conscious or through failure to alter nominal amounts in laws, can lead to substantial inefficiencies. Price controls enforced by the occupation troops in post-World War II Germany led to the effective abandonment of monetary exchange. The German "economic miracle" resulted from the unauthorized removal of these controls by the West German government. Restoration of money as a usable means of exchange and of prices as a guide to the allocation of resources to their most valuable use led to an increase of output of 50 percent in the last half of 1948 alone.[18] If a government enforces price controls, then lower inflation rates are the only way to avoid economic disaster. In the early 1970s, many Western countries tried price and wage controls with disastrous political results in subsequent elections for the parties which installed or advocated controls. A little experience rapidly dampens voter enthusiasm for such approaches.

THE COSTS AND BENEFITS OF UNANTICIPATED CHANGES IN THE INFLATION RATE

The period of adjustment to changes in the steady-state inflation rate has substantial costs and benefits.

Consider what happens if the trend growth rate of nominal base money is increased by, say, 3 percentage points. First there is a boom as aggregate

---

[18] Further discussion of this fascinating episode of literal mass starvation due to price controls is found in Jack Hirshleifer, *Disaster and Recovery: A Historical Survey*, No. RM-3079-PR, Santa Monica, Calif.: The Rand Corp., 1963; Horst Mendershausen, Prices, Money and the Distribution of Goods in Postwar Germany, *American Economic Review*, **39**: 646–672, June 1949; and Gustav Stolper, Karl Häuser, and Knut Borchardt, *The German Economy: 1870 to the Present*, London: Weidenfeld and Nicolson, 1967.

demand is increased. Whether it counts as a cost or benefit to trick people into taking jobs or selling products at wages and prices which would be otherwise unacceptable is a difficult question. But since people are indeed fooled into thinking they are better off than they really are, there is clearly a *political* benefit to those who engineer the increased nominal base-money growth just as there would be a political cost to those who dared to engineer decreased nominal base-money growth. The cost of moving to a lower trend growth rate of the nominal money supply could be reduced by advance public announcement. If a program of reduced money growth were believable—if it were incorporated in law, for instance—then expected growth in aggregate demand, prices, and wages would fall. This would reduce or eliminate the temporary increase in unemployment.

The other substantive implication is that as prices rise more rapidly than anticipated in previously agreed interest rates, creditors lose and debtors win. Interest rates rise as anticipations adjust so that this advantage is eliminated. But until the adjustment is completed, loans are made at what turn out to be unfavorable terms for the lender. In the case of a decreased growth rate of nominal base money, the tables would be turned in favor of the lender. Whether the debtors or creditors predominate, the arbitrary transfers of wealth involved in unanticipated inflations appear politically costly. So politicians do not explicitly endorse increased inflation,[19] but merely carry out policies which eventually lead to it.

THE COSTS AND BENEFITS
OF VARIABLE STEADY-STATE INFLATION RATES

The great difficulty with a fiat monetary standard such as now exists in the United States is the potential variability in the inflation rate. A political decision can select any growth rate of base money, but political decisions can be changed. The temptations to increase the growth rate of nominal base money because of an impending election are great. If there is an increase, by how much? The political costs of returning the nominal money supply to the previous growth path (and causing a recession) may well be sufficient to guarantee that it is never done.

Making a long-term contract becomes very risky. Therefore, these valuable contracts must either be forgone or more expensive alternatives used to allow adjustment of money sums to reflect the actual rate of inflation. As these arrangements become common, it becomes harder for the government to cause either a boom or recession by altering the growth rate of the money supply. But

---

[19] There have been political parties which openly advocated unanticipated inflations, but they have not been successful. The Greenback Party was founded in 1874. Its inflationist views were absorbed into the losing Democratic Party platform of 1896.

consider the price: Money loses its usefulness as a standard of value for transactions to be settled in the future and more expensive substitutes must be found.

Consider how the United States adopted a fiat standard with the trend inflation rate left to the discretion of the Federal Reserve System. In 1913 the United States was on a gold standard so that the price level was simply the price of gold in terms of all other goods and services. The relative price of gold would change from time to time with discoveries of new ore deposits or mining techniques, but advances in the production of other goods kept pace on average. So there was no persistent upward or downward trend to the price level.

The fractional reserve banking system led to recurrent panics and temporary drops in the money supply. The Fed was established to prevent the panics by issuing Federal Reserve Notes and maintaining the nominal money supply. So long as the Fed was constrained to redeem its notes for a fixed amount of gold, the value of the dollar remained tied to the value of gold in terms of goods. If the Fed increased the nominal money supply too rapidly, demands for redemption would reduce its gold holdings and the Fed would cut back its rate of issue. If it were to choose too slow a growth rate of the nominal money supply, gold holdings would grow until the Fed increased the rate of issue in nominal base money.

In 1933, the definition of a dollar was changed by law from 1/20.67 of a fine ounce of gold to 1/35 of an ounce. This altered definition implied a 70 percent increase in the equilibrium price level. The Fed, it will be recalled from Chap. 13, had ceased to play by the rules and did not adjust the nominal money supply accordingly. Instead the American gold stock grew steadily. Not until the middle of the Korean War was the American price level 70 percent higher than it had been during the 1920s.

By that time, the Fed had largely forgotten the rules of the gold standard. As inflation was continued at a reduced rate during the remainder of the 1950s, gold began to flow out of the United States. Concern over the balance of payments became severe during the early 1960s, and it appeared that the Fed would have to stop nominal-money-supply growth and thus engineer a recession to correct matters. In 1965, Congress repealed the law requiring the Fed to hold gold to the extent of 25 percent of deposits at the Fed and let the Fed know that the remaining requirement of gold against Federal Reserve Notes would be repealed when it became binding. This in effect removed all guidance from the gold standard to the determination of the price level. By 1968, the Fed ceased providing gold on demand even to foreign central banks, though it was not made official until 1971.

So the Fed is now free to decide the trend growth rate of the nominal money supply by any criterion it chooses, including political pressure from the President and Congress. Predicting the price level 20 years from now is a political guessing game, not the subject of economic analysis.

The question naturally arises whether this system of monetary control is politically stable. Why should the political attractiveness of a little faster nominal-money creation be less at 20 percent per annum inflation than at 5 percent per annum? The author of this book can see no reason.

There does not appear any way to establish a stable, predictable growth rate of the nominal money supply under a system of completely discretionary policymaking by the Fed. There appear to be two viable means of establishing a fixed-trend nominal-money-supply growth rate: a true commodity standard and a legally fixed growth path of the nominal money supply.

A commodity standard requires production and storage of a significant amount of some product—say gold—in order to provide at least a substantial fraction of the growth of real money balances. It is difficult to establish a central bank with powers sufficient to deal with a banking panic that cannot abuse those powers so that the commodity standard becomes ineffective. There are alternatives such as federal deposit insurance which can be used so that central bank powers need not be so great. But it must be acknowledged that commodity standards have not been generally retained in the face of the substantial costs that are involved.

An alternative that is increasingly popular with the Congress is setting by law or constitutional amendment a growth path of the nominal money supply. Such a legal rule would make the fiat monetary standard as predictable and stable as a commodity standard without the costs of production and storage or the danger of irresponsible central bank actions.

The Fed would be required to maintain the nominal quantity of money within a certain percentage of the stated growth path at all times. This would assure that the average growth rate of the nominal money supply over any substantial period of time must be very close to the growth rate used in establishing the stated growth path. The percentage of variation permitted would establish a margin for error and, if desired, a margin for short-run discretionary variations in money supply growth for reasons of stabilization policy. A similar proposal to limit the annual growth rate of the nominal money supply to a certain range provides a less predictable standard since the Fed might choose to always be at the high or low end of the permitted range. The differences from the central growth rate would then cumulate over time.

If America is to choose a steady-state inflation rate, a framework must be provided by which that choice may be expressed and enforced. If no choice is made, there is no reason to expect that the ills of continuing unanticipated increases in the growth rate of the nominal money supply will be avoided. The political temptation is too great to reduce the unemployment rate now and worry about the increased inflation rate when it happens after the election. Any inflation rate is consistent with either a commodity or fiat standard.[20] If no standard is explicitly adopted which limits the ability of the Fed to print money at will, the most likely prospect is continued accelerating inflation.

A difficult question is what steady-state inflation rate to choose. Some would

---

[20] The definition of the monetary unit can be steadily changed under a commodity standard.

urge an announced gradual reduction in the growth rate of the nominal money supply to one consistent with zero inflation. Others argue that the advantages of zero inflation over 6 or 8 percent are small at best and that the temporary increase in unemployment and arbitrary shift in wealth from debtors to creditors which are necessary to get to 0 percent outweigh any such gain. The research necessary to more accurately judge the magnitudes involved remains to be done.

That is how it is with macroeconomics. Answering one hard question leads to the posing of others. The work to be done grows at a positive rate.

SUMMARY

1 United States macroeconomic policy is determined by the federal government, given the predictable behavior of the banking system and state and local governments.

2 Macroeconomic analysis can show the short-run and long-run implications of various possible policies. Because of differences in value judgments concerning conflicting goals, different people may differ on which policy is preferable.

3 It is sometimes argued that because the electorate is largely ignorant of the long-run effects of macroeconomic policies, federal policymakers put undue weight on costs and benefits which occur before the next election.

4 Major goals which have influenced macroeconomic policy are "maximum employment, production, and purchasing power," as well as balance-of-payments equilibrium, low or stable interest rates, economic efficiency, economic growth, and environmental quality. In part these goals reflect a desire for increased economic stability—for a reduction in business fluctuations.

5 Because business fluctuations reflect unexpected shocks, a stabilization strategy must be chosen which reduces fluctuations on average. For a strategy to work, the effects of macroeconomic policy must work opposite to the effects of private-sector shocks on average, and the policy effects must not be so large as to add more instability than they offset.

6 The Lucas-Sargent-Wallace group of policy skeptics argues that any active macroeconomic policy is at best ineffective. Most macroeconomists, however, argue for either active or limited use of macroeconomic policy for stabilization.

7 With regard to monetary policy, there is general agreement that the Fed should offset the effects of fluctuations in the money multiplier on the growth rate of the nominal money supply. Some argue that any policy which varies the nominal-money-supply growth rate will be destabilizing because its effects will be generally unrelated to private-sector shocks. Others argue for varying money supply growth in response to fluctuations in either interest rates or some indicator such as the unemployment rate.

8 The effects of fiscal policy occur over a shorter period, so that it is potentially more useful as an offset to private-sector shocks. However, fiscal policy has proven very slow—and perhaps costly—to change.

9 Those who argue for a limited-policy strategy argue that past recessions have been caused by money-multiplier fluctuations and activist macroeconomic policy. Activists admit past policy errors but believe that we can now do better.

10 The steady-state level of real income can be increased through increases in the government surplus which raise the investment-income ratio σ. The adjustment to the higher investment-income ratio involves a period of reduced consumption levels, however. A nearly equivalent policy is the use of taxes to finance direct government investment.

11 Policies which leave the growth rate of labor unchanged will affect the growth rate of real income only during a temporary period of adjustment. They can affect the steady-state level of real income permanently, however.

12 The empirical evidence does not suggest that it makes a great deal of difference to the real economy what steady-state inflation rate is chosen within broad limits. The major costs of inflation are associated with the adjustment to changes in the steady-state inflation rate, not its level. Real effects of alternative steady-state inflation rates operate through economizing on money balances, alternative means of financing government, and the investment-income ratio. Attempts to suppress inflation by enforced price and wage controls and similar restrictions lead to reduced real income through abandonment of monetary exchange and misallocation of resources.

13 Maintaining a selected steady-state inflation rate is technically simple but the political temptations to do otherwise are great. American monetary arrangements leave the determination of the rate of inflation to the discretion of the Federal Reserve System. Political pressures for increased growth rates of the money supply prior to elections are likely to lead to accelerating inflation unless an explicit constraint on Fed decisions is imposed. Such a constraint might take the form of a return to a commodity standard or a legal rule establishing a prescribed growth path of the nominal money supply.

CONCEPTS TO KNOW

stabilization strategy   stop-go policy

QUESTIONS AND EXERCISES

1 What is the role of macroeconomic theory in the formulation of macroeconomic policy? Why can macroeconomics not tell whether a temporary increase in unemployment should be traded off for a permanent

decrease in the inflation rate? Why is a knowledge of macroeconomics nevertheless valuable in formulating both the question and its answer?

*2 Why is stabilization policy judged in terms of overall strategy rather than by whether a particular policy decision in fact moved the economy toward steady-state equilibrium?

3 The Lucas-Sargent-Wallace critique shows that effective stabilization policy can occur only if policymakers use more information than is used by individuals in forming anticipations. What does this imply for a plan to permanently reduce the unemployment rate by a series of unanticipated accelerations in the nominal-money-supply growth rate?

4 How can it be that active variation in the growth rate of the nominal money supply in light of current conditions may lead to less economic stability?

5 Why is it necessary that someone who advocates stabilization by active fiscal policy believe that fiscal policy can affect nominal income? Why do some people who believe that fiscal policy affects nominal income believe that fiscal policy cannot be used for stabilization? Is there any inconsistency in these views?

6 Why might an increased real government surplus imply an increased ratio of investment to income?

7 In Fig. 15.1, why does $\left(\dfrac{y}{k}\right)_0 = \left(\dfrac{y}{k}\right)_1 = \dfrac{\overline{\Gamma l}}{\sigma}$?

8 Why do macroeconomists not find much to choose from among alternative constant rates of inflation? Can you think of any reasons why an anticipated inflation is bad in and of itself?

*9 Why do attempts to suppress inflation through wage and price controls convert a relatively harmless situation into a major disaster?

*10 Suppose that a law is enacted requiring the Fed to maintain the actual nominal money supply within 1 percent of a "standard money supply" which grows at a rate of 4 percent per annum.

 (a) What is the highest legally possible average growth rate of the nominal money supply over a period of 6 months? Over a year? Over 5 years?

 (b) What is the lowest legally possible average growth rate of the nominal money supply over a period of 6 months? Over a year? Over 5 years?

 (c) Draw a diagram showing how the logarithm of the standard money supply grows over time. Indicate the range within which the Fed must maintain the actual nominal money supply.

 (d) On your answer to part (c), indicate the possible range of the actual nominal money supply if the law required instead that the Fed maintain the nominal-money-supply growth rate between 3 and 5 percent per annum. Why does the standard money supply law allow for more short-run policy but for less long-run discretion?

REFERENCES FOR FURTHER READING

Burns, Arthur F., and Paul A. Samuelson: *Full Employment, Guideposts and Economic Stability*, Washington: American Enterprise Institute for Public Policy Research, 1967.

Francis, Darryl R.: The Role of Monetary Policy in Dealing with Inflation and High Interest Rates, *Federal Reserve Bank of St. Louis Review*, **56**(8): 2–9, Aug. 1974.

Friedman, Milton: Contemporary Monetary Problems, *Economic Notes*, **2:** 5–18, 1973, no. 2.

———: The Role of Monetary Policy, *American Economic Review*, **58:** 1–17, Mar. 1968.

———: *A Program for Monetary Stability*, New York: Fordham, 1959.

Gramlich, Edward M.: The Usefulness of Monetary and Fiscal Policy as Discretionary Stabilization Tools, *Journal of Money, Credit, and Banking*, **3:** 506–532, May 1971.

Modigliani, Franco: The Monetarist Controversy or, Should We Forsake Stabilization Policies? *American Economic Review*, **67:** 1–19, Mar. 1977.

Simons, Henry C.: Rules versus Authorities in Monetary Policy, *Journal of Political Economy*, **44:** 1–30, Feb. 1936.

Tobin, James: *The New Economics One Decade Older*, Princeton: Princeton University Press, 1974.

Wriston, Walter B.: The Whale Oil, Chicken and Energy Syndrome, Address to The Economic Club of Detroit, New York: First National City Bank, 1974.

MATHEMATICAL APPENDIX

M.1 HOW TO USE THIS APPENDIX

This mathematical appendix is intended to give capsule reviews of the more forgettable parts of high school algebra which are used in the text. It is a tool to be used when and to the extent necessary for the individual reader. No attempt is made to cover any topic in greater depth than is required for understanding the text: For example, only a few simple and very useful properties of logarithms are discussed; the complications of computations with logarithms would only add irrelevant confusion.

Nearly all the Roman and a good bit of the Greek alphabet have been used in the text as symbols for particular macroeconomic variables. Rather than resort to the use of unfamiliar symbols, the Roman alphabet is used in this appendix without any reference to the variables which correspond to individual letters in the text. That is, y stands for any variable here and not just for real income. So the discussions apply generally to any variable with the properties specified.

M.2 FUNCTIONAL RELATIONSHIPS IN MACROECONOMICS

A *function* is a mathematical statement of how the value of one variable is dependent on (determined by) one or more other variables. The function assigns a value to the dependent variable for any possible combination of the determining variables. If any variable w is a function of the variables x, y, and z, say, this is written as

$$w = f(x, y, z) \qquad [\text{M.1}]$$

The *value* of the function $f(\quad)$ is w, and x, y, and z are its *arguments*. Often the function is denoted by the same symbol as the variable which it determines:

$$w = w(x, y, z) \qquad [\text{M.2}]$$

In macroeconomics, functions are used to describe generalizations about aggregate human behavior. Either because of imperfections in the data or in aggregation or in mathematical specification or because of omission of minor arguments, these behavioral functions will not hold exactly at all times. Instead they indicate the expected or average value of the function for the indicated values of its arguments. The actual value of the variable will vary around this indicated value in a random fashion. Needless to say, much macroeconomic research is aimed at improving the data and functional specification so that the range of this random error is reduced. Macroeconomists generally use the equals sign ($=$) for a relationship which is based on a behavioral function and therefore only holds on average. If a relationship holds exactly, due to the definitions of the data, the identity sign ($\equiv$) is used instead.

It is useful to be able to indicate whether an increase in one of its arguments will increase or decrease the value of a function. For some functions, say $w(\ )$, it is unambiguous that an increase in a particular argument, say x, always increases the value of the function. Then we would say that w is an *increasing function* of x. If an increase in one of the arguments, say y, always decreases the value of the function, say $w(\ )$, then w is a *decreasing function* of y. For some functions, increases in an argument will sometimes increase and sometimes decrease the value of the function, depending on the value of the argument and, perhaps, the value of other arguments. In that case no general characterization can be made.

The simplest numerical specification of a function such as [M.1] is a linear equation:

$$w = 1 + 2x - 7y + 3z \qquad\qquad\qquad [\text{M.3}]$$

If x were 3, y were 1, and z were 2, then the value of w would be

$$w = 1 + (2 \times 3) - (7 \times 1) + (3 \times 2) = 6$$

An increase in the value of x to 3.1, other arguments being the same, would increase the value of w to

$$w = 1 + (2 \times 3.1) - (7 \times 1) + (3 \times 2) = 6.2$$

Quite generally for any linear equation, the ratio of the change in the value of the function to the change in the value of one of the arguments is equal to the coefficient of the argument. In this case, for example, we have

$$\frac{6.2 - 6}{3.1 - 3} = \frac{0.2}{0.1} = 2$$

For this reason, the coefficient of a linear function is frequently used as a measure of the impact of an argument on the value of the function.

M.3 THE USE OF LOGARITHMS FOR SCALING

The graphical and mathematical analysis of many macroeconomic relationships is greatly simplified by using logarithms to scale the variables. Most
students will recall having been exposed to a confusing mass of tedious detail
on the use of logarithms in performing calculations. These details may remain
forgotten as far as this book is concerned. Using logarithms for scaling is much
more straightforward.

Logarithms are based on the idea that any *positive* number a can be written
as some other number greater than 1 raised to some power b. That is, if e is
greater than 1, it is possible to find a b such that

$$a = e^b \qquad\qquad [M.4]$$

This is also written as

$$\log_e a = b \qquad\qquad [M.5]$$

Any number greater than 1 would do, but there is one that arises naturally in
many important applications, and so it will be used exclusively in this book.
This number is in fact called e; it is the base of natural logarithms and has a
value of 2.71828....[1] The notation will be simplified by dropping the indication
of the base e:[2]

$$\log a = \log_e a \qquad\qquad [M.6]$$

The value of $\log a$ increases as a increases so that one and only one value of
$\log a$ corresponds to every (positive) value of a. The definition of logarithms
implies that $\log 1 = 0$, and that numbers smaller than 1 have negative logarithms and numbers greater than 1 have positive logarithms.[3]

Three very useful properties of logarithms are

1 If $a = bc$, then $\log a = \log b + \log c$.
2 If $a = b/c$, then $\log a = \log b - \log c$.
3 If $a = b^c$, then $\log a = c \log b$.

A great many macroeconomic relationships are multiplicative or involve ratios.
Converting these relationships by taking logarithms permits a discussion of a
simple linear relationship. This especially simplifies graphical illustrations.
Graphing $\log a$ instead of a is simply a rescaling to different units similar to

---

[1] Like the number $\pi = 3.14159...$, e is found in the solutions to many different kinds of real-world problems.
[2] Natural logarithms are indicated by some authors as ln a. Since no other bases are used, the notation "log a" is
generally used in economics.
[3] This is based on the fact that $e^0 = 1$ and $e^{-a} = 1/e^a$.

converting data collected in $ billion to units of $ trillion. The major difference is that the logarithmic transformation of the units converts the data so that if the ratio of two values, say a_2/a_1, is a certain number, say g, the algebraic difference of their logarithms (the *logarithmic difference*) will be a constant $\log g$ whatever the value of a_1. This occurs because

$$\log a_2 - \log a_1 = \log \frac{a_2}{a_1} = \log g \qquad [\text{M}.7]$$

Graphs of the logarithms of values are said to have *ratio scales* because of this fact.

It so happens that if g is close to 1 (say $0.8 \le g \le 1.2$), then

$$\log g \approx g - 1 \qquad [\text{M}.8]$$

This convenient approximation is illustrated in Table M.1 which gives the values of $\log g$ corresponding to selected values of g. Substitution of [M.8] into [M.7], shows that

$$\log a_2 - \log a_1 \approx \frac{a_2}{a_1} - 1 \qquad [\text{M}.9]$$

Table M.1 VALUES OF LOG g

g	$\log g$	$g - 1$	g	$\log g$	$g - 1$
0.10	− 2.3026	− 0.90	1.01	0.0099	0.01
0.50	− 0.6932	− 0.50	1.02	0.0198	0.02
0.80	− 0.2231	− 0.20	1.03	0.0296	0.03
0.85	− 0.1625	− 0.15	1.04	0.0392	0.04
0.90	− 0.1054	− 0.10	1.05	0.0488	0.05
0.91	− 0.0954	− 0.09	1.06	0.0583	0.06
0.92	− 0.0845	− 0.08	1.07	0.0677	0.07
0.93	− 0.0726	− 0.07	1.08	0.0770	0.08
0.94	− 0.0619	− 0.06	1.09	0.0862	0.09
0.95	− 0.0513	− 0.05	1.10	0.0953	0.10
0.96	− 0.0408	− 0.04	1.15	0.1398	0.15
0.97	− 0.0305	− 0.03	1.20	0.1823	0.20
0.98	− 0.0202	− 0.02	2.00	0.6932	1.00
0.99	− 0.0101	− 0.01	10.00	2.3026	9.00
1.00	0.0000	0.00			

for a_2/a_1 close to 1. Now the proportionate difference between a_2 and a_1 is

$$\frac{a_2 - a_1}{a_1} = \frac{a_2}{a_1} - 1 \approx \log a_2 - \log a_1 \qquad \text{[M.10]}$$

So logarithmic differences are an alternative measure of proportionate differences for proportionate differences between plus and minus 0.20 (20 percent).

M.4 RATES OF CHANGE AND GROWTH RATES

The rate of change and the growth rate of a variable are alternative means of measuring how the variable changes over time. Which concept is most useful depends on the variable and problem at hand.

The simplest measure of change in some variable, say a, is the difference between the value of the variable at the end and at the beginning of some period of time, say $a_1 - a_0$. To obtain a measure which is independent of the period of time, we divide by the length of the period, as explained in Sec. 5.1. The rate of change of any variable a is defined as

$$\Delta a \equiv \frac{a_z - a}{z} \qquad \text{[M.11]}$$

where z is the arbitrarily small period of time, and a is the current value of a and a_z is the value at the end of the period. This is also known as the time derivative of a. The rate of change Δa is measured in the units of a per annum. That is, if a is measured in base-year dollars, Δa is measured in base-year dollars per annum.

Many variables grow over time at a relatively stable proportionate rate. For example, real income might typically grow by R\$4 billion per annum over a year starting from a base of R\$100 billion per annum and by R\$40 billion per annum from R\$1,000 billion per annum. In either case, this is the same proportionate growth of 0.04 or percentage growth of 4 percent. It is often convenient to measure such variables in terms of their proportionate growth in a way which is independent of a particular period of measurement. For this purpose, the growth rate of any positive[4] variable a is defined as

$$\Gamma a \equiv \frac{a_z - a}{a \cdot z} \qquad \text{[M.12]}$$

---

[4] Growth rates are customarily defined only for variables which are measured upwards from a natural origin of zero.

where z, a, and a_z are as defined for [M.11]. Comparison of the definitions [M.11] and [M.12] shows that

$$\Gamma a \equiv \frac{\Delta a}{a} \qquad\qquad\qquad\text{[M.13]}$$

That is, the growth rate of a variable is its rate of change (per annum) as a fraction of the level of the variable.

Since a_z and a will be arbitrarily close in value for an arbitrarily short period z,

$$\frac{a_z - a}{a \cdot z} \equiv \frac{1}{z}\left(\frac{a_z}{a} - 1\right) \equiv \frac{\log a_z - \log a}{z} \qquad\qquad\text{[M.14]}$$

in view of [M.9]. The right-hand side of [M.14] is the definition of the rate of change of log a. Therefore for any variable a, we have

$$\Gamma a \equiv \Delta \log a \qquad\qquad\qquad\text{[M.15]}$$

The growth rate of a variable is the same as the rate of change of the logarithm of the variable.

Two rules on growth rates are used frequently in the text. The first is that the growth rate of the product of two or more variables is equal to the sum of the growth rates of these variables. First note that the rate of change of a sum of two or more variables is the sum of the rates of change of the variables.[5] Suppose that the product is $w \equiv xy$. Then take logarithms to obtain

$$\log w \equiv \log x + \log y$$

So

$$\Delta \log w \equiv \Delta \log x + \Delta \log y$$
$$\Gamma w \equiv \Gamma x + \Gamma y \qquad\qquad\qquad\text{[M.16]}$$

The generalization to more than two variables is straightforward.

---

[5] If $a = b + c$, then $a_z - a = b_z - b + c_z - c$. Therefore,

$$\frac{a_z - a}{z} = \frac{b_z - b}{z} + \frac{c_z - c}{z}$$

The generalization to more than two variables is obvious.

The second rule is that the growth rate of a ratio equals the growth rate of the numerator minus the growth rate of the denominator. Since in the case just considered we have $y \equiv w/x$, all that is needed by way of proof is to solve [M.16] for Γy:

$$\Gamma y \equiv \Gamma w - \Gamma x \qquad\qquad \text{[M.17]}$$

One other handy fact to know is that if any variable a has a constant growth rate g from time 0 to time t, then[6]

$$a_t \equiv a_0 \, e^{gt} \qquad\qquad \text{[M.18]}$$

An important example of this rule is continuously compounded interest (compare Eq. [3.9]).

M.5   ELASTICITIES

Economists frequently wish to refer to the responsiveness of the value of a behavioral function with respect to one of its arguments, other arguments being the same. This is sometimes expressed in terms of the ratio of the change in the value of the function, say a, to the arbitrarily small[7] change in the value of the argument, say b. This is called the derivative of a with respect to b. It is equal to the coefficient of b if a is a linear function of b and perhaps other variables.

For variables which are measured upward from a natural base of zero, it is often easier to think in terms of the ratio of the proportionate change in the value of the function to the arbitrarily small proportionate change in the value of the argument. Thus, the elasticity of a with respect to b would be defined as

$$\eta(a, b) \equiv \frac{(a' - a)/a}{(b' - b)/b} \qquad\qquad \text{[M.19]}$$

where b' is arbitrarily close to b and all other arguments of $a(\ )$ are held constant.

In view of Eq. [M.10] and the fact that if b' is arbitrarily close to b so will a' be arbitrarily close to a, we can equivalently write this elasticity as

$$\eta(a, b) \equiv \frac{\log a' - \log a}{\log b' - \log b} \qquad\qquad \text{[M.20]}$$

---

[6] The proof, which involves integral calculus, is based on the fact that if $\Delta \log a \equiv g$ is a constant, then $\log a_t \equiv \log a_0 + gt$. So $\log a_t \equiv \log a_0 + \log e^{gt} \equiv \log(a_0 \, e^{gt})$, from which [M.18] follows directly.

[7] We use an arbitrarily small change in b to avoid possible effects of the size of the change on the value of the ratio.

This comes in handy for functions such as $w = w(x, y, z) = x^a y^b / z^c$ which are linear in the logarithms:

$$\log w = a \log x + b \log y - c \log z$$

In this case, the coefficient of the logarithm of an argument equals the elasticity of the value of the function with respect to the argument. In this example, $\eta(w, x) = a$.

Figure M.1 Illustration of relationship between a and Δa. The upper panel illustrates the hypothetical behavior of some macroeconomic variable a between years 0 and 9. The lower panel illustrates the behavior of the rate of change of a, Δa, as found by computing the slope of the graph of a. The sign of Δa indicates whether a is rising $(+)$, neither rising nor falling $(\Delta a = 0)$, or falling $(-)$. The slope of Δa indicates whether the slope of a is becoming more positive $(+)$, neither more nor less positive $[\Delta(\Delta a) = 0]$, or less positive $(-)$. Note that the abrupt change in the slope of a at year 2 causes a corresponding abrupt change in the graph at Δa.

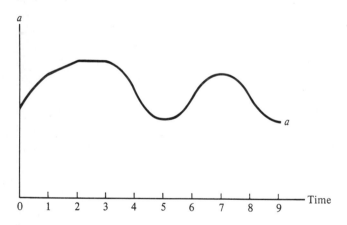

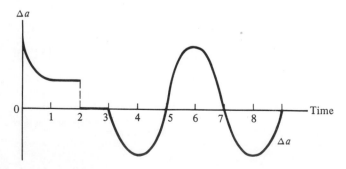

M.6 READING SLOPES FROM GRAPHS

We frequently graph the value of some variable, say a, measured on the vertical axis against time measured on the horizontal axis. The slope of a graph at some particular time is defined as the ratio of the change in a for an arbitrarily short period z to z. This is precisely the definition of the rate of change in [M.11]. So the slope of a variable plotted against time equals its rate of change.

There are six rules which are useful in relating the behavior of the graph of any variable a to its slope Δa:

1 Whenever a is increasing Δa is positive.
2 Whenever a is decreasing Δa is negative.
3 Whenever a is neither increasing nor decreasing, Δa is zero.
4 If a rises more rapidly or falls less rapidly over time, Δa rises.
5 If a rises less rapidly or falls more rapidly over time, Δa falls.
6 If a follows a straight line over time, Δa is a constant.

These rules are illustrated by Fig. M.1. From year 0 to year 2 and from year 5 to year 7, a is increasing and Δa is positive (Rule 1). From year 3 to year 5 and from year 7 to year 9, a is decreasing and Δa is negative (Rule 2). From year 2 to year 3, and exactly at years 5 and 7, a is neither increasing nor decreasing and Δa is zero (Rule 3). From year 4 to year 6 and from year 8 to year 9, a rises more rapidly or falls less rapidly as time goes on, so Δa rises (Rule 4). From year 0 to year 1, from year 3 to year 4, and from year 6 to year 8, a rises less rapidly or falls more rapidly as time goes on, so Δa falls (Rule 5). From year 1 to year 2, and from year 2 to year 3, a follows a straight line and Δa is constant (Rule 6). Note that the sudden change in the slope at exactly year 2 is represented by a drop in Δa.

The growth path of any variable a is the graph of log a against time. Its slope at any instant is $\Delta \log a \equiv \Gamma a$. So the slope of the *growth path* of a is the growth rate of a. This fact is used repeatedly in the text to infer the behavior of growth rates from growth paths and vice versa.

ANSWERS TO SELECTED EXERCISES

1.1 (a) $y_1 = y_0 + \$10$ billion $+ 0.5(y_1 - y_0)$
$(1 - 0.5)(y_1 - y_0) = \$10$ billion
$y_1 - y_0 = \$10$ billion$/0.5 = \$20$ billion.
(b) $(1 - 0.75)(y_1 - y_0) = \$10$ billion
$y_1 - y_0 = \$10$ billion$/0.25 = \$40$ billion.

1.4 No. They may think that government spending fluctuations have been small relative to fluctuations in money.

2.3 Profits are the residual between the NNP value added of the firm and payments to other income recipients and of taxes net of transfer. The inclusion of profits in income assures that the NNP value added of each firm will equal its payments to income recipients and of net taxes; thus output and income are exactly equal.

2.6 (a) The GNP value added = sales − raw materials = \$2,500,000 − \$750,000 = \$1,750,000. Note that accountants use the terms "net income" and "profits" interchangably.

(b) The NNP value added = sales − raw materials − depreciation = \$2,500,000 − \$750,000 − \$300,000 = \$1,450,000. Note that NNP value added also equals wages + interest + taxes + profits = \$1,100,000 + \$150,000 + \$120,000 + \$80,000 = \$1,450,000.

2.11 Firms are the site of production, but the income from production is paid to the owners of the factors of production and in taxes. Firms can make expenditures for final goods and services (invest) only if and to the extent that their owners increase their security holdings.

3.2 (a) $y_1 = Y_1/P_1 = 1000.00/1.000 = 1000.00$.

$y_2 = Y_2/P_2 = 1102.50/1.050 = 1050.00$.

$P_3 = Y_3/y_3 = 1212.75/1050.00 = 1.155$.

$y_4 = Y_4/P_4 = 1210.00/1.100 = 1100.00$.

(b) Year 3. Year 4. Year 3.

(c) Billions of base-year dollars per year. Current dollars per base-year dollar. (Year 1 appears to be the base year.)

3.6   Yes; because the person with $10,000 per year could hold $2,000 in currency and checking deposits while the $100,000-per-year person holds only $1,500 in these forms. The point is that one's money is neither one's flow of income nor one's total wealth, but rather one's holdings of the particular assets which are money.

3.13
$$L_0 = \frac{\$100}{1.10} + \frac{\$1,100}{1.10^2}$$

$$L_0 = \$90.91 + \frac{\$1,100}{1.21}$$

$$L_0 = \$90.91 + \$909.09 = \$1,000.00$$

Note that this is a 2-year coupon bond with a coupon amount ($100) equal to 10 percent of the face amount ($1,000). When the interest rate and the coupon rate are equal, the present value of the bond equals the face amount.

4.8
$$144 - 1000R = 100 + 100R$$
$$1100R = 44$$
$$R = 44/1100 = 0.04 = 4\%$$
$$s = 100 + 100(0.04) = 104$$
$$i = 144 - 1000(0.04) = 104$$

The equations for saving and investment correspond to the values in the table in Exercise 4.1; so direct solution gives the same equilibrium values of R, i, and s.

4.10 The goods and services one must give up to obtain a dollar or can obtain in exchange for a dollar are $1/P$. The interest rate paid by banks on deposits is the return per annum on holding money as deposits.

4.13 $Y_1 = P_1 y_1 = (1.25)(800) = 1000.$ $\phi_1 = M_1/Y_1 = 200/1000 = 0.2.$ All real variables including real income and fluidity would be unaffected by differences in the nominal quantity of money; so $y_2 = 800$ and $\phi_2 = 0.2.$ $Y_2 = M_2/\phi_2 = 300/0.2 = 1500.$ $P_2 = Y_2/y_2 = 1500/800 = 1.875.$ $M_2/M_1 = 300/200 = 1.5.$ $P_2/P_1 = 1.875/1.25 = 1.5.$ $y_2/y_1 = 800/800 = 1.$ $Y_2/Y_1 = 1500/1000 = 1.5.$ $\phi_2/\phi_1 = 0.2/0.2 = 1.$ (Can you generalize about the ratios of the nominal variables? Of the real variables?)

5.1   Most European countries during the dark ages; isolated tribal communities. There could be real economic growth with zero population growth if there is growth in the average quality of the labor force or in the participation rate. (Note that the model of this chapter is useful only where the growth rate of labor and the saving-income ratio are both positive.)

5.3   It is shown in Fig. A.1 (refer to Fig. 5.3) that the equilibrium labor-capital ratio is less in country 0 with the lower growth rate of labor. Since $y/l = f(k/l, 1)$ is an increasing function of k/l—see the derivation of [5.8]

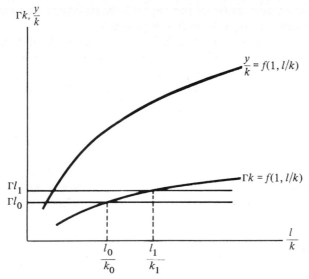

Figure A.1 Solution to Exercise 5.3.

for the reason—country 0 will have the higher income per unit of labor. Cannot say for per capita income: The higher growth rate of labor in country 1 may be due to higher growth rates of the participation rate and average quality in country 1 so that eventually the ratio of labor force to population is sufficiently higher in country 1 to offset the lower ratio of income to labor.

5.8   Yes. The comparative dynamics problem allows for the change in equilibrium real money demanded over a year's time (here, 2 percent) while the comparative statics problem applies to an instant of time for which the equilibrium quantity of money demanded is fixed.

6.2   (a)
$$\Gamma Y_S = \Gamma M_S - \Gamma \phi_S$$
$$\Gamma Y_S = 4\% - (-1\%) = 5\% \text{ per annum}$$
(b)
$$\Gamma Y_S = 8\% - (-1\%) = 9\% \text{ per annum}$$
(c) Work backward: To achieve a steady-state equilibrium ΓY must average the new ΓY_S of 9 percent per annum over the 4 years. The first 2 years averaged 7 percent per annum. So the next 2 years must average 11 percent per annum so that the average growth rate for the 4-year period is

$$\frac{2(7\%) + 2(11\%)}{4} = \frac{14\% + 22\%}{4} = \frac{36\%}{4} = 9\% \text{ per annum}$$

7.4   Firms would price their output higher if they correctly estimated the demand for their product; workers would search longer for higher wages if they were aware of the true distributions of wage offers. Instead firms draw down inventories at first which must later be rebuilt and workers supply more labor for firms to increase production.

8.2 $1,000 billion + 0.8($110 billion − $100 billion) = $1,008 billion. $10 billion/$100 billion = 0.1 = 10 percent. $8 billion/$1,000 billion = 0.008 = 0.8 percent.

8.4   Desired spending increases by only part of the tax decrease at the original levels of real income and interest rates compared to the whole amount of an increase in government spending. Further, a tax decrease may increase money demand at the original levels of income and interest rates and so tend to reduce spending.

8.8   The money multiplier decreases, other things equal, with increases in the reserve-deposit ratio. So a gradual increase in the actual reserve-deposit ratio toward the new desired level would decrease the growth rate of the money multiplier.

9.3   The units are

$$\frac{(£/\$)(\$/R\$)}{(£/R£)} = \frac{R£}{R\$}$$

where $R£$ is base-year pounds (pounds may be an index of all foreign moneys). This measures the amount of base-year pounds which can be obtained per base-year dollar. Suppose, for example, that $E = £0.4/\$$, $P = \$2/R\$$, and $P_F = £3/R£$. So $2 could buy $R\$1$ of goods and services domestically or it could be changed for $(\$2)(£0.4/\$) = £0.80$ and used to buy $£0.80/(£3/R£) = R£0.267$ of goods and services abroad. An increase in the ratio makes foreign goods cheaper to Americans and American goods more expensive to foreigners.

9.6   No, because the excess of purchases over sales will be made up by excesses of sales over purchases to other countries. No, for essentially the same reason.

9.12 Yes, because exchange rates and nominal interest rates will adjust to the extent that the small country chooses a rate of inflation different from that of other countries.

10.1 $R\$3,000 + (R\$100/\text{year})(1 \text{ year}) = R\$3100.$ $R\$3,000 + (R\$100/\text{year})(\frac{1}{2} \text{ year}) = R\$3050.$ $R\$3,000 + (R\$100/\text{year})(\frac{1}{4} \text{ year}) = R\$3,025.$ Since the flow of investment is small (typically 3 to 4 percent) relative to the capital stock, over a short period of time the percentage change in the capital stock is trivial.

10.3 (a) $R\$500 \text{ billion/year} + 0.3y + R\$500 \text{ billion/year} = y$

$$y - 0.3y = R\$1,000 \text{ billion/year}$$

$$(1 - 0.3)y = R\$1,000 \text{ billion/year}$$

$$y = \frac{R\$1,000 \text{ billion/year}}{0.7}$$

$$y = R\$1,428.57 \text{ billion/year}$$

(b) $y = (R\$1,100 \text{ billion/year})/0.7 = R\$1,571.43 \text{ billion/year}$.

(c) The MPC is 0.3. The change in $i + g + x = R\$100$ billion/year. The simple multiplier is $1/(1 - \text{MPC}) = 1/0.7 = 1.42857$. The change in income as computed in parts (a) and (b) is $R\$1,571.43$ billion/year $- R\$1,428.57$ billion/year $= R\$142.86$ billion/year. The multiplier times the change in $x + i + g$ is $(1.42857)(R\$100 \text{ billion/year}) = R\$142.86$ billion/year. It is called the *simple* multiplier because it is based on the simplifying assumption that $x + i + g$ equals a given number.

10.7 Short-period fluctuations in real income do not reflect proportionate changes in wealth or expected future income. So money holdings, a component of wealth, would generally not vary proportionately either. Persistent or permanent changes in income would change both wealth and the expected transactions proportionately and therefore money demand as well.

11.1 (a) Generally no, because there would be only five equations with which to determine six unknowns: y, R, a, m^d, m^s, and M^s.

(b) No, because this adds one equation for a total of six but adds a seventh unknown, P. Yes, because repeated substitution can be used to reduce number of equations by 5 (from 6 to 1), and the number of unknowns by the same amount (from 7 to 2). This functional relationship would be called the aggregate demand curve.

11.4 (a) A decline in investor optimism shifts the aggregate expenditure curve down and so shifts the IS curve down and to the left. It is seen in panel (a) of Fig. A.2 that the decline in investor confidence leads to a decline in real income from y_0 to y_1 and in the interest rate from R_0 to R_1.

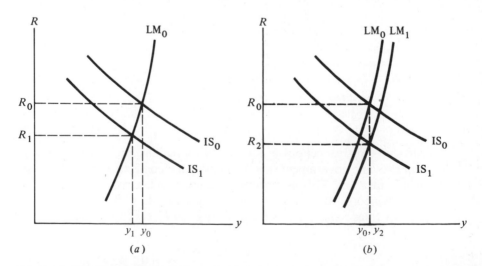

Figure A.2 Solution to Exercise 11.4.

(b) In panel (b), it is assumed that the Fed increases the money supply so that the LM curve shifts sufficiently to the right that the new LM and IS curves (LM_1 and IS_1) intersect at the same level of income $y_2 = y_0$ as initially (LM_0 and IS_0). This reduces the interest rate further to R_2. If fiscal policy were instead used to maintain the original income, the LM curve would be fixed at LM_0 so that the interest rate would be the same as before the decline in investor optimism.

11.10 A rate of change in a stock—here base money—does not alter the stock at any instant of time. Unlike investment, the growth rate of base money can be very high when growth is accomplished by reducing government debt. Thus substantial changes in money can in fact occur in short periods.

12.3 A tax reduction in this case shifts the LM curve to the left and the IS curve to the right. The interest rate would certainly rise, but whether real income rises, falls, or is unchanged depends on the relative size of the shifts in the IS and LM curves. Figure A.3 shows the case in which the

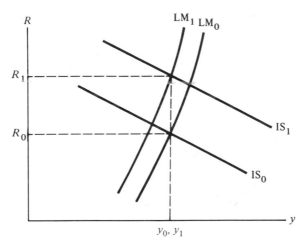

Figure A.3 Solution to Exercise 12.3.

two shifts just cancel out in their effect on real income. Since consumption rises and government spending and real income are constant, investment must fall. This is implied because the tax reduction increases private income and thus consumer expenditures while the increase in interest rates reduces investment for a given level of total income.

12.6 (a)
$$\phi = \frac{m}{y} = \frac{R\$200 \text{ billion}}{R\$1,000 \text{ billion/year}} = 0.2 \text{ year}$$

(b) The government increases its rate of borrowing by \$10 billion per annum.

$$\phi = \frac{m}{y} = \frac{R\$200 \text{ billion}}{R\$1,010 \text{ billion/year}} = 0.198 \text{ year}$$

(c)
$$\frac{0.200 - 0.198}{0.200} = \frac{0.002}{0.200} = 0.01 = 1\%$$

13.1   This is quite backward. Income falls to adjust (nominal) money demand downward because of previous decreases in nominal money supply. Nominal interest rates are low when the expected rate of inflation is low or negative and are not a good indicator of the impact of monetary policy. Desired fluidity moves contracyclically because money demand changes proportionately less than transitory fluctuations in real income and because of procyclical movements in nominal interest rates.

13.5   The idea is that the Fed relies on the liquidity effect to reduce interest rates, but this is canceled out over time by the (nominal) income effect, and the expectations effect eventually raises nominal interest rates above their initial level. Thus the initial increase in the growth rate of the money supply will soon prove insufficient to maintain "low" interest rates, and further increases will be required. (Can central banks perpetually use the liquidity effect to offset the other effects? Does the fact that high nominal interest rates are highly correlated with high trend growth rates of the money supply across countries and over time suggest an answer? If the Fed tried to follow such a policy, would it be likely that the expected rate of inflation would continue to be formed with such long lags as have been historically observed? *Hint:* Does the probability which one puts on a head occurring change when a double-headed coin is substituted for a fair coin?)

14.4   (a) Industries which produce goods for inventory and sell from inventory at an infrequently adjusted price—particularly producers of consumers' durable goods and investment goods (appliances, automobiles, etc.).

(b) They have skills specialized to their employer, accumulated seniority and pension rights, and the like, which would be lost if they changed employers. It would make it much longer. It would not be worthwhile to search if it were costly to do so and the probability of finding a better job before being recalled to the old job were low.

14.5   (a) $0.2 \text{ year} \times 0.2/\text{year} = 0.04 = 4\%$

(b) The rate at which people accept new jobs would be cut from $0.04/0.2$ year $= 0.2/\text{year}$ to $0.04/0.3$ year $= 0.133/\text{year}$; this is a fall of one third. The flow of people beginning to search remains at 20 percent of the civilian labor force per annum while only $13\frac{1}{3}$ percent per annum are getting new jobs. The difference of $6\frac{2}{3}$ percent per annum would add to the number of unemployed searching for jobs. It would rise to 0.3 year $\times$ (0.2/year) $= 0.06 = 6$ percent; then the rate at which people accept new jobs (0.06/0.3 year $= 0.2$/year) equals the flow of new searchers, and so the number unemployed neither rises nor falls.

(c) At first the difference between people looking for new jobs and those accepting new jobs would equal 0.25/year $-$ 0.133/year $=$ 0.117/year. So the search unemployment rate would rise faster than in part (b). It would also rise higher to 0.3 year $\times$ (0.25/year) $= 0.075 = 7.5$ percent.

15.2 In an uncertain world, bad luck might make a good decision turn out bad, and sometimes bad decisions will turn out well. Only hindsight is 20/20. So we must judge stabilization policy in terms of how well such policy turns out on average, given the way it is formulated.

15.9 Enforced wage and price controls prevent the use of money and prices as a means of coordinating and allocating inputs and outputs. There are no substitutes nearly as efficient. Hence the economy becomes either a command economy in which the government allocates inputs and outputs or a barter economy with reduced specialization of production. Both—particularly the latter—imply a considerable reduction in real income.

15.10 (a) The highest growth rate would occur if nominal money started out 1 percent below the standard money supply and ended up 1 percent above the standard money supply. This would increase the growth rate above 4 percent per annum by the 2 percent change divided by the length of the period. So the highest growth rates for $\frac{1}{2}$ year, 1 year, and 5 years, respectively, are

$$\frac{4\%}{\text{year}} + \frac{2\%}{0.5 \text{ year}} = 8\% \text{ per annum}$$

$$\frac{4\%}{\text{year}} + \frac{2\%}{1 \text{ year}} = 6\% \text{ per annum}$$

$$\frac{4\%}{\text{year}} + \frac{2\%}{5 \text{ year}} = 4.4\% \text{ per annum}$$

(b) Going from the top to the bottom of the permissible range would decrease the growth rate by 2 percent divided by the period; so

$$\frac{4\%}{\text{year}} - \frac{2\%}{0.5 \text{ year}} = 0\% \text{ per annum}$$

$$\frac{4\%}{\text{year}} - \frac{2\%}{1 \text{ year}} = 2\% \text{ per annum}$$

$$\frac{4\%}{\text{year}} - \frac{2\%}{5 \text{ year}} = 3.6\% \text{ per annum}$$

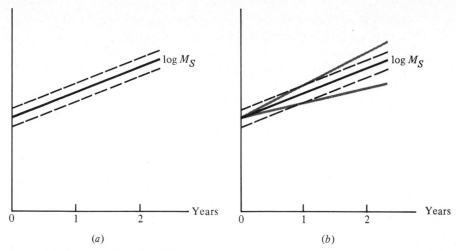

Figure A.4 Solution to Exercise 15.10.

(c) The standard money supply M_S is indicated by the solid line in panel (a) of Fig. A.4. The dashed lines are 1 percent (one-quarter of a year's growth) above and below the growth path of M_S.

(d) The growth rate range is indicated by the grey lines in panel (b) of Fig. A.4. During the first year, the standard money supply rule allows more discretion to the Fed. But the longer term range of discretion is less because 5 percent or 3 percent growth rates cannot continue indefinitely, as shown in parts (a) and (b) of this exercise.

GLOSSARY

Adjustment dynamics Analysis of the adjustment over time of the economy when it is away from steady-state equilibrium due to macroeconomic shocks.

Age-eligible population The number of persons 16 years of age and over who are residents of the United States or serving in the armed forces overseas and are not confined to institutions.

Aggregate demand curve Plots (for some short period) the combinations of real income and price level for which aggregate expenditures would equal income.

Aggregate expenditures Total income from the viewpoint of expenditures for goods and services by final users; consumer expenditures plus investment plus government expenditures plus net exports.

Aggregate production function The relationship which determines real output as a function of the inputs of labor and capital utilized.

Aggregate supply curve Plots (for some short period) the output y which producers would choose as a function of the price level P.

Aggregates Economywide totals or indices of such concepts as employment, output, prices, and money.

Arbitrage Making offsetting transactions in different markets to take advantage of price differences.

Arbitrageurs Those who carry out arbitrage.

Asset Any component of wealth; the source of an income stream; examples are money, government bonds, corporate securities, houses.

Asset demand for money The average holdings of money that serve as a reserve for emergencies.

Autonomous Refers to conditions which affect the macroeconomy but are not affected by it.

Autonomous demand shock (See **behavioral demand shock.**)

Average quality of labor The average number of potential raw-labor units per individual in the age-eligible population; a measure of human capital.

Backward-bending supply curve of labor A supply curve which indicates that increases in the real wage rate will decrease the quantity of labor supplied.

Balance of payments The amount of foreign money converted into domestic money (fixed exchange rates) or exchanged for domestic money by the monetary authorities (pegged exchange rates); net exports minus (private) net capital outflows.

Balance of trade (See **net exports**.)

Balanced budget When the government has taxes equal to expenditures so that the deficit is zero; may refer to individual governmental units or to government as a whole depending on the context.

Balanced-budget fiscal policy Government fiscal policy which leaves the deficit unchanged; equal changes in government spending and taxes.

Banking panic A cumulative process in which runs on banks become widespread due to fears that the failure of one bank will bankrupt other banks.

Barter The direct exchange of one commodity for another without the use of money.

Base money Currency, coins, and deposits at the Fed; that is, government issued money.

Base-year dollars($R\$$) The average amount of goods and services which could be bought with \$1 in the (arbitrarily chosen) base year. (See also **deflation of nominal amounts**.)

Behavioral demand shock A demand shock caused by an unexpected shift in macroeconomic behavioral functions.

Bond market The market for securities in the Keynesian model; equilibrium requires that the quantity of securities supplied equals the quantity demanded.

Bretton Woods Agreement An international agreement (1944) that established a system of pegged exchange rates in terms of the dollar.

Broad money supply (M_2) The narrow money supply (M_1) plus time deposits at commercial banks except for negotiable certificates of deposit of \$100,000 or more.

Business cycles Business fluctuations; the irregular alternation of expansions and contractions in business activity.

Cambridge identity The statement that nominal money is identically equal to the product of fluidity, real income, and the price level; $M \equiv \phi y P$. In compact form, nominal money is identically equal to the product of fluidity and nominal income; $M \equiv \phi Y$.

Cambridge k (See **fluidity**.)

Capital Refers, depending on the context, either to the capital stock or to the capital services which flow from the capital stock; assumption that the flow is proportional to stock permits choice of units so that flow and stock will have the same numerical value.

Capital consumption allowance The estimated amount of capital goods used up in production through depreciation, obsolescence, and accident.

Capital stock The stock of nonhuman resources of the economy; an aggregate index of the machines, buildings, and inventories which have been accumulated by past investment.

Cash-deposit ratio The ratio of cash (currency and coin) held by the public to bank deposits included in the money supply.

Catch-up period The portion of the adjustment period during which a variable offsets in the opposite direction an initial deviation between its actual and steady-state growth rates.

CDs (See **certificates of deposit.**)

Central rate The conversion rate implicit in a unified monetary system exclusive of the costs of conversion and shipping.

Certificates of deposit (CDs) Time deposits represented by certificates which are payable only at specified times; banks permit early withdrawal of some CDs subject to a substantial penalty.

Civilian labor force The number of civilians who have jobs, are looking for jobs, or are waiting to report to jobs; employed persons plus unemployed persons.

Commodity standard A monetary system in which money consists of a defined physical commodity, such as gold, or rights to such a commodity.

Comparative dynamics A method of analysis which compares the equilibrium values in a problem under alternative assumed growth paths of an exogenous variable, where growth rates explicitly enter into the solution.

Comparative statics A method of analysis which compares the equilibrium values in a problem under alternative assumed values of an exogenous variable, where growth rates either do not affect the equilibria or are assumed identical in each case.

Compound interest Interest which is computed as if paid and re-lent (compounded) at stated intervals. (See **continuously compounded interest.**)

Consol A perpetuity issued by the British government.

Constant price level assumption Assumption that the price level is given for the Keynesian model; this is the simplest of the various hereditary price or nominal wage assumptions which can be used to complete the Keynesian model.

Consumer expenditures Consumer purchases of goods and services; imprecisely referred to as consumption.

Consumer price index (CPI) Bureau of Labor Statistics index that measures the average levels of prices for commodities purchased by urban consumers.

Consumption Strictly, the use of goods and services by consumers; sometimes imprecisely used for consumer expenditures for goods and services.

Consumption function Keynes' terminology for the short-run consumer expenditure function.

Continuously compounded interest Interest computed as if the interval at which interest is compounded were arbitrarily short.

Contraction A period of general decline in economic activity; a recession.

Cost-push inflation Period when the inflation rate is increased by rapid increases in costs which are disproportionate to increases in demand.

Crowding out Reductions in private expenditures as a result of increases in government expenditures; nominal or real crowding out refers to whether nominal or real expenditures are considered; crowding out is partial, complete, or more than complete, according to whether the decrease in private expenditures is less than, equal to, or greater than the increase in government expenditures.

Cyclical unemployment Fluctuations of unemployment around the normal frictional unemployment due to business cycles.

Cyclical unemployment rate The difference between the actual unemployment rate and the natural unemployment rate.

Debt policy The decisions which determine the maturity structure of the government debt.

Deficit (See **government deficit.**)

Deflation A period of falling prices (negative inflation rate).

Deflation of nominal amounts Removing the effects of inflation from nominal stock or flow data by dividing by the price level; yields the corresponding real values in terms of base-year dollars.

Deflation rate Minus the inflation rate; $-\Gamma P$.

Deflator An alternative term for price index.

Demand deposits Bank deposits which are payable on demand and transferable by check.

Demand shock A macroeconomic shock which has its initial impact on the aggregate demand for goods and services.

Deposits A liability (legal obligation) of the bank to pay to the depositor a certain amount of currency and coin.

Depression A very severe contraction.

Dirty float A situation in which the government sometimes intervenes in the foreign exchange market without announcing any pegged exchange rate.

Discount bonds A bond that states only that a certain amount will be paid on a certain date; interest is implicit in the lower price paid for the bond. (See **Treasury bills.**)

Discounting Dividing a future payment by the amount to which $1 would then accumulate at compound interest; discounting a future amount gives its present value.

Discouraged-encouraged worker phenomenon The tendency for the civilian labor force to grow more rapidly than normal during booms and less rapidly during recessions.

Disequilibrium Period in which the economy is away from steady-state equilibrium.

Disposable personal income A national income accounts concept which measures cash (but not accrued) income receipts of individuals.

Distribution A curve indicating the probability of different values of a variable.

Dynamic Cambridge identity States that the growth rate of nominal money is identically equal to the sum of the growth rates of fluidity, real income, and the price level; $\Gamma M \equiv \Gamma \phi + \Gamma y + \Gamma P$. In compact form, the growth rate of nominal money is identically equal to the sum of the growth rates of fluidity and nominal income; $\Gamma M \equiv \Gamma \phi + \Gamma Y$.

Easy money Sometimes used to refer to a period in which nominal interest rates are low or falling.

Economic Stabilization Program (ESP) Richard Nixon's program of wage and price controls (August 1971–April 1974).

Elastic Displaying a nonzero elasticity.

Elasticity The ratio of the percentage (or logarithmic) change in one variable to the percentage (logarithmic) change in another variable which causes the change in the first variable. See also Sec. M.5 of the Mathematical Appendix.

Employed persons Number of persons who are either at work or have jobs but are not currently working due to vacation, illness, labor-management disputes, or bad weather.

Endogenous variables Variables which are affected in a predictable way by other endogenous variables and/or by the exogenous variables.

Excess fluidity The difference between the actual and desired value of fluidity; logarithmic excess fluidity is the difference between the logarithms of these values.

Exchange rate The number of units of foreign currency which can be exchanged for one unit of domestic currency; also used for an index of such individual exchange rates.

Exogenous variables Factors which are not themselves affected in a predictable way by economic variables and which affect economic variables themselves; can be used narrowly with respect to a limited list of economic variables.

Expansion A period of general growth in economic activity.

Expectation effect Tendency of the nominal interest rate to vary with the (tax-adjusted) expected inflation rate.

Exports Total sales of goods and services to households, firms, and governments in other countries. (See **net exports**.)

Factor services (See **inputs**.)

Factors of production The productive resources of the economy; the labor force and the capital stock.

Fed, the (See **Federal Reserve System**.)

Federal Deposit Insurance Corporation (FDIC) Insures depositors against loss from bank failures; important in preventing runs and banking panics.

Federal Reserve System The U.S. central bank; established by the Federal Reserve Act of 1913.

Fiat standard A monetary system in which money consists of pieces of paper and rights to pieces of paper.

Final goods and services Goods and services sold to final users; as opposed to intermediate goods and services sold to other firms for further processing.

Final users Purchasers of goods and services not for resale; consumers, government, firms for investment, and foreigners are the NNP final users.

Firing Termination of an individual's employment due to the decision of the employer.

Fiscal policy The decisions which determine the aggregate levels of government expenditures for goods and services and of taxes.

Fiscalists Macroeconomists who argued that fiscal policy has large affects on income but that monetary policy has weak effects.

Fisher equation States that the nominal interest rate equals the sum of the real interest rate and the expected inflation rate; sometimes amended to allow for effects of income taxes.

Fixed exchange rate An exchange rate permanently fixed by the definition of the moneys which are automatically convertible one into the other.

Fixed investment The rate of change in building, machines, and the like; investment less inventory investment.

Floating exchange rates An exchange rate determined by supply and demand forces in the foreign exchange market free of government intervention.

Flow variable A variable measured per unit of time; examples are income, expenditures, rates of change in stock variables.

Fluidity The ratio of money to income; $M/Y \equiv m/y$.

Foreign exchange market The market in which the money of one country is exchanged for the money of other countries.

Foreign exchange rate (See **exchange rate**.)

Frictional unemployment Unemployment due to the normal entry of new workers into the civilian labor force and to changes in relative demand and supply conditions; measured by the natural unemployment rate.

Full-employment real income The level of real income which would exist if the actual unemployment rate were to equal some specified "full-employment" unemployment rate; sometimes identified with natural-employment real income.

Function A mathematical description explaining how one variable is dependent on one or more other variables (the "arguments" of the function). See also Sec. M.2 of the Mathematical Appendix.

GNP deflator Commerce Department estimate of the price level; most readily available comprehensive price index.

GNP value added Sales revenue less costs of raw materials.

Gold exchange standard A term for the Bretton Woods system of pegged exchange rates, referring to the dollar being pegged to a weight of gold and the currencies being pegged to the dollar.

Gold standard An international commodity standard where countries are linked by fixed exchange rates as each money is defined as a specific weight of gold.

Goods market The market for goods and services in the Keynesian model; equilibrium requires that desired aggregate expenditures equal income.

Government deficit The difference between government expenditures and net taxes; the amount financed by government money creation and debt issuance.

Government expenditures Government purchases of goods and services, including labor services; excludes government transfer and interest payments. (See **taxes**.)

Government spending (See **government expenditures**.)

Great Depression The very severe contraction which occurred in the United States in 1929–1933.

Gross national product (GNP) The estimate of the total value of all goods and services produced in the United States and sold to GNP final users; the sum of purchases not charged to current expense by firms.

Growth path The graph against time of the logarithm of a variable.

Growth rate Measures the growth per annum of a variable as a fraction of the level of the variable; the ratio of the rate of change in a variable to its level. See also Sec. M.4 of the Mathematical Appendix.

High-powered money (See **base money**.)

Homogeneous of the first degree Denotes a function with the property that if all its arguments are multiplied by a given factor, its value is multiplied by the same factor.

Human capital A term for the real present value of our labor resources; human capital is increased by education and on-the-job training.

Implicit deflator for gross national product (See **GNP deflator**.)

Implicit function A functional relationship implied by an equation which sets a mathematical expression equal to zero.

Imports Total purchases of goods and services by households, firms, and the government from the rest of the world.

Income Total aggregate income; empirically measured by NNP.

Income effect Tendency of lagged increases (decreases) in real income and the price level in response to a stimulative (restrictive) monetary policy to increase (decrease) nominal money demand and hence nominal interest rates.

Income-expenditures identity A national income accounting identity which states that nominal income is identically equal to the sum of nominal consumer expenditures, nominal net investment, nominal government expenditures, and nominal net exports; $Y \equiv C + I + G + X$. Analogous forms appear in various simplified accounting schemes and in terms of real variables.

Inelastic A variable is inelastic with respect to another variable if its elasticity is less than one in absolute value; it is perfectly inelastic if the elasticity is zero (the other variable has no effect on the first).

Inflation A period in which the inflation rate is positive.

Inflation rate The growth rate of the price level.

Inputs The flow of productive services yielded by the factors of production; labor services and capital services.

Interest rate The ratio of the flow per annum of income from an asset to the value of the asset.

Intermediate goods and services Goods and services produced by one firm and sold to another for further processing and sale as intermediate or final goods and services.

International capital flows The exchange of existing or newly issued securities between residents of different countries.

International securities flows (See **international capital flows.**)

International shocks Demand shocks arising from trade and financial relations with foreign countries.

Inventory investment The rate of change in the stock of goods on hand; investment minus fixed investment.

Investment Rate of change in the capital stock; gross purchases of capital goods including additions to inventories less capital consumption allowances.

IS curve The graph of all combinations of real income and nominal interest rate for which the goods market is in equilibrium.

KE curve Capital market equilibrium curve; plots the combinations of labor and the real rental rate on capital for which the capital market is in equilibrium.

Keynesian Refers to ideas of John Maynard Keynes and his followers; especially the Keynesian or income-expenditures approach.

Keynesian revolution The revolution in macroeconomic thought inspired by John Maynard Keynes' *The General Theory of Employment, Interest, and Money* (1936). The Keynesian revolution stressed the importance of investment and fiscal policy in determining employment via the income-expenditures identity.

Labor force The stock of human resources in the economy.

Labor participation rate (See **participation rate of labor.**)

Laspeyres index A method for computing estimates of the price level which weights prices by the amounts of each good purchased in the base year.

Law of Diminishing Returns For fixed values of other inputs, unit increases in the variable factor of production will, at least beyond some point, cause decreasing increases in output.

Layoff The firing of a group of employees who are eligible to be rehired if demand conditions improve; some layoffs are expected to be permanent, others only temporary.

LE curve Labor market equilibrium curve; plots the combinations of labor and the real rental rate on capital for which the labor market is in equilibrium.

Liquidity effect Tendency of the nominal interest rate to fall (rise) at the beginning of a stimulative (restrictive) monetary policy as nominal money supply increases before real income and price level are affected.

Liquidity trap A horizontal segment of the money demand function hypothesized by Keynes to occur at some minimum interest rate at which people become indifferent between money and bonds.

LM curve The graph of all combinations of real income and nominal interest rate for which the money market is in equilibrium.

Long-run equilibrium The position of the economy when the temporary effects of unexpected change in macroeconomic conditions have been eliminated.

Lower rate (1) Under a unified monetary system, the central rate less shipping and conversion costs measured in foreign monetary units per domestic monetary unit; the exchange rate at which it pays to ship domestic money abroad and convert it into foreign money. (2) Under a pegged exchange rate, the exchange rate at which the central bank will buy as much foreign money as is offered.

M_1 (See **narrow money supply.**)

M_2 (See **broad money supply.**)

Macroeconomic shocks Unanticipated changes in underlying conditions which cause the economy to temporarily deviate from its steady-state equilibrium.

Macroeconomics The study of the determination of total employment, output, and the price level.

Marginal product of an input The increase in total output due to the addition of one more unit of the input (capital or labor) holding the other input constant.

Marginal propensity to consume (MPC) The ratio of the change in consumer expenditures to the change in private income.

Maturity (See **term to maturity.**)

Maturity structure The fraction of the total value of government bonds outstanding represented by each different term to maturity.

Microeconomics The study of the determination of relative prices and outputs of various industries and of the behavior of individuals and firms.

Monetarist revolution The revolution in macroeconomic thought following the 1963 publication of Milton Friedman and Anna J. Schwartz, *A Monetary History of the United States, 1867–1960*. The monetarist revolution stressed the relative dominance of nominal-money-supply shocks as a source of business fluctuations.

Monetarists Macroeconomists who argued that monetary policy has large effects on income but that fiscal policy is comparatively weak.

Monetary policy The various decisions of the central bank which determine the growth rate of the nominal money supply.

Monetary shock Unanticipated changes in the nominal-money-supply growth rate.

Money Those forms of wealth which are generally used to make ultimate payment for goods, services, and debts. (See **broad money supply, narrow money supply**.)

Money market The market for money in the Keynesian model; equilibrium requires that the quantity of money demanded equal the quantity supplied.

Money multiplier The ratio of money to base money.

Movement along a function A change in the value of a function due to a change in the value of one or more of its arguments.

Multiplier approach (See **simple multiplier approach**.)

Narrow money supply (M_1) The sum of currency, coin, and demand deposits held by the nonbank public.

National Bureau of Economic Research (NBER) An independent economic research organization which, among other things, pioneered the collection and analysis of national income accounts and other data on business fluctuations.

Natural-employment real income The level of real income which would exist if the actual unemployment rate were equal to the natural unemployment rate.

Natural unemployment rate The normal rate of unemployment due to the normal process of entry into the labor force and reallocation of workers.

Net capital outflows The value of securities bought from residents of other countries less the value of securities sold to them.

Net exports Exports less imports.

Net national product (NNP) The estimate of the total value of all goods and services produced in the United States and sold to NNP final users; GNP less the capital consumption allowance; total income.

Net taxes (See **taxes**.)

Neutrality of money Occurs if the level of the nominal money supply (for a given value of its growth rate) affects only nominal variables (such as nominal income and the price level) and not the real economy in long-run equilibrium. Compare with **superneutrality of money**.

New entrants People who have entered the labor force (either for the first time or after an absence) but have not yet found jobs.

NNP final goods and services Consumer expenditures, investment, government expenditures, and net exports.

NNP value added Sales revenue less costs of raw materials and capital consumption allowances.

Nominal Denotes that a variable is measured in terms of dollars; nominal flow variables are measured as dollars per year; nominal stock variables as dollars; nominal interest rates are the ratio of the nominal income stream to the nominal value of an asset.

Nonhuman capital (See **capital stock**.)

Nonmonetary demand shock A demand shock which does not alter the growth path of the nominal money supply.

Nonmonetary macroeconomic policy Fiscal policy and debt policy.

Normal unemployment rate (See **natural unemployment rate.**)

Okun's law Increases (decreases) in the unemployment rate are associated with abnormally low (high) real-income growth rates; $\Delta u = -a(\Gamma y - \overline{\Gamma y})$ where $a \approx \frac{1}{3}$ for the United States.

Output Total income from the viewpoint of final goods and services produced.

Overshooting Refers to the behavior of a variable during a catch-up period in which the actual growth rate exceeds the steady-state growth rate to offset a previous excess of steady-state over actual growth rate.

Paasche index A method for computing estimates of the price level which weights prices by the amounts of each good currently purchased.

Panic (See **banking panic.**)

Parallel shift A change in the graph of a variable so that the new graph is parallel to the old graph.

Participation rate of labor The fraction of the potential units of labor in the age-eligible population used in production of goods and services.

Pegged exchange rate An exchange rate set for the time being by a government and maintained by that government's willingness to exchange the foreign money for its own at the pegged rate.

Pegged interest rates A Fed policy to support the prices of government securities by buying all the securities offered or selling all the securities demanded at a certain pegged interest rate.

Permanent income The real private income normally expected from current real wealth; proportionate to real wealth and widely used as an index of real wealth in empirical work. (See **wealth, transitory income.**)

Perpetuity A bond or other asset which yields a constant flow of income forever.

Phillips curve A graphical representation of the statistical relationship between the unemployment rate and the growth rate of nominal wages for a particular period of time.

Policy demand shock A demand shock that is the result of a government policy decision.

Present value The value now for a given interest rate of an amount to be paid in the future. (See **discounting.**)

Price level The average level of prices; measured as the number of dollars per base-year dollar at current prices.

Private expenditures Consumer expenditures plus investment plus net exports.

Private income Total income minus taxes, transfers to foreigners, and statistical discrepancy; the latter two deductions are normally treated as approximately zero so that $Y_N \equiv Y - T$.

Probability The relative frequency with which an event would occur in a large number of trials.

Profits The difference between the sales revenues of firms and the sum of their payments for intermediate goods and services, wages, rents, interest, and taxes; the residual item in the income accounts.

Purchasing power parity The value of the purchasing power ratio that is consistent with given conditions and a particular steady-state balance of payments to income ratio.

Purchasing power ratio The exchange rate times the price level divided by the foreign price level; EP/P_F.

Quantity adjustment mechanism The hypothesis that firms adjust production to offset unintended investment in inventories; assures that the economy will move toward the equilibrium described by the Keynesian model.

Quasi-Phillips curve A graphical representation of the statistical relationship between the unemployment rate and the rate of inflation for a particular period of time.

Quit Termination of an individual's employment due to the individual's decision.

Rate of change Measurement of the change per annum of a variable in the units in which the variable is measured. See also Sec. M.4 of the Mathematical Appendix.

Real Denotes that a variable is measured in base-year dollars (that is, in terms of command over goods and services); real flow variables are measured as base-year dollars per year; real stock variables as base-year dollars; real interest rates are the ratio of the real income stream to the real value of an asset.

Real balance effect The tendency of consumer expenditures to increase, other things being equal, with an increase in real money.

Real rental rate of capital The average rate per annum earned on the use of R$1 of capital; usually implicit in the earnings of firms; the shadow price of capital.

Recession (See **contraction**.)

Reference cycle An expansion and the successive contraction of the economy.

Reference cycle peak The month in which an expansion ends and a contraction begins.

Reference cycle trough The month in which a contraction ends and an expansion begins.

Reservation wage The minimum nominal wage which an unemployed individual engaged in sequential search will find worthwhile to accept rather than continue searching.

Reserve currency A currency which is used by foreign countries to establish a pegged exchange rate and in which are denominated those countries' foreign exchange reserves used to maintain the pegged exchange rate.

Reserve-deposit ratio The ratio of bank reserves to bank deposits included in the money supply.

Reserve requirements Regulations set by the Fed requiring commercial banks to hold base money equal to certain percentages of the different types of deposits.

Restrictive monetary policy An unexpected decrease in the growth rate of nominal money.

Run on a bank Occurs when a large number of depositors lose confidence in the bank and demand payment of the amount of their deposits in base money.

Saving The difference between private income and consumer expenditures; $S \equiv Y_N - C$.

Search duration The average length of time that unemployed people can expect to spend searching for new jobs.

Search flow The annual flow of people beginning search expressed as a fraction of the civilian labor force.

Search unemployment rate The ratio of those unemployed and actively searching for jobs to the civilian labor force; excludes those unemployed who are on temporary layoff and not searching for jobs.

Secular Long-run trend.

Secular stagnation thesis Early Keynesian hypothesis that saving would rise over time relative to income and that investment opportunities were too limited for investment to do likewise; therefore income supposedly would fall short of natural-employment income unless government intervened.

Securities Claims to ownership of firms in the forms of debt and of residual ownership (equity); equal in value to the assets of the firms; securities held by households are equal in value to the capital stock.

Securities issues Rate of change in securities held by households; finances investment.

Sequential search Optimal search strategy involving acceptance or rejection of each job offer as received by comparison of expected costs and benefits of further search.

Shift in a function A change in the function so that its value changes for given values of all its arguments.

Shock-absorber role of money The use of money balances to adjust to the unexpected receipts and expenditures so that other plans do not have to be altered immediately.

Short period assumption Assumption that the Keynesian model is applied to a period sufficiently short that the effects of flows on stocks are negligible.

Simple multiplier approach Computation of the effects of an autonomous increase in aggregate expenditures by requiring equality of income and desired aggregate expenditures while assuming that the interest rate and price level are unchanged.

Speculative motive The desire to hold money instead of interest-bearing bonds because bond prices are expected to fall.

Spurious correlation The display of similar movements in two variables not because of the effects of one on the other, but because of the effects of a third variable on both.

Stabilization An increase in the stability of the economy so that it varies less around the steady-state equilibrium.

Stabilization strategy An overall plan or decision rule for making individual macroeconomic policy decisions; required because uncertainty makes questionable the contribution to stabilization of any given decision.

Stagflation Used variously to refer to (1) high inflation rates relative to recent past and slow real income growth, (2) high inflation rates and below-normal levels of real income and above-normal unemployment rate, and (3) rising inflation rates and unemployment and falling real-income growth rates.

Standard of living Real income divided by the population or, for convenience, by the age-eligible population.

Stationary state An economy in a long-run, steady-state equilibrium for which the growth rates of all economic aggregates equal zero.

Steady state Long-run equilibrium of an economy, such that all economic aggregates have constant growth rates; "steady-state" is used to refer to conditions which would exist were the economy in such an equilibrium.

Sterilization Offsetting of the effects on base money of central-bank purchases (sales) of foreign money by equal open-market sales (purchases) of government bonds by the central bank.

Stimulative monetary policy An unexpected increase in the growth rate of nominal money.

Stock variable A variable which can be measured at an instant without regard to the passage of time.

Stop-go policy The Fed's tendency to take action against inflation by reducing the growth rate of base money (slamming on the brakes), and to later reverse itself to take action against the unemployment increases that result from the previous action.

Superneutrality of money Occurs if the growth rate of nominal money does not affect fluidity or real income in long-run equilibrium; requires that desired fluidity be unaffected by changes in the nominal interest rate. Compare with **neutrality of money**.

Supply shock A macroeconomic shock which has its initial impact on the aggregate supply of goods and services.

Taxes Gross taxes less government transfer and interest payments.

Temporary layoff A layoff which is expected to be of short though perhaps uncertain duration until the workers are recalled to work.

Temporary-layoff unemployment rate The ratio of unemployed people who are on temporary layoff and not actively searching for work to the civilian labor force.

Term to maturity The length of time remaining until the final payment is due on a bond. (See **maturity structure**.)

Tight money Sometimes used to refer to a period in which nominal interest rates are high or rising.

Time deposits Deposits in commercial banks on which depositors can legally compel payment only at a certain time after notice or on a fixed date.

Trade deficit A negative balance of trade; imports greater than exports.

Trade surplus A positive balance of trade; exports greater than imports.

Transactions demand for money The average holdings of money used to separate expenditures and receipts.

Transfer payments Payments made other than in exchange for goods and services; government transfer payments (welfare, social security, veterans' benefits, and the like) are treated as negative taxes in computing aggregate taxes.

Transitory income Real private income minus permanent income; a measure of the rate of change in wealth due to windfall gains and losses.

Treasury bills Short-term (primarily 3-month) federal government discount bonds.

Undershooting Refers to the behavior of a variable during a catch-up period in which the actual growth rate is less than the steady-state growth rate to offset a previous excess of actual over steady-state growth rate.

Unemployed persons Number of people who are not employed, were available for work during the week, and either attempted to find jobs within the past four weeks or are waiting to report to jobs after layoff or to new jobs within 30 days.

Unemployment rate The total number of unemployed persons divided by the civilian labor force.

Unified monetary system A system in which two or more countries have fixed exchange rates.

Upper rate (1) Under a unified monetary system, the central rate plus shipping and conversion costs measured in foreign monetary units per domestic monetary unit; the exchange rate at which it pays to ship foreign money home and convert it into domestic money. (2) Under a pegged exchange rate, the exchange rate at which the central bank will sell as much foreign money as desired.

Value added (See **GNP value added, NNP value added**.)

Wage rate The average rate per annum earned by a unit of labor.

Wealth The total resources available to support current and future spending by consumers. (See **Permanent income**.)

Wholesale price index (WPI) Bureau of Labor Statistics index of prices charged to wholesale buyers for industrial and agricultural goods.

Yield to maturity The implicit interest rate which equates the sum of the present values of a bond's future payments to the price of the bond.

GLOSSARY OF SYMBOLS

The symbols used for macroeconomic variables and major parameters are listed below. These symbols are modified in the text by the addition of an overbar, prime, or numeric subscript to denote specific values of the variable or the variable in the indicated case. Subscripts e and S are used to indicate equilibrium and steady-state quantities respectively. The superscripts d or D, s or S and $*$ are used to indicate demanded (or desired), supplied, and expected quantities, respectively.

a	real aggregate expenditures
B	nominal base money
b	real base money
C	nominal consumer expenditures
c	real consumer expenditures
$\hat{c}$	real consumption (use flows, not expenditures)
CO	nominal net capital outflows
co	real net capital outflows
D	nominal government debt
d	real government debt
E	exchange rate
E_C	central rate
E_L	lower rate
E_U	upper rate
$f(\ \ )$	aggregate production function
G	nominal government expenditures
g	real government expenditures
I	nominal investment
i	real investment
k	capital

l	labor
M	nominal money
m	real money
M_1	according to the context, (1) the standard nickname for the narrow money supply, or (2) the value of nominal money (M) for a specified case 1.
M_2	according to the context, (1) the standard nickname for the broad money supply, or (2) the value of nominal money (M) for a specified case 2.
MPC	marginal propensity to consume
n	age-eligible population
P	price level
$\mathscr{P}$	probability of an acceptable job offer from a firm
P_F	foreign price level
q	average quality of labor
R	nominal interest rate
r	real interest rate
R_F	foreign nominal interest rate
R_L	nominal interest rate on long-term bonds
R_M	nominal interest rate on money
R^{min}	nominal interest rate at which liquidity trap occurs
r_p	the implicit real interest rate which relates permanent income to real wealth
R_S	nominal interest rate on short-term bonds
R$	base-year dollars
S	nominal saving
s	real saving
T	nominal taxes
t	real taxes
u	unemployment rate
u_N	natural unemployment rate
v	real wealth
W	nominal wage rate
w	real wage rate
W_r	reservation wage
X	nominal net exports
x	real net exports
Y	nominal income
y	real income

y_F	foreign real income
Y_N	nominal private income
y_N	real private income
y_P	permanent income
y_T	transitory income
Γ	denotes the growth rate of the variable which follows
Δ	denotes the rate of change of the variable which follows
λ	parameter indicating the speed of adjustment of actual to desired fluidity
μ	money multiplier
π	participation rate of labor
ρ	real rental rate of capital
σ	saving-income ratio
τ	marginal tax rate implicit in the bond market
ϕ	fluidity
Ω	stock of consumer durable and semidurable goods

INDEX

Page numbers in *italic* indicate illustration or tables.